# INDUSTRY STUDIES

## Third Edition

# INDUSTRY STUDIES

## Third Edition

edited by

## Larry L. Duetsch

**Library of Congress Cataloging-in-Publication Data**

Industry studies / Larry L. Duetsch (editor).—3rd ed.
    p. cm.
  Includes bibliographical references and index.
  ISBN 0-7656-0963-0 (hc : alk. paper) — ISBN 0-7656-0964-9 (pbk : alk. paper)
  1. Industries—United States—Case studies. 2. Industrial policy—United States—Case studies. 3. Competition—United
States—Case studies. 4. Industrial organization—United States—Case studies. I. Duetsch, Larry L.

HC106.8.I53 2002
338.0973—dc21

2002023102

Printed in the United States of America

The paper used in this publication meets the minimum requirements of
American National Standard for Information Sciences
Permanence of Paper for Printed Library Materials,
ANSI Z 39.48-1984.

BM (c)  10   9   8   7   6   5   4   3   2   1
BM (p)  10   9   8   7   6   5   4   3   2   1

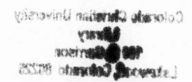

To the students (and colleagues) who have caused me to reexamine
my assumptions from time to time

# Contents

# List of Tables and Figures

**Tables**

**Figures**

# Preface

The U.S. economy, like that of other nations, is large, complex, and ever changing. Arguably, competition in many U.S. industries is particularly intense. To facilitate economic studies, products have long been classified according to a scheme that groups industries into broad economic sectors such as manufacturing and services (the two largest). These broad sectors gradually change in size and character as time passes and circumstances change. Over time, manufacturing, for example, has come to account for a smaller share of employment in the United States (and other developed economies) while services have come to account for a larger share of employment and output.

Since broad economic sectors encompass a great many industries, competition between the firms in a given sector is likely to be indirect at best. Direct competition between firms generally takes place within narrowly defined industries and markets. The fourteen studies in this volume examine well-defined industries, showing how firms compete directly with one another. Each study gives appropriate attention to government policies that have influenced competitive conditions in the industry. Each study is self-contained, examining a recognizable industry in the most appropriate manner.

It is noteworthy that, when taken together, the studies offer greater insight than they do individually. There are a number of reasons for this synergy. First, these studies deal with all of the major sectors of the U.S. economy. Five commodities and manufactured goods industries (both durable and nondurable) are examined, along with nine distribution and service industries (both financial and nonfinancial, including some that have been extensively regulated). The array of fourteen studies conveys a reasonably accurate impression of the relative importance of these sectors in recent years.

Second, taken together these studies draw attention to the interdependence of industries. The studies of steel and automobiles do this, of course, as do the studies of three health-related industries (health insurance, nursing homes, and pharmaceuticals). Developments in telecommunications and microcomputer platforms have had particularly far-reaching effects throughout the economy. In this regard, too, the studies convey an important aspect of the world around us.

Third, the need for careful design and assessment of public policies is underscored by a review of the many policy measures examined in these studies. Some policies can be deemed successful;

many cannot. Applications of antitrust law have been (and still are) an issue for broilers, airlines, banking, microcomputer platforms, motion pictures, and telecommunications. The traditional regulation of rates and/or entry has been relaxed—but not without controversy—in electric power and telecommunications. Environmental policies strongly affect the auto, steel, and electric power industries. The regulation of product safety has been problematic for autos and pharmaceuticals. Maintenance of desirable service standards continues to be an issue in regard to health insurance and nursing homes. Brewing and casino gambling are thought to exacerbate a variety of social problems. In every study, public policy considerations raise issues that demand attention.

Finally, these studies provide a broad array of "real" examples that give form and substance to the topics and issues commonly discussed in undergraduate industrial organization courses. The variety of organizational and behavioral patterns found in these studies will enrich any student's knowledge of the field. The difficulties that arise in delineating industries and markets, detecting market power, characterizing the behavior of firms, and evaluating performance are more easily understood after one examines the studies contained in this volume.

Kwoka's study of the automobile industry points to very basic reasons for its transformation since the 1970s—the failure to deliver value (price in relation to quality) and stress efficiency (in production operations). As a result, the largest early producers have lost market share, at first to imports and then to Japanese-owned U.S. assembly plants. The days of complacent oligopoly seem to be gone.

Greer's study of beer explores the structural changes in that industry since the 1950s. The industry has evolved into a tight oligopoly as strategic barriers to entry, especially those developed through product differentiation, have become more

formidable. Targeted price cuts, exclusive sports sponsorships, and exclusive distribution rights have been used to great advantage by the industry leaders.

The study of broilers by Rogers examines structure, conduct, and performance in turn. Consumers increasingly prefer convenient, more highly processed forms of chicken that seem more differentiable. But most chicken is still sold in unbranded forms to sophisticated buyers, so product differentiation is confined to the smaller fresh and processed market segments that involve branded sales.

My study of pharmaceuticals focuses on the role public policy has played in this industry. The degree of patent protection afforded to new biological/chemical entities, the extent of testing required of new products (even generic copies), the regulation of product labeling and promotion, and the ease with which generic substitution may be undertaken all affect the incentives firms have to innovate.

The study of steel by Barnett and Crandall emphasizes that increased competition in the United States has dramatically affected real wages and employment in the industry. In the 1960s, competition from imports led producers to seek trade restrictions; more recently strong competition from lower-cost minimills has forced integrated producers to retrench as the market share of minimills has grown.

Morrison's study of airline service gives special attention to the controversies deregulation has brought. After an initial spurt of entry, the passenger preference for large carriers has led to mergers and the development of hub-and-spoke route systems that yield better service for travelers based near smaller airports. Vexing sources of market power remain, generating calls for renewed public intervention.

The study of retail commercial banking by Adams summarizes extensive evidence that has been accumulated regarding structure-conduct-performance relationships in retail banking. The removal of legal restrictions on interstate banking has brought a wave of mergers that are having a profound effect on the structure of the industry and could adversely affect competition in local markets.

Pavalko's study of casino gambling points out that recent growth has brought greater acceptance of gambling as a form of mainstream entertainment. Naturally, both tribal and nontribal casinos find it increasingly difficult to sustain that growth in competition with other forms of entertainment. Growth has also brought greater recognition that more must be done to assist problem gamblers.

The study of electric power by Patton and Sinclair attributes the restructuring that has taken place to technological developments that enable us to monitor consumption throughout a distribution system, so that demand can be met by the transmission of power from the most economic generating site. Still, peak-load problems for the power grid as a whole have been difficult to manage equitably.

The study of health insurance by Mobley and Frech examines the linkage between specific insurance provisions and the cost of health care. Through more complete insurance coverage, people are induced to use more care and pay more for it. Greater cost sharing diminishes this effect. Reliance on health maintenance organizations has held down costs but has also limited patient choice.

Ornstein's study of motion pictures stresses that exclusive dealing and price discrimination are to be expected because of the industry's long-standing integration of production, distribution, and exhibition. Pressures for economic efficiency have now overridden earlier antitrust action, restoring vertical integration and relatively high concentration. Moreover, discriminatory pricing has persisted.

The study of nursing homes by Giacalone notes that the growth of nursing home capacity in the United States has not kept pace with the growth of the elderly population. Increasingly, providers have diversified to meet varied needs, ranging from skilled nursing care to adult day care. The prospect of rising costs has brought calls for limiting the extent of public financing for certain forms of long-term care.

Cottrell's study of microcomputer platforms examines the role of network externalities and technological change in the evolution of software competition. Although microcomputer platforms have now become standardized, Microsoft's position in the industry is daunting and seems unlikely to diminish soon. More competition could develop if applications focus increasingly on content rather than technique.

McMaster's study of telecommunications traces the evolution of competition since the 1984 breakup of AT&T. Both long-distance and local services have become increasingly competitive and the extent of state and federal regulation has greatly diminished. The key to maintaining a competitive environment seems to be the assurance of equal access to the communications network.

This review of the highlights of each study serves to describe the range of topics and issues that are addressed in the volume. The volume has been developed for use in undergraduate courses that deal with industrial organization and/or related public policy issues. The studies are presented in a highly readable form (without calculus) so that anyone with some background in economic principles can benefit from them. Although the studies have been prepared with economics students in mind, they will be of interest to anyone who wishes to gain a better understanding of competition in the U.S. economy.

# Acknowledgments

People at M.E. Sharpe—especially Esther Clark, Elizabeth Granda, Eileen Maass, Lynn Taylor, and Susan Rescigno—were very helpful to me during this project. Three people at the University of Wisconsin–Parkside—Erika Behling, Kimberley Brudny, and Darlene Safransky—assisted at various times as work proceeded on the manuscript. The project tested the patience of my wife Patricia (especially as the manuscript neared completion) and I must say she bore up well. Special thanks go to her.

# Part I

# Commodities and Manufacturing

Commodities, which are generally understood to be the most basic, relatively unprocessed products of agriculture, forestry, fisheries, and mining, have gradually diminished in relative importance in the United States since the 1950s. In terms of product value, commodities today account for little more than 5 percent of output, about half the level found in the 1950s.

Because commodities can be characterized as relatively homogeneous goods, these industries are more likely to have effective competition. One, the broiler industry, has remained effectively competitive despite a gradual increase in concentration, but is experiencing rapid growth in demand for more convenient forms of product that are more highly processed and more amenable to differentiation.

In terms of product value, the relative importance of the manufacturing sector in the U.S. economy has declined from just under 30 percent in the 1950s to less than 20 percent in the 1990s. In terms of employment, the relative importance of the manufacturing sector has diminished from just under 25 percent of the labor force in the 1950s to less than 15 percent today. Among the more developed nations, this pattern has not been unusual, as manufacturing has become more capital-intensive.

Although the manufacturing sector can be divided into broad subsectors or product groups, the lines drawn are seldom distinct. For example, durable goods are frequently distinguished from non-durable goods, despite the simplistic nature of this dichotomy. Direct competition between firms must be examined in more carefully defined industries and markets. In many well-defined industries throughout the manufacturing sector there is more effective competition today than there was in the 1950s. Increasing imports and antitrust actions have frequently made a difference.

Competition in each of four manufacturing industries—automobiles, beer, pharmaceuticals, and steel—is examined in the studies that follow. The automobile industry, long regarded as a tight oligopoly in the transportation equipment group, has become more competitive as the foreign-based transplants have applied superior managerial techniques in their U.S. manufacturing operations. Among the industries in the food products group, the brewing industry, which was once regarded as effectively competitive, has been transformed into a tight oligopoly through innovative marketing practices. For pharmaceutical producers, the rich technological opportunities for product innovation (to be expected in the chemical products group) have been offset (at least in part) by regulatory controls on the testing and marketing of new products. In steel, unlike some other industries in the primary metal group, ongoing process innovation by smaller firms (not the traditional leaders) has rejuvenated what had appeared to be a declining industry in the United States.

# 1

# Automobiles

## Products, Process, and the Decline of U.S. Dominance

*John E. Kwoka jr.*

Few inventions have transformed the planet as profoundly as the automobile. From the first mass production of thirteen cars in 1896 in the United States, annual production around the world rose to nearly 60 million in the year 2000. Roads now reach virtually everywhere, giving people and their goods a degree of mobility that was previously unimaginable. Autos and auto-related industries have become crucial to the economies of numerous countries, even as the automobile exacts a price in terms of pollution, land use, and vehicular injuries and deaths. And for most of the twentieth century no country was more closely associated with this sector than the United States—birthplace to the industry, home to the world's largest auto companies, and always the largest automobile market.

Over the past twenty-five years, however, it has been the auto industry in the United States that has been transformed. The role of the so-called Big 3 auto companies—General Motors, Ford, and Chrysler—has diminished and, indeed, Chrysler is now foreign-owned and fifth-ranked among world producers. A growing portion of the U.S. market has been ceded to Japanese companies, whose cars are increasingly preferred by consumers. Toyota, Nissan, and other Japanese producers are opening a growing number of plants in this country rather than exporting vehicles to the United States, creating a "transplant" sector of the U.S. auto industry that operates quite differently from traditional producers.

The magnitude of these changes is readily apparent. Table 1.1 reports shares of sales of passenger vehicles—cars plus light trucks—in the United States starting in 1969. In that year the Big 3 plus American Motors accounted for 89 percent of all vehicles sold, with GM by itself having a 46 percent share. Most imports were of European origin; about half of them represented Volkswagen's sizeable sales at the time, while Japanese products totaled less than 2 percent. But at each subsequent ten-year interval, U.S. companies accounted for an ever smaller share of total sales, falling to 66 percent by 2000.[1] GM by itself has lost 18 percentage points of market share and is now scarcely larger than Ford. Japanese vehicle sales soared to 18 percent of the market in 1980 and have continued to expand to their current 27 percent. Toyota now represents one-third of those, or 9 percent of the overall market.

In reality, the decline in the position of traditional U.S. producers is even greater. Figure 1.1 captures another major trend in the market—the dramatic shift of demand toward minivans, pick-

Table 1.1

**Shares of Cars plus Light Trucks**

|  | 1969 | 1980 | 1990 | 2000 |
|---|---|---|---|---|
| General Motors | 46.6 | 44.6 | 35.5 | 28.1 |
| Ford | 26.2 | 20.3 | 23.9 | 23.0 |
| Chrysler | 14.0 | 9.3 | 12.2 | 14.5 |
| AMC | 2.2 | 2.0 | — | — |
| Total U.S. | 89.0 | 76.2 | 71.6 | 65.6 |
| Toyota | 1.1 | 6.4 | 7.6 | 9.3 |
| Nissan | 1.8 | 5.6 | 4.5 | 4.3 |
| Honda | — | 3.4 | 6.2 | 6.7 |
| Total Japan | 2.9 | 18.4 | 24.0 | 25.5 |
| Total Europe | 7.2 | 5.6 | 3.4 | 6.1 |
| Total Korea | — | — | 1.0 | 2.7 |

*Source: Automotive News, Market Data Book*, various issues.

ups, and sport-utility vehicles (SUVs). Whereas twenty-five years ago these "light trucks" made up barely 20 percent of U.S. vehicle sales, they are now nearly one-half. U.S. producers' share of truck sales has changed scarcely at all over the past fifteen years, but its share of car sales has been falling at a rate of nearly 1.5 percentage points per year and it is now down to less than 53 percent. Clearly if not for this shift in the structure of demand, the U.S. overall sales share would be far smaller.

The effects of this shift in share have been both broad and deep. Production of cars and trucks by GM, Ford, and Chrysler (including AMC) in 2000 was no greater than it was in 1976, even as the total market grew by four million units. Imports from Japan accounted for most of the sales increment during the 1980s, whereas production at transplant facilities now comprises the bulk of the difference. Some ten Japanese (or joint Japanese–U.S.) assembly plants with a capacity of nearly three million vehicles have opened in the United

States since 1982, plus three more in Canada that are fully integrated into the U.S. market. This has forced the closure of approximately the same number of pre-existing U.S. plants, producing dramatic changes in the labor force, supplier relationships, and geographic locus of the new U.S. auto industry.

In what follows, we explore the nature, causes, and consequences of these changes in the U.S. automobile industry. We begin by examining the traditional U.S. industry and companies and then turn our attention to Japanese imports and the transplant sector. We shall see that the different experiences of these sectors over the past twenty-five years can be traced to differences in their business strategies. U.S. companies have always emphasized high-volume production of numerous constantly changing models, a strategy that has paid off very well when models were well designed and built, or when consumers had few alternatives. But weaknesses of their products combined with changing underlying conditions have made U.S. companies vulnerable, and the Japanese have been quick to take advantage. The Japanese automotive strategy focuses on a process of continuous improvement in the cost and quality of their vehicles. This slow-but-steady approach has produced fewer runaway product successes but, rather, long-term product and financial strength for Toyota, Honda, and other Japanese companies.

The above simplifies a richer, more complicated story. After all, the Japanese have had some outstandingly successful products such as the Honda Accord and Toyota's Lexus line. And the U.S. industry has made great efforts to emulate Japanese production systems, seemingly with some success as its market position stabilized during the 1990s. Despite such experiences, we shall see that the same underlying forces are still at work, and that they are likely to continue the transformation of this industry, which began many years ago.

Figure 1.1   **Percentage of Light Vehicles**

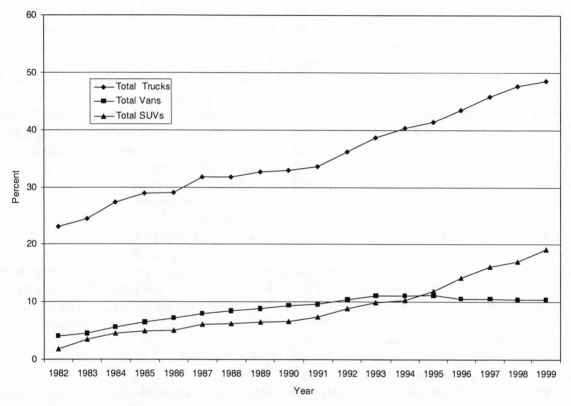

## The Traditional U.S. Auto Industry: Products and Volume

The U.S. auto industry is rooted in the vision of two individuals—Henry Ford and Alfred Sloan. With his pioneering emphasis on mass production of a single, unchanged utilitarian vehicle—the Model T—Ford made the automobile into a widely available good. When Sloan took control of General Motors in 1923, he recognized that consumers preferred various types of autos, not just a single one, and were prepared to pay for such variety. Moreover, consumers valued novelty in auto design and styling, so that periodic changes in the vehicle—again at some expense—stimulated demand and rewarded the company that offered such

changes. Sloan therefore instituted two novel marketing practices—the offering of multiple models and periodic style change.

Sloan's strategy proved to be outstandingly successful. By 1931 GM had overtaken Ford as the industry leader and its approach defined the course that the entire industry would pursue, with considerable success, for decades. In the post–World War II period, GM's market share fluctuated narrowly around 45 percent, and its profit rate on stockholders' equity averaged nearly 20 percent, twice the norm for all manufacturing companies. Ford's market share was on the order of 25 percent and its rate of return about 15 percent.

There were, however, two noteworthy aspects of this apparent success. First, not all companies shared in this success. Smaller companies in particular appear to have been placed at a disadvantage, and some observers suspected that was one of the reasons that larger companies adopted these strategies. Second, the development and production of appealing new models were by no means a sure thing. While auto companies in the past were at least partly protected from the consequences of poor products, that has changed over time. We shall discuss both of these issues more fully below, but first we need to delve more deeply into the economics of auto production, product variety, and style change.

### Economies of Mass Production

For a hundred years economies of mass production have been important in the automobile industry. Key aspects of the production process become cost efficient at volumes and costs that have risen over time to substantial levels. For example, it is generally agreed that a full-scale auto assembly plant now produces between 200,000 and 300,000 cars per year and costs over $500 million to construct. An engine or transmission plant ideally produces between 300,000 and 500,000 units of either component, at a construction cost of perhaps $500 million. These numbers obviously imply that auto production is an expensive undertaking requiring a market for perhaps a million units or more, depending upon the number and variety of models.

The principal U.S. auto companies have long been structured to achieve such economies. Major components like engines and transmissions are manufactured in large volume at central locations and then shipped, often over long distances, to assembly plants. Other parts and components might also be produced by the company or alternatively purchased from any of thousands of suppliers who periodically bid for manufacturers'

business. Assembly plants are scattered around the country, each dedicated to one or at most a few models. Finished vehicles are transported to thousands of dealers around the country who hold substantial stocks of cars for sale.

But if economies of scale have been important, it is also clear that the economies just described do not explain the differential size and performance of firms in this industry. After all, both GM and Ford have long operated well above minimum efficient scale, yet historically GM has enjoyed superior profitability. Chrysler and perhaps even AMC for a time achieved the seemingly necessary size, but neither achieved cost competitiveness or enduring market share. It therefore would seem that the historic advantage of size in this industry—at least past some minimum level—must lie elsewhere. We now turn to various nonproduction aspects of the auto business that in fact play crucial roles in the determination of size and performance.

### Multiple Models

Henry Ford is supposed to have said that customers could buy his Model T in "any color so long as it was black." While Ford's approach reflected his emphasis on high-volume standardized production, General Motors capitalized on consumers' desire for different varieties of car—different colors, sizes, capacities, or other attributes. Some of GM's offerings were similar to the Model T, while others were targeted at customers who preferred something quite different (a green car, say, or a larger car). This strategy served more customers better than any single vehicle could. Unable to compete with this product lineup, the Model T and its successor, the Model A, never recovered in the market. This strategy of multiple models became an integral part of all auto companies' marketing strategies. By the late 1940s, U.S. manufacturers collectively offered about 200 different models, a

Table 1.2

**Chrysler's Models** (1980)

| Vehicle names | Length (inches) | Variable cost ($) | Retail price ($) |
|---|---|---|---|
| Colt/Champ | 157 | — | — |
| Omni/Horizon | 165 | 4,836 | 5,806 |
| Aries/Reliant | 176 | 5,330 | 6,695 |
| LeBaron/Diplomat | 205 | 6,042 | 7,637 |
| Cordoba/Mirada | 210 | — | — |
| New Yorker/St. Regis | 221 | 7,135 | 8,875 |

*Note:* The paired names are those given to essentially the same vehicle sold by different Chrysler divisions.

number that grew to a peak of about 375 in 1970 before declining to the range of 250 to 300 in the 1990s. These products were arrayed in product "space" in a way that satisfied diverse customer preferences. For example, Chrysler's product lineup in 1980 consisted of six basic car lines, as shown in Table 1.2.[2] For simplicity, vehicle length is presented as the key product attribute; these car lines are located along this continuum from a length of 157 inches to 221 inches, spanning the range of customer preferences from quite small cars through full-size vehicles. They were spaced at intervals of 8, 11, 29, 5, and 11 inches—not quite even spacing but clearly designed to offer a vehicle close to each customer's preferred size. All manufacturers, including Ford, adopted this strategy of multiple product offerings.

The companies had several other reasons for offering product lineups consisting of carefully positioned vehicle types. One was that such lineups could help achieve an imperfect form of price discrimination among customers. While the cost of a large car is greater than the cost of a small one (see Table 1.2), that difference is considerably less than the increment in consumers' willingness to pay for a larger size. All auto companies therefore focused on large cars, striving to raise the price on

those cars to the level that extracted maximum profits from those customers who prefer this lucrative segment. The problem (to the company, at least) is that if a car's price rises, some customers may be induced to choose the next smaller car size at its now relatively lower price. To prevent this "downshifting," the company made the alternative smaller car less attractive by either raising its price or lowering its quality (size). The result is a product lineup designed to induce profit-maximizing self-selection by customers of vehicle types, with primary attention to the largest vehicle and higher prices, and lower quality for others.[3]

The auto companies have had at least three other reasons for marketing a variety of cars. First, small cars are generally car buyers' first purchases, and GM, Ford, and Chrysler have long believed that initial ownership creates loyalty to the brand (or at least to the corporation). This justifies a lower price for the car that creates those later sales and profits. Studies have shown, for example, that each Chrysler car that was purchased increased the probability of a subsequent purchase of a Chrysler product by 11 percentage points. The corresponding numbers for GM and Ford were 6 percent and 4 percent, respectively.

Second, despite the companies' preference for large cars, during the 1970s many consumers switched to small cars. The U.S. auto companies felt the need to offer the latter in order to avoid losing dealers from their network. Here, too, the real concern was with possible loss of sales of more profitable large cars if their dealer networks shrank, not with loss of sales of (unprofitable) small cars. And finally, with the advent of Corporate Average Fuel Economy regulations in 1975, each company had to produce enough small, fuel-efficient cars to average out (once again) against their more profitable, but "gas-guzzling" larger cars.

Clearly, offering multiple models fragments the market into ever-smaller-volume niches and thereby sacrifices economies of scale. This works to the special disadvantage of smaller volume companies and undoubtedly contributed to the demise of some. But all the auto companies have sought to limit any adverse cost effects from model proliferation by a strategy of parts "commonality." Commonality involves the use of identical parts and components across different models, permitting the realization of economies in component production even if a single vehicle model with that component does not sell at sufficient volume. So long as consumers do not know or care about the distinctiveness of, for example, the mufflers, wiring harnesses, or even transmissions in their vehicles, companies can achieve cost efficiencies while offering a wide array of apparently different models.[4]

## New Models, Style Change, and Advertising

The second aspect of Alfred Sloan's marketing strategy involved periodic introduction of new models and changes in the appearance of existing cars. This was intended to differentiate products over time, cater to the customer preference for newness, and stimulate replacement demand, the latter especially important as the overall market matured. There is abundant evidence that this works. During the 1970s and early 1980s, complete restyling of a vehicle raised an average model's sales by over 50,000 units, or 20 percent, in the first year. Interestingly, the sales gain diminished with each subsequent year, implying that the product went through a "life cycle" requiring further restyling in later years.

These strategies, however, were and are extremely costly. A complete makeover of an automobile's styling requires a new design and new dies with which to stamp the sheet metal into new shapes. These costs were estimated at about $700 per car in the late 1950s—a startlingly large number relative to car prices, which averaged about $2,500 at the time. In the 1990s, Chrysler spent $2.1 billion to restyle its full-size cars, $2.3 billion on its Jeep, and $2.8 billion on its minivans. Developing and launching a completely new vehicle is more expensive yet. Ford's innovative Taurus/Sable line cost in excess of $3 billion when it was introduced in 1986, and its more recent (and unsuccessful) effort to develop a "world car"—a basic vehicle that could be adapted to different countries—is reported to have cost $5 billion.[5]

Worse yet, such expenditures on new models and styling are basically high-stakes gambles, as customer reactions and sales are very uncertain. The failure of Ford's Edsel is legendary, but there are innumerable other examples of that uncertainty. Ford's radical redesign of its Taurus/Sable in 1996 was poorly received and the model quickly lost its position as the largest-selling car in the United States. Ford scrambled to soften the car's novel appearance. Ironically, at the same time Chrysler was redesigning its flagship minivans and, partly based on Ford's bad experience with dramatic change, decided to scale back some contemplated changes in the vehicle.[6] In this case, it was conservatism that proved to be a mistake, as Honda and others came out with more innovative minivans that took sales and share away from Chrysler. Clearly, there is no simple formula for success in this product strategy.

In addition to style change, marketing of autos is also characterized by an extensive amount of advertising. In dollar terms, the industry has long been one of the largest advertisers in the United States—the Big 3 media expenditures were $5.1 billion in 2000. There are, however, major differences among the companies in the extent of their advertising effort. While GM's total advertising expenditures are the largest, model-by-model data from the 1970s show that its advertising represented 1.85 percent of sales revenues, compared to 3.24 percent for Ford and 4.20 percent for Chrysler.[7] These figures support the view that scale economies in advertising allow the largest company to incur lower unit cost than its rivals, although more recently GM has increased its advertising expenditures substantially in an effort to sustain its sales.

Companies advertise and redesign vehicles in order to increase sales, of course, but with such enormous efforts by all companies simultaneously, one might ask whether or not the net effect of one company's advertising together with others' counter-advertising is an increase in total industry sales, and similarly how all their style change efforts affect total sales. If there is no effect, then advertising (and separately, style change) just leaves all companies with higher costs. The evidence in fact indicates that total advertising expenditure does have a positive effect on overall sales, so that counter-advertising by rivals does not cancel out a model's own advertising effort.[8] With respect to style change, however, the net effect appears to be that total sales in the market are essentially unchanged. This raises the question: Why have the companies persisted in this very expensive but ultimately self-canceling strategy? Certainly one possibility is that they may have been drawn into styling rivalry in the hope of unilateral sales increases, only to find they are trapped in a classic "prisoner's dilemma." That is, despite the collective futility of style change, each may find it difficult to retreat from the strategy, because doing so would yield sales to those who persisted in style change.

But it is also possible that style change had more mischievous purposes. To see this, assume that styling costs are fixed and that dies wear out and require replacement after production of a certain number of pieces. The company with the largest sales uses up its dies first and will replace them, either with the same type of dies or with dies designed for new sheet metal. As long as style change increases demand, clearly the company will choose new dies. But then smaller companies are confronted with the unpleasant choice between retaining their styling and losing customers or changing their styling and suffering higher costs, because with smaller production, their older dies are not yet exhausted.

So far, this predicament appears simply to describe economies of scale. But it may also be the case that the largest company can exploit and enhance this difference to its advantage. Rather than waiting until its dies are exhausted, the company can discard its dies early, incurring added expense to itself but imposing yet greater costs on its smaller rivals who must also change dies. With their higher costs, smaller rivals, are forced to raise their prices, thereby relaxing the pricing restraint on the leading firm.[9]

While it is very difficult to distinguish legitimate use of style change from its possible strategic and anticompetitive use, the latter possibility is at least suggested by the fact that the leading firm, GM, has always had the fastest pace of style change. Its product cycle dropped to shorter than three years during the 1960s. Moreover, during those periods in which GM chose to accelerate the pace of style change (the 1930s and again in the 1960s), smaller companies were forced out of the industry in large numbers.

### Asleep at the Wheel

For decades the U.S. auto industry settled into a behavior pattern based on Sloan's marketing and Ford's production principles. Competition was muted or absent with respect to some dimensions—notably, with respect to pricing. Prices were set in an annual ritual in which GM established the magnitude of the price change, at which point the other companies announced their changes or if they had previously announced tentative prices, revised theirs to bring them into line. With perhaps a few isolated exceptions, real price competition did not exist in the market.[10]

Another dimension on which competition did not focus was product quality. Autos were being built in ways that had changed very little from the methods set out by Henry Ford. Paramount importance was placed on maintaining continuous operation of the assembly line. To ensure that large numbers of all necessary components were held in inventory, extra workers were available to replace those absent or on break at any time, and repair stations were located at the end of each line to fix defective vehicles that came off the line. But the line itself never stopped.

This approach provided very little incentive for quality production, as ill-fitting parts could still be installed and poorly assembled vehicles would be attended to elsewhere. The results were a toxic mix of poor quality and high cost. In 1980, for example, GM's models were estimated to have 740 defects per hundred cars (a standard industry measure of quality), Ford 670, and Chrysler 810.[11] Chrysler's internal studies revealed a cost penalty from such defects of $274 per car. With sales of over 1 million units in 1979, the cost of poor quality to that one company was very large indeed.

Despite its emphasis on model proliferation and style change, management neglect of quality and cost, and the lack of price competition, the U.S. auto industry sustained itself for decades. Keys to its survival were two types of protection from the full consequences of its shortcomings. First, each manufacturer had a network of thousands of franchised dealers who dealt largely or exclusively with a single manufacturer. At their peak, the Big 3 had over 25,000 franchised dealers. Because of their dependence on the long-term success of the manufacturer, these dealers would make special efforts to ensure continued sales even in some years

when the vehicles were of poor quality or design. Second, apart from some expensive European vehicles, there were no real alternatives to Big 3 products. At most, prospective buyers could postpone their vehicle purchase, but there was no guarantee that next year's models would be any more satisfactory than this year's. Hence, most purchasers simply took what they could get.

In the period from 1950 into the 1970s, these factors lulled the U.S. auto companies into a sense of invulnerability. The reality, however, was that they had become a complacent oligopoly oblivious to the shocks that they were about to experience. In the remarkably candid words of a senior Chrysler executive, "The real problem is that the U.S. car industry went to sleep for twenty years. It was a 'gentlemen's market,' like a tennis match."[12]

## The Japanese Challenge: Imports, Transplants, and the Production Process

Beginning in the 1960s and accelerating during the 1970s, a series of events occurred that profoundly altered the environment in which the auto industry in the United States operated. Some of these were regulatory; vehicle safety standards took effect in the mid-1960s, emissions standards in 1968, and fuel economy standards in 1978, all over the strenuous opposition of the industry. Safety and emissions standards by themselves were estimated to add over $2,000 to the cost of a car in the mid-1980s, in the form of added hardware and maintenance, lower fuel efficiency, and reduced driveability.[13] But rising fuel prices and mileage standards ultimately had an even more profound impact on the domestic industry, as we shall see. The unpreparedness of the Big 3 companies and their inability to respond to these challenges provided an opportunity for Japanese manufacturers to enter the U.S. market, to develop dealer networks and consumer acceptability, and ultimately to dethrone the Big 3 from their dominant role.

## Fuel Prices and Small Cars

Concerns over fuel economy first arose as a result of the oil price shocks of 1973 and 1979. The rapid run-up in gasoline prices dramatically shifted sales toward smaller, more fuel-efficient cars. Although GM, Ford, and Chrysler had offered a few such cars, because of price and quality there was never much interest in them. By contrast, small imports were well positioned to satisfy this burgeoning demand. During the decade of the 1970s Japanese imports shot up from 285,000 to 1.9 million vehicles, at which time they represented 21 percent of the new-car market. Together with European imports, nearly 27 percent of the U.S. car market was being supplied from foreign sources.

The effects on the sales and profits of the U.S. companies were immediate and staggering. In 1980 GM lost three quarters of a billion dollars—and it was the most fortunate of the U.S. auto companies. Ford lost $1.5 billion and escaped bankruptcy only because of its profitable foreign operations. Ford, in turn, was more fortunate than Chrysler, which was plagued by both weak management and poor products. Chrysler managed to lose $1.7 billion in 1980, on top of a $1 billion loss sustained the year before, and required massive federal loan guarantees to save it from bankruptcy. Finally, there was AMC, which had been hanging on ever more tenuously in the market and was rescued by Renault through purchase of a half-ownership interest.

The U.S. companies did begin development of new small cars during this time, but they saw such cars as necessary evils that hopefully would go away as soon as fuel prices returned to historic levels. The companies spent years promoting a series of superficial, self-serving, and erroneous explanations for the success of Japanese imports. These included arguments that the problem was the dollar/yen exchange rate or the tax advantages of the Japanese companies, or a favorable industrial policy orchestrated by Japan's Ministry of International Trade and Industry (MITI).

When these explanations failed to convince skeptics, the industry contended that the problem was a temporary mismatch of demand and their product offerings. The industry was more successful with this argument, ultimately securing protection from imports. We shall discuss this policy next, followed by a closer examination of the problems afflicting U.S. auto companies' problems that they were all too slow to confront themselves.

## "Voluntary" Export Restraints

The U.S. auto industry argued that the shift of demand toward smaller, fuel-efficient cars had simply developed too rapidly and caught them by surprise. All three companies were about to introduce new small cars that they claimed would reestablish their position in the market. The companies therefore argued for "breathing room" in the form of import quotas until these new cars could prove themselves in the market. After extensive investigation, the International Trade Commission rejected their argument in 1980.[14] Undaunted, the companies pursued their campaign for protection in Congress and the executive branch and succeeded in getting the Reagan administration to impose quotas—euphemistically called "voluntary export restraints"—as of April 1981.

The voluntary export restraints (VER) limited Japan's exports to the United States to 1.68 million passenger cars for each of the following two years and to slightly more for an additional year. In 1985, the U.S. government declared that it would not request an extension, but Japan's MITI unilaterally restricted exports to the United States to 2.3 million units and held to that limit into the 1990s. Numerous studies have estimated the effects of the VER. The results of one typical study showed that Japanese car prices in the United States shot up nearly 20 percent between 1980 and 1981, conferring huge windfall profits on the Japanese companies.[15] But the point of the quotas, of course, was to assist the U.S. companies, not the Japanese. What actually happened is that GM, Ford, and Chrysler immediately took advantage of the import restraints to raise their own prices, by an estimated 11 percent on small cars and 16 percent on large cars. Moreover, the domestic companies actually appear to have reduced their output, probably the result of enhanced price coordination as they were now less constrained by imports. And indeed, the industry enjoyed a quick profit turnaround, earning $7.7 billion in profits in 1983.

There are two other noteworthy effects of the VER imposed on Japanese auto companies. First, the VER fixed a numerical ceiling on imports, and so the Japanese auto companies soon began shipping larger and more expensive cars to the United States to maximize profit on the fixed quantity. The percentage of "basic subcompacts" imported from Japan dropped from 55 percent in 1980 to 44 percent in 1984.[16] Ironically, then, the "protection" sought by U.S. auto companies hastened the day when Japanese producers entered the more important compact and larger car segments.

Second, when it became clear that the VER would remain in place for some time, the Japanese auto companies had either to settle for a lesser presence in the United States or to overcome their reluctance to set up operations outside their own country. They opted for the latter, with enormous effects on the U.S. market.

### The Japanese Response: Transplants

The entire Japanese auto industry produced only 165,000 passenger cars in 1960. By 1980, however, production had exploded to over 7 million, with 56 percent for export and nearly half of that going to the United States.[17] Pressure to invest in U.S. facilities grew intense, but supported by MITI, the Japanese companies resisted. This was due in part to Japanese concern about the unfamiliar relationships with labor and suppliers in the United States and in part simply to traditional Japanese insularity.

The company that eventually broke ranks was Honda, often the maverick. In 1979 Honda announced plans to add an automobile assembly plant at the site of its new motorcycle facility in Marysville, Ohio. The beginning of automobile production there in 1982 represented a watershed event for both the Japanese and U.S. automobile industries. Nissan followed with a pickup truck assembly plant in Tennessee in 1983 and began car production two years later. Toyota entered into a joint venture with General Motors and began assembly of cars for both companies in California in 1985. Mazda did much the same with Ford at a former Ford assembly plant in Michigan in 1987. In 1988, Chrysler and Mitsubishi began car production at a new joint venture in Illinois and Toyota's new car plant in Kentucky started up. The following year saw Subaru and Isuzu undertake a joint venture in Indiana and Honda start up its second U.S. assembly plant. By the year 2000, as shown in Table 1.3, Japanese transplants were able to produce about 2.7 million cars and trucks in the United States, with further expansions of at least 400,000 on the way, plus another 500,000 from their Canadian plants and 300,000 from Mexico.

The Japanese presence has grown well beyond assembly plants. These have been followed by an increasing number of facilities devoted to stamp-

Table 1.3

**Japanese Transplants in the United States**

| Company | Location | Start-up date | Capacity (thousands) |
|---|---|---|---|
| Honda | Marysville, OH | 1982 | 390 |
|  | East Liberty, OH | 1989 | 220 |
| GM-Toyota (NUMM) | Fremont, CA | 1985 | 375 |
| Nissan | Smyrna, TN | 1985 | 420 |
| Mazda-Ford | Flat Rock, MI | 1987 | 240 |
| Toyota | Georgetown, KY | 1988 | 490 |
|  | Princeton, IN | 1998 | 150 |
| Mitsubishi | Normal, IL | 1988 | 240 |
| Subaru-Isuzu | Lafayette, IN | 1989 | 180 |
| Total |  |  | 2,705 |

ing and the manufacture of transmissions, suspensions, and brake systems. All the Japanese companies now source additional smaller parts and components from U.S. companies or from Japanese companies that have set up operations here. Honda became the first company to achieve 75 percent domestic content

One notable implication of this growth of transplants is that their production has substituted for direct imports of cars from Japan. During the 1990s, Japanese-brand cars would constitute nearly one-third of all automobile sales in the United States, but in contrast to the previous decade, most of these would now come from U.S. facilities. Actual imports declined to little more than 800,000 units from a peak of about 2.4 million in 1986, and are increasingly limited to specialty vehicles. Transplant facilities now produce most of the high-volume Japanese vehicles sold in the United States.

For the U.S. industry, these transplants represent an entirely new breed of competitor, no longer subject to import quotas or exchange rate fluctuations, but firmly rooted in the domestic market. From the outset, these plants proved that small cars of high quality could be built and sold profitably in the United States. That burst several myths that

the Big 3 had relied upon and eventually led them to confront the real issues.

### The Japanese Production System

The first inkling of the extent of the problem that the U.S. companies faced emerged shortly after they introduced their own new cars. GM, Ford, and Chrysler expected their new cars to "drive the Japanese back to the sea" (as Henry Ford said), and in fact, GM's new X-body cars initially sold at the remarkable rate of nearly 1 million cars per year. In 1981, nearly half a million Ford Escort/Lynx models and 400,000 Chrysler K-cars were sold. But to the great surprise of the U.S. industry, Japanese car sales did not decline. Rather, early survey data showed that the new U.S. cars were substituting for sales of other domestic cars rather than succeeding as import fighters.[18] So the fundamental question was: Why were U.S. cars noncompetitive?

Part of the reason was already painfully evident to many consumers: The cars on which the U.S. companies were relying continued to be of inferior quality. Perhaps the most infamous example was GM's X-car itself, which initially appeared to have many attractive features. Yet fairly soon after its introduction, problems began to surface with respect to its engine and transmission, and then more serious concerns emerged over its brake system. Within a year of introduction, *Consumer Reports* had already pegged its repair record as "much worse than average."[19] GM only narrowly averted a government recall of many of the X-cars, but sales soon collapsed anyway. By the 1983 model year, all four X-body cars collectively sold only about 270,000, barely a quarter of the initial levels. In 1985, production of the series quietly ceased.

While the X-car story has its unique features, its low quality was common to U.S.-built cars. *Consumer Reports'* annual compendium of auto repair records for 1979 (a typical year) showed that fully 94 percent of Japanese-built models had a "much better than average" repair record, a rating not earned by a single U.S. car model. In fact, only 15 percent of all U.S. models were at all "better than average." And what consumers perceived was exactly correct—internal studies by the companies and some outside reports were showing that Japanese models had only 205 defects per hundred cars, whereas (as noted above) domestic cars had 700 to 800 such defects.[20] By a wide margin, the quality standard was being set by Japanese producers.

Compounding this was the even more shocking realization that the Japanese were producing these higher-quality cars at far lower costs than those of the U.S. companies. Early indications of major cost differences surfaced in the 1978–1979 period but went largely disbelieved, ironically because of the huge magnitudes they showed. When Roger Smith assumed control of GM in 1981, he ordered a cost comparison with GM's Japanese affiliate Isuzu. Since GM had access to verifiable Isuzu data, this would ensure that the numbers could be trusted. Smith was told that Isuzu could

build a car for $2,450 less than GM could.[21] The significance of this fact cannot be overstated. Since a U.S. small car at the time might cost $5,000 to produce, a Japanese car apparently cost barely half that. Even allowing for about $500 in transoceanic freight charges, the Japanese car would have a nearly $2,000 "landed" cost advantage—and moreover, it was likely to be of higher quality.

The auto companies gradually came to terms with this startling discovery and began to explore the sources of the cost differential. Here, too, there were unpleasant surprises. One of the earliest and most widely cited studies evaluated the relative importance of three factors—labor, technology, and management.[22] With respect to labor costs, it found that U.S. plants paid considerably higher wages than plants in Japan—perhaps by 40 percent—and, moreover, the problem went beyond the wage differential. U.S. plants also suffered from much higher absenteeism rates (6 to 8 percent in U.S. plants, compared to 2 percent in Japan), employed a costly and inefficient "tag" relief system (part of the emphasis on continuous line operation), and had union contracts that included numerous restrictive work rules that further inflated costs. For example, the workforce at U.S. assembly plants had as many as 90 finely divided job classifications, compared with three or four at typical Japanese facilities.[23] Nonetheless, studies found that labor was responsible for no more than one-fourth of the Japanese cost advantage.

Technology was even less of an issue, as there was essentially no difference between U.S. and Japanese auto plants. Automation played much the same role in both the United States and Japan. The sole exception appeared to be the process for changing dies in sheet metal stamping presses in order to make different parts. The technology for five-to-ten-minute die changes had been developed in the United States in the 1950s, but domestic companies continued to employ older systems that required eight to twelve hours by a four-person crew. In contrast, Japanese companies had seized the new technology, dramatically reducing downtime and improving the flexibility of their production process.

Thus, in contrast to the U.S. companies' belief that labor or capital were the problem, this study concluded that nearly two-thirds of the cost differential was due to "management systems," the manner in which management utilized these inputs. In contrast to U.S. production practices, for example, the Japanese companies utilized a tightly coordinated production system that constantly sought further improvement. Tight coordination was evident in such features as just-in-time inventory systems, in which parts and supplies were delivered from nearby suppliers every few hours. Compared to the U.S. system, this reduced freight costs, carrying costs, and space requirements and quickly exposed defective parts for corrective action. In addition, assembly line workers could stop the line as soon as any problems arose, also improving quality and virtually eliminating the need for repair stations. All of these measures reduced costs and improved quality, which in turn resulted in greater customer satisfaction and lower warranty costs.

Complementing this "lean" production approach was the principle of *kaizen,* or "continuous improvement." As pioneered by Toyota, this principle emphasizes that there is no point at which the production process is taken to be satisfactory, much less perfected. Rather, each task is continually reexamined by managers and workers to find ways that might further improve efficiency and quality. These improvements are sought regardless of current profitability or whether sales are growing, or constant, or declining.[24]

Managements of the U.S. auto companies were understandably reluctant to embrace these conclusions, as they raised the most serious questions about their own performance. Moreover, the problems could not be remedied simply by extracting wage concessions, installing more and better equipment, or even cutting excess management, although all of these were helpful and were tried. Rather, the remedy required a deep comprehension of the production system together with the willingness and flexibility to adapt as opportunities arose.

Thus the contrast between the Japanese and U.S. approaches to the automobile market was quite clear. The Japanese focused on producing very good—but not necessarily blockbuster—car models at ever-improving cost and quality. By contrast, GM, Ford, and Chrysler emphasized periodic new models whose greater sales would propel them to market leadership, but with less attention to cost and quality. This resulted in a "tortoise-and-hare"-type of competition between the two industries. While U.S. companies counted on new products to propel them into sales leadership, the Japanese were constantly refining their production process and thereby becoming ever-stronger competitors. For GM, Ford, and Chrysler to maintain sales leadership, they would need a constant string of product successes. But given the inherent uncertainty associated with new products, this was a gamble not likely to succeed again and again.

## The U.S. Companies: Costs and Quality

The challenge facing GM, Ford, and Chrysler in the 1980s was truly enormous. Their product quality was exposed as inferior and their costs far out of line. Their focus on new products was a hit-and-miss affair. Compounding this, a major recession drove U.S. companies' sales down from 9 million cars in 1978 to just 5 million in 1982, raising questions about the viability of the industry itself. But the companies did make substantial efforts to understand and implement aspects of the

Japanese production system and they did achieve some success. Yet, none found it possible to replicate the Japanese system, and all became distracted by other opportunities and activities.

### The Companies

Chrysler's predicament at the time was the most serious. Its market share fell below 9 percent in 1980 and, as noted earlier, it was saved from bankruptcy only by loan guarantees by the federal government. The conditions for those guarantees included union wage concessions, supplier price concessions, restraint in management salaries and staffing, and other important steps to cut company costs. Chrysler's new cars were launched in 1980 and, together with numerous derivatives, ultimately proved sufficiently successful to keep the company afloat. But it brought only one other new product to market during the entire decade, and instead, expended much of its resources on various nonautomotive businesses (though by acquiring American Motors from Renault, it also acquired the Jeep four-wheel-drive vehicle). By the early 1990s, these various other ventures plus another weakening of car sales had forced Chrysler to postpone or cancel new models, close three of its nine domestic assembly plants, and sell various assets including its share in a valued joint venture with Mitsubishi. Chrysler's car sales slipped behind both Toyota and Honda and its own assessment of its prospects is revealed by the fact that it actually sought to sell itself to Ford in 1991.[25]

Ford's early efforts to cut its costs were quite successful, with substantial cutbacks in nonessential personnel and facilities. It modernized many of its remaining plants and vigorously pursued development of such new products as its Taurus/ Sable line. Its share of the car market climbed back into the 20 to 22 percent range, and for three years in a row, it outearned GM, a feat it had not accom-

plished in the previous sixty years. Yet Ford, too, had spent billions in acquiring several companies in tangential and unrelated activities, capped by its $2.5 billion acquisition of Jaguar in 1990. This almost immediately proved to be a serious mistake both in terms of its price and the quality of the asset acquired. Like Chrysler, by the early 1990s Ford had become distracted from its core business and had a number of products in need of revitalization.

In some sense Chrysler and Ford were better off than GM simply by virtue of having to confront their problems earlier. With its greater size and resources, GM's Chairman Roger Smith sought to maintain the company's market position through an expensive multipart strategy—introduction of numerous new products, use of rebates and other devices to sustain sales and thus production at all of its facilities, a massive corporate reorganization, enormous emphasis on automation at several plants, and huge investment in the new Saturn car designed to "leapfrog" Japanese production techniques.

Unfortunately for GM, to varying degrees each of Smith's initiatives failed. Its new products were criticized for their styling per se and for the similarity of the versions offered in different divisions.[26] Its lineups within divisions were confused and confusing to consumers. GM encountered persistent quality and performance problems with its new cars. Its effort to maintain sales through the use of rebates led to very costly marketing battles. The huge internal reorganization of the company was ineffective at best and more likely counterproductive. Its expensive efforts to automate its factories reflected its longstanding, but mistaken, belief that automation was the key to higher productivity. Its Saturn project consumed eight years and $3.5 billion, and resulted in a car that eventually sold well but never became profitable.

Perhaps the most interesting initiative was General Motors' joint venture with Toyota. Located in California, this facility was managed by Toyota personnel to ensure maximum efficiency as well as to provide GM with the opportunity to observe the Toyota production system. It assembled a derivative of the Toyota Corolla that was sold through Chevrolet dealers as the Nova. The resulting vehicles were first sold in 1985 and were declared to be the best small cars in the United States. It was ironic, therefore, that the Nova did not sell well. Part of the reason was that the overall small car market declined, but sales of the Corolla routinely exceeded those of the Nova. Some speculated that the difference was due to the GM dealer network, others contended it was Chevrolet's confusing lineup of small cars, and yet others noted the U.S. reputation for poor quality.[27] Whatever the reason, the joint venture experience showed how difficult the comeback would be for the U.S. industry. The other motivation for the joint venture was to help GM gain insight into the Toyota production system. Here, too, the results were mixed: GM clearly learned some things, but the process was very slow and GM never fully realized the benefits that it had sought.

By the mid-1980s, GM had become the most inefficient U.S. auto company and also its biggest money loser. Its sales went into a freefall, its market share declining by 11 percentage points in a mere five years. Only slowly did GM begin to address its problems. In 1987 it began by closing a few plants to reduce its excess capacity. Over the next few years the company announced further plans to restructure, ultimately closing numerous engine, transmission, parts, and assembly plants, laying off over 200,000 workers, and reversing its 1984 reorganization. In 1991 this was capped by an historic coup by GM's outside directors, who replaced or demoted existing senior management in favor of a new team largely drawn from GM's more successful international opera-

tions. Despite this effort, the task of remaking GM had barely begun, and the outcome was anything but certain.

### New Models and Old Mistakes

Once they began to mount their efforts, the U.S. auto companies did make considerable progress in narrowing the cost and quality gap between themselves and their Japanese competitors. For example, in 1980 GM recorded 740 defects per 100 cars, but this fell to only 162 in 1989. Ford's defect rate fell from 670 to 143, and Chrysler's from 810 to 178.[28] Thus, U.S. auto companies had actually succeeded in surpassing the 1980 defect rate of 205 on Japanese cars, the rate on which those cars' reputation for high quality was based. On the cost side, one study of assembly plants, reported in Table 1.4, found that U.S. plants required on average 25 hours per vehicle. This was only about half the number of hours required ten years earlier—a remarkable improvement.

As it turned out, the U.S. auto companies were pursuing rapidly moving quality and cost targets. Measured by defects per 100 cars, Japanese defect rates fell from 205 in 1980 to 119 in 1990. Consumer Reports' repair ratings for 1990 vehicles (Table 1.5) confirmed that the quality of U.S.-built models continued to lag behind that of Japanese cars. In addition, despite productivity increases in U.S. plants, Japanese facilities improved as well and remained more than 30 percent more efficient, requiring only seventeen hours per car for assembly.[29]

The transplants presented an interesting contrast with both Japanese and traditional U.S. facilities. As shown in both Tables 1.4 and 1.5, the transplants were superior to U.S. plants but did not achieve quite the same standards as their parents in Japan. For example, only one-quarter of transplant cars in 1991 were "much better than average" in quality, compared to 43 percent for

Japanese imports. A direct comparison of 1987 Honda Accords made in the United States with Accords imported from Japan revealed that the former had 163 problems per 100, whereas Japanese Accords had only 93.[30] On the cost side, too, transplants achieved productivity levels intermediate between those of Japanese imports and conventional U.S. cars.

In short, the efforts made by GM, Ford, and Chrysler during the 1980s and early 1990s had brought them much closer to Japanese standards of cost and quality—closer, but certainly not equivalent. Closing the remaining gap would be far more difficult, if possible at all. But the U.S. companies were spared the need for that further effort by the extraordinary success of two new vehicles in the marketplace, the minivan and the sport-utility vehicle (SUV). Both were truly domestic products and for many years the near-exclusive province of U.S. companies. Their success generated enormous sales and profits for the U.S. companies, blunting the need to address the underlying problems. But as the Japanese began to develop good competing products and as sales of these new vehicles inevitably slowed, the erosion of the U.S. companies' market position resumed.

### The Minivan and Sport-Utility

Beginning in the late 1970s, Chrysler perceived the need for a larger and more versatile alternative to the station wagon. After some years of development, it introduced its hugely successful line of minivans in 1983. Ford and GM quickly adapted their existing small truck platforms to minivan production and began selling competing vehicles in 1984. Within ten years, total U.S. minivan sales grew to over one million units—about 11 percent of the overall passenger-vehicle market. Ninety percent of sales came from the Big 3, of which Chrysler's models represented over one-half.

Table 1.4

**Consumer Reports Repair Ratings for 1990 Cars**
(percent of models in each rating category by product origin)

|                          | U.S. | Japan | Transplants |
|--------------------------|------|-------|-------------|
| Much better than average | —    | 43    | 23          |
| Better than average      | 4    | 40    | 54          |
| Average                  | 51   | 17    | 15          |
| Worse than average       | 24   | —     | —           |
| Much worse than average  | 22   | —     | 8           |

Source: "Frequency of Repair Records, 1985–90," April 1991.

For most of this period the Japanese did not offer a truly competitive minivan. The early offerings by Toyota, Nissan, and Mitsubishi performed more like the trucks on which they were based. Others like the Toyota Previa were not as well designed for the family purposes that customers desired. In addition, Japanese sales were hampered by a 25 percent tariff on imported minivans—which, for customs purposes, were classified as "trucks"—as well as by Japanese companies' reluctance to market them aggressively in the face of trade complaints.[31]

During this time minivans were enormously profitable to the domestic industry. It has been estimated that Chrysler earned between $6,500 and $7,500 in variable margin on each minivan in the 1990s, accounting for virtually all of that company's total profits.[32] While less heavily oriented toward minivans than Chrysler, Ford and GM also derived huge profits from their sales of such vehicles. In 1994, for example, Ford earned $5.3 billion in profit while GM earned $4.9 billion, each on sales of over $100 billion. Chrysler's profit of $3.7 billion on less than half the sales revenue was even more impressive.

These sales were, however, a two-edged sword—while they provided the basis for the substantial success of the U.S. automobile industry

Table 1.5

**Assembly Plant Productivity** (hours per vehicle)

|          | U.S. | Japan | Transplants |
|----------|------|-------|-------------|
| Best     | 18.6 | 13.2  | 18.8        |
| Average  | 24.9 | 16.8  | 20.9        |
| Worst    | 30.7 | 25.9  | 25.5        |

*Source*: J. Womack et al., *The Machine that Changed the World* (New York: Macmillan, 1990), p. 85.

for ten or more years, that success diverted attention from underlying, persistent problems of cost and quality. Moreover, minivan sales could not be expected to expand and generate such profits forever—and indeed they did not. Rather, sales followed a fairly predictable product life cycle of initial rapid increase, followed by ever slower sales as the product exhausted its market.[33] That pattern is evident in Figure 1.2, which shows the percentage of total vehicle sales made up of all trucks, vans, and SUVs since 1982. Since full-size vans have not changed much from their initial 4.0 percent, the sales increment is due to minivans, and that peaked in 1995. Moreover, a growing fraction of those sales originate with Japanese producers. Honda and Toyota in particular have reworked their minivans until they equal or surpass U.S.-produced vehicles in cost, quality, and features. Sales from GM, Ford, and Chrysler were therefore in double jeopardy—slowing total sales, plus greater inroads by foreign competitors.

As it happened, any adverse consequences to the U.S. industry from changes in the minivan market were headed off by a second blockbuster product—the sport-utility vehicle (SUV)—that was also dominated by domestic companies. The first real SUV was the passenger-oriented version of the Jeep introduced in 1984, but sales of that vehicle remained modest throughout the 1980s. It was with Ford's new Explorer in 1990—a better riding, full-featured vehicle—that this segment

took off. As also shown in Figure 1.2, SUV sales grew in an even more dramatic fashion than did minivan sales. From 6.7 percent of the total vehicle market in 1990, SUVs accounted for fully 19 percent in 1999, with sales growth beginning to decelerate only in 2001.[34]

For many years after their introduction, SUVs remained very much a U.S. product, but by the mid-1990s Japanese producers were introducing competitive products at a rapid rate. Some of their SUVs were directed at the same market segment U.S. companies targeted, but they also found important new niches. In 1998 Toyota's Lexus division introduced its luxury SUV, the RX300. This product created a new and very profitable segment, one quickly occupied by models from Acura, BMW, and Mercedes but not (or at least not very successfully) by U.S. manufacturers.

This encroachment of Japanese products together with the inevitable slowing of overall truck sales eventually eroded the dominance of GM, Ford, and Chrysler. As it did, the same underlying forces that were driving changes in the car segment started to take over. Figure 1.1, shown at the outset, makes clear the implications of that traditional pattern—the U.S. share of strictly car sales has been declining for twenty-five years, and the U.S. share of total vehicle sales has been sustained only by the success first in minivans and then in SUVs. In the absence of yet another new blockbuster product (indeed, in the absence of a never-ending succession of them), the decline in the U.S. share of total vehicles would resume.

### Problems—Old and New

Throughout this period, the U.S. companies continued to make some progress in terms of cost and quality of their vehicles. Big 3 assembly plants reduced the number of hours required per vehicle by 17 percent between 1989 and 1994. Ford's

Figure 1.2    **U.S.-Produced Shares of Cars Versus Trucks**

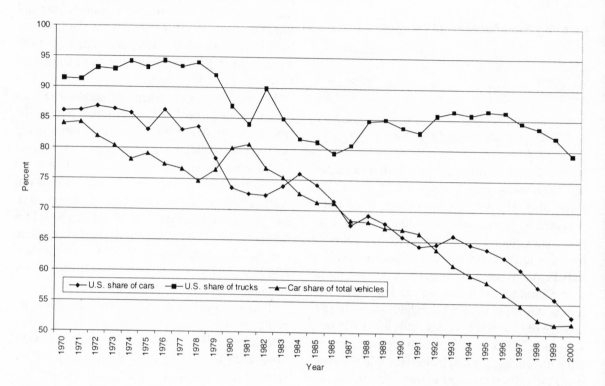

plants were the best of the Big 3 and were matching typical (but not best-practice) performance of the Japanese. Given the difficulty of the challenge, this was nonetheless a noteworthy achievement. Chrysler acquired an advantage in product development and engineering. Its adaptation of Toyota's "team approach" dramatically reduced the time and cost of bringing new products from the drawing board to market. On the quality front, Big 3 cars were vastly superior to those of earlier years and continued to get better. *Consumer Reports'* count of problems per 100 vehicles (measured differently from the methodology discussed above) showed a remarkable decline from 105 in 1980 down to 23 in the year 2000.[35]

For a time, this progress sufficed. Together with its success with minivans and SUVs, the U.S. industry appeared not just healthy but enormously so—Big 3 profits in 2000 totaled an unprecedented $20 billion. But beneath this appearance, renewed trouble was brewing. For one thing, despite the improvements cited above, the U.S. industry continued to suffer from cost and quality differentials. Table 1.6 summarizes the 1990 *Consumer Reports'* ratings of U.S., Japanese, and transplant vehicles, which continue to favor Japanese vehicles by a wide margin.

Perhaps more ominous, by the late 1990s new U.S. vehicles were not as well received as before, and some serious management weaknesses were becoming evident. For example, while General Motors had long sold both minivans and SUVs, GM has never offered a vehicle that led either segment. Its design, engineering, product launch, and production have all faltered repeatedly. Car and truck models have streamed out of the company, but with no discernable effect on its overall share. Management has been reorganized every few years since 1984, but the company remains more a reflection of its past history than an entity prepared for the future: It has too many divisions (one of which–Oldsmobile—it plans to shut down), too many vehicle models (twice as many as Ford, which sells nearly as many vehicles), and too many dealers (many in the wrong places).[36]

Ford's problems are different. It produced a number of successful car and truck designs dating back to the breakthrough Taurus/Sable line in 1986. Surveys of assembly plants showed Ford to be the most cost-efficient of the U.S. facilities, but more recently there have been signs of erosion in product quality. A J.D. Power survey ranked Ford's vehicles as worst among the seven major world car companies.[37] Its recent product launches have all been marred by recalls—in some cases, by several recalls of the same vehicle. Its warranty costs totaled $2.6 billion in 2000, exceeding even those of GM on a per-car basis. Its very profitable truck lines were coming under attack by Chrysler, GM, and foreign producers.

These concerns culminated in a bigger problem yet for Ford—the failure of Firestone tires installed on its crucial Explorer SUV. At a minimum, replacing the suspect tires was expected to cost Ford upward of $2.5 billion, and perhaps damage the reputation of the Explorer or other Ford vehicles. Compounding matters, Ford and Firestone engaged in a very public exchange over fault for the tire failure. The full consequences of this matter will take some time to assess, but the first—the firing of Ford's CEO—has already happened.

Due to its minivans and Jeep, Chrysler had enjoyed the best run of success of any of the Big 3 companies, but it also grasped the fact that its future was fraught with uncertainties. In 1998 it entered into what was called a merger with—but in reality was an acquisition by—DaimlerBenz, the German maker of Mercedes. Both companies were very profitable at the time, and the deal was intended to provide Chrysler with better access to international markets for its products, while Daimler wanted insight into Chrysler's low-cost product development process and its high-volume production methods. The parties claimed that the consolidation would generate $1.4 billion in gains in the first year and twice that in three to five years. One-third of this was to come from procurement savings, one-third from revenue gains, and the rest from combining product development and related activities.[38]

Within two years this merger encountered serious trouble. While Chrysler's performance had appeared to be outstanding, the reality was that its products were becoming stale, its marketing costs were rising, and its new-product pipeline was not as robust as thought. As Chrysler's share declined from nearly 15 percent to less than 12 percent and its profits evaporated, Daimler proceeded to take it over fully. Chrysler management was largely replaced (or quit), a number of factories were closed, and rigorous cost controls were put into place—hardly the vast synergies that were supposed to ensue. Whether these changes will produce their intended effects will take some time to determine.

Daimler's acquisition of Chrysler was part of a broader trend toward alliances and acquisitions among international auto companies. Indeed, Daimler proceeded also to acquire Mitsubishi, the fourth largest Japanese car company, in 2000. As with the acquisition of Chrysler, a number of problems were encountered. Other prominent recent arrangements, summarized in Table 1.7, include GM's equity purchase in Fiat and Daewoo, its acquisition of Saab, Ford's purchase of Volvo, and Renault's takeover of Nissan. Many observers an-

Table 1.6

**Consumer Reports Repair Ratings for 2000 Cars**
(percent of models in each rating category by product origin)

|                          | U.S. | Japan | Transplants |
|--------------------------|------|-------|-------------|
| Much better than average | —    | 62    | 37          |
| Better than average      | 6    | 21    | 32          |
| Average                  | 43   | 14    | 21          |
| Worse than average       | 18   | 3     | 11          |
| Much worse than average  | 33   | —     | —           |

*Source:* "Are Today's Cars More Reliable?" 2001.

ticipate the emergence of no more than five or six groups of international auto companies from the fifteen or so significant-sized companies that exist at present.

At the same time these various difficulties confronted the U.S. companies, their Japanese competitors were making steady progress. Toyota, Honda, Nissan, and others have started paying increased attention to the development of new models and the creation of the wider product lines characteristic of U.S. companies. For example, imports collectively offered 156 models in 1980, a total that doubled within ten years to the point that they outnumbered domestic models.[39] Many of these new products involved significantly larger cars than previously produced, as the Japanese sought to capitalize on the loyalty of their U.S. customers who were trading in their initial purchases of small cars for larger ones. Consequently, by the mid-1980s, it was the Honda Accord and Toyota Camry that set standards for compact/mid-size cars, and indeed, by the end of the 1990s the Camry would become the largest selling car in the United States.

Three Japanese companies also succeeded in cracking the lucrative market for luxury cars long dominated by very expensive European car lines. Honda first introduced its Acura line in 1986, followed by Toyota's Lexus and Nissan's Infiniti.

Both their sales and quality achievements were remarkable. While still praising the BMW and Mercedes, *Consumer Reports* concluded its first review of the Lexus by stating, "The Lexus adds up to the highest-scoring car we've ever tested, a new standard of overall excellence."[40] Consumer satisfaction surveys quickly showed the Lexus to be at or near the top, and sales soared.

All of these factors have created a sense of further imminent change in the traditional U.S. auto industry.

*Looking Ahead*

As the auto industry enters the new century, it is already encountering new forces for change. One of these is renewed concern over fuel economy as a result of gasoline price increases in the year 2000. Actual fuel economy of new vehicle sales in fact has been declining since 1987, primarily as the result of the increasing proportion of trucks in the sales mix. Trucks are generally heavier than cars and are not subject to the same stringent fuel-economy standards. But all the major manufacturers have long been researching alternative technologies for increased fuel efficiency, with a view to the possibly diminished role for the gasoline engine in cars and trucks in the future. Here, too, the choices made by U.S. and Japanese companies have resulted in different opportunities. While GM, Ford, and Chrysler have focused on fuel cells as a possible alternative power source, that technology has remained very problematic and is unlikely to be implemented anytime soon. By contrast, Toyota and Honda are already marketing so-called hybrid-power cars, which use a self-recharging battery to supplement a gasoline engine for portions of the drive cycle and get 45 to 61 miles per gallon of gasoline in city driving, more on the highway.[41]

A second issue concerns the apparent evolution of Japanese producers and their products. Whereas

Table 1.7

**Major International Auto Alliances**

| Asia | U.S. | Europe |
|---|---|---|
| Isuzu | *General Motors* | Saab |
| Suzuki | | Fiat |
| Fuji (Subaru) | | |
| Daewoo | | |
| | | |
| Mazda | *Ford* | Volvo |
| Kia | | Jaguar |
| | | |
| Mitsubishi | Chrysler | *Daimler* |
| Hyundai | | |
| | | |
| Nissan | | *Renault* |

*Note*: Italics denotes lead company in alliance.

Toyota, Nissan, Honda, and others originally focused their attention on smaller and less expensive cars, they now are mainstream auto companies with full product lineups vying for the large-volume family car segment. This strategy may have left open the opportunity for other manufacturers to go after the less expensive, small car segment, much as they themselves did a generation ago. And indeed, Korean exports to the United States—which were zero in 1986 and only about 100,000 as recently as 1995—now total nearly 300,000 or 3 percent of U.S. car sales. Hyundai itself has a 1.9 percent share, more than Mercury, Saturn, Mitsubishi, or Mazda.

Nissan and Honda also face other challenges. Nissan has suffered a series of setbacks in its home market that have distracted it from the United States. With the installation of a Renault manager in 1998, the company has rebounded quickly, but it remains to be seen if it can now put together the products, costs, and quality that once made it nearly as large as Toyota both in Japan and in the United States. Honda, as always, is pursuing its own strategy. Rather than seeking international partners, it is counting on new products and its technological

prowess to keep it independent, but others wonder whether it can survive the inherent uncertainties of that approach.

The third factor that is beginning to impact the U.S. auto industry, and may well become a major force, is the internet.[42] From a consumer perspective, the internet can provide information about vehicles they may be interested in; it can elicit bids from numerous dealers on a specific car; it can even operate like a buying service for that consumer, potentially replacing the traditional dealer function. Not surprisingly, dealers have opposed all but the information function for the internet, thus far preventing what appear to be opportunities for significant efficiencies in the sales and distribution of cars.

The impact of the internet on the production side may manifest itself more quickly. Manufacturers envision substantial cost savings from the development of supply exchanges, through which all their suppliers would have to bid and operate. The first of these, Covisint, has already been formed, but by doing so as a joint exchange among all of them, GM, Ford, and Chrysler have prompted antitrust concerns as to whether it might also be used for coordinating behavior among the companies. Beyond that, the companies are interested in moving to a "build-to-order" system for automobiles, whereby a customer's order would trigger the production of all the necessary parts and components, followed by their delivery to an assembly plant, and ultimately the delivery of the finished vehicle to a consumer or dealer within days of the initial order. This model would result in substantial savings in the costs of inventory and in better matching of vehicle production to demand.

## Conclusions

In his retrospective on General Motors, Alfred Sloan observed:

There have been and always will be many opportunities to fail in the automobile industry. The circumstances of the ever-changing market and
ever-changing product are capable of breaking any
business organization if that organization is unprepared for change—indeed, in my opinion, if it had
not provided procedures for anticipating change.[43]

It is ironic that the U.S. auto industry that Sloan
brought to maturity and strength has so often failed
to heed his advice. Of course, Sloan was an agent
of change in the formative period for the industry.
The half-century that followed was characterized
by stability—of industry membership, of technology, and of customer preferences. Led by GM, the
industry was a tightly knit group of profitable companies that did not need to compete on price or
cost and, indeed, lost the ability to compete. When
that competition came, GM, Ford, and Chrysler
were altogether unprepared and, as Sloan predicted, they have been transformed, if not broken,
by it.

Despite considerable efforts to address their
deficiencies—and indeed, significant progress in
doing so—all the traditional U.S. companies nonetheless face a future far less certain than anything
since the birth of the industry. GM is but a shell of
its former self, shrinking under the burden of widespread and seemingly intractable product, process,
and management problems. Chrysler has given up
its independence to Daimler, but even that has not
prevented its recent success from fading. Ford
seems best positioned to make the transition to the
new paradigm, but as has been true before, mis-
steps and mistakes are thwarting its efforts.

But there are auto companies in the United
States producing vehicles of high quality and well
suited to customers' preferences and whose production processes are lean and cost efficient. Those
companies, of course, are Honda, Toyota, and
Nissan. While they are still commonly termed
"transplants," the reality is that these are increasingly U.S. companies, producing vehicles built
almost entirely in this country and firmly situated
in U.S. product, labor, and supplier markets. It is
these companies that paradoxically appear to have
assimilated Alfred Sloan's advice about change
most fully, and it is these companies whose future
seems more favorable as a result.

## Notes

Thanks to Kimberly Young and Kamen Madjarov for research assistance.

1. The initial year 1969 was chosen, as 1970 data are
distorted by a major strike at GM.

2. Each carline actually consists of multiple body styles,
but for present purposes a simple examination of car lines suf-
fices. For further discussion of the underlying economics, see
F.M. Scherer, "The Economics of Product Variety," *Journal of
Industrial Economics* 28, no. 2 (December 1979): 113–34.

3. This implies, for example, that Chrysler's small Colt/
Champ line was deliberately made less attractive (smaller,
fewer amenities) in order to protect sales of the next larger
vehicle, and so on up the lineup. This discussion is adapted
from J. Kwoka, "Market Segmentation by Price-Quality
Schedules," *Journal of Business* 65, no. 4 (October 1992):
615–29.

4. Clearly, consumers care more about the distinctiveness of visible portions of the vehicle, but occasionally they
discover common internal components. GM was accused of
"engine-switching" when it installed engines produced in traditionally Chevrolet plants in higher-priced car lines such as
Buick. Despite public complaints, GM had much earlier consolidated its engine production across divisions, and the
Chevrolet label meant little.

5. F.M. Fisher, A. Griliches, and C. Kaysen, "The Costs
of Automobile Style Change Since 1949," *Journal of Political Economy* 70, no. 5 (1962): 433–51. "Can Detroit Make
Cars That Baby Boomers Like?" *Business Week,* December
1, 1997, pp. 134–41.

6. "Is It Bold and New, Or Just Tried and True?" *New
York Times,* July 16, 2000, p. 3-1.

7. *Automotive News Market Data Book: 2001* (Detroit:
Marketing Services, Inc., 2001); J. Kwoka, "The Sales and
Competitive Effects of Styling and Advertising Practices in
the U.S. Automobile Industry," *Review of Economics and
Statistics* 75, no. 4 (November 1993): 649–56.

8. Kwoka.

9. An allegation along these lines was first made by J.
Menge, "Style Change Costs as a Market Weapon," *Quarterly
Journal of Economics* 76, no. 4 (1962): 632–47. This story is

consistent with economic theories that now stress how dominant firms may raise their rivals' costs to their own advantage.

10. Details are provided in J. Kwoka, "Market Power and Market Change in the U.S. Automobile Industry," *Journal of Industrial Economics* 32, no. 4 (June 1984): 509–22.

11. *The Harbour Report: A Decade Later* (Detroit: Harbour and Associates, 1990).

12. Harold Sperlich, head of Chrysler's automotive operations, quoted in "Why GM Needs Toyota," *New York Times,* February 16, 1983, p. D-1.

13. *Ward's Automotive Yearbook* 1994 (Southfield, MI: Ward's Communications, 1994), p. 20. A good analysis of these regulations can be found in R. Crandall et al., *Regulating the Automobile* (Washington, DC: Brookings Institution, 1986).

14. This proceeding is further described in "The Internationalization of the Automobile Industry and Its Effects on the U.S. Automobile Industry," International Trade Commission Publication V12, June 1985, pp. 8–10.

15. R. Feenstra, "Voluntary Export Restraint in U.S. Autos, 1980–81," in *The Structure and Evolution of Recent U.S. Trade Policy,* R. Baldwin and A. Kruger, eds. (Chicago: University of Chicago Press, 1984), chap. 14.

16. Department of Commerce, "The U.S. Automobile Industry, 1984," December 1985, p. 8.

17. Motor Vehicle Manufacturers Association (Detroit). *World Motor Vehicle Data,* 1989 edition.

18. See "X-cars Stealing GM's Big-Car Sales," *Automotive News,* November 1979. Also, U.S. Senate Banking Committee, "Findings of the Chrysler Corporation Loan Guarantee Board," (Washington, DC: Government Printing Office, 1980), p. 163.

19. *Consumer Reports*, April 1981, p. 225.

20. *The Harbour Report: A Decade Later.*

21. "Another Turn at the Wheel," *The Economist* (March 2, 1985): 2.

22. This study, "Productivity and Comparative Cost Advantages: Some Estimates for Major Automotive Producers" by Harbour and Associates, Inc., was widely disseminated in 1980 and relied on by the U.S. auto companies.

23. "Foreign Investment: Growing Japanese Presence in the U.S. Auto Industry," General Accounting Office, March 1988, p. 52.

24. For further description of the Toyota production system, see "Why Toyota Keeps Getting Better and Better and Better," *Fortune,* November 19, 1990, p. 66; also, "How Toyota Defies Gravity," *Fortune,* December 8, 1997, p. 100.

25. "Ford Studied Possible Bid for Chrysler, Then Declined," *Wall Street Journal,* August 11, 1991, p. A-3.

26. "General Motors: What Went Wrong," *Business Week,* March 16, 1987, p. 102.

27. "An Unexpected Flop," *National Journal,* April 12, 1986. The antitrust aspects of this joint venture are described

in J. Kwoka, "International Joint Venture: General Motors and Toyota," in *The Antitrust Revolution*, 2d ed., J. Kwoka and L. White, eds. (New York: HarperCollins, 1994), pp. 46–75.

28. *The Harbour Report: A Decade Later.*

29. J. Womack, D. Jones, and D. Roos, *The Machine That Changed the World* (New York: Maxwell Macmillan International, 1990), p. 85. Details from this study also revealed the cost implications of differences in production philosophies. Japanese plants required 25 percent less floor space, two-thirds less repair area, and held less than one-tenth the inventory of U.S. companies' plants.

30. Cited in "The Americanization of Honda," *Business Week,* April 25, 1988, p. 92. Other studies have shown similar differentials.

31. The U.S. companies in fact filed a complaint against Japanese minivan producers in the early 1990s, but the International Trade Commission concluded that the U.S. industry had not been injured by them. ITC Investigation No. 731-TA-522, 1992.

32. "Slowing Minivan Sales Worry Struggling DCX," *Automotive News,* March 12, 2001, p. 3.

33. This model assumes there is a maximum number of potential purchasers of a product, based on the match between its characteristics and customers' needs. Sales of a newly introduced product initially grow rapidly toward that maximum, but as the number of new potential customers shrinks, sales slow. For a study of the role of product cycles in minivans, see J. Kwoka, "Altering the Product Life Cycle of Consumer Durables: The Case of Minivans," *Managerial and Decision Economics* 17, no. 1 (January/February 1996): 17–25.

34. "Rollback: America's Love Affair with Sport Utilities Is Now Cooling Off," *Wall Street Journal,* May 30, 2001, p. A-1.

35. "Are Today's Cars More Reliable?" *Consumer Reports,* April 2001, p. 12. As before, the Japanese were improving their products steadily as well, thereby maintaining a significant advantage over Big 3 quality.

36. "GM: 'Out with the Olds' Is Just the Start," *Business Week,* December 25, 2000, p. 57.

37. "Ford: Why It's Worse Than You Think," *Business Week,* June 25, 2001, pp. 80–87.

38. "Daimler-Chrysler Merger to Produce $3 Billion in Savings, Revenue Gains Within 3 to 5 Years," *Wall Street Journal,* May 8, 1998, p. A-1.

39. Automotive News *Market Data Book,* various issues.

40. *Consumer Reports,* June 1990, p. 410.

41. For discussions of these technologies, see "A Driving Force Behind Tomorrow's Greener Cars," *Business Week,* November 27, 2000, p. 34–35; also, "Hybrids Are Heading for Main Street," *Business Week,* July 9, 2001, p. 34.

42. This discussion is adapted from J. Kwoka, "Automobiles: The Old Economy Collides with the New," *Review of*

*Industrial Organization* 19, no. 1 (August 2001): 55–69.
    43. A. Sloan, *My Years with General Motors* (Doubleday: New York), p. 438.

## Selected Readings

Crandall, Robert W. *Regulating the Automobile.* Washington, DC: Brookings Institution, 1986. A comprehensive and careful evaluation of the impact of safety, emissions, and fuel economy regulation on the auto industry through the early 1980s.

Cusumano, Michael, and Nobeoka Kentaro. *Thinking Beyond Lean.* New York: Simon and Schuster, 1998. A description of new methods of product development in autos—especially Toyota's—that go beyond production-oriented "lean" principles.

Halberstam, David. *The Reckoning.* New York: William Morrow, 1986. A very readable account of the evolution, strengths, and weaknesses of the U.S. and Japanese auto industries from the vantage points of two major firms, Ford and Nissan.

Kwoka, John. "International Joint Venture: General Motors and Toyota." In *The Antitrust Revolution,* J. Kwoka and L. White, eds. New York: HarperCollins, 1994. An analysis of the antitrust issues raised by this joint venture, focusing on pricing and on efficiencies.

White, Lawrence. *The U.S. Automobile Industry Since 1945.* Cambridge, MA: Harvard University Press, 1971. A now classic study that examines the structure, conduct, and performance of the industry in the relatively stable period from World War II to 1970.

Winston, Clifford. *Blind Intersection.* Washington, DC: Brookings Institution, 1987. A collection of economic studies of auto market demand, costs and cost differentials with Japan, the effects of import restraints, and safety regulation.

Womack, James, Daniel Jones, and Daniel Roos. *The Machine That Changed the World.* Rawson, 1990. Provides data and insight on the relative productivity, costs, and quality of U.S., Japanese, transplant, and European auto production.

# 2

# Beer

## Causes of Structural Change

*Douglas F. Greer*

A few years ago *Consumer Reports* sponsored blind taste tests in which a panel of seventeen knowledgeable tasters (ranging from brewmasters to brewing students) graded dozens of brands of beer on thirty beer qualities.[1] Among the sixteen brands of regular American lager tested (including Budweiser, Michelob, and Miller Genuine Draft), the top-ranked beer was the *least* expensive, Old Milwaukee. The second-ranked beer, Stroh's, was also relatively cheap. The two brands judged poorest in this class were pricey—Miller Genuine Draft ("cooked-vegetable off-flavor") and Rolling Rock ("sulfury off-flavor"). Overall, the prices of these sixteen American lagers and their taste-test quality ratings were not significantly correlated. Paying more does not necessarily get you more when it comes to beer.

Contributing to this striking result is the fact that all regular American lagers taste very much alike, at least to nonexpert ordinary quaffers. Numerous blind taste tests confirm this. Hence, loyal "Bud" drinkers typically cannot correctly identify their brand over other regular lagers without the aid of that familiar Budweiser label.[2]

How can it be, then, that Anheuser-Busch (A-B), propelled by Budweiser, has grown from only 6 percent of the national market in 1950 to almost 50 percent in 2000? Why have many equal or bet-

ter tasting "regional" brands of lager beer with lower prices than Bud (e.g., Stroh's, Rainier, Schmidt, Blitz-Weinhard, Genesee, Old Style, Olympia, Hamm's, Pearl, Blatz, Grain Belt, Lone Star, and Narragansett) dwindled or totally disappeared from the scene? In economic terms, beer market concentration has risen immensely for reasons that are not obvious. There is a lot more to selling beer than brewing one that tastes good and is priced competitively.

This chapter explores the massive structural changes that the beer industry has experienced over the past five decades—their nature and their causes. Several other topics will also attract our attention. We will study distribution, for instance, but structural change will occupy center stage. Huge structural transformations over relatively brief periods occur rarely; hence, we will take advantage of the opportunity to study such a transformation in the beer industry.

### History and Background

#### Product Identification

Beer is a malt beverage. Indeed, it is *the* malt beverage. Its production relies on four main ingredients—malted barley grain, hops, yeast, and water.

Processing them has become rather standardized. Malting germinates the grains of barley, thereby developing enzymes that convert starch to sugar. Adding the malt to water, flavoring the resulting "mash" with hops (and with rice or corn, frequently, too), and then processing this mix yields "wort," which is brewed by cooking. Filtering follows. Yeast is then added for the fermentation stages. Several subsequent steps of filtration, carbonation, and storage are taken toward the end of production. Finally, regular canned and bottled beers are pasteurized to extend their shelf life, whereas so-called draft beers, like Coors and Miller Genuine Draft, rely on other means to curb perishability, such as constant cold storage throughout all stages of distribution.

Could soda pop be considered a close substitute for beer, close enough to be important economically? In 1986, the Coca-Cola Company argued that all beverages, including beer and even tap water, should be lumped together in one enormous product market for purposes of economic analysis. Coca-Cola was making this argument in defense of its proposed acquisition of the Dr Pepper Company. Shortly before Coca-Cola made its bid for Dr Pepper, its arch rival, PepsiCo, had announced its intention of acquiring 7-Up. If Coca-Cola and Pepsi had been allowed to buy Dr Pepper and 7-Up, together they would have gained nearly 80 percent of all carbonated soft drink sales through merger, a share offensive to U.S. antitrust law. Hence, Coca-Cola was arguing for an "all beverage" market in an attempt to reduce considerably the market shares involved in these proposed soda pop mergers. To support its contention, Coca-Cola argued that all beverages quench thirst and that the "human stomach can consume only a finite amount of liquid in any given period of time." Although these contentions were true, the federal district court considering the case rejected Coca-Cola's proposal in favor of a narrower market definition that included only carbonated soft drinks and excluded beer.

We agree with the court. Comparing the two products, we find distinct product characteristics, unique production facilities, many different consumers, distinct prices, and specialized vendors. It is not surprising, then, that the cross-elasticity of demand between beer and soda pop seems to be close to zero (meaning that changes in the price of one beverage have relatively little impact on the quantity of the other demanded). Moreover, estimates of the "own" price elasticity of demand for beer tend to be inelastic—in the range of 0.7 to 0.9. Price increases reduce the amount people wish to drink, but not sharply. This suggests more broadly that, in general, there are no really close substitutes for beer.[3]

Television ads for beer disclose that beer is not equally popular among all people. Senior citizens promote denture adhesives over the airwaves but not Bud. Matronly women endorse the "suds" in a box of Tide but not those in a can of Coors. Marketing studies confirm what you might suspect from these observations. Slightly less than half of the adult population in America drinks any beer at all.[4] Indeed, only 13 percent of the total adult population in America consumes over 80 percent of all beer produced. Those comprising this 13 percent are "heavy users" who drink more than five beers a week. And these heavy users are predominantly young males.

Demographics thus drive trends in aggregate beer demand. Figure 2.1 shows the age composition of the adult population over the last five decades. The population of young adults, aged 21 to 34, was rather constant during the 1950s and early 1960s. It then grew rapidly during the late 1960s through the mid-1980s. This was the "baby boom" generation. Those born just after World War II

## Figure 2.1    Age Composition of the U.S. Adult Population

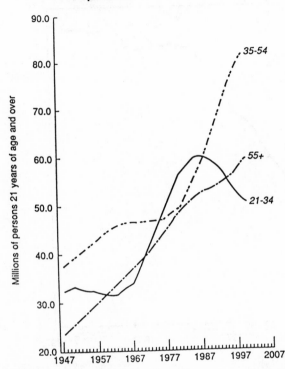

*Sources:* R.S. Weinberg & Associates, Brewing Industry Research Program.

reached drinking age in the mid-1960s, and those born during the 1950s began seriously consuming alcoholic beverages in the 1970s. Finally, during the 1980s, these people began to populate the 35 to 54 age bracket, causing an explosion there just as their aging deflated the 21 to 34 bracket.

The baby boomers thus moved through the population profile like a pig through a python—with a bulge, and with results for beer consumption easily seen in Figure 2.2. Total beer consumption remained rather stable at about 85 million barrels during the 1950s. Then the 1960s and 1970s witnessed brisk growth in consumption as the baby boomers began to imbibe. By the

1980s, demand leveled off at about 190 million barrels annually. At the turn of the century, sales were still not more than 200 million barrels, even though the babies of the baby boomers had reached drinking age.

### Geographic Markets

The product market is only part of the story. The field of competition among brewers may be further delineated geographically. Now, all the major brands are advertised, distributed, and sold nationally (i.e., Budweiser, Bud Light, Coors, and so on). This gives a national orientation to the industry that warrants the substantial attention we will be giving to nationwide statistics.

On the other hand, developments at the regional level are also of interest. As already noted, regional brands have played a major role in the industry in the past. Some, like Rainier (Washington), Old Style (Wisconsin), and Genesee (New York), remain notable today. Hundreds of craft brewers and microbrewers likewise operate regionally rather than nationally. More generally, the costs of transporting beer tend to be high relative to the value of the product because beer is, after all, mainly water. As a result, the major brewers have multiple production facilities spread throughout the country. Anheuser-Busch, for example, had twelve breweries in 2000 located in places like Houston, Los Angeles, and Newark, as well as in St. Louis, where A-B is headquartered.

### Structure: Concentration

We will consider four main elements of the beer industry's structure. Of these, concentration is the most intriguing because it has changed dramatically during recent decades. Once we trace these changes and the mergers that may have contrib-

Figure 2.2    **U.S. Total Malt Beverage Shipments, 1947–1996** (excluding exports, including imports)

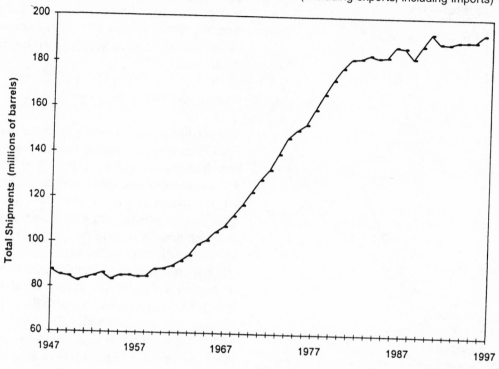

*Sources:* U.S. Brewers Association, *Brewers Almanac 1976; 1990 Beer Industry Update; 1996 Beer Industry Update.*
*Note:* Totals exclude nonalcoholic beers.

uted to them, we will consider barriers to entry in connection with economies of scale and then tackle product differentiation.

### National Market Concentration

In the late 1940s, most beer was supplied by small firms that never shipped to more than a few neighboring states. Now most beer is supplied by a few giant firms that ship throughout the nation. In 1947 there were over 400 independent companies operating a total of 465 separate plants (not counting microbreweries of less than 10,000-barrel capacity). Now just four companies operate 24 breweries

that together have an annual capacity exceeding 190 million barrels, enough to supply the consumption of all domestic beer (excluding imports).[5]

When translated into national concentration ratios, as shown in Table 2.1, the industry's transformation appears striking. The combined share of sales of the two largest firms rose from 8.8 percent in 1947, to 29.9 percent in 1970, and to 68.2 percent in 2000, an eightfold increase since World War II. Four-firm concentration jumped from 17.1 percent to 85.2 percent over these years. Thus a tightly knit oligopoly has emerged from what once could be considered a rather diffuse collection of relatively small brewers.

Table 2.1

**Two- and Four-Firm National Concentration Ratios in the Beer Industry, Selected Years, 1947–1996**

| Year | Two largest | Four largest |
|------|-------------|--------------|
| 1947 | 8.8 | 17.1 |
| 1950 | 11.9 | 22.0 |
| 1960 | 16.0 | 27.0 |
| 1970 | 29.9 | 44.2 |
| 1980 | 49.5 | 66.4 |
| 1990 | 65.2 | 83.0 |
| 2000 | 68.9 | 85.2 |

*Sources:* R.S. Weinberg and Associates, St. Louis, MO, consultants; *Beer Industry Update,* various years.

Table 2.2

**National Market Shares of the Present Top-Three Brewers, Selected Years** (percent)

| Year | Anheuser-Busch | Miller | Coors |
|------|----------------|--------|-------|
| 1947 | 4.1 | 0.9 | 0.5 |
| 1950 | 5.8 | 2.5 | 0.8 |
| 1960 | 9.6 | 2.7 | 2.2 |
| 1970 | 17.8 | 4.1 | 5.8 |
| 1980 | 28.4 | 21.1 | 7.8 |
| 1990 | 43.4 | 21.8 | 9.7 |
| 2000 | 48.2 | 20.7 | 11.1 |

*Sources:* R.S. Weinberg & Associates; *1995 Beer Industry Update; 1997 Beer Industry Update; 2001 Beer Industry Update.*

Table 2.2 illustrates some variability among the firms ranking in the very top. It shows the national market shares of the industry's three leading firms as of 2000 looking backward over selected years to 1947. Anheuser-Busch, producer of Budweiser, has enjoyed first place in the rankings since 1957 and has experienced the greatest growth. Now, with nearly 50 percent of the market, A-B is the dominant firm.

Miller, currently ranked second nationally, coasted along without much to distinguish it during the 1950s and 1960s. Thereafter, during the 1970s, Miller made a spectacular climb to 21.1 percent market share in 1980, a share that stabilized thereafter. Much of Miller's growth during the 1970s can be credited to the explosive popularity of Miller Lite.

Coors starts out especially small in Table 2.2 because its geographic spread was initially limited. Whereas Budweiser and Miller High Life were well established as national brands as early as 1950, Coors was confined to the western states as late as 1970. Now Coors has spread throughout the United States. Moreover, the sparkling achievements of its Coors Light brand have propelled the company (like a silver bullet) into third place behind Anheuser-Busch and Miller.

### *State and Regional Concentration*

Regional beers like Olympia, Lucky Lager, Blatz, and Falstaff at one time held top spots and large market shares in some states. They have now been thoroughly displaced by national brands. Moreover, regional concentration has risen substantially, so more than simple displacement has occurred.

Table 2.3 shows two-firm concentration ratios for several large states from 1960 to 2000. A comparison of these concentration ratios with those of Table 2.1 indicates that decades ago concentration was higher regionally than nationally. The 1960 two-firm ratios of Table 2.3 average 37.4 percent compared with the national figure of 16.0 percent for 1960. Thus, because regional concentration was ample to begin with, it could not have risen as much as national concentration has. Displacement has been at work. However, in every case Table 2.3 also shows that regional concentration has increased substantially, so the concentration trend cannot be dismissed blithely.

Table 2.3

**Concentration Ratios in Three Major States, Selected Years, 1960–2000**

| State | 1960 | 1981 | 2000 |
|---|---|---|---|
| California | | | |
| Top-two brewers | 30.6 | 66.2 | 62.7 |
| Texas | | | |
| Top-two brewers | 43.2 | 49.0 | 73.2 |
| Wisconsin | | | |
| Top-two brewers | 38.4 | 55.1 | 77.1 |

*Sources: Beer Statistics News; 1990 Beer Industry Update; 2001 Beer Industry Update; and industry sources.*

Anheuser-Busch is the chief beneficiary of this rising regional and state concentration. In 2000, A-B's market share exceeded 50 percent in two-thirds of all states for which data are available.[6]

## Structure: Mergers

Counting acquisitions of plants and brands as well as entire firms, we could tally more than 600 beer company mergers over the past five decades. These include Pabst-Olympia, Stroh-Schlitz, and most recently Pabst-Stroh.[7] By definition, merging among brewers reduces their number and increases concentration above what it would be otherwise. Hence, of all the possible causes of the trend toward fewer numbers and higher concentration, we should consider mergers first.

When we do, we find a paradox. Although brewing mergers have been voluminous, they have *not* contributed substantially to present-day concentration. This is because almost all the mergers have involved sharply shrinking brands and companies. For example, the latest combination of importance brought Pabst and Stroh together in 1999. During the fifteen years preceding their merger, each of these companies experienced massive declines in

their market shares and total annual shipments. Moreover, their sales were composed of many fading brands whose past troubles had provoked previous mergers—for example, Schlitz, Piels, Schaefer, Grain Belt, Rainier, Pabst Blue Ribbon, Blatz, and Lone Star. None of these previous mergers reversed the falling fortunes of these companies.

In contrast, today's top-three companies—Anheuser-Busch, Miller, and Coors—have not grown by merger but rather by internal expansion. They have created new brands rather than acquire them—brands like Miller Lite, Bud Light, Coors Light, Milwaukee's Best, and Genuine Draft. And their combined market shares constitute the high concentration now prevailing. Indeed, it could be said that the successes of these firms—especially Anheuser-Busch and Miller—contributed to the failures of the many companies that have sought shelter in mergers. So to a very large extent the intense merger activity in this industry has not been the cause of the concentration, but rather it has been symptomatic of larger, more sweeping forces that have created concentration more directly. The mergers, in other words, have been a by-product of deeper economic developments rather than an immediate cause. Hence much of the discussion that follows will attempt to analyze just what those developments have been.

## Structure: Economies of Scale and the Condition of Entry

Economies of scale could help to explain the concentration trend in beer. They may also influence the condition of entry into the industry.

Economies of scale are efficiencies associated with greater size, efficiencies that lower the per unit costs of production. That is to say, the long-run average cost curve falls as output capacity

Figure 2.3   **Economies of Scale in Brewing**

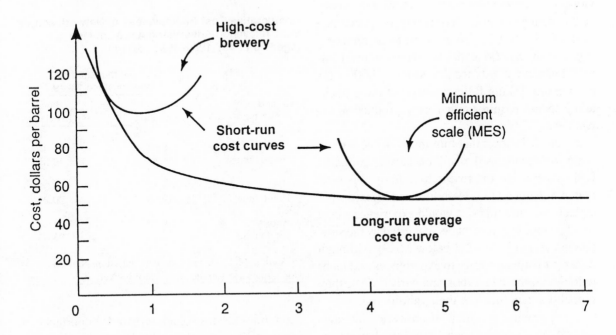

**Annual output, millions of barrels of beer**

expands if economies of scale are present.

Figure 2.3 shows two short-run average cost curves, together with the long-run average cost curve that would derive from the hypothetical collection of all possible short-run options. As brewery scale rises from 0.5 million barrels of annual output to 1.0 million barrels and to 4.5 million barrels, long-run average cost per barrel falls quickly at first and then more slowly. Beyond 4.5 million barrels of capacity, Figure 2.3 indicates there are no further gains in efficiency, so the long-run average cost curve levels off to become horizontal. The point at which economies end is called the *minimum efficient scale* (or MES). Figure 2.3 depicts economies as they might apply to a single plant. Multiplant economies are also possible.

*Plant Economies of Scale*

At the plant level, economies of scale can occur for a number of reasons:

1. *Specialization of labor*. As the number of workers multiplies with plant size, individual workers specialize, thereby becoming more productive.
2. *Specialization of machinery*. Small firms must often rely on multipurpose machinery.
3. *Increased dimensions of capital*. Pipes, tanks, vats, and other such equipment generate economies of scale because a doubling of their surface area more than doubles their capacity.

This last effect is the one that applies most obviously to brewing operations. However, appreciable plant economies also stem from specialized machinery. Bottling lines operate at amazing speeds—over 1,000 bottles filled per minute. Canning lines move at twice that speed—2,000 cans per minute. Taking full advantage of these packaging speeds requires rather large production capacities.

Figure 2.3 shows that minimum efficient plant scale in brewing is 4.5 million barrels annually. F.M. Scherer led the research yielding this estimate.[8] Scherer and his team further estimated that a plant one-third this size would experience a cost disadvantage of 5 percent (as suggested by the slow rise in costs in Figure 2.3 below MES). Although Scherer's estimates refer to experiences and technologies of the late 1960s and early 1970s, they probably retain much of their validity today.

The present population of breweries includes several that are well above 4.5 million barrels annual capacity—for example, Anheuser-Busch in St. Louis (14.5 million barrels), Miller in Albany, Georgia (10.3 million barrels), plus Coors in Golden, Colorado (20.0 million barrels). Still, one of Anheuser-Busch's newest breweries has an annual capacity of only 4.3 million barrels (in Fairfield, California), and the breweries of Stroh and Pabst, which averaged about 4.0 million barrels capacity, were efficient. Hence, the estimate of 4.5 million barrels for a minimum efficient scale plant seems reasonable.

## Multiplant Economies of Scale

Economies of scale at the firm level, associated with multiplant operations, might arise for beer from several possible sources—peak spreading, lot-size economies, and advertising. Of these, advertising is the most important source of multiplant

Table 2.4

**Comparative Cost Effectiveness of Network and Spot Television Advertising Aimed at Men (aged 18 to 49), 1980–1982** (dollars)

| Year and program type | Cost per thousand male viewers, aged 18–49 | |
| --- | --- | --- |
| | Network television | Spot television |
| 1980 | | |
| Sports | 8.71 | 15.34 |
| Prime time | 11.81 | 19.39 |
| 1981 | | |
| Sports | 9.19 | 19.35 |
| Prime time | 12.63 | 20.29 |
| 1982 | | |
| Sports | 9.70 | 21.54 |
| Prime time | 14.14 | 23.49 |

*Source*: McCann-Erickson data, based on Nielson television ratings and supplied to a major brewer.

economies because of advertising's importance to brewers. The advantages that large size imparts to a brewer's advertising potency come in several forms, as we will see in depth shortly. Regarding standard economies of scale in advertising, we may note that nationwide scope (which, as we have seen, entails multiplant operations) carries a cost advantage in television advertising over a more limited local or regional scope of operations.

In general, national network television advertising is substantially less costly than local spot television advertising. Estimates for coffee indicate that local spot advertising costs 10 to 40 percent more than national network advertising.[9] Estimates for beer run higher. The higher estimates arise apparently because beer drinkers occupy a narrower demographic spectrum than coffee drinkers. Viewer ratings for males aged eighteen to forty-nine are highest for sports and prime-time programming—in comparison to weekday daytime, late fringe, or evening network news.[10]

Hence, the data for sports and prime-time programs are most pertinent. Samples of these data are given in Table 2.4. Comparing the first and second columns of Table 2.4 shows spot television expense per male viewer to have been about 80 percent higher than network expense, on average, from 1980 to 1982.

One key factor explaining this is transaction costs: "Both spot and network advertising contracts involve negotiation, performance, and monitoring costs. For the spot alternative, many such contracts will be negotiated and monitored. In contrast, network advertising involves a single contract negotiation, requires substantially less monitoring, and may involve lower performance costs."[11]

Among brewers, Anheuser-Busch and Miller are in the best position to take advantage of these network economies, and they do. During 1994, for instance, Anheuser-Busch and Miller together spent nearly five times more on network television advertising than their next four largest rivals combined. This difference is disproportionately large relative to the market shares involved.[12] Moreover, the smaller brewers cannot easily overcome this spending advantage of A-B and Miller by investing more heavily in network advertising opportunities because of two impediments. First, the costs of network advertising opportunities are very high relative to the total advertising budgets of the smaller firms. Just one minute of advertising time on the Super Bowl, for instance, costs many millions of dollars. Second, exclusives have limited the access of small brewers to live sports events, the most important sponsorships for beer advertising. Mike Roarty, long-time senior vice-president of A-B, summarized the situation when he said that consolidation in the industry "happened as a direct result of the growth of [TV] that helped reenforce the national brands."[13]

Overall, then, multiplant economies of scale, especially those associated with national advertising, probably give a company with three or four plants substantial advantages over a firm with just one plant. This is the conclusion of Scherer, Beckenstein, Kaufer, and Murphy, who stated that the disadvantages of having just one large efficient plant as compared to several could be "severe," depending upon matters of "brand image."[14]

We can now compare these estimates of minimum efficient scale plant (4.5 million barrels) and minimum efficient-sized firm (four plants) with the scope of the market to see if the current concentration is "warranted" by economies of scale. Annual beer production nationally is roughly 180 million barrels. Hence a minimum efficient-sized plant of 4.5 million barrels would account for 2.5 percent of the national market, and a minimum efficient-sized firm with four efficient plants would account for 10 percent of the national market. By these numbers, scale efficiencies would justify two-firm concentration of 20 percent and four-firm concentration of 40 percent. Compared to the concentration observed in Table 2.1, these efficiencies would perhaps help to explain the concentration that occurred up to about 1965, when two-firm concentration was 20.1 and four-firm concentration was 34.4 percent. They cannot explain the concentration that has occurred since then. Two-firm concentration is now three times greater than what could be warranted by scale efficiencies.

These estimates of minimum efficient scales did not apply in 1950. Changes in production technology and the importance of TV advertising have changed the minimums. Hence, it would be more accurate to say that *changes* in minimum efficient scales have contributed substantially to changes in the industry's concentration, but huge fractions of actual concentration and changes therein remain to be explained by other factors.

Figure 2.4    **Classification of Beer Brands by Product and Price Segment**

| | Imports ($6.00) | Super-premium ($4.30) | Premium ($3.75) | Popular | |
|---|---|---|---|---|---|
| | | | | Low ($2.75) | Economy ($2.15) |
| Lager or Draft | Heineken<br>Molson Golden<br>Corona<br>Beck's | Michelob<br>Killian's Irish Red<br>Red Wolf<br>Rolling Rock | Budweiser<br>Miller Genuine Draft<br>Coors Original<br>Old Style | Old Milwaukee<br>Busch<br>Keystone<br>Stroh's | Schaefer<br>Milwaukee's Best<br>Blatz<br>Pabst |
| Light | Amstel Light<br>Molson Light<br>Corona Light | Michelob Light | Corona Light<br>Bud Light<br>Miller Lite | Keystone Light<br>Busch Light<br>Stroh's Light | Milwaukee's Best<br>Natural Light<br>Blatz Light |
| Ice | Molson Ice<br>Labatt Ice | | Bud Ice<br>Icehouse<br>Coors Arctic Ice | Old Milwaukee Ice<br>Pabst Ice<br>Busch Ice | |
| Malt Liquor | | Michelob Malt Liquor | Hurricane | Colt 45<br>Schlitz Malt Liquor<br>Olde English 800 | Magnum |
| Nonalcoholic | Excel<br>Clansthaler<br>Kaliber | | Sharp's<br>O'Doul's<br>Cutter | Old Milwaukee N.A. | |

*Source*: Various industry sources.
*Note*: Six-pack price is approximate average price for leading brands in 2000.

The impossibility of placing all the blame on economies of scale may be seen in a few added observations as well. First, top-notch efficiency has not saved a number of firms from failure. Schlitz is an example. Schlitz was so efficient that an industry report dated 1978 used Schlitz as its standard of efficiency.[15] Second, much of the efficiency that we have observed, especially at the firm level, relates more to image management than to production efficiency. Genuine production cost efficiencies typically favor large size because large firms can then cut price below levels sustainable by smaller, less efficient firms, thereby driving the smaller firms from the market. Economies in advertising or image maintenance act differently. They enable those possessing favorable images to *raise their prices* without losing, and perhaps even gaining, appreciable sales. Such image effects are best considered as an element of product differentiation, which is our next topic.

Finally, economies of scale of the magnitude experienced for the production of beer would normally pose a moderate barrier to new-firm entry. New entry is further thwarted by strong product differentiation. As a result, in the past five decades no one has entered the industry in a big way to challenge the industry's current leaders. Imports have grown, but they still account for only about 10 percent of total U.S. consumption and they occupy only the very highest price brackets. Similarly, brew pubs and other craft brewers have sprouted recently. But these instances of entry do not matter much economically from the industry's larger perspective. Independent craft brands accounted for only about 3 percent of total industry sales in 2000. Overall, then, Anheuser-Busch, Miller, and Coors need not be concerned that newcomers will significantly challenge their prominence.

## Structure: Product Differentiation

Product differentiation occurs when consumers perceive that a product differs from its competition on any physical or nonphysical characteristic, including price.[16] Any retailer's cooler case illustrates this definition with a dazzling variety of beer products and prices. Figure 2.4 tries to organize that variety on two dimensions, price level and basic product type (ignoring the craft brewers for the moment).

Brands fall into four main price categories—imports, super-premium, premium, and popular (with two subdivisions for these inexpensive brands). Historically, the largest of these categories was the popular category. In 1960, for example, over 76 percent of all beer sold in the U.S. was popular priced. By 2000, the overall share of popular-priced brands had dropped to only about 15 percent. The trend for premiums has been almost exactly the reverse. In 1960, premiums accounted for approximately 20 percent of total industry volume. Now, premium-priced beers, including premium-priced light beers and ice beers, account for over *60 percent* of total industry volume. (This means that consumers now willingly pay a lot more for brands that taste essentially the same as the much cheaper brands that previously led industry sales, a seemingly odd phenomenon that we will attempt to explain later with the concept of brand image.) The share of high-priced imports and super-premiums has also grown, though less sharply. In 1960, imports and super-premiums together accounted for about 1 percent of all consumption. By 2000, their combined share had risen to around 15 percent.[17]

As for the product types, American lagers have been the clear favorite historically and they still account for over 40 percent of all beer sold in the United States. In 1960, there were no light beers

whatever. But light beers have grown briskly since their introduction in the late 1960s to reach a rank just above lagers with about 43 percent of total volume. Most recently, during the 1980s and 1990s, lagers have also lost some ground to dry beers, ice beers, nonalcohol beers, and craft brews of various sorts. We will discuss these developments at length shortly; suffice it to say here that none of these latest developments could be considered truly revolutionary from the industry's overall perspective. Dry beers, ice beers, and nonalcohol beers had a spurt of interest, which has since dimished. Of all the recent developments, the craft brews, which are typically priced in the very highest ranges, are the most interesting and the most likely to succeed permanently, even though they accounted for no more than about 3 percent of all beer sales by volume in 2000. Hence, we shall focus on the craft brewers more intensively as we proceed.

To explore product differentiation more deeply and to introduce some economic theory, we may note that differentiation derives from three possible sources: (1) real product attributes, assuming full information and rational behavior on the part of buyers, (2) incomplete information, and (3) nonrational buyer behavior. Let's consider each in turn.

### Real Product Attributes

Assume for the moment that buyers are fully informed and act rationally. Variation in real product attributes may then be a source of product differentiation. The reason for this, as Lancaster stressed, is that people may buy a product or a brand not because of some sweeping subjective image of it, but rather because of the bundle of specific attributes the product or brand possesses.[18] Lancaster defined "attributes" as "those properties or characteristics of a product which are intrinsic to it, and are concretely observable, objectively measurable, and relevant to choice among alternatives." Product differentiation based on variations in such product attributes comes in two forms—horizontal differentiation and vertical differentiation.

*Horizontal differentiation* occurs when one brand contains more of some attributes but less of other attributes in comparison to another brand. When brands differ on strong and weak points in this manner, consumers having different preferences will select different brands if they have identical prices. Indeed, each consumer would be willing to pay extra to obtain his or her favorite brand.

In beer, one possible point of horizontal differentiation is flavor. Beers, or malt beverages generally, can vary considerably in their bitterness, ranging from something with considerable bite like Guinness Stout, to something rather airy like Coors Light. The second major flavor dimension is maltiness. Craft ales tend to be much more malty than light beers. When we consider both these flavor dimensions together, the result is seen in Figure 2.5. Craft ales like Samuel Adams Ale, Sierra Nevada Pale Ale, and Anchor Steam tend to be both rather bitter and quite malty. Craft lagers, like Samuel Adams Lager, Brooklyn Brand, Sterling, and Legacy are, on the whole, less flavorful. In contrast to the craft ales and craft lagers, regular lager beers (like Budweiser and Miller High Life) and light beers (like Bud Light and Coors Light) cluster in tight bunches toward the less bitter and less malty reaches of these flavor spectra.

Added points of horizontal differentiation among American beers concern alcohol and calorie content. In alcohol content most regular beers, like Bud and Coors, have 4.6 to 5.0 percent alcohol by volume while low-alcohol beers, like Sharps

and Cutter, have virtually none. In calorie content regular beers tend to have 140 to 150 calories per twelve ounces, while light beers have 105 to 115 calories per twelve ounces.

One implication of such objective horizontal differentiation is that the industry can be segmented into several "real" submarkets, as we have already seen in Figure 2.4. Another implication is that fully informed rational people would purchase different brands of beer according to their preferences in these respects, even if all beers were priced the same.

*Vertical differentiation* occurs when brands vary in real qualities such that all fully informed rational buyers would prefer a high-quality option to a low-quality option if both had identical prices. Among automobiles, for instance, all fully informed rational buyers would prefer a Mercedes-Benz over a Yugo if they had identical prices on their window stickers. Of course, in the real world, the prices of different quality brands do vary, as do buyer preferences and budgets. So, with low prices on economy models and high prices on premium versions, some people select the former while some choose the latter (without deviating from our current assumptions of full information and rationality). The price variations may match cost variations. However, firms often like to be strongly positioned in the premium levels of a market because they can be tremendously profitable. The higher price of the higher-quality product is often disproportionately high compared to the cost of the higher quality, yielding exceptionally high profit margins to the high-quality producers.

Is there vertical differentiation in beer? The answer is "yes" if we consider all beers, including the craft beers. The answer is "no" if we consider only the mass-produced lagers and light beers that compose the vast bulk of the American industry. Let's begin with "no."

Figure 2.5    **Horizontal Differentiation in Beer**

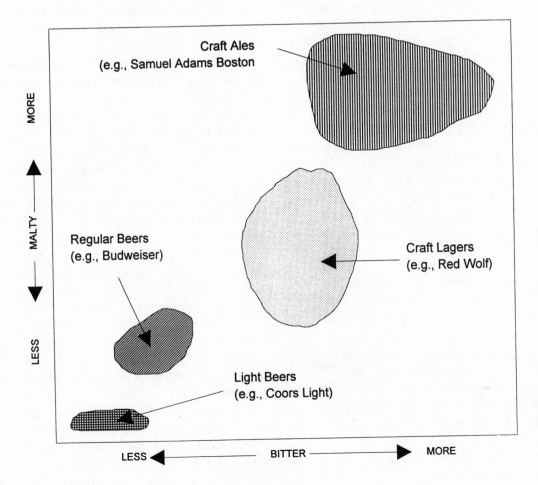

*Sources:* Adapted from *Consumer Reports*, June 1996, p. 15.

Among mass-produced lager and light beers there are some slight variations in quality across beers due to different qualities of barley, different degrees of care in the brewing process, and so on. However, these differences are extremely small among mass-produced beers. The cost of producing a super-premium beer like Michelob is only a few pennies a bottle more than the cost of producing a premium beer like Budweiser or a popular beer like Busch. For some companies, the cost differences between their different vertical qualities of product are apparently no more than a fraction of a penny per bottle.[19] Claimed differences, like beechwood aging, do not in the end make much real difference for mainstream American beers. Regarding water, for instance, all brewers process their water to achieve purity—even Coors, which is famous for its Rocky Mountain spring water. In January 1979, shortly after announcing the purchase of land in Virginia for a potential new brewery outside of Colorado, William K. Coors, chairman of the company at the time, told a group of beer wholesalers meeting in San Diego that "you could make Coors from swamp water and it would be exactly the same."[20]

The answer for mainstream lagers and lights remains no even after considering the wide range of prices for super-premiums, premiums, and populars. The notion that price is a signal of quality in brewing is largely imaginary, a word appropriately derived from *image*. The *Consumer Reports* blind taste-test noted at the beginning of the chapter illustrates this.[21]

If price-level differences in mass-produced beer are not grounded in quality (genuine vertical differentiation), then where do they come from? They derive partly from history. Virtually all of the regional lager beers of the 1940s through the 1950s were popular priced, while only the national beers of those years—Budweiser, Miller High Life, Pabst, and Schlitz—were premium priced. So-called super-premiums did not exist except for imports.

The national beers charged higher premium prices back at mid-century, but not because of their higher-quality ingredients or their special recipes. Rather they charged premium prices to cover the higher transportation costs they incurred when shipping their brew nationwide from only one plant (located in St. Louis for Budweiser or in Milwaukee for each of the other national brands). To persuade beer drinkers that these premium prices were worth paying, the national brands had to convince them that these products were somehow premium products. The premium quality was not conveyed in premium taste, at least not genuinely. As Henry King, former chief of the U.S. Brewers' Association, put it, "Most people can't distinguish the taste of one beer from another. Beer is a psychological choice more than anything else."[22]

The premium was therefore grounded on image and has been ever since. Miller's former president, William Howell, acknowledged this when he said, "The image you create very definitely establishes the product in the consumer's mind."[23] Hence, there is a "premium" image. After the national brewers built numerous plants around the country, their transportation costs fell. Their prices remained at premium levels, however, at least for a while. The premium prices enhanced profits and paid the costs of the immense advertising that the national brewers poured into maintaining their premium images. Today, Budweiser is the only original "national" brand that retains its premium image and premium prices. Pabst, Schlitz, and Miller High Life have all been repriced downward to the "popular" category, not as a result of any genuine quality changes, but rather as a result of image problems that produced falling sales volumes.

The importance of image to the price categories is illustrated by Lite. Miller first introduced Lite in 1973. Although it was not the first light beer, it was the first one to be mass marketed successfully. It contained less raw material, less alcohol, and less of everything else except water and packaging, thereby costing less to produce than regular beer. From the very start, however, Miller priced Lite as a premium beer rather than as a popularly priced beer. Other brewers followed with their high-priced lights. During the late 1970s, then, industry insiders said the cost of producing light beer was $2 to $3 a barrel less than the cost of producing regular lager beer and yet, like Miller, most sold for about $2.75 more.[24]

If the foregoing evidence answers the vertical

differentiation question with no, what prompted the companion yes answer? The craft brews. They are a source of genuine vertical differentiation. Their relatively high prices are, indeed, based on higher costs for higher quality ingredients and greater care in the brewing process, at least to some extent.

There are two main classes of craft beer. The first class is composed of brands like Anchor Steam, Full Sail Amber, Geary's Pale Ale, and Sierra Nevada Pale Ale, which are brewed in relatively small breweries and typically distributed to limited regional markets. (Oregon, Washington, and Maine are states where craft brews have been especially popular, approaching 10 percent of total beer volume sold in those states.) We shall call these craft regionals, not to be confused with the regular-beer regionals. The second class of craft beers is composed of brands that are brewed chiefly by fairly large breweries under contract to the companies that own the brand names. Samuel Adams and Pete's Wicked brands, are the main examples of this class. Their beer is produced by other brewers under contract (although Samuel Adams does have a tiny token brewery in Boston). Apart from the brewing process itself, these contract brewers typically handle all other aspects of their business, including recipe specifications, advertising, marketing, distribution, and even purchase of ingredients. In 2000, contract brewers sold 1.4 million barrels of brew, while craft regionals sold 3.0 million barrels.[25] (Strictly speaking, a micro brewery operates a plant producing less than 15,000 bbls. per year and a brewpub is a restaurant-brewery that sells most of its beer on-site. Together, these two types sold 1.5 million barrels in 2000.)

Figure 2.6 compares the costs of the craft brews with those of mass-produced premium lager beers in 1996. The ingredients of craft brews are 60 percent more costly than the ingredients of regular beer.

However, the absolute cost per six-pack is only about 10 cents greater, which is nowhere near enough to account for the huge differences in average final prices—$6.44 and $6.52 for the craft beers versus $4.01 for regular premium beer. The costs of packaging craft beers are likewise somewhat higher, but again not strikingly so. At brewer level (disregarding the huge differences in distributor and retailer markups), the largest cost differences relate to labor and production costs, advertising and marketing costs, and brewer profit margin per six-pack. Regional craft brewers have the highest costs of labor and production ($1.06 per six-pack). Given the importance of economies of scale, this is not surprising. Contract craft brewers have labor and production costs that match those of regular beers because the contracting gives them access to large efficient breweries. But their advertising, marketing, and management costs are enormous compared to the others ($1.35 per six-pack versus $.54 and $.33). Finally, brewer profit margins are much higher for both classes of craft beer compared to regular mass-produced beer.

In sum, the craft beers have some costs that are indicative of truly superior quality compared to regular beers—ingredients especially. Still, image is obviously at work as well. The high prices of craft beers are not closely connected to the quality-related costs. This is especially apparent when one craft beer is compared with another. The Spearman rank correlation between price and quality ranking in the *Consumer Reports'* blind taste-test of seventeen different craft ales is −.370, meaning that low-priced craft ales tended to rank *above* high-priced craft ales, on average, in the tasting panel's preference.

### Incomplete Information

When consumers have less than complete information, which is typical, differentiation need not,

Figure 2.6   **Cost Breakdown for Mass-Produced Beer and Two Kinds of Craft Beer**

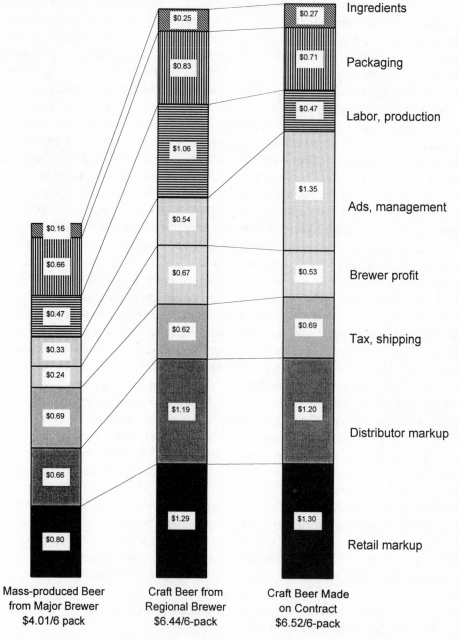

*Source:* Adapted from *Consumer Reports*, June 1996, p. 11 (based on data from R.S. Weinberg and Associates). See also *Beer Marketer's Insights*, November 27, 1995, pp. 2–3.

as we have just seen, be grounded on variations in objective product attributes. The main information deficiency concerning beer relates to quality. In such situations consumers often rely on cues to determine what they perceive to be the best buy. Although consumers may be acting rationally in relying on such cues, they may nevertheless be making poor choices. The main quality cues that beer drinkers rely on are price, seller's market position, and advertising.

Consumers use price level as an index of quality (even when they cannot taste any difference between brands, partly because they cannot taste any difference). J.D. McConnell demonstrated this in a controlled experiment he conducted on beer taste perceptions during the late 1960s. He made twenty-four home deliveries of six-packs of beer over two months to a large sample of beer drinkers. All the beer was identical in brand and brewery for the entire study, so absolutely no quality differences in fact existed. The consumers did not know this, however. They were kept uninformed because all the regular labels were removed. New labels that displayed neutral consonants from the middle of the alphabet were substituted—$P$, $L$, and $M$—with each used twice in each six-pack. The three newly labeled beers were said to be priced at $.99, $1.20, and $1.30 per six-pack, which corresponded to popular, premium, and super-premium price levels in those days. Asked to drink and assess the beers over the twenty-four deliveries, respondents rated the "high-priced" beer higher in quality than the other two beers by a wide margin. One drinker said of the brand he thought was cheap, "I could never finish a bottle."[26] Price can thus be a convincing cue.

Seller's market position, another cue poorly informed buyers rely on, is often exploited by sellers in general when they advertise "We're Number One." The uninformed buyer may assume (or

hope) that most other buyers are well informed about quality. Quick deduction then yields the conclusion that those other buyers have acted on their presumed knowledge by (1) bestowing large market shares and longevity on those sellers who offer good quality for the money, and (2) penalizing sellers of inferior quality by giving them small market shares and brief life spans. In a word, market position reflects reputation. Of course, the ignorant consumer's key assumption is that others are well informed. In fact, however, those others may likewise be ignorant and likewise acting on a false assumption that others are informed. The result would then be reputation levitation by a bandwagon effect.

When Budweiser claims that it is the King of Beers, it is obviously encouraging consumers to cue on market position. Other examples in beer relate to first-mover advantages—the good reputation a brand may have by being first in some manner. Miller's Lite beer was the pioneering light beer in the 1970s. It created the light category. And with the expansion of light beer, sales rivals followed with their light beers and vigorously promoted them. Yet Miller Lite continued to lead all rivals in the light category for two decades (capturing 40 percent of the segment in 1988, for instance). Experimental studies suggest that first-mover advantages often stem from consumer biases that develop as they gain quality information through experience. When qualities are ambiguous, as they apparently are in beer, the consumer's

[t]rial of the pioneer has an important role in the formation of preferences for all such brands. All are compared to the pioneer, the ideal is perceived as close to it, and the pioneer is perceived as prototypical—representative yet completely distinct. In this situation the pioneer occupies a favorable perceptual position that is difficult to imitate and costly to compete against, yielding a powerful competitive advantage.[27]

Given that incomplete information generates first-mover advantages, is it any wonder that Anheuser-Busch and Miller try hard to create new product segments—dry beer, super-premium dry, bottled draft, ice beer, and so on—in hopes of being perceived as pioneers if some segment sells well?

The third main cue that beer drinkers rely on in lieu of full information is, of course, advertising. For many years Coors captured huge market shares in the West, becoming at one point California's leading beer, all without much advertising. It had an amazing mystique. That was quite unusual, however, and Coors has long since reverted to the industry norm of relying on heavy advertising to convey a quality message.

### Nonrational Behavior

Brewer advertising does more than inform. It persuades. It builds images of pleasure, of belonging, and of other psychological benefits that can affect perceptions of quality in nonrational, subjective ways. For example, Jacoby, Olsen, and Haddock conducted an interesting experiment in which their subjects first tasted beers without labels and then with labels. The researchers found that adding the brand label to the "ultra premium" beer raised its average quality rating with subjects 24 percent, while brand identification of the "regional inexpensive" beer lowered its average rating 30 percent.[28]

Theories of product differentiation based on product attributes and information imperfections, as just discussed, are incomplete because they assume buyer "rationality" in the traditional economic sense. They focus on the functional needs of buyers to the neglect of more subjective, symbolic, and experiential needs:

*Functional needs* are those that motivate problem-solving product selections, based on objective at-

tributes such as fuel economy, nutrition requirements, and convenience.

*Symbolic needs* are desires for products that fulfill internally generated needs of self-enhancement, role position, prestige, group membership, or ego identification.

*Experiential needs* are desires for products that provide sensory pleasure, variety, or cognitive stimulation.[29]

On some occasions, people may perceive beer as meeting only functional needs (e.g., quenching thirst of someone who has mowed the lawn on a hot day). Inexpensive or unadvertised brands like Olympia, Schaefer, and Blatz fit this description. Brewers give other brands images of fulfilling symbolic needs. The advertising of these brands lacks information but brims with image-building expressions and scenes such as "This Bud's for You," or "The Night Belongs to Michelob," (August Busch IV pushed the Budweiser frog campaign because he thought it would give the beer a "hip" image.[30]) Finally, the existence of experiential needs explains why some beers, especially expensive ones, become faddish. An example of this is Corona, a Mexican import that had phenomenal success during the 1980s. The explosive popularity of craft beers can also be explained by experiential needs. Surveys show that even the most loyal craft beer drinkers consume only two-thirds of their beer in craft brands.[31]

Thus advertising, persuasive advertising in particular, has become extremely important to the beer business. Apart from the symbolic and experiential needs that certain brands can be portrayed as satisfying, advertising is influential in beer for other reasons also. Beer is a relatively inexpensive perishable "convenience good" as opposed to an expensive durable "shopping good" (like refrigerators), so consumers are less budget conscious and less motivated to collect objective information about beer than they would be otherwise.[32] Moreover, the persuasive effect of advertising is especially powerful when there is an interaction between the advertising and the consumer's experience, something that seems true of beer. The message and the trial interact to affect behavior.[33]

## Summary of Structure

The beer industry has experienced immense transformation. Concentration has risen dramatically at all geographic levels. Two companies of long-time national standing have been especially successful—Anheuser-Busch and Miller. They have more than displaced the regional brews that once held sway, except for Coors, which has expanded from its regional origins to rank third nationally. None of these three has grown appreciably by merger. Rather than contribute to concentration in this industry, mergers have served as a salvage mechanism, a refuge for failing brands and companies. Changes in economies of scale at plant and firm levels have contributed to the rising concentration among the large nationals and the declining conditions among the smaller noncraft regionals. However, economies of scale contribute no more than a partial explanation, and most of the multiplant economies observed relate to image-building efforts. This finding brought us to product differentiation, which, as we have seen, can be based on real product attributes varying horizontally and vertically, incomplete information among buyers, or nonrational subjective impulses driven by symbolic or experiential needs.

## Conduct

*Conduct* identifies what firms do and how they behave. In this section we will survey brewer pricing, advertising, product variation, and distribution. In the course of our survey we will highlight behaviors that have contributed to the industry's concentration. When discussing economies of scale, we saw that large size had certain advantages. Such economies could be called technical advantages because they derived chiefly from technical efficiencies. Now we will consider strategic behaviors that give large firms further advantages.

A firm possesses a strategic advantage when, by its conduct, it can enhance its market share and long-run profitability at the expense of existing or potential rivals. Such conduct may entail short-run sacrifices of profits, but sacrifices are often not necessary. Whatever the sacrifices of the firm conducting itself in this manner, strategic advantages mean that its rivals suffer from the behavior. Rivals experience falling revenues, or rising costs, or both simultaneously. With falling revenues or rising costs, their profits and viability shrink. This in turn implies long-term gains to those wielding strategic advantages.

Examples of strategic conduct from general industrial experience include limit pricing and preemptive capacity expansion. From an extensive questionnaire survey of American corporate executives, it has been found that strategies aimed at entry deterrence were "surprisingly important."[34] In particular, intensive advertising and product proliferation were the two strategies most often used. Anheuser-Busch and Miller fit this finding well. Structure causes conduct, and (conversely) conduct causes structure. The two-way causality can be confusing. The strategic behavior just mentioned illustrates variations in conduct affecting structure. In addition, we will consider cases of structure influencing conduct. For example, A-B's dominant market share promotes price leadership in the industry. Likewise, product differentiation in beer contributes to intensive advertising conduct.

## Price Conduct

As a general rule, Anheuser-Busch serves as price leader for the industry. Aside from selected situations when A-B discounts (to be discussed shortly), its aim is to set its prices as high as possible within the constraints of a growth objective. Of Anheuser-Busch's several brands, Budweiser, its biggest seller, is the key. Once the price of Bud has been set, the others fall into place depending on which rung of the price ladder they occupy (e.g., super-premium Michelob stands higher and popular-priced Busch sits lower). Most other brewers also key to Budweiser, usually matching Bud's price for premium and going somewhat above or below it for super-premiums and popular.

Anheuser-Busch's general tendency to exercise high-side price leadership is, according to the company, a "statesmanlike pricing position."[35] This "statesmanlike" leadership is made possible by the strong premium images of A-B's main brands as well as its colossal market share. Most of the industry's genuine price competition, therefore, centers on popular-priced brands. In the early 1980s, for instance, intense price competition broke out in the popular category among Stroh, Heileman, Pabst, and Miller, mainly because of Miller's efforts to market Milwaukee's Best and Meister Brau and because of Stroh's efforts to take Schaefer national and bolster the position of Old Milwaukee. Prices of populars fell so low at the time that some smaller brewers accused Miller of selling below cost.[36] A-B's role in this battle illustrates its premium power:

> Though it indirectly instigated the contest [by creating excess capacity at Miller and the others], Anheuser remains unscathed. "We can't play the price game," says A-B's president Dennis Long. It periodically discounts Budweiser. . . . But price competition in the premium and super-premium categories, where Anheuser has 94% of its sales, is rare—almost by definition.[37]

In other words, A-B simply cannot cut price vigorously and persistently without damaging its premium and super-premium images. As August Busch IV put it, price cutting on Budweiser is "the worst thing in the world for brand image."[38]

Anheuser-Busch's strategy includes cutting price to discipline rivals who are slow to follow its lead or to meet competition if that competition is gaining market share at A-B's expense or bringing A-B's growth below its desired level. It cuts *temporarily and selectively*. For example, when playing "statesman," Anheuser-Busch usually announces its price increases in January. After it did so in 1989, *Beer Marketer's Insights* routinely reported that "all [other brewers are] expected to follow."[39] They did not (not completely, anyway). Nine months later, in October, A-B announced aggressive discounts on its major brands, saying that "[Miller and Coors] have been following a policy of continuous and deep discounting for at least the past 18 months. . . . We cannot permit a further slowing in our volume trend."[40]

Anheuser-Busch's actual price cuts turned out to be milder than announced. It lowered prices in less than a third of its regional markets and made few changes where it was overwhelmingly dominant, such as in New England.[41] Thus, A-B targeted its discounts.

To the extent that Anheuser-Busch leads industry pricing upward, it does not pressure its rivals. It lifts an umbrella under which rivals may find some room to maneuver. From this one might conclude that pricing conduct has not contributed to A-B's burgeoning market share. But that would be incorrect. Miller and A-B have both priced strategically upon occasion to gain market share, especially in past decades when the (noncraft) regional brewers were more of a competitive force than they are today and when, correspondingly, A-B and Miller had lower market shares.

Their basic approach has been to target their price cuts in product type and geographic location so as to check their rivals while incurring minimum damage to themselves. In product type, A-B and Miller have introduced popular-priced brands—Busch, Natural Light, Meister Brau, and Milwaukee's Best—brands that can be sharply discounted for long periods without suffering any loss of premium image, because they have none. These can even be "fighting brands," as Milwaukee's Best seemed to be vis-à-vis Old Milwaukee. Because, historically, most of the regionals were strongest in popular-priced beers, instigations of vigorous price combat in this price category by A-B and Miller have probably contributed to the demise of the regular-beer regionals.

The industry's history is also replete with instances of price promotions targeted to particular regions. When used by large firms like A-B and Miller, this tactic may either be defensive or offensive, to preserve an eroding regional market share or to expand one greatly. Viewed in isolation, this phenomenon can be seen as the inevitable result of the competitive process. And in large part such competition is desirable and pro-competitive. But prolonged periods of fierce price combat in a particular region may sap the competitive vigor of firms operating entirely within the area, while having very little adverse effect on the overall strength of the national firm.

For example, during October 1953, after a costly union wage settlement that substantially increased labor costs, Anheuser-Busch attempted to lead a general price increase everywhere except Missouri (their base) and Wisconsin (the base of other large brewers). However, several regional brewers failed to follow. In an apparent attempt to discipline selected mavericks, A-B cut Budweiser's price in the St. Louis market from $2.93 a case to $2.35 a case, thereby eliminating the price premium A-B

maintained between Budweiser and popular-priced regional brands like Falstaff. Although failure to follow had not actually occurred inside St. Louis (because there had been no attempt by A-B to raise prices there), the maverick St. Louis brewers, Falstaff among them, sold beer outside St. Louis where price increases were attempted and ignored. Anheuser-Busch's motive may be inferred from President Busch's later testimony that A-B might not have "done anything" if these regional rivals had also raised their prices in October 1953. Anheuser-Busch's price cut in St. Louis lasted thirteen months, during the course of which its market share there jumped from 12.5 percent to 39.3 percent, a tripling at the expense of the mavericks. Note that this huge shift occurred even though the price of Budweiser *never fell below the prices of its rivals.* It fell only to *meet* their prices. Budweiser's premium image gave it the high ground in price warfare, so A-B could grab market share just by temporarily forgoing some profits rather than experiencing losses. Its rivals experienced the losses. In February 1955, A-B announced a 20 percent price increase. Not wanting to make the same mistake twice, the battered regionals raised their prices to the point of satisfying A-B.[42] In the end, A-B retained much of its market share gain, having 21.0 percent in July 1956, compared to 12.5 percent in December 1953.

**Advertising Conduct**

Given the importance of image, it is not surprising that advertising is crucial to brewer vitality. Grabowski's econometric analysis found a "statistically significant impact of advertising on market shares in both the short run and long run."[43] Kelton and Kelton concluded their econometric study of beer advertising by saying that "brand-shift probabilities are indeed sensitive to intra-industry advertising differentials." Moreover, they found that "Miller's advertising has exerted an especially significant effect on its transfer-purchase [brand-switching] probability and market share."[44]

You might suspect that advertising has contributed to the industry's concentration. That contribution has been made in two main ways: (1) the adverse forces of huge and escalating dollar outlays, and (2) the history of exclusives in live network television sports broadcasting.

### Advertising Expenditures

In general, consumer convenience goods get more advertising than other goods. By its nature, then, beer invites above-average amounts of advertising—just as do soda pop and breakfast cereal. There is more, however. Variations in industry advertising intensity are often associated with variations in industry concentration. Because beer has experienced enormous variations in concentration, it is appropriate to search for variations in advertising outlays that might be associated with these changes in concentration.

In general, a typical pattern of association between advertising intensity and concentration would display a positive relationship between them over a low-to-moderate range of concentration and a negative relationship between them over a moderate-to-high range of concentration.[45] In a positive range, movement from low to moderate concentration frequently causes the focus of competition to shift from price to nonprice efforts, thereby escalating advertising outlay. In the same positive range of association, higher advertising intensity may be causing higher concentration because of economies of scale in advertising or cost–price squeezes that force the weakest firms out of the industry. On the other hand, in the range of

negative association, very high concentration approaching monopoly levels may be expected to reduce advertising intensity as rivalry of all kinds weakens with some form of collusion or with one firm's achievement of dominance. Overall, the positive/negative pattern that emerges from cross-section studies of many industries yields a peak level of advertising intensity that varies but lies somewhere in the region of concentration reflecting moderate oligopoly (e.g., four-firm concentration ratios of 40 to 70 percent).[46]

The beer industry followed this typical positive/negative pattern from 1947 to 1970 but thereafter broke away as if on a rampage. Let's glance at events before 1970 and then explore what has happened since.

Beginning in 1947, when concentration in beer was low to moderate, advertising was just slightly above 3 percent of sales revenue. Promotion expense rose rapidly thereafter, as one firm and then another leapfrogged ad outlays relative to sales. The process of escalation was apparently aggravated by the advent of TV advertising, a decline in sales in taverns, the rise of package sales instead of tap sales, and the geographic expansion of many brewers. By the early 1960s, advertising relative to sales was near the 7 percent level, up 133 percent from what it was at the outset. Expenditures for packaging differentiation had also burgeoned. As a consequence, profits for all firms in the industry wilted and most smaller, weaker firms failed or merged.

The advertising of the large national brewers had greater potency in generating sales during the 1950s and 1960s than the advertising of the small regionals.[47] Exactly why the large nationals had the upper hand is unclear. However, their premium images, their large absolute outlays, and their ability to use cost-effective national network TV instead of higher-cost alternatives apparently helped.

In any case, the escalated advertising burden seems to have contributed to high concentration in the industry.

During the late 1960s, advertising outlays began to fall as concentration progressed to still higher levels. Relative to sales, outlays fell toward their 1947 origins, so by the early 1970s it appeared that the industry had traced the positive/negative pattern of advertising and concentration with uncanny precision. Leading the deescalation was top dog Anheuser-Busch, whose measured media advertising costs per barrel fell 23 percent between 1967 and 1970.[48]

After 1970, however, advertising outlays shot up once again. In constant (1987) dollars, industry advertising more than doubled over 1970 to 1988, rising from $325 million to $763 million. Industry outlays per barrel jumped from $2.69 to $4.58 (in constant 1987 dollars). Much of this explosion occurred during the 1970s, as reflected in William Coors's exclamation in 1978 that the major brewers have "gone berserk with advertising expenditures."[49]

Responsibility for the explosion appears in Figure 2.7. The vertical axis is a ratio indicating a firm's advertising intensity relative to all others in the industry. It is the firm's share of total industry advertising outlays divided by its share of industry sales. For example, a firm with 20 percent of the advertising and 20 percent of the market would have a ratio of 1.0. Equal shares of advertising and sales in this manner for all firms over time would place them all on the horizontal line of Figure 2.7 at 1.0. In fact, Figure 2.7 shows that some firms have been relatively aggressive, spending on advertising substantially more than what might be expected from their market shares. Miller's ratio soared above 1.0 during the early 1970s, signaling that Miller triggered the explosion by launching an especially aggressive advertising attack.

Anheuser-Busch responded defensively at first and then rather aggressively, maintaining an advertising-to-sales ratio well above the industry average during the 1980s. Those with ratios below 1.0 have been rather inhibited, spending proportionately less on advertising because of hesitant inclinations or tight budgets. Stroh and Heileman slipped below 1.0 after the early 1970s and then tumbled sharply during the 1980s. Coors presents a pattern of dramatic change. Until 1976, Coors relied on its mystique rather than on the media. Thereafter it joined Miller and A-B with stratospheric levels of advertising outlays.

What prompted Miller in the first place? It was acquired in 1969–1970 by Philip Morris Corporation, which immediately began marketing Miller's beers with the same skill and intensity that made it number one in cigarettes (Marlboro).[50] Estimates of Miller's media outlays leap 326 percent from $34.2 million in 1970 to $145.6 million in 1978 (in 1987 dollars). The money went mainly to introduce Lite and to reposition High Life. Both efforts were aimed at lifting Miller from its seventh-place ranking and 4.1 percent national market share at the time of acquisition. Miller successfully marketed Lite, using former athletes who argued over its attributes. High Life, on the other hand, had a "champagne of beers" image before 1970. This was attractive to upper-class people and women who were not heavy users. So Miller repositioned the brand. In the words of *Advertising Age*, Miller took High Life "out of the champagne bucket and put it into the lunch bucket without spilling a drop."[51] Miller's expenditures per barrel on High Life and Lite were 5 to 10 times those of Budweiser during the early 1970s. These outlays produced huge market share gains for Miller, from 4.1 percent in 1970 to 18.9 percent in 1978. The company rocketed to second place in the industry and began boasting that it would pass Anheuser-Busch.

Figure 2.7    **Ratio of Advertising Share to Market Share, 1970–1988**

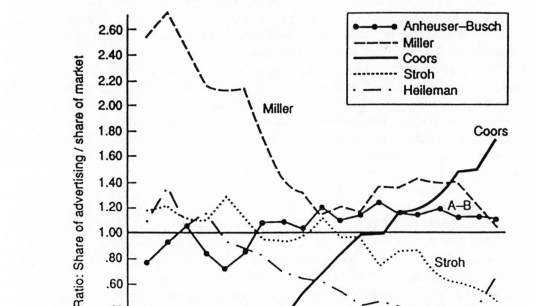

*Source:* Data supplied by R.S. Weinberg and Associates, Brewing Industry Research Program, 1990.
*Note:* 1.00 means percentage share of advertising outlay equals percentage share of industry sales.

Anheuser-Busch responded by doubling its outlays from $75.4 million to $153.8 million (in 1987 dollars). Advertising per barrel for Budweiser rose from $1.46 in 1975 to $2.20 in 1978 (1987 dollars). August A. Busch III, who had succeeded his father as CEO, challenged Miller in a *Business Week* interview: "Tell Miller to come right along, but tell them to bring lots of money." By 1985 A-B was sprinting ahead of Miller in the race for market share and in the boasting, too. Dennis Long, A-B's president at the time, claimed that A-B's success derived from its gigantic size in the mar-

keting arena: "Others just can't keep up with us when we move into a market. We have the ability to buy all."[52] In Figure 2.7, Miller's advertising/market share ratio falls after 1975 partly because of A-B's immense gains in advertising share.

Among the lesser brewers, only Coors has been able to keep up with A-B and Miller. Between 1975 and 1980, Coors increased its annual advertising outlays *662 percent* (in constant dollars). Its ad costs per barrel jumped *555 percent* during those years. Subsequently, during the 1980s, Coors more than doubled its total dollar outlays and per barrel expense. The company's efforts to expand nation-wide and to launch Coors Light motivated much of its surge.

After analyzing the beer industry's two bouts of advertising escalation from 1947 to 1964 and from 1970 to 1987, John Sutton concluded: "While it can indeed be argued that the initial impetus underlying the rising trend in concentration may be the changing degree of scale economics in the industry, *a central role in the evolution of structure was played by the process of competitive escalation of advertising outlays that occurred over these two crucial periods.*"[53] (Emphasis added.)

Since 1987 the advertising outlays of A-B, Miller, and Coors have remained relatively high. In 1996, outlays relative to sales were higher for beer than for all but a few other industries—for example, detergents, breakfast cereals, razor blades, perfumes, and cosmetics.[54] If seller concentration in the industry continues to rise and eventually stabilizes, advertising outlays may begin to fall to more moderate levels. A truce should be profitable. Advertising was very high in Canada during the 1980s. But after Molson and Labatt developed a duopoly in Canada (through mergers), they substantially reduced advertising outlays over the early 1990s.

### Advertising Exclusives

Anheuser-Busch and Miller had more of an advantage over their rivals during the 1970s and 1980s than simply the ability to outspend them. Anheuser-Busch and Miller obtained exclusives when sponsoring live network television sports broadcasts. An "exclusive" accompanies a brewer's purchase of program sponsorship when the brewer is given the right to exclude other brewers from advertising on the same program. For example, an A-B exclusive on Monday Night Foot-

ball would allow A-B to advertise Budweiser, Bud Light, Michelob, and all of its other brands during a game while excluding the advertising of other brewers during the game. Anheuser-Busch and Miller have held such exclusives for most live-action network sports programs—NFL football, NCAA football, major league baseball, the Olympics, the Indy 500, and so on. The problem for smaller brewers has been compounded by closed bidding, when sponsorship of a sports event (or schedule of events) has been offered only to A-B or Miller for negotiated sale.

The cost advantages A-B and Miller enjoyed from their TV sports exclusivities are suggested in Table 2.4. Earlier we compared the columns of Table 2.4 for a comparison of network and spot TV. Now we compare the two rows "Sports" and "Prime Time" for each year from 1980 to 1982. The sports sponsorships are less costly in every case (per thousand male viewers). Regarding network TV in 1982, for example, sports sponsorships were 31 percent less costly than prime time—$9.70 per thousand viewers versus $14.14.

The relevance of these cost comparisons for A-B and Miller in their battle against smaller rivals is seen most clearly in the fact that A-B and Miller acquired a disproportionate number of these cost-effective buys. In 1989, A-B and Miller together accounted for 90 percent of all beer category network sports outlays, an amount considerably greater than their 65 percent combined beer market shares at the time.[55] This raised their rivals' costs, as rivals then had to rely on more expensive media alternatives to make their pitch to consumers.

### Product Proliferation

The major brewers have hurled dozens of new products (or brands) at one another in recent decades, as well as abundant advertising. Indeed, new product launches incite extraordinary advertising expenses, so part of the explosion in advertising since 1970 can be attributed to a boom in new brand introductions.

During the early 1990s, there was a sharp escalation in new brand introductions. Beginning with sixteen new brands (in 1990), the pace quickened to sixty-nine (1991), sixty-five (1992), eighty-two (1993), and one hundred sixteen (1994). Zima, Red Dog, Old Milwaukee Draft, Keystone Dry, Miller Gold Draft, and O'Doul's were among the many launches. And during these years, ice beers apparently accounted for more new brands than any other category, for example, Bud Ice, Miller Lite Ice, and Ice House. In 1994 alone, *forty* new ice beers were introduced.[56] (Ice beers are produced at temperatures a few degrees colder than ordinary brew, which gives them a slightly higher alcohol content.)

During the 1990s, craft beer brands also proliferated. In addition to several hundred new craft beers recently introduced by small craft regionals, contract brewers, and microbrewers, A-B, Miller, and Coors have devised what might be called faux-craft beers, given the scale of these major players. A-B alone can be credited with more than a dozen faux-craft beers clustered in families—that is, Michelob Specialty Ales and Lagers, the American Originals series, Pacific Ridge Pale Ale regionals, and Ziegenbock. A-B also owns an interest in Redhook and Widmer. (Miller and Coors hide their identity through subsidiaries Plank Road and UniBev.) The high profit margins of the craft beers are too good for the big three to resist.[57]

New introductions, when undertaken aggressively, can be very expensive. A-B's launch of Bud Ice Draft in 1993, for example, cost $16 million in advertising and marketing, $2 million in consumer research, and $16 million in capital equip-

ment. Moreover, new brands are a risky business. Dry beers, ice beers, and clear beers (like Zima) have all gone through a rise-and-fall life cycle. Still, the proliferation of brands will continue, especially among the largest brewers. Jack McDonough, Miller's chairman, stated his strategy this way: "If we can hit a single, a double or a triple, profitably, we will. If something lasts only three years, hey, we were there first, we made some money, and if it disappears, well we didn't over-invest in it."[58]

Why has product proliferation occurred if it is so expensive? And why is size again so important? A brewer gains certain advantages from having multiple brand offerings. And large brewers probably gain disproportionately relative to small ones. *Some of these gains constitute strategic advantages that seem to have assisted the recent rise in beer concentration.*

First, one advantage to multiple brands has already been alluded to. It allows different price markups and thus an array of pricing strategies when the brands occupy different segments. In particular, multiple brands across price levels reflect the consumers' belief that price signals quality, and consumers believe in that signal partly because of this brand/price variation. Thus, Michelob probably helps the sale of Budweiser vis-à-vis popular-priced beers because Michelob's super-premium presence helps create the image that Budweiser is of sufficiently high quality to be worth more than popular-priced beers. Studies show that, in general, greater price range variability for brands causes consumers to accept price as a quality indicator more readily.[59]

Second, with multiple brands in this environment, A-B and Miller can pursue fighting brand strategies. Miller could not go after Stroh's Old Milwaukee by cutting the price of Genuine Draft without damaging Genuine Draft's premium image. But it could introduce Milwaukee's Best and price it cheaply. Such strategies extend to promotion expenditures as well. Popular-priced brands typically receive less advertising support than premium and super-premium brands. Yet A-B's Busch brand had advertising expenditures per barrel that have in the past been 26 percent to 93 percent greater than A-B's premium Budweiser brand. As a result, the Busch brand is by far the most intensely advertised popular-priced beer.

Finally, product proliferation by A-B and Miller pressures the smaller brewers. To the extent that new brands are established, retail shelf space for other brands often vanishes. The smaller brewers then feel compelled to defend their spaces by introducing their own new varieties. But A-B and Miller retain the advantage because the costs of proper introductions are to a large extent fixed and sunk.

The costs are fixed in the sense that they must exceed some minimum threshold, say $20 million, as a necessary but not sufficient condition for a modestly successful national launch. They are fixed because they are spent to gain minimum ad exposures and shelf space and to design the graphics and conceive the image to be portrayed. At the same time, these introductory costs are sunk because they cannot be recovered in the event of failure. The money spent on advertising to introduce what turns out to be a flop is money gone forever. It produces no asset that could be put to alternative uses.

The largest brewers—Anheuser-Busch and Miller—have advantages here in two ways. Their fixed costs can be spread over larger total volumes to reduce their costs per barrel compared to those of others playing the product proliferation game. Also, their greater size lets them carry the risk burden implied by sunkenness much more gracefully than the smaller firms can.

The craft brewers have been an exception to these basic economics. At retail level, they have taken significant shelf space away from the major brewers by giving retailers spectacular markup margins. As seen earlier in Figure 2.6, the retail markups on craft beers average about $1.29 or $1.30 per six-pack. These are 62 percent higher than the $.80 markups on regular beers. Unusually hefty wholesale markups also entice distributors into placing craft beers on their trucks and pushing them.

## Distribution

In all but a few areas of the United States, beer reaches consumers through a three-tiered system of (1) product production, (2) wholesale distribution, and (3) retail sales. Typically, the wholesale distributors are not owned by the brewing companies. These wholesale distributors receive their beer in large shipments from the brewery, warehouse it, and then distribute it as needed to retailers. They are also responsible for related services, such as advertising locally and rotating stocks. Distributors attempt to secure retailers' shelf space and promotional support, thereby assisting the brewer in securing consumer demand.

Two forms of vertical restraint commonly control brewer-distributor relations. First, informal exclusive dealing limits the freedom of many A-B distributors with respect to the brands they may carry.[60] Second, territorial exclusives imposed by virtually all brewers restrict distributors to certain assigned territories. We shall discuss the latter.

### Territorial Exclusives

Except in Indiana, where territorial exclusives are banned by law, distributors throughout the United States are commonly authorized by brewers to do business only within certain territories. This means that the sale of Budweiser to retailers in, say, Atlanta is the exclusive privilege of the A-B distributor authorized to do business in that area. The sale of Budweiser to Atlanta retailers by an A-B distributor assigned to some other territory would be "transshipping" in violation of the system. Each distributor's exclusive territory is the result of a "vertical" agreement between the brewer and the distributor, not the result of a "horizontal" agreement among the distributors themselves.

Formal or informal territorial exclusives have been common in the beer industry for a long time, partly because of state regulations.[61] However, express, nationally uniform, contractual territorial exclusives by Anheuser-Busch, Miller, and the other national brewers date only since the early 1980s·after the Supreme Court decided *Continental TV, Inc. v. GTE Sylvania* in 1977. The Court held that such restraints would be governed by a "rule of reason," under which illegality would depend on such factors as the market power of the manufacturer imposing the restraint and the purpose and overall effect of the restraint.[62]

The economic rationale for allowing territorial exclusives in most instances is fairly clear. A brewer's territorial exclusives limit the freedom of action of the brewer's distributors, but this does not necessarily limit competition in the market as a whole. A brewer's territorial exclusives inhibit what is called intrabrand competition because they prevent different distributors of the same brand (e.g., Pabst Blue Ribbon) from vying with one another when selling Pabst to retailers. But the territorial exclusives do not necessarily curb interbrand competition between, for example, Pabst and Budweiser, which is the kind of competition that is of greatest importance to competition as a whole. Indeed, a relatively weak brewer's territorial exclusives may actually enhance this

interbrand competition even as the exclusives restrain intrabrand competition because they may allow that relatively weak brewer to compete better with more powerful brewers.

One of the main procompetitive reasons a brewer would want to assign territorial exclusives is that territorial exclusives increase the likelihood that distributors will service all retail outlets—small 7–Elevens and corner taverns as well as huge supermarkets and discount liquor marts. Without territorial exclusives, distributors would tend to ignore small retail outlets and concentrate their resources and energies on bigger accounts—aggressively trying to attract the business of distant large retailers located outside their normal territory and defensively trying to preserve their business with large retailers inside their normal territory (who will be the targets of aggressive sales efforts by distant distributors whose normal territories lie elsewhere). With these aggressive motives spurring a distributor's distant efforts and defensive motives guiding a distributor's nearby efforts, small retailers may be neglected.

There are circumstances, however, in which a brewer's territorial exclusives could be, on balance, substantially anticompetitive. One possibility in this respect exploits the fact that territorial exclusives keep different geographic markets separate from each other. With transshipping prevented and isolation preserved, a large, powerful firm can use territorial exclusives to help implement anticompetitive price discrimination, lowering price in one territory to harass rivals there while maintaining prices elsewhere.

It is difficult to tell the exact extent of these anticompetitive possibilities, but A-B's and Miller's territorial exclusives may thus raise anticompetitive problems. The larger the market shares of A-B and Miller, and the stronger their premium images, the more serious these possibilities. Territorial exclusives among the distributors of Coors, Stroh, and the lesser brewers seem innocent by comparison. Indeed, the territorial exclusives of these firms could on balance be procompetitive.

## Summary of Conduct

Our study of conduct has revealed several strategic advantages associated with large size (and diversity) that further explain the industry's march toward higher concentration. Apart from their technical advantages of economies of scale, A-B and Miller have benefited greatly from their ability to target price cuts across geographic territories and across brand categories in such a way as to discipline or wear down their rivals. In advertising they have charged ahead of the field with skyrocketing absolute outlays (subsidized by cigarette profits in the case of Miller and by premium and super-premium price markups in the case of Anheuser-Busch). Their exclusives on national network television sports sponsorships have given A-B and Miller command of the most cost-effective media buys in the beer business. When it comes to product proliferation, A-B and Miller seem to have enjoyed the upper hand again. New brand launches incur immense costs when done effectively. Those costs tend to be both fixed and sunk, characteristics that can best be managed by the largest brewers. Having a constellation of brands helps A-B and Miller maintain their premium images, recover quickly when their brands stumble, and capture limited shelf space in retailers' refrigerators. Finally, territorial exclusives please the distributors more than the brewers. But even in this instance it appears that, among the brewers, A-B and Miller have been able to use their exclusives to good advantage vis-à-vis their smaller rivals. In particular, territorial exclusives assist geographic price

discrimination because they serve to separate markets regionally.

Apart from these several ways in which conduct apparently contributes to the industry's concentrated structure, we find instances where structure influences conduct. Note that the strategic advantages just mentioned would not be "strategic" without the degree of dominance that the two largest brewers—A-B especially—can bring to the task. More traditionally, we find top dog A-B serving as price leader and we find the industry's strong product differentiation prompting various promotional behaviors.

## Performance and Other Issues

By strictly economic standards, the performance of the beer industry is less interesting than its structure and conduct. One reason for this is the easy predictability of performance given what has been said thus far. It should be no surprise, for instance, that A-B is by far the most profitable firm in the industry and that it ranks well among all corporations in the economy. If we concluded that advertising expenditures and other promotional outlays for beer were not merely high but excessively high (creating an uneconomic level of cost that some have termed X-inefficiency), we would likewise probably be affirming your expectation rather than catching you unawares.

Noneconomic performance is something else altogether. The beer industry has come under attack by those fighting alcohol abuse. In 1990 a nationwide Roper poll of college students disclosed that they thought alcohol abuse was by far the biggest problem on campus. Nearly twice as many students (53 percent) cited it as a major problem compared to the next biggest problem—theft and violent crime.[63] The issue is thus one that permeates society.

An irony in this for beer is that, at least off campus, the campaign against alcohol abuse may in the end lift beer demand as people switch from hard liquor and wine to beer because beer is regarded as less troublesome in this respect than those other beverages.

## Summary

Returning to our opening question of what has caused beer concentration to soar since 1950, we find not one answer but many. Of the many, four stand out. First, technical economies of scale in production rose. Second, two explosions of advertising expenditures—one during the 1950s and early 1960s, and the other during the 1970s and early 1980s—rocked the industry, shaking the financial foundations of all but the biggest brewers because brand image is critical to success in this industry. Third, strategic behaviors of various sorts, such as price discrimination and product proliferation, have favored A-B and Miller over the others. Finally, several kinds of exclusivities have bestowed advantages on A-B and Miller. The story is a complex brew and an intriguing one.

## Notes

1. "Can You Judge a Beer by Its Label?" *Consumer Reports*, June 1996, p. 10.

2. R.I. Allison and K.P. Uhl, "Influence of Beer Brand Identification on Taste Perception," *Journal of Marketing Research* 2, no. 3 (August 1964): 36–39; S.H. Rewoldt, J.D. Scott, and M.R. Warshaw, *Introduction to Marketing Management* (Homewood, IL: Richard D. Irwin, Inc., 1973), pp. 177–90.

3. Thomas F. Hogarty and Kenneth G. Elzinga, "The Demand for Beer," *Review of Economics and Statistics* 54, no. 2 (May 1972): 197.

4. *1996 Beer Industry Update*, p. 278.

5. *2001 Beer Industry Update*, p. 248.

6. *2001 Beer Industry Update*, p. 92.

7. For a list of the major acquisitions occurring from 1950 to 1984, see Victor J. Tremblay and Carol Horton Tremblay, "The Determinants of Horizontal Acquisitions: Evidence from the U.S. Brewing Industry," *Journal of Industrial Economics* 37, no. 1 (September 1988): 21–45.

8. F.M. Scherer, Alan Beckenstein, Erich Kaufer, and R.D. Murphy, *The Economics of Multi-Plant Operation* (Cambridge: Harvard University Press, 1975), p. 80.

9. John C. Hilke and Philip B. Nelson, "An Empirical Note from Case Documents on the Economies of Network Television Advertising," *Review of Industrial Organization* 4, no. 1 (Spring 1989): 131–45.

10. For example, viewer ratings for men (aged 18 to 49) during the early 1980s were, not surprisingly, four times greater in sports than in weekday daytime. *1982 TV Sports Factbook* (New York: Backer and Spielvogel Bates Worldwide, 1983), p. 4.

11. Hilke and Nelson, p. 132.

12. *Jobson's Beer Handbook 1995* (New York: Jobson Publishing, 1995), 141–43.

13. *Beer Marketer's Insights*, September 20, 1994, p. 4.

14. Scherer, Beckenstein, Kaufer, and Murphy, pp. 241–42, 248–49, 259. Interestingly, they do not find this advantage specifically in network versus spot TV advertising (p. 247). Their research relates primarily to the late 1960s, however, so their findings date from a time when regional marketing was more important to the industry than it is now, simply because regional brands were stronger then.

15. Charles Keithahn, *The Brewing Industry* (Washington, DC: Federal Trade Commission, 1978).

16. Peter R. Dickson and James L. Ginter, "Market Segmentation, Product Differentiation, and Marketing Strategy," *Journal of Marketing* 51, no. 2 (April 1987): 4.

17. *2001 Beer Industry Update* (St. Louis: R.S. Weinberg and Associates, 2001), pp. 115–30.

18. Kelvin Lancaster, *Consumer Demand: A New Approach* (New York: Columbia University Press, 1971).

19. Charles G. Burck, "While the Big Brewers Quaff, the Little Ones Thirst," *Fortune*, November 1972, p. 106; *Wall Street Journal*, November 17, 1977, p. A-1.

20. *San Francisco Chronicle*, January 27, 1979, business section (quoted by editor, Donald K. White).

21. "Can You Judge a Beer by Its Label?" pp. 10–17.

22. *Los Angles Times*, December 15, 1985, part 4, p. 6.

23. "Miller Seeks to Regain Niche as Envy of Beer Industry," *Wall Street Journal*, December 3, 1986, p. A-6.

24. *Beer Marketer's Insights*, January 30, 1978, p. 3; August 28, 1978, p. 3.

25. *2001 Beer Industry Update*, p. 251

26. J.D. McConnell, "The Price-Quality Relationship in an Experimental Setting," *Journal of Marketing Research* 5, no. 3 (August 1968): 300–303. During a deposition on March 2, 1989, Leonard J. Goldstein, CEO of Miller Brewing Company said, "There are price segments in the marketplace—

premiums, super-premiums, imports, and the price of those products plays one part in how the consumer perceives that product." (*State of New York v. Anheuser-Busch et al.*, U.S. District Court, Eastern District of New York).

27. Gregory S. Carpenter and Kent Nakamoto, "Consumer Preference Formation and Pioneering Advantage," *Journal of Marketing Research* 26, no. 3 (August 1989): 285–98.

28. J. Jacoby, J.C. Olsen, and R.A. Haddock, "Price, Brand Name, and Product Composition Characteristics as Determinants of Perceived Quality," *Journal of Applied Psychology* 55, no. 6 (December 1971): 570–79.

29. C.W. Park, B.J. Jaworski, and D.J. MacInnis, "Strategic Brand Concept-Image Management," *Journal of Marketing* 50, no. 4 (October 1986): 135–45.

30. Patricia Sellers and Erin Davies, "Bud-weis-heir," *Fortune*, January 13, 1997, p. 92.

31. *Beer Marketer's Insights*, December 2, 1996, p. 3.

32. Michel E. Porter, "Consumer Behavior, Retailer Power, and Market Performance in Consumer Goods Industries," *Review of Economics and Statistics* 56, no. 4 (November 1974): 419–36; Alfred Arterburn and John Woodbury, "Advertising, Price Competition and Market Structure," *Southern Economic Journal* 47, no. 3 (January 1981): 763–75.

33. John Deighton, "The Interaction of Advertising and Evidence," *Journal of Consumer Research* 11 (December 1984): 763–70. Because most American beers taste alike, including different brands of a given brewer, it might seem that brewers often sell the same beer under different brands to exploit different images. This may happen occasionally, but to the present author's knowledge, this is not typical. For interesting examples of this behavior in cigarettes and cold remedies, however, see *Wall Street Journal*, March 3, 1990, pp. A-1, A-7; and February 1, 1991, pp. B-1, B-8.

34. Robert Smiley, "Empirical Evidence on Strategic Entry Deterrence" *International Journal of Industrial Organization* 6, no. 2 (June 1988): 167–80.

35. "A Struggle to Stay First in Brewing," *Business Week*, March 24, 1973, pp. 45–46.

36. *Los Angeles Times*, December 15, 1985, part 4, p. 7.

37. Ibid.

38. "A Whole New Game in Beer," *Fortune*, September 19, 1994, p. 86.

39. *Beer Marketer's Insights*, January 9, 1989, p. 2.

40. "For Customers, More Than Lip Service," *Wall Street Journal*, October 6, 1989, p. B-1.

41. "A Warning Shot from the King of Beers," *Business Week*, December 18, 1989, p. 120.

42. U.S. House, Select Committee on Small Business, *Hearings on Small Business and the Robinson-Patman Act*, vol. 2, 91st Cong., 1st and 2nd sess., 1970. Testimony of R.C. Brooks, Jr., pp. 721–38; *Federal Trade Commission v. Anheuser-Busch*, 363 US 536 (1960).

43. Henry G. Grabowski, "The Effects of Advertising on Intra-industry Shifts in Demand," Occasional Papers of National Bureau of Economic Research *Explorations in Economic Research* 4, no. 5 (1978): 675–701.

44. Christina M.L. Kelton and W. David Kelton, "Advertising and Intraindustry Brand Shift in the U.S. Brewing Industry," *Journal of Industrial Economics* 30, no. 3 (March 1982): 293–303.

45. D.F. Greer, "Product Differentiation and Concentration in the Brewing Industry," *Journal of Industrial Economics* 19, no. 4 (July 1971): 201–19.

46. Allyn D. Strickland and Leonard W. Weiss, "Advertising, Concentration, and Price-Cost Margins," *Journal of Political Economy* 84, no. 5 (October 1976): 1109–21; J. Sutton, "Advertising, Concentration and Competition," *Economic Journal* 84, no. 3 (March 1974): 56–69; A.J. Buxton, S.W. Davies, and B.R. Lyons, "Concentration and Advertising in Consumer and Producer Markets," *Journal of Industrial Economics* 32, no. 4 (June 1984): 451–64; D.F. Greer, "Advertising and Market Concentration," *Southern Economic Journal* 38, no. 1 (July 1971): 19–32.

47. Victor J. Tremblay, "Strategic Groups and the Demand for Beer," *Journal of Industrial Economics* 34, no. 2 (December 1985): 183–98.

48. D.F. Greer, "The Causes of Concentration in the U.S. Brewing Industry," *Quarterly Review of Economics and Business* 21, no. 4 (Winter 1981): 100.

49. *Beer Marketer's Insights*, October 16, 1978, p. 2.

50. For details on the Miller-Philip Morris Corporation, see Willard F. Mueller, "Conglomerates: A Nonindustry," in Walter Adams, ed., *The Structure of American Industry*, 6th ed. (New York: Macmillan, 1982), pp. 450–57.

51. "John Murphy of Miller is Adman of the Year," *Advertising Age*, January 9, 1978, p. 86.

52. *Los Angeles Times*, December 15, 1985, part 4, p. 6.

53. John Sutton, *Sunk Costs and Market Structure* (Cambridge, MA: MIT Press, 1991), p. 299.

54. "1996 Advertising-to-Sales Ratios for the 200 Largest Ad Spending Industries,"*Advertising Age*, July 1, 1996, p. 11. The reported figure, 6.2 percent, is not exactly comparable to the others because of unique excise taxes on beer. Adjusted for excise taxes, beer advertising as a percentage of sales would be about 7.8 percent.

55. *Adweek*, October 2, 1989, p. 6.

56. Patricia Sellers, "A Whole New Ball Game in Beer," *Fortune*, September 19, 1994, p. 80.

57. *Beer Marketer's Insights*, February 6, 1995, p. 2.

58. *Beer Marketer's Insights*, June 13, 1994, p. 3.

59. Susan B. Petroshius and Kent B. Monroe, "Effects of Product-Line Pricing Characteristics on Product Evaluation," *Journal of Consumer Research* 13, no. 4 (March 1987): 511–19; R. Rao Akshay and Kent B. Monroe, "The Effect of Price,

Brand Name, and Store Name on Buyers' Perceptions of Product Quality: An Integrative Review," *Journal of Marketing Research* 26, no. 3 (August 1989): 351–57.

60. In 1996–1997, A-B launched a program to get its distributors to deal exclusively with A-B's brands and those of selected "beer partners" like Redhook and Modelo. By 2001 the vast majority of A-B's volume was being handled by exclusive distributors. According to A-B's *1997 Annual Report*, the purpose of the program was to boost A-B's market share toward a goal of 60 percent, its share having stagnated at 44 percent over 1991–1995. By 2000 its share had jumped to 48.2 percent (*2001 Beer Industry Update*, p. 42). For further discussion of this program see the previous version of this chapter in the second edition of this book.

61. Peter C. Carstensen and Richard F. Dahlson, "Vertical Restraints in Beer Distribution: A Study of the Business Justifications for and Legal Analysis of Restricting Competition," *Wisconsin Law Review* (January/February 1986): 1–81.

62. *Continental TV, Inc. et al. v. GTE Sylvania, Inc.*, 433 U.S. 36 (1977).

63. *Beer Marketer's Insights*, October 11, 1990, p. 3.

## Selected Readings

*Beer Industry Update*. Published annually. Various volumes. West Nyack, NY: Beer Marketer's Insights, Inc.

*Beer Marketer's Insights*. Biweekly periodical. Various issues. West Nyack, NY: Beer Marketer's Insights, Inc.

Elzinga, Kenneth G. "The Beer Industry." In Walter Adams and James Brock, eds. *The Structure of American Industry*, 9th ed. Englewood Cliffs, NJ: Prentice-Hall, 1995.

Greer, Douglas F. "The Causes of Concentration in the Brewing Industry." *Quarterly Review of Economics and Business* 21, no. 4 (Winter 1981): 87–106.

Hoch, Stephen, and John Deighton. "Managing What Consumers Learn from Experience." *Journal of Marketing* 53, no. 2 (April 1989): 1–20.

Kelton, Christina M.L., and W. David Kelton. "Advertising and Intraindustry Brand Shift in the U.S. Brewing Industry." *Journal of Industrial Economics* 30, no. 3 (March 1982): 293–303.

Mueller, Willard F. Testimony in hearings on *Mergers and Industrial Concentration*, U.S. Senate, Committee on the Judiciary, Subcommittee on Antitrust and Monopoly, 95th Cong., 2nd Session, May 12, 1978.

Sass, Tim R., and David S. Saurman. "Advertising Restrictions and Concentration: The Case of Malt Beverages." *Review of Economics and Statistics* 77, no. 1 (February 1995): 66–81.

Sutton, John. *Sunk Costs and Market Structure*. Cambridge, MA: MIT Press, 1991.

Tremblay, Victor J., and Carol Horton Tremblay. "The Determinants of Horizontal Acquisitions: Evidence from the U.S. Brewing Industry." *Journal of Industrial Economics* 37, no. 1 (September 1988): 21–45.

# 3

# Broilers

## Differentiating a Commodity

*Richard T. Rogers*

*A chicken in every pot.*

—Herbert Hoover, 1928

A *broiler* is the industry's name for a young chicken grown for meat rather than for eggs. The name causes some confusion. The term *fryers*, the industry's first widely used term for young chickens sold for their meat, reflected the most common method of cooking chicken before health concerns reduced interest in fried foods. Kentucky Fried Chicken introduced fast-food chicken in the 1930s, and its growth made the Colonel's recipe famous worldwide, but it has changed its name to KFC to deemphasize the word *fried*. Even the National Broiler Council, an industry group formed in 1954, debated the name issue for years. First they began using the word *chicken* in all consumer promotions such as "September is National Chicken Month." Finally, in 1999 the Council agreed to replace the word *broiler* with the word *chicken* in its official name.

The chicken has a long history, with its first recorded reference being in China around 3300 B.C.[1] The ancestor to the modern chicken is thought to have come from Asia, and these colorful and aggressive birds still populate parts of Myanmar and Northern India. In ancient times cock fighting was the sport of choice among emperors, kings, and noblemen, as well as common folk. Prized fighters sold as thoroughbred racehorses do today. The birds were valued by armies, traders, and explorers for their minimal needs and many uses: eggs, meat, entertainment—even the feathers had great value. Cock fighting remains a popular gaming sport in many parts of the world, including within some regions of the United States, where it is illegal in all but three states.

Although chickens arrived in America along with the first European settlers, the raising of chickens primarily for their meat is a relatively new industry. In the early 1900s, the United States was still a country of small farms, and chickens were a sideline venture of most farms. Although the number of chickens on each farm was small, it was a huge business in the aggregate. Chickens were easy to raise, and the extra eggs, which were sold to local townspeople, provided supplemental money for the household. The cockerels (young male chickens) were sold in

Table 3.1

**U.S. Broiler Production, Exports, and per Capita Consumption**

| Year | Production Number (millions) | Production Liveweight (million pounds) | Exports (million pounds) | Per capita consumption (pounds) |
|------|------|------|------|------|
| 1935 | 43 | 123 | NA | 0.7 |
| 1940 | 143 | 413 | NA | 2.0 |
| 1945 | 366 | 1,107 | NA | 5.0 |
| 1950 | 631 | 1,945 | NA | 8.7 |
| 1955 | 1,092 | 3,350 | NA | 14.6 |
| 1960 | 1,534 | 6,137 | 93 | 23.5 |
| 1965 | 2,058 | 7,176 | 88 | 29.8 |
| 1970 | 2,770 | 10,074 | 94 | 36.9 |
| 1975 | 2,922 | 10,983 | 138 | 36.7 |
| 1980 | 3,929 | 15,531 | 567 | 46.9 |
| 1985 | 4,439 | 18,623 | 417 | 54.8 |
| 1990 | 5,841 | 25,550 | 1,143 | 69.1 |
| 1995 | 7,371 | 34,353 | 3,894 | 79.2 |
| 2000 | 8,261 | 41,294 | 5,548 | 89.6 |

*Source:* U.S. Department of Agriculture.

the spring as frying chickens, a seasonal treat for any family.

Farmers in rural areas close to major population centers like Philadelphia and New York City saw opportunities in the spring fryer business. Also, farmers from poor cotton-growing states, like Georgia and Arkansas, began to seek better returns from chicken farming than from struggling with cotton. New England states and the Delmarva Peninsula, a region formed by parts of the three states of Delaware, Maryland, and Virginia, started raising broilers for the big-city markets. There was sufficient money being made that the industry grew, and support services, like trucking, became viable businesses.

The New York City market was the center of poultry distribution early in the twentieth century. Its large Jewish population provided a ready market, since the Jewish faith required that Jews eat meat, preferably a luxury meat, on the Sabbath

and other holidays. Frying chicken was considered just such a luxury for most city people. New York City and poultry became inexorably linked with marketing terms like *New York dressed*, which were used by the entire industry.[2]

The two world wars were good for the chicken business. Both World Wars I and II provided high demand for poultry products, and input suppliers helped the industry gear up with "defense chicks" and feed supplies to contribute to the war effort. One enthusiastic feed supplier's ad proclaimed, "It is YOUR DUTY to help win this battle for increased production."[3] These were profitable years, but thereafter the industry suffered as the war demand vanished and beef rationing was ended. Although many enterprises cashed out after earning war-time profits, others braced for the hard times that would come. Those in the broiler industry were convinced that better times would return to the broiler industry.

Table 3.2

**Consumption: Pounds per Capita on a Boneless, Trimmed-Weight Basis**

| Year | Beef | Pork | Red meat total | Chicken | Turkey | Poultry total | Fish | Grand total |
|------|------|------|------|------|------|------|------|------|
| 1960 | 59.1 | 48.6 | 115.1 | 19.1 | 4.9 | 24.0 | 10.3 | 149.4 |
| 1965 | 70.4 | 43.6 | 120.1 | 22.8 | 6.0 | 28.8 | 10.9 | 159.8 |
| 1970 | 79.6 | 48.1 | 131.9 | 27.4 | 6.4 | 33.8 | 11.7 | 177.5 |
| 1975 | 83.0 | 38.3 | 125.4 | 26.4 | 6.5 | 32.9 | 12.1 | 170.5 |
| 1980 | 72.1 | 52.1 | 126.4 | 32.7 | 8.1 | 40.8 | 12.4 | 179.6 |
| 1985 | 74.6 | 47.7 | 124.9 | 36.4 | 9.1 | 45.5 | 15.0 | 185.4 |
| 1990 | 63.9 | 46.4 | 112.3 | 42.4 | 13.8 | 56.3 | 15.0 | 183.5 |
| 1995 | 64.4 | 49.0 | 115.1 | 48.8 | 14.1 | 62.9 | 14.9 | 192.9 |
| 2000 | 66.1 | 49.2 | 116.7 | 54.4 | 14.0 | 68.4 | 15.2 | 200.2 |

*Source*: U.S. Department of Agriculture, Economic Research Service; U.S. Department of Commerce; and National Marine Fisheries, Food Consumption, Prices, and Expenditures.
*Note*: All bone and fat normally trimmed before retail sale has been subtracted. The red meat total includes veal and lamb.

## Production, Consumption, and the Market

Herbert Hoover's 1928 slogan, "A chicken in every pot," was quite a political promise, one of the few that have been well filled. In 1935 broiler production stood at just 43 million birds and per capita consumption was only 0.7 pounds (see Table 3.1). Chicken was still a luxury item to most people. By 2000 per capita chicken consumption had increased to almost 90 pounds per person and rivaled beef for the highest per capita consumption of any meat. With both an increasing domestic population and the industry's success in export markets over this sixty-five-year period, production volume increased over 300-fold, a staggering growth rate.

### *Consumption*

By 1987 food writers were claiming that poultry (chicken plus turkey) had displaced beef as the most commonly consumed meat. Although per capita beef consumption has fallen since its record highs of the mid-1970s in contrast to poultry's growth, the headline writers were ahead of themselves. Red meats are sold with most of the bone and fat trimmed prior to retail sale, whereas chickens are often sold as whole dressed birds with much of the product discarded as waste (e.g., bones, necks, and so on) after the retail sale. On a boneless, trimmed-weight basis, it was not until the1990s that per capita poultry consumption matched that of beef consumption, and it still remains below all red meat consumption (see Table 3.2).

Per capita meat consumption has increased over time as expected in an affluent society. Since the various meats are substitutes for one another, each meat's future growth will be based on population growth, exports, and success at taking share from other meats. Poultry has taken a growing share, mainly at the expense of beef consumption. Pork consumption has been nearly stable since 1960, and fish consumption increased to sixteen pounds per capita in 1987, but has been unable to sustain the

Figure 3.1   **Broiler Price–Quantity Relationships, 1950–2000**

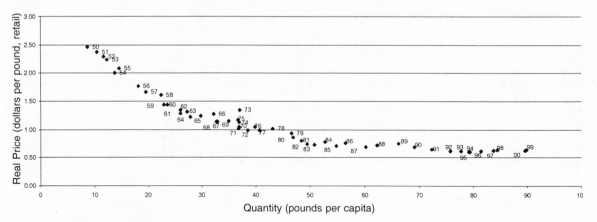

*Source:* USDA.

trend and remains at fifteen pounds per capita. Although much has been written about increased fish
consumption, turkey consumption is nearly as high
and has a higher growth rate. The new aquaculture
industry, especially the catfish segment, has many
similarities to the broiler industry, but success now
depends on consumer preferences.

*Price and Quantity*

To take market share from competing meats requires
increased consumer demand for a particular meat,
usually because of income changes, relative price
changes among the substitutes, and changes in tastes
and preferences. As the real price of broilers has been
lowered dramatically over time, consumption has
increased; but the negative relationship between real
price and per capita consumption has flattened, from
1950 to 2000 (see Figure 3.1). By the 1980s, increases
in per capita broiler consumption were occurring with
little or no decrease in broiler prices. This suggests
that either the price of substitutes was high relative
to that of broilers or a shift in consumer tastes and
preferences was taking place. Both explanations are
plausible, and there was also an income effect as more

affluent consumers purchased premium parts and
forms of chicken with higher value added.

The price of ready-to-cook chicken has increased
over time, with bone-in breasts leading the way, but
prices held steady in the 1990s, at just over $2 a
pound.[4] Beef prices, as measured by the price of
ground chuck, declined from 1980 to 1986, then recovered by 1990 and continued to increase to just
under $2 a pound. Chicken breasts are the premium
chicken part, with the bone-in breast selling at over
twice the price per pound of the while chicken. Currently, boneless and skinless breasts are the luxury
fresh chicken cut and usually sell at twice the price
of bone-in breasts. Chicken has lost some of its relative price advantage over other meats and the price
of its premium parts now rivals that of many red
meat cuts, further demonstrating the increased consumer appeal of chicken.

*Elasticities*

Research has shown that the income elasticity (the
responsiveness of demand to income changes) of
broilers has declined over time as it shifted from
that of a luxury item to that of a more common

meat item. Some studies done with 1950s data found estimates exceeding +1.0, while nine recent studies show an average income elasticity of +0.38.[5] Cross-price elasticities with beef and pork have shown more agreement, with most estimates around +0.20 for beef and +0.28 for pork. Research on the broiler own-price elasticity shows that the long-run price elasticity is inelastic and has become more inelastic over the last forty years, with an estimate between –0.2 and –0.6 supported by most recent studies. With the industry in the inelastic portion of its demand curve, expansion of production should reduce industry revenue by depressing price more than increasing consumption, unless other factors shift the entire demand curve.

## Consumer Preferences

Broiler consumption has benefited during the last decade from consumers' interest in health and concern over dietary fat. Compared to both beef and pork, chicken is generally a more healthful product, especially when the skin is removed and it is not fried. Since the mid-1950s, health associations have been warning people about the increased health risks of a high-fat diet. Although awareness has increased, average fat consumption remains above the recommended 30 percent of calories from fat. Fundamental change in consumer behavior is a long process. Consumers have made greater changes among the sources of fats than in reducing total fat intake. Red meat consumption has been reduced, but high-fat ice cream consumption increased. Butter consumption fell, but margarine and cheese consumption advanced.

Today's food consumer is changing. Fewer are educated in food selection, handling, and preparation. Consumers are busier and eat fewer meals in the traditional family setting. Consumers are often confused and hold misperceptions regarding their food choices. Media stories and marketing slogans often add to the confusion rather than provide clear information. A premium is placed on convenience, resulting in a shift of meal preparation tasks to food processors and store deli departments. The traditional family meal is less common in modern households, where children often zap their own meals in the microwave. New products emerge at a blinding pace, providing variety but making it more difficult to keep up with the latest consumer information. There are over 60,000 items in the modern supermarkets and consumers cannot be expert on all of them. They need help, and marketers and retailers are helping with store displays and shelf tags that provide consumer information. Consumer advocates prefer a neutral third party to be involved in this educational process and have called for changes in food labeling requirements that would reduce the marketing hype and provide easier access to information.

More meals are eaten away from home—almost half of consumer expenditures on food are in restaurants, fast-food outlets, and other food-service establishments. Consumers are provided with much less information from food-service firms than is found on the packages in the grocery store. Food-service firms, however, are getting a mixed message. For example, McDonald's was blasted by a wealthy industrialist in full-page advertisements in leading newspapers for its hamburgers' fat content, and the company launched the McLean burger with only 9 percent fat, but it failed in today's marketplace. Taste is still paramount in consumers' fast-food choices.[6]

## Production

### Regional Concentration

Broiler production is concentrated in the "broiler belt" of states, which starts at the Delmarva Peninsula and swings down through the Southeast to East

Texas (see Figure 3.2). California is the only top-ten state in production that is outside this region.[7] Most of these states were part of the original broiler industry, but the Northeastern states have declined as production movedSouth to lower costs of production. The leading ten states account for 75 to 85 percent of all broiler production. Although that figure has been stable for twenty-five years, continued growth in the industry has started to spill into adjacent states like Kentucky and Tennessee, and hence the top ten's percentage has slipped toward the lower end of the interval. Processing plants tend to locate close to broiler production as advances in transportation allow shipment of dressed broilers to the population centers.

*Vertical Structure*

Broiler processing is highly integrated, with the processors controlling the vertical stages in the broiler industry either by owning or contracting each stage of the vertical system—from breeding stock to market-ready products (see Figure 3.3). The vertical process begins with the eggs the breeder farms send to the hatcheries. The hatched chicks are then sent to the grow-out farms, where they will grow to market weight in six to eight weeks. Growers are usually under contract to the integrators. Feed is provided by the integrator and represents about 70 to 75 percent of the costs of grow-out. Feed costs are so important to the total cost of production that market analysts use feed costs as a proxy to forecast broiler prices and processors' returns.

Once the birds reach market weight, they are sent to a slaughtering plant, which is more sensitively called a processing plant, where they are processed into "dressed broilers." The live birds enter the plant to be hung by their feet, electrically stunned, and bled. Their feathers, feet, en-

trails, hearts, livers, and other parts are removed before they emerge as dressed broilers. Many birds are then ice packed or chill packed, either as the whole birds or as the cut-up parts familiar to all who shop the supermarket's meat case. Some others are quick frozen, either whole or as individual pieces, and some are shipped to another company-owned plant for further processing into value-added products.

Further-processing is the fastest growing segment of the poultry industry. Since fresh broilers are highly perishable commodities, processors would like to increase the shelf life and create additional value, which will make broilers less like a commodity. In 1962, over 80 percent of broilers were marketed as whole chickens, 15 percent were sold cut up in parts and only 2 percent were further processed.[8] By 2000, the percentage sold as whole birds had fallen to just 9 percent, and the percentages for cut-up and further processed were 46 percent and 45 percent respectively. Freezing is a traditional method of increasing shelf life, but consumers prefer to buy fresh chicken, which sells at a healthy premium. Nevertheless, many food-service companies prefer the product frozen since it gives them more control and less waste without negative reactions from consumers, who seldom even know the product was once frozen. Consumers are more accepting of frozen chicken when it is sold as value-added, convenience food such as a frozen entrée.

*Marketing Channels*

The final products are either sold to distributors or marketed by the processors in two main marketing channels—food service (combining institutions and restaurants) and retail grocery stores (see Figure 3.3). In 1995 the retail market accounted for 43 percent of broiler volume, food service 30 percent, and export markets 16 percent, with the remaining volume entering nonhuman

Figure 3.2  **Top Broiler States**

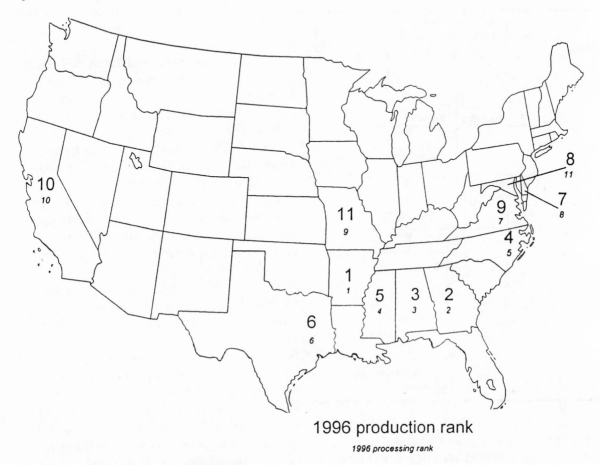

1996 production rank

*1996 processing rank*

*Source:* USDA and Census of Manufacturers.

consumption markets (e.g., feed and pet food).[9] The export market has grown from insignificance to about 20 percent of domestic production, exceeding 5.5 billion pounds in 2000 (see Table 3.1). Russia has gone from a nonimporter of U.S. broilers in 1988 to the number-one export destination, even with major trade disputes, devaluation of the ruble and subsequent distress in the Russian economy. China/Hong Kong is the number-two export market. Mexico is the third largest importer of U.S. broilers and, together with Russia and China/Hong Kong, account for 65 percent of U.S. exports. Japan (the previous leading importer of U.S. broilers) has slipped to the fifth largest importer of U.S. broilers, just behind Canada. The growing export market has been welcomed by the industry because it not only moves a significant amount of product but also helps balance the demand for different chicken parts. The Russians prefer legs while most Americans prefer breasts. In 1999, 23 percent of broiler products exported to China/Hong Kong were chicken feet (over 300

Figure 3.3 **Vertical Structure of the Broiler Industry**

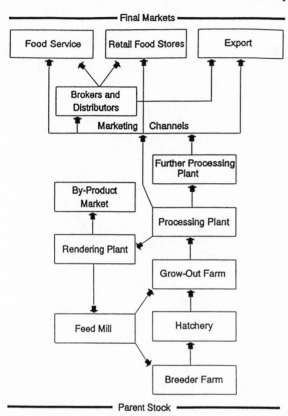

million pounds), a by-product destined for pet food in the domestic market but a delicacy in China.[10]

## *Defining the Market*

We have not yet provided a clear definition of the market. Market definition is complex, yet fundamental to meaningful analysis, and many antitrust cases bog down over market definition since it has a critical effect on such important economic concepts as market concentration. Market definition has two critical components—product definition and geographic definition. Economists want to include those products that compete directly with

one another in the same market. Unfortunately, the cross-price elasticities needed to check the degree to which products are substitutes are not available for most products.

We define our product market as broilers, but others could argue that this product definition is too narrow and should include at least turkeys and perhaps all meats. We choose to define the market as broilers and treat the other related products as imperfect substitutes. Once product form is included, the definition becomes less clear. Broilers are sold as whole birds, in parts, or in a value-enhanced form. Ground chicken, for example, probably competes more directly with ground beef than with chicken breasts. Although we will discuss such problems where appropriate, our primary focus will be on broilers.

The geographic scope of the broiler market is nationwide for the output market, but local for the input market, as the typical radius for a processor to acquire broilers is about twenty to fifty miles. Some firms, including leading firms, do not sell nationwide and maintain regional strategies, but modern transportation methods make national shipments possible, and the distance fresh broilers are shipped has dramatically increased over time, especially with laws allowing the shipment of super-chilled chicken (26 degrees) that can be thawed and sold as fresh. Frozen and canned chicken have always been shipped greater distances than fresh products. Imports from outside the country are minimal, and exports, although substantial, are treated as a factor affecting the domestic market rather than enlarging the geographic scope of the market.

## Market Structure

Market structure refers to the organizational characteristics of a market that largely determine where it falls on the competitive spectrum between monopoly and competition. Market structure has several important elements that reflect the competitive environment of the market. We will focus on four key elements: concentration, vertical integration, product differentiation, and conditions of entry. These elements of market structure have a strong theoretical justification, as well as a long empirical history as crucial determinants of market conduct and performance.

## Concentration*

The broiler market has been one of the most unconcentrated industries in the food system. The leading firms have not dominated the market. Although data on broilers alone are limited by availability and comparability over time, one can use the broader poultry industry to capture major trends as chickens dominated the early poultry processing industry. We examine data for the entire United States, despite evidence of regional markets existing in parts of the country.

Every four to five years the Department of Commerce takes a census of manufacturers. The first reported census concentration ratios (CR) were for 1935, and the four largest processors (CR4) accounted for 30 percent of the poultry industry. The next census, in 1947, showed 330 companies with $479 million in poultry shipments and a CR4 of 32 percent. The 1954 census reflected the postwar growth as the number of poultry processors more than tripled to 1,189 with shipments of $1,258 million, a growth rate exceeding 23 percent per year. This rapid growth and influx of new entrants reduced CR4 to 17 percent of industry shipments. In subsequent census years, the number of companies has continually decreased from the 1954 record.

Beginning with the 1954 census, concentration ratios were available for the major product markets comprising the poultry dressing industry, with separate data for both young chickens and turkeys. The last published census data are for 1982, but other data from the U.S. Department of Agriculture (USDA) federal inspection records and from the trade journal *Broiler Industry*, now *Watt Poultry USA*, compare well with the census data and provide annual concentration figures.[11]

Concentration in broilers remained very low from 1954 to the mid-1970s (see Figure 3.4). The CR4 was 18 in 1954, reached a low of 12 in 1958, and stayed nearly constant at 18 from 1964 to 1976. The CR8 followed a similar path, suggesting that the largest firms were just holding their share of a growing market. The CR20 advanced, suggesting that larger firms held a growing share, but a rising CR20 without an increasing CR4 or CR8 reflects a diminishing disparity among the top twenty firms as more firms reach a comparably efficient level of operation.

Starting in 1977, concentration began a slow increase, with CR4 crossing the important benchmark value of 40 in 1989. Many economists view a CR4 of 40 as a threshold level below which workable competition prevails.[12] The broiler industry was an unconcentrated industry until 1983, when it appeared to have become a low-grade oligopoly.[13] The industry CR4 reached 50 in 2001, yet concentration in broilers remains lower than the average for all food manufacturing industries. The increases in concentration were the result of mergers among the leading firms. It seems that the increase in concentration in broilers from 1977

---

*Concentration means share of shipments accounted for by largest four, eight, or twenty firms (e.g., sales of largest four divided by industry sales).

Figure 3.4    **Broiler Concentration, 1954–2001**

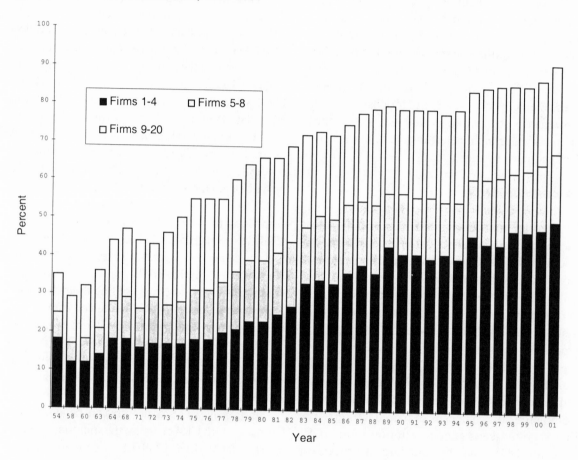

to 1989 was almost entirely due to mergers.[14]

Tyson Foods is now the largest broiler processor in the United States (see Table 3.3). Started in the 1930s as a family business trucking live broilers from other growers, the business grew as it achieved the efficiencies that accrue to those who coordinate the broiler operation. It grew by acquiring others; fifty of its first fifty-three plants were acquired.[15] Before the late 1980s the leading broiler processors held similar market shares. In 1989, after an acquisition battle with rival ConAgra, Tyson emerged as the acquirer of Holly Farms

Foods, acquiring its 6.9 percent of the market and the number one spot it still holds today. In July of 1995 Tyson acquired the poultry division of Cargill. It failed in its attempt to buy WLR Foods, Inc., the fourteenth largest broiler processor in 1996, but purchased the broiler operations of Hudson Foods in 1998. Tyson's most recent acquisition (September 2001) was IBP, Inc. the number one beef and pork packer in the United States.

Although Tyson has consolidated its hold on the number one position, the next three largest firms are similar in size and have traded positions

Table 3.3

**Leading Broiler Companies** (dollars)

| Name | 2001 Production | | 1998 Fresh chicken advertising | | |
| --- | --- | --- | --- | --- | --- |
| | Rank | Share | Rank | Share | Millions |
| Tyson Foods | 1 | 23.8 | 2 | 24.7 | 6.5 |
| Gold Kist | 2 | 9.2 | 7 | 1.8 | 0.5 |
| Pilgrim's Pride | 3 | 8.7 | — | — | 0.0 |
| ConAgra | 4 | 8.3 | 5 | 3.4 | 0.9 |
| Perdue Farms | 5 | 7.5 | 1 | 49.8 | 13.2 |

*Sources:* "Poultry & Egg Marketing," reprinted in *Food Institute Report*, May 21, 2001, p. 5; and Competitive Media, LNA/Media Watch, 1998.

among themselves over the years. Gold Kist, an agricultural cooperative, has been among the top four firms for decades. It was the second largest broiler processor in both 1977 and 1982, but fell to the third spot in 1990. It made no acquisitions, but grew internally, and returned to the number two spot in 1994, where it has remained.

ConAgra, a large diversified agribusiness firm, was the number one firm in 1982 before Tyson Foods made three major acquisitions. ConAgra was also actively engaged in mergers, and the fight with Tyson over control of Holly Farms was major business news for nearly a year, until ConAgra withdrew from the bidding and accepted a cash settlement. In 2000 it was the third largest broiler processor with an 8 percent market share, but by 2001 it had slipped to number four as it continued to shift its focus to noncommodity products. Pilgrim's Pride moved from fifth to third by purchasing WLR Foods, Inc. (the one that got away from Tyson Foods) in 2001. Perdue Farms entered the broiler business in 1968, has made two small acquisitions since 1977, and is just behind ConAgra and Pilgrim's Pride in market share. It has been among the top six broiler firms for over fifteen years. Even with the changes in the rankings, the firms behind Tyson's dominant share remain similar in size.

The mergers among leading firms have gone unchallenged under the antitrust laws because the broiler industry was unconcentrated. In 1984 the Department of Justice developed its merger guidelines based on the Herfindahl-Hirschman Index (HHI), which is calculated by summing the squares of each firm's market share (expressed as a percent). The guidelines state that mergers will not be contested in markets where the HHI is under 1,000. In 1988 the HHI for broilers was 511; in 1989 it had increased 200 points to 711, with Tyson accounting for 433 of the total; and in 2000 the HHI was 884, with Tyson accounting for 550 of the total.[16]

These HHIs were calculated for sellers in a nationwide market. If the appropriate market is regional, then the true HHI for each regional market is likely to be much larger. Also, mergers among broiler processors affect buyer concentration for the live broilers to process. Most broilers are raised under contract to the processors, and one would expect less favorable terms for the growers as the number of processors competing for growers' services declines. Since processors prefer a twenty-mile radius, and seldom reach beyond fifty miles for the assembly of live broilers, most growers face oligopsony or even monopsony buyer power.

The leading broiler companies in 1950 were quite different from the current leaders, with the large meat-packing companies holding the leadership positions in the poultry business.[17] The leader was Swift and Company, followed by C.A. Swanson & Sons, and then Armour & Company; also involved in 1950 were the General Foods Company, Wilson and Company, and the Cudahy Packing Company. Those companies no longer exist as individual operations. The Swift brand (and its Butterball turkey) was acquired by ConAgra when Beatrice Foods was broken up after a leveraged buyout. Swanson was acquired by the Campbell Soup Company, but the brand name remains a leader in the small canned poultry category. The Armour company was caught up in the conglomeration trend of the 1960s and 1970s and at one time was owned by Greyhound (the bus company), but ConAgra acquired the brand in 1983. In 1981 General Foods acquired Oscar Mayer (which in turn had acquired the Louis Rich Turkey Company in 1979), and all are now part of the Philip Morris Companies, the largest U.S. food company.

It was not just the large meat companies that once held leadership positions in the broiler business. Major feed companies, with their obvious interest in the growing broiler business, became major players in the industry. They began as suppliers of birds and feed to growers under business agreements that reduced the grower's risk but positioned the feed companies as the main coordinators of the industry. Once they organized the input side of growing broilers, it was a logical next step to become involved in processing.

Ralston Purina, Pillsbury, and Central Soya were such companies in the 1960s.[18] Ralston Purina came to own many broiler businesses that fell into financial trouble during the broiler depression in 1961 and was the largest broiler processor in the country by 1968.[19] In 1971 it announced that it would withdraw from the broiler business, citing volatility and the poor fit with the diversified food processor image it was cultivating in the investment community. The decision, which shocked the industry, came just after Ralston had announced an aggressive marketing plan for a branded line of broilers, including precooked and frozen products. Some former Ralston Purina people formed new companies that have since become successful. For example, Hudson Foods, formed by Red Hudson after leaving Ralston Purina, was ranked twenty-fifth in 1975 and fifth in 1996, before becoming part of Tyson in 1998.

The largest broiler companies are among the largest food manufacturing companies, especially when ranked by sales rather than value added. Based on 2000 sales data, ten of the largest broiler companies make the list of the 100 largest food manufacturers.[20] ConAgra is the second largest U.S. food manufacturer, behind the Philip Morris Companies, and is the only highly diversified firm among the broiler companies. The other broiler companies differ by being more specialized in poultry and closely related products. Many of the fifty largest broiler companies still carry the family name of the founders—names like Tyson, Perdue, Pilgrim, Townsend, Foster, and Zacky.

An additional feature of most of the broiler firms is regional specialization. Although both the Tyson and ConAgra brands are nationally distributed, most of the top fifty broiler companies are far more regional in their sales area. For example, Perdue is heavily committed to the Eastern Seaboard, and Foster Farms and Zacky are similarly committed to the West Coast markets. The further-processed part of the poultry industry is more concentrated than the fresh broiler market, despite having a larger number of companies. Most of the leading twenty broiler slaughterers own further-processing plants as well, but smaller companies do not.[21] Most of the growing number of companies involved in further-processing do not operate slaughtering plants and instead buy dressed broilers from others. Even Tyson supplies such firms with dressed broilers ready for further-processing, a practice it would like to stop because even though it likes the added volume, it dislikes supplying its rivals in the further-processed market.

In summary, output concentration of broilers has been among the lowest in the food system, but its continued rise suggests this will change. Tyson's near 24 percent national share, which is more than two and a half times that of its nearest rivals is the only anomaly in this otherwise very competitive market structure. Within some regions of the country, these firms hold leadership positions. Ironically, should Tyson's nearest rivals attempt to merge to match Tyson's national share, the antitrust laws would probably be used to prevent them from doing what Tyson was allowed to do earlier. Although the industry's output concentration ranks low in the food manufacturing sector, the input concentration is among the most concentrated in the agricultural sector, with growers facing near-monopsony market structures. The broiler processors sell, directly or indirectly, to an ever more professional, sophisticated, and concentrated retail sector that can place its own demands on the processors.

### Vertical Integration

The most distinctive feature of the broiler industry, compared to other agricultural industries, is the degree of vertical integration the processors have achieved. The modern broiler firm is often referred to as an integrator rather than as a processor, to underscore its involvement in the entire broiler subsector. Prior to the integrator, the broiler subsector shown in Figure 3.3 was linked by a series of cash markets. Growers bought chicks from hatcheries, who bought their eggs from specialized breeder stock companies, and then sold the live birds to the processor. The stages were linked by markets, with demand and supply determining the price at each stage. The growers disliked the risk posed by the volatile market price for live broilers, and others saw inefficiencies in markets providing the coordination function for the subsector. Firms saw opportunities to internalize the market's coordination role through vertical integration.

The feed companies, anxious to expand the market for their feeds, were the first to become involved in coordinating the broiler industry by supplying chicks to contract growers and eventually arranging for the processing of the birds. Farmer-growers were eager to reduce the price risk that was inherent in raising broilers and were receptive to the arrangements with feed companies that lowered their risk in exchange for more stable earnings. Further coordination efficiencies led feed companies into processing as well. Some feed companies reluctantly entered the grow-out stage when their affiliated farmers went under.

Over time most of the markets that linked the various stages of the broiler subsector were replaced by either internal firm transfers or by contracts. Processors seeking efficiencies and improved coordination took ownership control of almost all stages of the broiler subsector. They typically left the breeding of the parent stock to a few specialized firms, the most concentrated part of the subsector, but today most of the major companies have acquired this function as well. The integrators have basic breeding programs to produce the hatching eggs for their own hatcheries. The integrator then delivers the chicks to growers who raise the birds, called grow-out, in housing designed to the specifications of the integrator. Over 90 percent of the grow-out farms operate under contract to the integrator, with the remainder raised on company-owned grow-out farms. Under the usual contract arrangement, the integrator retains ownership of the birds, supplies the feed and medication, and provides supervisory field personnel. In return the grower is provided a payment for managerial skills, labor costs, and investments in housing and equipment. The contract often has incentives to encourage quality broilers with minimal feed. The major integrators typically own their own feed mills and customize the feed to their needs. The birds reach market weight in six to eight weeks and are loaded and transported by the integrator's employees. The integrator determines the timing of the next batch of chicks delivered to the grower.

The traditional part of the integrator's operation is the processing plant, where the broilers are "dressed" for market. The waste products from processing are sent to a company-owned rendering plant and processed into by-products, including pet food and feeds. Further processing of the value-enhanced products is done in either company-owned plants or in those of processors who do not have their own slaughtering plants. Some of the low-valued products like necks and backs are processed into mechanically deboned poultry meat for chicken hotdogs and luncheon meats. Plants are typically specialized for a primary product form, whether it be cutting, deboning, or preparing products for food-service companies.

### Product Differentiation

The degree of product differentiation is another key element of market structure that shapes market conduct and performance. In the absence of product differentiation, consumers consider the products from competing sellers as perfect substitutes and thus make their purchases based on price comparisons. As the degree of product differentiation increases, consumers view the competitors' products as imperfect substitutes, with the distance between competing offerings increasing with the degree of product differentiation. Sales of the differentiated brands are less sensitive to price changes, which provide sellers with some discretion in pricing their products that would not exist if products were homogeneous.

Product differentiation has both a market-structure and market-conduct component. The degree of product differentiation in a market is a structural fact of the market, although its precise measurement is difficult. Sellers of undifferentiated products cannot extract price premiums from informed buyers. However, firms often pursue conduct strategies to create a degree of product differentiation.

Physical differences provide a basis for product differentiation, but product differentiation may also arise from subjective attributes. Broiler processors have created both real and subjective product differentiation. The real product differentiation efforts have included product quality, product form, and the level of services provided the retailer. The latter is often called enterprise differentiation rather than product differentiation since its focus is on the retail buyer rather than the final consumer. This was the first form of product differentiation in selling broilers because processors realized that consumers had difficulty distinguishing one brand of chicken from another. Processors knew the importance of the retail buyer and sought a favored status by making the retailer's job easier or less expensive. In the early 1970s, Holly Farms was the first processor to interest retailers in receiving tray-packed chicken, the Holly Pak, ready for the meat case.[22] Although retail meat cutters and their unions disliked the loss of final preparation at the retail store, the tray-pack method has become a standard practice. The processor–retailer relationship continued to shift services from the retailer to the processor. Today it is common for a processor to apply the retailer's own scanner pricing labels to its order before it leaves the processor's plant.

Chicken sold through food-service markets (e.g., restaurants, fast-food outlets, and institutions) accounts for over 40 percent of domestic broiler volume. The food-service companies control product differentiation in this marketing channel, since the consumer will not know the identity of the broiler processor and will associate the product with the food-service company. The actual chicken product may be differentiated or may become so only through association with the outlet.

Clearly, KFC chicken and McDonald's McNuggets are differentiated products that have brand awareness, but the differentiation is not associated with the broiler supplier. The broiler processor achieves differentiation through services directed at the food-service company and can achieve a degree of enterprise differentiation by supplying a product that best meets the needs of the food-service company. Nevertheless, the product is being sold to professional buyers who will not pay price premiums that exceed the extra value they receive. In short, price will still be a critical factor in determining who supplies the account, but other services such as reliability, the willingness to supply specific products, and the commitment to the account will be considered.

Physical differences can provide a method of differentiating a product from the competition's offerings. In the fresh chicken market, skin color has been used to differentiate chicken. Consumer preferences for different skin color vary by region, with the South and West usually preferring a pale color and the Northeast a yellow color. Perdue Farms made the yellow color the first theme in its advertising campaign. It copied the idea from a Maine firm that fed its chickens marigold petals because the xanthophyll in the petals enhanced the skin's yellow color.[23] Of course others followed, and some even tried to turn the theme against Perdue. Holly Farms suggested in its advertising that Perdue's color was unnatural and also complained to the National Advertising Division of the Council of Better Business Bureaus that the Perdue ads were misleading, causing consumers to associate skin color with quality.

Fat content replaced skin color as the next physical difference that firms used to differentiate their products—my chicken is leaner than your chicken. The leaner birds did receive a price premium, as consumers responded to the healthful low-fat image. However, these physical differences could be matched by competitors and price once again became central to buying decisions.

Physical differences are not necessary for product differentiation to exist. In many cases, product differentiation stems from intangible differences. Although these illusory and subjective differences can have many sources, most are created by firms' advertising efforts.[24] Images are much harder to imitate, or to counter successfully, than physical differences. Engineers, chemists, and food scientists can usually duplicate actual differences, but a successful image advantage is more difficult to offset. Even firms that have been successful with one campaign can find themselves unable to repeat their past success. It is becoming increasingly rare in the food system to find differentiated products that are not advertised heavily.

Subjective product differentiation is less likely to prove an advantage when selling to knowledgeable buyers, since they will be able to debunk any hype and base any price premiums on true quality/service factors. Thus, such efforts are not employed in the marketing channels that sell to professional buyers. However, the modern household is a busy place, and no one person can be expert on the 60,000 items sold in a modern super-combo grocery store. It is in this marketing channel that subjective product differentiation, usually created and maintained through advertising, plays an important role.

This association between product differentiation and advertising suggests that brand advertising expenditures can be used as a proxy measure of the degree of product differentiation. Food products that do not lend themselves to product differentiation (such as fresh beef) usually receive little if any brand advertising. They may receive industry-supported generic advertising aimed at increasing market demand (and benefiting all sellers), but such industry-wide advertising campaigns have no effect on brand differentiation. Products that are differentiated so that individual brands are not perfect substitutes usually receive moderate to heavy amounts of brand advertising. For example, soft drinks are highly differentiated and are heavily advertised. Thus, we can array food products from undifferentiated to highly differentiated by using the advertising intensity associated with the products.

There are several reasons to expect less product differentiation in the broiler business than in many other food industries. First, processors pay for USDA graders to grade their broilers and almost exclusively sell USDA Grade A birds to consumers as fresh chicken. Although firms believe that quality variations still exist among Grade A birds, consumers have not shown strong preferences or even the ability to distinguish such differences. Most taste tests, whether done using professional food critics or average consumers, have revealed little to no difference between brands of chicken.[25] Second, although over 80 percent of

broiler processors offer branded fresh chicken, over half of the fresh chicken sold does not carry the processor's, or even the distributor's, brand.[26] Almost every retail store offers both processor-branded chicken and its own store label (private label) chicken. The store label is either the grocery chain's name or another name that is exclusive to the chain's stores. These store-brand labels emphasize price competition rather than product differentiation claims.

Product differentiation is further diminished because over 40 percent of chicken is eaten away from home in restaurants and fast-food outlets, where the consumer does not know the brand's identity. Thus, unlike soft drinks for which the consumer knows the brand served by the food-service establishment, the brand awareness of chicken is deemphasized by the food-service segment of the market. Finally, the large number of chicken processors and the relatively low market concentration should make price competition the primary competitive tool.

Despite these reasons to expect less product differentiation in broilers than in much of the rest of the food industry, firms have had some success in their efforts at brand marketing and product differentiation. During the 1950s and 1960s, the large food manufacturers who were in the broiler business attempted to achieve product differentiation. Ralston Purina, Swift, and Armour advertised branded chicken during this period, but the expenditures were quite minor; less than 0.1 percent of total broiler sales was spent on major media advertising.[27] During this period turkeys were more intensely advertised because, sold frozen, they provided a branded package and a longer shelf life. Campbell Soup advertised its frozen Swanson Fried Chicken and other frozen chicken dinners, including the traditional chicken pot pie, but these were all further-processed products.

During the 1970s, significant advertising was undertaken to create and maintain product differentiation for broilers. Frank Perdue of Perdue Farms is often credited with the first use of advertising to create product differentiation.[28] In 1972 major media brand advertising for broilers was less than a million dollars, with Perdue Farms accounting for over 40 percent of the total. In the same year, branded turkey advertising amounted to nearly $2 million—for an industry one-fourth the size of the broiler industry. By 1975 the broiler industry was outspending the turkey industry and doing so by an increasing margin in each successive year. By 1990 the industry was spending over $30 million to promote fresh broilers, and Perdue Farms was still the largest advertiser with a 41.6 percent share of the total expenditures. The $30 million figure was not sustained during the 1990s. In 1997, under $20 million was spent, but it rose to $26.5 million in 1998, with Perdue Farms accounting for about half of those expenditures, followed by Tyson's 25 percent share of the total.

The more a product is processed, the greater the opportunity for product differentiation. Further-processed poultry is more differentiated than fresh broilers for several reasons. Processed poultry has a longer shelf life because of added preservatives, freezing, or better packaging. Further-processed poultry carries a processor's brand name and is packaged, providing a way to distinguish it from the competition's offerings. In addition, much of the processing is aimed at creating differences. Much of the motivation for new product development is the hope to pioneer the next new market segment, and firms invest heavily in new product development and product differentiation.

The traditional processed products were modernized from the canned and frozen fried chicken of the 1960s to frozen nuggets, breaded microwaveable chicken sandwiches, marinated chicken strips, and fully cooked breaded chicken patties, as well as other convenient products. These more highly processed poultry products began attracting larger advertising expenditures. In 1972 they were the subjects of a million dollars worth of major media advertising. That figure grew to $52 million by 1987, but has fallen back to about half that amount in 1998. Some of the spending has shifted to promoting frozen dinners (e.g., Healthy Choice) that often include chicken as the meat item.

Although brand advertising expenditures grew from an insignificant amount in the 1960s to $30 million for fresh broilers and around $100 million for offerings of the broader poultry industry including turkey and further-processed products by the early 1990s, the totals are low relative to sales and compared to other food industries. Even in 1975 the broiler industry's advertising-to-sales ratio (A/S) was only 0.1 percent in major media advertising. This ratio increased to 0.3 percent in the late 1980s, but declined to 0.2 percent in 1992 and returned to 0.1 percent in 1997. As expected, the largest A/S ratio was in the further-processed poultry market, where the ratio increased from 0.3 percent in 1972 to 1.4 percent in 1987, but then fell back to under 0.5 percent in the 1990s. Frozen dinners (often containing chicken) became a larger recipient of some of the advertising dollars from poultry firms and this shift accounts for much of the reduction in broiler advertising.

These low A/S ratios reflect low levels of product differentiation in broilers. The fresh broilers A/S ratio of around 0.2 percent compares to the average for all food and tobacco industries of 2.0 percent. Nevertheless, the broiler industry has achieved a degree of product differentiation that is higher than in most food commodity industries. For example, brand marketing is quite rare in the fresh beef and pork industries, where USDA grades (e.g., USDA Choice) and the retail store's reputations for meats are the crucial factors influencing consumers. Both their A/S ratios round to 0.0 percent. Even in the canned tuna industry, where brands have a long history, product differentiation has waned over time as private label tuna has come to outsell the leading brands.

Despite the modest successes in creating product differentiation, the broiler industry remains near the bottom of the food industries in creating and maintaining product differentiation through advertising. The industry pales in comparison to those food industries known for high degrees of product differentiation. Food industries with the highest measured-media A/S ratios include chewing gum (16 percent), breakfast cereals (11 percent), chocolate candy (13 percent), and instant coffee (10 percent).

### Conditions of Entry (and Exit)

We now turn to entry conditions, a fourth major element of market structure—the most important element but also the most difficult to measure. Entry conditions are usually referred to as *barriers to entry* and include anything that provides established sellers with an advantage over potential entrants.[29] Barriers to exit, which also affect entry conditions, depend mainly on the extent to which fixed costs are sunk (or irretrievable), making exit more costly.

The impressive growth of the broiler industry has made both entry and exit easier than in much of the food manufacturing sector. In a growing market, exit decisions need not take place at depressed prices, whereas in a declining market few buyers are attracted until the asking price is reduced significantly. Even though the number of firms has continually fallen since the record high in 1954, entry barriers remain low in broiler pro-

cessing, and new firms have entered the market.

The relationship between average cost of production and firm output size is captured by the long-run average cost curve. Such cost curves show vital information about the production process and the likely competitive outcome. Much attention is focused on the lowest output level that minimizes a firm's average cost. This output size is called the *minimum efficient size* (MES) and is often presented as a percentage of the total market size. Unfortunately, it is no easy task to determine an industry's MES.

Such is the case with broilers, although some information is available. A 1964 study showed that processing costs decreased continually with output size, but after an output of 10 million birds per year the decrease was small.[30] One study concludes that an output of 10 million birds per year, representing 0.33 percent of 1969 broiler production, captured most of the efficiencies.[31] A more recent study, conducted to determine the feasibility of an integrated broiler operation in Michigan, concluded that a technically efficient and cost-effective processing plant should process 8,400 birds per hour.[32] Expanding this processing rate to an annual production volume results in an estimated MES value of 0.4 percent.

A totally different method using census plant data finds similar results. This approach estimates the MES value by the percentage of total sales made by a plant of median size and has proven to yield a reliable proxy.[33] The census-based MES estimate for the poultry industry in 1997 is 0.44 percent of total sales. These different methods of estimating MES all suggest that the MES in broilers does not represent a substantial barrier to entry. Using an MES estimate of 0.4 percent of output, the industry could accommodate 250 plants of an efficient size.

These MES calculations are for a plant, not a

firm. Less is known about estimating multiplant economies of scale. The Michigan study used only one processing plant for its cost-effective integrated broiler complex. Although most of the smaller firms among the fifty largest broiler companies operated just one slaughtering plant in 2000, the leading firms are multiplant firms.[34] Tyson operated forty-two slaughtering plants, the most of any firm. For the top ten firms, the number of slaughtering plants varied from three to Tyson's forty-two. Although leading firms are not necessarily the low-cost producers in an industry, their configuration suggests that efficient firms typically operate multiple plants. If one assumes that an efficient firm needs two to four plants that operate at the MES value of 0.4 percent, then the broiler industry has room for between sixty and one hundred twenty-five firms of an efficient size. Such a range estimate does bracket the current number of significant broiler companies and further suggests that barriers to entry are low in the broiler industry. Even though entry barriers are low, any entry into the broiler industry would still be likely to include acquisitions of existing firms to gain managerial talent, information, and instant market share.

## Market Conduct

Managers choose strategies based on their assessment of the market's basic conditions and structure. Firms in classic competitive markets offer managers little choice in matters regarding pricing and promotion. Managers of firms in oligopolistic markets face many more strategic decisions. All strategies must be selected with an eye on the competition since the interdependence of firms in oligopolistic markets makes each firm watchful of its rivals' actions. However, managements differ in their assessment of their market situation, and some will choose strategies that seem incorrect to others, though in time they may be viewed as brilliant moves that eventually improved the firm's prospects.

Our discussion of the broiler industry's market structure found low but increasing concentration, low product differentiation, and relatively low entry barriers. Such a structure predicts that firms will display competitive conduct strategies. Greater concentration, product differentiation, and growth were found in the more value-enhanced products, and hence we expect greater use of advertising strategies for these products.

There are submarkets within the broiler industry called *strategic groups*. These groups differ along two major dimensions—the marketing channel used and the extent of value-added processing involved. The two principal marketing channels for chicken are food-service and retail food stores. The extent of value-added processing varies from unbranded fresh whole chickens to the branded, value-enhanced products like breaded nuggets and marinated prime parts. Firms within a strategic group share similarities with one another and differ in important respects from nonmembers. Different strengths are needed to succeed in a particular strategic group. The theory of strategic groups contends that firms strive to drive other firms out of their strategic territory and to create mobility barriers that limit other firms' entry into their group. It has been suggested that "most strategic investments are entry- or expansion-deterring."[35] When strategic groups with high mobility barriers exist within an industry, then industry structure may prove misleading. According to one respected observer, "An industry need not be concentrated overall for a particular strategic group to have enormous market power."[36]

These two dimensions—the extent of processing and the marketing channel used—determine which strategic group a firm belongs to. Of course, some broiler processors, and all of the larger ones, operate in more than one strategic group. The firm's decision to emphasize a certain strategic group is itself a strategic choice. Since the market conditions and structural characteristics differ somewhat among the market segments, we expect to find different firm strategies being used.

### Product Strategy

A firm's product strategy depends on the strategic group in which it operates. The most competitive strategic group supplies value-added processors with basic dressed broilers and parts as inputs for their finished products. The characteristics of this strategic group are standardized quality, bulk shipments, no branding, less marketing emphasis, and selling to informed professional buyers. Price and service are critical for success in this strategic group, and this places efficient and low-cost operations at an advantage.

Marketing to food-service companies, especially the major chains, requires a commitment to meet their needs with dependable service. Some restaurants continue to buy whole broilers and do their own preparation in the restaurant, but the trend is to shift more of this preparation back to the processor, especially for the fast-food and chain-restaurant companies. This reduces labor costs and helps standardize the product—a repeat of the evolution that first took place in the retail food store's meat department. The food-service companies that sell a bone-in product prefer smaller broilers, while growers and processors prefer larger, more meaty birds, requiring companies like KFC, Popeye's, and Church's to contract directly with a processor for smaller birds suited to their needs. Other fast-food outlets that sell boneless products use meat from deboning plants. Suppliers to food-service companies must be price competitive since the profes-

sional buyers are fully aware of prices and qualities that exist in the marketplace. The processors that market to the fast-food sector often use the export market to help balance the excess chicken parts, usually legs and leg quarters.

Processors who supply food stores with unbranded or store-label chicken operate in a strategic group much like those that serve food-service companies. Their emphasis must be on price and service to the retail buyer. Processors who offer a line of branded chicken form a more marketing-oriented strategic group in which, although price and service are critical, other nonprice forms of competition become important—new product introductions, advertising support, and product differentiation.

The other dimension of product strategy is the degree of value-added processing to offer. As consumers get busier and less knowledgeable about food preparation, processors have stepped forward with complete "meal kits." Traditional food processors and retail food stores have lost food business to food-service outlets, and chicken products offer no exception. To stem the tide, many convenient forms of chicken are now sold in retail stores, including fully-cooked rotisserie chicken and the awkwardly termed home-replacement meal. Because value-added products offer processors the greatest product differentiation potential, greater advertising support is to be expected. Although a store's retail buyer is an informed professional, the final consumer is less knowledgeable than in years past. Price is not the key consideration; convenience, taste, and health also motivate these purchases and, unlike price, these other factors are more subjective and hence affected by perceptions as well as fact.

The more value-enhanced products are the fastest growing part of the business and offer more stable earnings, as they are less influenced by the whole-bird price fluctuations. Introductions of new chicken products continue to grow. The traditional chicken pot pie now competes with numerous frozen, microwaveable products. Processors now offer marinated, fully cooked chicken wings, precooked chicken patties, nuggets, fillets, strips, and tenders. The traditional luncheon meats and hot dog products have their chicken-based equivalent versions. Marinated chicken finger foods are offered in several spice flavors, and ground chicken now competes with hamburger. Premium frozen dinners also represent a major product category for processors.

A couple of niche markets in the traditional fresh chicken section of the grocer's meat case are of interest. First, kosher chicken, which has a longer history than conventional chicken, has gained wider consumer interest because of concern caused by factory-farming techniques. The kosher process, in which Jewish dietary law controls the methods, is slower than conventional practices and is meant to be more humane. Kosher chicken does cost more than conventional chicken and boasts a superior product as stated in an Empire Kosher Poultry advertisement: "Compared to kosher, ordinary chicken doesn't have a chance . . . [it] is more than rabbis blessing chicken. It's an incredibly strict process that produces the cleanest, healthiest, best-tasting chicken you can buy."[37] Unfortunately, the claim fails in product testing by *Consumer Reports*.[38]

The second niche is an attempt to benefit from consumer concerns over modern factory-farming methods. These firms claim a return to a more natural growing environment where the chickens are given fewer, if any, antibiotics or growth hormones. At present the effort seems more marketing hype than true reversion to barnyard farming. But these free-range chickens have their fans, including customers willing to pay $75 for a dinner of grilled free-range chicken.[39] Sunny southern

California is a perfect setting for one such venture, "Rocky the Range Chicken." Rocky's tag shows a macho chicken wearing a cowboy hat and boots with spurs and toting a gun. A reporter, however, found that Rocky's day is "not exactly a blaze of activity. . . . It's eat, drink, and sit down."[40] Despite the tranquil image, each chicken gets two square feet of space, about twice the conventional practice. The company has since added "Rosie the Organic Chicken" and claims to be the first to carry the USDA organic certification.[41] A newer entrant sells "Buddhist-style" chicken—the bird is sold with its head and feet still attached for twice the price of ordinary broilers and claims a 70 percent share of the chickens sold in New York's Chinatown.[42] The chickens are raised on soybeans and corn and take twelve weeks rather than the industry standard of six weeks to reach market weight.

### Firm Strategies

Don Tyson of Tyson Foods succinctly stated his company's strategy as, "Segmentation, concentration, and domination."[43] Tyson's success in outbidding ConAgra for Holly Farms in 1989 demonstrated its resolve. Holly's brands were leaders in the fresh broiler market, whereas Tyson's brands were leaders in food-service and in precooked and frozen value-added chicken products. The acquired leadership position in the fresh market segment enhances its image in its value-enhanced products. Tyson has not been shy about turning its economic success into political muscle. A long-time financial supporter and business advisor to Bill Clinton, a fellow Arkansan and former state governor and U.S. President, Don Tyson has been accused of buying influence. Mike Espy, a Clinton appointee as secretary of agriculture, was forced to resign when allegations that he had accepted cash and gifts from agricultural firms, including Tyson Foods, continued to mount.[44] Mr. Espy was eventually cleared in the courts, but Tyson's political efforts were exposed. Tyson Foods pushed hard for favorable legislation allowing it to ship "rock-hard," super-chilled chicken that could be sold as fresh despite protests from California processors. Except for never knowing the birds were once "frozen," consumers benefit by having more competitors reach the West Coast market segment.

Tyson entered the red meat business when it acquired Holly Farms and planned to expand its beef and pork business. It provided its food-service customers with a full meat line, and it saw additional opportunities in the red meat industries, especially if the techniques learned in marketing broilers were applied to red meat. Tyson found it difficult to repeat its broiler success and returned its focus to broilers by the end of the decade. It sold its fish operations, and rival ConAgra now owns the Louis Kemp fish brand. Tyson did maintain its other nonbroiler interest in the fast growing domestic tortilla market both as the major supplier to Taco Bell and as the marketer of its own brand, Mexican Original.

In September 2001, Tyson Foods returned to its vision, as articulated by Don Tyson some ten years earlier when he said, "We want to control the center of the plate for the American people,"[45] by completing the purchase of IBP, Inc., the nation's largest beef and pork processor. With that acquisition, Tyson Foods became not only the leading firm in broilers, but number one in beef and pork as well. Not everyone in the investment community applauded Tyson's second attempt to broaden its scope by adding other protein sources to its product array, but the merger was completed anyway.

ConAgra is the fourth largest broiler processor and a much larger company overall than Tyson— at least it was before 2001. ConAgra has been the nation's second largest food company for several years but now, with the addition of IBP's sales, Tyson will be roughly the same size as ConAgra in U.S. food sales. ConAgra was a major player in the restructuring of the beef industry during the 1980s.[46] It acquired its first beef plant in 1983 from Armour Food Company. By 1988 it was the second largest beef packer in the United States, with a 21.1 percent share of industry capacity. Had ConAgra won the merger battle for Holly Farms, it would have been the number one broiler processor. ConAgra became the country's largest turkey processor by acquiring Beatrice's Swift turkey operations in 1990 and its successful Butterball turkey line. It has attempted to transfer the success of the "Butterball" brand name from turkey to a line of chicken products. It also has pork and lamb processing plants as well as seafood and catfish operations. Its meat products range from fresh cuts to highly processed prepared meats (e.g., bacon, ham, hot dogs, lunch meat, and surimi). Its nonmeat food brands include Act II and Orville Redenbacher, LaChoy, Egg Beaters, Fleischmann's, Parkay, Blue Bonnet, Marie Callender's, Hunts, Peter Pan, Van Camp's, and Wesson. It is easily the most diversified of the broiler companies. ConAgra is heavily committed to the more processed, value-enhanced meat products. In broilers it has the complete line of fresh cuts that sell under the Country Pride label, but it has aggressively marketed prepared foods that emphasize convenience, taste, and health. It is a major player in frozen dinners with its Healthy Choice, Banquet, and Kid Cuisine labels—numbering over 350 branded products in total.

The Tyson Foods/IBP combination creates a firm similar in size to ConAgra, and these two companies seem ready for a strategic battle for "the center of the American plate." They differ in their present focus. ConAgra continues shifting its emphasis from commodity meats to more value-added products, especially frozen dinners, and Tyson Foods is dominant in the commodity markets ConAgra is leaving. Tyson is expected to expand beyond its leadership in fresh meats to more value-added products as well, but resources will be stretched thin as they digest their recent purchase, and modern meat plants require large volumes for efficient operation, likely forcing Tyson to sell meat inputs to further-processors for some time.

Handling farm inputs such as fertilizer and feeds, Gold Kist is an agricultural cooperative that operates businesses that support farmers. Among the farm outputs, it markets poultry products through its subsidiary, Golden Poultry Company, under the Young 'n Tender brand name. Golden Poultry also supplies private-label chicken to retail stores, a practice known as *dual branding*. Although Golden Poultry markets a full line of fresh chicken products, it has not expanded into the prepared and precooked, value-added products that characterize both Tyson's and ConAgra's broiler operations.

Perdue Farms is a privately held company that has remained specialized in poultry. It started as an egg company, expanded into broilers in 1968, and acquired a turkey operation in 1984. It was the first company to adopt the same mass-media marketing practices for fresh chicken that are used for branded, heavily differentiated products. Perdue has been a major innovator in new product development with its line of prepared, precooked breaded chicken products—nuggets, tenders, patties, cutlets, and spicy wings. Perdue was also one of the first companies to offer ground chicken and turkey.

Of the five leading broiler companies, ConAgra has the most strategies available to it, due to its diversification and the number of leading positions it holds in major markets. Its brands include many of the food industry's most recognized names. It can shift resources from stable, profitable opera-

tions to bolster other operations. Competitors fear such powerful firms because of their deep pockets. In addition, retailers may be influenced by the size and market presence of such a large diversified food firm and make concessions not made to specialized firms.

On the other hand, specialized firms can be tenacious competitors, willing to make huge sacrifices to survive. Private family-controlled operations can be more committed to the business than to earning the largest return possible on their investments. The largest broiler companies of the 1950s and 1960s were among the largest food marketers, but they exited in search of better returns and have been replaced by smaller, more specialized firms like Tyson Foods and Perdue Farms. ConAgra was the exception, but has now been joined by Tyson Foods—they are firms that must meet expectations of a diversified group of stockholders who often seek results in the short term. ConAgra has focused its commodity businesses on more value-enhanced products rather than on more traditional commodities. Most of the leading broiler firms have reduced their dependence on fresh chicken since it is the least profitable, most volatile side of the poultry business. Pilgrim's Pride adopted this strategy in the 1990s as it moved quickly toward selling value-added products rather than fresh chicken, and by 2000 made over 60 percent of its U.S. chicken sales in further-processed products.[47] Clearly, the leading broiler companies, with the exception of the farmer-owned cooperative, Gold Kist, are trying to use their broiler operations as input sources for their further-processed products.

### Advertising

Since broilers have little product differentiation and market concentration is moderate, advertising expenditures should be relatively low. Although some very modest advertising for broilers existed before the 1970s, it really began after 1970 when Perdue Farms began advertising and its major competitor, Holly Farms (now owned by Tyson), retaliated in a similar fashion. Since 1972 Perdue Farms has either led in advertising broilers or placed second to Tyson Foods. In 1998, Perdue Farms remained the leading major-media advertiser with a 49.8 percent share, Tyson Foods was second with a 24.7 percent share, and ConAgra fifth with 3.4 percent (see Table 3.3). These three firms dominate broiler advertising to a much greater degree than they do production, but ConAgra has reduced its advertising support dramatically over the last five years as it puts more dollars behind its frozen dinners. In 1995, it was the third largest broiler advertiser with a 19 percent share. Gold Kist, the agricultural cooperative, was the second largest broiler processor, yet ranked seventh in advertising with a 1.8 percent share. Nevertheless, that is a substantial increase in advertising for the cooperative as it was almost a nonadvertiser in prior years. The top two broiler advertisers are clearly Perdue and Tyson, and they have been so for over 30 years.

The advertising rivalry between Perdue and Holly Farms caught the imagination of several writers, who depicted the chicken ad wars in wonderfully written essays.[48] Such accounts need to be placed in perspective. The interest in the advertising was not due to its massive dollar amount, but was probably due to the novelty of pitching such a commodity as if it were a soft drink. The ads themselves were clever and quite successful in garnering attention in a cluttered advertising market. Frank Perdue was a hit as he starred in his own commercials, asserting that "It takes a tough man to make a tender chicken."[49] His advertising agency convinced him to be the company spokes-person, stating, "This was advertising in which Perdue had a personality that lent credibility to the product. If Frank Perdue didn't look and sound like a chicken, he wouldn't be in the commercials."[50] After twenty-three years of pitching his chickens, he introduced his son in a commercial by saying "He may even be tougher than I am."[51]

Although the advertising generated interest in the media and the budget for it was larger than previous advertising expenditures for fresh broilers, it was still relatively minor compared to that for most food products. In 1992, roughly twenty broiler processors advertised their fresh chickens in the major media, with combined expenditures reaching $27 million, but by 1998 only eleven firms advertised with expenditures of $26.5 million. KFC, owned by Tricon Global Restaurants, spent $161 million in media advertising, over five times that spent by all the broiler companies combined. Philip Morris Companies spent $214 million advertising just its beers. Thus, although much has been written about the advertising of broilers, it has been done only on a relatively minor scale. The interest has been generated by the industry's reliance on brand advertising, unlike the industry-wide generic advertising campaigns commonly used by the commodity groups such as the beef, pork, and dairy industries.

Despite the long rivalry between Perdue and Tyson and the addition of ConAgra to the marketing fray, product differentiation created and maintained through advertising remains very low for broilers. It exists to a greater extent among the more value-enhanced products as the leaders shift more of their advertising dollars to the further-processed products. In 1998 Tyson Foods spent $6.5 million advertising its fresh chicken and $8.8 million on its further-processed chicken entrées and similar frozen prepared chicken products. ConAgra is a much larger advertiser, spending nearly $100 million in media advertising in 1998, over six times Tyson's total, and has even more dramatically shifted its advertising dollars toward frozen dinners. In 1998, it spent about $1 million each on its fresh turkeys and chicken but $20.5 million on its several lines of frozen dinners. Unfortunately, the advertising data lack the detail necessary to separate dinners with chicken from the other dinners. Clearly the major broiler companies are allocating less advertising support to fresh broilers and more to the value-added products, especially frozen dinners.

## Pricing

Markets determine prices through the interplay of supply and demand. The resulting price is the best indication of the product's economic value. But not all transactions take place in public markets, where the resulting price is public knowledge. Price discovery, knowing the true economic value of a product, is difficult without open markets with many buyers and sellers. With the widespread practice of vertical integration in the broiler industry, a market price is not determined until the processor–retailer (or distributor) exchange. It is at this stage that basic supply-and-demand conditions finally generate an economic price. Processors and major retail buyers negotiate prices daily for ice-packed, ready-to-cook whole broilers. This price generates an important base price, which is widely reported through the twelve-city price reports of the USDA and the "Georgia Dock" price released weekly by the Georgia Department of Agriculture. Prices of processor tray-packed products, including cut-up broilers and the various chicken parts (e.g., breasts, thighs, legs, and wings), are often related to this whole-bird price by a formula. The prepacked form of marketing has grown in volume share over time, but it is estimated that nego-

tiated trades account for about half of broiler volume. Although there is some concern about the heavy use of formula pricing in the industry, the USDA twelve-city broiler price has wide acceptance as an accurate reflection of broiler values.

Because broiler prices are so volatile, in 1991 the Chicago Mercantile Exchange started trading a broiler chicken futures contract tied to the USDA price. The futures contracts allow hedgers, who seek to avoid the price risk associated with volatile markets, to transfer the chance to profit from the price volatility to speculators in exchange for a locked-in price. Thus, the speculators hope to profit from the price volatility that the hedgers seek to avoid. The futures contract has been discontinued due to limited interest since the broiler processors are willing to accept the task of managing the price risks involved.

The price reporting in the broiler industry provides a good evaluation of the price of the basic broiler commodity—the ice-packed whole bird. As the products become more processed, the price information weakens. Although there are useful formulas for determining the relative value of the major chicken parts (e.g., breasts and legs), as further processing is added (e.g., breaded nuggets and patties), market prices become less available. Many food-service firms have entered contract arrangements with processors or distributors, and the terms of the contracts are not disclosed, although some are known to be cost-plus formulas. Most food-service firms want stable menu prices, and hence the price volatility of the broiler market is a management problem that long-run contracts with processors help avoid.

The final price consumers face varies considerably in both product form and marketing channel. Those firms in the strategic group that supply whole birds for further-processing have little pricing discretion and are tied to the commodity prices.

Since they sell a standardized product (e.g., Grade A whole birds) to informed professional buyers, these firms make money by emphasizing cost efficiency and managerial skill in dealing with price risk.

Those firms in the strategic group that supply food-service accounts must be price competitive, but also need to meet tightly specified quality requirements, provide reliable service, and often show a willingness to tailor products to meet the needs of the buyer. Brands are not important, but the reputation of the firm in meeting the needs of the food-service buyer is critical. The food-service buyers are professionals who have an excellent knowledge of the industry and follow the commodity prices.

The firms that supply an unbranded or store-labeled product to the retail food stores operate in a similar manner to those that supply the food-service accounts. Price and service are the critical factors that determine success in this strategic group. Firms that supply the retail food stores with a branded product that has some national or regional product differentiation are able to earn a price premium over the commodity prices—ranging from 5 to 15 cents per pound for the basic broiler and standard tray-packs. Such firms still emphasize service to the retailer since, unlike Perdue, most do not have so much product differentiation that the retailer fears loss of the brand. Nevertheless, success in this strategic group goes beyond price competition to include such things as advertising support, new product development, and the ability to increase presence in the meat case.

Chicken prices in a retail food store vary dramatically with product form. It is not unusual for unbranded or store-label leg quarters to sell at prices as low as 49 cents per pound, lower than the price per pound of the whole bird. Breasts are sold in many forms—whole breasts, split breasts, with and without ribs, boneless and skinless—and carry the highest price of the chicken parts. Breaded chicken breast products and marinated chicken breasts carry the highest price per pound—exceeding $6 per pound for some marinated, skinned, boneless breasts. Such prices rival premium steak prices. The popularity of breast meat has created a supply problem since whole chickens have a fixed number of parts—a fixed proportions production function. Genetics has produced broilers that have more breast meat, but it remains a marketing challenge to move the nonbreast products. The industry has responded with numerous products that have proved popular. Marinated chicken wings, deboned thigh strips, and ground chicken have become important product forms. In addition, the export market has provided a valuable lesson in understanding and profiting from the diversity of consumer preferences. Not everyone prefers white meat. Mexico, Russia, and other members of the former Soviet Union have become major importers of U.S. chicken, especially important since they buy predominately the dark meat parts.

In summary, pricing is very competitive in the broiler industry, especially in the primary forms. The more value-enhanced products that have achieved some product differentiation have a reduced price sensitivity and more frequently compete on nonprice terms.

## Performance

Just as people in business look to the bottom line to evaluate firm performance, industrial organization economists look to market performance to evaluate how well a market has accomplished its task of coordinating society's resources to meet consumer demands. Our models predict that market performance is determined by the market's basic conditions, structure, and conduct, but confirmation of such predictions requires empirical assessment. The broiler industry does not deviate from expectations, as its performance is consistent with its competitive structure—low concentration, low product differentiation, vertical integration, and low barriers to entry.

Economists want market prices to reflect costs of production in the long run, whereas those involved in business could imagine no finer world than one where prices always exceed costs. Profit, and how industries react to profit, is central to the proper functioning of a capitalist system. When prices exceed costs, the industry is profitable and more resources should flow into the production of the good or service—through existing firms or new entrants. When the opposite happens, resources should flow out only until normal profits are restored. This market adjustment mechanism is essential to the free enterprise system. The system fails only when excessive market power, barriers to entry, and restrictive government policies interfere with the corrective mechanism. Profit is the driving force in this self-adjusting mechanism that aligns society's marginal benefits with the societal marginal cost of supplying the product.

### Allocative Efficiency

Economists note that the process by which supply and demand determine the market's price and output results in allocative efficiency, giving assurance that resources are put to their most desirable use. The key empirical check on a market's allocative efficiency is the industry's response to profits. When profits are above normal in a period, expansion is expected in the following period. When profits are below normal, contraction is expected. The broiler industry is a model of allocative efficiency, although expansion has usually been quicker than contraction. In general, the industry has experienced continual demand growth, putting upward pressure on broiler prices. Growth and attractive prices have encouraged firms to increase production, which, when combined with cost-reducing technology, expanded supply and lowered the real price to consumers. Over the years this process has been repeated many times, resulting in the relationship shown in Figure 3.1. However, the process is much more volatile than Figure 3.1 suggests.

Like most agricultural industries with a perishable commodity, the industry is somewhat cyclical; some analysts see a three-year chicken cycle. Firms within the industry respond to changes in supply and demand conditions that can vary greatly. Given the short production cycle of broilers, firms can change their output levels in three to nine months in response to market forces. The most significant demand changes emerge with changes in the supply and pricing of substitutes, with changes in export markets, and with changes in general economic conditions. On the supply side, the changes are usually more dramatic and unexpected. Weather and disease are the chief supply uncertainties. The weather affects both the cost of feed and the success of the grow-out stage of production. The latter is further affected by disease. When favorable cost conditions prevail, especially low feed costs, the industry is usually profitable. Although economists delight in markets that adjust to the interplay of supply and demand, the resulting price can swing erratically. Even a snowstorm that is expected to hit major cities will move prices upward temporarily as buyers increase order sizes in preparation for consumer stockpiling.

Broiler price volatility is a problem for management planning. All else equal, both business managers and consumers prefer stable prices to volatile prices in a market. Volatile prices, however, are often a sign of competition, one that most economists prefer to the price stability that results from supply management by firms with market power. In times of slack demand, firms with market power idle resources (e.g., lay off workers at a plant), reducing supply and offsetting the downward pressure on prices. No firms in the broiler industry possess such market power, and thus prices fall and rise with the unimpeded interaction of supply and demand.

Vertical integration improved the vertical coordination of broiler production but did not affect horizontal coordination. Firms take individual actions rather than collective actions. The usual outcome is that the sum of each firm's production increase exceeds the industry expansion consistent with stable prices; thus, price falls and most firms in the industry suffer poor returns until demand catches up and prices recover. The industry trade associations often appeal to their members to hold the line on expansionary decisions, warning that the collective outcome will hurt all, but there is a sufficiently large number of broiler firms so that mistrust of others and self-interest prevent the advice of the association from being heeded. Even Tyson has attempted to use its dominant position to signal the industry, and itself, toward higher prices from controlled expansion. In its 2000 annual report, John Tyson, chairman and CEO, wrote: "In recognition of the oversupply, last fall we announced a 3 percent production cut. Unfortunately, the industry did not follow our lead, and chicken supplies remained high."[52] Consumers are the beneficiaries.

## Technical Efficiency

Under competitive pressure, firms must adopt low-cost technologies to remain in business and invest in finding still better methods. The broiler industry has done an enviable job. The public sector (mainly the USDA, the departments of poultry science at the land-grant universities, and the Cooperative Extension Service) has assisted by providing sound information and improved scientific methods, but the firms in the industry have made rapid use of improvements and invested their own resources in further research and development.

The broiler industry has a remarkable record in reducing the real costs of producing a pound of broiler meat through the discovery, implementation, and diffusion of improved technology and management. Advances in genetics, health care, nutrition, housing, processing, and distribution have combined to give the U.S. processor the lowest production costs in the world.[53] Only Thailand and Australia compete with such low costs. The vertical integration enables management to coordinate the stages of production and respond quickly to needed changes.

The industry's feed conversion rate, a measure of productivity, has declined from over three pounds of feed to produce a pound of liveweight in the 1940s to slightly under two pounds today. The number of days required for a bird to reach market weight has declined from over seventy days in 1955 to under fifty days today, and the average market weight of a broiler has increased from 3.1 pounds to five pounds in the process. The marketing efficiency of the broiler industry is also impressive. The selling expenses are low, especially for broilers, but even among the value-enhanced, further-processed products the selling expenses are less than the average among food industries.

The overall consequence of allocative and technical efficiency is that prices should reflect costs. Hence, one indicator of market performance is based on the theoretical result that market price should equal marginal cost after all adjustments have occurred. The relationship between price and marginal cost has often been proxied empirically by calculating a price-cost margin (PCM) from census of Manufactures data. Although it is regarded as a crude proxy for industry profitability, the PCM can be calculated from census data for an industry by first subtracting total payroll and the cost of materials from the value of shipments and then dividing the result by the value of shipments. (This census PCM ignores several costs, such as taxes, corporate overhead, advertising and marketing, research, and interest.) The PCM cannot be expected to equal zero, but it does provide a useful benchmark to check how prices compare to costs and to compare industries.

Broiler processing has had one of the lowest PCMs in the food system. In 1997, the latest year for which data are available, the PCM was 22.4 percent for broilers, up from just 11.9 percent in 1992. The PCM for processed poultry products was higher at 28.9 percent in 1997 and the gap between the two has narrowed from previous census years. The average for all food and tobacco product classes was nearly 30 percent. In the more concentrated, differentiated food industries it was much higher—64.8 percent for breakfast cereals, 55.2 percent for chewing gum, 52.9 percent for beer, and 51.5 percent for corn chips, for example.

## Product Variety

The broiler industry has demonstrated remarkable technical efficiency in finding and adopting cost-saving technology. In addition, the industry has continually increased product variety as it responds to consumer demand for convenient food products and seeks profitable new outlets for broilers. The forms in which consumers can buy chicken today are overwhelming—seldom do we buy the whole bird anymore, unless it has been precooked on a rotisserie. Instead we select our favorite parts.

The demand for parts allows processors to charge more for the high-value cuts and less for the other parts not in high demand. These preferences are related to consumer income, and those consumers willing and able to pay premiums for breasts help reduce the price of leg quarters.

The demand for convenience foods also benefits processors by allowing them to increase the production of value-enhanced products that are less susceptible to price fluctuations and have provided better profits. This change should continue and holds both good and bad news for consumers. As the product form becomes more value-enhanced, product differentiation becomes more pronounced and market performance could suffer in the future. At present, the consumer is willing to pay for the added benefits of convenience and the excitement of new products. To date, the industry has been very responsive to both the retail buyers' needs and to consumer demand.

## Product Quality

Marketing a perishable food product is not easy, and it is especially difficult to market fresh meat products. A fresh broiler's shelf life is ten to fifteen days from the time it leaves the processor's plant until it reaches the consumer's plate. Most chicken in the grocers' meat cases is USDA Grade A, which helps to standardize quality. Lower-grade chickens are wholesome but are usually further processed into pot pies, soups, and similar products. Companies have emphasized brands more than the USDA grade as they attempt to create product differentiation.

Consumers have difficulty evaluating food quality, and taste can be a highly subjective matter. In many households today, no one is trained in food selection, handling, and preparation, and thus consumers often rely on informal cues that may or may not have any merit. The color of the broiler's skin is not a useful guide to product quality, yet many consumers continue to base preferences on the chicken's skin color.

Most of the taste-test studies done on fresh broilers by trained experts conclude that quality differences are minor and exist even within the same brand. *Consumer Reports* concluded their article on fresh chicken by noting that all of the sampled chickens were reasonably tender and the differences in flavor were small.[54] Brand names did no better in terms of taste or consistency. The article suggested that consumers should check for product freshness by examining the sell-by date and then shop by price, choosing the plumpest pieces for a given price.

Blind taste-tests often produce humorous results. A *Wall Street Journal* reporter found that four of six dinner guests preferred ordinary chicken to the pricey "Rocky the Range Chicken," with one guest claiming that the one she mistakenly thought was Rocky tasted "like a bird that flies around. It tastes happier."[55] Even the well-known chef of Los Angeles's Spago restaurant, Wolfgang Puck, who serves grilled Rocky at premium prices, preferred ordinary chicken over Rocky in a blind taste-test done in his restaurant. His response to the taste-test was, "I definitely think we should find out why they charge so much money."[56]

## Food Wholesomeness and Safety

The red meat industry has had continuous mandatory federal inspection since 1906, when Congress approved the Meat Inspection Act. (This followed publication of Upton Sinclair's novel *The Jungle*, depicting the horrors of Chicago's meat packing plants.) Poultry was excluded from the act because it was a minor industry then. In the 1920s voluntary poultry inspections began, triggered largely by a poultry plague that swept through New York City, poultry's leading distribution center at the time. In 1957, the Poultry Products Inspection Act brought mandatory inspection to the poultry industry for products to be sold interstate. The 1968 Wholesome Poultry Products Act expanded inspection to products marketed within a state's borders. Today there are over 7,000 federal inspectors monitoring the wholesomeness of poultry (and other meats) at federal expense.

The original meat inspection system was designed to detect diseases and infections since acute infections, often traced to animal products, were the leading cause of human death.[57] The resulting system relied on sight, touch, and smell checks performed by trained federal inspectors on every bird. Under the system, the inspector checks for abnormalities (e.g., broken bones, inflammations, tears, feces, tumors, and unusual color) as he or she examines the outside, inside, and organs of each bird, all in two or three seconds. When abnormalities are found, the inspector can direct an employee to trim or wash the problem areas or can condemn the entire bird. Condemned parts and birds that are not approved for human consumption are sent to rendering plants.

The system initially proved successful, but calls for its reform began in the late 1970s and continued until reforms were adopted in the late 1990s. Processors sought faster line speeds than were allowed with the continuous, every-bird inspection system, and in 1985 the National Academy of Sciences issued a report stating that the inspection system was outdated and unscientific.[58] The original infectious disease problems that the system was designed to detect were replaced by newer problems of microbial and chemical contamination that go unnoticed by the old inspection methods. Detection of these problems, like salmonella and campylobacter, require laboratory analysis.

Salmonella, campylobacter, and other food-borne illnesses present a troublesome problem.[59] Salmonella is a widespread natural pathogenic bacterium that causes flu-like symptoms in most people but can be fatal, especially in the old and the very young. Campylobacter has similar effects. Most people never know what made them ill, and few ever report it to medical professionals or health officials. This inability of the consumer to identify the source reduces the firm's incentive to control the problem since the benefit will not necessarily offset the cost. Cooking kills the bacteria; thus proper handling and preparation methods would eliminate the problem. However, consumers must be quite careful and their decreased knowledge of food preparation contributes to the problem. Contamination can occur when a used knife, cutting board, or even a drop of water from the chicken touches other surfaces or food items.

The 1980s and 1990s were a time of deregulation, and the political climate supported efforts to shift more of the inspection tasks from government to industry. Economic incentives exist for processors to improve quality control to reduce costs and improve product quality, as long as the buyer can identify and attribute the higher quality to the processor. Brands can serve this function by identifying the seller to the buyer. The poultry industry as a whole has an interest in protecting its reputation and retaining the public's trust and confidence in the wholesomeness of its products. The industry experienced the negative effect a major story can have when television's *60 Minutes* aired a special in 1987 on the salmonella problem that depressed poultry sales for some time. Hudson Foods encountered financial problems when it was asked to recall hamburger tainted with the *E. coli* bacteria in August 1997, and the financial fallout contributed to its selling its poultry division to Tyson in 1998 for $642.4 million.

The new inspection procedures started in 1997 in the industry's largest plants and now are in place for small plants as well. The new process requires poultry plants to implement a hazard analysis and critical control points (HACCP) approach to food safety.[60] The HACCP plan must include analysis to determine where safety hazards occur in processing, identification of critical control points for these hazards, and implementation of control methods to assure that hazards stay within critical limits. At least one bird must be tested for salmonella each day, and the plant must not have more than 20 percent of its chickens contaminated with salmonella or it must take actions to reduce the incidence or face possible closure. No testing is done for campylobacter.

The new HACCP plans are reducing salmonella in broilers; the latest USDA data show the percentage of broilers with salmonella has fallen to 9.1 percent for all plant sizes in 2000.[61] Larger plants do better than smaller plants. As recently as 1985, a USDA study concluded that 35 percent of chicken carcasses were contaminated with salmonella[62] and the 20 percent baseline above came from a USDA study in 1995 on average contamination levels. Testing by *Consumer Reports* support these reductions in average levels but found a range from 4 percent to 14 percent among four top brands.[63]

The improvement in salmonella numbers is of little comfort given the failure to control the even higher incidences of campylobacter. The 1994/5 USDA baseline study found that 88 percent of chickens were contaminated with campylobacter, and the recent testing by *Consumer Reports* found levels from 60 percent to 80 percent among four top brands. A March 1998 report in *Consumer Reports* found campylobacter in 63 percent of the tested chickens, salmonella in 16 percent, and both contaminants in 8 percent. Only 29 percent were free of both. They concluded that no brand was cleaner than another and that "as a group" the premium chickens, including free-range, were the most contaminated.[64] USDA has yet to set a standard and begin testing for campylobacter, although it is planning to.

Perhaps HACCP along with other new technologies can solve the problems without any new threat to food safety. Much remains to be done by both the industry and the consumer. Consumers need to relearn proper handling and cooking practices. The industry can limit antibiotics, increase monitoring throughout the vertical food chain, and continue research on vaccines and other treatments given to the chickens before processing. Irradiation of poultry has shown that it can reduce, or eliminate, salmonella and campylobacter.[65] It has been approved for use with poultry products and can extend the shelf life of raw chicken to sixty days. However, the industry is reluctant to use it because of its cost and fears of consumer reaction to the idea of radiation. To date, only one irradiation plant is treating poultry, and the meat is sold mainly to food-service companies. Estimates suggest that irradiation could add one to five cents per pound to the price of chicken. There is greater uncertainty regarding consumer attitudes toward buying products that have been treated with low-level doses of radiation. Some industry studies suggest that consumers are ready to try it, but it remains an open question whether consumers want irradiated chicken or just cleaner chicken. Once treated, the packages must be labeled "Treated with Irradiation." Also, as a former USDA official has said "(irradiation is) not a substitute for taking proper sanitation measures in processing plants. After all, sterilized poop is still poop."[66]

## Equity

Of the four major groups that share in the success of the broiler industry, consumers are the clear winners. They have benefited from a competitive industry that has lowered the real cost of its products and has responded to consumers' demands. Next, the owners and managers of the integrated broiler companies have been rewarded for their abilities and risk-taking consistent with a competitive industry. When a good year brings above-normal profits, current firms prosper but, since market power is not a problem, the industry adjusts to reduce future profits as expected. That is not to say that the top CEOs of the leading firms are not handsomely rewarded. John Tyson, of Tyson Foods, made $1.1 million in 2000 ($650 thousand in salary and the rest in long-term compensation). Bruce Rhode, CEO of ConAgra, made $3.4 million in salary and bonuses and $5.8 million in total direct compensation. David Van Hoose of Pilgrim's Pride made $922 thousand in 2000 from salary and bonuses.[67] Whereas all consumers have benefited and top managers are among the best paid in the food system, not all growers and laborers have shared in the industry's success. Whether the variability in success is attributable to skill level and job performance or to an inequitable sharing of the rewards is unclear, but the economic setting suggests that some groups are in the weaker position.

## Growers

Over time, the size of broiler farms has dramatically increased while the number of broiler farms has fallen substantially—by over 50 percent since 1959, if small farms of under 2,000 birds are not considered. In 1959 there were 42,185 broiler farms, but only 2,254 farms raising 100,000 or more birds per year accounted for 28.5 percent of broiler sales.[68] By 1997, a farm with under 100,000 birds was a small farm, as 98 percent of all sales were made by farms with at least 100,000 birds.[69] In just about forty years, the largest share of broiler sales had shifted from farms raising between 16,000 and 60,000 birds per year to farms raising between 300,000 and 500,000 birds per year. In 1997, 15.6 percent of the broiler farms had 500,000 or more birds, but they accounted for 48 percent of broiler sales.

These growers perform the grow-out function for the vertically integrated processors. Over 90 percent of the broilers are raised under contracts with independent growers, with the rest raised on company-owned farms. The grow-out stage represents about 50 percent of the total capital costs of a vertically integrated broiler firm. The main advantage of having independent growers raise the chicks to market weight under contract is to reduce the capital needs of the integrator while still maintaining control of the total operation. Integrators do not wish to tie up half of their assets in the grow-out function when better profit opportunities exist elsewhere, yet they want control of this important stage of the vertical system. Farmers who raise chicks to market weight have always been financially vulnerable. Originally, it was the market's price volatility that caused financial stress, and growers sought arrangements with feed companies to reduce the risk of raising broilers. Contracts were welcomed by the financially weak growers.

Even with contracts, growers remain vulnerable. The growers provide the land, buildings, equipment, labor, and management functions for the grow-out stage. The integrator provides the chicks, feed, medicines, and supervisory assistance. A major risk the grower faces is the sunk cost of the land, buildings, and equipment, since they have no good alternative uses. These sunk costs create a barrier to exit. The integrator decides how many batches of chicks the growers will get each year, with a substantial effect on the grower's income. In addition, the integrator can demand modern-

ization programs and changes in cultural practices, threatening to cut off a grower. Integrators have distanced themselves geographically from other integrators, and hence growers face either a local monopsonist or at best a tight oligopsony. The areas chosen for broiler production are often those with few, if any, economic alternatives. The areas are often characterized as "rural poor." Usually the land is not productive in an agricultural sense. The growers are not organized into collectives or bargaining units, and allegations have been leveled at integrators for cutting off growers who try to organize growers. Such an economic setting suggests that the contract growers are in a weak position, even though the processor has no desire to raise all the broilers under company ownership. Unfortunately, no publicly available data allow examination of grower returns to determine whether a problem exists and whether it is widespread or limited to marginal growers.

Such conditions have traditionally encouraged farmers to form cooperatives to vertically integrate into processing to eliminate market power abuses directed at farmers. In addition, cooperatives return any profits from the processing stage to the grower-members. Gold Kist is the only agricultural cooperative in the broiler industry, but it has set up an investor-owned subsidiary to process and market broilers, hence it no longer fits the classic model of a farmer-owned marketing cooperative seeking to maximize member returns from both the production and processing functions.

## Labor

The employees of the processing plants have not become prosperous, but have gained added job opportunities from processors locating in their rural areas. The processing plants are located close to the production areas and thus share the economically depressed conditions of these regions. The processing plant is likely to be one of the few employers in the area. Working conditions are often poor; worker safety violations are not uncommon and have had tragic consequences. Even in the better plants, the work is unpleasant and repetitive motion trauma is common. Most of the line workers are minority women, whereas most managers are white males. Union representation is low, estimated to be 25 percent of poultry workers, and union organizers are unwelcome. Of all the food industries, poultry workers earned the lowest average hourly wage rate in 1999 of all production workers—just $8.96.[70] The nearest rival for the bottom hourly wage was the fresh and frozen fish packing industry, at $9.27, which shares many characteristics with poultry processing. This contrasted sharply with the 1999 average for all food and tobacco industries of $12.07 per hour and with the $24.44 per hour earned in the beer industry, an industry that is both highly concentrated and unionized—two major factors related to high wages. Should wage rates rise in the poultry industry, however, processors will further automate their plants and also explore relocating—most likely in Mexico—as free trade continues to expand.

## Summary

Overall, the broiler industry is one of the most competitive in the food system. Its market structure is characterized by low concentration, low product differentiation, (vertically integrated) well-managed firms, and low barriers to entry that have resulted in lowering the real cost of broilers over time. Its firms compete on a price and quality basis. Objectively superior quality receives a premium consistent with the cost of the improved quality. Firms have responded to consumers' de-

mands for convenient, flavorful, and healthful products. To date that new demand has benefited firms as well, since they have been able to market value-added products that reduce their sensitivity to commodity price swings. Such competitive market structure and conduct have delivered outstanding market performance.

The industry is at a crossroads, however. Recent years have seen a marked increase in concentration, causing concerns, especially in input markets. The level of output concentration has reached the level that economists use to mark noncompetitive industries. The dominance of Tyson leaves the industry little chance of returning to lower levels of concentration. Its major acquisition of IBP, Inc. in late 2001, makes it the number-one firm in processing broilers, beef, and pork, allowing it even more strategic choices. If Tyson's next two largest rivals attempt to match Tyson's market share, the industry would become a tight oligopoly. The beef industry became a concentrated industry in less than ten years. If further mergers are challenged to prevent the broiler industry from following the beef industry to a more concentrated structure, then Tyson is likely to remain a dominant firm protected by the very antitrust laws that allowed it to acquire almost all of its assets.

The shift toward more value-enhanced products, although clearly driven by consumer demand, does allow for greater product differentiation and a lessening of price competition. The broiler companies have found it easier to increase market share than to differentiate basic broilers. To most consumers, chicken is still chicken and they do not hold strong brand loyalties among fresh suppliers. The increased concentration and a shifting of emphasis to processed products makes the broiler industry one to watch in future years.

Consumers have been the clear winners in an industry whose market structure and conduct delivered near-perfect market performance, albeit with some unpaid environmental externalities and below average worker compensation and protection. We can only theorize that a less-than-perfect market structure will bring a less-than-perfect market performance in the years to come as consumers trade rock-bottom, perfectly competitive prices for a dazzling array of product variety.

## Notes

Nyssa Schloyer provided research assistance. Eileen Keegan and Darleen Slysz assisted in manuscript preparation. The author thanks Gary Thornton of Watt Publishing Co. for providing data from the annual broiler survey.

1. Gordon Sawyer, *Agribusiness Poultry Industry* (Jericho, NY: Exposition, 1971), pp. 15–16.

2. A "New York dressed" broiler is slaughtered and bled, and the feathers are removed, but not the entrails.

3. Sawyer, *Poultry*, p. 76.

4. USDA, *Poultry Yearbook*, 2001 available at <http://usda.mannlib.cornell.edu/data-sets/livestock/89007/>.

5. *The U.S. Broiler Industry* (Washington, DC: U.S. Department of Agriculture, Economic Research Service [ERS], 1988), pp. 77–81.

6. William Robbins, "One Man with Purpose Takes on Heart Disease," *New York Times*, July 22, 1990, sec. 1, p. 6.

7. Available data now combine California's figures with those of other states to avoid business disclosure of two leading firms, which prevents an update of Figure 3.2.

8. "How Broilers are Marketed," <http://dpichicken.com/index.cfm"content=facts>, October 15, 2001.

9. *1995 Industry Survey.* (Washington, DC: National Broiler Council).

10. David Harvey, "Growth in Broiler Production Likely to Slow in 2001," *Agricultural Outlook*, November 2000; USDA, Economic Research Service, pp. 2–3.

11. Richard T. Rogers, "Structural Change in U.S. Food Manufacturing, 1958–1997," *Agribusiness* 17, no. 1 (2001): 3–32.

12. John M. Connor, Richard T. Rogers, Bruce W. Marion, and Willard F. Mueller, *The Food Manufacturing Industries* (Lexington, MA: D.C. Heath, 1985), p. 73.

13. Ibid., p. 148.

14. Bruce Marion and Donghwan Kim, "Concentration Change in the Selected Food Manufacturing Industries: The Influence of Mergers versus Internal Growth," *Agribusiness* 7, no. 5 (1991): 415–31.

15. Tyson Foods, Inc. *Annual Report*, 1990.

16. *Broiler Industry* (January 1997 and December issues of earlier years); *Watt Poultry USA, Survey 2001* (and earlier years).

17. "Value of Shipments Data by Product Class for the 1,000 Largest Manufacturing Companies of 1950," Staff Report to the Federal Trade Commission, January 1972.

18. *Organization and Competition in the Poultry and Egg Industries*, National Commission on Food Marketing, U.S. Dept. of Agriculture, Washington, DC. Technical Study No. 2, 1966.

19. Bruce Marion and H.B. Arthur, *Dynamic Factors in Vertical Commodity Systems*, Research Bulletin No. 1065. (Wooster: Ohio Agricultural Research and Development Center, November 1973).

20. Steve Ennen, "The 2001 Top 100 Food Companies," *Food Processing* 62, no. 5 (May 2001): 20.

21. *Broiler Industry*, December 1990, p. 32; *Watt Poultry USA, Survey*, 2001.

22. Marion and Arthur.

23. Thomas Whiteside, "Annals of Business," *New Yorker*, July 6, 1987, pp. 39–56.

24. Connor et al., p. 73.

25. More information on taste tests is presented in the performance section of this chapter.

26. David Amey, "Nation's Top Broiler Companies," *Broiler Industry*, December 1989.

27. Major media advertising is consumer oriented and is the main instrument for creating and maintaining product differentiation in food products. It includes advertising expenditures in network, spot, syndicated, and cable television (and radio), consumer magazines, including Sunday magazines, major newspapers, and outdoor billboards. It excludes advertising expenditures directed at trade buyers.

28. Charles D. Schewe and Reuben M. Smith, *Marketing Concepts and Applications*, 2d ed. (New York: McGraw-Hill), p. 10.

29. Connor et al., p. 91.

30. Clark R. Burbee and Edwin T. Bardwell, "Marketing New England Poultry—Economies of Scale in Hatching and Cost of Distributing Broiler Chicks," Agricultural Experiment Station Bulletin 483, University of New Hampshire, May 1964.

31. Marion and Arthur.

32. *The U.S. Broiler Industry*, pp. 65–69.

33. Rogers, *Structural Change.*

34. *Watt Poultry USA, Survey*, 2001.

35. Michael Spence, "Competition, Entry, and Antitrust Policy," in *Strategy, Predation, and Antitrust Analysis*, Steven Salop, ed. (Washington, DC: Federal Trade Commission, 1981), p. 75.

36. Michael E. Porter, "Strategic Interaction: Some Les-

sons from Industry Histories for Theory and Antitrust Policy," in *Strategy, Predation*, pp. 455–56.

37. Yochi Dreazen, "Advertising Kosher—Food Marketers Aim More Messages at Non-Jews," *Wall Street Journal*, July 30, 1999, p. B-2.

38. "Chicken, What You Don't Know Can Hurt You," *Consumer Reports*, March 1998, pp. 12–18; "A Fresh Look at Chicken Safety," *Consumer Reports*, October 1998, pp. 26–27.

39. Kathleen Hughes, "If Fitness Matters, Shouldn't a Chicken Do a Workout Too?" *Wall Street Journal*, July 16, 1986, p. 1.

40. Ibid.

41. Petaluma Web site <http://www.healthychickenchoices.com/chickens.html>, October 21, 2001.

42. "The Chicken, the Whole Chicken, and Nothing but the Chicken," *The Food Institute Report*, May 11, 1998, p. 6.

43. J.M. Koonce and Joe G. Thomas, "Differentiating a Commodity: Lessons from Tyson Foods," *Planning Review* 17 (September–October 1989): 24–29.

44. Kim Clark, "Tough Times for the Chicken King," *Fortune*, October 28, 1996, pp. 88–97.

45. "ConAgra in a Good Mood," *Food Business*, March 25, 1991, p. 12.

46. Marion and Kim, "Concentration Change."

47. Pilgrim's Pride annual report, 2000.

48. Whiteside, pp. 39–56.

49. Schewe and Smith, p. 11.

50. Whiteside, pp. 39–56.

51. *Wall Street Journal*, April 11, 1994, p. A-68.

52. Tyson Foods Annual Report, 2000.

53. *The World Poultry Market—Government Intervention and Multilateral Policy* (Washington, DC: U.S. Department of Agriculture, ERS, 1990), p. 10.

54. "Fresh Chicken," *Consumer Reports*, February 1989, pp. 75–77.

55. Hughes, p. 1.

56. Ibid.

57. Geoffrey S. Becker. *Federal Poultry Inspection: A Briefing*. Hearings before the Subcommittee on Livestock, Dairy and Poultry of the House Committee on Agriculture, 100th Cong., 1st sess., 87–432 ENR, May 8, 1987.

58. Ibid.

59. Gene Bruce, "Dirty Chicken," *Atlantic Monthly*, November 1990, p. 32; "Chicken: How Safe? How Tasty?" *Consumer Reports*, March 1998, p. 12; "A Fresh Look at Chicken Safety," *Consumer Reports*, October 1998, p. 26.

60. Jean C. Buzby and Stephen R. Crutchfield, "USDA Modernizes Meat and Poultry Inspection," *Food Review*, January–April 1997, pp. 14–17.

61. USDA, Food Safety and Inspection Service (FSIS), "Progress Report on *Salmonella* Testing of Raw Meat and Poultry Products, 1998–2000," Sal Comp Report 010411.pdf, received by request from FSIS in October 2001. Also see <http://www.fsis.usda/gov/OA/background/salmtest5.htm>, October 30, 2001.

62. Bruce, p. 32; "Chicken: How Safe?" p. 12; "A Fresh Look at Chicken Safety," p. 26.

63. "A Fresh Look at Chicken Safety," p. 26.

64. "Chicken: How Safe?" p. 12.

65. *Poultry Egg and Marketing*, November–December 1990, p. 17.

66. *Consumer Reports*, March 1998, p. 18.

67. "Hedging Their Bets," *Wall Street Journal*, April 12, 2001, p. R-1.

68. *The U.S. Broiler Industry*, p. 13.

69. *1997 Census of Agriculture*, volume 2, available at <http://www.nass.usda.gov/census>.

70. *1999 Census of Manufactures—Annual Survey of Manufactures* (Table 2).

## Selected Readings

Knoeber, Charles R., and Walter N. Thurman. "'Don't Count Your Chickens . . .': Risk and Risk Shifting in the Broiler Industry." *American Journal of Agricultural Economics*, August 1995: 486–96. An economic evaluation of how legal contracts can be written to replace some market incentives to improve vertical system performance.

Rogers, Richard. "The U.S. Food Marketing System." *Wiley Encyclopedia of Food Science and Technology*, 2d ed. Frederick J. Francis, ed. New York: Wiley, 2000, 2701–24. A broad overview of the food marketing system as it coordinates a vast array of economic activity involved in transforming and transporting an increasingly diverse set of producer's products to consumers—when, where, and how they prefer them. This vertical system is experiencing changes resulting from technological change; globalization; industrialization; consolidation; and an ever-changing, more affluent, and more diverse consumer population.

Rogers, Richard. "Structural Change in U.S. Food Manufacturing, 1958 to 1997." *Agribusiness: An International Journal* 17, no. 1 (2001): 3–32. The paper uses public and purchased census data to document increases in both aggregate and market concentration in U.S. food manufacturing industries.

Royer, Jeffrey, and Richard Rogers, eds. *The Industrialization of Agriculture: Vertical Coordination in the U.S. Food System*. Ashgate Publishing, 1998. The book consists of sixteen chapters written by leading experts on the economic and institutional aspects of vertical coordination and industrialization of the U.S. food system.

Sawyer, Gordon. *Agribusiness Poultry Industry.* Jericho, NY: Exposition, 1971. This classic book explores and records the early history and development of the U.S. poultry industry.

## Selected Web Sites

Delmarva Poultry Industry, Inc.: <http://www.dpichicken.org/>

National Chicken Council: <http://www.eatchicken.com/>

National Contract Growers Association: <http://www.web-span.com/pga/>

National Interfaith Committee for Worker Justice: <http://www.nicwj.org/pages/issues.Poultry.html>

USDA, Economic Research Service: <http://www.ers.usda.gov/Topics/View.asp't=103200>

USDA, Food Safety Inspection Service: <http://www.fsis.usda.gov/OA/FAQ/hotlinefaqindex.htm#5>

United Poultry Concerns: <http://www.upc-online.org/workers/>

# 4

# Pharmaceuticals

## The Critical Role of Innovation

*Larry L. Duetsch*

It is evident that innovation in the pharmaceutical industry generates social benefits of great magnitude. Mortality and morbidity rates for many diseases have fallen dramatically in the last half-century, extending our productive lives and improving the quality of life. With the introduction of new products, the duration of many diseases has been shortened and the cost of treatment has frequently been reduced. Hospitalization is much less often required to treat disease successfully.

Still, the economic cost of direct medical expenses and lost productivity caused by just six major diseases totals more than $600 billion annually. This enormous sum is the total of cost estimates prepared independently by governmental and nonprofit agencies that promote the study of Alzheimer's disease, arthritis, cancer, cardiovascular disease, diabetes, and stroke. The potential benefit (cost savings) from improved treatments for these (and other) diseases offers a tremendous inducement to intensify pharmaceutical research.

Although remarkable progress in the treatment of disease has been made since the 1940s, recent advances in biotechnology have now revealed especially promising approaches to the discovery and production of new drugs to treat disease safely and effectively. More can and should be done to facilitate pharmaceutical innovation. This study examines the nature of pharmaceutical research, the nature of competition in the industry, and the nature of the public policies that promote and/or discourage innovative activity in the industry. It concludes with an examination of the impact of current public policy on pharmaceutical innovation.

## Strategy and the Development of New Products

Many innovative new products are introduced each year in addition to new drugs. Although new drugs frequently become active ingredients in more than one product, combination products, new dosage forms, and duplicate generic products greatly increase the number of new products introduced annually. These derivative products have provided benefits of improved therapeutic action, greater convenience, or increased competition in therapeutic markets. Since new drugs become the basic components of the derivative products and may be regarded as the source of most progress, their development is of particular importance and deserves special attention.

The total amount of innovative activity in the pharmaceutical industry appeared to reach a low

Table 4.1

**Total Number of New Drugs Approved, 1940–1999**

| Period | No. of new drugs approved |
|--------|-------|
| 1995–99 | 185 |
| 1990–94 | 126 |
| 1985–89 | 108 |
| 1980–84 | 95 |
| 1975–79 | 83 |
| 1970–74 | 75 |
| 1965–69 | 104 |
| 1960–64 | 152 |
| 1955–59 | 248 |
| 1950–54 | 205 |
| 1945–49 | 125 |
| 1940–44 | 67 |

*Source:* Food and Drug Administration, 2000.

point in the 1970s. The number of new drugs introduced in the United Sates during the 1970s was about one-third of the number introduced during the 1950s, as Table 4.1 shows. The number of new drug introductions has risen since then, especially during the 1990s. This chronological pattern of new drug introductions does not mirror industry expenditures on research and development activity, which have risen continually in real terms. Instead, it appears that in the 1960s some worldwide phenomenon that could be described as a depletion of research opportunities contributed to a slowdown in the rate of progress. During the 1980s and 1990s, as industry spending on research and development intensified, the flow of new product introductions increased.

The spurt of innovative activity in the 1950s can be attributed to a research strategy that could not be sustained. The early strategy relied extensively on trial-and-error—systematic examination of the therapeutic properties of large numbers of chemical entities, especially closely related deriva-

tives of known entities that might have desired properties. One search conducted in this manner, for a drug that would be effective against tuberculosis, is said to have involved more than 100,000 such entities. The approach, sometimes derided as "molecule manipulation," occasionally led to the development of a significantly improved drug therapy. More than one-third of the most important advances in therapy introduced in the United States from 1944 to 1963 resulted from the examination of closely related chemical entities.[1]

Pharmaceutical research has achieved progress in treating nearly all forms of disease, but the degree of progress has been more striking for some disease classifications than for others. Very different patterns of progress can be seen when developments for different classes of disease are examined. In some instances one breakthrough discovery has led to a substantial improvement in therapy. More often, though, innovative improvements in therapy have been incremental, with each new product resulting in a marginal gain in safety or efficacy. Breakthrough discoveries have sometimes involved examination of chemically related drugs with therapeutic properties that were quite unexpected, having applications quite different from those originally sought. In some cases important uses for drugs with unexpected therapeutic properties went unrecognized for many years after their introduction.

The course of pharmaceutical research projects is still far from predictable. Nevertheless, since the 1960s the research strategy used to identify better therapeutic agents has grown more sophisticated. Progress no longer depends as heavily on trial-and-error techniques. Our understanding of pharmacological action in humans has advanced so that it is now possible to design chemical and biological entities to obtain desired therapeutic effects. Discovery-by-design techniques have

Table 4.2

**Domestic and Foreign Research and Development Expenditures of Research-Based Pharmaceutical Companies, Selected Years**

| Year | Domestic R&D in current dollars (millions) | Domestic R&D in constant (1999) dollars | Foreign R&D in current dollars (millions) | Ratio of foreign R&D to total R&D (percent) | Ratio of all R&D to global sales of ethical drugs (percent) |
|------|------|------|------|------|------|
| 2000 | 19,987 | 19,693 | 5,692 | 28.5 | 17.0 |
| 1995 | 11,874 | 12,628 | 3,334 | 28.1 | 19.4 |
| 1990 | 6,803 | 8,221 | 1,617 | 23.8 | 16.2 |
| 1985 | 3,379 | 4,776 | 699 | 20.7 | 15.1 |
| 1980 | 1,549 | 2,870 | 427 | 27.6 | 11.9 |
| 1975 | 904 | 2,420 | 158 | 17.5 | 11.3 |
| 1970 | 566 | 2,058 | 52 | 9.2 | 11.4 |

*Source*: Pharmaceutical Research and Manufacturers of America, *PhRMA Annual Survey*, 2001.
*Note*: R&D expenditures for ethical pharmaceuticals only.

greatly reduced the need for screening large numbers of potential therapeutic agents, making it possible to target the search for improved agents. Advances in biotechnology have contributed greatly to the recent increase in the number of new drug introductions.

The applied research that is carried out in the pharmaceutical industry today interacts ever more strongly with the progress of academic research carried out in hospitals, medical centers, and universities. There has always been a very strong complementarity between the product-oriented research done in industrial laboratories and the more problem-oriented research carried on in academic settings. By contributing to our understanding of the causes of disease and the pharmacological effects of chemical and biological entities, academic research has suggested new paths for applied research. At the same time, applied pharmaceutical research has frequently led to new products whose pharmacological action was unexpected, and the gaps in our understanding of that action have often been reduced through subsequent use of these products as tools in the ongoing academic investigation of cellular biology. The interaction between academic and applied research can best be described as mutually supportive.

*Investing in Pharmaceutical Innovation*

The investment in innovative activity in the pharmaceutical industry is more appropriately measured by the value of the resources that are committed to the development of new products than by the number of products that are eventually obtained. Annual expenditures on research and development are shown in Table 4.2. During the 1970s, real growth in the industry's domestic expenditures on research and development averaged just 3.4 percent per year of over the previous year, but real growth then increased sharply to 11.1 percent during the 1980s and 9.2 percent during the 1990s. Foreign expenditures by the industry grew more rapidly than domestic expenditures, more than doubling as a proportion of the industry's total research and development activity. Growth in the size of foreign markets and less

Table 4.3

**Distribution of Domestic Research and Development Expenditures by Function, Selected Years**

| Function | Percent of total | | | |
| --- | --- | --- | --- | --- |
| | 1975 | 1985 | 1994 | 1999 |
| Synthesis, extraction, biological screening, pharmacological testing | 39 | 32 | 32 | 27 |
| Toxicology and safety testing | 10 | 10 | 6 | 5 |
| Clinical evaluation | 25 | 29 | 35 | 45 |
| Dosage formulation, stability testing, bio-availability studies, process development | 23 | 24 | 23 | 19 |
| Regulatory expenses | 3 | 5 | 4 | 4 |

*Source*: Pharmaceutical Research and Manufacturers of America, *PhRMA Annual Survey*, various years.
*Note*: Expenses designated "other" were excluded.

stringent controls over testing in foreign markets contributed to this shift. Overall, the intensity of the industry's expenditures on research and development (relative to sales) showed no trend during the 1970s and then increased abruptly to a significantly higher level during the 1980s and 1990s.

These industry expenditures have been distributed among the functions that precede new product introductions in the proportions shown in Table 4.3. The product development process is complex, involving a number of distinct steps that must be carried out sequentially. It is apparent that during the past twenty-five years industry expenditures on new product development have grown most dramatically in the realm of clinical evaluation, driven by the need to demonstrate safety and effectiveness in order to obtain regulatory approval. The cost of clinical evaluation is now nearly half of the growing real expenditure on research and development.

## The Nature of Pharmaceutical Competition

Innovation plays a critical role in the competition that takes place within therapeutic markets. Good prospects for continued innovation enlarge the circle of potential competitors and make it more difficult for leading firms to sustain their market power. To assess market power at a point in time, the boundaries of relevant therapeutic markets must be identified, taking into account possibilities for substitution in production as well as in consumption. Leading firms throughout the industry derive their revenue primarily from products protected by patents and produced on an exclusive basis, without licensing their patents. These firms do not face competition in the sale of a given chemical entity until patent protection has expired and generic producers are allowed to enter.

Serious competition comes only from developers of other entities that offer comparable safety and efficacy. Although substitutable drugs could be developed by any of the firms that undertake substantial amounts of research, the record of new product introductions suggests that the circle of prospective competitors is typically not large. Most new drugs have been introduced by firms that already had some share of the therapeutic market in question, if only a small one. Leading firms have long sought to innovate in therapeutic groupings in which they held no share, but have had limited success. In the 1990s firms made a greater effort to develop broader portfolios of products in order to reduce their dependence on a few chemical entities.[2] Glaxo, one of the largest pharmaceutical producers, had just five or six new entities in development at any time in the early 1990s and sought to have twenty to thirty in development by the end of the decade. Merck, already among the leaders, sought to expand its portfolio of products from eleven therapeutic groups in 1992 to at least twice that number in 2002. Without acquiring other firms, such goals have proven elusive.

Despite the prevalence of patented products, industrywide concentration in pharmaceuticals has not been high. Table 4.4 shows that until the 1990s there was no trend in the share of total shipments accounted for by the largest firms that manufacture pharmaceutical preparations in the United States. During the last decade, merger activity has significantly increased the market share held by the four largest producers. More will be said about this later, but the increase in overall concentration does not seem to be problematic at this time.

It seems more appropriate to describe market power in the industry in the context of naturally separable therapeutic markets, since drugs in different therapeutic groups are generally poor substitutes for one another (e.g., cardiovascular drugs and vitamins). As one can see, concentration has been higher in the eight therapeutic classes that are shown in Table 4.3, but again in most classes there was no trend during the period for which data are available.

Still more narrowly defined therapeutic markets can be formed on the basis of pharmacological action alone (e.g., analgesics, antibiotics, diuretics, and oral contraceptives). In many of these narrower markets, the four leading firms have typically held higher market shares, ranging from about 50 percent to nearly 90 percent. As one might

expect, most prescriptions are written for one of a small number of patented products that offer the greatest safety and effectiveness for a particular diagnosis. On the basis of pharmacological action, the economic markets for many (perhaps most) prescription drugs can be characterized as quite highly concentrated.

Of course, a bit of judgment is required to draw the boundaries that delineate economic markets, and there is reason to believe that markets defined on the basis of pharmacological action alone may be too narrow. Somewhat broader therapeutic markets can be drawn more pragmatically by observing how physicians actually use products in treatment. Products with quite different pharmacological action are often used to treat a given diagnosis. When physicians prescribe in this manner, it would seem appropriate to group the products together to form a market for the purpose of examining the competitive behavior of producers. Over time, changing usage patterns can alter the boundaries of markets drawn in this manner. For example, Merck's Proscar, first introduced to treat enlarged prostates, seems to have found a new use in treating baldness. Johnson and Johnson's Topamax, first intended to treat epilepsy, also seems to be effective in treating obesity. Leading firms are likely to account for somewhat smaller shares of these more pragmatically defined (typically broader) markets.

## Cost and Risk in Drug Innovation

During the past thirty years the cost of drug innovation has increased greatly, driven largely by the increased cost of clinical testing. One study of new drugs approved for marketing in the 1980s found that, when one includes the cost of failed drugs, costs averaged $73 million (in 1990 dollars) prior to clinical testing on humans and $53 million dur-

Table 4.4

**Concentration Ratios for Pharmaceutical Preparations and Therapeutic Classes, Selected Years**

| | | Value of industry shipments (percent accounted for by) | | |
| | Year | Four largest companies | Eight largest companies | Twenty largest companies |
|---|---|---|---|---|
| Pharmaceutical preparations | 1997 | 36 | 50 | 71 |
| | 1992 | 26 | 42 | 72 |
| | 1982 | 26 | 41 | 67 |
| | 1972 | 25 | 43 | 73 |
| | 1963 | 22 | 37 | 71 |
| **Therapeutic class** | | | | |
| Preparations affecting neoplasms, the endocrine system, and metabolic disease | 1982 | 51 | 73 | 94 |
| | 1972 | 48 | 70 | 95 |
| | 1963 | 53 | 74 | 92 |
| Preparations acting on the central nervous system and the sense organs | 1982 | 41 | 59 | 86 |
| | 1972 | 43 | 63 | 38 |
| | 1963 | 44 | 65 | 83 |
| Preparations acting on the cardiovascular system | 1982 | 54 | 72 | 92 |
| | 1972 | 57 | 76 | 92 |
| | 1963 | 52 | 67 | 86 |
| Preparations acting on the respiratory system | 1982 | 38 | 61 | 88 |
| | 1972 | 48 | 70 | 90 |
| | 1963 | 39 | 58 | 80 |
| Preparations acting on the digestive or the genito-urinary system | 1982 | 32 | 47 | 79 |
| | 1972 | 35 | 53 | 80 |
| | 1963 | 30 | 50 | 72 |
| Preparations acting on the skin | 1982 | 32 | 51 | 77 |
| | 1972 | 35 | 56 | 77 |
| | 1963 | 33 | 47 | 70 |
| Vitamin, nutrient, and hematinic preparations | 1982 | 43 | 61 | 80 |
| | 1972 | 27 | 44 | 69 |
| | 1963 | 28 | 49 | 74 |
| Preparations affecting parasitic and infective diseases | 1982 | 43 | 62 | 92 |
| | 1972 | 45 | 67 | 93 |
| | 1963 | 47 | 72 | 95 |

*Source:* U.S. Bureau of the Census, *Census of Manufactures*, various years.

ing the clinical phase.[3] Because new drug trials now typically involve many more patients, the cost of clinical testing has risen quite dramatically in recent years. A more recent study indicates that the pretax cost of developing an approved new drug rose to more than $500 million in the 1990s, counting both the cost of failures and interest costs during the period of investment. Some would say this is an exaggerated cost estimate, but the time required to develop and test new drugs increased to such a degree that by the 1980s a typical new chemical entity could be expected to have less than ten years of patent protection remaining at the time of introduction. Great variability has characterized the expected returns (relative to costs) for pharmaceutical innovation. Less than 30 percent of the new drugs introduced in the 1970s appeared to produce sufficient returns to cover the cost of bringing them to market.[4] But the ten most successful new drugs were *very* successful, producing returns that exceeded costs (on average) by a factor of five. The degree of risk in this innovative process is clearly high. Larger pharmaceutical firms have been better able to bear the cost and risk of bringing new drugs to market.

More recently, the growing cost and risk associated with new product developments has led firms to pursue growth through merger and/or strategic alliances. With shorter product life cycles and growing pressure to pursue costly new research strategies, many of the largest firms made strategic acquisitions during the 1990s, as Table 4.5 shows. Short of mergers, strategic alliances are often struck to allow pharmaceutical firms to draw upon the research expertise of others, bring products to market more rapidly, or more effectively commercialize approved products. The number of alliances between domestic and foreign pharmaceutical companies, biotechnology firms, university research centers, and contract research organizations grew from about 100 in the mid-1980s to about 700 in the late 1990s.[5]

## Price Competition and Product Promotion

Industry critics frequently point out that the same products sell for very different prices in different countries. International drug-price differences are defended by the industry on the basis of differences in demand, for the most part. Much of the growth in U.S. spending on prescription drugs in recent years has resulted from the growing number of prescriptions filled, especially by the elderly. Moreover, in recent years the prices of generic products have risen more rapidly than those of branded products.

Some may suspect that innovative new pharmaceutical products, protected by patents and promoted intensely, are effectively insulated from price competition. However, indications of competition within U.S. therapeutic markets have been found in the pricing of new drugs both at the time of introduction and in the subsequent pricing of those products that must compete with generic entrants. Table 4.6 presents data on the pricing and therapeutic importance of 171 new drugs introduced from 1958 to 1975. When compared to the price of established products that they were expected to replace, new drugs that were expected to provide substantial therapeutic gains were more often priced well above the established products. In contrast, new drugs that were judged to provide little therapeutic gain were very likely to be priced at or below established products, presumably to penetrate the market. This strongly suggests that the price levels chosen for innovations vary with the degree of quality rivalry that is encountered. High initial prices were set for breakthrough products, for which demand was relatively inelastic.

Table 4.5

**Selected Recent Acquisitions in Pharmaceuticals**

| Year | Acquiring company | Target company | Apparent objective(s) |
|------|-------------------|----------------|------------------------|
| 1994 | Roche | Syntex | Painkillers, anti-inflammatory drugs, research pipeline |
| 1994 | American Home Products | American Cyanamid | Vaccines, antibiotics, generic drugs |
| 1995 | Glaxo | Burroughs Wellcome | Antiviral drug Zovirax, AIDS drug AZT |
| 1995 | Hoechst | Marion Merrell | Cardizem heart drug, Seldane allergy drug, generic drugs |
| 1995 | Pharmacia | Upjohn | Research pipeline |
| 1996 | Ciba-Geigy | Sandoz | Biotechnology products and research pipeline |
| 1998 | Zeneca | Astra | Ulcer drug Prilosec, expanded research program |
| 1998 | Sanofi | Synthelabo | Expanded research program |
| 1999 | Warner-Lambert | Agouron | HIV drug Viracept, biotechnology products |
| 1999 | Roche | Genentech | Biotechnology products |
| 2000 | Glaxo Wellcome | Smith Kline | Operational efficiencies, expanded research program |
| 2000 | Pfizer | Warner-Lambert | Anticholesterol drug Lipitor, cardiovascular and diabetes drugs, biotechnology products |
| 2000 | Pharmacia & Upjohn | Searle | Pain reliever Celebrex, research pipeline |
| 2001 | Bristol Myers Squibb | DuPont (pharmaceuticals) | Anticoagulant Coumaden, HIV drug Sustiva, research pipeline |

*Source: Wall Street Journal*, various issues.

The relative prices of established products have tended to decline later in the product life cycle as competitors introduce comparable or possibly superior products. Generally, the greater the market share achieved by new drugs, the greater the reduction in relative prices has been. In recent years competition has been promoted through the efforts of health insurance plans and hospitals to negotiate prices. Both brand-name and generic products are commonly discounted for large buyers. De-

Table 4.6

**Relative Price of New Drugs and Food and Drug Administration Rating, 1958–1975**

| Ratio of price of new entity to price of leading drugs | FDA rating | | | | | | | |
|---|---|---|---|---|---|---|---|---|
| | Important therapeutic gain | | Modest therapeutic gain | | Little or no therapeutic gain | | Total | |
| | no. | % | no. | % | no. | % | no. | % |
| Less than 1.0 | 7 | (24) | 12 | (35) | 53 | (49) | 72 | (42) |
| From 1.0 to 1.5 | 6 | (21) | 13 | (38) | 44 | (41) | 63 | (37) |
| Greater than 1.5 | 16 | (55) | 9 | (27) | 11 | (10) | 36 | (21) |
| Total | 29 | (100) | 34 | (100) | 108 | (100) | 171 | (100) |

*Source:* Adapted from W. Duncan Reekie, "Price and Quality Competition in the United States Drug Industry," *Journal of Industrial Economics,* 26 (March 1978), Table 1.

spite the pressure for price competition, price differentials can and do persist between products that appear to be good substitutes. Some brand-name drugs have been able to sustain both higher prices and higher market shares, besting generic competitors and even other branded competitors. While price competition certainly takes place, it does not always appear to be effective.

There is no question that the unique therapeutic value of some products has conferred substantial market power on innovators in some therapeutic markets. Patent protection has bolstered the position of firms that have achieved market dominance through innovation, although the duration of market dominance has been limited as much by successive innovations as by patent expiration. In some cases, even the eventual expiration of patents has not enabled the new generic producers to quickly erode the dominance of leading brands. Significant product differentiation advantages are often derived from the brand-name trademark that is retained indefinitely by the innovator. In some cases a branded drug has gained recognition as the first to offer a therapeutic advance, enabling the innovator to capitalize later on an apparent first-

mover advantage. In the often-cited case of a branded diuretic that was recognized as a major breakthrough at introduction, the innovator retained 33 percent of the market for more than ten years after ten other firms had introduced therapeutically equivalent drugs.[6] The innovating firm retained its leading share despite spending less on advertising and charging substantially more than the other firms. The potential risks of inappropriate substitution have made pharmaceuticals an extreme case in terms of the price differentials that have sometimes been sustained without great loss of market share.

Pharmaceutical firms cannot be described as the passive beneficiaries of first-mover status. The marketing of prescription drugs has long relied on brand names that are among the most heavily promoted in the United States. Pharmaceutical promotion has served two purposes, informing physicians of the existence and characteristics of new products and reinforcing their recall of established products, especially those that face competition. Until recently, there have been two primary types of promotion for prescription drugs: direct contact with physicians by drug salespeople (known as detailing) and advertising in professional journals. As a share of industry sales revenue, these expenditures can only be described as intense, but it has been found that comparable drug products used primarily in hospitals have been promoted much less intensely, presumably because selections were made by groups of practitioners who could pool their knowledge rather than by individual physicians.

The rules governing efforts to reach consumers (patients) through media advertising of prescription drugs limited the effectiveness of this form of promotion until 1997, when the rules changed. Companies are now allowed to cite the benefits of specific drugs in television advertising without listing all side effects and warnings. Only the main risks need be cited and details can be provided by means of a toll-free number or Internet address. In 1996 direct-to-consumer advertising totaled nearly $800 million, primarily for relatively vague messages that did not cite benefits but urged viewers to contact their doctors. With their greater freedom, drug producers roughly tripled their use of media in four years. During 2001, producers were expected to spend more than $200 million just to advertise the products used to treat anxiety and depression. Many of these firms have had a great deal of prior experience with intense television promotion of their over-the-counter (OTC) products. In 2000 spending on direct-to-consumer advertising still amounted to about half the amount spent on traditional physician-targeted advertising and detailing. Pharmaceutical product sampling, long relied on in the industry to create brand awareness and build product loyalty, remained the most costly form of product promotion in 2000, involving goods valued at nearly as much as the other forms of promotion combined.[7] Industrywide, spending on all forms of promotion combined amounted to just over 10 percent of global sales in 2000.

Intense promotional expenditures might be expected in an industry that presents physicians and patients with an ever-changing technology and thereby poses high costs of information. Many considerations impinge on the choice of the best drug therapy for particular circumstances. The effects of drugs are influenced by the patients' age, gender, weight, diet, work habits, and general condition. Other considerations include ease of administration, possible side effects, and compatibility with other medications. Pharmaceutical firms have a strong incentive to provide this information freely to physicians in order to increase the demand for their products. Even information regarding adverse side effects can increase demand by reducing the likelihood that physicians will show undue concern for adverse reactions. If the information provided to physicians proves unreliable, especially that provided through detailing, the firm may well lose access to physicians.

Among therapeutic categories there has been a great deal of variation in the intensity with which promotion has been carried on, much of it related to the need for information. As one would expect, more intense promotion has been undertaken in therapeutic categories in which more new products were introduced, in which advances have been more significant, and in which prescriptions are written sporadically. The average age (time elapsed since introduction) of the products that have been promoted through detailing is substantially less than the average age of products advertised in journals, presumably because physicians have greater need for information about newer products. For newer products, promotion has relied on detailing to a greater degree. Detailing is better suited to the provision of information that is specific to a physician's practice as well.

During the second year following introduction, new products have typically been promoted far more intensely than the targeted established product, although the target is usually promoted at much greater total expense. In response to entry, the established product is often promoted less intensely than it was prior to entry, which one would not expect if promotion was largely persuasive. These patterns suggest that product promotion has facilitated the entry of therapeutically important new drugs and has thereby provided the benefits of more rapid adoption of better drug therapy.[8]

**Innovation and Public Policy**

Pharmaceutical products promise consumers substantial therapeutic benefits and, at the same time, pose substantial risks. The increasing complexity of evaluating and comparing these benefits and risks creates an information imperfection if consumers are unable to obtain sufficient information to act in their best interest. New drugs in early stages of development can be particularly difficult to assess, but this may be true even of established products. Therapeutic benefits and risks depend on such things as dosage levels, interactive effects that occur when the product is administered in combination with other drugs, and idiosyncratic patient responses. In the case of new products, these benefits and risks remain uncertain if insufficient premarket testing has been completed. Since testing is costly and time-consuming, firms may have a tendency to complete too little of it before going to market. Firms may have a further tendency to overstate benefits and understate risks, even for established products, despite the threat of damage suits and loss of good reputation. To alleviate this information problem, the government has taken steps to make markets work better by directly controlling the flow of information. In an effort to ensure better information, public policy in the United States has evolved into a

system of strong regulatory controls over pharmaceutical testing and marketing.

The regulation of pharmaceutical marketing in the United States has long sought to ensure that claims made for products are not false or misleading. To this end, the powers of the Food and Drug Administration (FDA) have been strengthened on a number of occasions. The Food, Drug and Cosmetic Act of 1938 first required firms to obtain FDA approval of new drugs prior to their introduction. In turn, the FDA required firms to enumerate the uses of drugs and demonstrate their safety under the conditions for which usage was recommended. Prior to that time, consumers commonly engaged in self-medication without the advice of physicians. The required approval seemed likely to make self-medication safer and more effective. Proponents of the act claimed that it would actually encourage self-medication in this way.

Ironically, the implementation of other provisions of the act quickly and sharply curtailed the practice of self-medication, dramatically changing the marketing practices in the industry by creating a distinction between OTC drugs, which were required to carry detailed labels written for purposes of self-medication by lay people, and prescription-only drugs, which needed only technical labels written for health professionals. The FDA increased the amount of information drug labels were required to contain, but exempted prescription-only products from these requirements on the grounds that they posed no public health threat. Because pharmaceutical firms, with the consent of the FDA, have been able to market products on a prescription-only basis, consumers had no choice but to employ suitably licensed medical agents to select drugs on their behalf.

Until 1938, regulation had sought to improve the flow of information to consumers. The new regulations denied consumers ready access to information. The approach taken by the FDA seemed to presume that clear directions for self-medication could not be written for certain drugs or that consumers would not follow them. The basis for such a presumption remains unclear. The implication in regard to drug marketing was clear immediately. Whereas branded drugs had previously been promoted directly to consumers, the marketing of prescription drugs was now to be directed more and more at medical practitioners. These professionals became unusual customers. As agents of the consumer, they did not pay for the products they ordered and might even remain unaware of their cost. This arrangement certainly made the demand for most prescription drugs more inelastic than it would otherwise have been. Many new drugs would have had inelastic demand in any case; this made the demand for prescription drugs even more so.

At present the FDA effectively discourages informed choice by exempting producers of prescription drugs from the labeling requirements that are imposed on OTC drugs. To expand their markets, however, some firms have chosen to seek FDA approval of the labels and package inserts that are required to reclassify certain commonly used prescription products as OTC products for self-medication. Under the terms of 1984 legislation, the makers of branded prescription drugs generally have been given three years of exclusivity after gaining OTC approval, preventing other firms from making cheaper OTC copies even though cheaper prescription copies (generics) may be available. Of the ten top-selling OTC brands introduced from 1975 to 1992, nine were switches from prescription-only to OTC status.[9]

In recent years OTC status has been granted to a baldness treatment, Rogaine; a heartburn reliever, Tagamet; and the popular anticholesterol drugs, Mevacor and Pravachol. In 2001, an FDA review panel recommended OTC status for the allergy drugs Claritin, Allegra, and Zyrtec in an action sought by an insurance company that expected to reduce its payments for the drugs (and physician visits) by $90 million per year.[10] Producers initially resisted that change in status, apparently fearing that it would hurt their sales of prescription-only substitutes.

### Patent Protection

In 1948 the Patent Office ruled that drugs that were new and useful, including chemical modifications of natural substances, could be patented, as could the processes by which they were made. Consequently, until close substitutes could be developed through further innovation, firms could capitalize on protected market positions. Rather than licensing other firms to use their patents under royalty agreements that might have been difficult to enforce and would have been likely to foster public animosities, innovating firms in the 1950s more often chose to produce on an exclusive basis. Exclusive production was entirely compatible with marketing techniques that focused on a relatively small target group—medical professionals who could be reached through detailing and advertising in professional journals.

The payoff quickly proved to be substantial. The largest firms in the industry soon derived a high proportion of their sales from just a few products, and each of those products generated an even higher share of profits than of sales. Leading firms in the industry continue to derive high percentages of their total sales (and profits) from their best-selling products today. As one might expect, the high profits earned on some products have energized industry critics who, without success, have sought compulsory licensing of drug patents and prohibition of the use of brand names.

Table 4.7

**Drug Development Time** (Years) **from Synthesis to Approval by the FDA**

|                  | Approval in 1960s | Approval in 1970s | Approval in 1980s | Approval 1990–1996 |
|------------------|-------------------|-------------------|-------------------|--------------------|
| Approval phase   | 2.4               | 2.1               | 2.8               | 2.2                |
| Clinical phase   | 2.5               | 4.4               | 5.5               | 6.7                |
| Preclinical phase| 3.2               | 5.1               | 5.9               | 6.0                |

*Source*: Center for the Study of Drug Development, Tufts University, 1998.

The great success leading firms have derived from a few innovations has also brought a high degree of risk; their earnings have become dependent on the sales of a few products. Numerous recent examples of this have been reported. In a two-year period ending in June 2002, Merck lost its right to exclusively market four drugs that were generating $4.6 billion in sales annually. One, Vasotec, accounted for half of that total. Before 2002, Eli Lilly lost exclusivity for drugs that generated more than half of its 1996 U.S. sales. One of these, Prozac, accounted for 43 percent of Lilly's U.S. sales in 1996 and still accounted for more than 20 percent in 2001. By 2002, Schering-Plough lost exclusivity for drugs that generated well over half of its total 1996 U.S. sales. Loss of patent protection on key products is thought to have contributed to industry consolidation in a number of cases, leading Roche to acquire Syntex in 1994 and Upjohn to be acquired by Pharmacia in 1995.

The duration of the patent protection that has been granted to new and useful drugs since 1948 has been shortened by the length of time required to obtain FDA approval of the product that is developed. Because the Patent Office has almost always granted patents more quickly than FDA approval can be obtained, the period of market exclusivity has been shortened. In the 1950s the need to demonstrate safety usually shortened the period of exclusivity by a matter of months, not

years, as has later been the case. This diminishing period of exclusivity appears to have resulted from increasingly lengthy preclinical and clinical development times, as Table 4.7 shows. The time required for the preclinical phase of development had already increased by the 1970s and the time required for clinical trials has continued to increase since then. The time required for final FDA approval of a new drug application has changed little until recently, when a serious effort to speed up approvals began. More will be said about this later.

### Proof of Safety and Efficacy

In 1962 growing public concerns about the risks associated with the increasingly sophisticated products that were being introduced led to the passage of important amendments to the Food, Drug and Cosmetics Act. These amendments directly affected the process of drug innovation in two ways, requiring proof of efficacy for the approval of new drugs and establishing FDA control over the clinical testing of new drugs to demonstrate safety and efficacy. There are several distinct phases of clinical testing. In phase I, drugs are evaluated for safety in a small number of healthy volunteers, beginning with small single doses and progressing to larger multiple doses. Efficacy is the primary focus of phase II trials, conducted on a small number of patients instead of healthy volunteers. More extensive phase III trials evaluate safety and efficacy in 3,000 to 5,000 patients (a typical recent number—twice the number in the early 1980s), including the elderly, patients with multiple diseases, those who take other drugs, and patients whose organs are impaired. Drugs that are already on the market must continue to undergo surveillance to detect unforeseen adverse reactions and also to be tested to demonstrate efficacy for each new use.

Thus, new drugs had to meet high evidentiary standards after 1962. Testing guidelines were developed and formalized during the 1960s. To demonstrate efficacy, the FDA required that clinical testing make use of experimental and control groups in double-blind studies, where neither the patient nor the physician knows whether the patient is receiving the experimental drug or something else, possibly a placebo. The FDA regulations concerning the development of evidence of efficacy (and safety) led to large increases in the cost of gaining approval of new drug applications, especially for drugs whose effects are unavoidably subjective, as they are for drugs that alleviate pain or depression.

Before clinical tests on human subjects may begin, the FDA has required firms to submit a new drug investigational plan, providing the results of animal tests and laying out the procedures that are to be followed in human testing. After review, or at any time during clinical testing, the FDA can block execution or request modification of a plan that poses excessive risks to volunteer subjects or that does not follow sound scientific procedures. This active involvement of the FDA in the research and development process has contributed to higher development costs (in order to ensure safety) and made the clinical phase more time-consuming.

There is good reason to believe that the research strategies pursued by pharmaceutical firms were altered after 1962. Prior to that time the most successful research programs gave scientists significant latitude in choosing research projects. Scientists had generally emphasized medical need and research feasibility in determining the type of therapeutic research to pursue. These considerations corresponded reasonably well to the potential sales and development costs firms could expect. By the late 1960s, it became necessary to also consider expected regulatory costs and delays in choosing among research projects that could be pursued. The development of drugs to treat rare diseases was undoubtedly discouraged by the prospect of a diminished rate of return.

Firms were forced to limit the autonomy their scientists could be afforded when it became clear that the impact on product development of more stringent regulatory requirements was likely to be more pronounced for certain therapeutic classes of drugs. Proof of efficacy is inherently more straightforward and far less costly for drugs that fight infection, for example, than for drugs that reduce heart disease. Antiinfectives need only be shown to kill certain organisms and, since they are administered briefly, pose relatively few long-term hazards. Cardiovascular products are much more difficult to test because the disease mechanisms are much less well understood and, given the need to administer them over long periods, much more lengthy testing is required. Consequently, the development of cardiovascular products is comparatively costly. It has been estimated that the prospect of costly testing has significantly reduced overall research spending relative to levels that would have prevailed.[11] Undoubtedly the effect has varied among therapeutic classes.

The 1962 amendments to the Food, Drug and Cosmetic Act also empowered the FDA to control claims made in drug advertising and promotion. Advertising claims that firms made for their products had to be limited to those approved by the FDA for labels and package inserts. All ads were required to include the generic name of the drug. After 1962 the FDA even sought to control oral statements made during detailing.

### Generic Substitution

The 1962 amendments to the Food, Drug and Cosmetic Act further centralized decision-making authority with regard to new drugs, seeking to protect consumers by barring hazardous products from the market. This increase in the extent and degree of regulatory control has been quite costly to society, since some beneficial products were not brought to market when the time and expenditure that were required to meet regulations reduced the expected rate of return. This has been especially true for generic products that promised little or no advance in treatment, but instead promised price competition. Fewer generics have been introduced as a result. Among the 200 largest selling drugs in 1983, thirty-four of the fifty-two drugs with expired patents had no generic competition.[12] Among the top twenty, two drugs with combined sales of $200 million had no competition. In part, this situation developed after 1962 because firms that sought to introduce generic substitutes were required to furnish independent (duplicative) evidence of efficacy, not merely evidence of biochemical equivalency. Given the difficulty of displacing branded products that physicians had grown accustomed to and were persistently reminded of through advertising and detailing, the high cost of extensive clinical testing further deterred entry by reducing the expected rate of return on generic products. To gain entry, generic producers had to bear high costs of both testing and marketing.

Even before 1962, antisubstitution laws that had been passed by the states early in the 1950s had made entry more difficult for generic producers. To deter drug counterfeiting, state laws generally prohibited pharmacists from dispensing substitutes for the brand prescribed by the physician. Given the reluctance of physicians to prescribe generically, this greatly compounded the difficulty faced by firms that would introduce generic products, effectively forcing them to establish their own brand identification in order to gain entry. During the 1970s growing interest in cost containment programs for drugs led the states to begin repealing their antisubstitution laws, replacing them with provisions that would allow pharmacists to engage in substitution unless the physician has indicated that the prescription is to be dispensed as written.

Although these newer substitution laws differ in many details, two general approaches predominate. In some states, prescription forms have two signature lines, one permitting the pharmacist to substitute and the other requiring that the prescription be dispensed as written. Physicians consent to substitution by signing the permissive line. States that do not use the two-line form allow pharmacists to substitute unless the physician has indicated on the prescription that it is to be dispensed as written. The frequency with which physicians have allowed substitution has been found to differ markedly under these two approaches. In 1989, in states using the two-line form physicians allowed substitution on about 59 percent of all prescriptions, whereas in states without such a form substitution was permitted on 89 percent of all prescriptions.[13]

Some states have sought to require pharmacists to substitute lower cost drugs unless the physician has indicated otherwise. Most states have provided guidance to pharmacists by distributing either an approved list of drugs for which substitution is permitted or a list of drugs for which substitution is always prohibited. The frequency with which pharmacists actually substitute when allowed to do so has been found to vary greatly from state to state, from about 5 percent to about 50 percent. Reports suggest that, in the first year of substitution in Michigan, when substitution did occur, the average consumer saved 20 percent of the price of the drug prescribed.

The difficulties of verifying therapeutic equivalency and the potential liability that could result from inappropriate substitution have made it possible for branded drugs to maintain premium prices and sizable market shares after patent protection has expired. Not surprisingly, follow-on products —either generics or alternative drugs— are more likely to obtain substantial market shares when regulatory authorities have certified their therapeutic equivalence. Follow-on products have had notably greater success in obtaining a significant share of hospital purchases than of drugstore purchases, presumably because hospital formulary boards have better knowledge of alternative drugs and clearer incentives to economize. The strongest stimulus to substitution occurs when states allow pharmacists to retain a portion of the savings, provide pharmacists with certification of bioequivalence, limit the subsequent liability of pharmacists, and require physicians to do more than sign a form to prevent substitution.

By the early 1980s, with the repeal of anti-substitution laws, a major obstacle to the introduction of follow-on products that would stimulate price competition had been removed. This increased the likelihood that a dominant market position would be eroded more quickly after patent expiration. The time-consuming nature of clinical testing requirements, particularly for certain therapeutic categories, had already greatly reduced the effective length of patent protection for new drugs by delaying their introduction. Recall that the ex-

pected effective life of patents on new drugs had dropped to less than ten years by the 1980s. Together, greater ease of substitution and more extensive clinical testing undoubtedly reduced the expected return to drug research and weakened the incentives to do drug research.

## Patent Extension and Generic Competition

The Drug Price Competition and Patent Term Restoration Act of 1984 restored part of the patent life that had been lost in establishing proof of efficacy and has facilitated the introduction of generic products after patent expiration. The act sought to improve the incentives to pioneer new drugs and also sought to stimulate later price competition from imitators.

Under the provisions of the act, the life of a new drug patent has been extended by the length of time taken by the FDA to review the new drug application plus one-half of the clinical testing time, with a maximum extension of five years and no extension beyond fourteen years of effective life. Patent holders, who often obtain more than one patent to ensure their exclusive right to produce a new drug, may obtain an extension of the life of one patent of their choosing. Although this law extended the period of patent exclusivity for many new drugs, it is worth noting that products are likely to be supplanted in the market by newer products before their extended patents expire. Hence patent extension can never fully compensate patent holders for time lost in obtaining FDA approvals. The incentives to undertake research simply cannot be fully restored in this manner.

The act allowed generic producers to satisfy proof-of-efficacy requirements by performing relatively low-cost testing to demonstrate bioequivalency with the pioneer's product, so that the amount of generic entry and the intensity of price competition greatly exceeded previous levels. The impact of the act on generic introductions was dramatic, leading the FDA to approve about two thousand generic applications by 1991. In one example of post-patent entry, when Syntex patents expired in December 1993 on antiarthritics (Naprosyn and Anaprox) with combined sales of $700 million that year, two-thirds of all new prescriptions were filled by generics within a month and the price dropped more than 80 percent.[14] In another example, when Bristol Myers Squibb lost patent protection on Capoten (a heart medication) early in 1996, fourth-quarter sales dropped 83 percent as three-cent generic pills undercut the fifty-seven-cent branded product.[15] These are particularly striking examples involving products with large sales.

More generally, branded producers have maintained price in the face of generic entry while competition between a growing number of generics has driven their prices down. Branded producers curtail promotion and rely on habitual use of the brand name to maintain a significant market share. A study of eighteen drugs facing generic competition during the late 1980s found that generic prices averaged 61 percent of the branded price during the first month, 46 percent one year after entry, and 37 percent two years later.[16] The average generic market share rose from 9 percent in the first month to 35 percent after a year and 49 percent after two years.

Another study found that price competition among generic producers worked very strongly, with the generic price falling from 59 percent of the preentry branded price with one generic entrant to 50 percent with three entrants, and 29 percent with ten.[17] The study examined thirty drugs that lost patent protection during the period from 1976 to 1987 and found a marked increase in the rate of generic entry in the years (1985 to 1987) following passage of the act. Generic dispensing at retail pharmacies rose from 17 percent in 1980 to 30 percent in 1989. Taken together, the provisions of the act appear to have greatly stimulated generic competition and benefited generic producers more than pioneers. In 1999 generic producers accounted for nearly half of the prescription drugs sold, more than double their share at the time the 1984 act was adopted.

Whenever possible, drug companies now try to fend off generic competition by persuading physicians and patients (perhaps through free sampling) to switch to a newer branded product that is a bit more effective or more convenient to administer than the branded product that is about to become available generically. Every generic approved by the FDA has been shown to be precisely the same chemical, with the same dosage and equivalent absorption rate, and with the same manufacturing consistency as the branded product. Nevertheless, manufacturers of branded products (or their representatives) frequently file petitions with the FDA to oppose approval of generic drugs. Even when the petitions fail, they can keep generic drugs off the market for months or years. At least seventy petitions were filed between 1990 and 2001 in opposition to generic introductions. Less than 20 percent of these petitions have been found to have merit, but tactics such as this have made the average approval time for generic drugs about six months longer than for new drugs in recent years, despite the 1984 act.[18] Of course, the additional period of market exclusivity is often worth a great deal to branded manufacturers. Some branded manufacturers have even made contractual arrangements with generic manufacturers to delay the introduction of a substitutable product. The Federal Trade Commission has threatened civil actions recently to prevent producers from protecting the sales of branded products in this manner.

## An Assessment of Public Policy

The stringent regulatory controls that have governed the availability of pharmaceutical products have made it highly unlikely that unsafe or ineffective products will reach the market. This assurance is desirable, but must be weighed against the cost of obtaining it. The legislative mandate and regulatory procedures of the FDA have created a strong likelihood of bias regarding the two types of error that can be made in approving or blocking the introduction of new products. The first type of error the agency can make is to approve unknowingly the introduction of new products that are either unsafe or ineffective for certain patients. This type of error has become quite unlikely as a result of the careful attention that is given to the design and execution of clinical studies. The second type of error that the agency can make is to block introduction of new products that are reasonably safe and effective, usually because the number of patients affected is not too great. This may also seem rather unlikely if clinical studies are well designed, but there is reason to believe that this second type of error has become more likely than the first.

The need for good judgment by well-informed decision makers is at the heart of this matter. Since drugs are never completely free of adverse side effects and their effectiveness varies among patients and among clinical situations, judgments must be made regarding safety and efficacy. Therapeutic benefits must be weighed against therapeutic risks. The mandate and procedures of the FDA have induced extremely cautious behavior on the part of officials who can expect to bear heavy personal costs if their approval of a product is later regarded as ill advised. This prospect further motivates officials to impose testing standards that have significantly delayed the approval of all products, including very desirable products. The cost of delaying the introduction of desirable products has been borne primarily by patients and drug manufacturers who might have benefited, not by FDA officials. FDA officials have been unable to take a neutral stance with respect to the consequences of ill-advised approvals and ill-advised delays, being more amenable to delay because it is less likely to subject them to personal risk.

In evaluating pharmaceutical regulatory controls, we must weigh the costs of delay and decline in new product introductions against the benefits of greater safety and efficacy. By generating greater confidence in the safety and efficacy of drugs that do reach the market, stringent regulatory controls should facilitate their more rapid adoption. Still, the benefits derived from regulatory controls may be quite modest if the frequency with which unsafe or ineffective products reach the market is not much lower than it would have been without regulatory controls. There is evidence that the fraction of new prescription drugs that could be described as ineffective was about the same in the years following FDA certification of efficacy as in the years immediately preceding certification.[19]

Well-intended efforts to demonstrate efficacy may be quite costly to society if regulatory controls result in delays that deny patients substantial therapeutic benefits. The benefits that are forgone because of regulatory delay and the risk of ill-advised introductions are particularly difficult to trade off. Reasoned judgment supports the introduction of drugs that pose serious risks if they also offer benefits that outweigh their risk. When U.S. regulatory controls are compared to the less stringent controls of other developed nations, studies indicate that the United States has experienced sizable costs of delayed therapeutic benefits in exchange for relatively modest benefits of less exposure to drug toxicity.[20] Some drugs that have proven to be very useful for a limited patient population have not been introduced in the United States because the costs of obtaining FDA approval would exceed their expected sales revenues.

To restore incentives (at least in part) to develop drugs to treat diseases that affect fewer than 200,000 patients, the Orphan Drug Act of 1983 authorized the FDA to grant a seven-year period of market exclusivity following approval of an orphan drug and granted a 50 percent tax credit for certain clinical research expenses. To date, about 200 orphan drugs have been approved, compared to ten in the decade prior to 1983.

## Facilitating New Product Introductions

FDA officials have been well aware of the benefit/ risk trade-offs described here and have sought to shorten the time needed to gain approval of a new drug application. Since the late 1950s all drugs have been assigned a high, medium, or low review priority that accords with their anticipated therapeutic importance. Review procedures have been gradually modified to expedite and compress the review timetable as much as possible for new products that have been assigned high priority. The test data that are required in the new drug application can be submitted in summary form. Applicants can place greater reliance on foreign test data to obtain approval more quickly. Deadlines have been established for review decisions. More clearly specified mechanisms have been adopted for the resolution of scientific disputes between FDA officials and new drug applicants. These procedural modifications have brought incremental improvement in review timetables, but the process has remained lengthy. Furthermore, some important new

products are not quickly recognized as such and assigned an appropriate priority.

To their credit, by 1992 FDA officials had made special efforts to speed the review of drugs for disorders such as Alzheimer's disease and acquired immunodeficiency syndrome (AIDS), for which few therapeutic alternatives exist. In 1996 the FDA moved to reduce the review time for new anticancer drugs by authorizing approval for use on the basis of partial evidence, such as effectiveness in shrinking tumors. Until then, approval required demonstration of improvement in survival time and quality of life, which take much longer to evaluate.

The Prescription Drug User Fee Act of 1992 brought a concerted effort to reduce the time required for FDA review of new drug applications. Under the act, pharmaceutical firms were required to pay more than $300 million in application fees during the period from 1993 to 1997 thereby enabling the FDA to hire nearly 700 additional reviewers to reduce approval time to an average of twelve months without compromising safety standards. Approval times dropped sharply, as Table 4.8 shows, and the act was reauthorized in 1997 for five more years. Companies were expected to pay fees of nearly $700 million during that period (and about $135 million during 2002) to enable the FDA to obtain the resources to further reduce approval times to an average of ten months. Still, the agency has had difficulty achieving its desired timeline for review and approval.

The FDA Modernization Act of 1997 brought needed changes. The act legislatively established the mission of the FDA for the first time—to promote public health by the timely review of applications for new products and to protect public health by ensuring that regulated products are safe, effective, and properly labeled. The act authorized fast-track approvals for drugs that meet the (unmet)

Table 4.8

**Average Time** (Months) **for Approval of New Drugs by the FDA, 1987–2000**

| Year | No. of new drugs approved | Months to approval |
|------|------|------|
| 2000 | 27 | 17.6 |
| 1999 | 35 | 12.6 |
| 1998 | 30 | 11.7 |
| 1997 | 39 | 16.2 |
| 1996 | 53 | 17.8 |
| 1995 | 28 | 19.2 |
| 1994 | 22 | 19.7 |
| 1993 | 25 | 26.5 |
| 1992 | 26 | 29.9 |
| 1991 | 30 | 30.3 |
| 1990 | 23 | 27.7 |
| 1989 | 23 | 32.5 |
| 1988 | 20 | 31.3 |
| 1987 | 21 | 32.4 |

*Source*: Food and Drug Administration, 2001.

needs of patients with serious or life-threatening conditions. For such patients, the act also authorized expanded access to investigational new drugs. To improve the timeliness and/or quality of a review, the act authorized use of outside experts to advise the agency.

Two other features of the 1997 act deserve mention. First, the act authorized the FDA to extend the period of market exclusivity by six months for branded manufacturers that conduct clinical trials on children when the agency believes pediatric information is needed. Because such trials on children are relatively small and inexpensive, costing perhaps $1 to 2 million, and the payoff from extended exclusivity is often many times that amount (occasionally more than $100 million), this provision has brought a sharp increase in the amount of pediatric testing that is done before generics are allowed to enter. Second, the act authorized the FDA to oversee the distribution of information

about unapproved uses of approved drugs. When the FDA deems it appropriate, copies of peer-reviewed medical journal articles and other validated scientific information can now be distributed to physicians by producers. There seems to be little doubt that the omnibus 1997 act has brought a number of reasonable improvements in the regulation of pharmaceutical products.

More fundamental change in the regulatory review process is still called for by observers. The system of drug regulation has had an undesirable all-or-nothing character. To satisfy their mandate, FDA officials have generally attempted to complete their certification of new products as safe and effective before marketing is allowed to begin. This has fostered an undue conservatism in the approval process since the determination of safety and efficacy is unavoidably subjective. Recognizing this, it would be preferable to modify the FDA's mandate by allowing new products to be marketed sooner—as soon as significant preliminary evidence of safety and efficacy has become available. New products that are introduced at this early stage of testing could be granted an "approval pending" status, with close monitoring of the feedback from ongoing long-term large-population studies of safety and efficacy. Greater reliance on testing by means of post-marketing surveillance is common in other developed nations, resulting in more rapid availability of new products.

If products with this status are accompanied by suitable warnings, there seems to be little reason to limit this proposal to drugs for particularly life-threatening diseases like AIDS or certain forms of cancer. The FDA should retain authority to remove a product from the market quickly if the results of ongoing testing warrant such a step. Expert review panels, made up of respected academic scientists rather than FDA officials, could be used to approve, extend, or terminate the "approval pending" status for new products. Outside experts may be better able to balance benefits and risks associated with new products. Manufacturers, physicians, and pharmacists may bear some additional liability, but it seems likely that, with a minimal increase in risk to patients, more rapid introductions would increase the incentive for firms to pursue product development.

It may be desirable to consider a dramatic overhaul of drug regulation in the United States by reverting to the more limited role performed by government prior to 1938. At that time regulation sought to improve the quality of the information available to consumers, not to limit their choice. Perhaps government should again simply mandate that labels and package inserts fully inform consumers about the chemical and known therapeutic properties of drugs. Such an approach would explicitly recognize that the meaning of safety and efficacy varies from person to person, depending crucially on personal values and attitudes toward risk. The present system of drug regulation, which imposes collective choice on consumers, is inherently arbitrary in its impact on individuals. The basic authority of the FDA might be limited to ensuring that consumers are adequately informed of known risks, ending the agency's power to determine whether or when drugs can be made available.

Greater reliance on informed choice provides greater flexibility, allowing physicians and/or consumers to choose the degree of risk that the situation warrants. A policy of informed choice does not require that therapeutic benefits for one class of consumers be sacrificed in order to protect others. Realistically, of course, the prospects for a dramatic overhaul of the FDA's regulatory mandate seem to be nil.

## Notes

1. Larry L. Duetsch, "Research Performance in the Ethical Drug Industry," *Marquette Business Review* 17 (Fall 1973): 136.

2. "With Patents Expiring on Big Prescriptions, Drug Industry Quakes," *Wall Street Journal,* August 12, 1997, p. A-6.

3. Joseph A. DiMasi, Ronald W. Hansen, Henry G. Grabowski, and Louis Lasagne, "Cost of Innovation in the Pharmaceutical Industry," *Journal of Health Economics* 10 (July 1991).

4. Henry G. Grabowski and John M. Vernon, "A New look at the Returns and Risks to Pharmaceutical R&D," *Management Science* 36 (July 1990).

5. Pharmaceutical Research and Manufacturers of America, *Pharmaceutical Industry Profile 2001,* chapter 5.

6. Ronald S. Bond and David F. Lean, *Sales, Promotion, and Product Differentiation in Two Prescription Drug Markets* (Washington, DC: Federal Trade Commission, 1977).

7. Web site of IMS Health: <http://www.imshealth.com>, July 2001.

8. Keith B. Leffler, "Persuasion or Information" The Economics of Prescription Drug Advertising," *Journal of Law and Economics* 24 (April 1981): p. 54.

9. "More Firms 'Switch' Prescription Drugs to Give Them Over-the-Counter Status," *Wall Street Journal,* July 29, 1993, p. B1.

10. "FDA Panel Sets Allergy Drugs on OTC Path," *Wall Street Journal,* May 14, 2001, p. A-3.

11. Steven N. Wiggins, "The Impact of Regulation on Pharmaceutical Research Expenditures: A Dynamic Approach," *Economic Inquiry* 21 (January 1983): 117.

12. Henry G. Grabowski and John M. Vernon, "Longer Patents for Lower Imitation Barriers: The 1984 Drug Act," *American Economic Review* 76 (May 1986): 195.

13. "National Audit Finds Drug Substitution Rate Steady," *Drug Topics,* June 4, 1990, pp. 12–14.

14. "Price Wars, Patent Expirations Promise Cheaper Drugs," *Wall Street Journal,* March 24, 1994, p. B1.

15. "With Patents Expiring."

16. Henry G. Grabowski and John M. Vernon, "Brand Loyalty, Entry, and Price Competition in Pharmaceuticals After the 1984 Drug Act," *Journal of Law and Economics* 35 (October 1992): 336.

17. Richard E. Caves, Michael D. Whinston, and Mark A. Hurwitz, "Patent Expiration, Entry, and Competition in the U.S. Pharmaceutical Industry," *Brookings Papers: Microeconomics 1991,* p. 36.

18. "Drug Manufacturers Step Up Legal Attacks That Slow Generics, *Wall Street Journal,* July 12, 2001, p. A-1.

19. Sam Peltzman, "An Evaluation of Consumer Protection Legislation: The 1962 Drug Amendments," *Journal of Political Economy* 81 (September–October 1973): 10.

20. See Dale H. Gieringer, "The Safety and Efficacy of New Drug Approval," *Cato Journal* 5 (Summer 1985): 177–201; Henry G. Grabowski and John M. Vernon, *The Regulation of Pharmaceuticals: Balancing the Benefits and Risks* (Washington: American Enterprise Institute for Public Policy Research, 1983), pp. 37–47.

## Selected Readings

Caves, R.E., M.D. Whinston, and M.A. Hurwitz. "Patent Expiration, Entry, and Competition in the U.S. Pharmaceutical Industry." In *Brookings Papers on Economic Activity: Microeconomics 1991*. Washington, DC: The Brookings Institution, 1991. Analysis of patterns of competition surrounding patent expiration and subsequent generic entry in ethical pharmaceutical markets.

Comanor, W.S. "The Political Economy of the Pharmaceutical Industry," *Journal of Economic Literature* 44 (September 1986): 1178–1217. Excellent review of economic studies prompted by our evolving public policies toward pharmaceuticals.

Grabowski, H.G., and J.M. Vernon. *The Regulation of Pharmaceuticals: Balancing the Benefits and Risks.* Washington, DC: American Enterprise Institute for Public Policy Research, 1983. Review of evidence concerning effects of pharmaceutical regulation and examination of proposals for regulatory reform.

Temin, P. *Taking Your Medicine: Drug Regulation in the United States*. Cambridge, MA: Harvard University Press, 1980. Historical account of pharmaceutical regulation, calling into question the wisdom of restricting therapeutic choices.

# 5

# Steel

## Decline and Renewal

*Donald F. Barnett and Robert W. Crandall*

The American steel industry looms much larger in public policy discussions than its share of the overall economy might suggest. Once a large part of a growing U.S. manufacturing sector, steel now accounts for less than 0.4 percent of the gross domestic product and only 0.15 percent of the total U.S. workforce. Manufacturing has been in relative decline in the United States and other developed economies, but steel has declined even more than other industries. Many other manufacturing industries—computers, apparel, motor vehicles, or food processing, for example—account for a much larger share of manufacturing activity.

Ironically, it has been the steep decline in the steel industry that explains its prominent role in U.S. industrial, labor, and trade policy discussions. The industry has shed over two-thirds of its workforce since 1970, closing scores of plants in the industrial Midwest and Northeast and leaving vast industrial wastelands along the banks of the Monongahela and Mahoning Rivers in Pennsylvania and Ohio and along the shores of Lake Erie and Lake Michigan. Over the same period, dozens of new U.S. "minimill" steel companies have begun operations, mostly in formerly nonindustrial areas of Arkansas, South Carolina, Utah, Texas, and Nebraska.

For the student of industrial organization, the steel industry provides a fascinating case study of the evolution of an industry from monopoly to cooperative oligopoly to competition. Shortly after the beginning of the twentieth century, the U.S. Steel Corporation controlled nearly two-thirds of the industry's output, and imports were virtually nonexistent. By 2000, U.S. Steel's market share had fallen to less than 10 percent of domestic consumption, steel imports (both semifinished and finished products) were responsible for 22 percent of domestic steel consumption, and a new breed of small U.S. steelmakers—the minimills—accounted for 36 percent of the domestic steel market, and about 45 percent of domestic production. Meanwhile, many of the older, "integrated" companies–such as Wheeling–Pittsburgh, Bethlehem, LTV, and National Steel were either in bankruptcy or approaching it. It is not surprising that this remarkable evolution in market structure has had severe impacts on wages, prices, and the returns to steelmaking assets. In fact, there is little about the industry's current performance that resembles its performance in the first half of the twentieth century.

### Industry Overview

#### The American Steel Market

Steel is a basic building block for a modern industrial economy. It is used in the construction of buildings, roads, and bridges. Steel is also the principal material used in the production of appliances, motor vehicles, farm equipment, and machinery. Because of its weight, steel became less desirable with the rising energy prices of the 1970s and 1980s, leading to the substitution of aluminum, plastic, and other lighter materials for steel in many of its uses. However, steel has successfully won back many of these markets and developed new ones, such as housing, due to lower real energy prices and to recent changes in metallurgy that have resulted in high-strength steel products that require far less weight for each application.

Steel is produced in many shapes and sizes and in a variety of different qualities. Nearly 90 percent of all steel produced in the United States is carbon steel—an unalloyed product with relatively high carbon content. Steel may also be alloyed with nickel, chromium, or other metals in order to provide improved resistance to corrosion or surface appearance. When alloyed with chromium or nickel, it is called stainless steel. Alloy and stainless steels are generally produced in small quantities in electric furnaces and may sell for as much as seven times the price of carbon steel. Because the stainless and alloy producers are generally small firms whose products do not compete directly with the carbon steel products of the larger firms, this chapter concentrates primarily on the carbon steel industry.

In more highly developed economies, steel consumption increases less than proportionately with economic growth. As a country's infrastructure matures and its highways become saturated with motor vehicles, the steel market tends to grow more slowly than in more formative periods of national development. In the United States, steel consumption grew very slowly from the late 1960s as the automotive market matured and cars were downsized in response to the higher energy prices of the 1970s. Steel consumption peaked at 110 million tons in 1973 and 1974 during a period of soaring materials prices and did not return to this level for the next twenty years. During the 1986 to 1990 business expansion, for example, American steel consumption averaged only 96.5 million tons. Only recently, with the strong U.S. economy of the mid-1990s and steel's active role in recapturing lost markets and creating new markets, did steel consumption surpass its peak level of 1973 to 1974, rising to more than 130 million tons in the 1998 to 2000 period.

Two decades ago, the automotive industry was the biggest single user of steel, consuming nearly 20 percent of its output. Today, construction and motor vehicles each account for about 15 percent of shipments, with the remainder spread across various machinery, rail equipment, appliance, and energy markets (Table 5.1).

Until the 1960s, the United States imported very little steel. Tariffs on imported steel were modest, generally in the 7 to 10 percent range ad valorem, but shipping costs were generally high for this relatively low-valued product, and foreign producers did not have sufficiently low costs to allow them to absorb these high transportation costs. As a result, little steel moved across the oceans to the American border.

However, as the Europeans and Japanese recovered from World War II, they rebuilt their steel industries. Moreover, ocean shipping costs fell while U.S. steel prices rose rather rapidly in response to increasing wage and material costs. During the long 1959 U.S. steelworkers' strike, imports began to rise. Over the next decade imports rose rapidly, peaking at 17 percent of U.S. consumption in 1968 and remaining above 13 percent for the next decade. This import surge led the industry and its union to lobby the federal government for import protection in the 1970s, an effort that was rewarded in the last months of the Johnson administration. Voluntary restraint agreements (VRAs) were negotiated with the Japanese and

Table 5.1

**U.S. Steel Shipments by Market Sector** (thousands of tons)

| Sector | 1960 | 1974 | 1999 |
|---|---|---|---|
| Construction | 13,268 | 17,609 | 18,428 |
| Automotive | 14,610 | 18,928 | 16,771 |
| Agriculture | 1,003 | 1,859 | 761 |
| Containers | 6,429 | 6,429 | 3,842 |
| Rail transportation | 2,525 | 3,417 | 1,031 |
| Machinery | 3,958 | 6,440 | 1,722 |
| Electrical machinery | 2,078 | 3,242 | 2,267 |
| Appliances | 1,760 | 2,412 | 1,789 |
| Export | 2,563 | 3,961 | 2,408 |
| Other | 22,955 | 43,386 | 57,182 |
| Total | 71,149 | 107,683 | 106,201 |

*Source*: American Iron and Steel Institute, *Annual Statistical Report,* various issues.
*Note*: "Other" includes shipments to steel distributors and steel shipped for further processing.

European governments in 1968, limiting these countries' exports to the United States to a specified share of U.S. consumption. These agreements remained in place through 1974, when booming world demand for steel forced foreign steel producers to use most of their capacity to satisfy home market needs. However, when steel demand failed to rebound rapidly from the 1974–1975 recession that followed, the industry once again mounted a drive for trade protection. In 1977, new restraints were imposed in the form of minimum import prices—"trigger prices"—that remained until 1982 (Table 5.2).

Reeling from the 1982 recession and facing rising imports once again in the wake of a sharp increase in the value of the dollar, the U.S. industry once again petitioned for trade protection. In 1984 the Reagan administration responded by negotiating a new set of VRAs on steel imports. These VRAs remained in place through 1991, although they were not generally binding for the last three years due to the weakened dollar. Imports rose sharply in 1994 to nearly 25 percent of U.S. consumption in response to a strong dollar and a surg-

ing U.S. economy, then receded in 1995 as the dollar declined and rose again with the strengthening dollar in 1997. At the end of the 1990s, imports surged again to more than 27 percent of U.S. consumption in 1998 and 1999, before declining to 23.5 percent in 2001, leading to renewed pleas for trade protection. In 2001, the International Trade Commission responded by initiating an investigation under U.S. trade laws and recommending a variety of limitations on imported steel. Much of the surge in imports was reflected in semifinished steel—such as slabs—that the domestic producers use to make finished steel products. These low-cost semifinished products have enabled some domestic producers to increase shipments above the level permitted by their own primary steel capacity. In the late 1990s, imports of semifinished products had risen to about 25 percent of steel imports.

## Technology

Modern steelmaking is dominated by two distinct technologies. Large integrated works, operated by

Table 5.2

**U.S. Imports and Apparent Consumption of Steel Mill Products** (thousand tons)

| Year | Imports | Apparent consumption | Import share (percent) |
|------|---------|---------------------|------------------------|
| 1955 | 976     | 82,110              | 1.2                    |
| 1960 | 3,358   | 71,530              | 4.7                    |
| 1965 | 10,383  | 100,553             | 10.3                   |
| 1970 | 13,364  | 97,100              | 13.8                   |
| 1975 | 12,012  | 89,016              | 13.5                   |
| 1980 | 15,495  | 95,247              | 16.3                   |
| 1985 | 24,256  | 96,367              | 25.2                   |
| 1990 | 17,162  | 97,595              | 17.6                   |
| 1995 | 24,409  | 114,822             | 21.3                   |
| 1999 | 35,731  | 127,925             | 27.9                   |

*Source*: American Iron and Steel Institute, *Annual Statistical Report*, various issues.

*Note*: Imports for 1999 include 8.6 million tons of semifinished steel imported by U.S. steel companies.

the older companies, use a combination of smelting and refining[1] processes to produce molten steel that is poured into continuous casters (a device that enables you to form shapes as the steel cools) to form semifinished steel shapes. The newer minimills utilize electric furnaces to melt scrap or prereduced iron into molten steel which is also formed into semifinished steel products in continuous casters.[2] The electric furnace has been the focus of most of the innovations in melting technology in the past two decades.

The older integrated producers smelt iron ore into molten pig iron (raw, or "dirty," molten iron) with the use of coke and limestone in large blast furnaces. The largest of these blast furnaces is capable of producing as much as 4 million tons of "hot metal" per year, sufficient to supply 8 percent of the country's annual needs. This liquid pig iron is then transported to steel furnaces in which it is refined into molten steel by burning away impurities, controlling the carbon content, and adding various alloys. Modern steel furnaces employ oxygen to speed the refining process. These "basic oxygen" furnaces (BOFs) have the capacity to produce from 200 to 350 tons per heat (the process of firing up the furnace to obtain a batch of molten iron) in as little as twenty minutes. The Bessemer and open-hearth steelmaking technologies that preceded basic-oxygen steelmaking often required as much as eight hours per refined heat.

Once the molten steel is ready, it is transferred to continuous casters (which have replaced ingot-mold lines) by means of large refractory-lined ladles. Modern steel plants often perform further refining and heating in these ladles. Continuous casting is a process by which molten steel is formed directly into large slabs, blooms, or billets.[3] These slabs, blooms, and billets are then rolled into the various finished steel products listed in Table 5.3. Traditionally, the slabs utilized to produce the sheet products that include more than half of all steel consumed have been about eight inches thick. However, a new technology was pioneered by the new minimills (led by Nucor) in the early 1990s that allows these slabs to be much thinner, often as thin as 1.5 inches, so as to reduce the amount of rolling subsequently required to form the finished product.

Sheet steel is rolled from reheated slabs on large hot-strip mills—a set of powerful rolling stands through which the steel is generally reduced in thickness from eight inches—or, more recently, 1.5 inches—to less than a quarter of an inch. The largest of these mills are more than one-half mile long, cost more than $750 million to build and have a capacity of at least 3.5 million tons per year, or about 7 percent of the average annual U.S. consumption of sheet steel. The hot-strip mills used to roll the 1.5-inch slabs are much shorter and less expensive to build. Further finishing of hot-rolled sheets requires a variety of cold-rolling, anneal-

Table 5.3

**U.S. Steel Shipments, All Grades, 1999**

| Product | Tons (thousands) | Minimill share (percent) |
|---|---|---|
| Semifinished shapes | 1,128 | 4 |
| Wire rods | 5,241 | 100 |
| Large structural shapes and steel piling | 6,134 | 100 |
| Plates | 8,200 | 35 |
| Rails and railroad accessories | 634 | 65 |
| Hot rolled bars | 7,898 | 90 |
| Small structural shapes | 2,363 | 100 |
| Reinforcing bars | 6,546 | 100 |
| Cold-finished bars | 1,803 | 65 |
| Pipe and tubular products | 4,779 | 55 |
| Hot-rolled sheet and strip | 9,668 | 37 |
| Cold-rolled sheet and strip | 6,036 | 20 |
| Galvanized sheet | 21,309 | 10 |
| Tin plate and tin products | 3,771 | 0 |
| Other | 691 | 0 |
| Total | 86,201 | 47 |

*Sources*: American Iron and Steel Institute, *Annual Statistical Report, 1995;* Donald F. Barnett.

ing, and tempering facilities that need not be located in the same works as the hot-strip mill, but often are.

Thicker plates are generally rolled from slabs on specialized plate mills that have far lower minimum efficient scale. The longer steel products—bars, rods, small structural shapes, and large I-beams—are rolled from semifinished blooms, billets, or beam blanks, on a variety of rolling mills that are much less expensive to build than hot-strip mills and have a much lower minimum efficient scale. Most of these facilities produce from 250,000 to 600,000 tons per year.

Finally, the steel industry produces a variety of tubular steel products. Some are formed from plates or sheet and welded; others are produced by piercing round billets or blooms to obtain a seamless product.

Minimum efficient scale of an integrated steel works is dictated by blast furnace and hot-strip-mill technology. Because blast furnaces typically had to be shut down for several weeks every seven to eight years to replace or repair their brick linings, integrated works were usually designed to incorporate at least two such furnaces. Given that each must produce at least 3 million tons per year to be efficient, an optimal integrated steel plant would have about 6 million tons of molten pig iron capacity, or about 7 to 8 million tons of raw steel capacity. If only one 3 to 4 million ton blast furnace is built, the plant would be able to supply slabs to one efficient hot-strip mill, producing about 3.5 million to 4 million tons of rolled sheet per year. Modern technology now permits blast furnaces to operate for as long as fifteen years between relines, but new plants incorporating these blast furnaces are simply not being built because new integrated plants are no longer economically justifiable.

A minimill plant of minimum efficient scale that produces "long" products—various bar, rod, or structural products—will generally have one electric furnace, a continuous caster, and rolling mills with a capacity of less than 1 million tons per year. As electric furnace technology improves, however, many of these plants have been pushing beyond 1 million tons in annual output. Still, many long-product minimills produce between 450,000 and 750,000 tons of finished steel per year—or about 0.5 percent of the country's annual steel needs. Using the thin-slab casting technology, the newer minimill plants that are dedicated to sheet production generally have a capacity of 1 to 2.5 million tons of finished product per year.

### Raw Materials

The principal raw materials for integrated steelmaking are coking coal, limestone, and iron ore.

The major companies in the past generally integrated backward into the supply of each of these materials, often through joint ventures among themselves or with foreign companies. As late as the early 1950s these companies' control of iron ore supplies provided a formidable barrier to entry into the industry. By the late 1950s, however, new discoveries throughout the world and improved technology for using low-grade ores began to put downward pressure on ore prices.

After the 1970s OPEC oil shock, U.S. and Canadian steel companies began to worry about the adequacy of their iron ore supplies. As a result, they invested billions of dollars in new mining and iron pelletizing facilities that subsequently proved to be largely unneeded as steel demand weakened in the 1980s.

The United States has ample deposits of coking coal and limestone. Much of the coal is located in the Appalachian region and is supplied to the steel producers by independent coal producers and, to a lesser extent, by their own mines. Limestone is obtained from a large number of locations, generally fairly close to the integrated steel works.

Steel scrap—the raw material used by minimills and specialty steel producers in their electric furnaces—is obtained as a by-product of steel fabricating activities and from scrapped cars, trucks, appliances, and other steel products. Scrap prices vary with the strength of overall steel demand, and scrap supply is somewhat responsive to steel prices. Nevertheless, the growth of steel minimills is ultimately limited by the supply of scrap or scrap substitutes. To improve their product quality, minimills can also feed their electric furnaces with directly reduced iron (DRI) or pig iron (from countries such as Brazil and Russia with excess blast furnace capacity). DRI—iron purged of its oxygen—is based on production technologies that require substantial coal or natural gas and normally is less

capital-intensive than a new coke oven/blast furnace complex to make pig iron. Neither product is fully competitive with scrap until scrap prices rise to about $125 per ton, but both DRI and purchased pig iron are likely to be used increasingly in combination with scrap as electric furnaces continue to replace the blast furnace-BOF technology.[4]

### The U.S. Producers

As recently as 1970, there were fifteen integrated steel producers in the United States. This number has declined steadily since then. U.S. Steel is still the largest of the integrated producers, followed by LTV, Bethlehem, Inland, National, and AK Steel, a firm that was reconstituted from Armco's carbon-steel assets. There are three small midwestern companies that have endured a variety of ownership changes or reorganizations in recent years—Rouge Steel (formerly owned by the Ford Motor Company), Weirton, and Acme. Few of these companies will survive. As of 2001, Bethlehem, LTV, Wheeling-Pittsburg (WHX), and Acme were under Chapter 11 bankruptcy protection, and Geneva Steel had announced that it would close its plant entirely. A number of other companies, such as Sharon and Gulf States, had also suspended operations. Table 5.4 lists the producers, their estimated 2000 raw steel capacity and their market capitalization—the market value of their outstanding equity shares—as of the end of September 2001. The market capitalization of the integrated companies is now far less than the cost of one new efficient plant.

The largest minimill companies are Nucor—with eight steelmaking plants; North Star—with seven plants; Birmingham—operating five plants; AmeriSteel (formerly Florida Steel)—also with five plants; Co-Steel, a Canadian company, operating three long product plants and a flat product

Table 5.4

**Integrated and Minimill Steel Producers in the United States, 2001**

| Integrated firms | Raw steel capacity (millions of annual tons) | Market capitalization (millions, on 9/30/01) | Minimill firms | Raw steel capacity (millions of annual tons) | Market capitalization (millions, on 9/30/01) |
|---|---|---|---|---|---|
| Acme Steel | 1.2 | (B) | Atlantic Steel | 0.8 | NA |
| AK Steel | 4.4 | 910 | Bayou Steel | 0.8 | 8 |
| Bethlehem Steel | 8.5 | 167 (B) | Birmingham Steel | 3.5 | 31 |
| Geneva Steel | 2.4 | 4 (B) | Chaparral Steel (owned by Texas Industries) | 1.6 | NA |
| Inland Steel | 5.1 | 240 | AmeriSteel (formerly Florida Steel, owned by Geridau, Brazil) | 1.6 | NA |
| LTV Steel | 8.5 | 14 (B) | Gallatin Steel (owned by two Canadian cos.) | 1.4 | NA |
| National Steel | 7.1 | 48 | Georgetown Steel (owned by GS Industries) | 2.0 | NA |
| Rouge Industries | 4.0 | 20 | NS Group | 1.1 | 143 |
| U.S. Steel | 13.2 | 1,247 | Northwestern Steel and Wire | 2.4 | (B) |
| Weirton Steel | 2.9 | 16 | North Star (owned by Cargill Industries) | 3.0 | NA |
| WHX | 2.4 | 25 (B) | Nucor | 11.2 | 3,088 |
|  |  |  | Oregon Steel Mills | 2.1 | 138 |
|  |  |  | Quanex |  | 309 |
|  |  |  | Raritan River Steel (owned by Co Steel, Canada) | 0.8 | NA |
|  |  |  | Roanoke Electric |  | 130 |
|  |  |  | Steel Dynamics | 1.4 | 452 |
|  |  |  | SMI | 1.7 | NA |

*Sources*: Donald F. Barnett; Web site: <www.quote.yahoo.com>.
*Notes*: (B) denotes firm under bankruptcy protection; NA indicates data not available.

plant (in a joint venture with Dofasco of Canada); Steel SDI with one large flat mill and a structural mill under construction; IPSCO, of Canada, with three flat product minimills; and Chaparral—operating one very large plant in Texas and a second in Richmond, Virginia. Most of the new minimills have been built in the South, but a few have been built in every region of the country. The newer minimill companies are generally nonunion and have thus tended to avoid states with a large share of unionized workers, such as Michigan, Pennsylvania, or Ohio, preferring such states as South Carolina, Arkansas, Kentucky, and Alabama. Note that Nucor's market capitalization in late 2001 was greater than the combined value of all U.S. integrated companies. The minimills are clearly taking over the industry, powered by their greater operating efficiencies and lower capital costs.

There is now considerable foreign ownership of major American steel facilities. National Steel is now controlled by NKK of Japan. AK Steel is a new corporate entity that emerged from a joint venture between Armco and Kawasaki Steel of Japan. U.S. Steel has entered joint ventures at two of its works—one with a Korean company and one with a Japanese company. Inland is owned by a Dutch/Indian company and its large finishing facilities are joint ventures with Nippon Steel of Japan. Surprisingly, there are few foreign-owned minimills.

The only new steel plants built in the United States in the last 25 years are minimill facilities. There are now at least thirty minimill companies, producing both the long products—bars, shapes, rods, and small structural shapes—and a variety of sheet products. In fact, these smaller companies account for virtually all of the U.S. production of the standard grades of the long products and almost one-third of the sheet products. The minimills now completely control the large structural steel market as well, and they have moved rapidly into sheet production. Since 1989, ten minimill plants have been built in the United States to produce sheet and plate products, generally with thin-slab casting technology. The large integrated companies are left with only sheet, plates, and tubular steel products, and they are steadily losing market share in these products as well.

In the wake of the collapse in steel demand in the early 1980s and the relentless surge of the minimills, the U.S. integrated producers have retired more than half of their nearly 150 million tons of raw steelmaking capacity in the past two decades. Over this same period, the minimills have built more than 30 million tons of new capacity. The total amount of crude-steel capacity has been

Table 5.5

**U.S. Raw Steel Capacity, 1965–2000** (million tons)

| Year | Integrated firms | Minimills | Total |
|------|------------------|-----------|-------|
| 1965 | 143.7 | 4.5 | 148.2 |
| 1970 | 146.3 | 7.5 | 153.8 |
| 1975 | 142.9 | 10.2 | 153.1 |
| 1980 | 138.2 | 15.5 | 153.7 |
| 1985 | 111.8 | 21.8 | 133.6 |
| 1990 | 88.7 | 28.0 | 116.7 |
| 1995 | 71.9 | 40.5 | 112.4 |
| 2000 | 73.2 | 55.5 | 128.7 |

*Sources*: American Iron and Steel Institute, *Annual Statistical Report,* various issues; Donald F. Barnett and Robert W. Crandall, *Up From the Ashes: The Rise of the Steel Minimill in the United States* (Washington, DC: The Brookings Institution, 1986), Appendix C.

reduced by about 40 million annual tons because modern continuous-casting and rolling technologies generate far greater yields of finished steel from crude steel than was possible twenty years ago. The integrated facilities that remain are generally much more efficient than they were just a decade ago. Investments in new process controls, major changes in union work rules, and a shift to contracting out many routine maintenance functions to smaller independent firms have reduced labor usage. Moreover, the most inefficient plants have been closed permanently (Table 5.5).

As a result of this severe rationalization (i.e., moving to close inefficient facilities) and new entry by efficient minimills, the steel industry today is far more competitive with its foreign rivals than it was in the 1970s. Product quality is improving; labor productivity is rising sharply. Indeed, most of the improvement in productivity can be traced to the closing of plants that often required up to ten man-hours per ton of output, replacing them with minimills that require about one man-hour per ton.[5] But the large integrated firms are still only marginally profitable in a strong economy and very unprofitable in downturns, a situation that is reflected in the prices of their equities. In 2001, the average integrated steel producer's assets were valued by the stock market at less than $200 per ton—a far cry from the $1,200 to $1,500 per ton that would be required to build a new, efficient integrated works.

## The Structural Evolution of the Industry

U.S. Steel's early dominance of the American steel industry derived not from natural scale economies, but from acquisitions. Even at the beginning of the twentieth century, the minimum efficient scale in steelmaking did not require plants that were a large share of the U.S. industry's output. However, transportation costs loomed so large for this low-valued product that a number of concentrated regional markets soon developed, particularly after the merger wave at the turn of the century.

At first the industry was centered in western Pennsylvania, and U.S. Steel was the dominant firm, but Bethlehem Steel soon developed a base in eastern Pennsylvania from which it dominated the market in the northeast. As manufacturing grew in the Midwest, steelmaking gravitated to the Chicago area, with U.S. Steel building a mammoth works in Gary, Indiana, in 1906. In the 1920s, U.S. Steel expanded its steelmaking operations to Fairfield, Alabama, thereby establishing a southern base for the first time.

By the 1930s, the steel industry had become a set of regional oligopolies. In the east, Bethlehem Steel operated plants in Baltimore, Maryland, and Bethlehem, Pennsylvania. In the western Pennsylvania–eastern Ohio region, U.S. Steel competed with Pittsburgh Steel, Jones and Laughlin, Youngstown Sheet and Tube, and Republic Steel. In the Midwest, U.S. Steel, Inland, National Steel, and a few smaller companies (including Ford's Rouge

works) competed for the large sheet steel business. In Alabama, U.S. Steel's Birmingham works competed with Republic's Gadsden works for the southern market. The West had only the Colorado Fuel and Iron works in Pueblo and a few small works on the west coast.

Prior to World War II, the minimum efficient scale of an integrated steel works was much smaller than it is today. Blast furnaces had substantially less than 1 million tons of capacity, open-hearth steel furnaces had very low annual capacity, and hot-strip mills were much slower and narrower than those in operation today. Thus the regional concentration in steel that developed in the interwar period was not a reflection of large-scale economies. Rather, it was the result of acquisitions and the control of raw material supplies.

### Market Performance in the Interwar Period

The steel industry has been the subject of substantial Congressional and antitrust scrutiny because of its erstwhile central role in the economy and its concentrated market structure through the 1960s. U.S. Steel was formed from a series of mergers in 1898–1901 that gave it nearly 50 percent of the nation's steel capacity. In the first few years of the twentieth century, U.S. Steel accounted for about two-thirds of the country's raw steel output, thereby attracting the attention of the antitrust authorities. Shortly after the government's 1911 victories in the Standard Oil and American Tobacco antitrust suits, another major Sherman Act suit was initiated against U.S. Steel for monopolizing the U.S. steel industry. By the time the case was litigated, however, U.S. Steel's share of the American market had fallen to about 50 percent, a share that the courts ruled was too small to constitute monopolization.

After the U.S. Steel case was decided by the Supreme Court in 1920, the steel industry structure solidified into a set of regional oligopolies. These firms operated in a market driven by the demand for investment goods—a market that is more volatile than overall aggregate demand. During the long Depression of the 1930s, therefore, the steel industry suffered very low capacity-utilization rates.

Despite the volatility in steel demand, list prices for steel were remarkably stable in the interwar period, leading to a variety of governmental and scholarly investigations of the causes of this price rigidity. Attention focused on U.S. Steel's price leadership and the use of a delivered price system known as "basing-point pricing." Even before World War I, the chairman of U.S. Steel would regularly announce his company's view of what prices should be over the next few months or the next year. The other steel companies would follow, apparently reasoning that they would gain little in market share from undercutting U.S. Steel because the leader would quickly match their new price. The low price elasticity of steel demand also contributed to their reluctance to shade prices because the quantity demanded in the market could not be increased much by price competition. Given the large ratio of fixed to total costs in this industry, a price war that drove prices to short-term marginal costs could have had disastrous effects on profits—particularly in a recession or a depression.

The basing-point system was a uniform delivered price system that was apparently maintained noncollusively. Each steel producer would quote its prices in the form of a list price plus freight charges to the customer's facility. The freight charges would be calculated from the nearest basing point—Pittsburgh, Chicago, or Birmingham—regardless of where the steel was produced. As a result, a plant in Cleveland shipping to a customer in a nearby suburb would charge the list price of the steel plus freight from Pittsburgh—giving rise to allegations that the customer paid "phantom freight."

This basing-point pricing system was alleged by critics of the practice to be collusive, and it certainly reflected price discrimination. Different buyers paid different prices for steel because of their geographical location, not because of actual differences in freight costs. Defenders of this system alleged that it reflected the fact that steelmakers away from the major producing centers found it necessary to meet but not beat the prices charged by producers at the basing point. That these delivered prices were not undercut by steel producers located closer to the customer was simply a reflection of the large fixed costs of steel production and a reluctance to risk a price war that would result in prices falling to variable costs.

These steel pricing practices were never successfully prosecuted as collusive practices that would be illegal per se under Section 1 of the Sherman Act. Rather, they were successfully challenged by the Federal Trade Commission in 1948 as an unfair method of competition and thus a violation of Section 5 of the Federal Trade Commission Act. As a result, the formal adherence to basing-point pricing ended shortly after World War II, though delivered pricing continues to this day.

### The Post–World War II Era

After World War II, the steel industry began to raise prices steadily in response to increases in material costs—particularly iron ore costs—and wage rates. Because all but a few of the major producers bargained as a group with the United Steelworkers of America, they generally experienced the same wage increases. The conclusions of these bargaining rounds would be followed by virtually

Table 5.6

**Total Compensation for U.S. Production Workers, 1960–1999** (dollars/hour)

| Year | Steel | All manufacturing | Steel premium (percent) |
|------|-------|-------------------|--------------------------|
| 1960 | 3.82  | 2.87              | 33.1 |
| 1965 | 4.48  | 3.35              | 33.7 |
| 1970 | 5.68  | 4.90              | 16.0 |
| 1975 | 10.59 | 7.34              | 44.3 |
| 1980 | 18.45 | 11.99             | 53.9 |
| 1985 | 22.81 | 15.81             | 54.0 |
| 1990 | 25.62 | 19.07             | 34.1 |
| 1995 | 34.67 | 20.47             | 52.7 |
| 1999 | 35.34 | 22.77             | 55.2 |

*Sources*: For steel, American Iron and Steel Institute, *Annual Statistical Report,* various issues; for manufacturing, U.S. Department of Labor, Bureau of Labor Statistics.

simultaneous announcements of price increases, a practice referred to by one observer as the "annual rite of spring." Each year list prices rose regardless of demand, leading congressional investigators and some economists to worry about "administered-price" inflation.

One explanation for this wage-price spiral was that it allowed the steel producers to escape from the depressed prices created by World War II price controls without having to engage in formal collusion. Whatever the explanation, the steel companies apparently tired of the practice in 1959 when they acceded to a long strike rather than continue the wage-price spiral. By this time, many foreign steel industries—particularly in Europe and Japan—had recovered from the war, iron ore prices were falling in the wake of the development of new deposits, and shipping costs were falling.

During the 1959 strike, steel imports began to surge, and they continued to increase throughout the 1960s. As a result, the integrated U.S. producers faced a sluggish market throughout the early 1960s, inducing them to grant much more moderate wage increases. Between 1960 and 1970, average steelworker compensation fell from 133 percent of the U.S. manufacturing average to 116 percent (Table 5.6).

Until the outbreak of the Vietnam War, the industry operated with substantial excess capacity. By 1968 the industry was once again operating at nearly 90 percent of capacity, but the industry nevertheless succeeded in persuading the Johnson administration to negotiate the first VRAs (or quotas) on imported steel. Ominously, it was also about this time that the smaller minimills first began to expand into the domain previously controlled by the rigid steel oligopoly.

The concern over administered-price inflation continued into the 1960s and even the early 1970s. Stagflation became the major concern of economists in the late 1960s and early 1970s, leading President Johnson to institute "jawboning" of wage and price increases in various U.S. industries, and President Nixon to impose wage-price controls even before the 1973–1974 Arab oil embargo.[6]

Some of the concern over administered-price inflation may now be seen to have resulted from an illusion created by official statistics that rely on list-price quotes from concentrated industries. Transaction prices deviate from list prices, particularly when demand declines, but list prices may not be reduced in the face of declining demand. A study conducted in the 1960s, using price data obtained from buyers, concluded that in concentrated industries actual transactions prices do respond to demand changes, but they found that steel prices were among the most rigid in their sample.[7] The findings concerning steel prices for the period from 1957 to 1967 are now of little more than academic interest, given the changes in the structure of the steel industry and in the behavior of steel prices in recent years.

## Wages and Prices Since 1970

By 1968, imports of steel had risen to 17 percent of U.S. consumption. Minimills were beginning to take some of the lower grades of bar and small structural steel from the larger producers. The last new major integrated works—Bethlehem's at Burns Harbor, Indiana—was just opening, increasing the level of competition in the midwestern sheet steel market.

Because of the Vietnam War and the overheating of most developed economies between 1972 and 1974, the steel industry was to have one last burst of strong demand before sinking into deep decline. In 1973–1974, U.S. steel demand accelerated and prices rose substantially, particularly after the expiration of price controls in 1974. The integrated companies began to plan to expand capacity. U.S Steel and National Steel began to plan for large new plants on the southern Great Lakes just as the 1975 recession began. At that point, the integrated firms had more than 140 million tons of capacity, but government and Wall Street reports began to show that the Japanese industry, which was of comparable size, was far more efficient. By the end of the decade, the Japanese were able to produce a ton of sheet steel for about $90 less than the average U.S. integrated firm—a cost advantage that was far greater than the cost of exporting a ton of steel to the United States.[8]

Beginning in 1977, the integrated industry, which only two years earlier was anticipating the expansion of capacity, began to close plants. By 1985, these firms had permanently closed 35 million tons of capacity and more closures were still on the way. Imports peaked in 1984 at 26 million tons and then began to fall slowly because of the VRAs. The deregulation of trucking and partial deregulation of railroads combined with the low world shipping rates to increase competition for

virtually all steel products in the United States. Some companies imported slabs into the East or the West for rolling into sheets. Semifinished slabs produced by some U.S. mills were shipped relatively long distances for rolling by other mills. The new minimills began to expand into higher quality products, such as wire rods, special steel bars, and wider steel beams.

The demand for steel is very price inelastic, even in the long run. Research suggests that the price elasticity of steel demand is between $-0.2$ and $-0.3$.[9] With demand so inelastic and with large cyclical swings in demand, steel prices can become as volatile as some commodity prices. In fact, the post-1970 data on actual revenues per ton of steel shipments show a considerable rise in the volatility of steel prices, undoubtedly the result of sharp increases in domestic and import competition.

The movements in real annual average prices (nominal prices deflated by the GDP price deflator) for two major products are shown in Figure 5.1. Cold-rolled sheet is the most important integrated-company product, and hot-rolled bars were once a major product for integrated companies but are now dominated by minimill companies. Note that the minimill product, hot-rolled bars, until recently exhibited greater price volatility than cold-rolled sheet because the former has been produced under more competitive conditions and is more likely to be sold on a spot basis. A large share of cold-rolled sheet is sold to large buyers such as motor vehicle producers at contract prices. Nevertheless, even the sheet prices have become much more volatile in recent years due to greater competition from imports and domestic minimills, and all steel prices have been declining at an inflation-adjusted rate of about 3 percent per year since the late 1980s.

Given the behavior of prices since 1980, the decades-old concern about oligopolistic administered pricing simply disappeared, and, as a result,

Figure 5.1 **The Real Price of Cold-Rolled Sheet and Bars, 1973–2000**

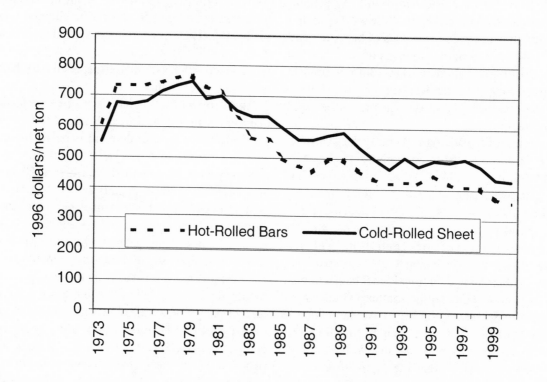

the antitrust concerns that had dogged the industry for decades have largely vanished. In 1958 the government had blocked the attempt by Bethlehem Steel to acquire Youngstown Sheet and Tube, a producer with plants in Youngstown, Ohio, and northern Indiana. In 1978 Jones and Laughlin was allowed to buy Youngstown Sheet and Tube, and then in 1983 J&L and Republic combined to become LTV Steel, the nation's second largest producer. The concern over monopoly power had diminished considerably by 1983, even in the sheet steels that Republic, J&L, and Youngstown produced for the midwestern market.

Most of the firms in the industry bargained as a single unit with the United Steelworkers until 1986. The 1973–1974 negotiations led to a sharp rise in steelworker real wages, due to a cost-of-living escalator and other guaranteed increases. By 1980, steelworkers were earning nearly 55 percent more than the average industrial worker. This premium has moderated since then because of the entry of nonunion minimills and the competitive pressure on the integrated firms.

By the mid-1980s, import competition was coming not only from Japan and Europe, but from Korea, Canada, and Latin America. Minimills were expanding rapidly, and steel demand was languishing about 10 to 15 percent below its 1973–1974 peak.

The integrated sector was forced to contract and to seek major reductions in labor and material costs. The resulting impact on wage settlements with the United Steelworkers was predictable—real wage rates began to decline in the 1980s.

In 1986 the industry bargaining cohesion broke down. Several companies negotiated agreements that provided for a variety of wage concessions, but U.S. Steel was unable to reach an agreement. In August U.S. Steel was closed by a strike (or a "lock-out," according to the union), the first such occurrence in Big Steel in more than twenty-five years. A settlement was not reached for more than six months.

The new union contracts and the continuing gravitation of steel production to minimills, most of which are nonunion, placed downward pressure on steel wages over the 1980s. Real wages in the steel industry in 1989 were 11 percent below their level in 1981. When the dollar declined in 1985–1987, the pressure on the integrated industry abated somewhat, and real wages began to rise once again in the 1990s, but at a modest rate of 2 percent per year. Steel employment, which had peaked at about 700,000 workers in the 1960s, fell to less than 300,000 by the late 1980s, and continued to decline to about 220,000 by 2000. As minimills continue to replace integrated plants, it likely that total steel employment in the United States will soon be far less than 200,000.

## The Cost Structure of Integrated Firms, Minimills, and Major Exporters to the United States

The labor agreements of the early 1970s had devastating impacts on the integrated firms' costs of production that were compounded by the restrictive union work rules and the obsolete facilities that combined to limit productivity growth. By the end of the 1970s, the raw material and labor costs of the integrated firms were far above those of the efficient producers in Korea, Japan, Brazil, and Canada. Since then, despite closure of half of the integrated industry's capacity and major cost-cutting efforts here, more successful cost-cutting efforts abroad, the rapid acceleration of post-employment benefit obligations, and a much stronger U.S. dollar have left the U.S. integrated companies at a substantial cost disadvantage in the production of cold-rolled sheet, compared with the average Korean, Brazilian, Japanese, or European producers. (See Table 5.7.) Moreover, the new minimills in the United States and abroad have substantially lower costs than their larger integrated brethren in producing the commodity and medium grades of cold-rolled sheet. There is no need to analyze cost differentials for bars, rods, and structural shapes; the U.S. integrated firms no longer produce them in any sizable quantity.

Given these cost differences, it is not surprising that most of the integrated firms are being forced to close plants, sell others, and downsize the remainder. Slowly, they have abandoned virtually all of the smaller diameter products—bars, rods, and structural shapes—to the new minimills. Most of the plants in the Pittsburgh and Youngstown areas have closed. Several medium-sized plants were sold to small consortia or to their employees, and many of these subsequently closed.

By 2000, the U.S. carbon-steel industry had evolved into two distinct groups of producers: (1) The large integrated companies; and (2) the minimills. The larger integrated companies' crude-steel capacity had fallen from about 145 million tons in 1975 to about 70 million tons in 2000. The minimills had more than 55 million tons of capacity by 2000.

The large integrated companies are now limited almost entirely to sheet and tubular products. The minimills dominate all of the smaller prod-

Table 5.7

**Total Operating Cost for Cold-Rolled Sheet and Wire Rod** (dollars/ton, excluding capital costs)

| | Cold-rolled sheet | | | | Wire rod | |
| --- | --- | --- | --- | --- | --- | --- |
| Year | Japanese integrated firm | U.S. integrated firm | Brazilian integrated firm | U.S. minimill | U.S. integrated firm | U.S. minimill |
| 1960 | 145 | 135 | * | NA | 125 | NA |
| 1970 | 150 | 180 | * | NA | 165 | 123 |
| 1980 | 355 | 410 | 295 | NA | 360 | 260 |
| 1990 | 405 | 400 | 310 | 285 | NA | 255 |
| 1995 | 435 | 405 | 310 | 310 | NA | 300 |
| 2000 | 365 | 425 | 270 | 275 | NA | 265 |

*Source*: Donald F. Barnett.
*Note*: Asterisk indicates data not available; NA indicates data not applicable because firm did not produce this product in the given year.

ucts, such as wire rods, reinforcing bars, small structural shapes, merchant bars, and large structural shapes. The most ominous development for the integrated firms, however, was the movement of the minimills into sheet products.

In 1990, Nucor began to produce sheet steel in its newest minimill located near Indianapolis, Indiana. This new plant utilized a revolutionary continuous caster that produces much thinner slabs than conventional casters and routes these slabs directly to the hot-strip mill with minimal reheating. This design allowed Nucor to invest in a less expensive hot-strip mill with lower minimum efficient scale and reduced energy requirements, while supplying its casting and rolling facilities with steel produced in electric furnaces. Since 1990 Nucor has built three more of these thin-slab plants, and six others have been built by various companies, including one Canadian consortium and one joint-venture of British, U.S., and Japanese companies. Each of these new plants uses electric furnaces to produce between 1.2 and 2.5 million tons of sheet products per year. Many also have cold-rolling and galvanizing capacity. By 2000, these minimill plants were shipping about 20 million tons of sheet steel, representing nearly one-third of the U.S. market for these products.

The inevitable effect of minimill expansion in the U.S. steel market has been a steady reduction in the capacity of the large, integrated firms' plants. U.S. Steel has closed entire facilities, including its Fairless, Pennsylvania, works. Sharon Steel and Gulf States, two smaller integrated firms, have disappeared. LTV, Geneva, and Acme have announced that they will close their plants. Many other integrated companies, such as LTV, Bethlehem, Weirton, Rouge, and Wheeling Pittsburgh (WHX) are unlikely to survive as independent entities. The competitiveness of even the most likely-to-survive sheet steel plants of the integrated companies is problematic, and they cannot match the minimills' costs from new thin-slab casting plants. However, the minimill plants are currently still limited to a lower-quality product niche by their reliance on scrap, and they are therefore expanding their use of directly reduced iron (DRI). Minimills also consume a significant amount of pig iron because of its superior metallurgical properties.

The success of the minimills had been mistakenly attributed to lower wage rates. Minimills often pay their workers as much per hour as the hourly pay at integrated plants (although they do not have the penalty of historic postemployment benefit obligations). They have been more successful than the integrated firms because of greater productivity. Minimill plants are designed to minimize costs, including labor costs, and are operated with fewer work-rule restrictions, generally a reflection of their nonunion status. Moreover, many provide strong work incentives in their labor compensation, paying workers in proportion to the output delivered and the profits earned by the company. As a result, the best minimills enjoy as much as a $100 per ton labor-cost advantage over integrated works, due almost entirely to their higher labor productivity.

Minimills also enjoy materials cost advantages over integrated firms because they do not need coal, iron ore, and limestone. However, most of this advantage is offset by the large electric energy requirements of the electric furnace. Finally, the capital costs of new facilities are about one-fourth of those of an integrated works (see below), but this difference is largely academic given the low probability of constructing new integrated plants in the United States or other developed countries.

### Investment and Efficiency: Too Much or Too Little?

For decades, it has been widely believed that the U.S. steel industry declined because it was too slow to invest in new steelmaking technology. In the late 1950s, as other nations were building basic-oxygen steelmaking furnaces, the U.S. industry continued to operate and even expand its open-hearth capacity, despite the much longer heat times required by this older technology. While some of

this criticism may have been justified, the U.S. industry was well advised to keep its open hearth capacity for some time because of the cost of replacing it, the constraints provided by existing plant layouts, and the open-hearths' ability to accommodate more scrap in their charge. Scrap prices have traditionally been much lower in the United States than elsewhere in the world.

In the 1970s, a similar story emerged—this time involving continuous casting. The traditional method of producing steel had required pouring liquid steel into ingot molds, cooling these ingots, then reheating the ingots for rolling into slabs, billets, or blooms, and final rolling. Continuous casters eliminated the reheating of ingots, the intermediate rolling step, and a substantial amount of yield loss associated with rolling ingots into semifinished shapes. By the mid-1970s, the Japanese had converted most of their capacity to continuous casting, but the U.S. integrated companies lagged far behind.

Similar differences exist in blast-furnace operations, direct rolling, and continuous finishing operations. Because of their antiquated plants and their poor cash-flow prospects for the past fifteen to twenty years, the integrated producers have been unable or unwilling to invest in many of these newer technologies. Surprisingly, those companies that were most aggressive in investing in their steelmaking and raw materials operations in the late 1970s and early 1980s were the ones to fall into insolvency. This apparent paradox in investment rates can be explained by the investment strategies employed by the large integrated firms. The investment outlays in the 1970s reflected the desire of steel managements to expand their ability to produce for peak demand. The 1970s had created an aura of impending scarcity of materials and recurrent booms in which prices would rise rapidly. The steel producers wanted to be ready to satisfy these peak demands, thereby holding back further surges by importers and, of course, earning large profits during these periods.

The investments that resulted from these scarcity fears were expansions of iron ore mines, iron pelletizing plants, and coke ovens. Investments in continuous casters, improved finishing mills, or ladle metallurgy facilities would improve quality or reduce costs, but they would not expand raw steelmaking capacity. As a result, these improvements were postponed. In the 1980s, the large integrated companies realized that they had overexpanded materials capacity while keeping far too many inefficient basic steelmaking facilities in operation. As a result, they began closing their most inefficient plants and modernizing their more efficient works. New continuous casters were installed in the large northern Indiana works of Bethlehem, USX, Inland, and LTV. Most of the remaining capacity around Pittsburgh, Youngstown, and Buffalo was closed.

In the 1990s the American market shifted from cold-rolled coil to coated products (galvanized steel). A few producers, such as AK Steel, found that large improvements in productivity were possible with new operating practices in some key facilities such as blast furnaces, hot-strip mills, cold mills, and coating lines. All producers attempted to emulate AK, expanding the throughput in these facilities while adding many new coating lines. These efforts, combined with the limited operational flexibility of BOF and caster capacity, led to the expansion of some blast furnaces and the closing of others. The integrated firms increased their purchases of semifinished steel, much of it from abroad, to fill up their expanded rolling and major new coating-line capacity. In the 1990s, the integrated industry was able to expand its shipments without expanding capacity, while almost 20 million tons of minimill capacity was being

added. During this period, employment reductions, new methods of financing, and the accumulation of postemployment benefit obligations (pension and health benefits) increased the integrated firms' fixed costs. These higher fixed costs would place the firms in financial difficulty if their production volume declined, as it did with a vengeance in 2001.

### The Long-Run Supply Elasticity of Steel in the United States

For almost two decades, no one asked how much it would cost to expand steel capacity and, therefore, how much the price of steel would have to rise to induce integrated steelmakers to expand capacity. The industry had far too much excess capacity to be interested in expansion.

The last new U.S. integrated plant was built by Bethlehem in the 1960s. The last new European plant was built in southern France in the 1970s, but was never completed as planned. The last new Japanese plant was completed in the late 1970s. The only integrated plants completed in the developed world since the 1970s are STELCO's Canadian plant on the northern shore of Lake Erie, opened in 1981, and Pohang Steel's large new complex at the southern end of Korea. Thus, there is very limited evidence on the current cost of building new integrated plants anywhere in the developed world.

In the mid-1970s, U.S. Steel was contemplating the construction of a new integrated works on the southern shore of Lake Erie. The estimated cost of this plant was about $750 per net ton of finished steel output. It is widely believed that the cost today would be about $1,700 per ton—an estimate based solely on inflation since the mid-1970s. At any realistic capital charge reflecting depreciation and the real cost of capital, the costs of operating such a plant would be prohibitive. For instance, assuming a twenty-five-year life and a 10 percent real cost of capital, the real capital cost per ton of output from such a facility would be $185, or nearly half the price of the typical finished product, cold-rolled sheet. Given the cost of materials, energy, and labor, no firm could build such a plant today.

Existing plants have no use other than the manufacture of steel, and they have very little scrap value. To justify replacing an existing plant, the new integrated works would have to achieve at least $185 in operating cost savings, clearly an impossibility. At most, such a new plant might achieve $60 in labor-cost savings and another $25 in energy and materials-cost savings. Even in good markets such as that of 1999, current plants have substantial difficulty in achieving positive cash flows above operating costs; therefore, prices would have to rise by at least $110 per ton above 2000 levels just to achieve a break-even performance, an unlikely scenario given the long-run real decline in steel prices.

The obvious alternative is the continued expansion of minimills to supply more and more of the nation's steel needs. A new minimill designed to produce a mix of hot-rolled and cold-rolled sheet from thin slabs costs no more than $200 per ton to build—but such a facility may not be able to produce the highest quality of the sheet products demanded by the automotive and appliance industries. At the steel prices realized in the mid-1990s, these minimills could be built and operated profitably, given the normal price of scrap and iron. Since scrap/iron accounts for about 30 percent of their costs, the elasticity of long-run supply for steel from such plants is about three times the supply elasticity of scrap. We estimate that the long-run supply elasticity of scrap is equal to 0.4; therefore the long-run supply elasticity of steel

from minimills is at least 1.2.[10] This means that if they are confined to scrap, minimills can expand supply by 1.2 percent for every 1 percent increase in price, all other things equal.

Minimills have been expanding their use of DRI, and especially pig iron, to supplement scrap. Given the essentially infinitely elastic supply of iron ore for such facilities, there is reason to believe that the supply of minimill products could itself be extremely price elastic. In the 1990s, the only impediment to the expansion of steel supply was the capacity constraints in iron pellet plants that provide the necessary feedstock to the DRI plants, but this does not appear to be an insuperable problem. Indeed, DRI capacity in the United States expanded rapidly—from just 0.6 million tons in 1995 to a projected 6 million tons by the year 1999 (before they all were forced to close by falling scrap and iron prices in 2000/2001).

### The Role Of Exchange Rates

The U.S. integrated industry's contraction may be attributed to the rise of more efficient competitors, but the speed of the decline in the 1980s and 1990s was surely related to exchange rates. In the early 1980s, the U.S. dollar appreciated by nearly 50 percent in real terms. As a result, imported steel fell in price relative to domestic steel, and U.S. export prices rose relative to home-market prices in the countries to which the United States exports. Although the dollar receded in the early 1990s, it rose once again from 1997 to 2000, leading to a new surge of imports.

Approximately 40 percent of the cost of a ton of steel in the major steel exporting countries is denoted in dollars because ore and coal contracts are generally based on the U.S. dollar. Thus, when the dollar appreciates, the price of materials to foreign steel exporters rises proportionately. Of their remaining costs, approximately half are dollar-related, comprising consumables that are exported into dollar markets. This leaves about 40 percent of the cost of foreign steel that is strictly local in cost, such as labor, and does not rise with the dollar. In some countries such as Canada and Mexico, however, even labor rates are very much related to U.S. wage rates and exchange rates. For example, up to one-third of Mexican workers are actually paid in U.S. dollars. The early 1980s appreciation of the dollar lowered the dollar costs of steel exported to the United States by more than 30 percent. This decline placed downward pressure on U.S. steel prices, further endangering the marginal facilities of the U.S. integrated firms.

The decline in the value of the dollar after 1985 removed some of the foreign pressure on U.S. steel prices and by 1989–1990 reduced exports to the United States to less than the VRAs allowed. In the late 1990s, the U.S. dollar rose as the U.S. economy expanded, triggering another increase in imports that was exacerbated by the Asian crisis of 1997–1998 and the steep decline in business activity in the former Soviet republics. With the dollar strong and demand weak in Asia and Eastern Europe, world steel prices collapsed. By mid-2001, the average (spot) export price of steel had declined to about $210 for hot-rolled coil, a $70 per ton decline since mid-1998, and to $285 for cold-rolled coil, an $85 per ton decline since mid-1998. Thus, in a world of fluctuating exchange rates and turbulent economic conditions, the U.S. steel industry remains vulnerable to future increases in the value of the dollar that might be caused by monetary or fiscal policies.

## Environmental Policy

The steel industries of the United States and most developed countries have suffered from the effects of heightened social awareness of the problems of environmental pollution in the past two decades. Blast furnaces, coke ovens, and steel furnaces are capable of generating enormous amounts of hazardous particulate air pollutants. Controlling these emissions can be very costly, particularly if the controls must be retrofitted to old facilities. Moreover, the steel industry uses enormous quantities of water to quench coke and cool steel as it is being processed. Controlling the runoff from these processes and recycling the water is also quite expensive.

In the late 1970s and early 1980s, the U.S. industry spent an average of nearly $500 million per year on environmental control equipment, or about one-sixth of its capital expenditures. These outlays have fallen in recent years as the industry has caught up with most of its current environmental obligations. However, there remain possible issues of historic environmental contamination and who will pay for any cleanups.

It is interesting that environmental control costs provide yet another advantage for minimills because they have no coke ovens or blast furnaces or historic site problems. Their major exposure to environmental control cost lies in the capture of dust from their electric furnaces and in the electric utilities' cost to control sulfur oxides. In the next decade, electric rates may be raised substantially by the 1990 Clean Air Act requirement that utilities reduce sulfur oxide emissions by about 10 million tons per year.

## The Burden of Postemployment Benefit Obligations

Most of the integrated companies in the U.S. industry have large, underfunded postemployment benefit (PEB) obligations (pension, health care, etc.). These obligations arose out of past labor contracts with PEB packages. In many cases, the troubled integrated firms did not fully fund these postemployment obligations at the time of the contract, and the funds to pay these obligations have evaporated with the declining stock-market performance of many of these companies. To vastly simplify the problem, each firm makes an actuarial calculation of how much is needed to pay for the PEB's to which they are committed when the workers retire and need the funds. They then use projected interest rates and stock returns to determine how much funding must be supplied in any given year to meet these obligations, given the funds already in place. These calculations of required funding can vary enormously from year to year because of changing financial market conditions. As a result, firms may not have sufficient funds in some years, but they may have a surplus in others. They are therefore allowed to defer or accelerate payments with changing market conditions. Over time, if the calculations of life expectancy have been underestimated or stock market returns have been overestimated, cash obligations in each subsequent year may rise. Similarly if more workers are "voluntarily" retired early to reduce current costs, PEB obligations will rise. If in these depressed market conditions, firms deliberately postpone funding these obligations, the unfunded PEB obligations increase. By 2001 many integrated firms had huge PEB obligations, exacerbated by a poorly performing stock market and the need to "voluntarily" retire many workers to cut costs and close facilities. While some integrated U.S. steel companies, such as USX, had funded their PEBs, most had not. On the other hand, the integrated firms' rivals, the minimills, had profit-sharing and defined-contribution plans, and therefore few had significantly underfunded PEBs.

To pay off the integrated producers' aggregate PEBs, while at the same time keeping sufficient facilities operating, the integrated steel companies' cash flows must improve dramatically, either through much higher prices or much lower costs. Lower costs will require a drastic industry restructuring, essentially reducing the workforce and, in turn, adding to the PEB obligations. Higher prices will come, to some degree, with market recovery, but U.S. steel prices are already among the highest in the world and cannot be expected to recover to anywhere near the mid-1990s levels, especially since these latter levels would bring new minimill entry. Regrettably, one must opine that there is no feasible combination of cost-cutting and likely price recovery that will enable sufficient cash generation by integrated producers to pay off their unfunded PEBs, meet their variable and fixed costs, and fund the minimal capital expenditures required to keep core facilities running. Indeed, it is problematic whether they will be able to pay the additional PEBs created each year.

This suggests that eventually either the retired workers will not receive their full health benefits or that the government must step in to guarantee they are paid what they are owed. Pension obligations, for instance, are insured by the government's Pension Benefit Guaranty Corporation. If the steel firms with large unfunded PEB obligations were relieved of these obligations, which could be equal to as much as 25 percent of current employment costs, this would drastically improve the competitive position of the integrated firms whose obligations are forgiven and alter the competitive playing field domestically as well as internationally. Needless to say this potential "unburdening" and how to pay for it, is a major point of contention in 2001 between funded and unfunded companies—the minimills and most integrated firms—and their respective workers or unions. The situation may get worse, and to facilitate the transition to a minimill-dominated industry, some relief may be forthcoming. However, even this relief will not allow the integrated firms to arrest the decline that has reduced them to about half of the current U.S. steel industry.

In late 2001, the Organization for Economic Cooperation and Development (OECD) convened a meeting of the world's largest steel-producing countries to discuss approaches to alleviating the problems of the world steel industry. With world steel prices at their lowest real levels in fifty years and substantial antiquated excess capacity overhanging the industry, the OECD was examining options for obtaining capacity reductions around the world. Given the large number of steel-producing countries and the large number of workers involved in steel production, such capacity reductions are likely to be difficult to obtain, particularly in the wake of the U.S. government's March 2002 decision to impose tariffs of up to 30 percent on imported steel. Nevertheless, some elimination of inefficient capacity that survives only because of government support would probably help ease the severe trade frictions that have developed over low-price steel.

## The Future of American Steel

Large integrated steel works are no longer a prominent fixture in the highly developed economies of the world. The enormous cost of constructing such works and the generally declining steel intensity of these countries have combined to render most of their integrated steel works quite unprofitable. There have been no new integrated steel works built in a developed country in more than a decade. None has been started in the United States in three decades.

The large integrated American steel companies have been forced to manage an accelerating de-cline by forming joint ventures with foreign companies, closing outmoded facilities, and modernizing those facilities that can still compete with foreign producers and domestic minimills. For the most part, this means that they have had to concentrate on sheet steels and tubular products because the minimills have lower costs than the large companies for most of the smaller-diameter products. In the next few years, many of these companies will fail and the remaining companies are likely to combine into two or three moderate-sized firms. This "combination" however is being made more difficult by unfunded postemployment benefits, and perhaps historic environmental clean-up issues.

The future of the American steel industry lies almost entirely with the minimills. As the United States and Canada settle into free trade with Mexico, the North American market will become even more competitive, further winnowing the remnants of U.S., Canadian, and Mexican steel giants. However, at any foreseeable future exchange rate, the entrepreneurial North American minimill companies should remain competitive and possibly even begin to expand export shipments.

## Notes

1. Smelting is the process of removing oxygen from a metal oxide ore. Refining is the process of removing impurities from the smelted metal. For very light metals, refining precedes smelting, but in steelmaking, smelting precedes refining.

2. Stainless steel producers also use electric furnaces, and even large integrated steelmakers have some electric furnace capacity. The minimills, however, have been pioneers in using high-powered electric furnaces to produce molten steel with maximum efficiency.

3. Slabs are semifinished steel shapes that have a cross-section of about eight to twelve inches by four to six feet in most cases. Billets generally have round or square cross sections up to six inches in diameter. Blooms generally have square cross sections in excess of six inches in diameter.

4. Most DRI is imported from Latin American countries

that have low natural gas prices and easy access to iron ore.

5. Robert W. Crandall, "From Competitiveness to Competition: The Threat of Minimills to Large National Steel Companies," *Resources Policy* 22 (1996): 107–18.

6. The steel industry had a rather acrimonious relationship with a number of U.S. presidents. President Truman tried to seize the industry during the Korean War to prevent a strike. President Kennedy had a major dispute with the industry over its wage-price behavior in 1962, and President Johnson was alleged to have locked industry and union negotiators in a room during the 1968 negotiations.

7. George J. Stigler and James K. Kindahl, *The Behavior of Industrial Prices* (New York: National Bureau of Economic Research, 1970).

8. The $90 differential is in operating costs. The Japanese had higher fixed costs than U.S. companies because of their newer plants, reducing the total-cost differential to $55 per ton. For competitive analysis in a period of general excess capacity, it is the difference in variable cost that matters.

9. Timothy J. Considine, "Economic and Technological Determinants of the Intensity of Material Use," *Land Economics* 67, no. 1 (February 1991): 99–115.

10. See Donald F. Barnett and Robert W. Crandall, *Up from the Ashes: The Rise of the Steel Minimill in the United States* (Washington, DC: Brookings Institution, 1986), Appendix C.

## Selected Readings

Barnett, Donald F., and Robert W. Crandall. *Up from the Ashes: The Rise of the Steel Minimill in the United States*. Washington, DC: Brookings Institution, 1986. An economic analysis of the growth of minimills and the decline of integrated firms in the United States. International comparisons of production costs.

Barringer, William H., and Kenneth J. Pierce. "Paying the Price for Big Steel," <http://www. aiis.org/newsletters/?file=newsletter07.htm> American Institute for International Steel, 2000. An analysis of the costs to U.S. consumers of repeated exercises of trade protection. Argues that large, integrated U.S. companies' problems derive from their inefficiency.

Deily, Mary E. "Investment Activity and the Exit Decision." *Review of Economics and Statistics* 70 (November 1988): 595–602. Examines the effect of scale economies and plant efficiency on the decision by integrated producers to retire capacity.

Howell, Thomas R., William A. Noellert, and Alan W. Wolfe. *Steel and the State: Government Intervention and Steel's Structural Crisis*. Boulder, CO: Westview Press, 1988. A detailed examination of state assistance to the steel industry in numerous countries. Argues that the U.S. industry's problems are largely related to foreign governments' subsidies to their industries.

Hufbauer, Gary Clyde, and Ben Goodrich. "Time for a Grand Bargain in Steel?" <http://www.iie.com/policybriefs/news02-1.htm>. Institute for International Economics, Washington, DC, January 2002. Analyzes alternatives for resolving trade disputes in steel and paying large post-retirement legacy costs of integrated steel companies.

Karlson, Stephen H. "Adoption of Competing Inventions by the United States Steel Industry." *Review of Economics and Statistics* 68 (August 1986): 415–22. An empirical investigation into the rate at which the BOF furnace was adopted in the United States. Concludes that early, small-scale adoption was a serious error.

Oster, Sharon. "The Diffusion of Innovation Among Steel Firms: The Basic Oxygen Furnace." *The Bell Journal of Economics* (Spring 1982): 45–56. Examines the impact of cost-saving and establishment size on the rate of adoption for the BOF furnace and the continuous caster.

# Part II

# Distribution and Services

The relative importance of distribution in the U.S. economy—the wholesale and retail trades taken together—has not changed much since the 1950s. In terms of the value of output, distribution today accounts for little more than the 15 percent share that it accounted for earlier.

Over time, the frequency with which tight oligopoly is found in distribution has diminished to such an extent that the sector can be characterized as effectively competitive, although exceptions can easily be found, especially in smaller local markets or in the distribution of specialized products. Steps taken to achieve greater reliability and efficiency through the reorganization of electric power generation have not yet reduced consumer vulnerability to sudden rate changes. Vertical restraints have been a concern in some channels of distribution, but in the motion picture industry vertical restraints appear to promote economic efficiency.

The service sector of the U.S. economy has grown substantially since the 1950s. Financial and nonfinancial services together accounted for nearly 30 percent of the value of output in the 1950s and today account for about 40 percent. Financial services (which include insurance and real estate) account for about half of this relative growth. Services account for well over half of total employment today.

Overall, there is more effective competition in the service sector today than there was in the 1950s.

The numerous instances of industry deregulation, along with a variety of antitrust actions, have accounted for the bulk of this increase in effective competition. Particularly striking examples can be found in the communication, financial services, and transportation subsectors.

Competition in seven service industries—airlines, retail commercial banking, casino gambling, health insurance, microcomputer platforms, nursing homes, and telecommunications—is examined in the studies that follow. In the transportation subsector, deregulation has brought lower fares and better service to the airline industry, yet airlines wield an unexpected degree of market power and industry critics have called for renewed government intervention. In retail commercial banking markets, performance has repeatedly been shown to be better when concentration is lower, raising concern about effective local competition as interstate banking continues to grow. Although most forms of gambling have grown rapidly during the past twenty years, the growth of riverboat and tribal casinos in certain regions of the United States has been particularly striking and only recently has begun to slow. Because the design of health insurance programs strongly affects the utilization (and cost) of medical services, the most rapidly growing programs in recent years have been those that succeed in containing costs. Also in the health sector, the rising cost of nursing home services has led firms to expand the range of services offered to tap new sources of revenue that might reduce their dependence on Medicare/Medicaid funding. The market for microcomputer platforms still seems likely to become more competitive as the development of new products continues, facilitated by hardware improvements. In telecommunications, despite greatly diminished state and federal regulation after the breakup of AT&T, telecommunication services have not yet become effectively competitive in certain respects.

# 6

# Airline Service

## The Evolution of Competition Since Deregulation

*Steven A. Morrison*

After forty years of tight regulation by the federal government, the airline industry was deregulated in 1978. Such a dramatic change in an industry's economic environment is bound to have significant effects, and the airline industry is no exception. Airlines provide an interesting example of how an industry evolves when freed from government regulation. After more than two decades of deregulation, this evolution is still not complete, although the form to which the industry is evolving is becoming clear.

This evolution has not been without controversy. Each zig and zag of the industry renews the debate about the wisdom of deregulation and the future of the industry. The industry has this high profile because many people are fascinated with aviation. Others devote attention to airlines because airline deregulation was the first of regulatory reforms in several fields (e.g., railroads, trucking, telecommunications, banking) in the late 1970s and 1980s. Analysts look to airlines, the oldest deregulated industry, for insight into other industries. Although the airline industry is a complex one, it is amenable to study because of the wealth of data—a legacy of regulation—the government continues to collect.

This study chronicles and explains the evolu-

tion of the domestic passenger airline industry since it was deregulated in 1978.[1] The next two sections provide a brief history of the government's involvement in the industry and the deregulation movement. The following section describes the technology of the industry and introduces some terminology that will be useful. After a discussion of the demand for air transportation, there is a discussion of what airline deregulation was supposed to accomplish and what it has accomplished. Finally, current trouble spots and policy options are identified.

### History of the Industry

The aviation age began in 1903 at Kitty Hawk, North Carolina, when Wilbur and Orville Wright performed the first power-driven, heavier-than-air, controlled flight. It was just eleven years later, in 1914, that scheduled commercial passenger service began. For $5 the St. Petersburg–Tampa Airboat Line carried passengers eighteen miles between Tampa and St. Petersburg, Florida. Significant growth in the industry would wait until after World War I, and then it was mail rather than passenger transportation that developed.

The first regular airmail service began in 1918,

operated by the Post Office. By 1927, the Post Office had contracted out all airmail service to private carriers. Private carriage was feasible because the federal government undertook the expense of constructing the air infrastructure (e.g., lighted civil airways and beacons for navigation).

Carriers were paid for carrying mail on the basis of its weight and the distance traveled (pound-miles). At one point, after several changes in postage rates and in payments to carriers, carriers received more for carrying mail than the cost of the postage. This posed financial problems for the Post Office and was exacerbated by the incentives carriers had to mail heavy packages to themselves. In 1930, partly in response to such problems, Congress passed legislation to base compensation on capacity and distance (space-miles) instead of pound-miles. Although this ended the problems with the pound-mile system, the space-mile system gave carriers an incentive to use larger aircraft and to use the extra space to carry passengers. Because passenger transportation was not financially feasible without a mail contract, the postmaster general effectively controlled entry into the industry. Thus subsidized passenger service began with the postmaster general as the regulator of commercial air transport.

Aviation continued to develop during the early 1930s, despite the Depression, because of significant technical advances in aircraft design and manufacturing. Reacting to new problems, in 1934 Congress passed an act that divided control of air transportation among three agencies. This also proved unworkable because carriers submitted ridiculously low bids to one agency (zero in at least one case) to win a mail contract, knowing that another agency had the power to raise rates that were too low. Finally, in 1938 Congress passed the Civil Aeronautics Act, which remained basically unchanged until deregulation in 1978.

The act, patterned after the Interstate Commerce Act of 1887 and the Motor Carrier Act of 1935, subjected the industry to public utility–type rate-of-return regulation. To implement the regulations, the act created what was to become the Civil Aeronautics Board (CAB). This legislation, enacted during the Great Depression, reflected the widespread distrust of market forces that prevailed then and the belief that government regulation could improve the market outcome.

The Civil Aeronautics Act required carriers to have a certificate of public convenience and necessity issued by the board. The sixteen carriers operating when the act was passed received "grandfather" rights and were granted certificates for the routes they served. Other applicants had to show that they were "fit, willing, and able" to perform the proposed service and that the service was "required by the public convenience and necessity."

The act allowed the entry of new carriers, but the CAB never granted a major (trunk) route award to a new entrant. However, the board did allow entry into other categories: "local service" carriers providing feeder service for the trunks (1943); air taxi and commuter airlines operating small aircraft, usually with fewer than twenty seats (1952); and supplemental charter carriers (1962). Nonetheless, from the beginning of CAB regulation in 1938 until one year before deregulation in 1978, the board did not permit entry on any route that already had two or more carriers.[2]

Initially, the CAB set air fares equal to prevailing first-class rail fares. Ultimately the board set fares as a function of distance so the industry would earn a 12 percent return on its rate base, assuming a 55 percent load factor (percentage of seats filled). The fare formula included a fixed terminal charge and a fixed amount per mile for each of several mileage segments. Because the board felt that cross-subsidization of short-haul routes by long-haul routes would foster the development of aviation, the formula was designed so fares for long routes were greater than costs and fares for short routes were less than cost. The board then allowed carriers to file for the fares called for by the formula.

Because fares were based on industrywide costs, they differed substantially from costs in many markets, even for the same distance. Although airlines were effectively prohibited from engaging in price competition, they were allowed to compete with quality of service, with emphasis on equipment and flight frequency, which were explicitly not under the board's control. Carriers added equipment and flights in the lucrative long-haul markets and reduced flights (to the extent allowed) in unprofitable short-haul markets.

There was also an interesting link between the board's entry policy and its fare policy. Because of the fare formula, an airline's profits depended to a large extent on its route configuration. The board was aware of this and awarded new routes to balance the advantages and disadvantages that its prior route awards and pricing rule had created.[3]

Besides regulating entry, the board also regulated exit. To exit a route, a carrier had to obtain CAB approval. Because the board's restrictive entry policy gave value to a carrier's right to serve a route, firms did not exit the industry through bankruptcy. Instead, they "exited" through mergers, which provided a convenient way for a healthy carrier to acquire route authority.

## The Deregulation Movement

Economists began criticizing CAB regulation as early as the 1950s. Gradually, more and more analysts accepted the position that the airline industry did not have characteristics that made economic regulation necessary. The critics argued that airline regulation had led to higher fares than would prevail in an unregulated market, yet the industry was not earning excess profits.

Since the Civil Aeronautics Act regulated "interstate air transportation," airlines operating entirely within one state were not subject to federal regulation. This aspect of the law set up an interesting "controlled" experiment of sorts: by comparing unregulated intrastate fares with fares on similar interstate routes, a measure of the effects of regulation could be obtained. One particularly influential study pointed out that in 1965 the fare charged by the intrastate carrier Pacific Southwest Airlines (PSA) between San Francisco and Los Angeles (338 miles) was $11.43, while the fare charged by CAB certified carriers between Boston and Washington, D.C. (400 miles) was $24.65.[4]

Going beyond the compelling case for deregulation provided by academic studies, a series of events during the 1970s set the stage for deregulation. First, the introduction of wide-body jets in 1970 coincided with a recession and led to excess capacity in the industry. The CAB responded by imposing a moratorium on new route cases and by allowing carriers to agree to capacity limitations on major routes. Both actions were widely criticized.[5] Next, in 1973 fuel prices soared in the wake of the Arab oil embargo. Regulatory reform was seen as a means of fighting inflation and eliminating government red tape.[6] Furthermore, a change in public attitude toward competition and regulation occurred during the decades since the CAB was created. By the 1970s, people viewed government regulation with the same suspicion with which competition had been viewed during the 1930s.[7]

In 1975, the Ford administration sought deregulation of the airlines. Shortly thereafter, during

1976 and 1977, the CAB began to loosen regulatory control by interpreting the existing statute more liberally, a trend that increased dramatically when economist Alfred Kahn was appointed chairman of the CAB in 1977. The resulting liberalizations, such as the board approval of American Airlines' proposed "Supersaver" fares in 1977, gave legislators an inkling of how a deregulated marketplace would function. Although the Congress was won over, airlines themselves—and airline labor groups—remained largely unconvinced of the wisdom of deregulation; most airlines and unions opposed deregulation.

Finally, in 1978, Congress passed and President Carter signed the Airline Deregulation Act. The overriding objective of the act was reliance on competition. Entry regulations were phased out; since 1982 carriers have been free to enter any route they desire, as long as they are fit, willing, and able. Exit regulations were eliminated; carriers can now exit at will. Fare regulation was also phased out. In 1983 the CAB's authority over fares was eliminated. Carriers can charge whatever fares they desire. Finally, in 1985 the CAB ceased to exist; its remaining functions (e.g., international aviation, consumer protection) were transferred to the Department of Transportation.[8]

## Technology and Terminology

Do large airlines have a cost advantage over small airlines? If so, small airlines would be unable to compete and the industry would come to be dominated by a few large firms. At the heart of the issue of cost advantages is the production technology of the airline industry. Because there are many ways to measure an airline's size, we must first address the issue of measuring airline output and then consider ways of measuring airline size.

At its most basic level, the unit of output of a passenger airline is transportation of passengers between cities. We could describe the output of an airline by listing the number of passengers it carries from New York to Los Angeles, the number of passengers it carries from Chicago to Denver, and so on. When viewed in this way, air transportation is a multiproduct industry. However, dealing with these multiple products at the disaggregate level would quickly become unwieldy—in 2000 the U.S. domestic airline industry produced more than 425 million (directional) passenger trips among approximately 660 airports, involving approximately 100,000 unique (directional) city pairs.

To summarize the list of outputs of an airline, several more-tractable aggregate measures have been developed. The simplest of these is a count of passengers. In particular, this measure is usually called revenue passengers enplaned (RPE) because it counts paying passengers each time they board a plane. Although it has some uses, it has two drawbacks. First, because it does not take trip distance into account, a short trip and a long trip both count as one enplanement. Second, if one passenger makes a trip without changing planes (a direct flight) while another passenger travels from the same origin to the same destination but changes planes (a connecting flight) the connecting passenger's trip would be counted as two enplanements, whereas the direct passenger's trip counts as only one enplanement. Thus, this measure of output is sensitive to the way in which the output was actually produced.

A measure of output that overcomes the first problem and could, in principle, overcome the second is revenue passenger miles (RPM). A revenue passenger mile is one paying passenger transported one mile. If an airline carried 100 passengers 500 miles, it would have produced 50,000 revenue passenger miles. Thus, this measure varies with distance flown. When passengers on connecting flights fly a greater distance than would be required by a nonstop flight, this measure also captures the way in which the output was actually produced. In principle (although seldom in practice), each trip could be counted as the minimum number of revenue passenger miles necessary to complete the trip.

There are analogous measures of an airline's capacity. One measure is aircraft departures. Like the RPE measure of output, it fails to take into account the distance flown or the size of the aircraft. The measure aircraft miles takes into account the miles flown but does not take aircraft size into account. The most frequently used measure of airline capacity is available seat miles (ASM). This is the number of seats available for sale times the distance the aircraft is flown. If an airline flies a 150-seat plane 1,000 miles, it has a capacity of 150,000 available seat miles.

Demand for air transportation varies from route to route, with further variation from day to day and hour to hour on a given route. In addition to the predictable component of demand, there is a random component. Because aircraft come in discrete sizes and cannot be stretched or shrunk to accommodate changes in demand, aircraft usually fly with some empty seats. A measure of how much of an airline's capacity is actually sold is the load factor—the ratio of RPM to ASM. Thus, if an airline flies 10,000 available seat miles and has 7,000 revenue passenger miles, its load factor is 0.70 or 70 percent.

With our measures of output now in hand, we can start to address the question of whether large airlines have lower costs per revenue passenger mile than small airlines. Answering this question seems straightforward. Compare the cost per revenue passenger mile of large carriers with that of small carriers. For example, in 2000 the largest

U.S. airline, United Airlines, produced about 127 billion RPM at a cost of $.147 per RPM. US Airways, the sixth largest carrier in the United States, produced about 47 billion RPM at a cost of $.197 per RPM. This certainly seems like evidence of increasing returns to scale. However, cost comparisons are not that simple.

To understand the economics of producing air transportation, start with the unrealistic assumption that there are no economies of aircraft size. In other words, assume that an aircraft with 100 seats is 100 times more costly to fly a given distance than an aircraft with one seat. If it were, the cost per available seat mile would be independent of aircraft size and efficient air transportation would allow each passenger to be transported in one-person aircraft directly from any origin to any destination at any time. If only airlines could operate that way! The reason they do not is that there are economies of aircraft size—larger aircraft are cheaper to operate per available seat mile than smaller aircraft.[9] (If they were not, there would be no reason to have large aircraft.) These economies are illustrated in Figure 6.1, which shows 1996 aircraft operating cost per seat mile as a function of the number of seats and distance. Herein lies a basic trade-off in any transportation activity: the trade-off between low operating costs and convenient service. Passengers prefer frequent service. But providing frequent service means using small aircraft, which have a higher cost per available seat mile.[10] Because of this, airlines do not "schedule" one-person aircraft to leave whenever each passenger wants to leave, and instead schedule larger aircraft to leave at various times throughout the day. This results in less convenient service to passengers, but it is less costly to produce.[11]

As more passengers travel on a route, it becomes possible to use larger aircraft (and have more frequent service), thus lowering the cost per avail-

Figure 6.1 **Aircraft Operating Cost per Available Seat Mile**

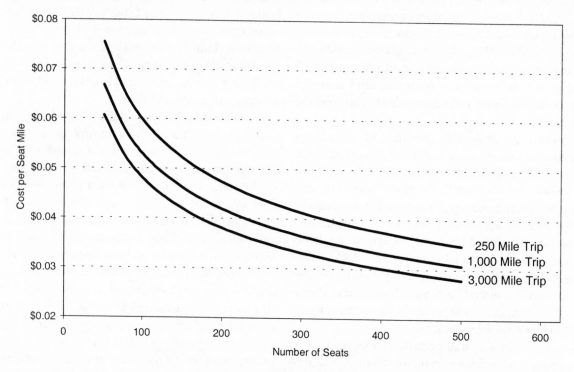

*Source:* Author's calculations using 1996 aircraft operating cost data from U.S. Department of Transportation, Form 41.

able seat mile. This is what transportation economists call economies of density, where density is measured by the number of passengers traveling on a route between two cities. Because of economies of aircraft size, air transportation has economies of density.[12]

But there is another aspect to the convenience/operating cost trade-off. Consider a city with many "thin" routes, that is, routes with very few passengers per day. Suppose these routes could each receive once-a-day service with small aircraft or once-every-other-day service with a larger aircraft. In either case, service would be expensive and inconvenient. But there is a third alternative. Why not combine all passengers from the thin routes

onto several large planes and take them to a centrally located airport? Once there, they change planes (with other travelers going to or from other such points) and fly to their final destination accompanied by passengers from many origins bound for the same destination. This is the basis for the hub-and-spoke route system. By combining passengers with many origins or destinations on the same plane, travelers receive the benefit of larger aircraft and the benefit of more frequent departures than they could have with point-to-point service. The downside is the increased travel time and the inconvenience of changing planes. If the number of travelers going from one city to another is large enough, the time and inconvenience costs outweigh the benefits of more frequent service and larger aircraft. Thus, dense routes receive point-to-point service, while less dense routes are combined and use the hub-and-spoke system.

Now we can answer the question of whether large airlines have lower unit costs than small airlines. By "large," we mean an airline that serves many cities. In particular, how do the costs of one airline producing a given number of passenger miles on its route system compare with the costs of another airline that produces twice as many passenger miles to twice as many cities?[13] Research indicates that the larger airline will have costs twice that of the smaller airline, so that unit costs are identical. Thus, the production of passenger transportation is characterized by constant returns to scale. Large airlines do not have cost advantages over small airlines. Observed variations in cost between large and small airlines are primarily due to differences in route density and route length.[14] On the production side, at least, there is no reason to believe that large airlines have an advantage.

## Demand for Air Transportation

Big airlines do not have a cost advantage over their smaller rivals, but do passengers prefer to fly on larger airlines, giving such airlines demand-side advantages? To investigate this possibility we must explore the nature of passenger demand for air travel.

The demand for air transportation is very peaked. Demand for travel differs from month to month, day to day, and hour to hour. In addition to the peaking, there are random fluctuations in demand that are hard to predict. For example, demand for this Friday's flight will differ from that for last Friday's. Compounding the airlines' problems, not everyone with a reservation actually shows up.[15]

Also, there are many different types of travelers.

The simplest breakdown of travelers distinguishes pleasure travelers from business travelers. As a generalization, pleasure travelers buy their own tickets and prefer a low fare to convenient service. Business travelers' tickets are purchased by their employers. They tend to be willing to pay a high fare to get convenient service on short notice.

Economists measure the sensitivity of demand to changes in price and income (or other factors) using the concept of elasticity of demand. In particular, demand elasticity is the ratio of the percentage change in quantity demanded to the percentage change in price or income. No one knows precisely what these elasticities are, but it is generally agreed that demand for air travel is very responsive to changes in income. In particular, the income elasticity of demand is probably around 1.5. This means that if passengers' income rises by 3 percent, with all other factors (price, etc.) constant, demand for air travel will increase by 4.5 percent. When the economy is growing, airlines do very well. However, this is a two-edged sword. During a recession, for example, if income falls by 2 percent, demand for air travel will fall by 3 percent. Because of the high income elasticity of demand, the airline industry is cyclical—so much so that it grows—and shrinks—faster than the economy as a whole.[16]

The response of demand to changes in price depends on trip purpose. Business travelers have a less elastic demand than pleasure travelers. Once again, precise estimates elude us, but as an approximation, pleasure travelers have a demand elasticity around 1.9, while business travelers have an elasticity of about 0.8.[17]

But do travelers have a preference for large airlines? The answer appears to be yes for at least three reasons.[18] First is information costs. Travelers tend to call the largest airline that serves their city because they know it is more likely to serve their destination and to have convenient departure times. (Alternatively, the largest carrier is likely to have more affiliated travel agents.) Second, passengers prefer the large integrated route systems of large carriers. This makes it possible to fly to many points worldwide on the same airline, with less chance of a lost bag or a missed connection. Finally, frequent flier programs also enhance the desirability of a large carrier. So even though there is no cost reason why large carriers should dominate the airline industry, passenger preference for large carriers does place small carriers at some disadvantage.

## Deregulation: What Was Supposed to Happen

The deregulation movement was based largely on the performance of the California and Texas intrastate airlines. These airlines were the model for what kind of industry the deregulated air transportation industry was supposed to become. Since there were thought to be no advantages to large-scale production, it was expected there would be entry of new airlines, offering low-fare service. These low fares would be possible because these carriers would have low labor costs. In addition, although these new entrants would fly conventional jet aircraft, they would fit them with more seats (i.e., less leg room) and would operate at high load factors (i.e., percentage of seats filled). Barriers to entry into the industry and into particular city-pair markets were thought to be small, so entry—or the threat of entry—would keep airlines from earning excess profits.[19]

## Deregulation: What Actually Happened

Before describing the changes deregulation has brought to the airline industry, we must address two methodological points. First, when did airline deregulation begin? The simple answer—although too simple—is October 28, 1978, when President Carter signed the Airline Deregulation Act. But, as mentioned earlier, the CAB began loosening the constraints of regulation as early as 1976. So comparisons that use 1978 as the starting point probably understate the effect of airline deregulation.

The second point is more subtle. Most evaluations of airline deregulation—including this one—simply compare the industry's performance "before" with its performance "after" and ascribe the difference to deregulation. In other words, such "factual" comparisons simply compare what was to what is. Such an approach assumes that the only changes in the industry were those induced by deregulation. For example, if fares rise (or fall) because fuel prices rise (or fall), one must ask whether this has anything to do with deregulation. The way around this problem is a counterfactual analysis, in which what is is compared with what might have been. For example, to see what effect deregulation had on fares, one could compare actual deregulated fares with (an estimate of) what regulated air fares would have been if regulation had continued. This is counterfactual because regulated fares never existed in the deregulated environment.

There is no question that factual comparisons can be illuminating. The comparisons provided in this chapter are factual. But you must always ask yourself whether something other than deregulation could have contributed to the observed changes.[20] The next six sections chronicle the changes in key areas that have occurred in the wake of airline deregulation.

### Industry Concentration

Figure 6.2 plots the domestic airline industry's four- and eight-firm concentration ratios, fre-

Figure 6.2 **Percentage of Domestic Scheduled Passenger Miles Flown by Largest Four and Eight Firms**

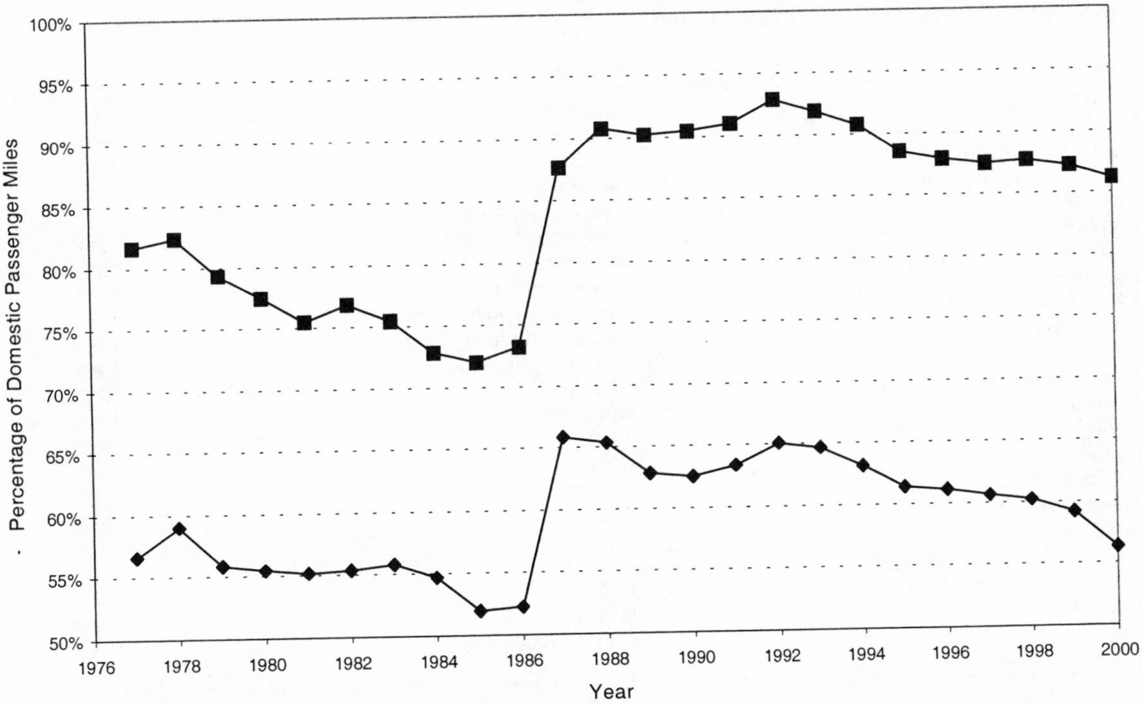

*Source:* Author's calculations using data from U.S. Department of Transportation, Form 41.

quently used measures of industry concentration.[21] In 1977 the eight largest airlines accounted for about 82 percent of total domestic revenue passenger miles and the four largest accounted for 57 percent. By 2000 the eight-firm ratio had risen somewhat to 86 percent while the four-firm ratio declined slightly to 56 percent. In the intervening years, until early 1986, the industry became less concentrated. But from mid-1986 until mid-1988, the industry became much.more concentrated because of the mergers that took place during that period.

Table 6.1 shows the important airline mergers, acquisitions, and failures that have taken place since airline deregulation. Although it took less

than a year after deregulation for the first two carriers to merge, the great merger wave occurred between June 1985 and October 1987, when fourteen mergers were consummated.

The use of concentration ratios based on revenue passenger miles gives a distorted impression of the degree of competition in the airline industry. The output of airlines is not really revenue passenger miles; that is just a simple way of aggregating the output of the industry into a single number. (Recall that the airline industry is a multiple-product industry producing and selling thousands of different products—travel between city pairs.) Thus, instead of looking at what has happened to competition in the "national market" for

Table 6.1

**Important Airline Mergers, Acquisitions, and Failures**

| Carriers | Resulting carrier | Year |
|---|---|---|
| North Central-Southern | Republic | 1979 |
| Republic-Hughes Airwest | Republic | 1980 |
| Northwest-Republic | Northwest | 1986 |
| Pan American-National | Pan American | 1980 |
| Pan American | Ceased operating | 1991 |
| Braniff | Ceased operating | 1982 |
| Texas International-Continental | Continental | 1982 |
| People Express-Frontier | People Express | 1985 |
| Texas Air-People Express | Texas Air (holding company) | 1986 |
| Texas Air-Eastern | Texas Air (holding company) | 1986 |
| Eastern Airlines | Ceased operating | 1991 |
| Southwest-Muse | Southwest | 1985 |
| Southwest-Morris | Southwest | 1993 |
| TWA-Ozark | TWA | 1986 |
| Delta-Western | Delta | 1986 |
| American-AirCal | American | 1987 |
| American-Reno | American | 1998 |
| American-TWA | American | 2001 |
| U.S. Air-PSA | U.S. Air | 1987 |
| U.S. Air-Piedmont | U.S. Air | 1987 |
| U.S. Air-Trump Shuttle | U.S. Air | 1992 |
| Midway | Ceased operating | 1991 |
| United-Air Wisconsin | United | 1992 |

revenue passenger miles, we should look at what has happened to competition at the route level. It is at the route level, after all, that airlines actually compete with one another. Revenue passenger miles produced between Cincinnati and Seattle do not "compete" with revenue passenger miles between Pittsburgh and New Orleans. Measures of the extent of competition at the route level tell a strikingly different story from that of the other more aggregate measures. In Figure 6.3 we see that in 1977, the year before formal deregulation, the average domestic airline route had about 1.7 "effective competitors."[22] This measure of competition rose steadily through 1986 when, due to mergers, the number of effective competitors per route declined and since 1991 has been relatively stable in the range of 2.2 to 2.3. Based on this route-level measure, airline competition is significantly

stronger than it was before deregulation. However, the figure also shows that all routes have not experienced the same gains. Long-haul routes (greater than 2,000 miles) have seen competition increase by 78 percent, while competition on short-haul routes (less than 500 miles) is unchanged from its level in 1977.

Another, perhaps more intuitive, way to look at the extent of route-level competition is to see what has happened to the percentage of passengers who travel on "competitive" carriers (i.e., those with a route market share less than 20 percent) and those who fly on "monopoly" carriers (i.e., those with a route market share greater than 90 percent). The percentage of passengers captive to monopoly carriers has been cut by nearly half—from 29 percent in 1977 to 15 percent in 2000. During that time, the percentage of passengers flying on com-

Figure 6.3   **Domestic Competition at the Route Level**

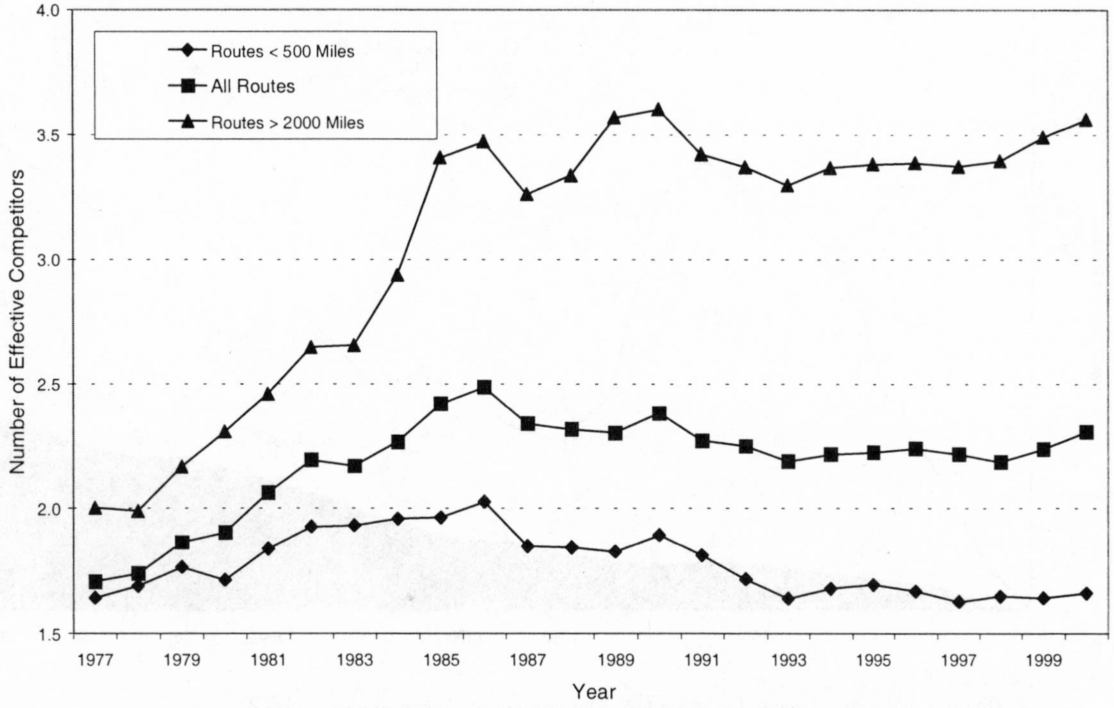

*Source:* Author's calculations using data from U.S. Department of Transportation, Data Bank 1A.

petitive carriers more than doubled, from 8 percent to 17 percent.

In addition to the number of competitors on a route, the identity of those competitors is also important. Deregulation allowed entry by existing airlines into new routes but it also allowed the entry of new, usually low-cost, low-fare airlines into the industry. The extent of competition provided by these new entrants is shown in Figure 6.4, which distinguishes between Southwest Airlines and other new entrants. Competition by new entrants began rising immediately after deregulation until it reached a peak in 1985 at about 18 percent of domestic passenger miles. The importance of new entrants declined from 1986 through 1988 due to

the acquisition of People Express by Texas Air Corporation in 1986 and the significant expansion of the pre-deregulation airlines. However, since 1989 the share of domestic passenger miles flown by new entrants has continued to increase and in 2000 reached 19 percent, its all-time high.

It should be noted, however, that the effect of a carrier, especially a low-fare carrier, extends beyond the routes it actually serves. A carrier may also influence fares on nearby routes that it serves that passengers view as reasonable substitutes for travel on the route in question. For example, Southwest Airlines serves the route from Providence, Rhode Island, to Baltimore-Washington airport in Maryland. These airports are sufficiently close to

Figure 6.4  **Percentage of Domestic Revenue Passenger Miles Flown by New Entrant Carriers**

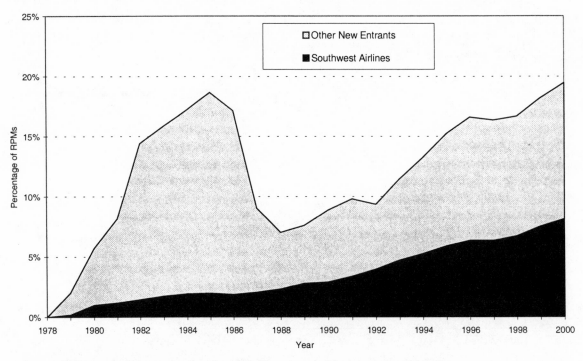

*Source:* Author's calculations using data from U.S. Department of Transportation, Form 41.

Boston and Washington Reagan National, respectively, that fares on Southwest also influence fares on that route. In addition, a carrier can provide potential competition on a route it does not serve if carriers that serve the route charge lower fares than they otherwise would to give other carriers less incentive to actually enter the route. Table 6.2 shows that these effects can be substantial, at least in the case of Southwest Airlines, the nation's premiere low-fare airline. In 1998, Southwest was the seventh largest domestic passenger airline with a 7 percent share of domestic scheduled revenue passenger miles. Despite its relatively small size, through its effects on the routes that it serves, on nearby routes, and on routes it is poised to serve, it influenced air fares on routes accounting for 94

percent of the domestic market. As shown in the table, in 1998 the fare savings attributed to competition from Southwest Airlines were over $12 billion.

Despite the increased competition in general at the route level and the increased role of low-fare carriers, there is a concern that in certain markets the dominance of a few firms makes it is easier for them to collude and raise fares. However, a study of pricing on thirty-three routes where United Airlines and American Airlines dominated the market (together carrying 75 percent or more of each route's passengers) found strong evidence against collusive pricing behavior.[23]

Another measure of post-deregulation concentration that is the focus of a lot of attention is the

Table 6.2

**Southwest Airlines' Impact on Fares in 1998**

| Category | Domestic passenger miles affected (%) | Fare savings (billions) |
|---|---|---|
| Actual competition | | |
| Routes served | 21.0 | 6.55 |
| Nearby routes | 23.7 | 3.03 |
| Potential competition | | |
| Serves both endpoint airports | 6.5 | 0.95 |
| Serves one endpoint airport, one nearby airport | 2.7 | 0.18 |
| Serves two nearby airports | 0.1 | −0.01 |
| Serves one endpoint airport | 30.7 | 1.76 |
| Serves one nearby airport | 9.4 | 0.42 |
| Total | 94.2 | 12.88 |

*Source*: Steven A. Morrison, "Actual, Adjacent, and Potential Competition: Estimating the Full Effect of Southwest Airlines," *Journal of Transport Economics and Policy*, 35 (May 2001): 239–56. Totals may not add due to rounding.

concentration at hub airports where one or sometimes two carriers account for a large share of airport activity. Table 6.3 shows the dominant carrier and its share of aircraft departures at sixteen airports (chosen from the top fifty) where one carrier had more than 50 percent of the passenger aircraft departures in 2000. For comparison, the share and dominant carriers are also shown for 1977. The dominant carrier's share of departures increased at all but one of these airports, with significant increases at some of them. Of course, these airports do not represent what happened to airports in general; these airports are worst cases. Figure 6.5 shows what has happened to airport concentration over time, as measured by all enplanements and originating enplanements.[24] In 2000, the average airport in the United States was more concentrated based on total enplanements (which include connecting passengers) and somewhat less concentrated based on originating enplanements (which include only those travelers who are beginning their outbound or return trips) than it was in 1977.

## Fares

Although there are other aspects of the industry that are also important—service quality, for example—fares occupy center stage in any discussion of the airline industry and deregulation's effect on it.

A simple way to look at the effect of deregulation on air fares is to see how air fares have changed relative to the overall price level. In particular, we can calculate real air fares by adjusting actual air fares by the changes in the Consumer Price Index (CPI). This is shown in Figure 6.6, which plots real airline yield from 1970 through 2000. (Yield is revenue per revenue passenger mile and is the standard measure of average air fares.) Real air fares have fallen under deregulation, regardless of when you consider deregulation to have started. As of 2000, air fares were 41 percent lower than their level in 1976. But can this decrease be attributed to deregulation? As the figure shows, yields had a downward trend even before the beginning of the deregulation movement. Here a counterfactual comparison would help. Results of such a

Table 6.3

**Leading Carriers at Large Airports**

| Airport | Leading carrier in 2000 | 2000 share | Leading carrier in 1977 | 1977 share |
|---|---|---|---|---|
| Atlanta | Delta | 56.4 | Eastern | 41.2 |
| Detroit Metro | Northwest | 55.8 | North Central | 21.3 |
| Minneapolis-St. Paul | Northwest | 56.7 | Northwest | 37.8 |
| Houston Intercontinental | Continental | 55.6 | Texas International | 22.4 |
| St. Louis | TWA | 58.2 | TWA | 34.4 |
| Denver | United | 54.0 | Frontier | 26.3 |
| Philadelphia | US Airways | 59.1 | Allegheny | 24.0 |
| San Francisco | United | 53.9 | United | 39.4 |
| Charlotte | US Airways | 87.2 | Eastern | 63.9 |
| Miami | American | 50.7 | Eastern | 38.3 |
| Pittsburgh | US Airways | 79.3 | Allegheny | 49.9 |
| Salt Lake City | Delta | 66.0 | Western | 37.5 |
| Memphis | Northwest | 60.3 | Delta | 34.8 |
| Houston Hobby | Southwest | 76.9 | Texas International | 95.0 |
| Oakland | Southwest | 68.0 | United | 43.7 |
| Dallas Love | Southwest | 82.0 | Southern | 40.9 |

*Source*: Author's calculations using data from U.S. Department of Transportation, Schedule T3, Data Bank 22.

*Note*: Airports among the fifty largest in 2000 (based on departures) where one carrier had more than 50 percent of departures in 2000. Shares exclude operations by regional affiliates operating under code-share agreements. Also, because intrastate airlines did not report data to the Department of Transportation in 1977, the leading carrier shown for 1977 is the leading certificated (i.e., regulated) carrier.

counterfactual for 1998 show that fares were 28 percent lower than they would have been had regulation continued.[25] For 1998, the annual fare savings to travelers attributed to deregulation amount to $24 billion (1998 dollars).[26]

As interesting as aggregate yield figures are, they may mask changes in how deregulation has affected different routes. Figure 6.7 shows real fare changes for 19,119 (origin-destination) routes for which fare data were available for the fourth quarters of both 1978 and 2000. As can be seen in the figure, there are considerable differences in fare changes among the routes, with about 73 percent of the routes (accounting for about 85 percent of passengers and about 94 percent of passenger miles) experiencing lower average real fares, and about 27 percent facing the same or higher average real fares. The (logarithmic) trend line shows that there is a pronounced relationship of fare

changes with distance; on average, short-haul routes have experienced real fare increases while real fares have fallen on long-haul routes. This finding is not at all surprising because the CAB had intentionally set long-haul fares above cost and short-haul fares below cost.

Another feature of fares under deregulation that is lost when looking at yields is the change in the distribution of fares charged on any given route. Even occasional air travelers are aware of the array of fares available, ranging from expensive unrestricted coach fares to deeply discounted fares with a host of restrictions. Airlines also vary fares and the number of discount seats available by time of day. When demand is high, fares are high; when demand is low, fares are lower. Table 6.4 illustrates how varied fares can be on a single flight. The extent of this variation over time is shown in Figure 6.8, which plots a measure of fare disper-

Figure 6.5  **Airport Concentration**

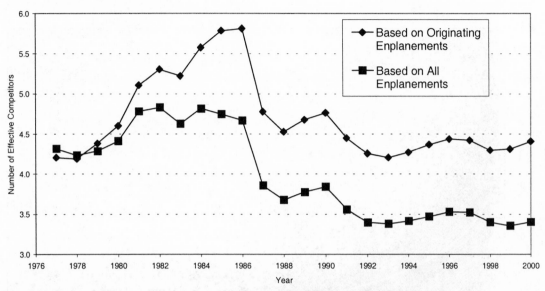

*Source:* Author's calculations using data from U.S. Department of Transportation, Data Bank 1A.

Figure 6.6  **Domestic Airline Yield Adjusted for Inflation** (2000 dollars)

*Source:* Author's calculations using data from the Air Transport Association.

Figure 6.7   **Real Fare Change as a Function of Distance: Fourth Quarters of 1978 and 2000**

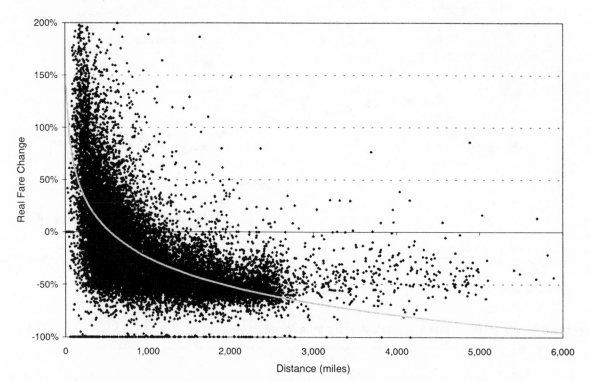

*Source:* Author's calculations using data from U.S. Department of Transportation, Data Bank 1A.

sion over time.[27] As is readily apparent in the figure, fares have become more dispersed since deregulation. In 1978, fares on each route showed relatively little variability and stayed that way for the next few years. Fare dispersion increased beginning in 1985 and peaked in 1991. After declining for the first half of the 1990s, dispersion increased then leveled off for the remainder of the decade. In 2000, fare dispersion was slightly higher than at its previous peak in 1991. It is important to point out, however, that not all this dispersion is due to price discrimination. Some of the dispersion reflects cost-based price differences, for example, peak versus off-peak fares. Also, business travelers, who pay high fares, have an easier time booking a seat at the last minute than pleasure trav-

elers because airlines carry a larger "inventory" of seats for business travelers (relative to their expected demand) than they do for pleasure travelers. The cost of these "extra" seats is reflected in the fares business travelers pay.

### Service Quality

Fares have declined, but what has happened to service quality? One aspect of service quality is how easy it is for a traveler to get a seat on the flight of his or her choice. This is (inversely) related to the load factor, the percentage of seats filled. A low load factor means that, on average, travelers will have a relatively easy time getting a seat on their preferred flight. As load factors in-

Table 6.4

**Airline Yield Management**

| Type of ticket | No. of passengers | Average fare ($) |
|---|---|---|
| First class (14 seats, all booked) | | |
|   Full first class | 5 | 909 |
|   Discount first class | 3 | 529 |
|   Paid/free upgrades | 5 | 248 |
|   Frequent flier awards | 1 | 0 |
| Coach (115 seats, all booked) | | |
|   Full coach | 38 | 530 |
|   7-day advance purchase fare | 7 | 64 |
|   14-day advanced purchase fare | 24 | 101 |
|   21-day advanced purchase fare | 5 | 186 |
|   Frequent flier awards | 6 | 0 |
|   Special discount fares (e.g., contract) | 35 | 362 |

*Source*: U.S. General Accounting Office, *Aviation Competition: Restricting Airline Ticketing Rules Unlikely to Help Consumers*, GAO-01-831, July 2001.

*Notes*: The fare data are from an actual flight. The average fare is the average one-way fare for each class of ticket based on the local fare for travelers flying between the origin and destination of this flight and is prorated for the fifteen travelers making connections. Because of differences in the fraction of travelers making a connection, the average seven-day advance purchase fare is lower on this particular flight than the average twenty-one-day advance purchase fare. If only local fares were used, the twenty-one-day fare would be lower than the seven-day fare.

crease, travelers face an increasing probability that the flight of their choice will be sold out, necessitating taking a flight with a less preferred departure time. As shown in Figure 6.9, load factors have increased under deregulation. In 2000 the load factor was nearly 73 percent, its highest level since World War II and its immediate aftermath.

Although average load factors have increased, this has not been uniform across routes. In particular, Figure 6.10 shows the average load factor as a function of distance for 1977 and 2000. Load factors have increased for all distances, but the increase for routes shorter than 900 miles was 9 percentage points, whereas the increase for routes longer than 900 miles was 19 percentage points. The relatively greater increase for long routes was expected and took place because, under regulation, long-haul fares were set above cost, which led to low load factors as carriers competed with flight frequency.

## Network Structure

Another change that is receiving a lot of attention is the increased reliance on hub-and-spoke route structures under deregulation. One often hears passengers complaining about having to take connecting flights rather than direct flights. One study found that in 1983 passengers were willing to pay nearly $75 to avoid one hour spent at a connecting airport.[28] Although the percentage of passengers who take connecting flights has increased from about 29 percent in 1977 only to about 32 percent in 2000, a dramatic change has occurred in the nature of those connections. In 1977, about half of all connections were interline connections, where passengers change airlines as well as planes. By 2000, interline connections had all but disappeared and were replaced by online connections, where passengers change planes but not airlines. In 2000, less than one-half of one percent of travel-

Figure 6.8   **Fare Dispersion in U.S. Domestic Markets**

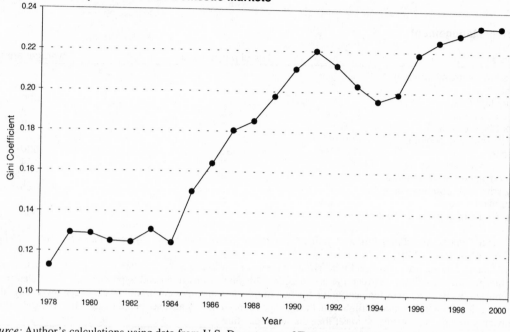

*Source:* Author's calculations using data from U.S. Department of Transportation, Data Bank 1A.

Figure 6.9   **Percentage of Seats Filled with Revenue Passengers**

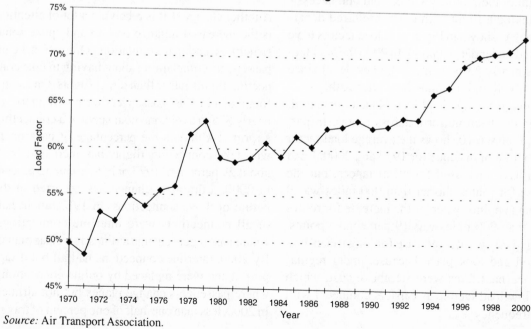

*Source:* Air Transport Association.

ers made interline connections. One study has estimated that travelers find online connections sufficiently more attractive than interline connections that they are willing to pay $33 (in 2000 dollars) more for online service.[29] But most important of all, the hub-and-spoke route structure gives passengers—from spokes and from the hub—more frequent service than would be possible with single-plane service. Because passengers bound for many destinations are flown in the same plane, more frequent service is possible than with single-plane service. In fact, one study of deregulation found that about two-thirds of the benefits to passengers from deregulation were from increased frequency of service made possible by the hub-and-spoke route structure.[30]

## Profits

Figure 6.11 shows the operating profit margin for U.S. scheduled airlines. Operating profit margin expresses operating profits (operating revenue minus operating cost, which excludes interest and taxes) as a percentage of operating revenue. As the figure makes clear, the industry is a cyclical one. During the recession of the early 1980s, industry operating profits were negative. They recovered in 1983 and 1984 and then hovered in the 3 to 5 percent range. In the early 1990s, due primarily to the recession, the industry sustained three years of losses. Since then, profits have improved significantly and rose to 8 percent in 1998 and declined for the next two years, although profits remained high by historical standards. However, these industry averages hide wide variations in profitability among firms. In 2000 operating profit margins for major carriers ranged from a negative 6 percent for Trans World Airlines to a positive 18 percent for Southwest Airlines.

## Safety

Airline safety invariably comes up in any discussion of airline deregulation. But safety was not deregulated. Safety standards continue to be enforced by the Federal Aviation Administration (FAA). However, some people believe that increased competition in a deregulated marketplace will cause airlines to be less safe by skimping on maintenance or by hiring less experienced pilots. Others counter that without the protection from competition afforded by regulation, a carrier that was unsafe—or even perceived to be unsafe—would not survive in a regime of free entry by other carriers. Both views make sense. Ultimately, it is an empirical question. What has happened to the safety record of airlines since deregulation? Figure 6.12 shows the probability of an airline passenger dying in an airline accident from 1975 to 2000. The safety record of airlines continues to improve in the deregulated era.[31]

## Possible Trouble Spots and Policy Solutions

Any change in an industry's environment as great as that caused by deregulation is bound to have unanticipated consequences. The trouble spots listed below (in no particular order) are not meant to be exhaustive, but they do cover the major areas of concern.

### Airport Gates

Before the 1930s, airports were often privately owned, but this ended with the Depression of the 1930s. Today all air carrier airports in the United States are publicly owned, usually by local government agencies. Although deregulation radically changed the airlines' environment, the system of providing airport services remains unchanged.

Figure 6.10 **Relationship of Load Factor to Distance: 1977 and 2000**

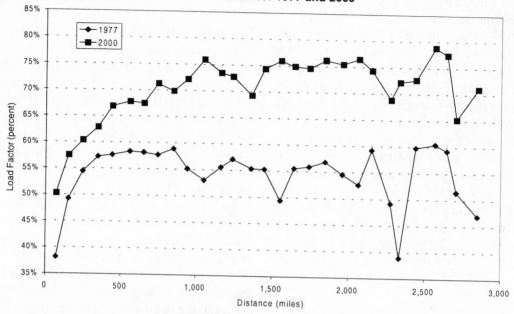

*Source:* Author's calculations using data from U.S. Department of Transportation, Service Segment data and Schedule T-100, Data Bank 28DS, Domestic Segment Data.

Figure 6.11 **Operating Profit Margin (All Services) of U.S. Scheduled Airlines**

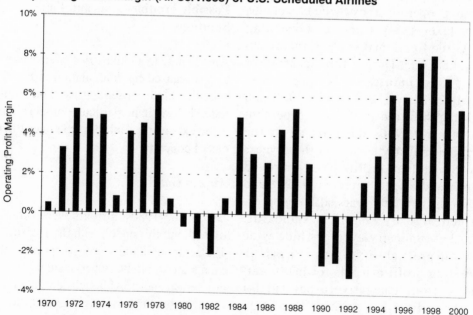

*Source:* Air Transport Association.

Figure 6.12 **Air Travel Safety**

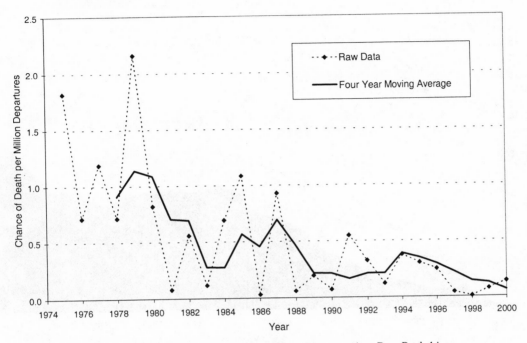

*Source:* Author's calculations using data from U.S. Department of Transportation, Data Bank 1A.

Airports still enter into long-term exclusive-use leases of airport gates with airlines, just as they did during regulation. The U.S. General Accounting Office (GAO) reports that 88 percent of the gates at 66 large and medium-sized airports are leased, and 85 percent of these are leased under exclusive-use terms, where the gate is effectively the property of the airline to use (or not use) as it sees fit.[32] These contracts and the difficulty of adding new capacity at airports may make it difficult for new carriers to enter airports. Post-deregulation airlines reported to the GAO that they had difficulty getting access to gates at Charlotte, Cincinnati, Detroit, Minneapolis, Newark, and Pittsburgh, where the share of gates under exclusive-use leases ranges from 84 percent (Newark) to 100 percent (Minneapolis).[33] The GAO found that the larger a carrier's share of leased gates at an air-

port, the higher its fares were. In particular, a doubling of a carrier's share of gates is associated with a 3.5 percent increase in that carrier's fares from that airport.[34] Another study found lack of availability of gates due to exclusive and preferential use lease provisions cost travelers $3.8 billion annually in higher fares.[35] Public policy should be directed toward making sure that airport resources are not kept artificially scarce by lease provisions. A few analysts believe that the best way to accomplish this is to sell airports to private operators who would run them to make a profit.

### Dominated Hub Airports

As shown in Table 6.3, some airports have come to be dominated by one or two airlines. A concern is that airlines will use their dominance at such

Figure 6.13   **Changes in Components of Actual Flight Time Since 1977**

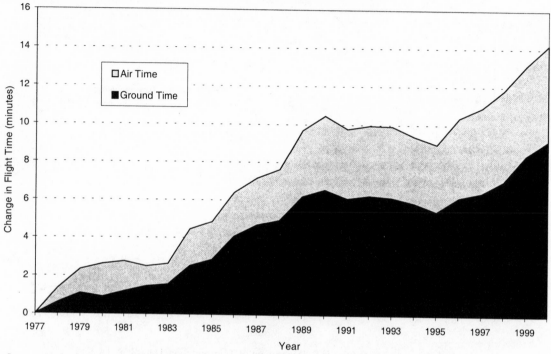

*Source:* Author's calculations using data from U.S. Department of Transportation, Service Segment data and Schedule T-100, Data Bank 28DS, Domestic Segment Data.

airports to raise fares. Indeed, the GAO found that fares in 1988–89 at fifteen dominated hub airports (where one carrier had 60 percent or more of passenger enplanements or two carriers combined had 85 percent or more of passenger enplanements) were 27 percent higher than at a control group of thirty-eight unconcentrated airports.[36] A subsequent study found, using the same definition of concentrated hub airport, in 1998 there were twelve concentrated hub airports and fares were 23 percent higher than fares at a control group of airports.[37] However, that study also found that when the control group of airports did not include airports served by Southwest Airlines, the hub premium vanished. Thus, what is called a hub premium appears to be a premium that airlines

charge in any market where they do not have competition from Southwest Airlines or other low-fare carriers. Clearly, the key to lower fares at hubs and at other airports as well is increased competition from low-fare carriers, which could be fostered, as noted above, by changes in the terms of gate leases.

### Perimeter Rules

Three airports have limitations on the length of flights or the origin/destination of flights that may use the airport. Such restrictions are referred to as perimeter rules. At New York's La Guardia Airport, the rule prohibits nonstop flights longer than 1,500 miles in order to shift long-haul traffic to Kennedy Airport. At Washington's Reagan National Airport

Figure 6.14  **Difference Between International Fares (U.S.–Foreign) and U.S. Domestic Fares Adjusted for Distance**

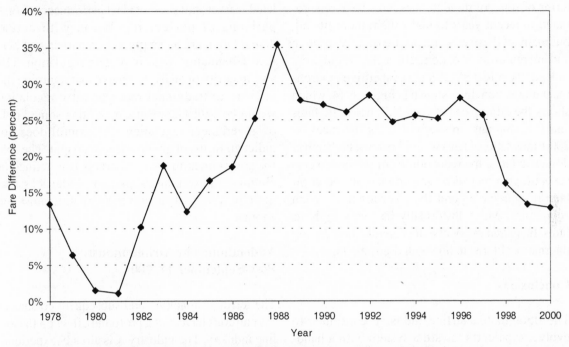

*Source:* Author's calculations using data from U.S. Department of Transportation, Data Bank 1A.

the limit is 1,250 miles and is designed to shift long-haul traffic to Dulles Airport. Enacted in 1980 to protect the then-new Dallas-Ft. Worth Airport, federal law (the Wright Amendment) prohibits airlines using aircraft with more than 56 seats from flying from Dallas Love Field to states other than Texas, Louisiana, Arkansas, Oklahoma, New Mexico, Mississippi, and Alabama. These restrictions have been estimated to cost travelers nearly $1 billion per year in higher fares.[38]

## Congestion

Figure 6.13 shows how aircraft flight times (actual, not scheduled) have increased since 1977, reflecting the increased congestion attendant with

the increase in aviation activity. In 2000, the average airline trip was about fourteen minutes longer than the same trip in 1977. For years, economists have advocated airport takeoff and landing charges that take congestion costs into account. In particular, such fees would equal the cost that an aircraft imposes on other aircraft (including the value of passengers' travel time) that are delayed. Such fees would be quite high at congested airports during peak periods and would be low—perhaps zero—during off-peak periods or at uncongested airports.

## International Aviation

Although domestic air travel was deregulated in 1978, international air travel remains governed by seventy-two bilateral treaties between the United States and the other countries involved.[39] The terms of some of these treaties have been renegotiated in recent years to make them more liberal, but many of these agreements are quite restrictive and are reminiscent of domestic airline regulation. Indeed, the effect of the less competitive environment internationally is shown in Figure 6.14, which shows the difference between U.S. domestic fares and U.S.–foreign fares (adjusted for distance). In 2000, international fares were 13 percent higher than domestic fares, the reduction from previous years reflecting the increasing importance of liberal bilateral agreements and the slowdown of Asian economies, which historically had very high air fares. Increased use of liberal bilaterals should bring international fares in line with domestic fares.

## Conclusions

The deregulated airline industry continues to evolve, apparently toward a system with a handful of large U.S. airlines serving domestic and international routes, with several smaller specialty carriers that serve particular market niches. The airline industry, like many others, is becoming increasingly global, and a similar evolution of other countries' carriers is also taking place.

Although most analysts still agree there are no advantages of large scale in producing available seat miles, it has become apparent there are significant economies of scale in marketing air transportation, that is, in producing and distributing information.

Although airline markets have not evolved in ways that analysts had predicted, the majority opinion is still that deregulated airline markets, with their imperfections, are better than regulated airline markets with their flaws. The studies of regulated and deregulated markets that have been conducted in the wake of industry deregulations

of the late 1970s and early 1980s have led to a greater awareness that both regulated and deregulated markets fall short of ideal performance. Comparisons of perfect regulation with actual deregulation are as empty as comparisons of perfect deregulation with imperfect regulation. The vast majority of analysts believe that returning the industry to traditional rate and entry regulation would be a mistake. But a belief that some kinds of government regulation are harmful does not indict all forms of government oversight. The role for government in airline markets is to reduce or eliminate those constraints and bottlenecks that limit the ability of carriers to compete against one another.

## Addendum: The Airline Industry Post–September 11, 2001

The terrorist hijacking and subsequent crashes of four aircraft have had a profound effect on the airline industry. The industry was already experiencing losses due to the slowing economy and the drop in profitable business traffic. A further softening of the economy as a result of the attacks combined with the fear of flying resulted in a steep drop in passenger traffic. Airlines, which before September 11 were expected to lose $3 billion for 2001, were then expected to lose an additional $2 billion because of reduced demand. Aircraft have been grounded and employees laid off. If demand does not rebound, the industry will likely undergo a round of consolidation. Even if traffic returns, the higher cost of increased security will ultimately lead to higher prices for consumers.

## Notes

1. Domestic and international freight transportation have also been affected, but they are not dealt with here. International passenger transportation is discussed briefly in the policy options section.

2. Elizabeth E. Bailey, "Deregulation and Regulatory Reform of U.S. Air Transportation Policy," in *Regulated Industries and Public Enterprise: European and United States Perspectives*, Bridger M. Mitchell and Paul R. Kleindorfer, eds. (Lexington, MA: Lexington Books, 1980).

3. Stephen Breyer, *Regulation and Its Reform* (Cambridge, MA: Harvard University Press, 1982).

4. Michael E. Levine, "Is Regulation Necessary? California Air Transportation and National Regulatory Policy," *Yale Law Journal* 74 (July 1965): 1416–47.

5. Melvin A. Brenner, James O. Leet, and Elihu Schott, *Airline Deregulation* (Westport, CT: Eno Foundation for Transportation, Inc., 1985).

6. Bailey, "Regulatory Reform."

7. John C. Panzar, "Regulation, Deregulation, and Economic Efficiency: The Case of the CAB," *American Economic Review* 70 (May 1980): 311–15.

8. The Department of Transportation was also responsible for merger review until 1989 when that authority was turned over to the Antitrust Division of the Department of Justice.

9. There are two reasons for this. First, there are some factors of production that are fixed regardless of aircraft size. For example, the number of pilots and the number of radios and fuel gauges. The second reason is based on aerodynamics. The drag on an aircraft (the force resisting forward motion) is roughly proportional to the surface area of the aircraft. If surface area doubles, drag and fuel costs double, but the capacity (volume) of the aircraft more than doubles. Thus, a larger aircraft has a lower cost per unit of capacity than a smaller aircraft.

10. In 1996, travelers on routes involving "non-hub" communities (those enplaning less than 0.05 percent of the nation's total) would have had 62 percent fewer departures if they had the same aircraft size and load factor as large-hub communities (those enplaning 1 percent or more of the nation's total). See Steven A. Morrison and Clifford Winston, "The Fare Skies: Air Transportation and Middle America," *Brookings Review* 15 (Fall 1997): 42–45.

11. Those travelers who place a very high value on convenience can charter a plane, which is very convenient—and very expensive.

12. For example, it has been found that if the number of passengers an airline carries increases by 1 percent (holding the number of cities served constant), total cost increases by less than 1 percent (0.80 percent). See Douglas W. Caves, Laurits R. Christensen, and Michael W. Tretheway, "Economies of Density versus Economies of Scale: Why Trunk and Local Service Airline Costs Differ," *Bell Journal of Economics* 15 (Winter 1984): 471–89.

13. Because passengers and cities both double, route density remains constant. Thus, this definition of the concept of scale does not confuse density economies with scale economies.

14. See Caves et al., "Economies." In the foregoing United–US Airways example, the average passenger on United traveled 1,513 miles compared with 783 miles for a passenger on US Airways.

15. On average, about 20 percent of travelers with reservations do not show for their flight. As a result, airlines sell more tickets than there are seats available because they know that not everyone with a reservation will show up. Of course, sometimes more people show up than there are seats available, in which case airlines ask for volunteers to give up their seats for some remuneration.

16. As a consequence, airline stocks are relatively volatile and are characterized by a high "beta," a measure of a stock's volatility relative to the stock market as a whole. Airline betas for the nine largest publicly traded passenger airlines have averaged 1.07, with a range from 0.77 (Alaska) to 1.42 (American). A beta of one indicates that a stock is as volatile as the stock market as a whole.

17. A survey of estimates of the price elasticity of demand for air transportation reports that the most likely range is 1.10 to 2.70 for vacation trips and 0.40 to 1.20 for nonvacation trips. See Tae H. Oum, W.G. Waters II, and Jong Say Young, "A Survey of Recent Estimates of Price Elasticities of Demand for Transport," The World Bank, Working papers, Transportation Division, WPS 359, January 1990.

18. See Michael W. Tretheway, "The Characteristics of Modern Post-Deregulation Air Transport," Working paper, Faculty of Commerce, University of British Columbia, 1991.

19. The idea that the threat of entry will keep firms from earning excess profits is known as the contestable markets hypothesis.

20. Although the results presented below do not constitute a counterfactual because other factors (e.g., technological change) may be at work, the conclusions drawn are strongly suggestive and qualitatively consistent with the few rigorous counterfactuals that have been performed for the airline industry using less recent data.

21. The *n*-firm concentration ratio is the percentage of the market accounted for by the largest *n* firms. In this case, the market is defined in terms of domestic scheduled revenue passenger miles.

22. The number of "effective competitors" is the inverse of the Herfindahl index. The Herfindahl index, rather than simply counting the number of carriers in a market, adjusts for unequal market shares by summing the square of each airline's market share. When market shares are expressed as fractions rather than percentages, the Herfindahl index approaches zero in the competitive case with a large number of small firms, and equals one in the monopoly case. If two airlines each had a 50 percent market share on a route, the Herfindahl index would equal one-half. Inverting this gives two (effective competitors). Similarly, if there were three

unequal-sized competitors, with the largest serving two-thirds of the market and the other two each serving one-sixth of the market, the Herfindahl index would be one-half, which also translates into two effective competitors. Thus, "effective competitors" has a more intuitive interpretation than the Herfindahl index.

23. James A. Brander and Anming Zhang, "Market Conduct in the Airline Industry: An Empirical Investigation," *Rand Journal of Economics* 21 (Winter 1990): 567–83.

24. There are many measures of airport activity. Two frequently used measures are aircraft departures and revenue passengers enplaned. These are good measures of the extent of use of overall airport resources. However, at hub airports the share that a carrier has of enplanements or departures is not a measure of how captive originating travelers are to that carrier. A carrier that hubs at an airport will always have a greater share of total enplanements than it does of originating enplanements.

25. Of course, one has no way of knowing for sure what regulated fares would be. However a good guess can be made with an updated version of the fare formula that the CAB used during the last few years of regulation. See Steven A. Morrison and Clifford Winston, "The Remaining Role for Government Policy in the Deregulated Airline Industry," in *Deregulation of Network Industries: What's Next?* Sam Peltzman and Clifford Winston, eds. (Washington, DC: AEI-Brookings Joint Center for Regulatory Studies, 2000).

26. It should be noted that this figure does not take into account that the lower fares that most travelers enjoy today come at the expense of restrictions (e.g., minimum stay of a Saturday night) that are much more prevalent than during regulation.

27. The measure used is the Gini coefficient. This measure has an intuitive interpretation in that twice the Gini coefficient is equal to the expected difference in fares from two randomly selected tickets on a route expressed as a fraction of the average fare on that route. For example, if the Gini coefficient on a route is 0.25 and the average fare is $100, the expected difference in price between two randomly selected tickets would be $50.

28. Steven A. Morrison and Clifford Winston, "Enhancing the Performance of the Deregulated Air Transportation System," *Brookings Papers on Economic Activity: Microeconomics* (1989): 61–112.

29. Dennis W. Carlton, William M. Landes, and Richard A. Posner, "Benefits and Costs of Airline Mergers: A Case Study," *Bell Journal of Economics* 11 (Spring 1980): 65–83. The authors estimated that the value of single-carrier service ranged from $14.10 to $17.75 in 1980 dollars. The figure in the text is the average of these figures expressed in 2000 dollars.

30. Steven A. Morrison and Clifford Winston, *The Economic Effects of Airline Deregulation* (Washington, DC: Brookings Institution, 1986).

31. It cannot be ruled out that the accident record would have improved even more if airlines were still regulated. This question could, in principle, be answered using a counterfactual model of airline safety. However, developing such a model would be extremely difficult. Nonetheless, it is true that air travel is safer than it used to be.

32. See U.S. General Accounting Office, *Airline Competition: Industry Operating and Marketing Practices Limit Market Entry*, GAO/RECD-90–147 (Washington, DC, August 1990).

33. See U.S. General Accounting Office, *Airline Deregulation: Barriers to Entry Continue to Limit Competition in Several Key Domestic Markets*. GAO/RCED-97–4 (Washington, DC, October 1996).

34. See "Effect of Airline Entry Barriers on Fares," Statement of Kenneth M. Mead, U.S. General Accounting Office, GAO/T-RECD-60–62, April 5, 1990.

35. See Morrison and Winston, "The Remaining Role."

36. U.S. General Accounting Office, *Airline Competition: Higher Fares and Reduced Competition at Concentrated Airports*, GAO/RCED-90–102 (Washington, DC, July 1990).

37. See Morrison and Winston, "The Remaining Role."

38. Steven A. Morrison and Clifford Winston, "Foul Regulatory Weather Grounds Airline Competition," *Wall Street Journal*, December 3, 1997, p. A-1.

39. See U.S. General Accounting Office, "International Aviation: DOT's Efforts to Increase U.S. Airlines' Access to International Markets," Statement of John H. Anderson, GAO/RCED-96–32, March 14, 1996.

## Selected Readings

Levine, Michael E. "Airline Competition in Deregulated Markets: Theory, Firm Strategy, and Public Policy," *Yale Journal on Regulation* 4 (1987): 393–494. The author, having served as an airline executive, airline regulator, and academic, presents his views on the way deregulated markets function and how government policy may improve upon it.

Morrison, Steven A., and Clifford Winston. *The Economic Effects of Airline Deregulation*. Washington, DC: Brookings Institution, 1986. This study compared regulated airline markets in 1977 with a counterfactual model of the fares and service quality deregulated airlines would have offered in that year.

Morrison, Steven A., and Clifford Winston. *The Evolution of the Airline Industry*. Washington, DC: Brookings Institution, 1995. This study traces the evolution of the airline industry from before regulation to the present. It presents an empirical profile of the industry and examines the role of government policy in the airline industry. Transportation Research Board. *Entry and Competition in the U.S. Airline Industry: Issues and Opportunities*, Special Report 255. Washington, DC: National Research Council, 1999. This report, mandated by Congress, examines the functioning of the deregulated airline marketplace and address whether increased federal oversight or regulation is warranted.

# 7

# Retail Commercial Banking

## An Industry in Transition

### *Robert M. Adams*

The size and scope of the commercial banking industry, together with the unique role it plays in our economy, make it a particularly important industry to consider in any analysis of competition. The industry has over $6.0 trillion in financial assets (compared with $4.0 trillion in the insurance industry) and 2.1 million employees (more than the motor vehicle, steel, and petroleum industries combined). Banks provide essential deposit services; perform many payment functions; and lend funds to individuals, businesses, and governments.

This chapter focuses on competition in retail commercial banking, the provision of basic financial services to households and small businesses by depository institutions chartered to operate as commercial banks. This subset of depository institutions does not include thrift institutions such as savings banks or savings and loan associations, or credit unions. The chapter does not address the "corporate" (or "wholesale") banking market, the set of services typically demanded by large corporations or other banks. The distinction between retail and wholesale is essential for both policy and analytical purposes. At this time, the retail banking industry is especially interesting because it is in the throes of major changes resulting from the removal of legal barriers to entry, an unprec-

edented merger movement, and the adoption of electronic technology in the provision of some services.[1]

The various changes underway in retail banking raise questions about competition, barriers to entry, and public policy that are of interest to students of industrial organization and policy makers. This chapter seeks to use empirical evidence and some of the basic concepts of industrial organization to put these changes into perspective and examine some of the implications for competition analysis and public policy in the industry.

## Motivation for Banking as a Laboratory for Study

Banking in the United States has traditionally been a regulated industry. Consequently, teachers of industrial organization tend to place it in a special class with other regulated industries that are regarded as not very useful for studying general questions and hypotheses about competition, firm behavior, and performance. It is assumed that regulation inhibits or distorts the normal functioning of the marketplace so that any pricing behavior or firm interrelationships found to exist are not applicable to other industries in general, but are unique to the regulated industry under review. This is a mistaken view of the banking industry.

While banks are subject to various regulations, particularly involving portfolio risk, they have a wide range of discretion in their behavior and in the extent to which they compete for business. Most notably, banks' prices and profit rates are not subject to review, approval, or other constraints as is the case for public utilities. Consequently, banks may adopt whatever prices local supply-and-demand conditions will allow them to charge (or require them to pay), whether for checking accounts, savings deposits, student loans, safety deposit boxes, or any other bank service.

Entry and exit in banking, while not absolutely free from regulatory review, are clearly indicative of an environment where broad opportunity for discretionary behavior exists. For example, each year from 1990 to 1999 there were around 400 bank mergers, between 50 and 200 new banks were chartered, 1,700 to 2,700 new branch offices were opened, and 600 to 1,500 branch offices were closed (Table 7.1). Thus, it is apparent that entry and exit provide important vehicles for competition and strategic behavior within the retail banking industry.

Nonprice or quality competition is an important avenue for discretionary behavior by banks. While the basic services provided by retail banks (i.e., insured savings deposits, checking accounts, and loans) may be viewed as relatively homogeneous, nonprice competition among banks is common. For example, to differentiate itself from its competitors, a retail bank may choose to offer greater service by providing more tellers, extended evening and weekend hours, drive-through windows, banking-by-telephone, twenty-four-hour deposit and cash-withdrawal facilities through automated teller machines (ATMs), and a wide range of products such as safety deposit boxes, Christmas club ac-

counts, and other "improvements" in quality.

It is evident that retail banks have a wide range of opportunity for discretionary strategic behavior in pricing, entry and exit, and product/service quality competition. Despite certain elements of regulation in banking, market forces are the primary determinants of prices, output, and quality. Hence, retail banking provides a reasonable alternative to the manufacturing or retail sectors for investigating hypotheses derived from economic theories about the functioning of markets in a free market system.

Moreover, in several practical respects the retail banking industry provides an attractive laboratory for research on industrial organization. First, detailed, high-quality balance sheet and income statement data in digital form are available for all 8,000–plus banks in the industry. Second, the data are essentially comparable across all banking firms. Third, the data are available annually and are largely comparable over time. Fourth, unlike firms in the manufacturing sector generally, and even within specific manufacturing industries, retail banks produce fairly homogeneous outputs. Finally, retail banking is essentially a local-market industry, so many different geographic markets exist containing multiple firms in the same industry for which good data are available. This permits cross-sectional studies of the banking industry that do not need to hold factors constant across highly diverse industries as do studies of manufacturing; the researcher is not forced to do time-series analysis within a single industry in order to avoid such research problems.

In sum, despite its regulated status, the retail banking industry provides an excellent laboratory for research because of the wide latitude for discretionary firm behavior and the operation of market forces, the unusual detail, quality and availability of data, and the basic nature of these

Table 7.1

**Entry and Exit in Commercial Banking, 1987–1998**

| Year | No. of new state and national charters | No. of failures | No. of mergers | No. of branches Opened | No. of branches Closed |
|------|------|------|------|------|------|
| 1987 | 219 | 184 | 649 | 953 | 941 |
| 1988 | 229 | 200 | 468 | 1,502 | 1,042 |
| 1989 | 192 | 206 | 350 | 1,726 | 683 |
| 1990 | 165 | 168 | 366 | 2,719 | 878 |
| 1991 | 105 | 124 | 345 | 2,266 | 1,425 |
| 1992 | 72 | 120 | 401 | 1,642 | 1,656 |
| 1993 | 61 | 42 | 436 | 1,935 | 1,729 |
| 1994 | 49 | 13 | 446 | 2,710 | 1,147 |
| 1995 | 101 | 6 | 345 | 2,521 | 1,486 |
| 1996 | 145 | 5 | 392 | 2,487 | 1,870 |
| 1997 | 188 | 1 | 384 | 3,122 | 1,636 |
| 1998 | 194 | 3 | 518 | 2,384 | 1,485 |

*Sources*: Failure data are from the *Annual Report* of the Federal Deposit Insurance Corporation and statistical releases. Mergers and acquisitions data are from Stephen A. Rhoades, "Bank Mergers and Banking Structure in the United States, 1980–98," *Staff Study*, No. 174 (Federal Reserve Board, August 2000). New bank and branch openings and closings are from the *Annual Statistical Digest*, Federal Reserve Board, relevant years. For the 1990–1995 period, new bank and branch data include industrial banks.

firms and their scope of operations. Not surprisingly, industrial organization research done on the retail banking industry finds relationships and yields results similar to those found for the manufacturing sector.

## The Industry and Its Characteristics

An understanding of the key characteristics of the banking industry is needed before we can examine the ramifications of important recent policy changes affecting retail banking. A common first step used in any analysis of competition is to define the industry, the appropriate product, and the geographic markets. In other words, we must have a basic understanding of which firms are competing, what they are producing, and where they are competing.

In industrial organization, these questions are answered by analyzing consumer preferences and substitution patterns across firms, products, or geographic areas. For example, if many consumers are willing to change their banking relationships from local banks to more distant banks in reaction to minor changes in their services (i.e., local banks pay a slightly lower interest rate on deposits), then it is probable that the geographic market is relatively large. We should note that in the event of any change in services, some customers will switch. We need to know *how many* will switch and whether the likelihood of switching would deter a bank from changing its services (i.e., would it make the change unprofitable). The Department of Justice has solidified this notion of market definition in the "Merger Guidelines."[2]

## Retail Banks Versus Other Intermediaries

Banks are financial intermediaries that play a key role in the saving and investment process within the economy. Such institutions take in money from many individuals in the form of deposits or insurance premiums. They pool these funds and lend them to, or invest them in, companies as well as consumers who would generally find it to be very difficult and inefficient (if not impossible) to raise funds directly from other individuals. Moreover, banks provide the institutional mechanism used by the Federal Reserve to increase or decrease the money supply when it attempts to influence interest rates and thereby influence economic activity. A change in the money supply can be accomplished through banks because banks are required to hold in reserve only a fraction (say, 20 percent) of the money that is deposited with them, while the remainder (up to 80 percent) can be loaned out. Thus, when the Federal Reserve conducts open market operations by purchasing (selling) government securities, the money received by the sellers (paid by the buyers) of securities is deposited in (withdrawn from) banks, effectively increasing (decreasing) the reserves of the banking system. The money supply can increase (decrease) by a multiple of the original sale amount (say $1,000) because the bank (Bank 1) in which the $1,000 is deposited need to hold only 20 percent ($200) in reserve. Bank 1 can make a loan equal to 80 percent of the original deposit ($800). That loan, a newly created deposit completely divorced from the original deposit, will be spent and deposited by the second seller into Bank 2. Bank 2 can make a second loan of 80 percent ($640) of its new deposit. That second loan will be spent and Seller 3 will deposit the amount ($640) in Bank 3, and so on.

This view of banks as financial intermediaries and the agents for the transmission of monetary policy, while accurate, puts banking into a somewhat abstract macroeconomic perspective. Such a perspective is not very useful for analyzing the competitive behavior and performance of firms in the banking industry. In fact, this perspective does not even provide us with a good picture of what it is that banks do to make a profit. So, what do banks do? Very simply, they provide a number of basic financial services that most households and small businesses use, namely federally insured checking accounts, federally insured savings accounts, and various kinds of loans (e.g., for a car, a home, or school tuition). The firms that compete for the consumer's dollar by providing these and some other financial services constitute the retail banking industry. Some nonbank firms (e.g., automobile finance companies and mortgage banks) also offer some of these services, but none offers the full range of services (especially federally insured deposits) that are offered by commercial banks, thrifts, and credit unions.

A recently popular view is that traditional commercial banks do not form a distinct industry but are simply part of a broader "financial services" industry. That view, however, is too sweeping because of the wide array of activities and types of firms it includes, such as insurance companies, investment banks, depository institutions (like banks), finance companies, and brokerage firms. While a single financial conglomerate could undoubtedly provide all of the financial services produced by these different types of firms, these services are used for different purposes, are often purchased by distinct sets of customers, require different expertise to produce, and can be produced efficiently by separate firms. To lump them together as one broad industry would perhaps be comparable to treating all firms in the manufacturing sector that produce internal combustion engines as one industry. Such an industry would include firms that produce automobiles, trucks, chain saws, boat motors, lawnmowers, bulldozers, tanks, airplanes, rockets, and so forth. To treat such a diverse group of manufacturing or financial activities as one industry would make a meaningful industry analysis almost impossible. Indeed, as will be shown later, even within the overall commercial banking industry firms have become sufficiently different that a meaningful analysis requires us to distinguish between the wholesale and retail banking industries.

Moreover, thrifts and credit unions are typically distinguished from retail banks because either they do not offer the full palette of services offered by commercial banks (as is typically the case with both thrifts and credit unions) or they provide financial services to a limited group of people, i.e., membership is limited to a specific class of customers, as is the case with credit unions.

While recognizing that nonbank firms provide varying degrees of competition for specific services, we will treat retail banking as a distinct industry within the financial services sector. To define the industry then: retail banking encompasses a set of relatively homogeneous firms producing a fairly standard set of financial services used regularly by consumers and small- to medium-sized businesses.

## The "Cluster" of Banking Services

Banks offer a wide variety of services to customers. Individual banks differentiate their set of services from those of other banks not only by offering different interest rates, but also by differing fees, minimum balances, overdraft protection, and so forth (note that branch location is a form of differentiation). To determine which

products (or groups of products) are in the same market, an economist would consider consumer preferences and switching patterns. However, in 1963 the U.S. Supreme Court decided that the product market for banking is represented by a "cluster of products and services." In other words, banks offer a core set of services to individuals and businesses that other types of financial institution cannot provide.[3] Because of this decision, many banking regulators (including the Federal Reserve) use the banking cluster for public policy decisions. The Department of Justice, however, rejects the cluster approach and instead uses an approach that separates household consumers from small-business customers, because household preferences differ from small-business owner preferences. While the product market as defined by the banking cluster has not found universal empirical support, it does have the benefit that it simplifies an analysis of the industry.[4] This chapter uses the banking cluster as a definition of the product market.

### Retail Banking Versus Wholesale/ Global Banking

Having gained some idea of the product market for retail banking, we should compare retail banking and wholesale/global banking to further distinguish retail banking as a separate industry. This is more than just a pedagogical exercise, because all commercial banks (both retail and global) traditionally have been lumped together in the same industry. To do so today, however, can lead to poor analysis and poor public policy.

Firms that provide global banking services must have the financial resources and offer the specialized financial services needed by large national and international (foreign or domestic) corporations. These firms may also provide retail banking services, but retail banking customers differ dramatically from global banking customers with regard to the financial services that they need.

Another indication that these are indeed separate industries is that global banking service providers face competition from a greater variety of sources than do providers of retail banking services, because large corporate customers have special financing and information requirements. For example, providers of global banking services face competition from the commercial paper market and investment banks, but providers of retail banking services do not.

The geographic market for many wholesale bank customers is at least national in scope and often global. In contrast, the geographic market for the retail banking industry is still largely local in nature, roughly metropolitan statistical areas (MSAs) or non-MSA counties, and there is no indication that the preference of bank customers for local services is likely to change any time soon, since it is presumably caused by the lower information and transaction costs of dealing with local firms. Recent news articles indicate that local branch networks are still an important aspect of bank competition.[5] Bankers are keenly aware of this preference and treat retail banking as a very local activity requiring a local presence. As noted earlier, the number of banking offices in the United States increased from 57,000 to 73,000 between 1985 and 2000, even as the number of banks and banking organizations declined dramatically. The local market nature of community banking may (to some degree) also reflect higher information costs facing nonlocal financial firms.

Simply lumping together firms that provide such distinct products and services to such distinct customers would not define a particularly homogeneous industry and would make analysis difficult. Poor public policy would result because what might be good policy for the wholesale banking industry might be poor policy for the retail banking industry and vice versa. However, when a provider of global banking services provides retail banking services through a local branch network, that provider is included as a competitor in the retail part of the banking market.

### The Local Geographic Market

A key feature of any industry is the geographic scope of the market(s). If firms compete in a national market, it means that they compete more or less directly with all other firms in their industry throughout the country. In contrast, if firms compete in a local market, they compete directly with only those firms in the same geographic area, and price and output changes by firms in other areas will not significantly influence their behavior. Determining whether a particular industry is composed of a single national market or many local markets is crucial for meaningful analysis of an industry, but is often a source of confusion. The problem is that when some of the firms in an inherently local market industry such as bagel baking, operate across the nation (e.g., Lender's), that industry is often presumed to operate in a national market. That presumption is not correct.

Formally, geographic markets are defined by consumer preferences (i.e., price elasticities). Because price elasticities in banking are very difficult to estimate, we rely on other indirect evidence to define the geographic market. We consider the geographic market to be local rather than national in scope if customers generally purchase the service or product locally rather than from a distant area, or firms are able to operate at an efficient scale by producing only what can be sold within a local market (like a doughnut producer) rather than having to sell their output nationally (like automobile manufacturers) in order to achieve an efficient scale of production. Using these criteria, we can conclude that retail banking is basically a local market industry. Hence, the most important structural data for analyzing competition will be based on local geographic markets.

## Empirical Evidence on the Local Banking Market

Empirical evidence indicates that local market areas are generally the appropriate focus for analysis of the competitive effects of bank mergers. In particular, surveys of both households and small businesses continue to support the relevance of local geographic areas. The 1998 Survey of Consumer Finances shows that 95.2 percent of households that used any financial institution identified a local institution as their primary institution. Sixty-five percent of primary institutions were local commercial banks; savings and loan associations and credit unions accounted for an additional 26 percent of households served by a local primary financial institution.[6] The distance traveled to the financial institutions by households was remarkably small. For example, 50 percent of households obtained checking accounts, savings accounts, money market deposit accounts, and certificates of deposit within three miles of their home or workplace. Seventy-five percent obtained these same services within fifteen miles of their home or workplace. The majority of households also typically obtained credit of various kinds within a short distance (three to twenty miles) of home or work.[7]

The costs of obtaining price and service information, switching among financial service providers, and traveling significant distances for financial services are likely to be substantial for some households. In addition to information and transactions

costs, the need for quick local access to funds for contingencies seems likely to be a particularly important factor in the behavior of some households.[8]

The 1993 Survey of Small Business Finances reveals that local institutions are also the primary suppliers of financial services to small business.[9] The data show that 96 percent of small businesses used a local institution as their primary financial institution, with 84 percent using a local commercial bank and another 9 percent using thrifts. Small businesses relied on institutions located very close to their place of business. Fifty percent of small businesses obtained twelve of the thirteen financial services studied (except leasing) within seven miles, and for eight of the thirteen services, the distance was four miles or less.

Survey data for households and small businesses indicate that the demand for financial services has a strong local orientation. Bank branching behavior is also consistent with the view that local market areas are relevant for analyzing the competitive effects of bank mergers. In particular, the number of banking offices steadily increased from about 57,000 in 1985 to over 73,000 in 2000, even as the number of banking organizations and banks declined sharply from over 11,000 and 14,000, respectively, to about 6,500 and 8,200 (Table 7.2). These data, combined with the fact that many mergers expand the geographic office networks of banks, are a strong indication that banks continue to believe that a physical local presence is required in order to supply retail banking services effectively. Whether these changes reflect a response to the demands of retail customers or banks' efforts to reduce their own information and transactions costs in the provision of some retail services is not clear, but the importance of a local presence is. Finally, the continuing success and viability of smaller, basically local banks is a market indicator of the local nature of banking markets.[10]

Table 7.2

## Changing U.S. Banking Structure, 1985–2000

| Year | No. of banks | No. of banking organizations | No. of banking offices | Local deposit concentration: average HHI | | National deposit concentration: percent held by largest firms | | | |
|---|---|---|---|---|---|---|---|---|---|
| | | | | MSAs | Non-MSAs | Top 100 | Top 50 | Top 25 | Top 10 |
| 1985 | 14,268 | 11,021 | 57,417 | 1990 | 4,357 | 52.6 | 37.1 | 29.1 | 17.0 |
| 1986 | 14,051 | 10,512 | 58,181 | 2022 | 4,345 | 55.6 | 42.4 | 29.6 | 17.6 |
| 1987 | 13,541 | 10,100 | 58,820 | 2015 | 4,334 | 57.4 | 44.1 | 31.1 | 18.1 |
| 1988 | 12,966 | 9,718 | 59,568 | 2020 | 4,316 | 59.9 | 47.5 | 33.2 | 19.2 |
| 1989 | 12,555 | 9,455 | 61,218 | 2010 | 4,317 | 60.5 | 48.1 | 34.1 | 19.9 |
| 1990 | 12,194 | 9,221 | 63,392 | 2010 | 4,291 | 61.4 | 48.9 | 34.9 | 20.0 |
| 1991 | 11,790 | 9,007 | 64,680 | 1977 | 4,257 | 61.3 | 49.6 | 37.5 | 22.7 |
| 1992 | 11,349 | 8,730 | 65,121 | 2023 | 4,222 | 62.6 | 51.7 | 39.2 | 24.1 |
| 1993 | 10,867 | 8,318 | 63,656 | 1994 | 4,234 | 64.6 | 53.8 | 41.0 | 25.0 |
| 1994 | 10,359 | 7,896 | 65,097 | 1976 | 4,208 | 65.9 | 54.6 | 41.5 | 25.2 |
| 1995 | 9,855 | 7,571 | 68,073 | 1963 | 4,171 | 66.9 | 55.8 | 43.0 | 25.6 |
| 1996 | 9,446 | 7,313 | 68,694 | 1991 | 4,145 | 68.6 | 59.0 | 46.8 | 29.8 |
| 1997 | 9,064 | 7,122 | 70,698 | 1973 | 4,119 | 69.1 | 59.6 | 47.0 | 29.9 |
| 1998 | 8,697 | 6,839 | 71,231 | 1975 | 4,088 | 70.9 | 62.6 | 51.2 | 36.7 |
| 1999 | 8,506 | 6,742 | 72,562 | 1935 | 4,064 | 70.6 | 62.3 | 51.6 | 36.5 |
| 2000 | 8,239 | 6,676 | 73,553 | 1921 | 4,019 | 71.3 | 62.7 | 51.4 | 36.1 |

*Source*: Summary of Deposits data from the FDIC and Federal Reserve Board.

## Structure of the U.S. Banking Industry

The evidence leads to a clear conclusion that local markets are generally the relevant focus for analyzing competition. We now turn to a discussion of local banking markets. Many banking markets are already somewhat to very highly concentrated.[11] For example, 141 out of 318 (54 percent) metropolitan statistical area (MSA) markets had a Herfindahl-Hirschman index (HHI*) greater than 1,800 in the year 2000.[12] Rural markets (counties) are substantially more concentrated with 2,073 out of 2,266 such markets having an HHI exceeding

1,800.[13] In the aggregate, the average HHI for MSAs is 1,921 and for rural markets is 4,019, with corresponding three-firm deposit concentration ratios of 64 percent and 87 percent, respectively.[14]

The number of banking organizations provides another perspective on the structure of local markets. For example, about 1,073 non-MSA counties (or 48 percent) have four or fewer banking organizations, and 79 percent have seven or less.[15] Only about 13 percent of MSAs have ten or fewer banking organizations, but nearly 57 percent have 18 or fewer.

The large number of retail banking markets that are highly concentrated and have few banks obvi-

*HHI is the sum of the squared market shares of every firm in the industry (can range from 0 to 10,000). Values greater than 1,800 are often thought to be worrisome in antitrust matters.

ously cannot be casually dismissed simply as a phenomenon unique to relatively sparsely populated rural areas. Indeed, over one-half of MSAs also have an HHI greater than 1,800 as well. Moreover, 22 percent of the U.S. population live in the non-MSA rural areas and another 29 percent of the population live in small MSAs with populations less than one million.[16] The competitive effects of bank mergers in local retail markets, both urban and rural, may be significant and warrant careful attention.

## Recent Changes: Mergers, Interstate Banking, Barriers to Entry, and Electronic Technology

Major changes in retail banking with implications for competition are examined below. These changes have had a major effect on the structure of the industry during the past decade.

### Mergers

Legislation by individual states during the 1980s and 1990s, along with recent federal legislation allowing full nationwide banking, have led to ongoing unprecedented merger activity and massive structural changes in the banking industry.[17] From 1980 to 1998, over 7,900 banks were acquired, involving about $2.4 trillion in acquired assets, and several mergers occurred that were larger, in real terms, than any previous U.S. bank mergers.[18] This merger movement resulted in a very large decline in the number of banks between 1985 and 2000 (14,268 to 8,239) and a large increase in the share of nationwide banking deposits held by the largest fifty banking firms (37 percent to 62 percent). However, the average concentration ratio (and Herfindahl-Hirschman index) over all *local* banking markets has remained remarkably stable

throughout the period (Table 7.2). Given the importance of market concentration for competition and the relevance of local markets for retail banking, it would appear that, to date, the unprecedented merger movement in banking has not adversely affected the competitive structure of local retail banking markets.

The extraordinary amount of merger activity in banking since 1980 is mainly a response to the removal of legal barriers to geographic expansion, both within and across states, that began in earnest in the mid-1980s and culminated in passage of legislation allowing full nationwide banking in 1994. The largest mergers may be, in part, a response to the globalization of large-scale wholesale banking.

Mergers provide a vehicle for banks to expand into a now-permissible nationwide banking environment. The move toward interstate banking is illustrated in Table 7.3. The data show that there was very little interstate banking in the early 1980s, with an average of only 2.4 percent of commercial bank deposits held by out-of-state banking organizations in 1980 and 3.6 percent in 1984. In the mid-1980s, interstate banking picked up momentum so that by 1990 an average of 15.6 percent of the states' deposits were held by offices of banking organizations that were headquartered in other states. By 1996, that figure had risen to 25 percent; by 2000, it had risen to 52 percent. There is great variation among the states, with North Carolina, for example, having only 1.7 percent of its deposits in 2000 held in North Carolina offices of banks headquartered elsewhere. In contrast, the comparable figures for Arizona and South Carolina are 93.3 percent and 63.7 percent, respectively. The recent trend involves adjustments away from an artificial, legally created industry structure made up of fifty separate banking structures—one in each state.

There are, of course, various motives for mergers, some of which appear to reflect managers' best interests while others reflect stockholders' best interests. The motives include increasing profits, empire building, developing the capacity to implement new technology, increasing size to avoid being acquired, increasing size to become an attractive acquisition target, positioning for entry into an area by other banks, employing what is currently perceived to be the smart business strategy (like the "financial supermarket" vogue of the early-to-mid-1980s), reducing costs, increasing market share to gain control over prices, obtaining more core deposits, and diversifying loan originations.

Whatever the motives for individual mergers and despite the fact that mergers may not generally result in improved performance,[19] economists would generally applaud the removal of barriers to entry for facilitating a more efficient allocation of resources, and, of course, many bankers are pleased with the opportunity to expand their operations. However, as the industry moves toward nationwide banking, it is essential that the antitrust laws that apply to bank mergers be seriously enforced. Otherwise, any social benefits from deregulation may be offset by social costs from increased market power.

## Interstate Banking

While the removal of legal restrictions on interstate banking has a variety of possible implications for competition and barriers to entry in retail banking, it is important to analyze the evidence concerning these phenomena rather than assume that the possible effects have materialized.

It has been suggested that increased geographic expansion and multimarket operation by banks may cause the geographic market for retail competition to expand beyond the local level. The import of any such tendency, however, can easily be exaggerated, because some of the basic forces creating local markets are not fundamentally altered simply by the expansion of firms into additional local markets.

The relevance of competition within a local market context, even when multimarket firms are common, is not unique to banking. An analogy to grocery retailing may be useful. From the demand side, virtually everyone shops for groceries locally because of transactions costs. The fact that there are numerous large grocery chains (e.g., Kroger, American Stores, Safeway, A&P, and Winn-Dixie) operating in many local markets throughout the country or in broad regions, does not make the relevant geographic market for analyzing competition in grocery retailing a national or regional market. That there may be a substantial number of multimarket grocery retailers in Chicago, for example, is of little use to the consumer in downstate rural farming communities such as White Hall, where at most one or two such firms might operate. Furthermore, firm entry and exit into grocery retailing in any location is neither costless nor instantaneous. So distant retailers are likely to have (at most) a limited influence on pricing and service quality of grocery retailers in a small town.[20]

Another specific example of national chains that compete in local markets is the market of office supply superstores. The three major competitors with national networks, Staples, Office Depot, and OfficeMax, price their products according to the competition in local markets. Evidence from the Federal Trade Commission, presented in its review of the proposed merger between Staples and Office Depot, showed dramatic differences in advertised prices between markets where all three competitors were located and those where only a single firm was present.[21]

Table 7.3

**Interstate Banking Activity by State, Selected Years, 1980–2000**
(percent of banking deposits held by out-of-state banks)

| State | 1980 | 1984 | 1987 | 1990 | 1993 | 1996 | 2000 |
|---|---|---|---|---|---|---|---|
| Alabama | 0 | 0 | 0 | 0.5 | 3.8 | 5.1 | 8.1 |
| Alaska | 0 | 1.8 | 15.8 | 23.1 | 22.9 | 21.3 | 9.7 |
| Arizona | 27.9 | 27.2 | 55.3 | 63.0 | 89.2 | 95.1 | 93.3 |
| Arkansas | 0 | 0 | 0 | 2.2 | 2.0 | 22.6 | 30.1 |
| California | 0.9 | 0.7 | 0.7 | 0.1 | 1.0 | 2.9 | 40.4 |
| Colorado | 3.8 | 9.6 | 8.7 | 14.9 | 55.6 | 56.9 | 57.1 |
| Connecticut | 0 | 0 | 21.7 | 17.8 | 24.6 | 8.6 | 91.7 |
| Delaware | 0 | 46.3 | 48.6 | 67.6 | 37.4 | 29.9 | 52.1 |
| Dist. of Columbia | 0 | 9.4 | 63.3 | 66.6 | 58.7 | 60.6 | 65.5 |
| Florida | 0 | 6.3 | 31.8 | 40.8 | 48.1 | 54.4 | 79.3 |
| Georgia | 0 | 0 | 26.0 | 23.3 | 42.2 | 50.9 | 51.0 |
| Hawaii | 0 | 0 | 0 | 0 | 0 | 0 | 39.5 |
| Idaho | 37.5 | 38.5 | 37.2 | 49.9 | 56.7 | 91.5 | 82.2 |
| Illinois | 0.6 | 0.9 | 4.9 | 10.0 | 14.8 | 18.0 | 18.2 |
| Indiana | 0 | 0 | 21.4 | 25.2 | 53.0 | 48.8 | 51.2 |
| Iowa | 7.3 | 6.9 | 7.0 | 8.6 | 23.2 | 29.3 | 32.9 |
| Kansas | 0 | 0 | 0 | 0 | 9.6 | 29.9 | 26.2 |
| Kentucky | 0 | 0 | 17.0 | 33.5 | 35.5 | 44.0 | 45.7 |
| Louisiana | 0 | 0 | 0 | 3.7 | 5.1 | 22.0 | 37.1 |
| Maine | 0 | 28.6 | 47.0 | 44.6 | 46.1 | 36.5 | 38.4 |
| Maryland | 2.0 | 2.3 | 21.9 | 25.8 | 24.5 | 44.3 | 47.6 |
| Massachusetts | 0.1 | 0.1 | 2.1 | 8.2 | 17.0 | 4.2 | 10.2 |
| Michigan | 0 | 0 | 1.3 | 3.3 | 3.6 | 22.9 | 34.7 |
| Minnesota | 0 | 0 | 0.5 | 2.5 | 3.2 | 4.6 | 30.5 |
| Mississippi | 0 | 0 | 0 | 2.5 | 2.2 | 10.5 | 22.2 |

Thus, the fact that firms increase the number of local markets in which they operate does not by itself alter the basic supply-and-demand conditions of the industry. Consequently, it seems unlikely that simply because a bank expands into more local market areas, it will be less responsive to local supply conditions (e.g., the number of competitors, cost of labor, and cost of deposits) and local demand conditions (e.g., consumer preferences for services and growth in demand). The profit-maximizing bank would be expected to price its services to reflect the local supply-and-demand conditions. For example, it would not seem to be

profit-maximizing behavior for a bank to charge the same prices in small rural towns that it charges in markets such as San Francisco, Chicago, or New York City.

In some cases, it may not be profitable to vary prices across local markets. In fact, the evidence indicates that some multimarket banks do not vary deposit rates across local markets, but rather only across states.[22] Does this mean the geographic market is best represented by the state, and not by MSA or rural county? If consumer preferences have not changed and people still rely on local branches, then the geographic market is still local in scope.

Table 7.3 *(continued)*

| State | 1980 | 1984 | 1987 | 1990 | 1993 | 1996 | 2000 |
|---|---|---|---|---|---|---|---|
| Missouri | 0 | 0 | 0 | 0.3 | 0.4 | 2.5 | 37.0 |
| Montana | 41.2 | 39.0 | 38.7 | 35.9 | 31.1 | 36.2 | 26.5 |
| Nebraska | 7.8 | 8.7 | 7.7 | 8.4 | 10.2 | 22.1 | 24.7 |
| Nevada | 49.3 | 49.9 | 54.0 | 63.4 | 89.0 | 85.7 | 88.6 |
| New Hampshire | 0 | 0 | 0 | 11.6 | 10.5 | 18.0 | 90.5 |
| New Jersey | 0 | 0 | 2.7 | 13.7 | 32.2 | 41.8 | 50.0 |
| New Mexico | 13.0 | 11.0 | 10.2 | 8.8 | 36.0 | 59.2 | 64.6 |
| New York | 0.8 | 0.8 | 0.7 | 4.2 | 5.1 | 11.7 | 17.5 |
| North Carolina | 0 | 0 | 0.5 | 0.7 | 0.2 | 1.2 | 1.7 |
| North Dakota | 29.3 | 29.2 | 26.3 | 31.3 | 30.7 | 24.9 | 38.3 |
| Ohio | 0 | 0.1 | 1.4 | 6.2 | 3.4 | 2.5 | 21.7 |
| Oklahoma | 0 | 0 | 3.9 | 4.8 | 12.3 | 18.4 | 19.9 |
| Oregon | 29.5 | 34.7 | 46.8 | 44.9 | 47.4 | 41.6 | 75.9 |
| Pennsylvania | 0 | 0 | 3.8 | 12.2 | 9.8 | 12.9 | 30.4 |
| Rhode Island | 0 | 0 | 33.2 | 27.0 | 21.7 | 17.9 | 87.7 |
| South Carolina | 0 | 0 | 44.9 | 41.8 | 64.2 | 69.2 | 63.7 |
| South Dakota | 34.9 | 58.0 | 51.7 | 55.8 | 53.0 | 50.1 | 46.3 |
| Tennessee | 1.9 | 2.5 | 19.5 | 30.8 | 29.1 | 28.0 | 37.5 |
| Texas | 0 | 0 | 8.4 | 41.0 | 52.1 | 51.9 | 54.6 |
| Utah | 0 | 10.2 | 22.0 | 31.2 | 27.5 | 23.5 | 9.5 |
| Vermont | 0 | 0 | 0 | 0 | 3.4 | 1.8 | 33.4 |
| Virginia | 4.7 | 10.4 | 12.4 | 13.1 | 29.8 | 29.1 | 63.9 |
| Washington | 8.4 | 32.0 | 32.5 | 64.2 | 64.2 | 58.6 | 71.5 |
| West Virginia | 0 | 0 | 0 | 3.5 | 22.8 | 24.3 | 27.4 |
| Wisconsin | 3.0 | 2.7 | 3.2 | 18.3 | 15.1 | 14.9 | 17.0 |
| Wyoming | 13.6 | 13.3 | 11.3 | 32.0 | 40.4 | 66.3 | 67.7 |
| National Average | 2.4 | 3.6 | 9.2 | 15.6 | 21.2 | 25.0 | 52.0 |

*Source:* Summary of Deposits.
*Note*: Zero means literally 0 or a negligible amount of out-of-state deposits.
Data reflect deposits held by insured commercial banks through June of each year.

Multimarket banks could be pricing deposits uniformly within a state because the costs of researching each individual market in order to tailor prices to local market conditions outweigh the gain in profits from doing so.

Furthermore, large multimarket banks may establish list prices for various services for all of their offices. These prices would serve to provide guidance to local offices, maintain some centralized control over prices for various services, and implement strategies that may emphasize certain

services or customers over others (e.g., increase mortgage loans and decrease business loans, or increase core deposits and reduce purchased money).[23] However, the profit-maximization objective suggests that banks, like other retailers, would not adhere rigidly to list prices, but would give local offices the latitude to account for local market conditions in setting prices. Indeed, this matter has received considerable attention recently in connection with "overages," that is, the practice of encouraging mortgage loan officers to set interest rates above the bank's base (or list) price by compensating them with some percentage of the difference. Such overages not only provide incentive compensation, but are also a way to account for local supply-and-demand conditions. This pricing strategy for mortgages is particularly notable because mortgages are often cited as an example of a bank service for which the relevant market is no longer local. Mortgage originations, however, continue to be influenced significantly by local market conditions, despite the evolution of nationwide mortgage lending firms and a large market in mortgage-backed securities.

Many years ago a study of branch banking and pricing found evidence of flexible pricing in banking. Based on interviews with officials in large branch banking systems, it was noted that

> Branch banks frequently claim to follow a policy of maintaining the same prices at all offices. However, optimal prices in the head office city, where there are many competitors, are generally lower than the profit-maximizing prices at the small-town branch offices. Even banks that profess to follow a policy of uniformity do deviate from this policy when they find it profitable and administratively feasible to do so.[24]

There is no obvious reason that a profit-maximizing pricing strategy would be different today.

Finally, it is worth remembering that multimarket banking is nothing new. It has been around for many years, first within individual states, by way of both branch banking and multibank holding companies, and since the early 1980s among groups of states under regional interstate banking compacts between states. In fact, by 1987, 9.2 percent of U.S. bank deposits were held by out-of-state organizations and by 1990 the figure had risen to 15.6 percent (Table 7.3). There is no particular reason to suppose that simply broadening such multimarket activity to a national scale should al-

ter what has heretofore functioned as a local market industry where competition takes place at the local level in response to local supply-and-demand conditions.

A study of MMDA and SuperNOW deposit rates in local markets (MSAs and counties) in California and six other Western states with extensive branching found significant differences in SuperNOW account rates among local markets within states.[25] Although these intermarket differences within states were small compared to interstate differences in rates, they are indicative of local markets for SuperNOWs. The MMDA rate did not exhibit intermarket differences, a fact that may be attributable to the high (unmeasured) service component, charges, and minimum fees not reflected in the interest rate. The services analyzed in that study are, of course, only two of many services that seem likely to have similar characteristics. These findings for California raise doubts that geographic expansion by banks alone will enlarge the size of the market for retail banking services, because California has had extensive statewide branch banking for years, is geographically very diverse, and accounted for 10 percent of U.S. bank deposits at the time of the study.

One factor that may create more homogeneity in (or among) local markets is the reduction of legal barriers to entry associated with interstate banking. Especially as interstate branching proceeds, banks may need to adjust their pricing behavior to account for increased potential for entry. Nevertheless, differences in competitive conditions among local markets will almost surely persist for the foreseeable future, in view of the costs of entry and exit, varying market attractiveness across local markets, and the fact that much of the so-called entry from geographic expansion is by way of merger so that the number of firms and market shares in a local market are not affected. It is notable that an empirical analysis of bank deposit prices in California indicates that, despite extensive branching and the lack of legal barriers to entry, banks in California pay lower interest rates on various deposit accounts than banks in other states, after controlling for costs, local market concentration, and other factors.[26]

Clearly legal barriers to entry have declined in retail banking, since the passage of federal legislation allowing interstate banking. However, it would be bad economics and bad public policy to assume that the substantial elimination of legal barriers have eliminated barriers to entry in general in retail banking. This point cannot be too strongly emphasized because there has been a tendency during the past decade for many economists to presume that in most industries there are no barriers to entry or no market imperfections other than those created by laws, and thus there is little need to enforce antitrust laws. Under the circumstances, it is important to address barriers to entry directly because barriers to entry play such an important role in the competitive process. Claims made about the demise of barriers to entry due to deregulation, electronic technology, or international competition cannot substitute for careful analysis of the relevant data.

### Barriers to Entry

It is clear that recent legislation allowing interstate banking has reduced legal barriers to entry into local retail banking markets. However, both economic theory and empirical evidence indicate that market-based barriers to entry continue to be significant in retail banking. Thus, the assumption that barriers to entry have generally disappeared because interstate banking is now allowed would lead to a misguided competition policy toward bank mergers, and the possible public benefit from bank mergers in the aggregate may be offset by adverse effects on competition in retail banking markets.

The conditions of entry are very important for analyzing competition and the concept has a venerable history in classical microeconomic theory (beginning with Adam Smith) and in empirical research.[27] In classical microeconomics, freedom of entry and exit is one of the conditions that must hold in order for a market to be perfectly competitive.[28] If no entry barriers exist, a market is either already competitive or "contestable," that is, regardless of the structure of a market, monopoly pricing cannot take place because monopoly profits will immediately be "contested" away by new entrants.[29] The authors of the concept of contestability state that "Perfectly contestable markets can be viewed as a benchmark for the study of industry structure—a benchmark based on an idealized limiting case."[30] The other theoretical extreme is that entry is blockaded and no new entry is possible. Real-world markets may be characterized by varying degrees of legal and economic barriers to entry and therefore may be less than perfectly competitive.

A number of the basic characteristics of retail banking appear to be sources of market imperfections that could directly or indirectly create barriers to entry. These include the existence of relatively uninformed buyers, information and transactions costs for buyers and sellers, a local market size that allows for only a small number of efficiently sized sellers, and the existence of sunk costs and frictions associated with entry and exit. At least five barriers to entry may be attributed to market characteristics.

*Economies of scale relative to market size* apply especially to smaller markets in which a new entrant must achieve a large percentage of the market's output in order to operate at a reasonably efficient scale. A potential entrant is likely to recognize that any attempt to acquire a large share of a market will significantly affect all incumbent firms, who will compete aggressively in reaction to such a threat. The possibility of such a response to new entry may well cause potential entrants to avoid entering smaller markets. In fact, evidence indicates that there is far less entry in small banking markets than in large markets, suggesting that economies of scale relative to market size may be of importance in retail banking.[31] Furthermore, there are many small banking markets in the U.S.; nearly one-half of the U.S. population lives in rural counties and small MSAs.

*Switching costs* are incurred by customers (e.g., information and transactions costs) when changing suppliers. Switching costs contribute to barriers to entry by making it difficult and costly for new entrants to attract customers away from incumbent firms. The adverse effects of imperfect information on the functioning of markets and its contribution to market power has long been a topic of study by economists.[32] In retail banking, the relatively wide range of fees and interest rates, especially in relation to the small size of many transactions, suggests that the search costs of obtaining information that would enable customers to compare banks may be significant relative to the benefits.[33] Furthermore, the great importance of physically convenient (nearby) bank office locations to households and small businesses suggests that transactions costs are very important to retail customers.[34] Finally, a significant contributor to switching costs in retail banking may be that bank customers are typically tied to a specific bank through one or more ongoing relationships, especially checking accounts, various forms of savings accounts, and automatic direct deposit and billing arrangements. Consequently, in order to switch current service purchases to a new bank, a customer must, among other things, go to the time and trouble of closing out relationships with the current bank. In contrast, to purchase many products such as sporting goods, appliances, clothes, groceries, and electronic equipment, the consumer can switch to a new provider without having to disentangle an ongoing relationship. Each purchase provides an opportunity to switch.

*Strategic barriers to new entry* result from a conscious strategy by established firms to deter entry.[35] An example of such behavior outside of banking is the brand proliferation by major breakfast cereal makers to use up limited shelf space in grocery stores.[36] A significant opportunity for entry deterrence may be emerging in retail banking as major banks establish exclusive contracts to place minibranches in the major grocery or other retail chains in a given market. For example, in the 1990s, Mellon Bank Corp and NationsBank (now Bank of America) began major moves into supermarket branches.[37] NationsBank signed a multiyear agreement with a grocery chain in Charlotte, North Carolina, to install twenty in-store banking centers and negotiated major contracts to do the same thing in several other states.[38] Other banks have signed similar exclusive agreements. This practice will increase the difficulty for a new bank to enter and achieve a sufficiently low cost structure and an effectively competitive market presence. The potential importance of grocery stores as an entry vehicle has been noted in connection with Minneapolis-based TCF's expansion into Colorado. An investment analyst observed, "I've always thought the grocery store was a cheap way to enter a new market and build a customer base. It makes it easier to make an acquisition later."[39] Such exclusive contracts for minibranches would seem to have the potential to be an effective vehicle to restrict new entry, or at least to make it more costly.

Another possible entry-deterring strategy in retail banking might be site preemption, whereby new offices are opened by incumbents somewhat ahead of demand requirements in a market. Thus, established firms with intimate knowledge of the upcoming growth areas in a local market could open up new offices in such areas even before the demand for additional banking services becomes apparent to outside firms. By the time the demand becomes apparent, incumbent firms would occupy the best (most convenient) sites and entry would be less attractive to potential entrants. Such behavior would be facilitated to the extent that incumbent firms (plausibly) have more information than potential entrants regarding demand conditions and likely future developments in the market.

More generally, retail banking appears to be characterized by conditions that are conducive to employing a strategy of entry deterrence. These conditions include asymmetric information between incumbents and potential entrants, prices that can be changed quickly by incumbents in response to new entry, and the possibility of preemptive investments involving sunk costs or yielding product differentiation (as in new offices). Thus, it appears that the opportunity for strategic entry deterrence behavior exists in retail banking.

*Asymmetric information* can create barriers to new entry because potential entrants, knowing less about cost and demand conditions in the market than incumbent firms, may consider entry into the market to be risky.[40,41] Furthermore, incumbents may take advantage of the information asymmetry to set prices that mislead potential entrants by causing them to believe that either demand or the marginal cost of the incumbent firm is lower than is actually the case. The potential entrant would be led to underestimate expected profits after entry. The possibility of such strategic behavior increases the risk of entering a market. However, although asymmetric information between incumbents and potential entrants occurs in retail banking, its practical importance as a barrier to entry has not been determined.

*First-mover advantages* exist when there are distinct advantages to being one of the first (or at least one of the established) firms in a market. Such advantages may make new entry more difficult and costly.[42] In retail banking, first-mover advantages may stem from the existence of customer switching costs (which are of some significance in retail banking), name recognition and an established reputation in the community, and the reluctance of customers (especially small businesses) to stop dealing with an established bank that has proven to be a dependable source of credit and other services. First-mover advantages appear to be sufficient to impede some entry but the extent of their impact has not been determined.

**The Empirical Evidence**

We have summarized various basic attributes of retail banking that may impede entry into local banking markets, but we must look to empirical research to determine whether such barriers are actually effective. A number of empirical studies suggest that local banking markets are affected to varying degrees by such barriers.[43] The existence of barriers to entry may be inferred from evidence of less than competitive behavior, behavior that presents opportunities for an incumbent to earn supra-normal profits. Such a situation cannot exist for very long unless entry is impeded.

1. Research in retail banking generally finds a significant relationship between profits or prices and measures of structure such as concentration and the number of competitors. That is, research indicates that when concentration measures, such as the Herfindahl-Hirschman index (HHI), are

higher, loan rates and profits tend to be higher, while deposit rates tend to be lower. This finding suggests that barriers to entry prevent supra-normal prices and profits from being quickly competed away.[44]

2. Several studies find substantial inefficiency in the industry not associated with size per se, but presumably related to managerial skill (so-called x-inefficiency). Such research finds substantial cost disparity among firms within various size classes of banks. The existence of widespread cost inefficiencies suggests that existing competition is insufficient to force banks to operate efficiently, and hence that entry barriers exist that inhibit new entry.[45]

3. Some studies have found that high local-market deposit growth over a period of three to four years is associated with relatively high profits, suggesting that competition from incumbent firms is not sufficient to drive high growth-related profits to normal levels fairly quickly and also suggesting that barriers to entry are inhibiting new entry in response to the high growth and profits.[46]

4. Studies have also found that the adjustment of some rates paid by banks to retail depositors is asymmetric. Deposit rates tend to adjust in response to downward changes in general market rates more quickly than to upward changes—an asymmetry that benefits the banks, not their customers. More important, this asymmetry is more pronounced in more highly concentrated markets,[47] an indication of insufficient competition, especially in concentrated markets, to force banks to raise deposit rates quickly in response to generally rising interest rates. Such evidence also suggests that entry barriers inhibit new entry that would otherwise have forced banks to adjust deposit rates in a competitive fashion in response to changes in general market rates.

5. One study has analyzed switching costs, that is, the costs to customers of changing suppliers, and found evidence that they exist.[48] In markets with higher switching costs, deposit rates are relatively low.[49] The inverse correlation between low deposit rates and high switching costs suggests that such costs weaken competitive forces among firms already in the market and raise barriers to entry of new firms. Although switching costs are not directly associated with concentration, their existence imposes a barrier to the entry of new firms.

In summary, legal barriers to entry into local banking markets have declined substantially since 1980.. It appears, however, that there continue to be various underlying economic barriers to entry into retail banking, including imperfect information and switching costs. Furthermore, a large and varied body of empirical research suggests that barriers to entry in retail banking markets exist. At a minimum, it is safe to say that local retail banking markets are not "contestable." Once a market assumes a clearly noncompetitive structure, it seems unlikely that firms will behave in a competitive fashion, or that the market will soon become competitively structured. Under the circumstances, the decline in *legal* barriers to entry in recent years should not be taken as a sign that all barriers to entry in retail banking have vanished. They clearly have not. Bank merger policy should take their existence into account as the industry continues its major consolidation.

Moreover, as shown earlier, the opportunity for operating over a wider geographic area that is offered by interstate banking does not alter the basic local market nature of retail banking. Greater multimarket banking does not mean that local markets are irrelevant and bank mergers affecting local market structure will have no effect on competition. Therefore, while interstate banking may indeed have important implications for retail banking structure and competition, these implications require analysis and should not be casually assumed.

## Electronic Technology

Electronic banking technology has in recent years been hailed as the wave of the future. Indeed, today virtually all back-office and bank-to-bank operations are performed electronically. Such technology could have profound effects on retail banking and on the competitive effects of bank mergers. If it becomes unnecessary for banks to enter local areas with a physical presence in order to attract customers and provide them with the full range of bank services, local markets will no longer be the relevant areas for analyzing competition. Customers will not be significantly constrained by information and transactions costs in selecting and conducting business with distant banks. Distant suppliers, however, may continue to have higher information costs than local suppliers, at least for some services. For example, a local bank may be able to better monitor the success of a local small business.

The dramatic growth of ATMs is sometimes cited as an indication of the emergence of retail electronic banking. Indeed, the number of ATMs grew from around 800 in 1972, to about 18,500 in 1980, 61,000 in 1985, and 227,000 in 1999. Similarly, the dollar volume of ATM transactions grew from $49 billion in 1980 to $741 billion in 1999 (Table 7.4). ATM activity, however, must be viewed in perspective. ATMs are used primarily as cash dispensers and basically constitute a convenience offered by many banks to their customers. ATMs are not a substitute for a branch and are not the broad-based retail platform for the delivery of banking services that will ultimately constitute retail electronic banking. The limitations of ATMs are suggested by simple facts. Even as

Table 7.4

**Number of ATMs, ATM Transactions, and Dollar Volume, 1985–2000**

| Year | No. of ATMs | ATM transactions (billions) | |
|---|---|---|---|
| | | No. of | $ volume |
| 1985 | 61,117 | 3.6 | 228 |
| 1986 | 64,000 | 3.6 | 232 |
| 1987 | 68,000 | 4.1 | 263 |
| 1988 | 72,492 | 4.5 | 297 |
| 1989 | 75,632 | 5.1 | 330 |
| 1990 | 80,156 | 5.8 | 383 |
| 1991 | 83,545 | 6.4 | 429 |
| 1992 | 87,330 | 7.3 | 482 |
| 1993 | 94,822 | 7.7 | 515 |
| 1994 | 109,080 | 8.5 | 558 |
| 1995 | 122,706 | 9.7 | 651 |
| 1996 | 139,134 | 10.7 | 717 |
| 1997 | 165,000 | 11.0 | 745 |
| 1998 | 187,000 | 11.2 | 762 |
| 1999 | 227,000 | 10.9 | 741 |
| 2000 | 273,000 | 13.2 | NA |

*Source:* Adapted from *Bank Network News,* various issues.

the number of ATMs exploded from 1980 to 2000, the number of brick and mortar banking offices continued to increase (from about 57,000 to about 73,000) along with the number of checks written (from 35 billion to 68 billion). At the same time, some banks aggressively established banking "centers" in grocery stores, where overhead is low and customer shopping traffic is very high and very regular. This recent trend toward establishing a physical presence in grocery stores is another clear indication that full electronic banking is not yet a substitute for a physical presence.

Personal computers (PCs) may have more potential than ATMs to serve as the retail platform to replace branches. Currently, online banking software can offer a fairly standard range of services, including account histories, bill payment, stop payment, loan applications, and various other financial transactions. Pure online banks (i.e., banks without any branch presence) were established in the late 1990s in an attempt to take advantage of the PC as a retail platform. Thus far, pure online banks have not become a viable alternative to traditional banks. In midyear 2000, fewer than 25 pure online banks existed, capturing only 5 percent of the U.S. online banking market, and less than 1 percent of all Internet banking customers consider a pure online bank to be their primary bank. Growth in online banking comes primarily from the introduction of online Internet banking services by traditional banks who view online banking as another way to bring greater convenience to their customers by increasing the number of contact points (branches, ATMs, and now the Internet).[50]

While online banking provides increased convenience for consumers and reduces costs for some banking-type of services, online banking is not a general substitute for a bank branch. Moreover, there is anecdotal evidence that some electronic services actually increase switching costs. Electronic services such as direct deposit of paychecks and direct debit of regular payments such as mortgages, utilities, and so forth, are costly to change. If an individual changes banks, then each formal arrangement for electronic banking services must be changed as well. As long as most banking customers still choose banks with local branches, retail banking markets will continue to be local.

As of mid-2001, the evidence indicates that pure retail electronic banking is not here yet. Indeed, if the past is any guide, there is also reason to believe that it may not arrive for some time. Over thirty-five years ago an acknowledged expert and governor of the Federal Reserve Board predicted that "within the discernible future . . . check usage as we know it will have largely disappeared."[51] Instead, the total number of checks written has in-creased from 10.5 billion in 1965 to 68 billion in 2000. There continues to be great uncertainty about the form retail electronic banking will take. For example, while there are those who extol PCs and the Internet as representing the future of retail banking, at least one industry expert believes the Internet will never be secure enough and the future of retail banking will be tied to "fast telecommunications geared to 'smart cards.'"[52] The hyperbole associated with the displacement of branches by electronic retail banking is finally being strongly questioned in recognition of market realities.[53] An article in the *Wall Street Journal* observed, "Don't expect too much from home banking, like most other things about computers, the hype far exceeds the reality."[54] There appear to be good reasons to have doubts about the immediacy of full-fledged electronic retail banking. Many things will need to come together in order for this to take place. The convenient, simple, full-service electronic device will need to be in most homes and small businesses; basic changes in customer behavior will be needed to get customers to be comfortable with banking electronically and to feel secure about having all of their funds moved around as electronic impulses; equipment in homes, banks, and stores will need to be ubiquitous and compatible; and prices of the electronic services will need to be attractive.[55]

Overall, despite the availability of applicable technology and the great potential for electronic retail banking, electronic banking has a long way to go before it becomes a significant factor in analyzing the competitive effects of bank mergers. In spite of its seeming inevitability, fully electronic retail banking may not be here for a very long time. Economic research and public policy on bank mergers must recognize these market realities in analyzing the competitive effects of bank mergers without getting carried away in the enthusiasm and hyperbole associated with this exciting technology.

## Summary

The retail banking industry is clearly undergoing a major transition, as is suggested by the dramatic decrease in the number of banks and the very large increase in nationwide banking concentration. The transition is being driven by the removal of restrictions on interstate banking, an unprecedented merger movement, the installation of thousands of ATMs, and initial experiments with as yet limited forms of electronic "home" banking.

In the future, electronic banking may have a fundamental effect on the analysis of competition in retail banking by making a national market (rather than local markets) the appropriate focus for analysis. However, a variety of evidence indicates that electronic banking has not yet had much effect in this respect. At this time, ATMs, PCs, and telephone banking have provided great convenience for some bank customers, but they have not proven to be good substitutes for local offices or to have significantly reduced the local orientation of the great majority of retail bank customers.

The merger movement is having the most immediate and substantial affect on retail banking in the short run. To some extent, bank mergers may be motivated by the uncertainty caused by the factors associated with the industry's transition. However, the removal of legal barriers to geographic expansion is probably the primary motivation for the merger movement as the industry adjusts to nationwide banking from a legally created fragmented market characterized by fifty separate state banking structures. Whatever the reason, mergers are having a profound effect on the structure of the industry and have the potential to affect competition in retail banking for better or worse.

If public policy toward bank mergers assumes that deregulation of geographic restrictions on entry has eliminated all barriers to entry into local markets and will thus ensure that local markets will remain competitive regardless of the effect of mergers on local market structure, then competition will be adversely affected. Such a presumption would reflect a failure to recognize that market-based barriers to entry may be significant in retail banking, as suggested by economic theory and empirical evidence. If, on the other hand, the existence of barriers to entry and the potential for mergers to affect local structures and weaken competition are recognized, it should be possible to maintain competition in local banking markets even as the transition of the industry continues. This would allow customers to enjoy the benefits of competition along with other possible benefits of interstate banking such as increased efficiency, greater competition, and an increase in the diversity of banks represented in local markets.

## Notes

This chapter is a revision of the chapter by Stephen A. Rhoades in the previous edition of this book. The views expressed herein are those of the author and do not necessarily reflect the views of the Federal Reserve Board. This chapter borrows heavily from three articles by Stephen A. Rhoades: "Competition and Bank Mergers: Directions for Analysis from Available Evidence," *Antitrust Bulletin* (Summer 1996), pp. 339–64; "Have Barriers to Entry in Retail Commercial Banking Disappeared?" *Antitrust Bulletin* (Winter 1997); and "Bank Mergers and Banking Structure in the United States, 1980–98," *Board of Governors of the Federal Reserve System Staff Study* 174 (2000). Excerpts from the first two articles are reprinted with permission of Federal Legal Publications, Inc.

1. See, for example, a special issue of the *Review of Industrial Organization* entitled "Industrial Organization Topics in Banking" (February 1997).

2. U.S. Department of Justice, "Merger Guidelines" (April 1997). See <http://www.usdoj.gov/atr/public/guidelines/horiz_book/hmg1.html>.

3. *U.S. v. Philadelphia National Bank et al.*, 374 U.S. 321 (1963).

4. Alan S. Blinder, "Antitrust and Banking," *The Antitrust Bulletin* 41, no. 2 (Summer 1996): 447–52.

5. See Matthias M. Bekier, Dorlisa K. Flur, and Seelan J. Singham, "A Future For Bricks and Mortar," *McKinsey Quarterly*, no. 3, 2000; and Gerald D. Verdi, "Traditional Banks Should Integrate Web Banking with the Branch Network," *American Banker*, June 16, 2000, p. 116.

6. An institution is defined as local if the institution office used most often is within thirty miles of the home or workplace of the people using the institution. The Survey of Consumer Finances, sponsored by the Federal Reserve Board, is a major national survey of consumers' finances. The survey is managed by Arthur Kennickell, who, along with Gerhard Fries, kindly provided these data. Institution types in the survey include depository institutions (commercial banks, savings and loan associations, savings banks, and credit unions), finance companies, brokerage firms, and "other" financial insitutions.

7. Survey of Consumer Finances (1998). I thank Gerhardt Fries for providing these data. These data include checking, savings, leasing, lines of credit, four categories of loans, transactions services, cash management, trust, brokerage, and credit-related services.

8. Despite the introduction of electronic services, local branch networks are still an important factor of bank competition. See note 5.

9. The Survey of Small Business Finances (1993), cosponsored by the Federal Reserve Board and Small Business Administration, is a major national survey of small business finances. Small businesses are defined as those with fewer than 500 employees. A financial institution is defined as local if it is within thirty miles of the firm. Preliminary evidence from the 1998 Survey of Small Business Finances points to little change in the results. See Marianne P. Bitler, Alicia M. Robb, and John D. Wolken, "Financial Services Used by Small Businesses: Evidence from the 1998 Survey of Small Business Finances," *Federal Reserve Bulletin*, April 2001. John Wolken, who manages the survey, kindly provided these data.

10. The success of small banks is evident from Stephen A. Rhoades and Donald T. Savage, "Post-Deregulation Performance of Large and Small Banks," *Issues in Bank Regulation* (Winter 1991): 20–31; and William B. English and Brian K. Reid, "Profit and Balance Sheet Developments at U.S. Commercial Banks in 1994," *Federal Reserve Bulletin* (June 1995): 545–69.

11. MSAs and non-MSA counties are widely used as rough initial approximations for local banking markets.

12. These figures are based on banks only. Inclusion of thrift institution deposits at 50 percent in making the HHI calculation results in 96 out of 318 MSA markets with an HHI greater than 1,800. The Federal Reserve generally includes thrift deposits at 50 percent when calculating HHIs to assess the competitive effects of proposed bank mergers.

13. Inclusion of thrift institution deposits at 50 percent results in 2,001 out of 2,266 rural markets with an HHI above 1,800.

14. The average HHIs with inclusion of thrift institution deposits at 50 percent are 1,628 and 3,765.

15. Based on 2000 Summary of Deposits data from the Federal Deposit Insurance Corporation and the Federal Reserve Board.

16. Based on 2000 census surveys.

17. Congress passed the Interstate Banking and Branching Efficiency Act, also known as the Riegle-Neal Act, in September 1994. That law permits nationwide banking through bank holding companies as of September 29, 1995, and nationwide branching as of June 1, 1997.

18. Stephen A. Rhoades, "Bank Mergers and Banking Structure in the United States, 1980–98," Staff Study, no. 174 (Federal Reserve Board, August 2000).

19. The performance effects of mergers in general is discussed in Nanette Byrnes, Paul C. Judge, Kevin Kelly, and David Greising, "The Case Against Mergers," *Business Week*, October 30, 1995, pp. 122–38; and in banking, Stephen A. Rhoades, "A Summary of Merger Performance Studies in Banking, 1980–93, and An Assessment of the 'Operating Performance' and 'Event Study' Methodologies," *Staff Study*, no. 167 (Federal Reserve Board, July 1994).

20. It has been found that there is substantial variation in grocery prices across local markets and that variation is directly associated with the concentration of grocery supermarkets. See, for example, Ronald W. Cotterill, "Market Power in the Retail Food Industry: Evidence from Vermont," *Review of Economics and Statistics* (August 1986): 379–86.

21. See *Federal Trade Commission v. Staples, INC. and Office Depot, INC.*, Civ. No. 97–701.

22. See Lawrence J. Radecki, "The Expanding Geographic Reach of Retail Banking Markets," *Federal Reserve Bank of New York Economic Policy Review* 4, no. 2 (June 1998): 15–34; and Erik A. Heitfield, "What Do Interest Rate Data Say about the Geography of Retail Banking Markets?" *Antitrust Bulletin* 44, no. 2 (Summer 1999): 333–47.

23. See, for example, a customer-segmentation strategy used by NationsBank in Carey G. Gillam, "Less Profitable Customers May Just Have to Wait," *American Banker*, April 24, 1997, p. 1.

24. Paul M. Horvitz and Bernard Shull, "Branch Banking, Independent Banks and Geographic Price Discrimination," *Antitrust Bulletin* 14, no. 4 (Winter 1969): 835–36.

25. Michael C. Keeley and Gary C. Zimmerman, "Deter-

mining Geographic Markets for Deposit Concentration in Banking," *Economic Review* (Federal Reserve Bank of San Francisco, Summer 1985): 25–45.

26. See Jonathan A. Neuberger and Gary C. Zimmerman, "Bank Pricing of Retail Deposit Accounts and 'the California Rate Mystery,'" *Economic Review* (Federal Reserve Bank of San Francisco, Spring 1990): 3–16.

27. See Adam Smith, *Wealth of Nations*, Edwin Cannan, ed. (Chicago: University of Chicago Press, 1976), ch. 7; Edward H. Chamberlin, *The Theory of Monopolistic Competition*, 1st ed., 1933 (Cambridge: Harvard University Press, 8th ed., 1965), pp. 200–201; and William J. Baumol, John C. Panzar, and Robert D. Willig, *Contestable Markets and the Theory of Industry Structure* (San Diego: Harcourt Brace and Jovanovich, 1982). For some early empirical work, see Joe S. Bain, *Barriers to New Competition* (Cambridge: Harvard University Press, 1956). For a more recent treatment of barriers to entry, see Richard J. Gilbert, "Mobility Barriers and the Value of Incumbency," in *Handbook of Industrial Organization*, vol. 1, Richard Schmalensee and Robert Willig, eds. (New York: North-Holland, 1989), ch. 8.

28. The other conditions required for perfect competition to exist include (a) the existence of a large number of firms such that no one firm can influence price, (b) a homogeneous product (no product differentiation) so that buyers are indifferent about which firm they patronize, and (c) perfect knowledge by consumers and producers, which forces competitive prices to exist.

29. The concept of contestable markets is based on very strong assumptions, including that entry and exit are instantaneous and frictionless, there are no sunk costs resulting from entry and exit, and a new firm can enter and become fully established before incumbent firms can initiate a price response.

30. W.J. Baumol, J.C. Panzar, and R.D. Willig, "On the Theory of Perfectly Contestable Markets," in *New Developments in the Analysis of Market Structure*, Joseph E. Stiglitz and G. Frank Mathewson, eds. (Cambridge: MIT Press, 1986), p. 339.

31. Dean F. Amel and J. Nellie Liang, "Determinants of Entry and Profits in Local Banking Markets," *Review of Industrial Organization* 12, no. 1 (February 1997): 59–78.

32. See, for example, Tibor Scitovsky, "Ignorance As a Source of Oligopoly Power," *American Economic Review* 40, no. 2 (May 1950): 48–53; and Joseph E. Stiglitz, "Imperfect Information in the Product Market," *Handbook of Industrial Organization*, vol. 1, Richard Schmalensee and Robert Willig, eds. (New York: North-Holland, 1989), ch. 13.

33. The number of fees and charges associated with basic banking services such as NOW accounts, noninterest checking, and savings accounts is impressive. See Timothy Hannan, *Annual Report to Congress on Retail Fees and Services of Financial Institutions* (Federal Reserve Board, 1996).

34. Data on the distance between retail bank customers and their financial service suppliers were collected in the 1993 and 1998 National Survey of Small Business Finances and the 1998 Survey of Consumer Finances, sponsored by the Federal Reserve Board. For a summary of findings on the distance of consumers from their financial service providers, see Myron L. Kwast, Martha Starr-McCluer, and John D. Wolken, "Market Definition and the Analysis of Antitrust in Banking," *Antitrust Bulletin* 42, no. 4 (Winter 1997): 973–95.

35. The issue of strategic entry deterrance has received a lot of attention. See, for example, Richard J. Gilbert, "Preemptive Competition," *New Developments in the Analysis of Market Structure*, Jospeh E. Stiglitz and G. Frank Mathewson, eds. (Cambridge: MIT Press, 1986), ch. 3; and Jean Tirole, *The Theory of Industrial Organization* (Cambridge: MIT Press, 1988), pp. 338–52.

36. An analysis of this behavior may be found in Richard Schmalensee, "Entry Deterrance in the Ready-to-Eat Breakfast Cereal Industry," *Bell Journal of Economics* 9, no. 2 (Autumn 1978): 305–27.

37. See Brett Chase, "Mellon Deal Hints More In-Store for Northeast," *American Banker*, September 13, 1996, p. 4; and "NationsBank, Grocer Plans Banking Centers," *American Banker*, November 8, 1996, p. 4.

38. See "NationsBank, Grocer Plans Banking Centers," and Olaf de Senerpont Domis, "Wells Fargo to Expand Supermarket Strategy in the Midwest," *American Banker*, September 3, 1999.

39. Brett Chase, "TCF Financial Using Grocery Store Chain to Expand into Colorado," *American Banker*, November 19, 1996, p. 4.

40. In the literature on the theory of the banking firm, asymmetric information between investors (depositors) and intermediaries (banks) is a key reason for the existence of the intermediaries, which can capitalize on the information they have for evaluating and investing in assets. A parallel argument could be used to explain, at least partially, the existence of local banking offices and their advantages over distant providers. See, for example, Anthony M. Santomero, "Modeling the Banking Firm: A Survey," *Journal of Money, Credit, and Banking*, part 2 (November 1984): 576–602. A more recent discussion directed specifically at information advantages of local banks is in Leonard I. Nakamura, "Small Borrowers and the Survival of the Small Bank: Is Mouse Bank Mighty or Mickey?" *Business Review* (Federal Reserve Bank of Philadelphia, November/December 1994): 3–15.

41. The implications of asymmetric information were recognized by Adam Smith, *Wealth*, ch. 7 and have received considerable attention, especially since Paul Milogrom and John Roberts, "Limit Pricing and Entry Under Incomplete Information: An Equilibrium Analysis," *Econometrica* 50, no. 2 (March 1982): 443–59. See Tirole, *Industrial Organization*,

p. 306, and David Encaoua, Paul Geroski, and Alex Jacquemin, "Strategic Competition and the Persistence of Dominant Firms: A Survey," in *New Developments in the Analysis of Market Structure*, Joseph E. Stiglitz and G. Frank Mathewson, eds. (Cambridge: MIT Press, 1986), p. 59.

42. The opportunities for first movers to engage in strategic nonprice behavior to deter entry are discussed in Encaoua, Geroski, and Jacquemin, "Strategic Competition," ch. 2.

43. Research also suggests that legal barriers did significantly affect local market competition in the past. See, for example, Dean F. Amel and J. Nellie Liang, "The Relationship between Entry into Banking Markets and Changes in Legal Restrictions on Entry," *Antitrust Bulletin* 37, no. 3 (Fall 1992): 631–49.

44. For a review of price-concentration studies in banking, see Leonard W. Weiss, "A Review of Concentration-Price Studies in Banking," in *Concentration and Price*, Leonard W. Weiss, ed. (Cambridge: MIT Press, 1989), pp. 219–65. Also see Timothy Hannan, "The Functional Relationship between Prices and Market Concentration: The Case of the Banking Industry," *Empirical Studies in Industrial Organization*, D.B. Audretsch and J.J. Siegfried, eds. (Dordrecht, Netherlands: Kluwer Academic Publishers, 1992), pp. 35–59; Stephen A. Rhoades, "Market Share Inequality, the HHI and Other Measures of the Firm-Composition of a Market," *Review of Industrial Organization* 10, no. 6 (December 1995): 657–74; Allen N. Berger and Timothy H. Hannan, "Using Firm Efficiency to Distinguish Among Alternative Explanations of the Structure-Performance Relationship in Banking," *Managerial Finance* 23 (May 1997): 6–31; and Steven J. Pilloff, "Multimarket Contact and Competition: Evidence from the Banking Industry," *Review of Industrial Organization* 14, no. 2 (March 1999): 163–82.

45. See, for example, Allen N. Berger and David B. Humphrey, "The Dominance of Inefficiencies over Scale and Product Mix Economies in Banking," *Journal of Monetary Economics* 28 (1991): 117–48; and Simon H. Kwan and Robert A. Eisenbeis, "An Analysis of Inefficiencies in Banking: A Stochastic Cost Frontier Approach," *Economic Review*, no. 2 (Federal Reserve Bank of San Francisco, 1996): 16–26.

46. See, for example, Stephen A. Rhoades, "Market Share Inequality," pp. 657–74.

47. See David Neumark and Steven A. Sharpe, "Market Structure and the Nature of Price Rigidity: Evidence for the Market for Consumer-Deposits," *Quarterly Journal of Economics* 107, no. 2 (May 1992): 657–80; Timothy H. Hannan and Allen N. Berger, "The Rigidity of Prices: Evidence from the Banking Industry," *American Economic Review* 81, no. 4 (September 1991): 938–45; and William E. Jackson III, "Market Structure and the Speed of Price Adjustments: Evidence of Non-Monotonicity," *Review of Industrial Organization* 12, no. 1 (February 1997): 37–57.

48. Steven A. Sharpe, "The Effect of Consumer Switching Costs on Prices: A Theory and Its Application to the Bank Deposit Market," *Review of Industrial Organization* 12, no. 1 (February 1997): 79–94.

49. Switching costs are proxied by the mobility and turnover of the population in a market. It is notable that because non-MSA markets tend to experience relatively little population mobility and turnover, switching costs are likely to be generally more important in non-MSA than in metropolitan markets.

50. See Robert DeYoung, "The financial performance of pure play Internet banks," *Economic Perspectives* (first quarter 2001); and Karen Furst, William Lang, and Daniel E. Nolle, "Internet Banking: Developments and Prospects," Economics and Policy Analysis Working Paper, September 2000 (U.S. Treasury, Office of the Comptroller of the Currency).

51. George W. Mitchell, "Effects of Automation on the Structure and Functioning of Banking," *American Economic Review*, Papers and Proceedings (May 1965), p. 160.

52. Clifford L. Brody, "Internet Simply Isn't Safe Enough for Banking," *American Banker*, November 1, 1995, p. 17.

53. See, for example, Walter S. Mossberg, "Banking by PC Doesn't Do Enough to Ease a Grim Task," *Wall Street Journal*, December 7, 1995, p. B-1; James R. Krause, "Despite Reports of Its Demise, the Branch Is Still on the Rise," *American Banker*, December 5, 1995, p. 1; Karen Kepper, "Branch-Only Customers Churn Out Most Retail Profits, Study Suggests," *American Banker*, December 5, 1995, p. 16; Timothy J. Ryan, "Branch Role Remains Critical," *Bank Management*, November/December 1995, p. 71; Peter L. Venetis and David Slackman, "Satisfying Diverse Customers Will Keep the Branch Relevant," *Community Banking*, April 4, 1997, p. 9; and Jeffrey Cutler, "Reed: Tech Revolution Won't Occur Overnight," *American Banker*, September 20, 1996, p. 1.

54. Mossberg, ibid.

55. For a discussion of the challenges that these uncertainties create for bankers, the continuing critical role of branches as a retail platform for the banking industry, and a possible strategy to employ as we move (perhaps very slowly) toward a world of retail electronic banking, see Stephen A. Rhoades, "Bank Mergers and Industrywide Structure, 1980–94," *Staff Study*, no. 169 (Federal Reserve Board, January 1996), p. 26.

## Selected Readings

*Antitrust Bulletin* 44, no. 2 (Summer 1999). *Antitrust Bulletin* is published by Federal Legal Pubs, Inc., New York. This special issue includes several articles on the definition of banking markets and the calculation of market shares. Other articles discuss the bank merger movement, ATM network mergers, and some general antitrust topics such as entry and exit, and predation.

*Review of Industrial Organization* 12, no. 1 (February 1997). *Review of Industrial Organization* is published by Kluwer, Boston. This special issue on banking provides a good illustration of the traditional industrial organization topics on which research is conducted in the context of the banking industry. Among the topics analyzed are the determinants of entry, the effect of switching costs on prices, and the relationship between market structure and performance.

*Antitrust Bulletin* 41, no. 2 (Summer 1996). This special issue on banking examines antitrust policy toward banking, competition issues surrounding ATM networks, and the views of key policymakers on antitrust policy toward banking.

*Antitrust Bulletin* 37, no. 3 (Fall 1992). This special issue on banking examines various antitrust policy issues in banking. It also presents research on industrial organization topics, including the effects of mergers on efficiency and the relationship between entry and legal barriers to entry.

Rose, Peter S. *The Changing Structure of American Banking*. New York: Columbia University Press, 1987. This book provides a very useful historical perspective on industry structure and institutional developments in commercial banking. It also provides a fairly extensive overview of research on a fairly wide range of topics related to banking competition and structure.

# 8

# Casino Gambling

## Competing with Other Forms of Entertainment

*Ronald M. Pavalko*

Until quite recently, casino gambling was not seriously considered to be an integral part of the American economy. A number of factors have contributed to this, including a moralistic view of gambling as a sinful activity and casino gambling's historic connection with organized crime. However, casino gambling is coming to be seen not as a peripheral anomalous activity, but as a significant part of the leisure/entertainment industry.[1]

The expansion of all kinds of legalized gambling represents a major social change in the United States. This change began in 1963 when New Hampshire legalized the first lottery of the twentieth century. It accelerated in 1977 when New Jersey legalized casino gambling in Atlantic City, grew in the late 1980s and early 1990s as midwestern and southern states legalized riverboat and dockside casinos, and received an enormous boost following congressional approval of casino gambling on Native American reservations in 1988.

This chapter will examine many aspects of the casino industry, including its place in the overall gambling industry, its size, the variety of venues and corporations that make it up, taxation, regulatory issues that affect it, internal and external competition, consolidation within the industry, and the industry's future.

## The Place of Casino Gambling in the Broader Gambling Industry

Prior to the early 1960s, legal gambling outside the state of Nevada was limited largely to horse and dog racing and charitable bingo. By the end of 2001, forty-seven states and the District of Columbia had legalized gambling of some kind. Only Hawaii, Utah, and Tennessee had no legal gambling. But, in November 2002, voters in Tennessee will cast their ballots on a lottery, and proposals for casinos in Hawaii surface regularly in that state's legislature.

Although the focus of this chapter is on casinos, it is important to have an understanding of casino gambling's position within the overall legal gambling industry. Between 1982 and 2000, gross gambling revenues (the amount of money wagered minus the amount paid to the players) increased from $10.4 billion to $61.4 billion, with an average annual increase of about 10 percent. Gross gambling revenues can also be regarded as the money that gamblers lose at different games. In 2000, consumers spent more on legal gambling than they spent on movie tickets, recorded music, theme parks, spectator sports, and video games combined.[2] How does "Gambling USA" (my name for the fictional holding company representing all legal gambling enterprises) compare to more familiar businesses? According to the 1999 Forbes Sales 500, it ranked tenth in sales in 1999, just ahead of Boeing and just behind Philip Morris.[3]

Using data on gross gambling revenues, Table 8.1 presents a summary overview of the growth of different components of the legal gambling industry in the United States for selected years from 1982 to 2000.

## Pari-Mutuels

Betting on horse and greyhound dog races and jai alai make up the "pari-mutuel" segment of the gambling industry. What these forms of gambling have in common is that gamblers are betting against one another rather than against the "house" (e.g., a casino). Gambling on horse races occurs at more than 150 tracks in forty-two states,[4] on dog races at about forty-nine tracks in fifteen states, and on jai alai at frontons in Florida, Rhode Island, and Connecticut.[5]

Pari-mutuels have performed very poorly compared to other gambling activities during the past twenty years. Although not shown in Table 8.1, revenue from betting at tracks on live races and at jai alai frontons has declined since the early 1980s as a result of competition from lotteries and casinos. The only things keeping pari-mutuel tracks in business are off-track betting (OTB) and inter-track wagering (ITW) which is also referred to as "simulcast" wagering. OTB facilities are legal in twenty-four states and, in the case of horse racing, more money is actually bet at OTBs than at tracks.[6] At tracks that have ITW facilities, gamblers can bet on live, televised horse and dog races being run at other tracks. As of 1999, thirty-eight states had legalized ITW.[7]

## Lotteries

State operated lotteries experienced substantial growth from 1964, when New Hampshire began the first legal lottery of the twentieth century, to the mid-1990s. Since then lottery sales have stabilized with, on average, very modest growth, although some states have experienced significant declines and others significant increases. The lackluster performance of lotteries is due, in part, to the increased availability of casino gambling. In Michigan, for example, Detroit's three casinos began operating in mid-1999, and the state's lottery sales declined in 2000 compared to 1999.[8]

By 2000, thirty-seven states and the District of Columbia were operating lotteries.[9] In Table 8.1, "traditional" lottery games refers to weekly and daily drawings, scratch-off cards, and pull tab games. Video lottery games refer to slot machine-like games operated by state lotteries and located in a variety of places including restaurants, bars, convenience stores, and truck stops. Despite their decreased popularity and increased competition from casinos, lotteries accounted for 28 percent of the revenues of the entire gambling industry.

## Card Rooms

Card rooms are primarily a California phenomenon, although they are legal in fourteen states. While they can be found throughout the state of California, they are concentrated in the southern part of the state, especially in the Los Angeles metropolitan area. Since the mid-1990s, card rooms have been added to a number of California racetracks, creating an unusual hybrid gambling venue. Card rooms are not casinos, since players do not play against the card room owner/operator. Rather, they play against one another, with the card room charging a fee for providing a neutral, nonplaying dealer and a place for players to come together. As Table 8.1 indicates, card rooms have experienced modest growth in revenues since the early 1990s.

Table 8.1

## Gross Annual Gambling Revenue, 1982–2000 (billions)

| | 1982 | 1990 | 1992 | 1994 | 1996 | 1998 | 2000 |
|---|---|---|---|---|---|---|---|
| Pari-mutuels | | | | | | | |
| Horses | 2.25 | 2.90 | 2.91 | 2.94 | 3.15 | 3.31 | 3.34 |
| Greyhounds | 0.43 | 0.70 | 0.69 | 0.63 | 0.50 | 0.49 | 0.46 |
| Jai alai | 0.11 | 0.11 | 0.09 | 0.07 | 0.05 | 0.04 | 0.05 |
| Total pari-mutuels | 2.79 | 3.71 | 3.69 | 3.64 | 3.71 | 3.84 | 3.84 |
| Lotteries | | | | | | | |
| Traditional games | 2.17 | 10.19 | 11.21 | 13.66 | 15.34 | 15.40 | 15.56 |
| Video lotteries | NA | 0.10 | 0.24 | 0.46 | 0.88 | 1.28 | 1.66 |
| Total lotteries | 2.17 | 10.29 | 11.46 | 14.13 | 16.22 | 16.68 | 17.22 |
| Card rooms | 0.05 | 0.66 | 0.66 | 0.73 | 0.68 | 0.74 | 0.95 |
| Bingo | | | | | | | |
| Charity | 0.78 | 1.02 | 1.09 | 1.04 | 0.95 | 1.00 | 0.99 |
| Tribal | NA | 0.39 | 0.43 | 0.45 | 0.63 | 0.95 | 1.20 |
| Other charity games | 0.40 | 1.19 | 1.30 | 1.36 | 1.48 | 1.60 | 1.48 |
| Casinos | | | | | | | |
| NV/NJ slots | 2.00 | 4.89 | 5.83 | 6.60 | 7.29 | 8.01 | 9.15 |
| NV/NJ tables | 2.20 | 3.41 | 3.12 | 3.57 | 3.78 | 3.83 | 4.41 |
| Riverboats | NA | NA | 0.42 | 3.26 | 5.54 | 7.29 | 9.01 |
| Indian reservation | NA | 0.10 | 1.07 | 2.97 | 4.73 | 7.21 | 9.24 |
| Bookmaking | | | | | | | |
| Sports | 0.01 | 0.05 | 0.05 | 0.12 | 0.08 | 0.08 | 0.12 |
| Horse races | 0.02 | 0.08 | 0.05 | 0.09 | 0.01 | −0.01 | 0.01 |
| Total book | 0.03 | 0.13 | 0.10 | 0.21 | 0.09 | 0.07 | 0.13 |
| Deepwater cruise ships | NA | 0.26 | 0.30 | 0.36 | 0.43 | 0.26 | 0.28 |
| Cruises to nowhere | NA | NA | NA | NA | NA | 0.28 | 0.34 |
| Land-based and other | NA | 0.16 | 0.47 | 1.58 | 2.10 | 2.52 | 3.16 |
| Internet | NA | NA | NA | NA | NA | 0.65 | 2.21 |
| Total casinos | 4.23 | 8.95 | 11.31 | 18.54 | 23.96 | 29.47 | 35.72 |
| Grand total | 10.41 | 26.21 | 29.93 | 39.90 | 47.62 | 54.28 | 61.40 |
| Casinos as a percent of grand total | 40.6 | 34.1 | 37.8 | 46.5 | 50.3 | 54.2 | 58.2 |
| Percent increase of grand total over preceding year | NA | 9.4 | 12.0 | 15.0 | 5.6 | 6.6 | 5.4 |

*Sources*: Eugene Martin Christiansen and Patricia A. McQueen, "1992 Gross Annual Wager, Part II: Revenue," *International Gaming and Wagering Business* 14 (August 15, 1993–September 14, 1993): 12; Eugene Martin Christiansen et al., "1994 Gross Annual Wager," *International Gaming and Wagering Business* 16 (August 1995): 40; Eugene Martin Christiansen et al., "1996 Gross Annual Wager," *International Gaming and Wagering Business* 18, no. 8 (August 1997): 24; Eugene Martin Christiansen, "The 1998 Gross Annual Wager Reflects the Strong I.S. Economy, as Consumer Spending on Gaming Hits Record Figures," *International Gaming and Wagering Business* 20 (August 1999): 24; and Eugene Martin Christiansen and Sebastian Sinclair, "U.S. Growth Rate Disappoints," *International Gaming and Wagering Business* 22 (August 2001): 1, 32.

*Notes*: NA indicates data not available or activity did not exist. In some cases data in columns will not add to the total because of rounding. Revenues from internet gambling are not included in the totals for 1998 and 2000 since Internet gambling is international.

Data for deepwater cruise ships included "cruises to nowhere" before 1998.

## Bingo and Other Charity Games

It is important to distinguish between two types of bingo games—charity bingo and bingo games operated by Native American tribes. Charity bingo refers to bingo games operated by churches, fraternal organizations, and other nonprofit charitable organizations. Charity bingo is legal in forty-six states and the District of Columbia. Bingo games operated for profit by Native American tribes are usually part of a casino complex, although there are some "stand alone" tribal bingo parlors. Compared to charity bingo, tribal bingo usually offers bigger jackpots, longer hours of play, and more continuous play. Charity bingo revenues peaked in 1992 and have hovered around $1 billion annually in recent years. On the other hand, tribal bingo has grown consistently since 1990, and in 2000 produced revenues of $1.2 billion.

"Other charity games" refer to casino games operated on behalf of charitable organizations (essentially the same organizations that can operate charity bingo games). They are often advertised and promoted as "casino nights" or "Las Vegas Nights." Such events are legal in forty-two states and the District of Columbia. Revenues from charity games grew consistently from 1982 to 1998, but declined in 2000. It is possible that as commercial and tribal casinos have grown and become more readily accessible, smaller-scale charity games have less appeal.

## The Casino Industry

Casino gambling is clearly the largest component of the gambling industry. As the bottom row of Table 8.1 indicates, in 1982 casino revenues accounted for 40.6 percent of total gambling industry revenues. By 1990 they had dropped to 34.1 percent, in all likelihood because of the growth of lotteries. By 1990, thirty-three states were operating lotteries and presented casinos with serious competition for gambling dollars.[10] Since 1990, casino growth has accelerated and casino revenues have continued to increase relative to total gambling revenues. By 2000, casino revenues accounted for 58.2 percent of total gambling industry revenues. The explanation for this is the increased availability of casino gambling opportunities. Riverboat and tribal casinos came on line in the early 1990s, and large destination resort theme parks with casinos grew in Las Vegas throughout the 1990s (and into the 2000s). In the years ahead, casino revenues can be expected to represent an even larger share of gambling industry revenues.

The term "casino gambling" subsumes a great variety of gambling activities that vary in terms of location, size, ownership and management, regulation, and the extent to which they are tied to other leisure activities (e.g., casinos on cruise ships). The remainder of this section identifies these different kinds of casinos.

## Nevada and Atlantic City Slots and Table Games

Despite the growth of tribal and riverboat casinos since the early 1990s, Nevada and Atlantic City remain the major gambling centers of the casino industry. A conventional way of identifying the scope of gambling in Nevada and Atlantic City is to examine data on revenues for slots and table games in these two locations combined.[11] As the data in Table 8.1 indicate, in 1982 Nevada and Atlantic City casinos derived slightly more revenues from table games than from slots. However, since 1990 that pattern has reversed. By 2000, revenues from slots were twice as large as revenues from table games.

Slot machines have come to dominate U.S. casinos. Approximately 80 percent of the typical casino floor is devoted to machine games. In 2000, about 70 percent of the money spent in nontribal casinos was accounted for by machine games.[12]

### Riverboat/Waterborne/Dockside Casinos

Riverboat and other waterborne casinos are an important recent development in the gambling industry. The term "other waterborne" is needed to fully describe some of these casinos since they now include Indiana-licensed vessels on Lake Michigan and "dockside" casinos in Mississippi that do not actually cruise anywhere. For simplicity, these will all be referred to as "riverboat casinos."

Riverboat casino revenues have been growing very rapidly in recent years. On the basis of percentage increase in revenues since their appearance in the early 1990s, riverboats, along with tribal casinos, have been the fastest growing part of the casino industry. As Table 8.2 indicates, riverboats are a middle-American phenomenon. With the exception of Indiana, they operate in states that border the Mississippi River. As of spring 2001, eighty-eight riverboat casinos were operating in these six states. During the early and mid-1990s there were serious movements to legalize riverboat casinos in Minnesota, Wisconsin, Ohio, and Pennsylvania, but proposals have failed to make it through the legislative process or have been defeated by voters in referenda.

### Tribal Casinos

In October 1988, Congress passed the Indian Gaming Regulatory Act (IGRA) which recognizes gambling as a means by which Native American tribes could achieve "tribal economic development, self-sufficiency, and strong tribal governments." Since the late 1980s Indian tribes throughout the nation have developed casinos. As "dependent sovereign nations," the relationship between the tribes and states is somewhat unique. An activity that is illegal in a state cannot be legal on a reservation located in that state (this is the operational meaning of "dependent"). It also means that tribes cannot be prohibited from engaging in activities that are legal in the state in which they are located (because of their "sovereignty"). Where states have legalized lotteries, bingo, and particularly casino games for charitable organizations, tribes have been able to develop casino gambling, as intended by IGRA. This relationship between tribes and states accounts for why tribes in Utah, for example, do not have gambling. Since no form of gambling is legal in Utah, none of the tribes in the state can have any kind of gambling enterprise.

To further complicate matters, while tribes can operate gambling enterprises on reservations, they can also operate them on off-reservation "tribal trust lands"—land that a tribe purchases but which is held "in trust" by the Bureau of Indian Affairs (BIA). The BIA has taken the position that it will approve the establishment of gambling enterprises on tribal trust lands only if there is local approval for the gambling project and if the project is approved by the governor of the state in which the land is located. Since 1988, there have been eighteen land acquisitions put in trust for the purpose of constructing gambling facilities on them.[13]

It is important to realize that tribal casinos (and bingo halls) are not owned by individuals who happen to be Native American entrepreneurs. Rather, they are owned by tribal governments, just as state lotteries are owned by state governments. Nontribal casinos are sometimes referred to as "commercial" casinos in order to maintain this private sector/government ownership distinction.

Table 8.2

**Riverboat Casinos by State, Spring 2001**

| State | No. of casinos | Year begun | No. of tables | No. of slots |
|---|---|---|---|---|
| Iowa | 10 | 1991 | 314 | 8,380 |
| Illinois | 9 | 1991 | 316 | 9,168 |
| Mississippi | 29 | 1992 | 1,270 | 27,104 |
| Louisiana | 12 | 1993 | NA | NA |
| Missouri | 9 | 1994 | 564 | 15,157 |
| Indiana | 10 | 1995 | 677 | 16,423 |

*Sources*: "North American Gaming Report, 1997," *International Gaming and Wagering Business* 18 (July 1997): S3–S38; "Revenue Review, February 2001," *Casino Journal* 14 (June 2001): 17; Mississippi Gaming Commission Web site: <www.msgaming.com>, June 2001; and Missouri Gaming Commission Web site: <www.mgc.state.us/annual>, June 2001.
*Note*: Mississippi has seventeen riverboat casinos and twelve "dockside" casinos located in Biloxi and Gulfport.

As of June 2001, Native American tribes in twenty-nine states were operating a total of 266 casinos.[14] As Table 8.1 indicates, revenues from Native American casinos have increased sharply since the early 1990s. One tribal casino, Foxwoods, located in Ledyard, Connecticut, and owned by the Mashantucket Pequot tribe, has the distinction of having the largest casino slot floor in the world, with approximately 6,400 machines as of July 2001.[15]

*Bookmaking*

Bookmaking refers to the placing and accepting of bets on sporting events and horse races that occur in the sports and race "books" of Nevada casinos. While wagers placed on sporting events and races are quite different from the play that occurs at other casino games, they can be viewed as a casino activity since most of the books are physically located in casinos. Bookmaking makes a very small contribution to total casino revenues. However, revenues from sports books have been growing in recent years, while revenues from race books have been weak (like the racing to which they are linked). Visitors from states with racing

(and off-track and inter-track wagering) who come to Nevada are less likely to gamble on something that they can gamble on "at home" than on something like sporting events that they cannot legally gamble on elsewhere. Race books actually lost money in 1998. Casinos may be operating them more as a service to their race bettors (and a way of getting them into the casino) than as a source of revenue per se.

*Deepwater Cruise Ships/Cruises to Nowhere*

Deepwater cruise ships refer to ocean-going cruise ships with casinos that offer a variety of machine and table games once the ships are in international waters. Cruises to nowhere are ships that are simply floating casinos (with amenities like restaurants, bars, and gift shops). Operating out of many U.S. ports, they too become "instant casinos" as soon as they are in international waters. One thing these two types of casinos have in common, and that distinguishes them from most other types of casinos, is that they are completely unregulated, and their revenues are not taxed by any political jurisdiction. Clearly, they are a very small part of the overall casino industry, with 2000 combined revenues of only $620 million.

### Land-Based and Other Casinos

"Land-based and other casinos" refer primarily to casinos in Deadwood, South Dakota; Cripple Creek, Central City, and Black Hawk, Colorado; New Orleans; and Detroit. While revenues for these casinos are small compared to riverboats (let alone Atlantic City and Nevada), they represent important regional gambling centers. Their popularity is attested to by a very substantial increase in revenues between 1990 and 2000 (see Table 8.1). The increase for 2000 is due almost entirely to the fact that Detroit's three casinos were open during all of 2000.[16]

### Internet Casinos

Since making their first appearance in 1995, online "virtual" casinos (and sports books) have grown phenomenally. In January 2001, the author went to the Internet site <http://www.internetcasinolist.com/> and found 687 Internet casinos listed. About 200 of these also offered betting on sporting events. In March of 2000, a similar exercise had produced a count of 283 such casinos. Such sites are constantly being added, others go out of business, and the number fluctuates a great deal. In January of 2001, a study of Internet gambling sites by Christiansen Capital Advisors and the River City Group, two companies that follow developments in the gambling industry, identified 1,400 "gaming sites."[17] This larger number probably includes casinos, casinos with sports books, sports books only, and government-operated lotteries located outside the United States.

Internet gambling sites are illegal in the United States. They operate mainly out of Caribbean and Central American countries where they are licensed but unregulated. Given the absence of regulation, it is difficult to identify with any precision how many people gamble at them and how much money is being wagered. However, estimates have been made that hint at the scope of Internet gambling. For example, one sports book called "Interops.com," based in Antigua, reported that it took 875,000 bets on U.S. football games during the 1998 season, and over 1 million bets during the 1999 season before the NFL playoffs began. They estimated that they would accept at least 92,000 bets on the 2000 Super Bowl.[18] Another analysis estimated that 4.5 million Americans have gambled at an Internet site at least once, and that at least one million make a visit to an Internet gambling site every day.[19]

Since Internet gambling is such a recent phenomenon, revenues have been estimated only since 1998. It is apparent from Table 8.1 that these revenues are relatively small compared to those of the rest of the casino industry. However, the potential for growth is phenomenal. Internet gambling has the potential for making gambling accessible to people regardless of the distance they live from a "bricks and mortar" casino. There are a number of reasons why it can be very attractive to particular segments of the population. People with physical limitations and disabilities can gamble online from their homes. Bad weather need not be a deterrent to playing casino games. Once an account with an Internet casino has been established, credit cards and ATM accounts can be used to place bets. Betting from home is a way for nonsmokers to avoid the ever-present cloud of smoke that fills most casinos. Moreover, people with children do not need to worry about arranging for childcare while they are gambling. One person who follows this segment of the gambling industry estimates that gross revenues will be $10 billion by

2003, up substantially from the estimated $2.21 billion in 2000.[20] Christiansen Capital Advisors, an economic analysis company that closely follows the gambling industry, makes a more cautious estimate of $6.3 billion by 2003.[21]

As Internet gambling appeared and expanded in the mid-1990s, the established brand-name casinos strongly opposed their legalization in the United States. However, their popularity and the success they have had in gaining a foothold among gamblers have led many casinos to rethink that position. By 2001, many (if not most) of the larger, established casinos have done a 180-degree turn on this issue and have been promoting the legalization of Internet gambling, regulated by state gaming commissions that would issue Internet licenses to the established casinos.[22]

## The Relative Importance of Different Casino Venues

The casino industry clearly consists of many different components, but what are the most important venues, the ones that drive the industry? The primary measure used to address this question is the one that has been used earlier, gross gambling revenues. The components of the casino industry can be thought of as serving different markets. Table 8.3 presents gross gambling revenues for nontribal casinos in the different markets for which these data are available. These revenue data are for one month, March 2001.

When most people think of casino gambling, the first place that comes to mind is Nevada. Consequently, it is somewhat surprising that riverboats actually produce the largest proportion of total casino revenues (42.3 percent). Nevada is next, with 33.0 percent, with most of the revenue generated at the Las Vegas "strip" casinos. Atlantic City is the next most important market with 17.7

percent of total revenues, just a little over half the revenues generated in Nevada. Mississippi is the third most important single casino venue, producing 12 percent of total nontribal casino revenues. Land-based casinos in Colorado, Detroit, and New Orleans generate only a small proportion of total revenues.

Gross gambling revenues are not the only measure on which different markets can be compared. Although riverboats are the largest producer of revenues, they are (after all) spread around six different states. As far as specific locations are concerned, the Las Vegas strip and Atlantic City are the nation's most important "traditional" casino gambling venues. There are two standard measures on which these venues can be compared: number of machine games and number of table games. Atlantic City has 37,004 machine games, and 1,326 table games, while the strip has 60,103 machines and 2,634 table games.[23]

## Casino Industry Effects on Employment and Tax Revenues

### Employment

In the 1990s, the prospect of creating employment opportunities was an important factor in the decision of many states to legalize casino gambling. This was particularly true in the case of riverboats. Indeed, the casino industry has become an important employer.

Table 8.4 presents data on employment in tribal, land-based, and riverboat casinos for 1999. Clearly, Nevada casinos employ more people than casinos in any other state. New Jersey and Mississippi rank second and third. Note that tribal casinos in California rank fourth, only slightly behind Mississippi. The National Indian Gaming Association estimates that about 25 percent of tribal casino

Table 8.3

**Gross Revenues of Major Nontribal Casino Markets, March 2001**

| Market | Gross revenues (millions) | Percent of grand total |
|---|---|---|
| Nevada | | |
| Las Vegas Strip | 434,457 | 21.4 |
| Reno | 71,203 | 3.5 |
| Downtown Las Vegas | 63,853 | 3.1 |
| Laughlin | 54,591 | 2.7 |
| Lake Tahoe | 26,063 | 1.3 |
| North Las Vegas | 21,360 | 1.1 |
| Total Nevada | 671,527 | 33.0 |
| Atlantic City, NJ | 361,020 | 17.7 |
| Riverboats | | |
| Iowa | 55,413 | 2.7 |
| Illinois | 158,563 | 7.8 |
| Mississippi | 243,225 | 12.0 |
| Gulf Coast | 97,452 ⎫ | 4.8 |
| Rest of State | 145,773 ⎭ | 7.2 |
| Louisiana | 138,464 | 6.8 |
| Missouri | 95,667 | 4.7 |
| Indiana | 169,843 | 8.3 |
| Total Riverboats | 861,175 | 42.3 |
| Colorado | 31,757 | 1.6 |
| Detroit | 86,262 | 4.2 |
| New Orleans | 22,339 | 1.1 |
| Grand Total | 2,034,080 | 100.0 |

*Source*: "Revenue Review, March 2001," *Casino Journal* 14 (July 2001): 39.

employees are Native Americans. When all three types of casinos are combined, the casino industry employs over a half million people. While casino jobs range a good deal in terms of wages and salaries, during the late 1990s the average annual income of casino employees was about $26,000.[24]

## *Tax Revenues*

While tribal (or off-reservation) casinos cannot be taxed by the states in which they are located, they do contribute to the cost of a variety of regulatory activities and infrastructure services provided by states and local communities. In addition, many make voluntary contributions to local governments, nonprofit organizations, and charities.

Along with employment, the enhancement of state and local government tax revenues was part of the rationale for casino legalization in the 1990s. In the eleven states that have legalized nontribal casinos, tax rates vary a good deal, and they are subject to change over time. States also vary in terms of the governmental entities (state or local government) that receive the tax revenues.

Table 8.5 presents a summary of the tax-rate formulas used by states and the amount of tax dol-

Table 8.4

**Casino Employment, by State and Type of Casino, 1999**

| Tribal casinos | | Nontribal casinos | |
|---|---|---|---|
| California | 33,800 | Land-based | |
| Connecticut | 17,000 | Nevada | 198,992 |
| Washington | 14,375 | New Jersey | 47,366 |
| Minnesota | 14,000 | Colorado | 5,923 |
| Michigan | 10,000 | Michigan | 4,895 |
| Wisconsin | 10,000 | South Dakota | 1,402 |
| | | | |
| Louisiana | 6,200 | | |
| Arizona | 5,700 | Subtotal | 258,578 |
| New York | 5,550 | | |
| New Mexico | 5,500 | | |
| Mississippi | 5,000 | Riverboat | |
| Oregon | 4,500 | Mississippi | 36,306 |
| Florida | 3,400 | Louisiana | 15,432 |
| North Carolina | 3,000 | Indiana | 13,880 |
| South Dakota | 2,800 | Missouri | 12,000 |
| North Dakota | 2,100 | Illinois | 10,566 |
| Iowa | 2,000 | Iowa | 9,550 |
| Kansas | 1,750 | | |
| Oklahoma | 1,500 | Subtotal | 97,734 |
| Idaho | 1,200 | | |
| Colorado | 700 | | |
| Texas | 700 | | |
| Nevada | 600 | | |
| Montana | 150 | | |
| Alabama | 114 | | |
| Wyoming | 26 | | |
| Nebraska | 23 | | |
| | | | |
| Total | 151,688 | Total | 356,312 |

*Source*: American Gaming Association, *State of the States: The AGA Survey of Casino Entertainment*, (Washington, DC: American Gaming Association, 2000), 5.

lars generated by casinos in 1999. Given the variations in rates and various "options" that exist, it is difficult to say precisely which jurisdictions have the highest and lowest tax rates. However, Nevada does appear to have the lowest rate (although it generates the most tax dollars), and Illinois and Iowa seem to have the highest rates. Despite this variation, it is important not to lose sight of the bottom line—in 1999 taxes on gross gambling revenues were a little over $3 billion.

**Has the Gambling Industry Reached Market Saturation?**

Although gross gambling revenues have been growing, some analysts of the gambling industry have suggested that this growth has been slowing and may indicate that the commercial gambling market in the United States is becoming saturated. During the two most recent years for which data are available, increases in gross gambling revenues

Table 8.5

**Tax Rates and Tax Revenues, Nontribal Casinos, 1999**

| State | Tax rates | Tax revenues (millions) |
|---|---|---|
| Colorado | Graduated rate with a maximum of 20 percent of GGR | 72,800 |
| Illinois | Graduated rate from 20 to 35 percent of GGR | 419,000 |
| Indiana | 20 percent of GGR | 425,000 |
| Iowa | Riverboat: 20 percent of GGR; racino (race track with slots): 28 percent of GGR, increasing 2 percent per year to a maximum of 36 percent | 214,000 |
| Louisiana | Riverboat: 18.5 percent of GGR; land-based (New Orleans): 18.5 percent of GGR or $100 million annually, whichever is greater | 324,000 |
| Michigan | 18 percent of GGR, plus a municipal (Detroit) services fee of 1.25 percent of GGR or $4 million annually, whichever is greater | 30,000 |
| Mississippi | Graduated rate with a maximum state tax of 8 percent of GGR; up to 4 percent tax on GGR may also be imposed by local governments | 302,000 |
| Missouri | 20 percent tax on GGR | 275,000 |
| Nevada | Graduated rate with a maximum of 6.25 percent of GGR | 635,000 |
| New Jersey | 8 percent of GGR plus a community investment tax of 1.25–2.5 percent of GGR | 330,000 |
| South Dakota | 8 percent of GGR | 3,700 |
| Total | | 3,030,500 |

*Source*: American Gaming Association, *State of the States: The AGA Survey of Casino Entertainment*, (Washington, DC: American Gaming Association, 2000): 7–18.
   *Note*: GGR refers to gross gambling revenue.

have not exceeded increases in personal income the way they did during the 1980s and most of the 1990s. For example, between 1998 and 1999, gross gambling revenues increased 6.01 percent, only slightly more than personal income, which increased 5.9 percent. Between 1999 and 2000, gross gambling revenues increased 5.39 percent, trailing the 7.3 percent rise in personal income.[25] This contrasts dramatically with the period from 1982 to 1997, when gross gambling revenues increased by 389 percent while personal income increased by only 157 percent.[26] The increases in gross gambling revenues for 1998–1999 and 1999–2000 (6.01 and 5.39 percent, respectively) are extremely weak compared to the period 1982–1998, during which gross gambling revenues increased an average of 10.4 percent per year.[27]

Another indicator that supports the saturation argument is the proportion of personal income that is spent on gambling. Between 1982 and 1997 the percent of personal income spent on gambling increased from 0.390 percent to 0.740 percent. In other words, people were spending a larger proportion of their growing income on gambling. However, the figures for 1998, 1999, and 2000 were 0.748 percent, 0.748 percent, and 0.735 percent, respectively.[28]

The Mississippi Gulf Coast offers an example of saturation. This area consists of twelve casinos, some with high-rise hotels, ranging from Biloxi to Bay St. Louis near the Louisiana border. As we saw when looking at revenues, this is one of the nation's major casino markets, and by some measures the third largest market after Las Vegas and Atlantic City. These twelve casinos generated $1.1 billion in revenues in 2000, and the region attracts about 22 million visitors per year, with about one-third of them spending at least one night in the 17,000 hotel and motel rooms that are available.[29]

Despite these impressive figures, the area may have reached saturation. The "drive-in market" (defined as a 300-mile radius of the casinos) has become saturated, and gambling revenue growth has declined from 24 percent between March 1999 and March 2000, to only 4 percent between March 2000 and March 2001. According to an industry analyst, the coastline is overbuilt and the market is saturated.[30]

Part of the problem in this area is infrastructure. Highways and the local airport have not expanded, not many tourism attractions besides casinos have developed, and large, "destination resort" hotels of the kind that have proliferated in Las Vegas have not developed. Consequently, the potential of the area for becoming a multiday destination resort has not been realized.

Adding to concerns along the Gulf Coast is the possibility of competition from expanded gambling in nearby states. In neighboring Alabama, legislation has been introduced that would allow slot machines at the state's pari-mutuel racetracks. In nearby Florida (an important source of visitors to Mississippi Gulf Coast casinos) the Seminole Tribe has turned to the federal courts to break a stalemate with the state over the negotiation of agreements to allow tribal casinos. Based on past actions of the federal courts in cases in other states, it is likely that the tribe will get the casinos it wants. The growth of such new forms of gambling in either state would mean serious competition for the Gulf Coast.

## The Casino Corporations

The businesses that make up the casino industry include both privately held and publicly traded corporations, although the latter are much more important to the industry than the former, especially in terms of the volume of business they do. In the 1960s and 1970s, the creation of publicly traded corporations was an important strategy for transforming the tourist-oriented Nevada casino industry from an industry run by organized crime syndicates to one with greater public acceptance.[31] Indeed, Nevada casino regulators created the most restrictive system of licensing and regulation to be found anywhere in the American economy and one that has served as a model for other states.[32]

The present discussion will deal only with the publicly traded corporations since more information is available about them. The corporations that operate casinos are only part of the picture. There are a number of businesses that supply the gambling industry (especially the casino sector) with a variety of goods and services. These businesses also include privately held and publicly traded corporations. Here too, only the publicly traded ones will be discussed.

In Table 8.6, gambling industry operators and suppliers are ranked by market capitalization (stock price times number of shares outstanding). Not all of them are directly connected to the casino segment of the gambling industry. For example, among the operators, Churchill Downs, Penn National Gaming, and Canterbury Park Holding Corporation are primarily in the racing segment of the gambling industry. However, their diversification makes for some overlap with the casino segment. For example, Penn National Gaming operates racetracks in West Virginia that include slot machines.

Anyone who has visited a casino destination resort such as Las Vegas, Reno, Atlantic City, or the Mississippi Gulf Coast will probably see many familiar names in Table 8.6. However, there are also corporations that will be unfamiliar because

Table 8.6

**Market Capitalization of Publicly Traded Gambling Facility Operators and
Gambling Industry Suppliers, July 1, 2001** (millions)

| Operators | | Suppliers | |
|---|---|---|---|
| Large | | Large | |
| MGM Mirage | 4,635 | International Game Tech. | 4,224 |
| Harrahs Entertainment | 3,452 | GTech Holdings | 1,062 |
| Park Place Entertainment | 3,268 | Global Payment Tech. | 1,044 |
| Mandalay Resort Group | 1,914 | | |
| Medium | | Medium | |
| Sun International | 916 | WMS Industries | 883 |
| Station Casinos | 861 | Alliance Gaming | 346 |
| Anchor Gaming | 825 | Shufflemaster, Inc. | 275 |
| Argosy Gaming | 741 | Daktronics | 268 |
| Aztar Corporation | 442 | | |
| Churchill Downs | 363 | | |
| Penn National Gaming | 359 | | |
| Ameristar | 347 | | |
| Boyd Gaming | 322 | | |
| Isle of Capri Casinos | 292 | | |
| Pinnacle Entertainment | 181 | | |
| Hollywood Casinos | 167 | | |
| Small | | Small | |
| Gametech International | 53 | Multimedia Games | 95 |
| Trump Hotels and Casinos | 44 | Mikohn Gaming | 85 |
| Blackhawk Gaming and Dev. | 44 | Casino Data Systems | 61 |
| Jackpot Enterprises | 34 | Acres Gaming | 38 |
| Century Casinos | 28 | Innovative Gaming Corp. | 20 |
| Canterbury Park Holding Corp. | 25 | PDS Gaming | 12 |
| Alpha Hospitality Corp. | 14 | Int'l Lottery and Totalizator | 10 |
| Sands Regent | 12 | Trans Lux Corporation | 8 |
| President Casinos | 2 | | |

*Source*: Web site: <www.finance.yahoo.com>, July 10, 2001.

they do not have a casino with the same name. They are essentially holding companies that have engaged in the acquisition of particular casinos. A prime example of this is Park Place Entertainment, which owns a number of "brand name" casinos including Caesars, Ballys, Paris, Flamingo, and Hilton. Like many of the larger casino corporations, it owns casinos in several jurisdictions (Nevada, New Jersey, Mississippi), and in other countries, including Canada, Australia, Uruguay, and South Africa.

The largest casino corporation, MGM Mirage, was formed through a recent merger of MGM and Mirage. In addition to the MGM Grand and the Mirage, from which the company takes its name, it also owns Bellagio, Treasure Island, and Holiday Inn Boardwalk Casino in Las Vegas, and casinos in Detroit, Australia, and South Africa.

The second largest corporation, Harrahs Entertainment, illustrates diversification, a characteristic of a number of casino companies. Harrahs has casinos in Atlantic City as well as Las Vegas, Reno,

Tahoe, and Laughlin, Nevada. It also operates a racetrack and riverboat casinos and is involved in the management of tribal casinos.

Mandalay Resort Group, the last of the "large" operators in Table 8.6, was once known as "Circus Circus." It's best-known brand-name casinos are in Las Vegas and include Mandalay Bay Resort, Circus Circus, Excalibur, New York New York, Luxor, and Monte Carlo. Like other corporations, it too has diversified and has a casino in Detroit and riverboat casinos in Mississippi and Illinois.

Two of the corporations in Table 8.6—Station Casinos and Jackpot Enterprises—are of interest because they represent different kinds of market specialization. Both can be considered "niche" corporations in the sense that they have identified a particular kind of demand that they seek to fill. Station Casinos operates four casinos in Las Vegas, but they are not located on the Strip to which most out-of-town visitors go. Station has developed what are referred to as locals casinos. Rather than compete for tourists with the big name-brand casinos, Station courts local Las Vegas residents who prefer to gamble closer to home and away from the crowded Strip area. While locals casinos are Station's primary business, they (like many other corporations) also exhibit diversification, operating two Missouri riverboats and a "slot route" in Nevada that competes with the premier slot route operator, Jackpot Enterprises. Jackpot Enterprises is almost exclusively a slot route operator. A slot route refers to the slot machines that are located in grocery stores, restaurants, bars, and so forth, throughout the state of Nevada.

The growth of riverboat casinos in the 1990s created an opportunity for casino ownership and management that many large, established Nevada casinos took advantage of. However, a number of new corporations developed to serve this special-ized market, and existing corporations branched out to enter the riverboat market. Examples include Argosy Gaming, which operates riverboat casinos in Missouri, Illinois, Louisiana, and Iowa, and Hollywood Casinos, with riverboats in Illinois, Mississippi, and Louisiana. Although it operates casinos in Nevada and Colorado, as well as a racetrack in Florida, Isle of Capri Casinos also is important in the riverboat market, with riverboats in Mississippi, Louisiana, Iowa, and Missouri. Many smaller casino operators were able to compete successfully with the larger Nevada-based companies in part because riverboat casinos could be started with a smaller initial capital investment than that required to start a large land-based casino in Nevada or Atlantic City.

Several of the gambling industry suppliers listed in Table 8.6 are involved in the design, manufacture, and sale of machine games and table game equipment. These include International Game Technology, the world's leading manufacturer of machine games, WMS Industries, Acres Gaming, Mikohn Gaming, and Innovative Gaming Corporation of America. Others are partially involved in machine game design and manufacture but have carved out other specialty niches as well. For example, Shufflemaster manufactures automatic card shuffling machines, but it also manufactures the tables for table games and software for slot machines. Some of the companies listed under "suppliers" also do business in the "operator" category. For example, besides manufacturing machine games, Alliance Gaming owns two casinos and owns machines installed in other casinos and shares in the revenue from them.

Several supplier corporations perform relatively specialized roles. One of the larger corporations, Global Payment Technologies, specializes in providing electronic processing of financial transactions. While it provides these services for non-gambling businesses, the casino industry is a key part of its business. Multimedia Games designs and manufactures bingo machines and video lottery terminals, and specializes in marketing them to tribal bingo halls and casinos. PDS Gaming specializes in the financing and leasing of gambling equipment, and the sale of reconditioned gambling machines. Two corporations, Daktronics and Trans Lux Corporation, are involved in the design, manufacture, leasing, and sale of large-scale programmable multi-color video displays of the kind found both inside and outside casinos.

One of the largest gambling industry suppliers has little to do with the casino segment of the industry per se. GTech Holdings' core business is providing information technology services for lotteries (in the United States and around the world).

Besides the businesses discussed in this overview of suppliers, a wide variety of businesses provide goods and services to the casino industry. These include accounting firms, banks, computer manufacturers, security and surveillance equipment manufacturers, advertising firms, architects and designers, and the manufacturers of lighting displays and specialized casino furniture, to name but a few.

## Casino Industry Issues

Two issues faced by the casino industry deserve special mention. One is problem gambling and underage gambling. The other involves the future of the industry—whether gambling is to be the core of the industry, or whether it will become a more broadly focused entertainment business. While these issues affect other parts of the gambling industry, they seem to be most keenly felt in the casino segment.

### Problem Gambling and Underage Gambling

While the majority of people who gamble do so with no adverse consequences, a small minority become addicted to gambling. Problem gambling is a potential achilles' heel for the gambling industry, and especially the casino segment. It is possible that if a backlash against legalized gambling were to occur, it could develop around the issue of problem gambling. It is beyond the scope of this chapter to present a thorough discussion of the nature of problem gambling.[33] A brief discussion of problem gambling and its implications for the casino industry will have to suffice.

Problem gambling is an addiction—as real as addiction to alcohol or other drugs. Problem gamblers' lives are dominated by gambling (actually gambling, planning the next gambling venture, getting money with which to gamble). Like drug addicts, problem gamblers develop tolerance and experience withdrawal symptoms. They lie to family members about their gambling and go to great lengths to conceal what they are doing. When they have exhausted their borrowing options, they will commit crimes (especially white-collar crimes like embezzlement) in order to get money with which to gamble or pay off their gambling debts.

Based on a national survey conducted in 1998, it is estimated that about 1.2 percent of the adult population (about 2.5 million people) are "pathological gamblers," another 1.5 percent (about 3 million people) are "problem gamblers," and an additional 7.7 percent (a little over 15 million people) are "at risk" of becoming problem gamblers.[34] Pathological gamblers are those who meet at least five of the American Psychiatric Association's (APA) ten diagnostic criteria for pathological gambling. Problem gamblers are those who meet three or four of the APA criteria, and those who meet one or two criteria are "at risk" of becoming problem gamblers.

The gambling industry has, in recent years, slowly and grudgingly acknowledged the reality of problem gambling and has begun to promote the idea of "responsible gambling" (the industry prefers the word "gaming"). Since the late 1980s Harrah's has operated a problem gambling education, awareness, intervention, and counseling program for its employees. It has also taken the initiative (followed by several other casino corporations) with casino signage encouraging people to "Gamble with your head, not over it," and "Know when to stop before you get started." Recently, it has been exploring ways of intervening with customers who show signs of problem gambling.

The most significant development on this issue has come from the American Gaming Association (AGA). This is the gambling industry's national trade and lobbying association, created mainly at the initiative of the larger casino corporations. In 1966 the AGA created the National Center for Responsible Gaming. The center's main function is to promote research and collect information on problem and underage gambling. The center also has made some headway in promoting an awareness of problem gambling within the casino industry.

Clearly, it is in the casino industry's self-interest to acknowledge the reality of problem gambling and take steps to reduce its impact on peoples' lives. Compared to the late 1980s, considerably more attention is being given to the issue today. For example, a discussion of problem gambling can be found as part of the programs of most gambling industry conferences and trade shows. Perhaps the most visible change is the presence of brochures about problem gambling and signs with the "help line" numbers of nonprofit state "councils" on problem gambling that can be found in most casinos. These are toll-free numbers that people who experience trouble with gambling can call to get information and referrals to counselers and Gamblers Anonymous meetings.

Underage gambling is an issue that the gambling industry (especially casinos) has embraced even more readily than problem gambling. In most jurisdictions it is illegal for anyone under eighteen to gamble, and in some states the legal gambling age is twenty-one. Gambling is very popular among young people. Research conducted in the United States and Canada between 1984 and 1999 has found that from 20 to 91 percent of adolescents have gambled for money during the past year, with higher percentages reported in more recent years.[35]

The most popular form of gambling among young people involves betting on cards, dice, and board games with family and friends, followed by games of personal skill played with friends, and then sports betting, with bingo last. However, playing the lottery (especially scratch-off and pull-tab games) is the favorite form of gambling among young people who live in jurisdictions with a lottery.

One study of Atlantic City high school students in the mid-1980s found that 42 percent of fourteen-year-olds and 88 percent of ninteen-year-olds had gambled in Atlantic City casinos.[36] While only a small proportion of youth gambling occurs in casinos, it is sufficient to be a serious concern to casino operators. The biggest risk that casinos face is the possibility of being fined or closed down, or (in extreme cases) of losing their licenses for allowing underage persons to gamble. Consequently, screening out underage potential gamblers at the entrances to casinos with identification checks when age is problematic is a major responsibility of casino security.

## Looking to the Future: The Gambling/ Entertainment Mix

There is no doubt that casino gambling has become a staple in the American entertainment menu. Casinos have gone through a complex transformation, and there is no reason to think that they will not continue to do so. The only question is the direction that changes will take.

Although the U.S. casino industry is quite diverse, there is no doubt that the industry is driven by what happens in Las Vegas. In other words, "As goes Las Vegas, so goes the casino industry." Consequently, a glimpse into the future needs to look at what has happened and is happening there.

Since the 1950s, Las Vegas has been transformed from mob-controlled gambling halls with a few hotel rooms to destination theme park resorts where casino gambling is just one item on the entertainment menu. The first step, accomplished by the late 1970s, was for the casinos to become publicly traded corporations.

The 1980s marked the next phase, the development of the theme parks, which has continued up to the present time. Since 1989, virtually every Strip project has been built with entertainment in mind. This movement was led by the (then) Circus Circus Corporation and the construction of the Mirage by the visionary Steve Wynn. The theme parks have made a conscious effort to market themselves as "family" entertainment, stressing the idea that Las Vegas was all about entertainment, not just gambling. Indeed, they successfully competed with Disney and similar destination resorts for the family entertainment dollar. Not everyone in the Las Vegas casino industry bought into this model, however. While the theme parks flourished on the Strip, the older, established, downtown casinos retained their "old-time gambling hall" character on the premise that gambling is what Las Vegas is

all about. While theme parks have not developed downtown, the casinos did develop a spectacular light show that draws more than just serious gamblers to the downtown area.[37]

The next big issue for Las Vegas and, by implication, the casino industry, is just how far it will move toward the "pure entertainment" end of the continuum. What happens will probably depend on the extent to which entertainment companies like Disney, AOL Time Warner, and MCA Universal develop a stake in the Las Vegas theme parks through mergers, acquisitions, and strategic partnerships. Once linked to the theme parks' parent companies, other casino venues (Atlantic City, the Mississippi Gulf Coast, and riverboats) would be candidates for more entertainment development. While such linkages are still at the discussion stage, a new round of California tribal casinos are being built with the idea of competing with the Las Vegas theme parks.[38]

Opinions differ on the prospects of casino corporations becoming the subsidiaries of entertainment conglomerates. Henry Gluck is the former chairman of Caesars World and currently cochairman of Transcontinental Properties, a company involved in a community development project in Henderson, Nevada. In Gluck's view, "Either the gaming companies will become bigger in the entertainment area or the entertainment companies will come into the gaming area." James Murren, president of MGM Mirage, shares this perspective. Indeed, his company has already partnered with Disney, which opened its "ESPN Zone" dining/entertainment facility at MGM Mirage's New York New York property in July 2001.[39] Others are more skeptical. Andrew Zarnett, a gambling industry analyst for Deutsche Bank, thinks the big entertainment companies will shy away from the casinos because they are so different from the kinds of businesses they are used to operating. As Zarnett puts it, "Gaming is very different from operating a theme park in Florida." Similarly, Mandalay Resort Group president Glenn Schaeffer argues that the theme park resorts have done very well without the entertainment companies and do not really need them.[40]

Just how this issue gets resolved will clearly shape the future of the casino industry. It is also possible that just as Las Vegas serves two markets (family entertainment theme parks on the Strip and more gambling-focused establishments downtown), the casino industry nationally may continue to develop with this dual orientation.

### Recession and Travel Safety

A final factor that may affect the casino industry is the ability and willingness of people to travel to destination resorts like the Las Vegas theme parks. The casino industry is not recession proof.[41] An economic recession, uncertainty about employment prospects, or anything that affects people's financial resources could lead them to reevaluate how they spend the entertainment dollars that might otherwise be spent on gambling. Concerns about the safety of air travel could have similar effects. For example, following the September 11, 2001, terrorist attacks on New York and Washington, D.C., air travel throughout the United States came to a halt. As flights resumed, many potential passengers were reluctant to fly because of concerns about safety. The impact on Las Vegas was swift and strong. A week after the attack, the hotel occupancy rate in Las Vegas was about 50 percent (compared to a normal occupancy rate in the 90 percent range), hotel room rates were 52 percent lower than they had been two weeks prior to the attack, and most major hotel/casinos were trying to decide how many people to lay off.[42]

A decrease in the ability or willingness of people to travel to destination resorts could clearly have an adverse effect on venues like Las Vegas. However, the beneficiaries of such a shift would probably be riverboat and tribal casinos. If gambling close to home became preferable to getting on a plane and traveling to a destination resort to gamble, riverboats and tribal casinos would become the casinos of choice. Atlantic City casinos would probably not be significantly affected, since they already rely mainly on "day-trippers" rather than people flying in for extended stays. If concerns of this kind adversely impact the Las Vegas casinos, they are likely to become even stronger advocates of the legalization of Internet gambling licenses for already licensed, established casinos.

### Notes

1. Eugene M. Christiansen, "Gambling and the American Economy," *The Annals* 556 (March 1998): 36–52.

2. Eugene M. Christiansen and Sebastian Sinclair, "U.S. Growth Rate Disappoints," *International Gaming and Wagering Business* 22 (August 2001): 1, 32.

3. Eugene M. Christiansen, "Mixed Results," *International Gaming and Wagering Business* 21 (August 2000): 15–17.

4. John Lyman Mason and Michael Nelson, *Governing Gambling* (New York: Century Foundation, 2001).

5. National Gambling Impact Study Commission, *Final Report*, Web site: <htpp://www, ngisc.gov> (June 1999).

6. Ronald M. Pavalko, *Risky Business: America's Fascination With Gambling* (Belmont, CA: Wadsworth, 2000).

7. National Gambling Impact Study Commission, *Final Report*.

8. Christiansen and Sinclair.

9. Patricia A. McQueen, "North American Gaming at a Glance," *International Gaming and Wagering Business* 20 (September 1999): 40–46.

10. Pavalko, p. 42.

11. Although the terms "slots" and "slot machines" are part of our everyday language, they are not entirely accurate. A technological revolution has made old-time reel slot machines an anachronism. The "machine games" (slots, video poker, and other games) that one encounters in contemporary casinos are really small computers designed to look like old slot machines. A more accurate term for these machines would be "electronic gambling devices" (or EGDs) and is beginning to come into vogue. However, since most reports on

gambling industry revenues use the term "slots," and most readers are familiar with this term, it will be used in the remainder of this chapter.

12. Janet Plume, "Slots are King," *Casino Executive Reports* (June 2001): 22–26.

13. National Indian Gaming Association, Web site: <http://www. indiangaming.org/members/casinos> (June 19, 2001).

14. Ibid.

15. "Watching Over the World's Largest Slot Floor," *Slot Manager* (July 2001): 12, 37.

16. Christiansen and Sinclair.

17. Sue Schneider, "Growing Pains Online," *International Gaming and Wagering Business* 22 (January 2001): 41.

18. Anick Jesdanun, "Internet Gambling on the Rise as Super Bowl Nears," *The Tallahassee (FL) Democrat,* January 29, 2000, p. 1B.

19. "Vegas After Piece of Net Gaming Pie," *Milwaukee Journal Sentinel,* August 7, 2001, pp. 1M–2M.

20. Marian Green, "All Wired Up, No Place To Go: America Lags Behind in the Global Internet Gaming Race," *International Gaming and Wagering Business* 20 (November 1999): 1, 32–36.

21. "Vegas After Piece of Net Gaming Pie," *Milwaukee Journal Sentinel.*

22. Sue Schneider, "Nevada Wades Into Internet Waters," *International Gaming and Wagering Business* 22 (July 2000): 40.

23. "Revenue Review, February 2001," *Casino Journal* 14 (June 2001): 17.

24. American Gaming Association, "Casino Industry: Myths and Facts," Web site: <http://www.americangaming.org> (September 2001).

25. Christiansen and Sinclair; Christiansen, "Mixed Results."

26. Christiansen, "Gambling and the American Economy."

27. Christiansen and Sinclair, "U.S. Growth Rate Disappoints"; Christiansen, "Mixed Results."

28. Christiansen, "Gambling and the American Economy"; Christiansen and Sinclair, "U.S. Growth Rate Disappoints."

29. Dave Palermo, "Southern Saturation: Gulf Coast Casinos Grow Out of Adolescence and Face the Challenges of a Maturing Market," *International Gaming and Wagering Business* 22 (May 2001): 13, 16–17.

30. Ibid.

31. For a more detailed account of this transformation, see Pavalko.

32. For a history of the Nevada regulatory system see Jerome H. Skolnick, *House of Cards: The Legalization and Control of Casino Gambling* (Boston: Little Brown, 1978).

33. For a more complete discussion of this topic see Ronald M. Pavalko, "Problem Gambling: The Hidden Addiction," *National Forum* 79 (Fall 1999): 28–32;

Pavalko, *Risky Business*; Pavalko, *Problem Gambling and Its Treatment: An Introduction* (Springfield, IL: Charles C. Thomas, 2001); and Rachel A. Volberg, *When the Chips Are Down: Problem Gambling in America* (New York: Century Foundation, 2001).

34. National Opinion Research Center, Gemini Research, The Lewin Group, and Christiansen/Cummings Associates, *Gambling Impact and Behavior Study: Report to the National Gambling Impact Study Commission*, Web site: <http://www. norc.uchicago.edu> (April 1999).

35. Durand F. Jacobs, "Juvenile Gambling in North America: An Analysis of Long-Term Trends and Future Prospects," *Journal of Gambling Studies* 16 (Fall 2000): 119–152.

36. A.F. Arcuri, D. Lester, and F.O. Smith, "Shaping Adolescent Gambling Behavior," *Adolescence* 20: 935–938.

37. For a more detailed history of these events see John M. Findlay, *People of Chance: Gambling in American Society from Jamestown to Las Vegas* (New York: Oxford University Press, 1986); Pavalko, *Risky Business*; and Jack Sheehan, *The Players: The Men Who Made Las Vegas*, (Reno: University of Nevada Press, 1997).

38. Matt Connor, "Breaking New Ground," *Indian Gaming Business* (Summer 2000): CA2–CA5.

39. Matt Connor, "Will They or Won't They?" *International Gaming and Wagering Business* 22 (July 2001): 1, 28–29.

40. Ibid.

41. Christiansen, "Gambling and the American Economy."

42. David Strow, "Hundreds of Casino Workers Laid Off," *Las Vegas Sun,* September 19, 2001, pp. 1C, 2C.

## Selected Readings

Goodman, Robert. *The Luck Business*. New York: Free Press, 1995. A highly critical examination of the economic impact of the gambling industry, including (but not limited to) casinos.

Mason, John Lyman, and Michael Nelson. *Governing Gambling*. New York: Century Foundation, 2001. This book examines public policy and regulatory issues as well as the economics of the gambling industry with an emphasis on lotteries and casinos.

Sheehan, Jack, ed. *The Players: The Men Who Made Las Vegas*. Reno: University of Nevada Press, 1997. A very readable and entertaining account of the development of Las Vegas as the gambling capital of the world, told by focusing on the role of key individuals, ranging from mobsters to corporate executives.

*The Annals* 556 (March 1998) was devoted to gambling. Four of the thirteen articles in this issue deal with the

Four of the thirteen articles in this issue deal with the economics and economic impacts of the gambling industry. The articles are: Eugene M. Christiansen, "Gambling and the American Economy," 36–52; William R. Eadington, "Contributions of Casino-Style Gambling to Local Economies," 53–65; Ricardo Gazel, "The Economic Impacts of Casino Gambling at the State and Local Levels," 66–84; and Audie Blevens and Katherine Jensen, "Gambling as a Community Development Quick Fix," 109–23.

Three monthly trade magazines published by Gem Communications, Las Vegas, NV, report on issues and trends in the gambling industry. *International Gaming and Wagering Business* deals comprehensively with the gambling industry on a worldwide basis. As its name implies, the *Casino Journal* follows developments primarily in the North American casino industry. *Casino Executive Reports* focuses on issues of practical importance to casino managers such as security, hospitality, marketing, competition, and new technologies.

# 9

# Electric Power

## Generating Controversy

*David B. Patton and Robert A. Sinclair*

The electric power industry is one of the most visible industries in the economy. Aside from the everyday convenience of electricity that reminds us of the services delivered by the local electric company, evidence of electric utility activity is ubiquitous. Utility poles, street lighting, high-voltage power transmission lines, and power generating plants are easily recognizable and their basic function is understood by almost everyone. Moreover, tens of millions of consumers deal directly with their utility every month when they pay their electricity bills.

In recent times, public awareness of the utility industry has deepened beyond simple recognition of the utility and its functions. During the last several years, as policymakers have debated and implemented policies to introduce some measure of competition into the utility industry, high-profile events in the industry have raised public awareness significantly. Most notably, of course, considerable attention was directed at the extraordinary difficulty California faced in early 2001 with its electric power supply.

In order to gain an understanding of the state of the electric power industry in the United States, this chapter provides an introduction to the basic elements of this industry. It includes a discussion of the structure of the electric power industry, its historical regulatory framework, the events leading to the move toward reform in the 1990s, and a discussion of the emerging competitive generation markets.

## Utility Industry Structure and History

The electric power industry is composed of three primary sectors: generation, transmission, and distribution. The generation sector consists of generating plants (and to some degree various fuel supply infrastructures like railroad lines and pipelines). Generating plants produce electricity using a variety of technologies and fuels. In the United States about 50 percent of total electricity output is generated by large coal-fired power plants that boil water to run steam-driven electricity-generating turbines. Nuclear power technology is the second-largest source of electric power in the United States (about 18 percent of total output) and, like coal-fired generation, nuclear-power generators boil water to move large turbines. These two types of generating units (along with certain types of natural gas-fired generators) are generally the lowest-cost suppliers and therefore tend to generate electricity under all market conditions.

Table 9.1

**Fuel Used by U.S. Generating Plants**

| Fuel | Percent of total |
|------|------------------|
| Coal | 51.4 |
| Natural gas | 15.7 |
| Hydro | 9.3 |
| Nuclear | 18.6 |
| Petroleum | 3.1 |
| Other | 2.0 |

*Source*: Energy Information Administration, *Electric Power Annual*, 1998.

For this reason these generating resources are referred to as "base-load" resources while higher-cost resources that only run under high-demand (and higher price) periods are referred to as "peaking units." In some regions, such as the Northwest, hydroelectric plants supply a significant portion of power-supply needs. These "hydro" plants use the momentum of flowing water to turn generating turbines. Table 9.1 shows the breakdown of the fuels used by various generating plants in the United States.

Electric generating plants generally are not located near electricity consumers. This is primarily because people prefer not to live, shop, or work in the vicinity of large power plants, and therefore plants tend to be located outside of residential and commercial districts. In many instances this is because community efforts have been successful at preventing plants from being built near residential areas. Instead, because they generate less opposition, industrial or rural plant sites have been chosen. Plants may also be located away from residential and commercial areas because it is economical to locate them near fuel sources. For instance, coal-fired plants often are located near coal mines so transport costs of the heavy coal can be minimized. These are referred to as "mine mouth" plants. Safety concerns (usually associated with nuclear power plants) also create a tendency to locate plants away from population centers.

The ability to locate plants away from the location of demand or "load centers" is possible because of high-voltage transmission facilities that can carry power long distances. These facilities consist mostly of conductors (i.e., power lines) and other equipment that help direct and regulate power flows. A challenge in providing efficient electricity supply is that a portion of the electricity is lost when it is required to flow over conductors for long distances. However, these electrical losses can be minimized if electrical voltage is increased. Voltage can be thought of as a measure of the force causing the flow of electricity over a conductor. It is similar to pressure, as one might think of it in terms of water pressure or gas pressure in a pipeline—the higher the pressure the more water or gas that can be transported at any instant. When voltage is increased, the current required decreases and the electrical losses resulting from transmission over long distances are decreased. High-voltage transmission systems were built in order to efficiently tie together geographically dispersed generation plants and load centers, allowing more favorable location of generation in relation to load. Such an interconnected system also facilitates reliable power supply as generators can be used to back each other up in the event of an outage.

Distribution facilities are similar to transmission facilities to the extent they are systems of conductors that allow power to flow. Distribution facilities, however, are more localized, being used to distribute power among the various customers in a local area. Voltage is the primary factor differentiating transmission facilities from distribution facilities. Although there is no standard delineation between transmission and distribution lines, transmission line voltages usually range between 69,000 volts and 765,000 volts, while distribution lines generally have voltages less than 69,000 volts. In addition to low-voltage power lines that carry electricity along neighborhood streets, the electric distribution facilities include transformers that step-down power to levels that are low enough to connect to the retail customers' premises.[1] This "service drop" is actually visible to many customers as a thick black wire that runs from a nearby utility pole onto the customer's premises. The service drop is connected to a meter (usually at the exterior of the premises) to measure how much electricity is delivered to the customer and then to a junction box inside the premises. A junction box contains breaker switches (or on older ones, fuses) that shut off power flow when electrical equipment inside attempts to draw too much power. This prevents dangerous amounts of electricity from entering the customer's premises. For larger customers, more specialized equipment might be installed to allow particularly large amounts of power to be used or to regulate its quality for specialized purposes.

## Regulation and Restructuring

### Cost-of-Service Regulation

Until very recently, most of the electricity in the Unites States (about 75 percent) was supplied by investor-owned utilities that performed all three functions—generation, transmission and distribution—within a single enterprise.[2] For a long time, utilities' retail prices and other activities were closely controlled by the states under comprehensive cost-of-service regulation, while wholesale prices (prices that utilities charge each other) were subject to federal regulation. Under cost-of-service regulation, utilities sold electricity to end users at regulated rates. These rates were set at a level com-

mensurate with the utilities' costs, defined as prudently incurred variable expenses like fuel and labor, as well as capital costs such as depreciation, interest, and an approved return on invested capital. In addition, cost-of-service regulation generally entails allocation of fixed monopoly service territories (i.e., the prohibition of free entry by other electricity providers).[3] This form of industry structure existed from about 1900 until the recent move toward restructuring.[4]

Cost-of-service regulation, indeed, regulation in general, is premised on the conclusion that free competition will not achieve outcomes that are economically efficient or otherwise desirable. Policymakers generally justify this form of state intervention as necessary to "protect the public interest." In fact, in the first part of the twentieth century much of the legal framework for instituting comprehensive regulation allowed the intervention of state governments in the regulation of various businesses to manage prices and restrict entry.[5] Although the public interest is cited as the justification for regulation, it has long been understood that regulation often benefits the industry participants themselves by limiting competition. Indeed, the regulatory framework in many industries was originally sought by the industry itself, including the electric utility industry.[6] For most of the existence of electric power industry, the question of whether utilities should be regulated was not given as much attention as how they should be regulated.

It is fair to say that the premise of regulation is that it is meant to be a substitute for market forces when certain market conditions fail to achieve desired results. In the case of electric utilities, it was argued that without regulation undesirable outcomes would emerge. Due to economies in constructing large generating plants, transmission facilities, and distribution networks, it was believed that a single firm could most economically provide electricity service to an area—that is, it was believed that electricity was a natural monopoly. Such a monopoly, if not regulated, could give rise to exorbitant prices for a product as essential as electricity. In fact, the economies of scale were thought to make competition infeasible as multiple rivals, after having sunk large investments in infrastructure to enter the market, would drive prices to levels such that no supplier would be able to cover its large fixed costs. This would leave no single supplier economically viable, until only a natural monopoly remained. The elements of this historic debate could not be given adequate attention without committing much of this chapter to it, but it is important to understand how utilities have been regulated. This helps in understanding the limitations of regulation and the motivation for moving away from comprehensive regulation. It also helps in understanding the historic and continuing need to regulate various elements of the industry and the degree to which regulation has been and will be appropriate and desirable in the future.

Cost-of-service regulation provides a regulated utility with the exclusive right to serve all retail customers in its franchised service territory. Historically, this service was vertically integrated—including the right to generate, transmit, distribute, and meter the electricity to end users. Under this regime, regulators intervene in the management of the utility in several respects. Foremost, all rates and charges to end users require regulatory approval, usually by a state public utility commission.[7] In addition, many managerial decisions—for example, whether and what kind of power plant to build, whether and how to upgrade transmission and distribution systems, and whether and how to implement new metering technology, new billing systems, and other major decisions—are also subject to regulatory scrutiny.[8]

While these latter functions of the regulatory agencies have an impact on the operation and performance of the utility, the primary focus of these agencies is price regulation. This is generally a process in which prices are set based on the cost incurred to provide the service. Thus, the traditional regulatory pricing model is the cost-of-service model. The cost-of-service model is largely an accounting exercise that attempts to sort out the allowable costs incurred in running a utility and then develops rates to recover costs in accordance with various formulae.

### Components of the Cost-of-Service Model

A utility's cost of service comprises two major cost areas: (1) operating and maintenance (O&M) costs and (2) capital costs. O&M costs cover fuel and other materials and supplies as well as labor necessary to keep the various electric facilities operating and maintained. The primary O&M cost is fuel expense. Labor costs are the second largest O&M expense. Capital costs are related to the investment to build or upgrade new plant or equipment. These assets constitute the utility's capital base and are what is called the utility's rate base. Hence, capital costs consist of the interest, amortization, depreciation, and (importantly) the return on the firm's invested capital (i.e., equity) associated with the rate base.[9]

In a cost-of-service regulatory proceeding, all costs incurred by a utility in its cost-of-service filing can be challenged by regulators or other parties to the proceeding. If regulators find an operating cost or a rate base item to be imprudently incurred, then it can be disallowed and the utility is not permitted to include these costs in its rates. Moreover, even capital expenditures that were prudently incurred, but are no longer used and useful by the utility in providing utility service, can be removed from the rate base and their associated capital costs not recovered. Of course, in some instances extensive debate follows certain controversial cost and rate base items. During the 1970s, nuclear power plant construction cost overruns were the subject of intense debate in rate proceedings.

## Cost Allocation

Once they are identified, the allowable costs are spread among the utility customers in the cost-allocation and rate-design phase of the cost-of-service proceeding. The rate-design phase is an attempt to allocate the utility costs among the various customers served by the utility. Each of the utility's customers uses the utility service in different ways. Perhaps the most extreme example is the case of some large industrial customers that receive power at transmission-level voltages and bypass the distribution grid. It would not be justified for such customers to pay for the cost of the distribution grid if they do not use it. But in most instances, the cost "caused" by a customer is less obvious. For example, some customers may consume a disproportionate share of their power needs during peak times when additional capital must be used to provide the peak requirements of the system.

Various principles have been developed that are used to address these allocation issues. The primary challenge is to divide total cost between those related to total energy usage and those related to usage at peak times. Once this division is made (which is usually controversial), then the total energy usage of each customer class is used as the basis of allocating energy-related costs while the usage of the customer class at system peak times is used as the basis for allocating peak-related

costs. What constitutes energy costs versus peak-related costs is the subject of a long-standing controversy. One common procedure is to classify all variable costs as energy-related and all capital costs as peak-related. Hence, energy-related costs are allocated to customer classes based on each class's energy usage and capital costs are allocated to each class based on each class's usage during peak demand periods. While this approach is simple, it ignores the fact that some capital investments are made to reduce overall energy costs. For example, large, base-load generating plants are designed and installed to run most of the time in order to reduce overall energy costs. It seems reasonable then, that some of the capital costs of such a plant should be deemed energy-related. In the cost allocation process, these controversies must be resolved. Another common allocation issue is the allocation of costs to the generation, transmission, and distribution functions of the utility. These costs can be difficult to separate and identify since joint costs are often incurred to provide multiple services. The separation of transmission costs from other services is particularly important since these costs are recovered through transmission rates regulated by the Federal Energy Regulatory Commission (FERC).

## Rate Design

After each class of customers is allocated a share of total costs, rates must be designed to recover these revenues from each member of the class. The question is how power prices should be structured —for example, through a large fixed charge each month or through a volumetric (i.e., per kilowatt hour [kWh]) charge. In making this choice, policymakers sometimes consider the incentives that alternative rate structures would provide to customers. Certainly a volumetric charge encourages conservation, while a fixed charge does not. In practice, rates are typically assigned in two parts—a fixed monthly charge and a charge related to volume consumed. Larger customers are sometimes also charged in relation to their maximum consumption during the month; for example a large industrial plant may have a maximum demand of 200 kW during some hour of the month. This type of pricing structure is designed to reflect the customer's contribution to the peak demands of the utility.

Sometimes the volumetric rate changes at different levels of consumption. For example, the first 500 kWh might cost eight cents while the next 500 kWh might cost twelve cents. This kind of rate increase with volume is called an inverted-block rate structure. When rates decline with usage, the rate is part of the declining-block structure. Proponents of conservation generally advance an inverted-block rate structure that charges more to customers that consume large amounts of power. Such a structure also shifts the total cost recovery responsibility to relatively large users who may have higher incomes and buy more electricity to heat and cool larger houses, run more appliances, and so forth. Such pricing may be consistent with particular social goals. These various alternative rate structures create additional controversy in the rate-making process.

Regulatory economists generally support structuring rates to charge higher rates to those customers whose demand is the least sensitive to the price (i.e., price inelastic). This pricing structure, known as Ramsey pricing, has been shown to be economically efficient, maximizing social welfare.

## Cost of Capital

While a host of issues are associated with accounting for the total costs of utility service, a key component of regulatory cost accounting is the cost of capital, or the price that utilities pay to borrow funds. Recall that this is only part of total costs. Other cost areas include variable expense such as fuel and labor and other capital costs such as interest and depreciation. We focus on cost of capital because it determines the appropriate rate of return for the utility to earn on its invested capital, which can be a substantial portion of the total rate. Hence, the cost of capital tends to be very controversial.

Cost of capital is the cost utilities incur to finance long-term projects (and, to a limited degree, their short-term expenses)—that is, it is the cost of borrowing money. For an individual consumer, this would be the interest rate on a loan or credit card. For utilities, it is more complicated as they can finance their operations in several ways. Investment capital can come from retaining earnings, borrowing from a bank, borrowing from the public in the form of corporate bonds, or by issuing equity ownership in the company in the form of preferred or common stock. Typically a utility (indeed, any large company) will use a combination of all of these methods of financing. The optimal mix of these forms of financing may differ, depending on various economic and technical factors facing an enterprise.

Aside from what is an optimal capital structure, the costs of each of the financing instruments for the utility is evaluated in a cost-of-service proceeding. These include interest on bank loans, interest on short- and long-term bonds, and the return on common equity. Determining the interest rates is a rather straightforward exercise, generally looking to the various indices that track market rates for comparably termed loans. Determining the allowable return on common equity is a more involved task with much more attendant controversy. Because common equity is a share of the firm's profits, the value of holding the equity is based on the discounted cash flow of future profits. Consequently, the potential appreciation along with the dividend must be sufficient to attract investors. Hence, in its simplest form, this discounted cash flow model calculates the implicit return on equity, given stock prices and dividends of similar firms. This exercise allows regulators to establish an appropriate return on equity for the regulated company.

### Infirmities of Cost-of-Service Regulation

As revealed in the preceding discussion, the rate-making process is subject to substantial debate and controversy. This can occur at many junctures: the cost-accounting area where disallowances might be disputed; the cost-allocation area where customers may attempt to shift costs to others; the rate-design area where utilities will seek a rate structure to maximize their profits prior to their next rate case; and the cost-of-capital area where the parties will debate proper capital structure and rate of return. This adversarial process does not lend itself to the development of economically efficient rates. Because resources are expended by the utility, its customers, and regulatory agencies, the cost of doing business also increases.

But besides the costs of regulation, cost-of-service regulation also creates inefficient incentives. Because utilities are able to recover most costs incurred in the prudent provision of service, the incentive to find ways to reduce costs or achieve operational efficiencies is limited. Since rates are based on an estimate of the cost of providing service, any reduction in costs results in lower rates at the next rate-making proceeding. This has the obvious impact of focusing the regulated enterprise away from intensive efforts to control costs. For

example, if an up-front investment must be made to increase some aspect of efficiency, the future benefit of the investment could be reduced if the resulting cost savings are simply passed on in the form of lower rates. Especially if the benefits show up after some lag, the incentive to take the risk of investing in cost-reducing technologies is undercut because the investment may be disallowed if it subsequently fails or may be appropriated in lower rates if it succeeds. While it is true that regulators have oversight and other watchdog-type groups like consumer advocates are permitted to intervene and participate in rate hearings, such intervention cannot replace efficient managerial incentives (i.e., rewards for good decision making) for the utility. Perhaps the most significant problem with cost-of-service regulation is the effect of the regulatory incentives over the long run on capital investment. A utility's primary source of revenue and profit is the return regulators allow on its invested capital. Since this return generally exceeds the utility's cost of capital (because equity returns are higher than the other components of the cost of capital), the utility will invest as much as it is able to defend as prudent—leading to overcapitalization. This can occur in rather subtle ways. For example, in choosing the technology for a new generator, the utility may chose a technology with higher investment costs and lower operating costs (such as base-load coal or nuclear plants) even though technologies with lower investment costs and higher operating costs (such as natural gas generators) may be relatively more economic. This tendency is the well known Averch-Johnson effect.[10] It is now understood that the consequence of a regulated rate that is too high may be overinvestment. When a regulated rate of return is too low, a reverse Averch-Johnson effect can occur, which results in undercapitalization.

## Restructuring

A major reason for the current move to deregulate the electric utility industry is related to the recognition of the shortcomings of traditional cost-of-service regulation, but other factors have played a key role as well. Without going too far back in time, it is fair to say that the transition away from comprehensive cost-of-service regulation began in the late 1960s. It might be traced to November 1965 when a protective relay in Canada near Niagara Falls failed, causing cascading outages at other elements of the electrical system and triggering the Great Northeastern Blackout. The blackout left most of the large population centers in the northeastern United States without power. The failure of the electric system in the northeast to withstand this transmission line failure accelerated important changes in the utility industry. One of the most important changes was the establishment of reliability councils, which began as groups of utilities within various regions that established standard protocols and procedures to help coordinate generating and transmission systems. As discussed below, in many important instances, these reliability organizations were the forerunners of the large transmission organizations that constitute the key entities in today's restructured electric power industry.

These reliability organizations made it easier for utilities to draw on one another's generating resources in times of emergency to avoid disastrous blackouts when generators or transmission lines went out of service unexpectedly. To achieve their reliability goals, utilities strengthened transmission interconnections to accommodate the transfer of electricity between systems. Historically, reliability councils were voluntary organizations that shared engineering and planning information—each transmission system being operated independently by the transmission-owning utility. As explained below, in the restructured environment transmission systems are to be operated on a regional basis as consolidated single systems by independent operators. Before discussing these entities in more detail, it is useful to understand how the rise of coordinated systems contributed to the move toward competition.

### The Move Toward Competition

The strengthening of transmission coordination among utility systems made it easier to trade power for other purposes than reliability, such as for economic reasons. These so-called "economy transactions" were undertaken to reduce overall generation costs. A utility did this by replacing the output of some of its own plants with the output of other utilities' plants that were cheaper to run but not being used at the time to satisfy their own demand. Utilities also began to trade power when it happened that one utility could supply power in order to allow another utility's plants to be shut down for maintenance. The trading also occurred on a longer-term basis when one utility had excess capacity and another had shortages. Under these circumstances, one utility can supply another utility with generation on a long-term basis through contracts that sometimes last many years.

As utilities became adept at the physical and financial sophistication required to accommodate these exchanges, it became apparent that other types of wholesale power transactions (i.e., sales for resale) were feasible and economically desirable. Municipal and cooperative utilities, which often do not own generation plants themselves but do own distribution systems, have to purchase power from generation-owning utilities. These municipal and cooperative entities were among the first to recognize how the interconnected transmission networks could be used to create competition among generators.

In some regions of the country, formal relationships were formed to facilitate economic trading of power between utilities. These relationships, called power pools, served as important precursors to competitive wholesale power markets. Power pools generally consisted of a group of utilities in a region that agreed to transfer some operating control of their generating plants and transmission facilities to a centralized pool.[11] Each utility was required to own or have entitlement, under long-term contract, to enough capacity to meet the expected load of its customers. (Recall that prior to restructuring utilities undertook all three functions of electric power supply to their customers—generation, transmission, and distribution.) The pool then ran or dispatched the entire fleet of plants on a least-cost basis, that is, serving load by using lower-cost plants ahead of higher-cost plants. In this way, it operated the combined assets of the pool members as an individual utility would operate its own assets. But a pool required that utilities settle accounts after energy was produced. This is because at any time, some utilities would be supplying more power to the pool than they needed to serve their load while others would be supplying less than they needed. When this happened, the utility that was "underproducing" paid the utility that was "overproducing" in accordance with the cost of generation. Hence, the operation of a power pool required the processing of generation and transmission data, as well as other supply data, just as stand-alone utilities required for optimal generation dispatch. But in addition, pools also required settlement mechanisms to ensure that participants were compensated for selling power for other members.

## Utility Technology Changes

Technological phenomena also accelerated the move toward competition. By the 1970s, the use of computer information technology led to advances in energy management systems. The basic motivation behind energy management systems was to improve the monitoring and control of various elements of an electric system. Utilities had always attempted to collect information about system conditions in order to operate at least cost and maximum reliability. Information about customer loads, the availability of transmission, and the status of electric generating units assist the utility in making more effective operating decisions. For example, when customer load increases, a utility is able to adjust its generation output to meet the increased demand. And it can do this in the most economical way if it can track the status of the various generating facilities and can use the most efficient plants available to meet the incremental increase in load. Energy management systems and other data control technology also allow a utility to respond to unexpected generating facility and transmission facility outages. In instances when such outages occur and output from generating facilities is interrupted, electric system information collected and processed by energy management systems can assist in "redispatching" other generation facilities in order to replace the interrupted supply quickly and at least cost.

These technological improvements happened in tandem with other key developments. A chief development was the growing acceptance among policymakers that competition might achieve efficiencies and provide a more effective means of protecting the public interest than regulation. By the 1980s, major sectors of the economy were undergoing deregulation, including the transportation industries (led by the airline industry) and the long-distance telephone industry. The energy crisis of the 1970s was also a key factor in moving electric restructuring forward. Under President Jimmy Carter, the Energy Department was formed and the Public Utility Regulatory Policy Act of 1978 (PURPA) was passed. PURPA legislation was a key development in the move toward replacing regulation with competition. As a result of its requirement that utilities purchase power produced by certain nonutility generators, it effectively ended utility monopoly over the generation of electricity. It also reinforced the growing perception that multiple generators using utility transmission systems could promote a competitive generation sector.

In addition, the movement of the industry away from large central-station power plants toward smaller gas-fired generators promoted competition among generators. As demand growth slowed in the 1970s, the economics of the large base-load coal and nuclear generators that had been the predominant form of new generation up to that time changed substantially. A number of these projects were declared to be imprudent when forecast demand growth failed to materialize, raising "regulatory risks" along with the construction costs and environmental costs of these technologies. At the same time, new gas-fired technologies emerged whose efficient scale was less than one-tenth the size of the base-load technologies and whose investment costs were a fraction of those of the older technologies. These technological changes made the entry of new suppliers much easier, helping to pave the way for competition among generators.

The only remaining barrier to full competition among generators was the fact that independent generators had limited rights to use the transmission network to deliver their power to wholesale or retail customers.

## Fundamentals of Power Flows

Before discussing how this barrier was overcome and before describing the new institutions that are developing in electric markets to govern competition as it emerges, it is important to devote some attention to the physical characteristics of the electric market and how it differs from most other markets. One of the defining characteristics of electricity is that it relies on a physical network for its delivery from suppliers to consumers. In this respect, it is not unlike many other industries that rely on other types of networks. However, the electric network has a number of attributes that together differentiate it from any other industry. First, the electric network is a displacement network. That is to say, it does not "deliver" the actual product that is produced by the supplier. The only requirement is that the quantity removed from the network at the delivery point be equal to the quantity supplied (adjusting for losses). Second, the flow of electricity on the network is governed by physical laws that are unlike those governing any other network. For example, in most networks, such as a gas pipeline network, the flow of the product can be controlled and directed. Electricity, however, travels through an interconnected electric network by flowing over every transmission line or path in proportions dictated by laws of physics.[12] Generally, the proportion flowing over each path is related to the electrical resistance of that path, determined by the length of the path and the voltage of the lines. For example, Figure 9.1 shows a network with three lines that have the same physical characteristics and are equal in length. The electrical flows shown correspond to a transfer of power from node A to node B. Two-thirds of the power flows directly from A to B while only one third of the power takes the more indirect route from A to C to B because the latter path is twice

Figure 9.1    **Power Flows over a Three-Line Network**

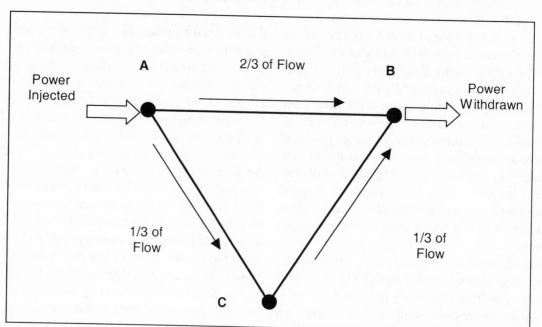

the distance. Similarly, on more complex interconnected networks, any power transaction causing an injection at one point and withdrawal at another will create flows on every line that is interconnected with those points. For example, a transaction in California will create small but measurable flows on lines in Montana. This phenomenon is known as "loop flow."

A third characteristic of electrical networks is that each line or facility has a limit that constrains the amount of electricity that may flow over the line or facility at one time. These limits may be related to the heat caused by the power flows (i.e., a thermal constraint) or by the voltage effects of the power flows (i.e., a voltage constraint). When these constraints are binding, the system is said to be congested. Without transmission congestion, the loop flow would be a relatively trivial issue. However, transmission constraints on one part of a network can affect transactions in other parts of the network. To examine how this may happen, Figure 9.2 shows a 60 MW transfer from A to B on the network from the previous example. The transmission constraints are noted as the limit of the network and the actual flows are shown as the flows of the network. In this example, 60 MW is the maximum amount of power that can be injected at A and withdrawn at B with one-third of the power traveling from A to C to B, and two thirds traveling directly from A to B (as explained above). Since the line from C to B has reached its 20 MW limit, 60 MW is the maximum amount that can transferred from A to B even though there is unused capacity on the line between the two points. Not only can no additional power be sent from A to B, but no additional power can be transferred

Figure 9.2    **Effects of a 20 MW Transmission Limit on the C to B Path**

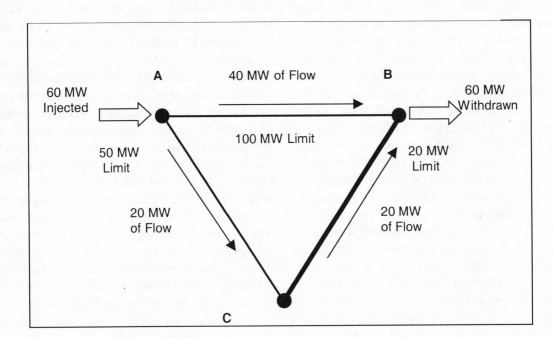

from C to B or from C to A because both of those transfers would cause additional flows on the C to B line. These network interactions create substantial economic issues, including network externality issues, transmission property rights and pricing issues, and transaction costs issues.

Finally, there is currently no economically viable method for storing electricity, so generation must satisfy demand in real time. The consequences of a significant imbalance between supply and demand on an electrical network are voltage problems that can damage generating units and destabilize the transmission network. Consequently, market prices will fluctuate to clear the market in real time as demand and supply conditions change. When demand is high or some large generating units are unavailable, higher-cost generating units must be run and market prices will

rise. Alternatively, market prices fall when demand is lower and can be met by lower-cost generating units. This pricing issue is developed in more detail below.

Each of these characteristics play an important role in determining the nature of competition in these markets, the incentives for utilities to merge, the potential for market power, and the methods to mitigate such market power. In addition, they ultimately play a key role in determining the new institutions that will be necessary to facilitate competition and minimize transactions costs.

*"Wheeling" and the Development of
Wholesale Competition*

By 1990, the term "wheeling" was widely used to describe third-party use of the transmission system by a power producer other than the transmission-owning utility. Some utilities that had excess generating capacity might seek to use the transmission system of other utilities to deliver power to municipal systems that were connected to the transmission system of another utility. Some utilities also might seek to "wheel across" another utility's transmission system to sell power to a utility not directly interconnected with the selling utility. Until 1992, these transactions generally required the approval of the transmission system owner. In some instances, the transmission-owning utility had the incentive to block such transactions in order to profit by keeping the power sale for itself. This obviously frustrated competition and was one of the issues addressed by the Energy Policy Act of 1992 (EPAct).

EPAct authorized FERC to require utilities to allow other power producers access to their transmission systems for wheeling power. But the law applied only to sales that involved the purchase by other utilities, as opposed to the purchase by end-use, retail customers (retail wheeling). In other words, the act mandated use of transmission systems only for wholesale transactions, that is, sales for resale. The limitation in the EPAct to wholesale (as opposed to retail) transactions arises from the fact that the electric power industry is regulated at both the state and federal levels. Generally, federal law governs wholesale electricity sales and access to utility transmission systems, whereas state laws govern the retail sale of electricity.

Among other changes, EPAct abolished the Federal Power Commission, transferred its authority to the FERC, and gave FERC broad authority to implement open-access transmission policies. Initially, requests by sellers of wholesale power for access to utility transmission systems were handled on a case-by-case basis, with FERC considering what terms and conditions were reason-

able based on specific circumstances. This changed in 1996 when FERC issued its open-access rules in FERC Order No. 888 and No. 889. Order No. 888 required all utilities under FERC jurisdiction (which means just about all transmission-owning utilities in the country) to offer open-access transmission tariffs. These were general-purpose tariffs that set terms, conditions, and rates so that wholesale buyers and sellers could gain access to utility transmission systems, essentially regulating transmission systems as common carriers. Order No. 889 helped facilitate Order No. 888 by requiring utilities to use Internet technology to disseminate information about the amount of transmission capacity available on each transmission system. Order No. 889 created the FERC's Open-Access Same-time Information System, known as "OASIS." Using OASIS, wholesale power suppliers were able to determine quickly the availability of transmission capacity for their power transactions, greatly facilitating wholesale power trading. The open-access policies of FERC allowed wholesale buyers and sellers throughout a broad geographic region to transact over a transmission network that heretofore had been largely unavailable to them. Wholesale transactions that had been price regulated by the FERC are now largely deregulated, except when FERC determines that a market area lacks the potential for effective competition.

The competition emerging at the wholesale level includes a variety of different types of buyers and sellers that can be clustered in five categories:

1. Traditional electric utilities generate 70 percent of all electricity consumed in the United States, most of which is used to serve their retail customers. These entities are also active buyers and sellers in the wholesale markets to maximize the value of their generating assets. Such utilities

generally operate under state regulation with an exclusive franchise to serve the retail customers in a given area. However, in a number of states that have moved toward retail competition, the traditional utilities have sold some or all of their generating assets to other suppliers.

2. Power marketers buy, sell, and broker electricity, typically owning few assets themselves. Power marketers generate profits by realizing arbitrage opportunities and taking speculative positions in the power markets, operating in much the same way as traders do in other industries. In some cases, marketers are active in competing to sell power to retail electric customers.

3. Municipal utilities generally rely on power purchase contracts with traditional electric utilities or marketers to serve retail customers. They typically do not own a substantial amount of generating assets.

4. Independent power producers own generating assets, but have no retail customers that they must serve. Instead, they generally arrange power sales contracts with electric utilities or marketers. Independent power producers obtain generating assets by building generating units themselves or by purchasing assets divested by utilities.

5. Large customers may buy electricity from the suppliers described above. In general, most retail customers that purchase electricity for their own use are subject to state regulation requiring them to purchase from the franchise electric utility serving their area. However, in some cases, their geographic location or specific regulatory exceptions allow certain large customers to purchase power competitively.

The array of different participants in the wholesale power markets is made more complex by the fact that participants are often affiliated with one another via sophisticated ownership or contractual relationships.

While open-access transmission policies developed in the early 1990s were a major stride toward more effective wholesale competition, the fact that most individual transmission-owning utilities retained control of their transmission systems continued to present concerns. One major concern was the fact that many power traders wanted to make transactions that required the use of two or more intervening transmission systems. If a transaction requires the use of more than one system, parties to the transaction may have to pay multiple transmission charges, referred to as "pancaked" charges. Pancaked transmission charges can limit the area within which competition develops by making long-distance transactions uneconomic. There were also continued concerns regarding operational control of the transmission system by utilities that also used the same facilities to compete in wholesale generation markets. While open-access policies prohibited some specific discriminatory conduct, transmission-owning utilities retained operating discretion that could be used to hinder development of free trading among market participants.

Lastly, due to the interdependence of the transmission systems caused by the loop flows described above, it quickly became apparent that increased coordination among the transmission owners' systems was needed.

### New Institutions to Facilitate Competition

As deregulation has begun to take shape in electric markets, new institutions have developed to address these concerns and ensure that competition will, in fact, emerge in these markets. In particular, the concept of a Regional Transmission Organization (RTO) was developed by FERC. Under an RTO, a number of utilities in a region turn over operational control (but not necessarily ownership) of their assets to an independent entity. The independent entity operates the amalgamated transmission system as a single system with the duty to facilitate trading and maintain reliability.

RTO functions include scheduling generation; resolving transmission congestion; coordinating schedules for taking generation and transmission facilities out of service for maintenance; administering the applicable system of transmission property rights; coordinating the expansion and upgrades of the transmission system; ensuring that there are sufficient reserves of generating capacity to maintain the reliability of the system; and providing a means for participants to settle "imbalances" (when a generator produces more or less electricity than is demanded by its load). FERC has also required RTOs to take on the role of market monitor with the authority to impose various sanctions on firms attempting to exercise market power. The appropriate division of roles among the RTOs, the regulators, and the antitrust agencies is still being developed by FERC.

By improving the coordination of transactions and power flows in a region, RTOs are able to facilitate fuller and more efficient utilization of the transmission network. In addition, by removing operational control of transmission systems from the utilities, the incentive for the utilities to use control of the transmission system to favor their own generation is lessened. And requiring utilities to consolidate operational control on a regional basis broadens the effective trading area by eliminating the need to pay pancaked transmission charges when crossing more than one transmission system.

To meet the requirements listed above, RTOs have begun implementing formal auction-based markets for electricity and operating reserves. The first RTOs to form and implement these types of markets emerged from former power pools that had operated in the Northeast. The FERC's open-access policies required power pools to change–opening the membership to all market participants. In this process, the power pools became known as Independent System Operators (ISOs) and replaced their former cost-based coordination with bid-based markets.

The most important such market is the spot electricity market. This market provides a means for settling imbalances (as required by FERC under its RTO policies), facilitating short-term trades between participants, and efficiently dispatching generating resources to respect the constraints on the transmission system. The spot markets are typically auctions for short-term power that result in hourly market-clearing prices. Some markets are designed to account for transmission congestion by establishing different market-clearing prices (i.e., quantity demanded is equal to quantity supplied at that price) at different locations on the electric network. When transmission congestion prevents lower-cost generating units in one area from being dispatched, while forcing higher-cost units to be run instead, then prices at the two locations should diverge. Other spot markets, most notably the New England Power Pool and the British electric market, set a single market price for the region and make payments to more expensive generators that must run due to transmission congestion. The payments are generally financed with a fixed charge to customers on the system called an "uplift charge."

It is essential to examine spot markets for two reasons. First, the nature of competition will be strongly influenced by the presence and structure of the spot market. Spot markets ensure that all efficient transactions are executed and all possible gains from trade are realized, subject to the bidding of the market participants. This ensures that the markets achieve an equilibrium, even in the very short term. Without a spot market, market participants must transact in a decentralized manner without the benefit of the full information that an auction provides. In addition, a spot market facilitates long-term contracting that existing firms and potential entrants can use to manage their risk more effectively. By creating a liquid spot market with visible prices, the power exchange provides the necessary price signal to properly value long-term contracts, futures contracts, options, and other derivatives.

Second, the spot markets provide a means of efficiently managing congestion and using the transmission system. The requirement to balance supply and demand on a real-time basis (through the imbalance market), while accommodating all transmission constraints, makes explicit coordination essential. This coordination is easily accomplished by the RTO through an auction that utilizes bids from each generator and provides full information regarding the transmission system. Some have argued that active short-term trading by participants could achieve outcomes similar to those of the auction market. In reality, however, transaction costs and the fact that participants lack full information about demand, the output of other generators, and the state of the transmission system hinders efficient short-term trading. The auction market overcomes these problems and helps ensure that the transmission system is efficiently utilized.

In addition to the spot markets, RTOs generally operate various forms of operating-reserve markets. These markets provide generating capability for reserves (ready to operate in response to unexpected system events) to ensure that customers continue to receive electricity reliably. For those markets to operate well, they should be run in conjunction with the spot electricity market to ensure efficient economic trade-offs are made between those generators that are held in reserve versus those that produce output. Making these trade-offs efficiently is necessary to set accurate prices for the operating reserves. As in all cases, designing the markets to send accurate price signals is essential for establishing efficient incentives for market participants and ensuring that competitive markets deliver promised benefits.

### Retail Competition

As competition has emerged at the wholesale level, states have begun to allow competition at the retail level. This is generally accomplished through state legislation or, in some cases, policy mandates of the state regulatory commissions. However, these actions have been taken at a very uneven pace, even between neighboring states in the same region. As we shall see, some states have pursued aggressive policies to mandate divestiture of generation to create rival suppliers in the state. These efforts have generally been accompanied by policies that allow access by alternative suppliers to the majority of the retail load. However, only a few states have pursued retail competition this aggressively with notable success. In the meantime, most other states have only implemented very limited pilot programs or investigations of the potential benefits of retail competition. The problems that arose in California have caused many states to slow the pace of deregulation of retail competition.

The limited success of retail competition to this point is due to a number of factors. First, robust competition at the retail level may require that suppliers compete to serve retail customers across relatively large regions, as they do at the wholesale level. Hence, introducing retail competition on a state-by-state basis may not be possible. This is especially true since each state has an incentive to promote imports and restrict exports (since this will tend to minimize prices in their state). Ultimately, a strong federal role may be needed to establish competitive retail markets in multistate regions.

Second, the wholesale commodity component of most retail rates is no more than 30 percent of the total rate–with the other 70 percent related to fixed costs that do not vary by supplier (taxes, distribution facility charges, etc.). Hence, even if alternative suppliers offer power to retail customers with a commodity cost that is 20 percent less than that of the incumbent utility, the overall rate reduction would only be 6 percent (i.e., 30 percent times 20 percent). Therefore, it is difficult for competitive suppliers to offer power at prices substantially lower than those of the existing utility.

Third, the prices prevailing in the wholesale markets are often higher than the commodity price embedded in many regulated retail rates. This makes the regulated rates relatively attractive to the retail customers. Because it is politically unpalatable to adjust the current regulated retail rates to reflect the commodity costs prevailing in the wholesale markets, customers have no incentive to consider alternative suppliers.

Lastly, even when alternative suppliers do acquire low-cost resources that would allow them to compete to make sales to retail customers, they may be able to maximize their profits by selling their output at the wholesale rather than the retail level. The reason for this is that the marketing and administrative expenses of selling power to individual retail customers can be substantial—overwhelming any additional profits that can be made selling power at the retail level.

For these reasons, the transition to full competition at the retail level may take a considerable amount of time. Indeed, unless federal lawmakers succeed in establishing a mandate and standard-ized guidelines for the states, full retail competition may never be fully achieved.

## Status of Regional Transmission Organizations

The transition to competitive wholesale markets has varied from one region of the country to another. To a significant extent, these differences stem from the structure of the regional electricity markets prior to the transition. For example, because three power pools already existed in the Northeast, that region now has three RTOs that emerged from the power pools. These three RTOs are the ISO New England (ISO-NE), the New York ISO (NY-ISO) and the Pennsylvania-Jersey-Maryland ISO (PJM-ISO). RTOs are forming in other parts of the country at a slower pace because they generally lack the advantage of building on an existing power pool. An important exception is California, where legislators and regulators mandated the creation of an RTO (CAL-ISO) and required their largest utilities to sell off most of their generating assets. In the Midwest and Northwest the RTO structures are designed explicitly to encourage bilateral contracting where buyers and sellers of power negotiate directly with one another.

Several RTOs have already commenced full operation, including CAL-ISO, ISO-NE, NY-ISO and PJM-ISO and Electrical Reliability Counsel of Texas (ERCOT-ISO). Others are in various stages of development. An analysis of each RTO follows, including a detailed discussion of the California experience.

### ISO-NE

ISO-NE was established by restructuring the existing New England Power Pool and began operating on July 1, 1997, following its approval by

FERC. It manages the transmission grid as well as a bid-based market for electricity and operating reserves. The market mechanism for trading in ISO-NE is an auction market that sets one price for the entire market. The market is cleared by ordering the bids in ascending rank and then matching the offered supply associated with these bids against the hourly demand. In general, the lowest-cost bid not selected to meet actual demand sets the market-clearing price for electricity, and all buyers who purchase power from the market will pay this price. If a higher-cost resource in one area must be dispatched to resolve congestion, these additional costs are recovered through an uplift charge. The specifics of these auction-based mechanisms are an important element of the restructured power industry. A closer examination of these features is undertaken in the next section.

## PJM-ISO

The PJM ISO began operating on January 1, 1998, following approval by FERC. Like ISO-NE, PJM-ISO is based on an existing tight power pool. PJM is an independent body that operates the ISO, administers PJM's open-access transmission tariff, operates the spot energy market, and approves regional transmission expansion plans. PJM-ISO operates throughout major portions of five mid-Atlantic states and the District of Columbia. The FERC has authorized PJM to operate a bid-based spot market for electricity and imbalances. The PJM market sets prices equal to the marginal cost of serving load at each location on its transmission grid (and hence the price varies by location to recover the costs of transmission congestion). The PJM markets also include the sale of transmission rights that allow participants to hedge congestion costs, but do not include competitive

markets for operating reserves. In October 2000, PJM filed to achieve FERC RTO status.

## NY-ISO

The New York ISO began operating December 1, 1999. Like NE-ISO and PJM-ISO, NY-ISO was based on an existing tight power pool. The ISO operates a bid-based power market that is very similar to the market in the PJM, whose prices vary by location to reflect transmission congestion. However, the New York markets also include competitive markets for operating reserves that are solved jointly with the spot electricity market. In this regard, the New York ISO currently operates the most complete set of power markets in the country. In addition to these markets, the New York ISO also issues and facilitates trading of financial transmission rights that are similar to those rights in PJM. These rights are very important due to their role in facilitating wholesale trading and allowing participants to hedge congestion costs.

Like the other ISOs, the New York ISO has filed to be granted RTO status by the FERC. However, FERC is currently considering the potential benefits of merging the Northeast ISOs into a single, larger RTO. The costs and benefits of such a requirement have been the subject of much debate and analysis.

## Midwest ISO

The nonprofit Midwest ISO (MISO) was founded in 1996 as a voluntary association of transmission owners. MISO has experienced fluctuating membership, with some members leaving to join the Alliance RTO. Unlike the Northeast, which is characterized by tight power pools, wholesale power in the Midwest is generally transacted bilaterally, with no centralized clearing market or centralized dispatch. MISO's responsibilities include maintaining OASIS information, calculating transmission capability, coordinating and scheduling requests for transmission service, and coordinating ancillary services. MISO planned to begin operation in early 2002. While it would not operate a spot market initially, it was developing a proposal to implement an auction market later that would resolve congestion and provide a settlement mechanism for imbalances.

### Alliance RTO

In December 1997, First Energy, Detroit Edison, and Consumers Power left the MISO to start their own ISO, the Alliance RTO. American Electric Power and Virginia Power joined later. While most RTOs are nonprofit entities, the Alliance RTO is seeking approval to become a for-profit RTO. FERC is currently considering the appropriate roles and functions for such an entity. By December 2000, nine additional members of MISO asked FERC for permission to leave MISO to join the Alliance RTO. Whether these petitions should be granted has become a hotly contested issue, with many arguing that the MISO and Alliance RTO should be merged into a single RTO. MISO and Alliance were forming separate RTOs, although recent decisions by FERC encourage the Alliance RTO to join with the MISO.

### The Southwest Power Pool

The Southwest Power Pool (SPP) was created in 1941 and now has fifty members. It serves customers in eight states. Even though the SPP describes itself as a power pool, it is not a tight, centrally administered power pool like the PJM-ISO, ISO-NE, and NY-ISO. Wholesale power purchases in the Southwest are bilateral, with no centralized

clearing site, power exchange, or centralized dispatch. It is mainly a group of utilities that share transmission interconnections to facilitate certain region-wide transfers. On October 13, 2000, SPP filed with the FERC seeking formal recognition as an RTO. In a separate filing, Entergy sought approval to transfer its transmission assets to a for-profit independent transmission company. Entergy also filed to have the transmission company operate under the management of the SPP, although it now seems likely that Entergy will join an organization in the Southeast and SPP will join MISO in some fashion.

### Electric Reliability Counsel of Texas (ERCOT) ISO

ERCOT is a bulk electric system, located completely within Texas, that handles about 85 percent of the electrical load within the state. FERC's jurisdiction over ERCOT is limited because the ERCOT system operates only within Texas and is largely isolated from the rest of the country. The Public Utility Commission of Texas (PUCT) created the ERCOT ISO in August 1996. The ISO has responsibility for the security of the ERCOT bulk power system, market facilitation (including operating the ERCOT OASIS), and coordination of transmission planning in ERCOT.

In May 1999, the Texas senate passed a bill that provides the framework for open access transmission and the implementation of retail competition. The effective date for retail choice was January 1, 2002, with some pilot programs beginning sooner. The PUCT decided not to establish a government-sanctioned power exchange, but instead chose to rely on bilateral contracts for power exchanges among distribution firms. While not creating a central market, the PUCT merged the nine ERCOT control areas into one ISO control area.

## Developments in the Southeast

The southeastern part of the United States has not moved forward with restructuring at the same pace as the Northeast, Midwest, and California. Part of the explanation for this is the low power costs in the Southeast (with the exception of Florida) and the perception that competitive benefits to consumers will not be as great as in the other parts of the country. There are two unique federal entities operating in the Southeast—the Tennessee Valley Authority (TVA) and the Southeastern Power Administration, which markets electric power generated at reservoirs owned by the U.S. Army Corps of Engineers. Certain federal restrictions on the activities of the TVA have been a barrier to the development of competitive markets in the Southeast. TVA has stated it is not required to file an open-access transmission tariff with the FERC, even though it provides comparable transmission service through its Transmission Service Guidelines.

In addition to the TVA transmission grid, there are three proposed RTOs in the region—GridSouth, the SeTrans Grid Company, and GridFlorida. All were proposed in RTO filings on October 16, 2000. GridSouth, a for-profit transmission company, will serve much of the Carolinas. The three GridSouth members would operate 22,000 miles of transmission lines, but would not operate a bid-based spot market. The Southern Company proposed SeTrans Grid Company as a for-profit transmission company that would operate transmission facilities in Alabama, Georgia, Mississippi, and Northern Florida, an area basically corresponding to the service areas of the Southern Company's operating subsidiaries. The proposed RTO would maintain a systemwide transmission tariff and be the sole provider of wholesale transmission service. The proposed GridFlorida RTO would be a for-profit transmission company that would be operated in peninsular Florida by the four public utilities that operate there.

## Developments in the West

The western grid covers fourteen states and is administered by one regional reliability council—the Western Systems Coordinating Council (WSCC). The WSCC is divided in turn into four subregions and thirty load control areas. With the exception of the California ISO, which is discussed separately below, RTO formation in this region is at the early stages and now includes two RTOs—Desert STAR and RTO West.

RTO West was proposed in October 2000 by nine electric utilities serving eight western states. Six of the utilities also decided to form an independent for-profit transmission company, TransConnect, that would own and operate the transmission assets of the utilities. The transmission company would in turn be a participant in the RTO. Desert STAR has a target date of late 2002 for commencing RTO operations. There were earlier activities that led to the proposed RTO West. Between 1996 and 1998, twenty-one utilities in the region worked to develop an independent grid operator named IndeGO. While an IndeGO proposal did not go forward to the FERC, the foundation was established for RTO West.

### California Markets

Restructuring in California began in 1994 with the California Public Utility Commission (CPUC) recommending far-reaching retail choice reforms. By 1996, these reforms were enacted into law by the California State Legislature and signed by Governor Pete Wilson. The California plan was aggressive and comprehensive, requiring several major structural changes. First, it created the California ISO (CAL-ISO) that would operate the transmission systems of the state's main three utilities: Pacific Gas & Electric (PGE), Southern California Edison (SCE), and San Diego Gas & Electric (SDGE). The ISO was given the responsibility for scheduling the delivery of power and also the authority to purchase short-term power for system reliability. A second main structural change was the strong incentives for the three main utilities to sell large portions of their generating assets. Since restructuring, the California utilities have sold more than two-thirds of their generating capacity to nonutility entities. The third major component of California restructuring was the creation of the California Power Exchange (CAL-PX). The CAL-PX was separate from the CAL-ISO and responsible for conducting a day-ahead auction for electricity.

Under the restructuring plan, PGE, SCE, and SDGE customers' rates were to be capped until that point in time when the utilities had recovered all of their "transition costs."[13] The utilities were under the obligation to procure generation supplies for these retail customers in the wholesale market using the CAL-PX. In fact, the restructuring plan required the three utilities to sell all of their generation output and purchase all of their requirements through the CAL-PX.[14] Other suppliers also sold into the CAL-PX, and some large buyers purchased power there. For the most part, however, it was anticipated that until large numbers of retail customers sought alternative power supply options through third parties, most customers would continue to purchase generation service from PGE, SCE, and SDGE under price caps.

The restructuring rules and mechanisms under California restructuring are numerous and complex. Stakeholders, the various parties connected to restructuring (like utilities, power marketers, and industrial and customer groups), designed them.

The processes, rules, regulations, and mechanisms were hammered out over many months of collaboration and were approved by the CPUC, the California legislature, the governor, and the FERC.

Despite the time and resources invested in designing these markets, the markets began to fail in 2001, the PX was closed, and the state began moving away from the model originally proposed. This started after sharp price "spikes" began to emerge during the summer of 2000, when prices at times in California shot up to over $800/MW per hour (MWh), compared to peak rates in the previous two summers of less than $100/MWh.

Later in 2000 and into 2001, dramatic rises in natural gas prices, supply shortages due to low rainfall in the west, sustained growth in load without significant investment in new supplies, and alleged withholding by some generators in California are likely to have contributed to sustained periods of very high prices. In addition, substantial flaws in the design of California markets contributed to these price spikes. Although the markets had operated relatively smoothly prior to this episode, market design flaws are much more visible and significant when the market is under stress (i.e., high demand, supply shortages, or both). These conditions were also exacerbated by the reluctance of out-of-state suppliers to make sales to the California utilities due to the utilities' poor credit rating.

The high wholesale prices were financially disastrous for SCE and PGE. The state's utilities agreed to sell power to retail customers at prices that were not to exceed retail caps, even though they had divested much of their generation and were required to purchase power from the CAL-PX. Hence, as power supply costs in the CAL-PX increased, PGE and SCE were purchasing their wholesale power at increasingly high prices, but had to sell it to retail customers at the lower, capped rate.[15] This started a downward spiral. As the wholesale PX price exceeded the retail cap, PGE and SCE began to incur a steady stream of losses that threatened their financial solvency. The precarious financial situation faced by PGE and SCE probably contributed to scarcity of supply as external generators began to worry that the utilities' financial situation could result in defaults on power supply liabilitites. As power supplies became scarce in spring 2001, interruptions in select parts of the transmission grid (called rolling blackouts) were required to prevent dangerous voltage drops and more widespread blackouts. PGE ultimately filed for bankruptcy protection.

The California experience has fundamentally slowed the industry restructuring process, particularly at the retail level among the states. However, substantial new generation facilities are being built and planned throughout the country. This, together with fairly well-behaved prices throughout the country during summer 2001, may signal that the industry is moving toward a long-run equilibrium—addressing those areas where investment failed to keep pace with load growth.

## Operation of Deregulated Markets

### General

Given the move toward deregulated electricity markets described above, some understanding of the common features of the deregulated markets and how these market structures might affect performance will conclude this overview of the industry. There are two standard characteristics of electricity markets that drive conclusions about how restructured markets might be expected to perform. From the demand-side, customers use electricity in significantly different amounts depending on the time of day, the day of week, and the season of the year. On the supply-side, because electricity is not storable, generating capacity of different types is required to stand ready to meet the fluctuating levels of demand. This results in the need to utilize a range of plants types in order to meet load efficiently.

For example, for the few hours when demand is at its peak, it is optimal to use peaking plants with high operating costs, but relatively low capital costs. In other hours, these plants are available as producers of operating reserves. Large plants with low operating costs, but which are expensive to build, are used during both peak-demand periods and off-peak periods. The additional capital required to build base-load plants with lower operating costs is justified, given the production cost savings that are achieved by running these units extensively.

From an operating perspective, the first decision that must be made is what units to "turn on" to meet demand over the next day or week, generally referred to as the "unit commitment" decision. The decision takes into account the start-up costs, the time required to start up, the amount of time the unit must run once it is on, and other factors. Like the investment decision described above, it may sometimes be optimal during lower-demand periods to rely on peaking generators with higher operating costs but low start-up costs to meet the peak demand for the day—saving the relatively high start-up costs of one of the base-load units. Given the unit commitment decision, the optimal "dispatch" of the various types of on-line capacity to meet fluctuating load is accomplished by operating plants in ascending order of marginal cost as demand grows. This is known as merit-order dispatch. As explained below, this dispatch is optimal regardless of the capital costs associated with each unit. This principle of merit-order dispatch guided the dispatch of the utilities' own generation prior to restructuring. But, as explained further below, a merit-order dispatch should also occur in a deregulated regional market where suppliers compete to serve load.

### Restructured Markets

There are a number of common features across the various restructured electricity markets in the United States. Primarily, of course, they share the goal of using market forces to improve performance by facilitating better trading, generation, and consumption decisions in the short run and investment decisions in the long run. This goal has been pursued following two common themes. First, market designs have sought to align power production with load efficiently as well as to ensure safe and reliable operation of the transmission system. Hence, market structures and rules were developed to facilitate buying and selling electricity to satisfy demand and to provide "ancillary services" (such as operating reserves) that ensure transmission security. These market structures generally include the use of auctions for accomplishing these objectives, as described below. A second common theme in restructured electricity markets has been reliance on market monitoring and certain restrictions on bidding practices in the auction markets. These provisions are designed to ensure that newly created wholesale markets operate competitively and efficiently.

### Market Structure

The fundamental issues that determine market performance relate to the basic structure of the market and the behavior of participants in the market. Economists use the term market structure to refer to the essential demand and supply attributes of a particular market. Key market-structure characteristics on the supply side include the

number of firms operating in a market, the relative sizes of these rivals, and the production costs of the units controlled by each supplier. On the demand side, key variables include the degree to which demand responds to price (price elasticity) and the degree to which the product is durable and/ or storable. In some markets, explicit rules defining the interaction of buyers and sellers are established. For example the market for stock equities is conducted in accordance with rules and regulations designed by the New York Stock exchange, the NASDAQ, and a number of regional and international exchanges. Likewise, many commodity products are bought and sold through formal market mechanisms.

In restructured electricity markets, a substantial portion of the wholesale trading of electricity occurs through forward contracts–generally bilateral agreements between market participants. However, due to the costs and information problems associated with trading efficiently in very short time frames, spot markets are increasingly relying on auctions or other formal market mechanisms to govern spot trading. In fact, recent decisions by the FERC indicate that they will likely require RTOs to implement standardized auction-based spot markets.

### Wholesale Electricity Auctions

The general market mechanism that has been used in the design of spot electricity markets is an auction that sets market-clearing prices in time frames ranging from five minutes to one hour. The prices that emerge from these auctions provide transparency and are referred to as market-clearing prices because they are the price at which all offers to sell and bids to purchase have been satisfied. In other words, no additional sales or purchases are possible given the bid prices of the suppliers and demand. In most cases, demand is relatively fixed in the spot market since wholesale purchases are typically made by utilities on behalf of customers whose electricity consumption is beyond the utilities' control. Hence, the market-clearing price will generally equal the highest bid accepted to meet the demand.

In simplified auctions that do not reflect the realities of the transmission network, a single clearing price is established for the entire market (e.g., the spot market facilitated by the ISO New England). However, it is now widely acknowledged that it is much more efficient for the auction markets to incorporate the limits of the transmission network by setting market-clearing prices that vary by location.

These locational prices are market-clearing prices that reflect the marginal costs to the system of serving load at each location. Hence, the locational prices implicitly reveal the economic value of transmission congestion on the system. In the short run, locational prices provide accurate incentives for generators to operate when needed to resolve transmission constraints. In the long run, the locational prices provide efficient signals to investors regarding where to build new generation or transmission facilities.

## Incentives in Wholesale Electricity Auctions

When suppliers lack market power—having no ability to affect market-clearing prices—the clearing-price auction structure gives each supplier the incentive to offer its resources at their marginal costs. A supplier's marginal costs are the total costs of producing additional output.[16] Clearly, if the supplier will receive a higher clearing price than its incremental cost of producing, then it should realize the additional profit by producing. This margin earned by the generating units in hours that they are running allow them to cover their fixed costs of remaining in operation, as well as the investment costs for new generators. Competitive markets will create efficient incentives for investment in new generation when supplies become scarce or when new generating technologies can enter to displace older, less-efficient existing generation. As this investment cycle continues, the competitive market prices should converge to a long-run equilibrium at levels that will sustain investment in the least-cost new generator.

## Market Power in Wholesale Electricity Markets

When suppliers respond to these incentives by bidding their marginal costs, the spot market will produce an efficient dispatch of the generating resources. However, the predicate that suppliers lack market power does not always hold. For example, transmission constraints can isolate relatively small areas with limited competition. In some cases, individual generators must run to satisfy the requirements of the system. These conditions create a relatively extreme form of market power since the bids of the "must-run" generator must be accepted. However, market conditions may also result in less extreme forms of market power.

Since the benefits that are expected from deregulation are predicated on vigorous competition in the emerging electricity markets, policies to detect and address potential market power issues have become important. In general, strategies to raise prices by exercising market power would involve withholding generating resources from the market in one of two ways. First, a supplier may physically withhold its supplies from the market by simply not allowing them to operate. Second, a supplier may economically withhold the resource by substantially raising its bid in an auction-based spot market above its marginal costs.

In both cases, the withholding will cause the output of lower-cost resources to be replaced by higher-cost resources. Under most market conditions, substantial resources with similar marginal costs are available so that the market price is not significantly affected—that is, the supply is relatively elastic. However, under other conditions, withholding may cause resources with significantly higher bids to be dispatched, resulting in a concomitant increase in the market-clearing price.

Economic withholding can be effectively addressed by applying a bid cap to suppliers that limits their ability to raise their bid prices when market conditions would otherwise allow them to exercise market power. Each of the northeastern ISOs that conducts an auction-based spot market employs some form of bid cap to address economic withholding. One advantage of the bid cap is that it allows the auction to continue to function without restricting legitimate price fluctuations. For example, in periods of shortage when prices must rise substantially to clear the market, a generator-specific bid cap will not hinder these price movements.

Physical withholding is somewhat more difficult to address effectively. While economic withholding can be detected and remedied in real time, physical withholding can be identified only after the fact. A generator that is not running when it would appear to be economic to do so can often be explained by legitimate technical or economic justifications. These justifications can be evaluated only ex post facto, and therefore the only available remedy is some form of penalty. The level of such penalties must be high enough to serve as an effective deterrent against attempts to withhold resources physically.

Of course, any remedies designed to address economic or physical withholding are inferior to structural solutions that would remove the incentive of suppliers to withhold generating resources. Examples of structural solutions include divestiture of generation to increase the number of effective competitors, and upgrading the transmission system to expand the import capability into constrained areas of the network. However, because these structural solutions may not be possible in all cases or politically feasible, market monitoring and market power mitigation will continue to be a key RTO function.

## Conclusions

This chapter has described an industry in the midst of a dramatic shift from regulation to competition at both the wholesale and retail levels. In fact, meaningful competition at the wholesale level is a necessary prerequisite for establishing competitive retail markets. However, the development of regional transmission organizations and other institutions necessary to facilitate vigorous competition at the wholesale level has met with varying degrees of success. These institutions are generally at a relatively formative stage, and substantial additional development is needed. FERC is attempting to accelerate this development through a number of regulatory initiatives. Most important, it is attempting to do this by using the lessons that have been learned through the successes and failures of the current ISOs to develop standardized guidelines for the wholesale markets emerging nationwide.

At the retail level, deregulation is proceeding at different rates across the various states. The California experience has caused many states to take a much more cautious approach to deregulation. However because electricity markets are generally regional markets, successful retail competition may need to be predicated on a consistent regional approach to deregulation. For this reason, numerous attempts have been made at the federal level to develop legislation that would establish a common framework for retail deregulation. However, efforts to develop and pass such legislation have yet to be successful.

## Notes

1. Residential and small commercial customers have power delivered at 220 volts while commercial and industrial customers take power at higher voltages, depending on the intended use. Some large industrial customers, like steel mills or railroads, sometimes "take delivery" at transmission voltages.

2. A smaller amount of electricity is provided by public power—publicly-owned municipal and cooperative utilities. These utilities are run by local municipal governments or by cooperative organizations that are basically nonprofit and self-regulated.

3. In the case of utilities, there are a number of other regulatory interventions that occur. We focus here primarily on price regulation. Utilities, like a large number of other industries, are also subject to other types of regulatory intervention such as air and water quality protections, standard labor laws, and local zoning laws.

4. Cost-of-service regulation is still prevalent in most aspects of utility regulation. The move toward restructuring was an effort to inject more market-based mechanisms into the generation sector. Traditional cost-of-service principles still largely apply to transmission and distribution.

5. See *Nebbia v. New York* (291 U.S. 502), at 536–37: "[T]he phrase 'affected with the public interest' can, in the nature of things, mean no more than that an industry, for adequate reason, is subject to control for the public good."

6. See G. Stigler, "The Theory of Economic Regulation," *Bell Journal of Economics and Management Science* 2, no. 1 (Spring 1971): 3–21; S. Peltzman, "Toward a More General Theory of Regulation," *Journal of Law and Economics* 19 (August 1976): 211–40.

7. In many important instances, retail customers buy power from publicly owned utilities. For example, the Los Angeles Department of Water and Power is a city-owned utility. Retail rates for these entities are generally set by the utility itself. Of course, in such a case the utility is run by the city government, which can intervene at a political level to correct any perceived problems. Many electricity consumers in the Tennessee Valley receive power produced by the Tennessee Valley Authority (TVA) that is not subject to state regulation. The TVA operates under guidelines developed by the federal government.

8. There were very high profile and contentious regulatory cases in 1960s and 1970s over the regulatory wisdom of building nuclear plants.

9. Expenditures on rate-base items are accumulated in the plant accounts, and the amount in the plant accounts is assumed to be paid over a number of years by way of depreciation and/or amortization expenses. The depreciation rate is supposed to correspond to the useful life of the capital asset to which it applies. This of course can create further controversy when opinions differ as to what constitutes useful life. Ultimately regulators approve the depreciation and amortization rates.

10. See H. Averch and L. Johnson, "Behavior of the Firm Under Regulatory Constraint," *American Economic Review* 52 (December 1962): 1052–69

11. In some power pools, referred to as "tight" power pools, many of the operational and planning responsibilities are centrally administered. Other power pools, organized more loosely, are referred to as "loose" power pools.

12. The laws of physics that describe how electricity flows in an interconnected network are known as Kirkoff's Laws.

13. Transition costs consisted of so-called stranded costs, which are capital costs that utilities claimed would be unrecoverable in competitive markets. Under regulation, electricity rates included the costs of operating power plants and also the costs of building and maintaining them (capital costs). The utilities claimed they could not recover all of their operating and capital costs if they were forced to compete at market rates. Therefore, the restructuring plan allowed much of the outstanding capital cost to be recovered through a fixed "transition charge" on all customers' bills regardless of whom the customer purchased its power supplies from. As long as these transition charges were in effect, the plan required retail customers' rates to be capped.

14. Because the restructuring legislation induced substantial generation divestiture, the utilities no longer retained enough generation to serve all of their retail customers. Therefore, their purchases from the PX are substantially higher than their sales into it.

15. In accordance with the restructuring plan, SDGE is no longer under a price cap since it no longer collects a transition charge.

16. Marginal costs include the generator's variable costs, as well as other costs such as environmental costs associated with emission limits or other restrictions, costs of lost opportunities to sell in other markets or future time periods, maintenance costs, and incremental risks the generator may face when operating at very high levels.

## Suggested Readings

Kahn, Alfred E. *The Economics of Regulation—Principles and Institutions.* Cambridge, MA: MIT Press, 1998. A comprehensive treatment of issues encountered throughout the history of regulatory institutions.

Kwoka jr., John E. *Power Structure—Ownership, Integration, and Competition in the Electric Utility Industry.* Boston: Kluwer, 1996. A multifaceted statistical study of utility costs that sheds light on how costs are affected by ownership structure, regulations, and other market factors.

Chao, Hung-po, and Hillard G. Huntingdon, eds. *Designing Competitive Electricity Markets.* Boston: Kluwer, 1998. Essays providing details about a variety of market design concepts that are being developed and used in the restructured electric utility industry.

# 10

# Health Insurance

## Designing Products to Reduce Costs

*Lee R. Mobley and H.E. Frech III*

A health insurer contracts to pay all or a portion of bills for medical services deemed "necessary" in return for a fixed premium. Consumers demand this service because it reduces risk. The cost of this service is the difference between the premium and the expected benefits, which is known in the industry as the loading charge. The degree of competition affects the size of the loading charge and the amount of innovation insurers will undertake to minimize the administrative costs that underlie it.

But efficiency in the provision of health insurance involves more than just minimizing administrative costs. Insurance also profoundly affects the rate of use and price of health services. When much of the cost of medical services is covered by insurance, more services will be used and patients will devote less effort to seeking providers with lower prices. These harmful effects of insurance on the provision and pricing of medical care services have led insurers to design policies to lessen its impact. These policies have included increasing the use of deductibles and coinsurance and, more recently, selective contracting between insurers and medical providers and extensive review of the medical necessity of services. The degree of competition in the health insurance market influences how much insurers use such policies. Thus the degree of competition affects not only

the resources that go into administering insurance but, much more important, it affects the resources that go into medical services.

Up until about the early 1980s, insurers largely ignored their adverse impact on medical costs. Since then, the health insurance market has become more competitive and, partly as a result, cost-containment efforts have increased markedly. In the first section of this study, we discuss the health insurance market in the early days, up to about 1980. In the following sections, we stress changes since 1980 that have made insurance markets more competitive. We conclude with some thoughts on what the market will be like in the future.

### The Early Days, Up to About 1980: Traditional Insurance Firms

In the United States, both public and private firms provide health insurance. The public providers are Medicare (federal health insurance for the elderly) and Medicaid (federal and state insurance for the poor and disabled). In the recent past, two major types of firms sold most U.S. private health insurance—commercial insurers and nonprofit organizations. First were the commercial health insurers, both profit seeking and mutual, who made up about half of the private insurance market in 1975. The other half of the

Figure 10.1 **Persons Covered by Blue Cross/Blue Shield (BCBS) and Commercial Insurers, Expressed as a Proportion of the Total Number of Persons with Private Insurance Protection, 1970–1996**

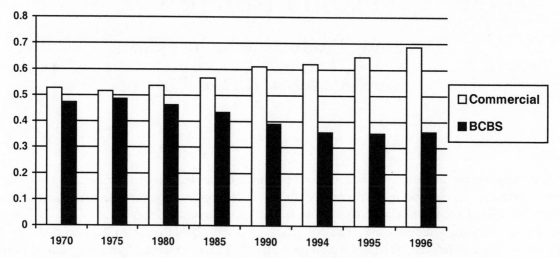

*Source*: Health Insurance Association of America, *Source Book of Health Insurance Data, 1999/2000*, p. 39.

market was covered by the mostly nonprofit Blue Cross and Blue Shield insurance.

The commercial market was populated by hundreds of firms, none of which had a market share of more than 1 or 2 percent. Entry was easy, and firms entered (and exited) at a high rate. Concentration ratios among the commercial firms were comparatively low.[1] As over 85 percent of individuals insured for hospital expenses were covered under group policies, it is probable that informed buyers dominated the market. Indeed, it is best to think of the commercial insurers as competitively providing a schedule of prices for various types of insurance. The consumer (or more commonly a union or employer representative) chose from this competitively determined schedule. Thus, the commercial part of the market seemed to be characterized by conditions favorable to competitive behavior. However, as we discuss below, competitive conditions varied

considerably across geographic regions, depending upon the degree of local dominance by the Blue Cross and Blue Shield plans.

In 1975, the other half of the industry comprised the Blue Cross and Blue Shield plans. The Blue Cross plans were organized by hospitals to provide hospital insurance, and the Blue Shield plans were organized by physicians to provide physician services insurance. The Blues were organized (and largely still are) as legally nonprofit public service firms. These firms were controlled by boards of directors with heavy representation of hospital and physician interests, in contrast to nonprofit mutual insurers that are nominally controlled by the policyholders. In many cases, the original boards of directors were completely controlled by hospitals or doctors. Typically, the Blues were organized under special enabling acts so that additional entry was not allowed. Thus, Blue Cross/ Blue Shield plans had considerable market power by about 1975. This contrasted sharply with the field of commercial insurance, where entry was relatively easy and common (Figure 10.1).

There were two sources of market power for the Blues. First, they were regulated and taxed more favorably than their competitors. Second, for both historical and continuing reasons, the Blues could often obtain discounts from doctors and hospitals that were greater than those of their competitors.[2]

One might expect these regulatory and discount advantages to lead to a complete monopoly for the Blue plans, but this is not what one observes. Rather than a steady increase in market share for the Blues, what one observes in fact is a long period of stability, followed by a recent trend toward declining market shares. The Blues' combined share of the national private health insurance market was quite stable from about 1940 to about 1975, hovering near 50 percent. Based on the percentage of people covered, it slowly declined to about 36 percent by 1994.

There are several explanations for the fact that the Blues did not come to monopolize insurance markets. One is that it was more convenient for employers to deal with one insurance firm or agent for all of their insurance needs. This would give an advantage to commercial insurers, who usually sell many types of insurance. Also, the regulatory advantages conferred on the Blue plans were used to "purchase" two items of value to those controlling and influencing the plans. The first was administrative slack/inefficiency. Second, the absence of a residual claimant and consequent pointlessness of earning a profit meant that the cost of these nonpecuniary aspects of compensation was low.[3]

The second item purchased was more complete insurance. While the Blues' all-or-nothing pricing did induce some consumers to purchase overly complete insurance, others chose to purchase a policy with more cost-sharing and could purchase such insurance only from commercial insurers. Commercial insurers survived largely because (1) their Blue competitors were inefficient and (2) the Blues left a portion of the market to them by refusing to sell insurance with large consumer copayment.

### The Impact of Blue Cross/Blue Shield Market Power on Medical Care Costs

The effect of the high market power of Blue Cross and Blue Shield is more serious than one might think, because of the linkage of the policies of the Blue plans to the cost of health care. The Blues had leverage in affecting medical care costs. The traditional Blue plans preferred more complete insurance with less consumer cost sharing (such as deductibles and coinsurance). There are two reasons for this.

First, more complete insurance raises the demand for medical care. The medical providers who controlled or influenced the Blue plans obtained higher revenues as a result. A second reason for the preference of the Blue plans for complete insurance was ideology—the belief that there should be no "financial barriers" to medical care. Howard Berman, a former vice president of the American Hospital Association (which controlled the Blue Cross trademark until recently) put it this way:

> As a matter of philosophy, Blue Cross Plans have from the outset been committed to provision of service benefits and comprehensive benefits. This commitment is . . . one of the factors that distinguishes Blue Cross Plans from commercial insurers. . . . There is no question that this is the Blue Cross Plan goal.[4]

The mechanism by which more complete insurance was induced is a special kind of discriminatory price—an all-or-nothing price. Consumers were confronted with an attractive price because of the regulatory advantages, but only very complete insurance was offered. One could not buy the entire possible menu of insurance plans from the Blues. Large deductibles (say $1,000 to $5,000) were especially rare.

The Blues' practice of promoting policies with minimal cost-sharing led to a lower level of cost-sharing in the overall market. Many consumers were led to purchase plans that included less cost-sharing than the plans they would have purchased otherwise, because the Blues offered an attractive premium for plans with full coverage.

## Moral Hazard: Insurance Raises Use

Economists have criticized the use of overly complete insurance because of its subsidy effect. When the patient pays only a small fraction of the cost of medical care, there is an inducement to utilize more care and pay a higher price for it. Consumers wind up demanding medical care that has less value to them than it costs to produce. This is called the moral hazard effect (i.e., encouraging wasteful behavior) of insurance. It is a problem for all types of insurance, but a worse problem for health insurance than for most.

Most insurance offers an objectively fixed dollar payment contingent on a loss. Often the dollar payment is equal to the value of the loss. For example, automobile collision insurance pays the value of the loss as determined by claims adjusters and estimates from body shops. The consumer is free to use the insurance payment to do whatever seems best. The consumer may decide to fix the car completely or partially or to replace it. The insurance payment is not conditional on what he or she chooses.

Health insurance is different because there is no objective way to determine the magnitude of the loss incurred by the patient. Instead, the insurance pays all or part of the cost of the health care.

The insurance payment reduces the effective price of the health care to the consumer. Thus, the consumer slides down the demand curve, demanding more at the lower effective price. This subsidy causes consumers to buy more health care, including some health care that is worth far less to them than it costs to produce.

Given the moral hazard problem, there is an optimal extent of insurance coverage (less than 100 percent coverage) that balances the moral hazard welfare (i.e., the well-being of the group) loss of more insurance against the risk-reduction benefits of more insurance. In a completely free, competitive, and undistorted market, consumers would purchase such optimal insurance.[5] The problem for the health care economy is that there are two major distortions pushing consumers in the direction of excessively complete health insurance. The first is the tax treatment of health insurance. Employer payments for health insurance are deductible as costs of doing business. At the same time, these payments are not taxable as income to employees. Thus, there is a tax subsidy toward purchasing more health insurance equal to the sum of the federal and state marginal income tax rates. This is a large subsidy, varying from 28 to about 50 percent.[6] The second distortion is the market power of the Blue Cross/Blue Shield plans, which attempts to promote even more complete health insurance.

Phelps states that the health sector could be about 10 to 20 percent smaller without the tax subsidy for health insurance, which is equivalent to about 1 to 2 percent of the gross national product.[7] Feldstein has studied the problem of the U.S. consumer who has excessively complete health insurance and estimates a welfare loss in the billions of dollars from the use of overly complete health insurance.[8] Since the Blue plans induce purchase of more complete insurance, consumer welfare losses of overinsurance are exacerbated.

## Consumer Choice and Search: Insurance Raises Prices

Health insurance reduces the incentives for consumers to search for and choose low-priced physicians and hospitals. Because of the insurance coverage, most of the savings from searching out and choosing the low-price provider accrue to the insurer, not to the consumer. This effect is at its worst for 100 percent coverage. All the benefits from the choice of a low-price seller benefit the insurer entirely, not the consumer who must perform the search and make the choice. These consumers will rationally select the most preferred doctors and hospitals, regardless of cost. Furthermore, they cannot be wooed away by price competition. Indeed, there can be no price competition at all for consumers with such insurance.

The moral hazard effect of insurance is still strong for the popular 20 percent coinsurance plan. Here, for each $100 saved by seeking out a low-price provider, the insurer keeps $80 of the savings, while the consumer obtains only $20. Even though coinsurance improves incentives when compared to full coverage, the incentives are still weak.

Only one type of traditional health insurance preserves correct incentives for consumer search and choice of low-price providers. This is the type sometimes called indemnity insurance (though the term is used loosely and inconsistently). Here, the benefit is a fixed dollar amount per unit of service. As long as the benefit amount is set below most providers' prices, the consumer keeps the entire gain if he or she finds a less expensive provider. If the consumer finds and chooses a doctor who charges $100 less for a procedure, he or she keeps the entire difference. Consumers with no insurance also have such ideal incentives.

Consider the impact of health insurance on the degree of price competition among doctors and hospitals. When customers have more complete coverage, the provider has less incentive to reduce price. The price-cutter will pick up a few new customers who will switch, but only a few. On the other hand, if the provider raises price above competitive levels, he or she will lose only a few customers. Thus, traditional health insurance reduces the incentives for providers to compete on price. This is a major reason that health care is so costly.

Another link between insurer market power and medical care costs is through restrictions on administrative cost-control activities. Lawrence G. Goldberg and Warren Greenberg documented the successful efforts of the Oregon Blue Shield to stop commercial insurers from controlling costs through an activist claims review process.[9]

Some observers (most notably Landes) clearly believe that the Blue Cross/Blue Shield system is procompetitive because it raises the output of health insurance.[10] This, in turn, raises the output of health care. In most industries, this would indeed indicate a procompetitive influence. However, in health care, the problem for both the private sector and for public policy is that many people have too much insurance coverage and consume too much medical care, not too little. Competition among insurers mostly takes the form of trying to reduce medical care use and insurance coverage, while retaining the risk-reducing benefits of insurance. Thus, procompetitive developments in health insurance would reduce output, the reverse of the usual case. The social problem of less competition among insurers is precisely that it increases output for those people who are insured.

## Modern Trends, Since About 1980: New Forms of Insurance

In the mid-1970s, traditional insurance (commercial insurances and the Blues) covered about 93

Figure 10.2   **Managed Care Plans (HMOs and PPOs) as a Percentage of the Private Group Insurance Business**

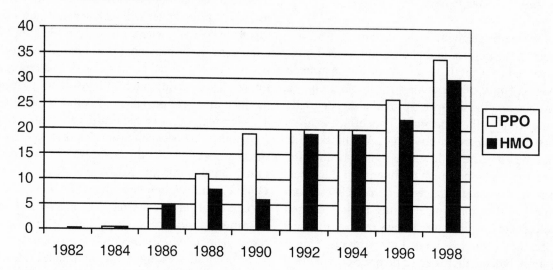

*Source*: Health Insurance Association of America, annual issues of *Source Book of Health Insurance Data,* 1992 to 1999/2000.

percent of those people who were privately insured. Almost all of the remaining 7 percent were covered by health maintenance organizations (HMOs) and preferred provider organizations (PPOs). By 1994, the HMO and PPO plans provided serious competition to the traditional insurances, serving almost 40 percent of privately insured individuals; this grew to almost 90 percent by the year 2000 (Figure 10.2).

The insurance market has changed dramatically in recent years. Newer organizations such as PPOs have begun to transform the nature of fee-for-service health insurance, and HMOs have become a more significant part of the health insurance market. The PPOs and HMOs greatly alter the incentives and the type of competition observed in the market.

Another change is that most large employers are now self-insured. When an employer self-insures, it typically hires either an insurer or a firm specializing in claims processing—known as a third-party administrator—to process claims. So the term "self-insurance" is a misnomer. The employee is still insured by someone else, not by himself or herself. But the risk is borne by the employer or union group rather than an insurance company.) Although many employers use commercial insurers and Blue Cross/Blue Shield plans as administrators, insurers must compete with third-party administrators (TPAs) for employer business. Employers have taken a more active interest in the benefit structure and administration of their plans. More important, self-insurance is a means of avoiding costly state regulations of private insurance coverage.

Because most of the nonelderly population is insured through employment-based group policies, the rising cost of medical care has been felt by employers as insurance premiums have increased. Between 1970 and 1980, the amount of insurance

Figure 10.3  **Growth Rate (Annual Percent Change) in Group Health Insurance Premiums**

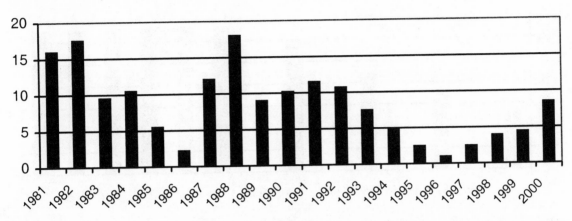

*Source*: Health Insurance Association of America, *Source Book of Health Insurance Data, 1992*, p. 29; Prospective Payment Assessment Commission, *Medicare and the American Health Care System: Report to Congress, June 1996*, p. 19; J. Gabel et al., "Job-Based Health Insurance in 2000: Premiums Rise Sharply While Coverage Grows," *Health Affairs* 19, no. 5 (2000): 144–151.

premiums paid by U.S. employers for group insurance policies rose 352 percent. During the mid-1980s, premium increases averaged 6 to 8 percent annually, but by 1990 they again reached double-digit levels, dipped in the mid-nineties, and then increased again by 2000 (Figure 10.3).

In order to slow premium growth, employers have shifted employees from traditional insurance plans into managed care plans, with premiums 9 to 12 percent lower. Most employers continue to offer traditional insurance as a choice among insurance plans for employees, but many are dropping this option. Also, employers are increasing consumer cost-sharing to control the moral hazard that causes premiums to rise over time. To do this, employers have increased the share of the premium paid by employees, and raised coinsurance and deductibles.[11] These recent changes in insurance have made insurance markets more competitive and were somewhat successful in slowing the growth rate in group health insurance premi-

ums in the nineties, although the recent upswing in premiums is troubling. As discussed below, anticompetitive legislative acts, such as insurance mandates, may have contributed to rising premiums in the late 1990s.

## Managed Care

Increased cost sharing is a simple and reliable way to reduce health benefit costs, but it has not been the only method of cost containment used by third-party payers. Insurers and employers are increasingly using administrative mechanisms to review the appropriateness of use of services. One technique that is now common is preadmission certification, a procedure that determines, before hospitalization, whether a hospital stay is appropriate. Many plans also review individual cases during a hospital stay to limit time in the hospital. Some plans require second opinions for surgery. Some insurers have given administrators discre-

Figure 10.4 **National Health Expenditures as a Percent of GDP**

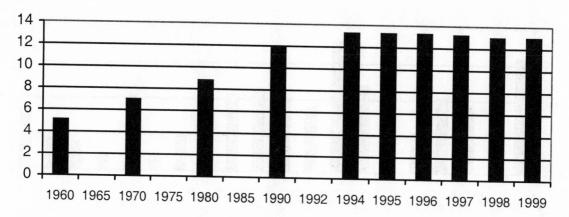

*Source:* Health Care Financing Administration Web site: <http://www.HCFA.gov/stats> (June 2001).

tion on a case-by-case basis to expand coverage to new services for a specific case if there is a likelihood of reducing overall treatment costs for a patient. These activities are called managed care.

These other cost-containment methods, along with increased cost-sharing, have apparently been effective in containing rising health care costs. The growth of spending on health care as a percentage of gross domestic product (GDP) rose steadily from 5.1 percent in 1960 to about 12.2 percent in 1990, causing considerable alarm and generating the impetus to better manage health care spending. In the 1990s, national health expenditures leveled off at about 13.2 percent of GDP, as Figure 10.4 shows, and industry experts attribute this new stability to the spread of managed care practices. (A quick glance back at Figure 10.2 shows that managed care insurances really became a significant force in the 1990s.)

National savings from managed care practices derive from several sources: (1) relatively slower growth in managed care premiums, (2) reduction in premiums for other insurers competing with managed care plans, and (3) slowing in the adop-

tion of cost-increasing medical technology. These savings are so large that the estimated cost of eliminating managed care would be about $329 billion between 2002 and 2005, which translates into about $3,600 per household. This is about 8 percent of private health insurance costs. In addition, about 6.4 million people would lose medical insurance, through premium increases, if managed care were eliminated.[12]

Traditional insurance plans have responded to the new competition from managed care plans by developing their own managed care plans (for example, the Blue Cross and Blue Shield plans had 78.7 million enrollees in managed care plans in 2000, as compared to industry giant Aetna U.S. Healthcare, at 19 million enrollees).[13] Traditional insurances have also adopted many managed care techniques to control costs in their traditional plans, techniques such as utilization review, preadmission screening, and use of financial incentives to encourage people to use more efficient physicians and hospitals. Insurers have moved quickly to develop the ability to provide these services, often by purchasing small firms that already had such expertise. Indeed, the effectiveness of managed care, which is much more difficult to measure than other aspects of an insurer's services, enables insurers to differentiate their products more than in the past.

Increased product differentiation is usually thought to reduce the competitiveness of a market, but in the case of managed care, other factors work in the opposite direction. Managed care services might reduce the importance of Blue Cross regulatory advantages. For example, a commercial firm that pays a higher premium tax might still attract business through superior cost control. Moreover, managed care does not have to be bundled with the health insurance product. As long as the employer is large enough to be experience-rated (or self-insured), managed care services do not have to be purchased from the insurer. Instead, the employer can hire utilization management firms to perform these services, and the employer can benefit directly from reduced claims. The ability to split managed care from traditional insurance services limits any reduction in competition that might result from product differentiation. The growth of managed care insurance has made the insurance market more competitive and has reduced the overall costs of insurance. Managed care increases administrative costs, but this is more than compensated for by a reduction of insurance-induced overuse of services. Overall costs have declined substantially.[14]

### Health Maintenance Organizations

Health maintenance organizations combine the insurer with the doctors and hospitals to eliminate the moral hazard incentive to overuse medical care that is inherent in traditional third-party insurance.[15] Profits for HMOs are higher if fewer services are provided, since revenue comes from premium payments made in advance. Thus, the HMO's incentive to supply fewer services opposes the HMO subscriber's incentive to demand many services because the out-of-pocket price is zero or near zero. Health maintenance organizations restrain utilization by nonprice rationing. The necessity of competing for members in the future prevents HMOs from providing too few services.

The recent growth of HMOs has been rapid (see Figure 10.2). They increased their market share from just 0.3 percent in 1982 to about 19 percent in 1994, with the greatest gain occurring in the latter half of the period. By 2000, HMOs served about 43.5 percent of the private group market. This growth has increased the competitiveness of the health insurance market in several ways. First, the growth of HMOs means that additional competitors have entered the market. These new competitors are particularly valuable for competition because many of them come from backgrounds other than traditional health insurance and because they have introduced a different product into the market. Because of their ability to channel patients to providers with whom they contract, even HMOs with small market shares have been able to negotiate substantial discounts.

Empirical evidence from as early as 1987 shows that employers whose employees chose HMOs as their health insurance paid substantially lower premiums, and that there was a lower profit margin on HMO insurance. This means that HMOs were a significant competitive force in health insurance markets by the late 1980s.[16]

Pressure from HMOs has led to competitive responses from traditional insurers. First, insurers have become more innovative in the design of traditional policies by developing PPOs and introducing managed care into traditional insurance policies. These responses have worked to reduce the quantity- and price-increasing effects of health insurance. Second, some of the larger traditional insurers have gone into the HMO business. Insurers bring to the HMO business access to capital, underwriting and claims processing experience, and extensive marketing organizations. Insurer entries to the HMO market have accelerated the growth of HMOs, thus magnifying the competitive impact of this development.

### Self-Insurance and Third-Party Administrators

While the insurance industry has become more competitive and many new products have been developed to meet employers' demand for more consumer cost-sharing and slower premium growth, consumer and physician groups have retaliated against managed care. Most states have passed laws that regulate the health insurance industry, mandating coverage and conditions for competition within the state.[17] These regulations hinder the ability of markets to produce the full range of insurance products that are demanded.

Large employers that are self-insured are exempt from state insurance regulation under the Federal Employee Retirement Income Security Act (ERISA) of 1974. Thus, large firms may avoid the market regulations by covering employees with group insurance plans designed specifically for their employee pool. Self-insurance is attractive because of improved cash management (employers pay claims directly rather than paying a premium in advance), exemption from state insurance regulation (both premium taxes and restrictions on benefit structures), and increased control over the design of the health benefit plan.

Being able to avoid the state regulations by custom-designing insurance for employees gives these firms a cost advantage over firms that purchase regulated insurance. This advantage has induced many more firms to self-insure than would otherwise be the case. By 1990, about 58 percent of all group coverage was through self-insured plans; in 1980 this was less than 25 percent.[18]

Increased use of self-insurance increases the competitiveness of the insurance market in several ways. First, as employers gain more control over their plans, cost-containment initiatives are likely to be incorporated more rapidly. The ability to pursue a benefit structure with cost-sharing is facilitated, since the Blue Cross/Blue Shield advantage based on exemption from premium taxes is eliminated. Second, self-insurance has opened the insurance market to an additional type of competitor, the third party administrator. The entry of this new type of competitor is providing an additional spur to competition and innovation with group insurance.

### Preferred Provider Organizations

Preferred provider organizations are contracts among insurers (or TPAs), providers, and consumers. The providers agree to serve PPO consumers on preferential terms, offering a lower price and agreeing to cooperate with utilization review restrictions. In turn, consumers are given financial incentives (such as reduced coinsurance and additional covered services) to favor PPO providers. For the PPO to be successful, a significant number of patients must change their source of medical care to preferred providers.

Preferred provider organization contracts can be additional provisions in traditional insurance policies or separate special policies. In either case, a lower premium or coverage of additional services can be used as an incentive. Preferred provider organizations differ from HMOs in that services from providers outside of the preferred panel are still covered (though with more cost-sharing) and providers are not usually at risk for the volume of services used by patients.

The ability to receive some payment for care received from nonplan providers is a significant attraction of the PPO plan. Observing this, some HMOs are experimenting with partial coverage of care received from providers who are not members of the HMO. If this catches on, it will probably make the HMOs more attractive in the market, but it will blur the distinction between HMOs and PPOs.

Preferred provider organizations reduce the tendency of insurance to raise prices of medical services. They not only provide an acceptable way for consumers to be given incentives to choose a low-priced, low-cost provider, but facilitate the consumer's search process by providing a directory of preferred providers. Through utilization review, PPOs also often reduce the impact of insurance on the use of services.

The development of PPOs has proceeded rapidly from their inception in the early 1970s. By 1988, PPOs insured about 11 percent of those with group insurance. By 1994, this had grown to about 20 percent, and by 2000, to about 45.3 percent, almost the same share as held by HMOs (see Figure 10.2). This rapid development made the market for health insurance more competitive. The entrance of PPOs has allowed new entrants, such as TPAs, to build market share. Preferred provider organizations have also lessened the importance of the traditional discounts of Blue Cross/Blue Shield plans. A superior PPO can give an employer a good reason to switch insurers.

### Declining Tax and Regulatory Advantages of Blue Cross/Blue Shield

The tax advantages of the Blues have been eroding. As budgets tightened, governments questioned whether public policy goals were being accomplished with the foregone tax revenue. In 1986 the federal government sharply curtailed the exemption of the Blues from federal income tax. State governments have increasingly monitored the public service activities that the plans perform and have insisted on minimum levels of activity if tax advantages are to be retained. A few Blue plans have concluded that the costs of public service activities they are expected to undertake exceed the resources available from tax advantages and have reincorporated as mutual or commercial insurers.

There has also been a trend toward Blue Cross/ Blue Shield plans competing with each other. Under antitrust attack from state attorneys general, collusion among the Blue Cross/Blue Shield plans is weakening. For example, using the antitrust laws, the state of Maryland sued the Maryland and District of Columbia Blue plans to end their explicit agreement dividing the state of Maryland.[19] In Ohio, several plans compete statewide as a result of an antitrust settlement with the state attorney general. A continuation of this trend will increase competition among insurers.

### Why Insurance Has Become More Competitive

The previous section discussed a number of developments that have changed the degree and nature of competition in the health insurance market. This section attempts to identify the forces behind these developments.

### Changing Attitudes of Employers

During the last few years, top corporate management has taken a more active interest in containing the costs of employee health benefit programs.

A study in 1981 showed that corporate purchasers of health care had little interest in cost containment.[20] There is substantial evidence now of increased leadership in cost containment at the top levels of corporate management and an upgrading of the position of employee benefits manager. Why did the change occur at this time?

Perhaps the central reason is the growth in the proportion of compensation costs going toward health benefits, which increased from 1.6 percent of wages and salaries in 1965 to 5.3 percent in 1985. By 1998, employers spent an average of $4,100 per employee on health care, which was about 36 percent of all nonwage employee benefits, totaling about $291 billion.[21] When more dollars are involved, sharp increases in premiums are more likely to capture the attention of top management. While health benefit costs had been growing relative to other compensation for some time, the sharply rising proportion in the 1980s made health care cost containment a more important source of cost savings.

The relatively severe recession of 1982 may have contributed to the acceleration of these trends. Although standard economic models state that firms are constantly seeking to reduce costs, the business and historical literature suggests that managers work harder to reduce costs when profits have declined or when the viability of the firm is at stake. As the level of health benefit costs increased sharply, many firms chose to reduce them in response to declining profitability. The 1981 federal tax cut that reduced individual income tax rates also contributed to increased employer and employee interest in cost containment. Recall that because employer-paid premiums are paid from pretax dollars, the income tax system subsidizes health insurance. Lowering income tax rates reduced the magnitude of the tax subsidy, thus increasing the rewards for cost containment. The

further reduction in marginal tax rates from the 1986 tax reform has further improved incentives. Most research finds the demand for employment-based health insurance is sensitive to changes in marginal tax rates.[22] While estimates of the magnitude of this relationship have varied widely, all predict an increase in cost-sharing in response to declining tax rates.

More recently, employer provision of health insurance has declined in non-core jobs and in smaller firms, as premiums for private insurance soared at the end of the nineties. The Bush administration's proposed reduction in the marginal federal income tax rate is expected to reduce incentives for private insurance coverage even further.[23]

The curtailment of health insurance benefits and tightening of control by employers over utilization and coverage has led to a popular backlash against managed care, which culminated in legislation introduced in February 2001 (HSR 526, the Bipartisan Patient Protection Act of 2001, also known as the "patient bill of rights"). One provision in the bill is expanded liability, which would enable larger lawsuits by patients against their health insurers and employers. Industry insiders fear that the expanded liability would further reduce employer-provided health insurance.[24]

### Medicare and Medicaid Policies

Budgetary concerns led to important policy developments in the Medicare and Medicaid programs, which in turn led to changes in the market for private health insurance. From the perspective of private insurers, the most critical development in Medicare policy has been the prospective payment system, and the most critical development in Medicaid has been the tightening of eligibility requirements. In addition, both programs have expanded enrollments in managed care options: managed care plans served about 54 percent of Medicaid and about 17 percent of Medicare enrollees in 2000.[25]

Both the prospective payment system and tightened Medicaid eligibility have made private purchasers (employers and insurers) more sensitive to the issue of cost shifting—that is, the idea that hospitals respond to lower Medicare or Medicaid payments by raising prices to private patients. Medicare's prospective payment system (PPS) has private payers worried that Medicare could reduce its payments below cost, so that the shortfall would be shifted to them (cost shifting) through increased markups of charges over costs. Actually, the opposite occurred during the first few years of PPS—profits on Medicare service increased. But the pressure of the federal deficit has led most observers to conclude that the generous Medicare reimbursement under early PPS will not last. Medicaid eligibility reductions have led to similar risks for private purchasers. Many people who are no longer eligible for Medicaid due to tighter real-income standards for welfare eligibility are still admitted to hospitals, and some of them are not insured. Since charitable contributions have shrunk to practically nothing in recent years, hospitals can recoup the costs of caring for these uninsured patients only by charging other patients more (if they have sufficient market power).

Private purchasers have taken two courses in response to the specter of increased cost shifting. First, some have organized politically to support state government actions to reduce payment differentials. These actions have included traditional state rate-setting efforts, policies regulating payment differences, and policies that directly address uncompensated care. The latter category includes selective Medicaid eligibility extensions and the development of mechanisms to make payments to hospitals that provide significant amounts of uncompensated care. Such payments are often funded through taxes on hospital revenues from all private patients. While this funding mechanism does not help private patients as a group, it protects the commercial insurers from bearing more of the costs of uncompensated care than the Blue Cross.

Second, private purchasers have tried to obtain discounts from full charges for both hospital and physician services. The key to obtaining favorable prices is the ability to channel patients to providers that agree to a discounted price, hence the development of PPOs and HMOs.

### Professional Standards Review Organizations

The professional standards review organization (PSRO) program was mandated by Congress in the late 1960s but has been phased out by now. It mandated a system of claims review designed to reduce medical care and especially hospital care use. These agencies might be seen as public sector precursors to the current managed care revolution that is taking place in the private insurance market. Perhaps because local physicians and hospitals controlled the local PSRO organizations, research studies found them to be ineffective.

Nonetheless, the PSROs may have contributed to the development of more effective utilization review in both the private and public sectors. The program gained practical experience and stimulated the interest of policymakers in developing better techniques. What was learned from the PSRO program was not lost, since many of the organizations continued as private peer review organizations and since the staffs of those that disbanded often found employment with insurers and other private-sector organizations offering utilization review services. The PSRO experience also conditioned providers to utilization review activities.

## Antitrust Enforcement in Health Care

For years, the growth of innovative health insurance schemes (such as HMOs) was delayed by boycott threats from physician groups. However, the development of antitrust law and the attention of antitrust law enforcement agencies has reduced the barriers to new forms of financing.

Prior to 1963, national hospital accreditation standards conferred great economic power on local medical societies. To be accredited, hospitals were required to exclude from their medical staff physicians who were not members of their local medical societies. By ejecting HMO physicians from medical society membership, local medical societies were able to block or hinder the development of these organizations.[26] In 1963, a court decision eliminated the requirement of local medical society membership as a prerequisite to hospital access.[27] We believe that this uncelebrated court decision is the key to understanding the decline of the ability of organized medicine to hinder physician and hospital competition. Furthermore, it also led to the weakening of the American Medical Association's influence on national health policy.

Groups of physicians have also boycotted insurers who used new cost-control measures. For example, in objection to utilization controls, the Michigan State Medical Society boycotted the local Blue Shield plan. The eventual result was a cease and desist order from the Federal Trade Commission in 1983.[28]

More recently, physicians have mobilized to seek exemption from tough antitrust laws that prohibit their collusion against managed care plans. Federal legislation was introduced in 1999 (HR 1304, the Quality Health-Care Coalition Act of 1999) that would enable physician groups to form with the intent to safeguard quality of care from competitive pressures to cut costs. Industry experts estimate that the cost of these physician antitrust waivers would be an increase in private insurance premiums of about 13 percent, which is substantial. This in turn would further reduce the enrollment in private insurance, increasing the ranks of the uninsured.[29]

A recent example of antitrust enforcement involved a new PPO in the small cities of Modesto and Turlock in Stanislaus County, California. The county medical society formed its own PPO and quickly signed on most of the local physicians. The Medical Society's PPO prohibited its member doctors from signing up with any other organizations, thus effectively denying competing PPOs and HMOs entry into the Modesto and Turlock markets. Only when threatened with an antitrust suit by the U.S. Department of Justice did the Stanislaus County Medical Society disband its PPO.[30]

## New Third-Party Administrators

Since employers do not usually have specialized knowledge of the health care market and of health insurance, they have sought outside help in managing their self-insured plans. Originally, this function was undertaken by TPAs such as Dual-Plus or AdMar in Los Angeles, Affordable Health Care Concepts in Sacramento, and Martin E. Segal Co. in Denver. These firms smoothed the transition to self-insurance and doubtless saved both money and managerial headaches. But more important for the evolution of a more competitive and efficient marketplace, these small independent firms, most of which began as either benefit or actuarial consulting firms, invented the modern PPO and provided the necessary expertise for its early growth.

One might have expected the established insurance firms to be the innovators. Instead, these small new TPAs and consultants provided the necessary entrepreneurship that transformed the entire industry. As Havighurst observed, the health insurance industry has been all too willing to strive for consensus and avoid innovation.[31] The entry of the new TPAs has changed that. Under the pressure of this new competition, commercial insurers and Blue Cross/Blue Shield plans have begun to offer TPA services and organize PPOs.

The process recalls Joseph A. Schumpeter's theory that most competition is likely to come from new products or ideas rather than from producing old products at a slightly lower cost. Through "creative destruction," newer firms offering new products displace once-dominant firms.[32] On the other hand, Schumpeter expected large firms operating in concentrated, oligopolistic markets to be especially innovative. Among health insurers, then, one would expect the Blue Cross/Blue Shield plans to be the most innovative, followed by the commercial carriers. That is not at all what has occurred. The innovations have come from small TPAs and consulting firms.

### More Physicians

The physician/population ratio is rising rapidly. The number of graduates of U.S. medical schools doubled from 1965 to 1981, and the number of foreign-trained physicians has also grown.[33] This raised the number of physicians from 1.68 per 1,000 in 1970 to more than 2.0 by 1980. The ratio rose steadily during the 1980s, reaching an all-time high in 1989 of 2.61. There was a sharp dip in 1990, to 2.16, and then continued growth by 1996, to 2.6.[34] A neglected benefit of this growth has been easier development of innovative health insurance schemes and a general growth of price competition.

New physicians are especially likely to charge low prices to increase their patient loads, either directly or by joining a PPO. Since new physicians have fewer regular patients, low prices are more likely to increase their revenues. In addition, they have not yet formed a network of friendships and working relationships with other doctors and thus are less susceptible to subtle professional pressure to avoid competing too sharply. The net result is more competition and lower physician incomes.

Managed care has also had an impact on the mix of physicians, by encouraging growth in the family and general practice areas and reducing the demand for specialists. The average physician earned almost 4 percent less in 1994 than in 1993, the first drop in earnings since 1982 (when current income statistics were first collected). But the averages conceal considerable variation in the income changes by physician specialty from 1985 to 1994. Physicians at the upper end of the income distribution (specialists) saw a larger than average drop in income, while those at the bottom (general care and family practice physicians) saw healthy increases in income. The narrowing of the income gap between primary care physicians and specialists can largely be attributed to growth in managed care plans. In 1986, only 43 percent of physicians provided some services to managed care plans. In 1995, more than 83 percent of all patient-care physicians had at least one managed care contract.[35]

### Competition in the Future

The health care financing system is still in transition. The current system will continue to respond to powerful forces for change. Of course predicting the future is difficult, and predicting the direction of the health care system is no exception.

Figure 10.5   **HMO Penetration by State, 2000**

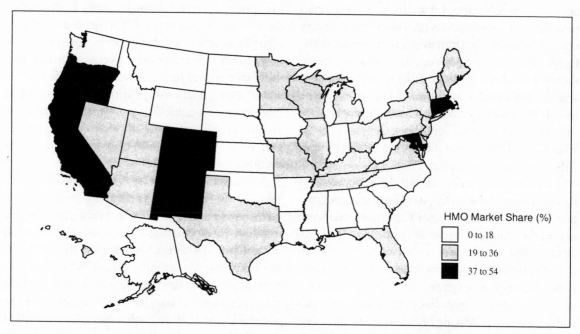

*Source*: *The Interstudy Competitive Edge: HMO Industry Report* 10.2, Interstudy, St. Paul, Minnesota, January 1, 2000.

Because of this transitional state, there is considerable variation across regions in the types of health plans and health care available. For example, there is considerable variation in the geographic penetration of HMOs, as Figure 10.5 shows. This is partly responsible for the geographic variation in medical treatments that is observed across regions. This variation in treatments for the same diseases across regions means that some patients are getting too much care, while others may not be getting enough. Either situation can place the patient at risk and increase costs.[36] The insurance industry and the federal government are currently devoting considerable resources to exploit this geographic variation, by studying the observed variation across regions. Once this variation is better understood, we will have better information at hand for designing health care systems that are both efficient and more uniformly effective.

Two factors make prediction about health care markets particularly uncertain. One is that the system is at the early stage of a cycle of innovation. Some of the current innovations may be discarded, and some of those that will ultimately succeed may not have appeared yet, or at least may not have been widely noticed yet. The second factor concerns the reaction of the public sector. To date, public officials have generally applauded the degree of innovation in the private financing of health care. However, the popular view could quickly change.

One early indication of public opinion regarding recent developments was a provision in the

Omnibus Budget Reconciliation Act of 1986 that limits the degree to which hospitals and HMOs can offer incentives to physicians to cut utilization. More recently, in September 1996, the federal government enacted direct federal controls on the content of health insurance benefit packages. These federal mandates represent major change in federal policy toward health insurance. Even more recent proposed regulation—one piece aimed at expanding liability for insurance companies and employers, and another piece aimed at loosening antitrust constraints facing physician groups—continues to threaten managed care. The literature shows large cost savings from managed care practices, thus there is a tremendous cost of eliminating it.[37]

## Why Mandates are Bad Economic Policy

Two new federal mandates force insurers to cover mental health benefits with the same policy limits (coinsurance, deductibles, etc.) as other health care services and force insurers to pay for at least forty-eight hours of inpatient care for mothers and newborns. These federal mandates supersede the ERISA exemption from state law through self-insurance that large employers have used to avoid similar state regulations. Thus the federal stance has shifted from one that protected employer groups from state health insurance mandates, to one that subjects them to federal insurance mandates.

There is wide agreement among health economists that insurance mandates reflect the lobbying of legislators by special interest groups (e.g., the American College of Obstetricians and Gynecologists and the National Mental Health Association) to obtain off-budget regulatory transfers. Transfers of income go to the providers of the regulated services and do not show up in state or federal government budgets. The mandates thus allow

legislators to reward special interest groups without generating any obvious costs. The costs show up later in the form of higher insurance premiums, less consumer choice over alternatives, and increasing numbers of uninsured individuals, among other things.

The new federal regulations are harmful in several ways: (1) they limit consumer choice, (2) they limit the utilization control for a service (obstetric care) that is quite price-responsive, and (3) they limit the ability to control utilization and fraud abuse for a service (mental health care) for which "need" is difficult to verify objectively. Thus they inhibit the workings of the market, impeding its ability to supply desired products efficiently.

Between 1970 and 1996, the number of state mandates increased 25-fold. State mandated benefits raise the cost of insurance and may increase the numbers of uninsured individuals; recent estimates show that one-fifth to one-fourth of uninsured individuals now lack coverage because of mandates.[38] But there has been a small offsetting effect, helping to contain health care costs. This happened as mandates led more firms to self-insure than would otherwise be the case, which increased competition in the insurance industry.

## Antitrust Enforcement in Health Care

Federal antitrust enforcement in health care is unlikely to change. Even the Reagan administration's relatively permissive antitrust policy did not reduce vigilance toward the health care industry. The Bush and Clinton administrations have kept the pressure on health care.

There is some recent evidence that managed care has affected the structure of the health care industry by causing greater integration of hospitals with physician groups to facilitate contracting with managed care plans.[39] In 1993, less than

25 percent of community hospitals were integrated with physician groups, but this is expected to increase. Hospitals affiliated with multihospital chains and larger hospitals were much more likely to have integrated. Because physicians are the key components in the production of health care services, hospitals that vertically integrate with groups of physicians have more power in bargaining with insurance plans.

Horizontal mergers and consolidations in the health care industry reached record numbers in the 1980s and have escalated to set new records in the 1990s, with no signs of abatement. The HMO industry was engaged in a major wave of mergers in the 1990s, and consolidation in this industry may give them greater clout in bargaining with hospitals in some regions. With continued consolidation in the industry, communities and regulators are becoming increasingly concerned about whether the public interest is being served. With the elimination of excess hospital capacity through merger and consolidation, insurers will find themselves in a weaker bargaining position. The integration of the hospital with physician groups enables the hospital to increase its market power. One way that insurers can regain leverage as the hospital industry consolidates is through similar (counteractive) consolidation.

## Other Factors Affecting Change in the Future

The forces that have caused change are likely to continue. The supply of physicians will continue to increase for the foreseeable future. Although federal government subsidies to medical school expansion are a thing of the past, few would predict public efforts to reduce class sizes.

Employers will continue to look for ways to contain health care costs. With marginal tax rates substantially lower as a result of the 1981 and 1986 tax reforms, incentives to contain the costs of health benefit programs are now stronger. Furthermore, a cap on the amount of employer contributions to health benefit plans that can be deducted from taxes might be enacted within the next few years. All of the proposed health care reforms in 1993 included some limitations. A philosophy of reducing marginal tax rates (or avoiding future increases) through broadening the tax base is now widely accepted in Congress. With such incentives, employers are likely to continue increasing cost-sharing and experimenting with managed care and PPOs. The control of medical care cost inflation is far from perfect today, due to the separation of the purchaser (the employer) and the consumer (the employee). In the future, the HMO/PPO contract to control consumer use is expected to become much more specific, more effective in containing costs, and more prevalent.[40]

A tightening of Medicare prospective payment rates for hospitals over the next few years appears inevitable. Hospitals have found Medicare patients to be highly profitable under PPS. This has resulted both from errors in setting initial rates and from faster than expected responses by hospitals to the new incentives. Reductions in Medicare payments relative to costs will increase the incentives for private payers to negotiate prices with hospitals through HMOs and PPOs. Like airline passengers after deregulation, it could be a rare patient who pays list price.

The force most difficult to predict is the policy response to the increasing proportion of patients that are uninsured. While health insurance coverage in the public sector remained relatively stable between 1979 and 1997, private insurance declined from about 71.9 percent to about 64.5 percent. Coverage provided by employers has declined, and there has been an increase in employee contribution to premiums. Workers in peripheral jobs (temporary and part-time) are increasingly less likely to have insurance than those in core (long-term, full-time) jobs. Health insurance enrollment has declined in industries composed of small firms and those with large minority workforces.[41] The combination of Medicaid eligibility restriction and changes in the economy has resulted in a larger proportion of the population without health insurance. The competitive pressures on providers who are losing the wherewithal to cross-subsidize patients has probably reduced access to charity care. As noted earlier, charitable contributions to hospitals are very minor now. Furthermore, they are often targeted toward research, not care for the uninsured.

The policy response to this problem is likely to affect health insurers and their new competitive tools. Some policies to help the uninsured would not harm health insurance competition (e.g., expanding Medicaid to cover more of the uninsured).[42] However, one possible reaction to the uninsured problem would be uniform national health insurance. Most forms of this would eliminate the current competitive, innovative health insurance system and replace it with some kind of highly regulated private or government system (e.g., one of the national health insurance plans proposed in 1993). Such a uniform plan is not necessary to deal with the plight of the population that does not have insurance, but it has some political or ideological appeal. A uniform national health insurance plan would narrow the choices in the current market and would end competition to reduce costs through innovative health insurance. This would be both unnecessary and unfortunate.

## Notes

1. Argus Chart of Health Insurance (Cincinnati: National Underwriter Co., various years).

2. H.E. Frech III and Paul B. Ginsburg, "Competition Among Health Insurers," in Competition in the Health Care Sector: Past, Present, and Future, W. Greenberg, ed. (Germantown, MD: Aspen Systems Corp., 1978); H.E. Frech III, "Monopoly in Health Insurance: The Economics of Kartell v. Blue Shield of Massachusetts," in Health Care in America: The Political Economy of Hospitals and Health Insurance, H.E. Frech III, ed. (San Francisco: Pacific Research Institute for Public Policy, 1988), pp. 293–322; Killard W. Adamache and Frank A. Sloan, "Competition Between Non-Profit and For-Profit-Health Insurers," Journal of Health Economics 2 (December 1983): 225–43; Roger Feldman and Warren Greenberg, "The Relation Between the Blue Cross Share and the Blue Cross 'Discount' on Hospital Charges," Journal of Risk and Insurance 48 (1981): 235–46: and H.E. Frech III, Competition and Monopoly in Medical Care (Washington, DC: AEI Press, 1996).

3. See Frech and Ginsburg; H.E. Frech III, "The Property Rights Theory of the Firm: Empirical Results from a Natural Experiment," Journal of Political Economy 84 (February 1976): 143–52; Ronald J. Vogel and Roger D. Blair, Health Insurance Administration: An Economic Analysis (Lexington, MA: Heath, Lexington, 1975); H.E. Frech III, "Blue Cross, Blue Shield, and Health Care Costs: A Review of the Economic Evidence," in National Health Insurance: What Now, What Later, What Never, Mark V. Pauly, ed. (Washington, DC: American Enterprise Institute for Public Policy Research, 1980), pp. 250–63.

4. Howard Berman, "Comment," in Greenberg, ed., Competition in the Health Care Sector (Germantown, MD: Aspen Systems Corp., 1978), p. 191. For a more recent reaffirmation of the Blue Cross/Blue Shield philosophy, see William Landes, "Affidavit: Blue Cross and Blue Shield Association v. Community Mutual Insurance Co.," Case No. C 85–7872, U.S. District Court, Northern District of Ohio, Western Division, August 28, 1986, pp. 31–32.

5. H.E. Frech III, "Market Power in Health Insurance," Journal of Industrial Economics 27, no. 1 (September 1980): 55–72. The optimality of competitively supplied insurance with moral hazard holds, since there is no governmental or public policy that can reduce the moral hazard. This is called constrained Pareto optimality—that is, the unavoidable existence of the moral hazard is the constraint. See also Peter Zweifel and Willard Manning, "Moral Hazard and Consumer Incentives in Health Care," in Anthony J. Culyer and Joseph P. Newhouse, eds., Handbook of Health Economics (Amsterdam: Elsevier, 2000), pp. 409–59.

6. Mark V. Pauly, "Taxation, Health Insurance and Market Failure in the Medical Economy," Journal of Economic Literature 24, no. 2 (June 1986): 629–75.

7. Charles E. Phelps, Health Economics (New York: HarperCollins, 1992), p. 303.

8. Martin S. Feldstein, "The Welfare Loss of Excess

Health Insurance," *Journal of Political Economy* 81, no. 2 (March/April 1973): 251–80.

9. Lawrence G. Goldberg and Warren Greenberg, "The Emergence of Physician-Sponsored Health Insurance: An Historical Perspective," in *Competition*, Greenberg, ed., pp. 231–54.

10. Landes, "Affidavit," p. 5.

11. Prospective Payment Assessment Commission, *Medicare and the American Health Care System: Report to Congress*, June 1996, p. 19.

12. H.E. Frech III, James Langenfeld, and Michaelyn Corbett, "Managed Health Care Effects: Medical Care Costs and Access to Health Insurance," Working paper in Economics no. 12-00, University of California, Santa Barbara, November 2000.

13. Managed Care Online Web site: <http://www.mcareol.com/factshts/mcolfact.htm>, June 2001.

14. Frech III et al. "Managed Health Care Effects."

15. H.E. Frech III and Paul B. Ginsberg, *Public Health Insurance in Private Medical Markets: Some Problems of National Health Insurance* (Washington, DC: American Enterprise Institute for Public Policy Research, 1978), chap. 5.

16. W. David Bradford and Lee R. Mobley, "Employment-Based Health Insurance and the Effectiveness of Intra-Firm Competition Between Insurance Providers," study using the 1987 Medical Expenditure Panel Study (MEPS) data, working paper (April 2001) available from W. David Bradford, E-mail: bradfowd@musc.edu.

17. Fred Hellinger, "The Expanding Scope of State Legislation," *Journal of the American Medical Association* 276 (October 2, 1996):1065–70.

18. Gail Jensen, Kevin Cotter, and Michael Morrisey, "State Insurance Regulation and Employers' Decisions to Self-Insure," *The Journal of Risk and Insurance* 62 (1995): 185–213.

19. *State of Maryland v. Blue Cross and Blue Shield Assn.*, 620 F. Supp. 907 (1985).

20. Harvey Sapolsky, Drew Altman, Richard Greener, and Judith D. Moore, "Corporate Attitudes Toward Health Care Costs," *Milbank Memorial Fund Quarterly* 59 (1981): 561–75.

21. U.S. Chamber of Commerce, *Employee Benefits 1985* (Washington, DC: U.S. Chamber Research Center, 1986); <http://www.uschamber.com/_labor+day+facts.htm>.

22. Charles E. Phelps, "Large-Scale Tax Reform: The Example of Employer-Paid Health Insurance Premiums," Working paper no. 37, Department of Economics, University of Rochester, March 26, 1986. Phelps finds that the elasticity of demand for premiums with respect to price (including tax benefits) is approximately –2. (An elasticity of –2 means that a 5 percent reduction in the marginal tax rate would reduce demand for health insurance by about 10 percent.) Others have found smaller elasticities, but Phelps argues that these estimates suffer from bias from using household data to model decisions made at the employment group level.

23. Martin Feldstein, "Board of Contributors: Bush's Tax Plan Is Even Better Than the Campaign Says," *Wall Street Journal*, March 28, 2000.

24. Statement by Chip Kahn, president, Health Insurance Association of America (HIAA), in a press release March 21, 2001: "HIAA Encouraged By President Bush's Concern About Unlimited 'Patient Protection' Liability" (Health Insurance Association of America Web site: <http://www.hiaa.org/news/news-current/press-releases/release6.html>, June 2001); the U.S. Chamber of commerce opposed this bill (U.S. Chambers of Commerce Web site: <http://www.uschamber.com/_political+Advocacy/Issues+Index/Health+Care/Managed+Care/default.htm>, June 2001).

25. Health Care Financing Administration (HCFA), "Medicare Managed Care Market Penetration Report, All Plans," June 2000 and "Medicaid Enrollment and Medicaid Managed Care Enrollment by State," December 31, 1999 <http://www.mcareol.com/factshts/mcolfact.htm>, Managed Care Online Web site, 6/2001).

26. Clark C. Havighurst, "Professional Restraints on Innovation in Health Care Financing," *Duke Law Journal* 2 (1978): 303–87.

27. *Griesman v. Newcomb Hospital*, 40 N.J. 384, 192 A.2d 817 (1963).

28. In re Michigan State Medical Society, 101 F.T.C. 191 (1983).

29. Monica Noether, "The Cost of Physician Antitrust Waivers," Charles Rivers Associates, March 3, 2000, available in pdf file Health Insurance Association of America Web site: <http://www.hiaa.org/pubs/pubs-titles/Research.htm> (June 2001). The U.S Chamber of Commerce opposes this legislation, see press release Monday, January 10, 2000: "Doctors Should Not Receive Collective Bargaining Power, Antitrust Exemption: Proposal Would Drive Up Costs, Increase Number of Uninsured Americans" (U.S Chambers of Commerce Web site: <http://www.uschamber.com/Press+Room/2000+Releases/January+2000/00–6b.htm>, June 2001). Also see H.E. Frech III and James Langenfeld, "The Impact of Antitrust Exemptions for Health Care Professional on Health Care Costs," LECG, Inc., Santa Barbara, CA, June 23, 2000.

30. Jon Gabel and Dan Ermann, "Preferred Provider Organizations: Performance, Problems, and Promise," *Health Affairs* 4 (Spring 1985): 24–40.

31. Havighurst, "Professional Restraints."

32. Joseph A. Schumpeter, *The Theory of Economic Development* (Cambridge: MA: Harvard University Press, 1934).

33. Monica Noether, "The Effect of Government Policy Changes on the Supply of Physicians: Expansion of a Competitive Fringe," *Journal of Law and Economics* 29, no. 2 (October 1986): 231–62.

34. Source: *Statistical Abstract of the U.S.*, various years; the American Medical Association (AMA), "Socioeconomic Characteristics of Medical Practice, 1996," August 1998 <http://www.HCFA.org>.

35. Carol Simon and Patricia Born, "Physician Earnings in a Changing Managed Care Environment," *Health Affairs* 15 (1996): 124–33.

36. Frech III et al., "Managed Health Care Effects."

37. Ibid.

38. Gail Jensen and Michael Morrisey, "Mandated Benefit Laws and Employer Sponsored Health Insurance," HIAA, January 1999 (Health Insurance Association of America Web site: <http://www.hiaa.org>, June 2001); Michael Morrisey, "Mandates: What Most Proposals Would Do," *The American Enterprise* 3 (January 1, 1992): 63–65; H.E. Frech III, "Risks That Rise With Health Mandates," *Washington Times,* October 22, 1996, p. A-15; Fred Hellinger, "The Expanding Scope."

39. Michael Morrisey, Jeffrey Alexander, Lawton Burns, and Victoria Johnson, "Managed Care and Physician/Hospital Integration," *Health Affairs* 15, no. 4 (1996): 62; Gail Jensen and Michael Morrisey, "Mandated Benefit Laws and Employer Sponsored Health Insurance," HIAA, January 1999 (http://www.HIAA.org).

40. Clark Havinghurst, *Health Care Choices: Private Contracts as Instruments of Health Reform* (Washington, DC: AEI Press, 1995).

41. Henry Farber and Helen Levy, "Recent Trends in Employer-Sponsored Health Insurance Coverage: Are Bad Jobs Getting Worse?" Working paper no. 402, Princeton University, July 1998; Lisa Cubbins et al., "Economic Change and Health Benefits: Structural Trends in Employer-Based Health Insurance," *Journal of Health and Social Behavior* 42, no. 1 (March 2001): 45–63.

42. Press release by Chip Kahn, HIAA president, April 5, 2001, "Senate Amendment A Victory For Millions Of Uninsured Americans," stated: "Today's Senate action—together with President Bush's tax package—indicates that there is growing momentum in Washington for helping the nearly 43 million Americans who lack health coverage. It also is important that both measures complement the employment-based health insurance system, which more than 170 million Americans depend upon to pay for their health care." (Health Insurance Association of America Web site: <http://www. hiaa.org/news/news-current/press-releases/release1.html> June 2001)

## Suggested Readings

Frech, H.E. III. *Competition and Monopoly in Medical Care*. Washington, DC: AEI Press, 1996. This book surveys and synthesizes a wide range of research on competition in health care.

———. "Preferred Provider Organizations and Health Care Competition." In *Health Care in America: The Political Economy of Hospitals and Health Insurance*, H.E. Frech III, ed. San Francisco: Pacific Research Institute for Public Policy, 1988. This essay provides more details on PPOs, with emphasis on how they affect health care markets. It explains why small PPOs with no market power can get large discounts from providers. Other essays in this volume examine other aspects of health care competition.

Frech, H.E. III, and Paul B. Ginsburg. "Competition Among Health Insurers." In *Competition in the Health Care Sector: Past, Present, and Future*, Warren Greenberg, ed. Germantown, MD: Aspen Sytems Corp., 1978. This essay provides details about both commercial and Blue Cross plans, focusing on the time period prior to 1977. It includes statistical evidence that regulatory advantages of Blue Cross/Blue Shield plans lead to higher market shares and higher administrative costs and that higher Blue Cross/Blue Shield market shares lead to higher hospital costs and prices. Other essays in this volume cover other aspects of competition in the health care sector.

Gabel, Jon, and Dan Ermann. "Preferred Provider Organizations: Performance, Problems, and Promise." *Health Affairs* 4, no. 1 (Spring 1985): 24–40. This essay provides more details on PPOs. In particular, it examines what types of organization founded the early PPOs.

Havinghurst, Clark C. "Explaining the Questionable Cost-Containment Record of Commercial Health Insurers." In *Health Care in America: The Political Economy of Hospitals and Health Insurance*, H.E. Frech III, ed. San Francisco: Pacific Research Institute for Public Policy, 1988. This essay examines the question of why aggressive insurer cost controls have been rare until recently. The main answer seems to have been opposition by organized providers.

Havinghurst, Clark. *Health Care Choices: Private Contracts as Instruments of Reform*. Washington, DC: AEI Press, 1995. This book examines the reasons for failure in cost-containment measures that depend upon contracts between insurers and employers. Contracts between insurers and individual consumers are discussed as a solution to the contract failure that exists, and are posed as an important area for future health care policy reform.

Hay, Joel W., and Michael J. Leahy. "Competition Among Health Plans: Some Preliminary Evidence." *Southern Economic Journal* 50, no. 3 (January 1985): 831–46. This study examines the effect of higher Blue Cross/

Blue Shield market share on hospital costs and prices. Using different data and techniques, it confirms the results found by Frech and Ginsburg.

Pauly, Mark V. "Taxation, Health Insurance and Market Failure in the Medical Economy." *Journal of Economic Literature* 24, no. 2 (June 1986): 629–75. This essay covers the interactions between health insurance and health care. In particular, it examines the effect of the favorable tax treatment of group health insurance.

Phelps, Charles E., "Large-Scale Tax Reform: The Example of Employer-Paid Health Insurance Premiums," Working paper no. 37, Department of Economics, University of Rochester, March 26, 1986. This paper examines the price elasticity of demand for health insurance. It surveys statistical research and suggests a historical test for statistical results.

# 11

# Motion Pictures

## Competition, Distribution, and Efficiencies

### *Stanley I. Ornstein*

The history of the motion picture industry spans over 100 years. During that period the industry has endured competitive challenges from network television, cable and satellite, massive corporate reorganizations, and years of government and private antitrust attacks. Since the passage of the Sherman Antitrust Act in 1890, few industries have been so drastically altered by government antitrust action as the motion picture industry. But it has survived, gaining prosperity through technological improvements in filmmaking and exhibition, and by capitalizing on new channels for distributing movies. Born of innovations in the photography of moving objects and the projection of images onto a screen, the industry rose from humble beginnings in the 1890s. The first theatrical screening took place in New York City in 1896, following a vaudeville act. Movie viewing was widespread by 1910 and reached enormous popularity in the 1920s, 1930s, and 1940s. In the 1930s and 1940s upward of 400 feature films were produced per year in the United States, and theater attendance in many years reportedly averaged 85 to 90 million per week, or over 4 billion annually, well above contemporary attendance levels of approximately 1.4 to1.5 billion.[1]

Following World War II, the vertically integrated structure of the top movie distributors, with common ownership of production, distribution, and exhibition, was dissolved by government antitrust actions and, under court order, many of the industry's well-established marketing and distribution practices, such as "block booking," "blind bidding," and exclusive dealing franchise arrangements were prohibited.[2] Movies then faced the challenge of network television, which some believed would destroy the movie business. With declining theater attendance, thousands of motion picture theaters were closed. However, over the last thirty years the industry has rebounded, capitalizing on the introduction of videocassettes, DVDs, and pay cable television; experiencing huge growth in foreign revenues; and attaining a post–1970 peak in North American theatrical admissions in 1998 of almost 1.5 billion.

This study offers an overview of the industry's evolution—its organizational structure, marketing and distribution practices, alleged antitrust transgressions, responses to forced dissolution, and contemporary economic performance. Industry studies provide an opportunity to broaden our understanding of economic practices. The motion picture industry provides vivid examples of prominent economic phenomena, including vertical integration, exclusive dealing, price discrimination, and adaptations to inherently risky investments.

The courts' dissolution of the industry's vertically integrated structure and curtailment of various distribution practices in 1948 provides a natural before-and-after experiment for examining the factors leading to vertical integration and the consequences of abandoning such integration. Price discrimination has been an integral part of the motion picture industry for more than seventy-five years. As we will see, the demand for movies lends itself to price discrimination, and practices arose to exploit this opportunity. Finally, the movie business is very risky. The box office outcome of any given movie is highly uncertain. The risk of investing in movies has had a substantial effect on the industry's business practices, structure, and evolution.

### Production, Distribution, and Exhibition

The movie industry traditionally operates at three levels: (1) production—the financing, development, and making of motion pictures; (2) distribution—the licensing, distribution, and promotion of movies; and (3) exhibition—the screening of movies. All three stages are obviously highly dependent on one another. Until the 1950s, the top five studios were vertically integrated companies, combining production, distribution, and exhibition. In 1948 the U.S. Supreme Court, in effect, required the top five studios to divest their ownership of movie theaters and halt a variety of distribution practices for violations of the Sherman Antitrust Act, destroying an integral part of their organizational structure and thereby increasing the costs of distributing movies.[3]

Table 11.1 lists the major studio-distributors of films in 2000 and their relative shares over time of domestic box office revenues (known as "rentals"). Columbia, Twentieth Century Fox, MGM/

UA, Paramount, Universal, and Warner Brothers have been major distributors since at least the 1920s and 1930s. As seen from the changing shares, the distributors' fortunes have risen and fallen over time, as blockbuster movies have propelled first one and then another distributor to the top in various years. However, as noted, the success of movies is uncertain, with the majority of movies losing money. The major hit movies must earn enough to compensate for the many losing investments. Generally distributors are unable to maintain a number one position for more than a few consecutive years, indicating how difficult it is to produce and distribute hit movies consistently. As one example, Sony (Columbia/Tri-Star) reported a $3.2 billion loss on its movie operations in 1994.[4] Sony had a series of poorly performing movies, gaining only 9 percent of theater rentals. However, Sony scored with major successes in 1997, propelling it to a top rental share of 20 percent. The hits disappeared after 1997, and Sony's share fell back to approximately 9 percent. Similar large swings are evident in the box office shares of other major studios.

Motion pictures are rented under license to exhibitors, with the box office receipts divided in an agreed proportion between distributor and exhibitor. The distributor receives a percentage of box office receipts, with the percentage declining the longer the movie runs. In one type of first-run movie license the distributor receives 70 percent of box office receipts for the first week or two of the run, with the percentage declining weekly thereafter. Under another formula for first-run movies, the theater owner receives a negotiated sum to cover overhead expenses, and the box office is split 9:1 for the distributor in the first few weeks, with the distributor's share declining over time. For second-run screenings, the distributor's share is typically between 30 and 35 percent or

Table 11.1

**North American Theatrical Rental Shares of Distributors**

| Year | AOL Time Warner (Warner Bros.) | Disney (Buena Vista) | Dream-works | News Corp (20th Century Fox) | MGM/UA | MIRAMAX | New Line | Sony (Columbia) | Viacom (Paramount) | Vivendi (Universal) |
|---|---|---|---|---|---|---|---|---|---|---|
| 2000 | 12 | 15 | 10 | 10 | 1 | 6 | 5 | 9 | 11 | 15 |
| 1999 | 14 | 17 | 4 | 11 | 4 | 4 | 4 | 9 | 12 | 13 |
| 1998 | 11 | 16 | 7 | 11 | 3 | 6 | 8 | 11 | 16 | 6 |
| 1997 | 11 | 14 | 2 | 11 | 3 | 7 | 6 | 20 | 12 | 10 |
| 1996 | 16 | 21 | | 13 | 5 | 4 | 5 | 11 | 13 | 8 |
| 1995 | 16 | 19 | | 8 | 6 | 4 | 7 | 13 | 10 | 13 |
| 1994 | 16 | 19 | | 9 | 3 | 4 | 6 | 9 | 14 | 13 |
| 1993 | 19 | 16 | | 11 | 2 | 3 | 3 | 11 | 9 | 14 |
| 1992 | 20 | 19 | | 14 | 1 | 1 | 2 | 13 | 10 | 12 |
| 1991 | 14 | 14 | | 12 | 2 | 1 | 4 | 9 | 12 | 11 |
| 1990 | 13 | 16 | | 14 | 3 | 1 | 4 | 13 | 15 | 14 |
| 1985 | 18 | 3 | | 11 | 9 | | 1 | 10 | 10 | 16 |
| 1980 | 14 | 4 | | 16 | 7 | | | 14 | 16 | 20 |
| 1975 | 9 | 6 | | 14 | 11 | | | 13 | 11 | 25 |
| 1970 | 5 | 9 | | 19 | 9 | | | 14 | 12 | 13 |

*Sources: Variety*, January 18, 1989, January 13, 1993, and January 6–12, 1997; Standard & Poor's, *Industry Surveys, Movie and Home Entertainment*, April 18, 1996, February 27, 1997, and May 10, 2001; and National Association of Theater Owners, *2000–2001 Encyclopedia of Exhibition*.

*Notes:* Other distributors at various times included Lorimar, Embassy Pictures, Gramercy and Orion. MIRAMAX was acquired by Disney in 1993. New Line was acquired by Warner in 1996. Sony includes Tri-Star since 1984.

less. These revenue shares are important since most movies earn the majority of their box office receipts within the first three to four weeks. On average, studio-distributors receive approximately 50 percent of box office receipts, although this can vary widely over movies and time. Profits from theater concession sales (popcorn, candy, soft drinks, video games, etc.) go solely to the exhibitor.[5]

Leading exhibitor firms in 2000 are shown in Table 11.2. The top ten exhibitors account for approximately 56 percent of all screens in North America, and the top fifteen, for 64 percent. Exhibition has experienced large-scale consolidation through mergers and acquisitions since the early 1980s and through internal expansion by the largest exhibitors. The largest theater chain in 2000, Regal, began in 1989, grew primarily by acquisition until the mid-1990s, and then grew by constructing new theaters. Loews Cineplex resulted from the 1998 merger of Sony's Loews Theaters, with approximately 900 screens, and Cineplex Odeon, with approximately 1,600 screens. Others, such as Cinemark USA and National Amusements, have also grown through acquisitions. As a result of differences across firms in acquisitions and new theater construction programs, the size ranking of exhibitors has shifted dramatically since the 1980s, and further concentration in screen ownership has occurred.

The growth in the number of screens has outpaced the rise in attendance for years. This was especially true in the 1990s. A construction boom in theaters from 1995 to 2000 added close to 10,000 new screens. The leading firms incurred large debt, which resulted in a series of theater firm bankruptcy filings in 1999 and 2000. Leading firms falling into bankruptcy reorganization included Regal, Carmike, Loews Cineplex, United Artists, and General Cinema; major regional firms like

Edwards and Silver Cinemas; and smaller chains.[6] Some chains planned over 20 percent reductions in their total screens. With large excess capacity in screens and efforts through bankruptcy reorganization to regain profitability, hundreds of older screens were closed.

These two tables illustrate the dynamic nature of the motion picture industry. Intense competition and the vagaries of individual movie success change the rankings of distributors, generally from year to year. In theater exhibition, changes in ownership due to acquisitions and bankruptcies have fostered greater concentration in ownership and dramatically changed the fortunes of individual firms. We will return to contemporary industry developments and performance later in the study. However, we start with industry history, for to understand the industry today one needs to examine its historic development.

**Early History**

At the inception of the industry, manufacturers of motion picture cameras and projectors produced the movies, for in order to sell their equipment they had to supply movies.[7] The movies were short, one-reel episodes, five to twenty minutes in length. They could be drama, westerns, comedy, or outdoor scenic movies. Movies were sold outright to exhibitors and viewed by individuals in penny arcades or in theaters along with vaudeville acts. Movies soon graduated to modest theaters for showings, known as nickelodeons for their five-cent admission fee, and thousands of nickelodeons opened throughout the country. Exchanges arose to facilitate movie trading among exhibitors who sought variety in movie viewing for their customers and a means to reduce the costs of acquiring movies. Exchanges evolved into early versions of modern day distributors, acquiring movies from

Table 11.2

**Top North American Theater Chains**

| | Number of screens | | |
| --- | --- | --- | --- |
| | 1994 | 1997 | 2000 |
| Regal Cinemas | 722 | 1,978 | 4,449 |
| Carmike Cinemas | 2,035 | 2,590 | 2,821 |
| AMC | 1,636 | 1,930 | 2,736 |
| Loews Cineplex | | | 2,726 |
| Cineplex Odeon | 1,643 | 1,550 | |
| Sony Theatres | 912 | 988 | |
| Cinemark USA | 1,214 | 1,459 | 2,227 |
| United Artists Theatre Circuit | 2,204 | 2,237 | 1,858 |
| National Amusements | 848 | 898 | 1,076 |
| General Cinema Theatres | 1,221 | 1,202 | 1,060 |
| Hoyts Cinemas | 519 | 817 | 967 |
| Act III Theatres | 568 | 703 | |
| Famous Players | 441 | 511 | 868 |
| Edwards Theatres | | 426 | 743 |
| Century Theatres | | 408 | 722 |
| Wallace Theater Company | | 132 | 544 |
| Silver Cinemas | | 153 | 540 |
| Kerasotes Theatres | | 404 | 521 |

*Sources*: *Variety*, January 4, 1987, and January 20, 1988; Standard & Poor's, *Industry Surveys, Leisure Time*, April 6, 1995 and Standard & Poor's, *Industry Surveys, Movies and Home Entertainment*, February 27, 1997; National Association of Theater Owners, *1997–1998 Encyclopedia of Exhibition* and *2000–2001 Encyclopedia of Exhibition*.

*Notes*: Loews Cineplex was formed by the merger of Cineplex Odeon and Sony Theatres in 1998; Regal Cinemas acquired Act III Theatres in 1999; Viacom, owner of National Amusements, acquired Famous Players of Canada in 1994.

producers and renting them to exhibitors. By 1911 there were a reported 150 exchanges (distributors) and 11,500 movie theaters in the United States. There were also dozens of motion picture producers. Movie theater chains were forming, and where they dominated local markets through movie booking agencies, some thought they exercised monopsony power, using that power in bargaining with distributors on movie rental rates.[8]

Feature-length films four- and five-reels long, which replaced the short one-reel movies, were widespread by 1913. To attract larger audiences, theaters became more lavish in architecture and size and provided patrons with amenities and comforts. Distributors, in turn, grew more sophisticated in selecting theaters for each movie and in setting rental rates according to theater size and location.

At the same time that theaters and distributors were multiplying rapidly, ten manufacturers of patented movie equipment formed the Motion Picture Patent Company (referred to here as the Patent Company) in 1908 as a means of eliminating what had been years of intra-industry patent infringement lawsuits and also in an attempt to exclude competition in the production, distribution, and marketing of movies.[9] The Patent Company's attempts to monopolize the industry failed; however, it pioneered in various aspects of movie distribution. In 1910 in an attempt to monopolize distribution, the Patent Company vertically integrated into distribution by forming the General Film Company, which acquired most of its former independent distributors. For the first time the General Film Company established a national distribution system of film rentals, classifications of theaters, time periods or "runs" for first-, second-, third-run, (and so forth) movies; and geographic zones or "clearances," which amount to exclusive exhibition territories for a given movie. Although it was innovative in distribution practices to maximize revenues, the company failed to move into feature film production, hastening its demise. The Patent Company was dissolved in 1918, after being found guilty in 1915 of attempting to monopolize the motion picture industry and after losing major patent lawsuits. Long before its dissolution, however, numerous new entrants had successfully challenged the Patent Company in all phases of the business: in the manufacturing of cameras and projectors and in movie production, distribution, and exhibition.

As one example of new entry, Paramount Pictures was formed in 1914 by combining five distribution-exchanges and regional distributors. Paramount secured contracts to distribute movies for three leading production companies. For its distribution services, Paramount retained 35 percent of the box office receipts it received from exhibitors, similar to the fees charged by distributors today. Paramount secured exhibitors for its producers, forming franchise or exclusive dealing relationships with exhibitors who screened Paramount's full line of movies. Paramount also helped finance new production by providing advances to producers against box office receipts and by contracting with exhibitors for future play dates.[10]

By 1914, blocks of movies for an entire year (block booking) were being licensed to distributors and exhibitors, requiring exhibitors to take lesser movies in order to receive movies scheduled to have appearances by the leading movie stars of the day. In addition to Paramount, other national distributors included Mutual, Universal, and Fox. As noted, the Patent Company's early attempt to monopolize failed primarily due to widespread entry from rival producers, distributors, and exhibitors. But the company pioneered in vertical integration between production and distribution and in the distribution practices—runs and clearances—that provided the basis for price discrimination.

## Vertical Integration

From 1915 to the 1930s there was large-scale vertical integration into production, distribution, and exhibition. Movie production studios integrated forward into distribution and exhibition, distributors integrated into production and exhibition, and exhibitor groups integrated backward into distribution and production. In 1916 the Famous Players-Lasky studio bought Paramount, the distribution company, and in 1919 started vertically integrating into theaters, acquiring 300 theaters by mid-1921. In 1917 theater owners organized the First National Exhibitors Circuit to act as a purchasing agent for movies, and vertically integrated into distribution and movie production. By 1920 over 600 theaters were in the group. Eventually its best theaters were acquired by Famous Players-Lasky-Paramount, which became Paramount Pictures. Other theater chains integrating backward into distribution and production included Fox, which became Twentieth Century Fox in the 1930s, and Loews Theaters, which first acquired Metro and in the 1920s put together the studios that became Metro-Goldwyn-Mayer (MGM). In the late 1920s, Warner Brothers, which pioneered in the first sound motion pictures, invested heavily in theaters, acquiring 500 theaters by the mid-1930s. A fifth vertically integrated studio, RKO, was

Table 11.3

**Theater Ownership by the Top Five Major Distributors, 1945**

| Firm | Theaters owned | Joint ownership with independent owners | Total |
|---|---|---|---|
| Paramount | 1,395 | 993 | 2,388 |
| Twentieth Century Fox | 636 | 66 | 702 |
| Warner Bros. | 501 | 20 | 521 |
| Loews | 135 | 21 | 156 |
| RKO | 109 | 187 | 296 |
| Joint ownership with top five firms | 361 | | 361 |
| Total | 3,137 | 1,287 | 4,424 |

*Source*: Michael Conant, *Antitrust in the Motion Picture Industry, Economic and Legal Analysis* (Berkeley and Los Angeles: University of California Press, 1960).

formed in 1929 by the Radio Corporation of American (RCA) in order to sell sound equipment to movie producers, and it eventually acquired approximately 200 theaters.

These studios—Paramount, Twentieth Century Fox, Loews (MGM), Warner Brothers, and RKO—controlled the bulk of first-run theaters in large and small cities in the 1930s and 1940s through ownership, leases, or franchise (exclusive dealing) contracts with independent theaters. The five major theater-owning studios cross-licensed one another's movies in cities or areas where they did not own theaters. Theater ownership as of 1945, both individual and joint, is shown in Table 11.3. The number of theaters owned by the vertically integrated firms represented about 24 percent of the approximately 18,000 U.S. theaters in 1945. The top five distributors accounted for 70 percent of first-run theaters in the ninety-two largest market areas (100,000 population and above), and approximately 60 percent of first-run theaters in cities of 25,000 to 100,000, generating the vast majority of movie revenues. The top eight distributors, which included Columbia, Universal, and United Artists (although these firms did not own theaters), accounted for 95 percent of film rental

payments to distributors over the period 1935 to 1944.[11]

Vertical integration was adopted during a period of intense competition, as a more efficient means of distributing and marketing movies. Numerous firms challenged the Patent Company during its attempt to monopolize the movie industry. Producers competed for major stars to enhance box office appeal, in the quality of movies produced, and for the best distributors and exhibitors. Exhibitors and distributors competed for box office receipts and for the best movies. Firms sought to reduce costs and enhance demand by integrating into two or all three levels of production, distribution, and exhibition. A variety of factors drove this movement to vertical integration. First, producers integrated into distribution, seeking greater control over the licensing, promotion, and theater placement of their movies. Second, according to some commentators, producers and distributors became concerned about contracting for exhibition outlets, fearing they would be foreclosed from the best outlets once exhibitors integrated backward into production, as in the case of the First National Exhibitors Circuit. By integrating into exhibition, producers had a secure network of outlets in at least some parts of the country. With guaranteed distribution and exhibition, producers could more easily finance movie production. In similar fashion, exhibitors were concerned about gaining an adequate supply of movies when producer-distributors integrated forward into exhibition, fearing they would lose movies to the distributor-owned theaters. By integrating backward into production and distribution, exhibitors sought to gain a secure supply of movies. However, such concerns were largely irrational. Self-sufficiency in the supply of movies for exhibition is not a tenable competitive position. Exhibitors and distributors want the best movies, regardless of source. No firm with exhibition outlets has ever been able to rely solely on its own movies as a source of supply.

Third, revenues to support the industry came from box office receipts and exhibitors controlled the box office. Dishonest exhibitors had many avenues to cheat on rental agreements and the distribution of box office receipts. Among the practices used were: understating tickets sold, delaying payment, screening at more than the authorized location, and reproducing movie prints. Such cheating was widespread, requiring large expenditures to monitor exhibitor behavior. Ownership of theaters and exclusive dealing arrangements could drastically reduce these losses. Such integration also ensured the setting of admission prices consistent with the distributor's wish to maximize box office receipts through price discrimination. Fourth, some producer-distributors believed they could operate first-run theaters more economically under ownership than by contracting with numerous independent exhibitors. Licensing movies is costly, requiring individual negotiations with exhibitors, transportation of prints, advertising, and the monitoring and collection of box office receipts. Ownership could possibly reduce some of

these costs, such as those of contracting and monitoring box office receipts.

In addition, "adjustments," a type of financial settling-up, are regularly made to contract terms when movies either do poorly or exceptionally well at the box office. Adjustments change the terms of the initial license, such as length of run, percentage shares of box office rentals, and advertising expense-sharing between exhibitor and distributor. Rather than have a movie play to a relatively empty theater, negotiations can shorten a run or move the film to a smaller theater. Since distributors and exhibitors must work together on a long-term cooperative basis, it is in the distributors' interest not to impose prohibitive losses on exhibitors. Adjustments have been part of the distribution process at least since the 1930s. Theater ownership internalizes certain costs, such as licensing and adjustments and, in principle, can reduce the overall cost of distribution and exhibition.

## Price Discrimination

From approximately the World War I era onward, movies were released to theaters in a tightly controlled, temporal pattern.[12] Motion pictures first appeared for a specific number of days in first-run theaters, then were moved to second-run theaters, next to third-run, and so forth. Admission prices varied by run, with the highest price for first-run, next highest in second-run, and so on. Movies were licensed or rented to theaters for a specific run, measured in days. From the 1920s into the 1940s, 75 percent of first-run films had runs of more than twenty-eight days, and some ran up to 100 days or more.[13] Theaters were granted geographic zone clearances, guaranteeing the theater an exclusive territory for screening; that is, the movie could not be shown by another theater within a prescribed distance. For example, approximately two-thirds of first-run theaters had geographic clearances of ten miles or more. Studio-distributors designated which theaters were first-run, generally reserving that status for their own theaters and those of their top rivals. As indicated, the majority of first-run theaters in major population centers were owned or partially owned by the top five studio-distributors: Paramount, Warner Brothers, Twentieth Century Fox, MGM, and RKO. Other first-run exhibitors were affiliated with the major distributors through exclusive dealing franchise arrangements. Since the majority of box office revenues came from first-run movies, many exhibitors sought first-run status for their theaters. Distributors also engaged in resale price maintenance, setting minimum admission prices for theaters in their rental contracts.

In addition to time and zone clearances, resale price maintenance on admission prices, and block booking, movies in the 1930s were typically rented to exhibitors "blind," with no advance information on the movies' contents. In the 1930s, a year's supply of films for exhibitors was acquired in a block during a two- or three-month buying (rental) season. Exhibitors were required to take blocks of films with no prior knowledge of the film's actors, storyline, and so forth, from various distributors for the following year's screenings. The films were yet to be staffed and produced. Theaters contracted for various numbers of films depending on their run status, with first-run theaters contracting for fewer films than, say, third-run theaters, since the latter would change films more frequently, sometimes two or three times in a week. Bulk purchasing (rental) through block booking provided exhibitors with films and distributors with assured outlets for their films. It also aided in minimizing movie inventory costs and, given that the movies were rented in advance, it ensured their financing.

The system of controlling exhibition prices by time and zone clearances and through resale price maintenance was clearly designed to maximize box office revenue by capturing the maximum area under the demand curve for movies. Prices were set according to individual consumer segments of demand, with differential pricing across each demand segment. Consumers with the highest demand viewed movies in first-run theaters and paid the highest admission price; then came consumers with a somewhat lower demand, viewing movies in second-run theaters at lower prices; then came consumers for third-run theaters, and so on. This method of differential pricing, matching price to relative consumer demand, produced far greater admission revenues for distributors and exhibitors to share than a uniform price for all consumers would have achieved. Maximization of box office receipts was further aided by resale price maintenance. Since exhibitors gained all concession profits and split box office receipts with distributors, they had an incentive to sacrifice box office receipts to increase concession sales. Fixing minimum admission prices in licensing contracts protected the distributor's interest in maximizing box office receipts.

## Antitrust Charges Related to Distribution

Few industries have been subject to more antitrust lawsuits than the motion picture industry. From approximately 1912 to the present, a variety of distributors and exhibitors have been embroiled in either a major government antitrust suit or in suing one another in one of literally hundreds of private suits. Government suits typically alleged some form of collusive activity and monopolization by either distributors or exhibitors. Private suits, often by exhibitors against distributors or against other exhibitors, generally alleged some form of anticompetitive discrimination in issuing licenses or some practice that foreclosed rivals from competing for movies.

From at least the 1920s onward, independent movie theater owners objected repeatedly to the control of first-run movie theaters by studio-distributors and the rental of movies by block booking and blind bidding. Many independent theater owners sought first-run movie status from distributors only to be denied the opportunity. Numerous examples exist of first-run status being granted only after a theater sold out or sold a partial interest to one of the top five producers.[14] When advance information about a movie was made available, theater owners also objected to being forced to take undesired movies through block booking in order to receive those they preferred, while the major studios' theaters allegedly escaped such pressure. Independents also objected to contracting for movies without receiving information about the contents or an advanced screening.

Believing themselves victimized by unfair discriminatory competition, disaffected independent theater owners sought protection from distributors, turning first to the Federal Trade Commission (FTC) and then to the Department of Justice (DOJ). The FTC filed a complaint against the (then) major studios in 1921, charging them with unfair competition through block booking and the control of first-run movie houses.[15] Following a lengthy investigation, the FTC concluded that block booking was an unfair trade practice and issued a cease and desist order, which was never enforced. Again responding to exhibitors' complaints, the DOJ brought an antitrust case against the eight largest studio-distributors in 1938, charging them with monopolizing the motion picture industry through their control of production, distribution, and exhibition. As a remedy, the DOJ sought the divestiture of theater ownership from production and

distribution. After one week at trial, the parties retreated to negotiate, which led to a consent decree in November 1940 whereby the five major producers agreed to limit block booking temporarily to five films at a time and to end blind bidding by having trade screenings for exhibitors. Curiously, despite years of complaints against blind bidding, few exhibitors attended the trade screenings.[16] The government, in turn, agreed not to pursue the forced divestiture of theaters for a three-year period.

The DOJ reopened the case in 1944, again seeking the divestiture of theaters as a remedy for alleged monopolization. In June 1946, a district court found that the top eight distributors had engaged in an illegal restraint of trade.[17] The court prohibited the firms from: (1) fixing admission prices; (2) agreeing to maintain uniform clearances; (3) engaging in excessive or unreasonable clearances, formula deals, or master agreements;[18] (4) pooling arrangements in exhibiting movies;[19] and (5) block booking. The court concluded that competitive bidding on a picture-by-picture, theater-by-theater basis, would solve the problem of discrimination against independent exhibitors, but it rejected the government's request for movie theater divestiture.

On appeal to the Supreme Court, the defendants were found to have monopolized the exhibition of first-run movies in major cities through vertical integration and complex licensing contracts and distribution practices.[20] Monopoly was found to exist at the exhibition level, as evidenced by the percentage of first-run theater ownership and domestic movie rentals controlled by the defendants. Theater control through vertical integration and franchising was held to exclude competition in the distribution and exhibition of movies. The Court agreed with the lower court that the solution was theater-by-theater licensing of individual pictures, but it rejected competitive bidding in favor of the divestiture of theaters and the end to franchising, and it directed the lower court to reconsider divestiture as the appropriate remedy. The Supreme Court also held that clearances and runs were not illegal as long as a fixed and uniform system of clearances did not prevail across all distributors. Final lower court decisions required the top five distributors to divest ownership in their domestic theaters and the new theater circuits to sell some of their theaters. By February 1953, all of the firms but Loews had spun off their theater circuits. Loews followed belatedly in 1959.[21]

The government spent the next twenty-five years reviewing all proposed acquisitions by the successor theater companies. An estimated 500 petitions for acquisitions were reviewed for their potential anticompetitive consequences. Maurice Silverman, the DOJ lawyer in charge of the reviews, spent the remainder of his career working on petitions.[22] In 1968 the successor to Twentieth Century Fox Theaters, National General Theaters, sought to acquire Warner Brothers Studios for $500 million, but Silverman blocked the acquisition. Most acquisitions were of a lesser magnitude, involving the acquisition of a few theaters. In 1974 the government stopped reviewing acquisition petitions, and in 1985 the DOJ effectively terminated the 1940 consent decree.

## Post-Divestiture Performance

The Court-ordered massive restructuring of movie distribution and exhibition provides a basis for testing the government's position that the industry's structure and complex distribution practices were adopted as part of a conspiracy to monopolize motion picture production, distribution, and exhibition by blocking competition from independent exhibitors and producers. It also pro-vides a basis for examining the distributors' use of vertical integration, by ownership or by contract in the form of exclusive dealing. We first look at the charge of monopolization.

### Tests of Monopolization

Assuming the eight firms had behaved monopolistically, by raising rental shares and admission prices above the competitive level, then after the court-imposed restructuring a return to lower competitive prices should have been evident. Admission prices and rental shares should have declined and output should have risen. An unambiguous test of this proposition is clouded, unfortunately, by the fact that the demand and supply of movies was changing. Movie admission revenue fell from $1.69 billion in 1946 to $1.12 billion in 1957.[23] Paid indoor movie theater admissions fell from 3.35 billion in 1948 to 1.96 billion in 1954 and 1.28 billion in 1958.[24] A number of factors contributed to the decline in movie attendance. A high birthrate following World War II limited leisure time for young families. People moved in large numbers to the suburbs, away from the (then) main concentration of downtown movie theaters, although this was offset in part by the growth of drive-in theaters. Drive-ins grew in number from approximately 300 in 1946 to 4,500 in 1956.[25] Of major importance was the spread of television ownership from 1948 onward and its effect on the demand for motion pictures. In 1949 approximately 12 percent of homes with electricity had a television set. At the end of 1957, 86 percent had a television set.[26] Nevertheless, it is instructive to examine the available evidence on changes in price and output.

Did distributors' rental shares of box office receipts fall, as a return to competition would predict? Distributors calculated that their average revenue share rose after the divestitures, from 26 percent in 1947 to 35 percent in 1953.[27] Exhibitors estimated a more modest distributor rental share rise, from 32.6 percent in 1947 to 35.9 percent in 1955. A third study indicates a distributor share increase from 30.4 percent in 1948 to 39.5 percent in 1954.[28] These results are inconsistent with the view that the eight firms were acting as a monopolist, extracting economic rents from independent exhibitors, since a return to competition would lower rental shares.

If the courts were correct, a return to competition in exhibition would also be reflected in lower admission prices. Resale price maintenance was prohibited, removing the floor on admission prices, and more theaters competed for first-run movie customers, which should have lowered prices. However, the average admission price, in real terms, rose from $.46 in 1948 to $.61 in 1950, a 33 percent rise, and remained near $.60 in real terms until the 1960s.[29] Lower demand for movies due to television and a return to competition should have reduced admission prices. One possible explanation for the price rise is that as more low-priced subsequent-run theaters closed, and more theaters shifted to first-run competition, the overall average price of admission rose.

Under monopoly, output is restricted and price is raised. The output of films by the top nine distributors first rose from 249 in 1947 to 320 in 1951, consistent with a prior monopolistic restriction on output, but it then fell to 301 in 1953 and 215 in 1955.[30] More broadly, film production declined from an average of 421 new releases per year in the United States in the 1940s to 338 new releases per year in the 1950s.[31] To the extent that television reduced the demand for movies, the total number of new movies would fall. In addition, the end to block booking, which tied grade B movies to grade A movies, would also tend to reduce total

production unless there were offsetting price discounts, since exhibitors would move toward fewer, better-quality films. The evidence on monopolization is thus far from clear, but whatever the possible competitive gains from ending vertical integration and the other offending distribution practices, they were not reflected in lower prices to consumers or a larger revenue share for exhibitors.

## The Restructuring of Distribution

The government claimed that the basis for monopolizing production, distribution, and exhibition was provided by the complex system of distributing movies through agreements involving theater ownership, exclusive dealing, block booking, runs and clearances, theater pooling arrangements, and resale price maintenance. Missing from the government's position was any awareness of whether there were, in addition, efficiency gains that would be lost by eliminating this complex structure of distribution. The contested practices began as early as World War I, during an era of intense competition in the industry, suggesting the practices were a response to competitive pressures to reduce costs and enhance the demand for movies. If so, ending the practices, whatever the effects on competition, would raise the costs of distribution.

Before analyzing distribution practices after the divestitures, some background information on movie licensing is needed. Motion picture licenses are granted in one of three ways: competitive bidding, competitive negotiations, and noncompetitive negotiations.[32] In competitive bidding, distributors send formal letters to competing exhibitors requesting bids on a forthcoming movie. Terms may include a nonrefundable rental guarantee, an advance payment against box office receipts, percentage terms for sharing box office receipts, cooperative advertising expense sharing, boundaries for geographic clearances, length of run, and the opening date. For peak-demand periods, the summer months and Christmas, bids are often requested six months or more in advance. Competitive bidding by exhibitors on a movie-by-movie basis is costly, in terms both of preparing bids and of evaluating bids from a variety of exhibitors in different locations. It also shifts the risks of a movie's failure to the exhibitor since adjustments to license terms after the opening date would defeat the purpose of competitive bidding. If exhibitors knew that license terms would be adjusted, their bids could be grossly overstated since overbidding would have no harmful consequences.

In competitive negotiations, a distributor negotiates with a few exhibitors in an area for the right to license a movie, rather than opening competition to all exhibitors. In noncompetitive negotiations, a distributor negotiates with a single exhibitor in an area. This took place under exclusive dealing contracts with exhibitors and by necessity in one-exhibitor towns. It also took place in earlier periods when exhibitors banded together to form booking agencies in order to gain leverage in negotiating movie rental terms with distributors and to capture the cost advantages of economies of scale.

Unavoidably, distributors and exhibitors must negotiate with one another and work to resolve conflicting interests over hundreds of movies from year to year. Numerous issues can divide the parties. Distributors want secure play dates during peak-demand periods when available screens may be scarce. Exhibitors want the best movies, at peak-demand as well as other times, and are always concerned over the risk of a box office flop, especially when they must guarantee payment in advance. Both sides seek to maximize their share of box office receipts. They may sustain significant costs when a movie fails, and each has an incentive to shift the costs to the other party. The process of licensing itself can be costly, involving negotiations over the numerous issues indicated above—revenue sharing, advertising expense sharing, length of run, geographic clearances, coverage of theater overhead expenses, and up-front financial guarantees by exhibitors. Any cheating on license terms is costly to distributors.

Organizational arrangements involving ownership and contracting arose to minimize the various costs of distribution and the potential conflicts between distributors and exhibitors. For example, block booking of yet-to-be-produced movies greatly reduced the costs of movie distribution relative to movie-by-movie distribution. With block booking, distributors dealt with about 10,000 contracts per year. Under individual-movie, theater-by-theater contracting in the 1950s, distributors handled hundreds of thousands of contract negotiations per year.[33] In the 1950s, when exhibitors found the cost of dealing on a movie-by-movie basis much higher than the cost of block booking, they returned to booking movies in groups.[34] As stated earlier, block booking also assured distributors of future exhibition and play dates, allowing the financing of future movies.

Vertical integration and exclusive dealing also served to reduce distribution costs. They provided long-term, stable relationships between distributors and exhibitors, where reputation and trust could be established through repetitive dealing. In block booking, for example, exhibitors learned to trust the overall quality of a studio's movie production. By standardizing licensing between a distributor and a network of closely affiliated exhibitors, conflicts could more easily be avoided and the costs of distribution reduced. Conflicts over post-licensing adjustments, made when a movie does poorly, are internalized under vertical integration since a single owner bears the costs of low revenues. In regard to cheating on license terms, which according to one estimate took place at 20 to 25 percent of theaters in 1947,[35] there is little incentive to cheat on license terms under vertical integration since only theater owners, not employee-managers, can benefit directly from violating license terms. Long-term exclusive dealing relationships or franchising served to reduce exhibitor cheating and overall conflicts with distributors. Cheating on license terms could result in termination of an exhibitor, and the loss of these benefits to exhibitors placed a restraint on their incentives to violate license terms. Franchise contracts also covered rental terms over an extended period, at least one movie season, saving the costs of negotiating on a movie-by-movie basis. Exclusive dealing also provided a secure source of future movies.

One reflection of an increase in distribution costs is the extent of conflicts between distributors and exhibitors. Evidence showing an increase in the number of conflicts between distributors and exhibitors after the divestitures supports the view that integration, either by ownership or by exclusive dealing contract, served to reduce the costs of distribution. The record shows that hundreds of private lawsuits were filed in the 1950s between distributors and exhibitors, based on alleged cheating on license terms agreed to by exhibitors and on alleged discrimination across exhibitors on license terms granted by distributors.[36] The Antitrust Division of the DOJ reported in 1953 that they had received about 1,000 complaints from exhibitors and that about one-third of all correspondence received was from exhibitors complaining about distributors on such issues as runs, clearances, and the criteria used for choosing ex-

hibitors.[37] As further evidence of increased conflict between distributors and exhibitors, Congress held hearings to investigate the motion picture industry in both 1953 and 1956 in response to complaints by exhibitors of unfair treatment and that distributors were violating the terms of the *Paramount* consent decrees.[38] This explosion of complaints appears to be: (1) a direct result of eliminating vertical integration and exclusive dealing, which served for many years to reduce disputes between distributors and exhibitors and thus reduced the costs of distribution and (2) a reflection of exhibitor and distributor attempts to adapt to new rules of movie licensing following *Paramount*. Thus, whatever anticompetitive behavior can be attributed to vertical integration in the motion picture industry, it also contributed to reducing the costs of distributing and exhibiting motion pictures.

If vertical integration and exclusive dealing provided the most efficient means of dealing with the conflicts between distributors and exhibitors and of minimizing the costs of movie distribution, their loss would cause distributors to develop alternatives. Two other organizational arrangements arose to replace vertical integration and exclusive dealing. One was a sub rosa form of exclusive dealing, known in the industry as "tracking" or a "marriage." In tracking, a distributor deals with the same exhibitor in a city or area on a long-term basis, but no formal exclusive dealing or franchising contract exists. The parties are committed voluntarily to a long-term relationship since it is in their mutual self-interest to reduce the costs of distribution.

A second form of distribution that flourished in the 1950s is known as "film splitting."[39] In split agreements, exhibitors in an area agree to rotate the selection of upcoming movies among themselves, avoiding competitive bidding. Exhibitors decide which exhibitor will negotiate with a distributor for a given movie. Distributors send bid letters to all the exhibitors in an area, but only the designated exhibitor negotiates for the movie. If an agreement cannot be reached, the distributor can negotiate with a second designated exhibitor or turn to an exhibitor outside of the split agreement.

Split agreements appear to be a blatant form of exhibitor collusion, intended to avoid competing for movie licenses. However, their use as an anticompetitive tactic remains something of a mystery. Splitting was widely adopted by the industry in the 1950s and for thirty years it was condoned by the DOJ, possibly because it helped protect small exhibitors and thus was in the spirit of the *Paramount* decision. Even more significantly, those most likely harmed by an exhibitor cartel, the distributors who could have stopped split agreements by private antitrust actions, fully accepted and participated with exhibitors in the split agreements. Acceptance of split agreements by distributors from the 1950s onward indicates that the agreements provided economic efficiencies such as savings in distribution costs, benefiting both exhibitors and distributors. Not until 1985 and 1986 did the DOJ take decisive action against exhibitors, filing thirteen lawsuits against split agreements throughout the country.

Tracking and split agreements dominated movie allocations to exhibitors after the court-ordered divestitures. Competitive bidding, the district court solution to exhibitor problems in 1946, was largely rejected by both sides. Loews reported that for an average picture with 15,000 theater bookings in 1955, competitive bidding was used in only 3.2 percent of the licenses.[40] Universal Pictures had a similarly low rate of competitive bidding. In contrast, tracking represented a form of integration and allowed for noncompetitive negotiations. Tracking provided the efficiencies of long-term

distribution relationships, achieved through repetitive dealing and subsequent settling-up through adjustments, but without vertical integration through ownership or formal exclusive dealing arrangements. Tracking also avoided the costs of competitive bidding and reduced the incentives for exhibitor cheating since, unlike competitive bidding, it allowed for adjustments. The benefits from split agreements in the 1950s appear to be a more or less assured exhibitor for a movie, an avoidance of the transaction costs and higher risks of competitive bidding, and a reduced likelihood of lawsuits by exhibitors charging distributors with discrimination in license terms since each exhibitor was given an equal opportunity to receive good movies. Splitting provided a weak form of block booking. Implicit in distributors' participation in split agreements was that some exhibitor would screen their movie, reducing the risks of production. Since distributors could have ended split agreements, the end result must have been that rental shares to distributors under split agreements were no less than alternative approaches to licensing.

Distributors and exhibitors have shifted between tracking, splitting, and competitive bidding as the relative costs and benefits of each licensing method have changed over time. In the 1950s, splitting and tracking dominated distribution. In the 1970s competitive bidding dominated distribution. According to General Cinema and Disney, between one-half and two-thirds of all distribution in the 1970s was achieved by competitive bidding.[41] According to another commentator, in the early 1990s there was little competitive bidding.[42]

The relative costs and benefits of alternative forms of distribution change over time with shifts in the supply and demand for movies, changes in the technology and cost of distributing movies and monitoring exhibitors, and changes in the law on distribution. For example, splitting is probably rare today because it was found to be per se illegal under the Sherman Antitrust Act in the 1980s.[43] Competitive bidding increased in frequency as the supply of movies decreased relative to the number of screens for viewing. The average annual supply of movies was 338 in the 1950s, but only 246 in the 1970s. The number of new releases fell from 282 in 1971 to 167 in 1977, rising to 232 in 1983.[44] From 1971 to 1977 the number of screens increased by 14 percent, from 14,055 to 16,041, while the annual output of new movies over the same period fell by 40 percent. It is not surprising to find that competitive bidding dominated distribution during this period. The number of new movies in the 1990s has far exceeded levels of the 1970s, at over 400 movies annually, consistent with less use of competitive bidding.

## Current Trends in Industry Performance

Contemporary indicators of industry performance and the demand for first-run movies in theaters are shown in Table 11.4. In the modern era, domestic box office admissions bottomed out in 1971 at a headcount of 820 million and have grown slowly since then, reaching a high in 1998 of 1.48 billion and declining to 1.42 billion in 2000. As an indicator of the demand for movies, total admission is misleading since it measures only theater attendance. Aggregate movie demand includes videocassettes, DVDs, pay television, and network and syndicated television. Nontheatrical revenues represent approximately 60 percent of total movie sales.

Domestic box office gross was relatively flat in the early 1990s, but it grew subsequently with rising attendance and average ticket prices. Again, a focus on exhibitor performance alone overlooks the much larger demand for movies in nontheatrical channels of distribution.

While admissions have grown slowly, paradoxically, the total number of screens, as indicated earlier, rose at a phenomenal rate in the 1990s. The number of screens grew by 34 percent in the short period of 1995 to 2000. Given the long-term growth in number of screens and slow growth in attendance, admissions per screen have fallen sharply since the 1970s.

New multiplex theater construction, sometimes with twenty screens or more, has been growing for years. As replacements for the large single-screen and small multiscreen theaters of an earlier era, they offer a number of economic advantages. Movies can be moved to different-sized theaters within the complex, depending on audience demand. Centralized operations, such as ticket sales and admission, concession goods sales, and restrooms, can service a large number of individual theater screens, achieving economies of scale in facilities and staff relative to separate theaters. Furthermore, by offering a variety of movies, exhibitors reduce their risk relative to dependence on a single movie. For patrons, a wide variety of movies are available at a single location, providing convenience and possibly reduced search costs, and blockbuster movies can be shown on two or three screens, further accommodating movie customers.

Although the price of motion picture admission is often complained about, average ticket prices in real terms remained relatively flat from the late 1960s to the early 1980s, when prices began to rise slowly. The basis of the price series in Table 11.4 changed in 1989, so price comparisons pre- and post-1989 are most likely not warranted. The price series from 1989 onward, however, shows a surprising fall in real ticket prices from 1990 to 1996, but real prices have risen in recent years. In addition, it is important to keep in mind that the quality of exhibition, in terms of seating, sound, and movie technology, has improved greatly and the price series is not adjusted for quality changes.

This study has focused on domestic economic and competitive performance, since that is of greatest public policy interest. However, the industry is international in scope, with U.S.-produced movies generating foreign revenues for distributors comparable to those produced in the United States. In 2001, U.S. distributors earned approximately $8 billion in revenues, with half coming from the United States and Canada and half from the rest of the world.[45] The main revenue-generating countries outside the United States are Japan, Germany, France, Canada, United Kingdom/Ireland, Spain, and Australia. Foreign market sales are huge and in the aggregate rival those produced in the United States.

### Channels of Distribution

The rise of new technologies in delivering movies has drastically altered distribution channels. Until the introduction of television in the late 1940s, movie receipts came exclusively from box office admissions. Television allowed home viewing of movies. Television networks became a substantial source of movie revenues starting in the 1960s. In the 1980s, VCR ownership spread rapidly, as did cable system and pay movie channel subscriptions.

Table 11.5 shows the dramatic shift in movie-generated revenues in the 1980s from box office sales to videocassette rentals and sales. Starting with virtually 100 percent of movie revenues in the 1940s, box office receipts fell to a little more than 50 percent of total domestic receipts by the early 1980s. Cable television pay channels were second to box office revenues, followed by videocassettes, which still lacked large-scale VCR penetration in U.S. television households. By 1984 theatrical box office accounted for less than 50

percent of domestic movie revenues for the first time in history. Videocassette revenues grew rapidly with the spread of VCR ownership. In 1980 about 2 percent of U.S. households with televisions had a VCR. This rose to 50 percent in 1987 and 80 percent by 1992.[46] In 1992 videocassettes accounted for over 50 percent of movie receipts for the first time. U.S. consumers spent approximately twice as much to watch movies on videocassettes as they did to view movies in theaters. Nevertheless, theater exhibition remains the key to a movie's future success in other distribution channels. Future demand is built on theatrical box office success, favorable reviews, word-of-mouth advertising, and promotion and advertising for theatrical and home viewing release.

### Price Discrimination

In the early years, distributors price-discriminated through the timed releases of movies from first-run to second-run to third-run theaters and so forth. Gone are most second-run theaters and all subsequent-run theaters. Along with temporal price discrimination by run, there has long been daily differential pricing, between early and evening screenings and across classes of customers, such as discount prices for children, students, and seniors. The modern equivalents of price discrimination are timed releases of movies to first-run theaters and then, in sequence, to hotels and airlines, pay television, home video, network television, and syndicated television. As in the earlier era, prices decline with later releases, reflecting differing segments of the demand for movies. For over seventy-five years, distributors have attempted to capture the maximum revenues from movie rentals and sales by price discrimination according to differing demands for movie viewing. With each new technology that allowed view-

Table 11.4

## Admissions, Screens, Average Admission Price, and Box Office Gross, 1967–2000

| Year | No. of admissions (millions) | Percent change | No. of screens | Percent change | Admissions per screen | Percent change | Average ticket price | Average ticket price (constant dollars) | Percent change | Box office gross (millions of dollars) | Box office gross (millions of constant dollars) | Percent change |
|---|---|---|---|---|---|---|---|---|---|---|---|---|
| 1967 | 926.5 | | 13,000 | | 71,269 | | 1.20 | 2.95 | | 1,110.0 | 2,727.3 | |
| 1968 | 978.6 | 5.62 | 13,190 | 1.46 | 74,193 | 4.10 | 1.31 | 3.05 | 3.33 | 1,282.0 | 2,981.4 | 9.32 |
| 1969 | 911.9 | -6.82 | 13,480 | 2.20 | 67,648 | -8.82 | 1.42 | 3.14 | 3.12 | 1,294.0 | 2,862.8 | -3.98 |
| 1970 | 920.6 | 0.95 | 13,750 | 2.00 | 66,953 | -1.03 | 1.55 | 3.26 | 3.87 | 1,429.2 | 3,008.8 | 5.10 |
| 1971 | 820.3 | -10.90 | 14,055 | 2.22 | 58,364 | -12.83 | 1.65 | 3.30 | 1.13 | 1,349.5 | 2,699.0 | -10.30 |
| 1972 | 934.1 | 13.87 | 14,428 | 2.65 | 64,742 | 10.93 | 1.70 | 3.30 | 0.03 | 1,583.1 | 3,074.0 | 13.89 |
| 1973 | 864.6 | -7.44 | 14,420 | -0.06 | 59,958 | -7.39 | 1.76 | 3.33 | 0.79 | 1,523.5 | 2,880.0 | -6.31 |
| 1974 | 1,010.7 | 16.90 | 14,417 | -0.02 | 70,105 | 16.92 | 1.89 | 3.32 | -0.16 | 1,908.5 | 3,354.1 | 16.46 |
| 1975 | 1,032.8 | 2.19 | 15,030 | 4.25 | 68,716 | -1.98 | 2.05 | 3.31 | -0.46 | 2,115.0 | 3,411.3 | 1.70 |
| 1976 | 957.1 | -7.33 | 15,832 | 5.34 | 60,454 | -12.02 | 2.13 | 3.27 | -1.05 | 2,036.0 | 3,127.5 | -8.32 |
| 1977 | 1,063.2 | 11.09 | 16,041 | 1.32 | 66,280 | 9.64 | 2.23 | 3.27 | -0.21 | 2,372.0 | 3,472.9 | 11.04 |
| 1978 | 1,128.2 | 6.11 | 16,251 | 1.31 | 69,423 | 4.74 | 2.34 | 3.25 | -0.32 | 2,644.0 | 3,677.3 | 5.89 |
| 1979 | 1,120.9 | -0.65 | 16,901 | 4.00 | 66,322 | -4.47 | 2.52 | 3.29 | 0.95 | 2,821.0 | 3,678.0 | 0.02 |
| 1980 | 1,021.5 | -8.87 | 17,590 | 4.08 | 58,073 | -12.44 | 2.69 | 3.22 | -2.06 | 2,748.5 | 3,287.7 | -10.61 |
| 1981 | 1,067.0 | 4.45 | 18,040 | 2.56 | 59,146 | 1.85 | 2.78 | 3.09 | -4.11 | 2,956.6 | 3,281.5 | -0.19 |
| 1982 | 1,175.4 | 10.16 | 18,020 | -0.11 | 65,228 | 10.28 | 2.94 | 3.06 | -0.74 | 3,452.7 | 3,596.6 | 9.60 |
| 1983 | 1,196.9 | 1.83 | 18,884 | 4.79 | 63,382 | -2.83 | 3.15 | 3.15 | 2.75 | 3,766.0 | 3,762.2 | 4.61 |
| 1984 | 1,199.1 | 0.18 | 20,200 | 6.97 | 59,361 | -6.34 | 3.36 | 3.24 | 2.86 | 4,030.6 | 3,883.0 | 3.21 |
| 1985 | 1,056.1 | -11.93 | 21,147 | 4.69 | 49,941 | -15.87 | 3.55 | 3.29 | 1.64 | 3,749.4 | 3,474.9 | -10.51 |
| 1986 | 1,017.2 | -3.68 | 22,765 | 7.65 | 44,683 | -10.53 | 3.71 | 3.32 | 1.04 | 3,778.0 | 3,385.3 | -2.58 |
| 1987 | 1,088.5 | 7.01 | 23,555 | 3.47 | 46,211 | 3.42 | 3.91 | 3.39 | 2.01 | 4,252.9 | 3,688.6 | 8.96 |
| 1988 | 1,084.8 | -0.34 | 23,234 | -1.36 | 46,690 | 1.04 | 4.11 | 3.42 | 0.75 | 4,458.4 | 3,706.1 | 0.47 |
| 1989 | 1,262.8 | 16.41 | 23,132 | -0.44 | 54,591 | 16.92 | 3.99 | 3.15 | -7.68 | 5,033.4 | 3,979.0 | 7.36 |
| 1990 | 1,188.6 | -5.88 | 23,689 | 2.41 | 50,175 | -8.09 | 4.23 | 3.19 | 1.29 | 5,021.8 | 3,792.9 | -4.68 |
| 1991 | 1,140.6 | -4.04 | 24,570 | 3.72 | 46,422 | -7.48 | 4.21 | 3.04 | -4.79 | 4,803.2 | 3,470.5 | -8.50 |

| | | | | | | | | | | | |
|---|---|---|---|---|---|---|---|---|---|---|---|
| 1992 | 1,173.2 | 2.86 | 25,105 | 2.18 | 46,732 | 0.67 | 4.15 | 2.92 | -4.13 | 4,871.0 | 3,423.0 | -1.37 |
| 1993 | 1,244.0 | 6.03 | 25,737 | 2.52 | 48,335 | 3.43 | 4.14 | 2.84 | -2.64 | 5,154.2 | 3,535.1 | 3.27 |
| 1994 | 1,291.7 | 3.83 | 26,586 | 3.30 | 48,586 | 0.52 | 4.18 | 2.78 | -1.93 | 5,396.2 | 3,595.1 | 1.70 |
| 1995 | 1,262.6 | -2.25 | 27,805 | 4.59 | 45,409 | -6.54 | 4.35 | 2.83 | 1.50 | 5,493.5 | 3,569.5 | -0.71 |
| 1996 | 1,338.6 | 6.02 | 29,690 | 6.78 | 45,086 | -0.71 | 4.42 | 2.78 | -1.71 | 5,911.5 | 3,715.6 | 4.09 |
| 1997 | 1,387.7 | 3.67 | 31,640 | 6.57 | 43,859 | -2.72 | 4.59 | 2.84 | 2.08 | 6,365.9 | 3,933.2 | 5.86 |
| 1998 | 1,480.7 | 6.70 | 34,186 | 8.05 | 43,313 | -1.24 | 4.69 | 2.85 | 0.66 | 6,949.0 | 4,229.8 | 7.54 |
| 1999 | 1,465.2 | -1.05 | 37,185 | 8.77 | 39,403 | -9.03 | 5.08 | 3.06 | 7.36 | 7,448.0 | 4,493.5 | 6.24 |
| 2000 | 1,420.8 | -3.03 | 37,396 | 0.57 | 37,993 | -3.58 | 5.39 | 3.20 | 4.36 | 7,661.0 | 4,546.3 | 1.17 |

*Sources:* National Association of Theater Owners, *2000–2001 Encyclopedia of Exhibition*; Motion Picture Association of America, *U.S. Economics Review*, 1992, 1997, and 2000; Goldman Sachs, *Movie Industry Update—1993*, April 7, 1993; and U.S. Department of Labor, Bureau of Labor Statistics, Producer Price Index data at <http://www.bls.gov>.

*Notes*: Average ticket prices and box office gross for 1967 through 1996 were deflated using the entertainment CPI, 1982–84 = 100. The entertainment CPI covers products beyond movies, including theater, opera, concerts, sporting events, sporting equipment, toys, hobbies, and reading materials. Average ticket prices and box office gross for 1997 through 2000 were deflated using the recreation CPI, 12/1997 = 100. The Bureau of Labor Statistics discontinued the entertainment CPI in 1997. The recreation CPI began in 1993 to take the place of the entertainment CPI.

Table 11.5

## Distribution of Domestic Theatrical Revenues

Gross revenue (millions) and percent of total

| | 1983 | | 1984 | | 1985 | | 1986 | | 1987 | | 1988 | | 1989 | | 1990 | | 1991 | | 1992 | |
|---|---|---|---|---|---|---|---|---|---|---|---|---|---|---|---|---|---|---|---|---|
| | $ | % | $ | % | $ | % | $ | % | $ | % | $ | % | $ | % | $ | % | $ | % | $ | % |
| Box office rentals | 1,700 | 54 | 1,800 | 47 | 1,635 | 40 | 1,650 | 38 | 1,830 | 38 | 1,920 | 35 | 2,165 | 35 | 2,260 | 32 | 2,160 | 29 | 2,100 | 26 |
| Pay TV | 550 | 17 | 600 | 16 | 635 | 15 | 600 | 14 | 575 | 12 | 630 | 11 | 670 | 11 | 725 | 10 | 750 | 10 | 770 | 9 |
| Home video | 400 | 13 | 950 | 25 | 1,335 | 32 | 1,630 | 37 | 1,915 | 40 | 2,460 | 45 | 2,760 | 44 | 3,220 | 46 | 3,760 | 50 | 4,230 | 52 |
| Television | 410 | 13 | 410 | 11 | 450 | 11 | 450 | 10 | 425 | 9 | 425 | 8 | 525 | 8 | 600 | 9 | 650 | 9 | 675 | 8 |
| Other | 100 | 3 | 60 | 2 | 56 | 1 | 62 | 1 | 65 | 1 | 90 | 2 | 105 | 2 | 150 | 2 | 220 | 3 | 370 | 5 |
| Total | 3,160 | 100 | 3,820 | 100 | 4,111 | 100 | 4,392 | 100 | 4,810 | 100 | 5,525 | 100 | 6,225 | 100 | 6,955 | 100 | 7,540 | 100 | 8,145 | 100 |

*Source*: Adapted from Goldman Sachs, *Movie Industry Update–1993*, April 1993.

ing at home—network television, cable pay channels, and videocassettes and DVDs—the channels of distribution have changed, but the same differential pricing strategy to maximize revenues has always prevailed.

## Industry Restructuring: Vertical Integration and Conglomerate Organization

### Vertical Integration

Four major distributors—Paramount, Warner Brothers, Columbia, and Universal—returned to theater ownership in the mid-1980s. A relaxation of consent decrees under the Paramount decision allowed Paramount and Warner Brothers to vertically integrate once again into theaters. Columbia and Universal were not bound by Paramount consent decrees, since they did not own theaters in the 1940s. In the mid-1980s the parent company of Universal, MCA, purchased 50 percent of Cineplex Odeon, including about 500 screens in Canada. Columbia/Tri-Star, later acquired by Sony, purchased the former Loews and USA Cinema theater chains. Sony acquired Cineplex Odeon in 1998, forming Loews Cineplex. Viacom, purchaser of Paramount in 1994, and Time Warner, formed by the merger of Time Inc. and Warner Communications in 1990, were partners in Cinamerica theaters, with over 300 screens, which they sold to WestStar Cinemas. In 1988 National Amusement theaters affiliated with Viacom. In addition, Viacom owns Famous Players, an 800–screen chain in Canada. With these acquisitions and continued new theater building programs, these studios accounted for approximately 4,500 screens, or 12 percent of North American screens.

Vertical integration for anticompetitive purposes, the view that dominated the government's thinking up to the 1980s, cannot explain this return by distributors to ownership of theaters. With only 12 percent of all screens, the distributors could not possibly collude to effect monopoly pricing and foreclosure of rivals. Only the expectation of fundamental efficiency advantages can explain this rebirth of vertical integration. These cost advantages include those mentioned earlier—control of box office receipts, adjustments in license terms after a movie opens, promoting movies, and reduced transaction costs between distributor and exhibitor in licensing movies. However, not all distributors believe the gains from domestic theater ownership are large enough relative to the investment cost and risk. Such large sophisticated companies as Disney and Twentieth Century Fox have not integrated into theaters in North America.

### Conglomerate Ownership

The major studio-distributors are generally part of massive, highly diversified conglomerate firms, with ownership of a broad class of entertainment and information products. A prominent current exception is Dreamworks, an independent company producing for movies, television, and music. Table 11.6 shows leading movie studio-distributors, their parent companies, and main areas of product ownership and production. Each firm in Table 11.6 produces movies and television shows, and many own television stations, cable systems, cable channels, theme parks, publishing and newspaper operations, professional sports teams, music firms, and retail outlets.

Conglomerate firm ownership of movie studio-distributors is not a new phenomenon. Gulf and Western, one of the largest conglomerate firms formed in the 1960s, with such diverse business lines as agriculture, apparel, automotive parts, and financial services, purchased Paramount Pictures

Table 11.6

## Conglomerate Operations Including Studio/Distributors

| Area | AOL Time Warner (Warner Bros.) | Disney | News Corp. (Twentieth Century Fox) | Sony Corp. (Columbia) | Viacom (Paramount) | Vivendi (Universal) |
|---|---|---|---|---|---|---|
| New movies | * | * | * | * | * | * |
| Film library | * | * | * | * | * | * |
| Theaters | * | | | * | * | * |
| TV shows | * | * | * | * | * | * |
| Broadcast TV station(s) | * | * | * | | * | |
| Broadcast TV network(s) | * | * | * | | * | |
| Basic cable network(s) | * | * | * | | * | * |
| Pay cable network(s) | * | * | | | * | |
| Cable or satellite systems | * | | * | | | |
| Recorded music | * | * | | * | | * |
| Theme parks | * | * | | | | * |
| Pro sports | * | * | | | * | * |
| Publishing | * | * | * | | * | |
| Audio players | | | | * | | |
| Video players | | | | * | | |
| Retailing | * | * | | | * | |
| Internet access | * | | | | | |

*Source*: Standard & Poor's, *Industry Surveys, Movies and Home Entertainment*, February 27, 1997, and May 10, 2001.

in 1967. Also in 1967, Avco, another major conglomerate, acquired Embassy, a long-time movie producer. Warner Communication was acquired by Time Inc. in 1990, but Warner was a diversified firm prior to the acquisition, with interests in movies, music, books and magazines, cable television, and video games. Twentieth Century Fox, before being acquired by News Corp., the international newspaper publisher, had ownership interests in movies, television stations, music, publishing, soft drink bottling, and ski resorts.

More recently, Sony, the producer of home electronic equipment, acquired CBS records in 1988 and Columbia, previously owned by Coca-Cola, in 1989. In 1994 Viacom Inc., owner of cable channels and theaters, acquired both Paramount Communications and Blockbuster Video, the retail chain. In June 1995, Seagrams, the beverage company, acquired 80 percent of MCA, owner of Universal, from Matsushita, the Japanese conglomerate, and then sold to Vivendi in 2000. In February 1996, the Disney Co. acquired Capital Cities/ABC, owner of ABC television, newspapers, and 80 percent of ESPN, the cable sports channel. Some of this acquisition activity has been encouraged by the relaxation of rules limiting joint ownership of television stations and newspapers, and allowing television networks to own programming for syndication.

A popular reason given for conglomerate ownership is that reaping the gains from a diversified portfolio of assets with relatively uncorrelated income streams, reduces the overall business risk of the firm. As noted, motion picture production has long been regarded as a relatively high-risk business. The popular view was that out of every ten movies, six or seven lost money, one or two broke even, and two or three made money. Combining movie-making with some countervailing steadier stream of income offers a means of reducing overall risk. A commonly offered explanation for combining various forms of entertainment products with media firms is that joint ownership facilitates intrafirm promotion and marketing of entertainment products by utilizing a variety of complementary distribution channels. For example, cable and television channels can promote one another's programming; movies can enhance related book and music sales; and movie characters can improve retail sales. Another common explanation for conglomerate ownership is to capitalize on the synergistic capabilities of management skills.

Whether the expected synergistic effects of conglomerate ownership of movies will materialize for present owners is yet to be determined. Some past movie studio owners, such as Coca-Cola, Matsushita, and Seagram's, sold out after disappointing performance in the production of movies. As in all competitive endeavors, some mergers and acquisitions prove successful in stimulating demand and lowering costs, and others do not, leading to divestiture. Some firms are more skillful than others in combining firms with different corporate cultures and in gaining from synergistic opportunities. However, many highly diversified firms formed in the conglomerate merger wave of the 1960s, such as Gulf & Western, International Telephone and Telegraph, Litton Industries, and Teledyne, ultimately failed to provide the expected stock market performance predicted by conglomerate ownership and were split up in the 1980s. These and other conglomerate firms divested hundreds of disparate firms in the 1980s, returning to a core set of businesses. Whether a similar fate awaits current firms with motion picture divisions is unclear. For now, conglomerate ownership rules the movie business.

## Conclusions

Government can alter the structure and conduct of an industry through regulation and lawsuits, but under open-market competition, fundamental economic principles and forces shape the structure and conduct of an industry.[47] The history of the motion picture industry provides a vivid example of this process.

The industry's structure and conduct were drastically altered through antitrust action, putting an end to the vertical integration of distributors into theaters, formal exclusive dealing arrangements, and numerous other distribution practices. Hundreds of theaters became first-run houses overnight, and hundreds closed in the ensuing years. Yet distributor–theater relationships continued to be ruled by competitive pressures for economic efficiency. Distribution by tracking was used as a means to capture the gains formerly provided by exclusive dealing arrangements. Split agreements were adopted to avoid the costs and risks of competitive bidding. Even after block booking was ruled to be anticompetitive, many theaters chose to book in small blocks in order to lower licensing costs.[48] And when, after many years, distributors were given the freedom to own theaters again, some distributors chose to reintegrate into theater ownership. Since merger for monopoly in exhibition was impossible in the 1980s and 1990s, the efficiency gains to vertical integration guided distributors back to theater ownership. The government's 1948 decree against theater ownership was, in a sense, overridden in the 1980s and 1990s by the efficiencies of vertical integration.

Moreover, despite the best efforts of government in 1948 to protect small theatrical owners by deconcentrating first-run exhibition, exhibition has returned to a relatively concentrated structure. The top five exhibition firms owned or controlled approximately 24 percent of the 18,000 screens in 1945 (see Table 11.3). In 2000, the top five exhibition firms owned 40 percent of the approximately 37,000 screens in North America (see Table 11.2). Small neighborhood theaters were eliminated by home viewing of movies via network television, cable, and videocassettes, as well as by the economic efficiencies of multiplex theaters. Government intervention surely had a profound effect on the structure of exhibition in the 1950s, but, in the long term, economic forces have reshaped exhibition to be even more concentrated than before the government's intervention.

As in the case of the persistent drive for efficiency in distribution, neither government intervention nor major changes in channels of distribution have altered the industry's ability to price differentially across consumers. Most revenues now come from nontheatrical sources, primarily videocassettes, DVDs, and cable television. This reverses the historic flow, in which first-run theaters produced the majority of revenues. Nevertheless, the timed release of movies and differential pricing have been utilized for over seventy-five years to capture the greatest amount of revenues.

During the industry's golden era in the 1930s, few could have foreseen the rise of television in the 1950s and its impact on the industry. In the 1960s few could have foreseen the rise of videocassettes in the 1980s and the great influx of revenues they generated. What technological changes will sweep the industry in the next twenty years— given digitalization of movies, distribution over the Internet, and unknown future innovations— and their impact is a story yet to be told. But, as in the past, industry structure and conduct will be conditioned by the competitive drive to increase the demand for movies and to gain efficiencies in their distribution.

## Notes

1. See Table 11.4 and Harold L. Vogel, *Entertainment Industry Economics* (Cambridge, England: Cambridge University Press, 1986), Table S2.2.

2. In block booking, large groups of movies, a year's supply, were licensed to exhibitors during the fall booking season. In blind bidding, exhibitors rented movies without advanced screening and, in earlier years, without knowledge of the movie's story, writers, and actors. In franchising, the exhibitor agreed to rental fees and typically had exclusive rights to license the distributor's movie for a year or more.

3. *United States v. Paramount Pictures, Inc.*, 344 U.S. 131 (1948); 85 F. Supp. 881 (S.D.N.Y., 1949).

4. *Los Angeles Times*, July 11, 1997, p. D-1.

5. Nat D. Fellman, "The Exhibitor," in *The Movie Business Book*, Jason E. Squire, ed. (Englewood Cliffs, NJ: Prentice-Hall, 1983), 313–22.

6. *Los Angeles Times*, March 7, 2001, p. C-1.

7. This section draws on the history presented in Mae D. Huettig, *Economic Control of the Motion Picture Industry* (Philadelphia: University of Pennsylvania Press, 1944); Ralph Cassady Jr., "Monopoly in Motion Picture Production and Distribution, 1908–1915," *Southern California Law Review* (Summer 1959): 325–90; Michael Conant, *Antitrust in the Motion Picture Industry: Economic and Legal Analysis* (Berkeley and Los Angeles: University of California Press, 1960); and Arthur De Vany and Ross D. Eckard, "Motion Picture Antitrust: The Paramount Case Revisited," *Research in Law and Economics* 14 (November 1991): 51–112.

8. *Federal Trade Commission v. Stanley Booking Corp.*, 1 FTC 212 (1918).

9. Robert Anderson, "The Motion Picture Patent Company: A Reevaluation," in *The American Film Industry*, Tino Balio, ed. (Madison: University of Wisconsin Press, 1985), 133–52.

10. De Vany and Eckard, 70–71.

11. Conant, 49–50.

12. Ibid., 61–76.

13. Ibid., 66.

14. Ibid., 55 and 64.

15. *Federal Trade Commission v. Famous Players-Lasky Corp.*, 11 FTC (1927).

16. Conant, 99.

17. *United States v. Paramount Pictures, Inc.*, 66 F. Supp. 323 (S.D.N.Y., 1946).

18. A formula deal involved a distributor and theater chain setting rental terms on the basis of a percentage of the national theatrical gross for a movie. One advantage of a formula deal was that it reduced the incentive for an exhibitor to cheat on reporting box office receipts. Master agreements

based the share of box office receipts on all the theaters in a chain, rather than on a theater-by-theater basis.

19. In pooling arrangements, independent exhibitors joined together, much like a cooperative, to gain the advantages of economies of scale. Managed by a member or committee of members, they booked movies and provided such services as bookkeeping and auditing. Pooling arrangements among the top five firms' theaters allegedly entailed the pooling of profits as well, as would take place in a cartel. They were found to be illegal.

20. *United States v. Paramount Pictures, Inc.*, 344 U.S. 131 (1948).

21. The consent decrees applied only to domestic theaters. At the time, Paramount controlled over 400 screens in Canada, and Twentieth Century Fox and Warner Brothers each controlled over 400 theaters abroad, with large holdings in England.

22. Ed Cray, "Hollywood Unchained," *California Lawyer* 6 (February 1986): 33–35, 54.

23. U.S. Department of Commerce, *National Income Supplement to Survey of Current Business*, 1954, 206–8; U.S. Department of Commerce, *U.S. Income and Output*, 1958, 151.

24. U.S. Bureau of the Census, *Census of Business, Selected Services, Summary Statistics*, 1948, 1954, and 1958. This source reports movie admission revenues falling from $1.25 billion in 1948 to $838 million in 1958.

25. *Film Daily Yearbook of Motion Pictures*, 1959, p. 106. The *Film Daily* was an industry daily newspaper published between 1915 and 1970. The *Film Daily Yearbook* was an annual published by Film Daily, New York, between 1918 and 1969.

26. *Electrical Merchandising*, McGraw-Hill Publishing Co., Inc., January 1951–January 1958, as reported in Conant, *Antitrust in the Motion Picture Industry*, p. 13.

27. Motion Picture Distribution Trade Practices, 1956: Hearings Before a Subcommittee of the Select Committee on Small Business, 84th Congress, 2d Sess., p. 305.

28. Robert W. Crandall, "The Postwar Performance of the Motion-Picture Industry," *Antitrust Bulletin* 20 (Spring 1975): 49–88.

29. Stanley I. Ornstein, "Motion Picture Distribution, Film Splitting, and Antitrust Policy," *Hastings Communications and Entertainment Law Journal* (Winter 1995): 415–44.

30. *Film Daily Yearbook*, 1949 and 1959.

31. *Film Daily Yearbook*, various issues.

32. For discussion of licensing see, *United States v. Capital Services, Inc.*, 586 F. Supp. 134 (E.D. Wis. 1983) and 756 F. 2d 502 (7th Cir. 1985); Fellman, "The Exhibitor," pp. 315–22; Ralph Cassady Jr., "Impact of the Paramount Decision on Motion Picture Distribution and Price Making," *Southern California Law Review* 31 (1958): 150–80.

33. 1956 Hearings, statement of Charles L. Feldman, Vice President, Universal Pictures (see n. 27).

34. Conant, *Antitrust in the Motion Picture Industry*, p. 145, n. 136.

35. Ibid., p. 71.

36. Ibid., pp. 178–79; James S. Gordon, "Horizontal and Vertical Restraints of Trade: The Legality of Motion Picture Splits Under the Antitrust Laws," *Yale Law Journal* 75 (1965): 239–60.

37. *Motion Picture Distribution Trade Practices: Hearings Before Select Subcommittee on Monopoly of the Senate Select Committee on Small Business*, 83rd Congress, 1st Session, 1953, p. 14.

38. 1953 and 1956 hearings (see nn. 27, 37).

39. Ornstein, "Motion Picture Distribution."

40. 1956 Hearings, pp. 372 and 474.

41. *General Cinema v. Buena Vista Distribution Company*, 532 F. Supp. 1244, 1271 (E.D. Cal. 1982).

42. D. Barry Reardon, "The Studio Distributor," in *The Movie Business Book*, 2d ed., Jason E. Squire, ed. (New York: Simon and Schuster, 1992), 309–19.

43. *United States v. Capital Services*, 756 F. 2d 502 (7th Cir. 1985).

44. Vogel, *Entertainment Industry Economics*, p. 45; Thomas Guback, "Theatrical Film," *Who Owns the Media? Concentration of Ownership in the Mass Communication Industry*, 2d ed., Benjamin M. Compaine, ed. (White Plains, NY: Knowledge Industry Publications, 1979), 179–249.

45. *Movies and Home Entertainment*, Standard & Poor's Industry Surveys, May 10, 2001.

46. *Arbitron Ratings/Television Updates* Quarterly Reports.

47. Stanley I. Ornstein, "Antitrust Policy and Market Forces as Determinants of Industry Structure: Case Histories in Beer and Distilled Spirits," *Antitrust Bulletin* 26 (Summer 1981): 281–313.

48. In 1950, after block booking supposedly ended, 3,700 theaters booked Paramount Pictures movies in blocks, with a right to cancel 20 percent of those booked. Conant, 145, n. 136.

## Selected Readings

Conant, Michael. *Antitrust in the Motion Picture Industry: Economic and Legal Analysis*. Berkeley and Los Angeles: University of California Press, 1960. This book has long been the definitive study of competitive conditions in the motion picture industry up to the 1960s. The author presents a strong case in support of the courts' *Paramount* decisions.

De Vany, Arthur, and Ross D. Eckert. "Motion Picture Antitrust: The Paramount Case Revisited." *Research in Law and Economics* 14 (November 1991): 51–112. This paper presents economic efficiency and pro-competitive explanations for the many distribution and licensing practices found to be illegal in the *Paramount* decisions, including vertical integration, block booking, blind selling, clearances and runs, franchising, formula deals, and master agreements.

Ornstein, Stanley I. "Motion Picture Distribution, Film Splitting, and Antitrust Policy." *Hastings communications and Entertainment Law Journal* (Winter 1995): 415–44. This papers summarizes the main types of motion picture licenses, provides economic efficiency explanations for film splitting and block booking, and tests for the competition-enhancing benefits of the *Paramount* decisions.

Vogel, Harold L. *Entertainment Industry Economics*. 5th edition. Cambridge, UK: Cambridge University Press, 2001. This book includes chapters on the motion picture industry, covering such topics as the financing, marketing, distribution, and financial accounting of movies, as well as providing historical data on the industry's economic performance.

# 12

# Nursing Homes

## Rising Costs and Added Forms of Service

*Joseph A. Giacalone*

The nursing home industry must be viewed in the context of the total health care delivery system. In this way, it is possible to assess the interrelationships of the industry with the other components of the overall system and consider the potential impact of changes and trends. This chapter begins with a look at the totality of health care expenditures and then proceeds to an analysis of the nursing home industry and related financial issues.

### Overview of Health Care and Nursing Home Spending Patterns

National health expenditures reached $1 trillion for the first time in 1996 and amounted to $1.2 trillion in 1999, the most recent year for which data are available. This represents spending of about $4,350 per capita. Despite their large absolute size, health care expenditures experienced a marked deceleration in growth during the 1990s. The double-digit year-to-year growth rates that marked the period from 1960 to 1990 gave way to single-digit rates that reached a low of 4.8 percent in 1998. The growth rate rose to 5.6 percent in 1999, however, and appeared to have begun an upward trend in the first years of the new century. Health expenditures, which accounted for 5.1 percent of gross domestic product (GDP) in 1960, rose

to 12.2 percent in 1990 and 13.0 percent in 1999. This measure has been relatively stable since 1993 but recent projections foresee a rise to almost 16 percent of GDP by 2010.[1] Higher private health insurance premiums, increasingly sophisticated treatment techniques, and the continuing surge in the cost of prescription drugs seem to be the major factors in this scenario. The move from a fee-for-service environment to a managed care environment was the most significant factor in slowing the growth of overall health care spending in the early 1990s.

In 1999, expenditures of $90.0 billion for freestanding nursing home care represented 7.4 percent of national health expenditures. The "freestanding" designation is important because the data on national health expenditures often do not include skilled-nursing care provided by hospital-based facilities. Such nursing care expenditures are included in the hospital care component of national expenditures. Table 12.1 shows the trends in spending for nursing home care in freestanding facilities in absolute terms and as a percentage of national health expenditures. The growth rate for nursing home spending has declined from 14.8 percent in 1988 to 2.3 percent in 1999, the smallest growth rate in almost four decades. This has been partially attributed to the expanded use of alternative care

Table 12.1

**Nursing Home Expenditures in the Aggregate and as a Percentage of National Health Expenditures (NHE), Selected Years** (billions)

|                  | 1960 | 1970 | 1980  | 1990  | 1999    |
|------------------|------|------|-------|-------|---------|
| NHE              | 26.9 | 73.2 | 247.3 | 699.5 | 1,121.7 |
| Nursing home care| 0.8  | 4.2  | 17.6  | 50.9  | 90.0    |
| Percent of NHE   | 3.0  | 5.7  | 7.1   | 11.2  | 7.4     |

*Source:* Health Care Financing Administration, Office of the Actuary, National Health Statistics Group.

settings (such as home and community-based care and assisted living), a slower rate of medical price increases, and cutbacks in federal Medicare spending due to the Balanced Budget Act of 1997.

We can more fully account for the extent of nursing home spending by isolating the nursing home care component from overall spending on hospital care. For the 1990 to 1996 period, hospital-based skilled-nursing care added from $3.7 billion to $9.0 billion to total expenditures on nursing home care. When such hospital-based care is factored in, it accounts for 6.8 percent to 10.3 percent of combined expenditures. Moreover, the growth rate of spending in the hospital-based facilities averaged 15.9 percent annually, compared with 7.5 percent for freestanding units over the period. The deceleration of spending growth was significant for freestanding facilities but small for hospital-based units.

## Overview of Health Care Financing Patterns

The key distinction in the funding of health care expenditures is between private and public sources. Private sources primarily consist of insurance and out-of-pocket payments; Medicare and Medicaid are the most important public sources. Since 1990,

the shares of health spending financed by private and public sources have been moving closer together. Private sources funded just 54.7 percent of spending in 1999; 45.3 percent was financed by public sources. These figures compare with 59.5 percent and 40.5 percent, respectively, in 1960.

It is noteworthy that after four years of declining growth, Medicare spending on nursing home care increased by over 26 percent in 1997. In an effort to control Medicare spending in this industry, the 1997 Balanced Budget Act mandated the introduction of a prospective payment system for skilled-nursing facilities, similar to that enacted for hospitals in 1983.

Medicaid, which is funded jointly by the federal and state governments, amounted to more than $108 billion in 1999. Medicaid is the largest third-party payer for nursing home care, financing around 46 percent of all nursing home care in 1999. Table 12.2 shows the financing of nursing home care since 1960.

Many studies have projected future U.S. expenditures on health care over both long-term and short-term time horizons, using different demographic and economic assumptions. In every case, the projections point to continuous increases in both overall health care expenditures and spending on nursing home care.

## A Brief History of the Nursing Home Industry

Today, the nursing home is at the center of long-term care in the United States. Yet as an industry, it has a relatively brief economic history. Its economic evolution has been largely a function of federal legislation in the areas of income maintenance and health policy. In general, nursing homes were never the specific focus of these legislative initiatives. Unquestionably, the Social Security Act

Table 12.2

**Nursing Home Expenditures by Source of Funds, 1960–1999, Selected Years** (billions)

|                            | 1960 | 1970 | 1980 | 1990 | 1995 | 1999 |
|----------------------------|------|------|------|------|------|------|
| Total                      | 0.8  | 4.2  | 17.6 | 50.9 | 75.5 | 90.0 |
| Private funding            |      |      |      |      |      |      |
| Out-of-pocket              | 0.7  | 2.3  | 7.4  | 22.0 | 25.1 | 23.9 |
| Private health insurance   | 0.0  | 0.0  | 0.2  | 2.1  | 3.7  | 7.5  |
| Government funding         |      |      |      |      |      |      |
| Medicare                   | NA   | 0.1  | 0.3  | 1.8  | 7.8  | 9.6  |
| Medicaid                   | NA   | 0.9  | 8.8  | 23.1 | 35.5 | 42.4 |

*Source*: Health Care Financing Administration, Office of the Actuary, National Health Statistics Group.
*Note*: Numbers may not add because of rounding.

of 1935 and its subsequent amendments have been responsible for much of the industry's development. Federal legislation has provided a substantial portion of the income for purchasing nursing home services and for developing the industry's physical capacity. Legislative developments have accounted for the pluralistic provider structure, with proprietary, voluntary (not-for-profit), and public facilities. Moreover, though the industry's capacity (measured both by number of homes and number of beds) is largely privately controlled, the industry's revenues derive primarily from public sources. Public programs such as Social Security retirement benefits provide a portion of the funds used for private payments.

Going beyond the welfare approach that is implicit in these income maintenance programs, the biomedical acute care model and decentralization have been important developments for the nursing home industry. American health care policy is centered on the primacy of the physician and the hospital as the dominant institutional provider of health services. The medical model, for better or worse, has been extended to the nursing home industry. Within broad guidelines, each state has considerable discretion in the determination of eligibility requirements and the services covered.

This decentralization accounts for the substantial interstate variation in the quantity, quality, and cost of nursing home care. This variation will be observed in most of the major industry components that will be addressed in subsequent sections.

The passage of the Social Security Act in 1935 was critical to the economic viability of the nursing home industry. Nursing homes were not addressed in the statute at all, but the income maintenance programs that were created provided purchasing power for the consumption of nursing home care. Later amendments to the act specifically targeted health care services and their financing. Whereas the income maintenance aspects of the Social Security Act significantly impacted the demand side of the industry, other legislative developments of the 1940s and 1950s influenced the supply side.

### The Medicare/Medicaid Era

The 1965 amendments to the Social Security Act were (and continue to be) the cornerstone of United States health policy. Although falling short of national health insurance, the Medicare and Medicaid programs represented a pivotal breakthrough for the public financing of health care. Since 1965, as reported earlier, consumer expenditures for health care and the cost of delivering that care have accelerated rapidly. Although all segments of health care expenditures experienced significant increases, nursing home care registered very large increases.

## Medicaid and the Nursing Home Industry

The provision of nursing home care was not a major objective of the 1965 Social Security Act amendments. Medicare, which targeted acute, physician-directed, hospital-based care, was the primary focus of the changes. Medicaid later became the key program for the nursing home industry because of 1967 amendments that provided the authority and conditions for nursing home participation in Medicaid.[2] The determination of eligible services and the manner of reimbursement quickly became (and continue to be) major issues for the industry and the government. The problem of cost containment derives from the fact that Medicaid was established as an open-ended program. Unlike Medicare, which was primarily an insurance program, Medicaid was a welfare program. The federal–state financial responsibility was shared, but the states were allowed to define "medical indigence" and determine covered services. The unlimited nature of this financial commitment coupled with the high cost of services ultimately led to the reconsideration of long-term care (LTC) arrangements and their financing.

## The Quality Issue Emerges

The quality-of-care issue came to the forefront in the nursing home scandals of the early 1970s. Legislative investigations, most notably in New York, revealed many cases of patient abuse, mistreat-

ment, inadequate services performed by underqualified personnel, theft of residents' funds, and manipulation of the reimbursement system for personal profit.[3] Not surprisingly, these revelations unleashed a wave of regulations designed to improve the situation. The regulatory process included standards, inspection, and sanctions. Federal standards for Medicare and Medicaid participation established minimums that states may exceed, but rarely do. Higher standards and their enforcement raises costs, thereby creating a dilemma for many states that would find the additional financial burden to be problematic. Even minimal existing standards are enforced unevenly by state and municipal jurisdictions.[4]

## Cost Containment: The Issue of the Eighties and Beyond

As the American population has aged and the demand for nursing home care has increased, the cost of providing that care has risen significantly, along with other medical care costs. Private and public ability to pay have not kept pace with those costs. Increasing life expectancy considerably diminished the adequacy of private funds. The exhaustion of private funds has forced many people to become "medically indigent." Meanwhile, federal and state fiscal problems have put severe constraints on public funding. In a totally proprietary industry, market forces should keep costs in check. But even with about 60 percent of the facilities and beds in the industry under proprietary control, market forces are obscured by the fact that about two-thirds of the industry's revenues derive from public sources.[5] Thus, covered services and the method of reimbursement have a critical effect on costs.

Cost-related reimbursement for nursing homes replaced flat-rate systems. Originally, cost-related reimbursement was retrospective, based on the expenditures incurred in the provision of services. Since no prior limits were set, retrospective systems were inherently inflationary. In an effort to hold down costs, many states switched to prospective reimbursement systems where the rates are set prior to the delivery of services. Although there are several versions of prospective systems, each essentially tries to preprice individual services based on some formula derived from historical costs and trends.

Cost containment and the financing of LTC was complicated by the 1987 Omnibus Budget Reconciliation Act, which contained provisions mandating significant nursing home reform. Various sections, especially those dealing with survey inspection procedures and training for nursing aides, raised the cost structure of the LTC facilities. Ultimately, cost containment came into conflict with quality improvement.

### Trends in the Nineties

On the supply side, the development of corporate nursing home chains in the 1980s continued to have a major impact on the industry's structure. By the mid-1990s, investor-owned chains controlled about 20 percent of facility capacity. Although the chains are largely composed of skilled-nursing and health-related facilities, many have diversified into newer aspects of the LTC industry. The early part of the decade was marked by considerable merger activity. Prior to the growth of corporate chains, small, individual ownership with thin capitalization had always characterized the industry, even in the proprietary sector. The corporate chains brought more sophisticated management to the industry as well as the latest in computerized information systems. Scale economies, especially in purchasing, provide cost-control advantages not attainable by small, independent units. Although the

industry suffered some major reversals in the late 1990s, the role of the chains remains significant.

### Balancing the Federal Budget

The concern over the cost of U.S. health care grew in intensity in the early 1990s. High on the political agenda was balancing the federal budget and a prime target was government spending on Medicare and Medicaid. By the mid-1990s, both political parties were committed to slowing the rate of growth or reducing outright this element of government expenditure. Any changes in Medicare and Medicaid funding arrangements and levels can be expected to have a major impact on the LTC industry.

The Balanced Budget Act, passed in 1997, included significant limits on federal government outlays for Medicare throughout the health care system. There were several provisions relating to skilled-nursing facilities, the most important of which was the institution of a prospective payment system similar to that mandated for hospitals in 1983. As will be seen, this and related financial constraints proved overly severe and led to a partial reversal.

As a potential offset to fiscal pressures on government financing, LTC insurance became a new initiative in private payment but has had little impact thus far. Although the health insurance industry sees good market potential for such policies and federal legislation has provided some deductibility for premiums since 1996, LTC insurance is still in an early stage of its development and its future as a significant payment mechanism is far from established.

### The Continuum of Care

There is significant interest in developing alternatives to institutionalized care that proponents argue would be less expensive and improve the well-being of the elderly population. The expansion of home care, assisted-living arrangements, social/health maintenance organizations, and adult day care are among the more widely discussed alternatives. Expenditures on home care delivered by home health agencies have experienced tremendous growth in the 1990s. The expansion of home health care can forestall institutionalization in a nursing home. At the same time, the nursing home industry has diversified its services by delivering a variety of subacute care services previously provided in a hospital setting. Moreover, many nursing home firms have begun to provide assisted living, which combines the provision of housing for the elderly with the delivery of certain LTC services that may culminate in placement of the elderly patient in a skilled-nursing facility. Adult day care is also being provided by many nursing homes. Thus, the nursing home industry is adapting to the "continuum of care" environment and redefining itself as the twenty-first century begins with a predictably large demographic expansion of the elderly population.

## Elements of Nursing Home Demand

There are numerous differences in the demographic, ethnic, cultural, and geographic characteristics of the population that affect care needs and the suitability of nursing home services provided. Since the vast majority of nursing home residents are at least sixty-five years of age, the general trends in the nation's population are important variables.

As can be seen from Table 12.3, the oldest age segments are projected to increase through the year 2050 both in absolute number and as a share of the total U.S. population. The 2000 estimated population of 34.7 million people aged 65 and over

would grow to 39.4 million by 2010 and the percentage share of this group will increase from 12.6 percent to 13.2 percent. By 2050, however, the elderly would number almost 79 million and represent 20 percent of the population.

Large increases in the oldest portion of the elderly population will occur because of greater life expectancy and the growing size of the birth cohorts that are approaching the oldest age group. In fact, all of the increase in the sixty-five plus age group after 2030 can be attributed to increases in the number of persons aged seventy-five years and older. After 2000, the eighty-five plus population segment is expected to double in number by 2030 and increase more than fourfold by the year 2050, to 18.2 million. The population 100 years and over, though numerically small, is projected to grow to 0.2 percent of the total by 2050. The 2000 centenarian population of 72,000 will grow to 214,000 in 2020, and to over 800,000 by 2050.

The combined effect of decreased mortality and larger birth cohorts will significantly impact the long-term care system just one decade into the twenty-first century. A study of the lifetime use of nursing homes has found that 27 percent of all persons over the age of twenty-five can anticipate at least one episode of nursing facility use in their lifetime.[6] There can be little doubt that the aging population will require substantial quantities of LTC services, including (though not limited to) those provided by nursing homes.

### Chronic Disease, Disability, and Institutionalization

Changing rates of morbidity and disability from chronic diseases can greatly affect demographic projections of demand for acute and LTC services. The prevalence of chronic disability can even be viewed as a "leading" indicator of health changes

Table 12.3

**Elderly Population by Age and Percent Distribution: 1990–2050**
(thousands, based on Middle Series projections, U.S. Bureau of Census)

| Year | 65 years and over | Percent of U.S. population | 85 years and over | Percent of U.S. population | 100 years and over | Percent of U.S. population |
|---|---|---|---|---|---|---|
| 1990 | 31,235 | 12.5 | 3,057 | 1.2 | 37 | 0.0 |
| 1995 | 33,543 | 12.8 | 3,634 | 1.4 | 54 | 0.0 |
| 2000 | 34,709 | 12.6 | 4,259 | 1.6 | 72 | 0.0 |
| 2005 | 36,166 | 12.6 | 4,899 | 1.7 | 101 | 0.0 |
| 2010 | 39,408 | 13.2 | 5,671 | 1.9 | 131 | 0.0 |
| 2020 | 53,220 | 16.5 | 6,460 | 2.0 | 214 | 0.1 |
| 2030 | 69,379 | 20.0 | 8,455 | 2.4 | 324 | 0.1 |
| 2040 | 75,233 | 20.3 | 13,552 | 3.7 | 447 | 0.1 |
| 2050 | 78,859 | 20.0 | 18,223 | 4.6 | 834 | 0.2 |

*Source*: Adapted from Table F and Table G in Day (1996), U.S. Bureau of Census, *Current Population Reports*, pp. 25–1130.

in the elderly population. It foreshadows most shifts in the total distribution of acute and chronic health care costs among the elderly.[7] Since institutionalization in a nursing home is the outcome of serious disability due to the incidence of chronic disease, it is important to understand the nature of dependency based on disability. The demand for nursing home care or some alternative form of LTC is closely linked, not only to the aging of the population, but to the incidence and trends of chronic disability. As will be seen, this has important economic ramifications.

*Disability Trends*

Numerous studies have carefully examined data from the periodic National Long-Term Care Surveys pertaining to disabilities and institutionalization rates. Statistically significant declines in the prevalence of disability in the U.S. elderly population have been found over the 1982–1994 period. Moreover, the declines in disability from 1982 to 1989 not only continued through 1994 but accelerated and were pervasive for all age groups

and disability levels.[8] These findings counter the widespread negative assumption that industrialized, economically advanced countries present social and public health problems that increase the risks of chronic disease and mortality.

*Economic Implications of Disability Trends*

Since persons with chronic disabilities tend to have higher per capita Medicare, Medicaid, and other acute and chronic health care costs than nondisabled persons, reductions in chronic disability at late ages may have important direct and indirect effects on the future growth of U.S. health care expenditures.

The ongoing controversy and uncertainty about the long-term solvency of the Medicare Trust Fund and overall Medicare costs can be linked directly to the variation in projections about the future distribution of chronic diseases and disability in a rapidly growing U.S. elderly population. Some projections call for substantial downward revisions in estimates of the size of the chronically disabled elderly population with elevated health service demands and costs.

This implies that the standard economic support ratios made by the Social Security Administration for the purpose of pension benefits need adjustment. Based on an expectation of steadily declining rates of chronic disability, a continuation of an acceptably high economic support ratio can be projected. In 1994, when the Hospital Insurance Trust Fund was in approximate balance, there were twenty-two workers for each recipient, far above pessimistic forecasts that were as low as eight to one. The more optimistic scenario suggests that increased life expectancy and more disability-free years can relieve pressure on the Social Security and Medicare Trust Funds.

## Structure of the Nursing Home Industry

There is some ambiguity about the precise definition of nursing homes. The terminology has evolved over time and the only terms that have precise meaning are those that are tied to regulations and reimbursement and even these have some variation from state to state. The preferred definition is the one used by the National Center for Health Statistics, which defines a nursing home as a facility with three or more beds that is either licensed as a nursing home by its state, certified as a nursing facility under Medicare or Medicaid, identified as a nursing unit in a retirement center, or determined to provide nursing or medical care.

Skilled-nursing facilities (SNFs) are considered the key entities in the industry. Such facilities provide the greatest degree of medical care since every patient is under the supervision of a physician and the facility has a transfer agreement with a nearby hospital. Twenty-four-hour nursing care is provided in skilled-nursing facilities. "Nursing facility" is often used as a synonym for "nursing home." Though in most cases this definitional ambiguity is not a problem, the reported data on the industry should be evaluated for the purpose at hand.

Both the federal and state governments regulate nursing homes. Each state licenses nursing homes but licensing requirements, reimbursement policies, regulations, classification systems, and terminology are not uniform from state to state. Moreover, other state departments may impose separate licensing requirements when the nursing home owns or operates related LTC facilities such as, for example, assisted-living units and adult day care facilities.[9]

The baseline source of data for the industry is the National Nursing Home Survey, a continuing series of national sample surveys of nursing homes, their residents, and their staff. These surveys have been conducted periodically by the National Center for Health Statistics since the early 1970s. The data are regularly updated and supplemented by the Health Care Financing Administration (HCFA). Much of the HCFA data is compiled in connection with the administration of the Medicare and Medicaid programs. Additionally, HCFA maintains a data network in cooperation with the state survey agencies. Their Online Survey, Certification and Reporting System compiles comprehensive information about the operation, census, and regulatory compliance of nursing facilities.

### Nursing Facilities: Selected Characteristics

The 1997 National Nursing Home Survey identified about 17,000 nursing home facilities, with 1.8 million beds, and 1.6 million residents. (See Table 12.4) The number of homes, number of beds, average number of beds per nursing home, and num-

Table 12.4

**Distribution of Nursing Facilities by Selected Characteristics, 1997** (percent of facilities)

| | |
|---|---|
| Ownership | |
| Proprietary | 67.1 |
| Voluntary nonprofit | 26.1 |
| Government | 6.8 |
| Certification status | |
| Medicare/Medicaid | 77.7 |
| Medicare only | 4.7 |
| Medicaid only | 13.6 |
| Not certified | 4.1 |
| Bed size | |
| Less than 50 beds | 12.9 |
| 50–99 | 37.2 |
| 100–199 beds | 42.2 |
| 200 or more beds | 7.7 |
| Census region | |
| Northeast | 17.3 |
| Midwest | 34.2 |
| South | 31.8 |
| West | 16.8 |

*Source*: Adapted from Table 1 of C.S. Gabrel, *An Overview of Nursing Home Facilities: Data from the 1997 National Nursing Home Survey,* No. 311 (Hyattsville, MD: National Center for Health Statistics, March 2000).

ber of residents have all increased since the first (1973–74) survey of this kind. However, the number of homes has declined from a historical peak of 19,100. Between the first survey and the 1997 survey, the average number of beds per facility rose from seventy-five to 107. Although the heavily urbanized Northeast region accounted for a relatively small number of facilities, its average of 135 beds per nursing home exceeded that of the other census regions. Just over 61 percent of the nursing homes were located in Metropolitan Statistical Areas (MSAs). Not surprisingly, these urban facilities had an average bed size of 120 versus eighty-six for those in non-MSA areas. Although the average number of beds per facility has been rising steadily, a slight majority of facilities still have fewer than 100 beds. Facilities with less than 50 beds, however, declined from 40.8 percent of the total in 1973–74 to 12.9 percent in 1997. Most of this change is accounted for by the increase in facilities with beds in the range of 100 to 199 whose share went from 20.4 percent to 42.7 percent over this period.

The extensive size of the proprietary sector is evident from Table 12.5. This sector has the largest number of facilities and the most beds, and serves the greatest number of residents. On the other hand, the average bed size of proprietary facilities falls between that of the voluntary and government sectors and its occupancy rate is the lowest, though the differences from the other sectors are not large.

*Multifacility Chains*

In 1997, 56 percent of the nursing facilities were owned or operated by a multifacility organization that may be a company, an individual, or a not-for-profit entity. The remainder were independently owned or operated. Hospital ownership or operation accounted for 14 percent of the total facilities, though hospital ownership is not mutually exclusive of either multifacility or independent ownership. The involvement of hospital organizations in ownership and operation grew from just under 10 percent in 1993. The trend here is clear. By 1995, multifacility ownership or operation surpassed independent ownership and the gap has been widening.[10] By 1998, the 32 largest nursing home chains controlled 20.9 percent of all SNFs and 22.3 percent of all SNF beds. Ownership patterns vary widely by state. Independent ownership and operation ranged from 86 percent in New York to 28 percent in South Carolina. The involvement of hospital organizations in ownership or operation of nursing facilities ranged from a low of 2

Table 12.5

**Sector Comparisons on Selected Characteristics, 1997**

|                          | Proprietary | Voluntary | Government |
|--------------------------|-------------|-----------|------------|
| Number of homes          | 11,400      | 4,400     | 1,200      |
| Percent of homes         | 67.1        | 26.1      | 6.8        |
| Number of beds           | 1,213,900   | 465,400   | 141,500    |
| Percent of beds          | 66.7        | 25.6      | 7.8        |
| Average number of beds   | 106.2       | 104.7     | 122.5      |
| Number of residents      | 1,054,200   | 422,700   | 131,700    |
| Percent of residents     | 65.5        | 26.3      | 8.2        |
| Occupancy rate           | 86.8        | 90.8      | 93.1       |
| Dual certification       | 9,100       | 3,400     | 700        |
| Medicare only            | NR          | NR        | NR         |
| Medicaid only            | 1,600       | 700       | NR         |
| Uncertified              | NR          | NR        | NR         |

*Source:* Adapted from Tables 1, 2, and 3 in C.S. Gabrel, *An Overview of Nursing Home Facilities: Data from the 1997 National Nursing Home Survey,* No. 311 (Hyattsville, MD: National Center for Health Statistics, March 2000).
*Note*: NR indicates data not reported because of statistical unreliability.

percent in Connecticut to a high of 44 percent in Montana.

Of the fifty largest nursing facility chains ranked by number of beds, all but six were in the for-profit sector. The six not-for-profit entities have primarily church-related ownership. Twenty of the for-profit organizations were publicly traded companies by 1998, while the others were privately held.

*Mergers and Acquisitions*

In recent years, the industry has experienced a strong merger trend. The timing here is important. The 1998 consolidations were down from an even greater number in 1997. However, most of the 1998 consolidation activity was the result of deals arranged before the imposition of a prospective payment system on SNFs as of July 1, 1998. The reimbursement restrictions that followed have forced the nursing home industry into a severe cost-cutting mode. Several major chains declared bank-

ruptcy in 1999, and this has dampened the interest in mergers and acquisitions significantly. Revival of the consolidation movement may have to wait until the transition to the prospective payment system is completed.

*Industry Concentration*

When a small number of firms dominate a market, the industry is said to be concentrated. A high degree of concentration conveys market power to the larger firms and is thought to diminish competition. Despite the wave of mergers that the nursing home industry has experienced in the 1990s, the industry cannot be said to be highly concentrated nationally. Traditional measures of market power are the four-firm and eight-firm concentration ratios that measure the market shares of the top four and top eight firms in an industry. In this industry, firm size can be based on either the number of facilities or the number of beds a firm controls. Based on the number of facilities, the four-firm and eight-firm concentration ratios for 1998 were 10.3 percent and 16.4 percent, respectively. Based on the number of beds, the comparable ratios were 11.0 percent and 19.0 percent. Though industry concentration was slightly higher based on bed capacity, these are low concentration ratios. In 1998, the largest firm, Beverly Enterprises, controlled 562 facilities (3.3 percent of the total) and 62,293 beds (a share of 3.4 percent).

It is important to point out, however, that these concentration ratios are for the United States as a whole. Since states are heavily involved in regulating the nursing home industry, especially in their role as payers, they frequently put restrictions on new construction and expansion. This serves as a real barrier to entry in some local and regional markets and thereby places limits on direct competition. Thus, certain firms have substantial market shares in markets where new entry is not freely permitted.

On the other hand, competition also comes from substitute products and services. In the nursing home industry, these substitutes are represented by the so-called "continuum of long-term care." In local or regional markets where a few certain nursing home firms have a large market share, competition often derives from other LTC services.

## Nursing Facility Beds and Residents

HCFA reported 1,834,820 total nursing facility beds in the United States in 1998, about the same number recorded in 1997. The average number of beds per facility in 1998 was 108. In 1997, the number of beds per thousand elderly aged sixty-five to eighty-four was sixty-one while the number of beds per thousand elderly aged eighty-five and over was 474. The five states with the largest number of beds are California, Texas, New York,

Ohio, and Illinois, all states with very large populations. New York has the highest average number of beds per facility at 179, followed by the District of Columbia, New Jersey, Connecticut, and Nevada.[11]

A growing trend in nursing facilities has been the steady increase in the number of "special care" beds. These are beds are dedicated to residents requiring highly specialized services such as rehabilitation, ventilator care, AIDS care, hospice care, and treatment for Alzheimer's disease.

Overall, occupancy rates remain high. In the aggregate, the mean and median facility occupancy rates in 1998 were 84 percent and 90 percent, respectively. Facility occupancy rates and state occupancy rates are indicators of the tightness of bed supply. Although the median facility occupancy rate has dropped slightly in recent years, it remains at a level that indicates bed shortages in many nursing facilities.

The 1995 National Nursing Home Survey estimated there were 1,548,600 residents of nursing facilities, while the 1997 survey reported 1,608,700 residents.[12] In both years, about 72 percent of residents were female and the racial composition of these residents was overwhelmingly white. Of the approximately 12 percent who were nonwhite, about five out of six were African-American. The elderly, aged sixty-five and over, accounted for 91.5 percent of the residents in the 1997 survey, up from 89.1 percent in 1995. In 1995, they were distributed by age group as follows: 15.6 percent aged sixty-five to seventy-four years, 37.6 percent aged seventy-five to eighty-four years, and 35.8 percent aged eighty-five and over. The comparable percentages for 1997 were 12.3 percent, 32.8 percent, and 45.9 percent. The shift toward the oldest age category is notable.

According to the 1995 survey, the average age of the residents on admission was eighty-two years, with women typically older than men. Sixty-six percent of the residents were widowed, though women outnumbered men in this category by two to one. Forty-one percent of the elderly residents came directly from hospitals while 37 percent entered the nursing home from a private residence. Other distributional characteristics of the nursing facility residents are shown in Table 12.6.

Nursing homes provide care for persons with both post-acute and chronic conditions. Post-acute care is usually rehabilitative, recuperative, or terminal and tends to involve short lengths of stay. The care of chronic conditions is associated with longer lengths of stay. Experts believe that the average resident length of stay has decreased in recent years as a result of an increased use of nursing facilities by hospitals that discharge medically complex or intensive rehabilitation patients to the less costly setting of a SNF. Such patients, though requiring more intense care, have shorter stays, thereby shortening the overall length for all residents.

### Industry Employment and Staffing

Total employment in nursing and personal care facilities rose from approximately 1.3 million in 1983 to over 1.8 million in 1999. Of these employees, more than 80 percent are in the nonsupervisory category. In 1999, females constituted 87 percent of the industry workforce, about the same percentage as in 1983. African Americans, Hispanics, and other minorities accounted for about 30 percent of industry employment. Between 1988 and 1999, the percentage of industry employees with part-time status declined slightly from 25 percent to 24 percent, while the median years of schooling per employee rose slightly from 12.3 years to 12.7 years. Table 12.7 shows the mean hourly wage and mean weekly wage for industry employees in current dollars.

Table 12.6

**Distribution of Nursing Facility Residents by Selected Characteristics, 1995 and 1997 Nursing Home Surveys** (percent of residents)

|  | 1995 | 1997 |
| --- | --- | --- |
| Ownership |  |  |
| Proprietary | 64.0 | 65.5 |
| Voluntary nonprofit | 27.0 | 26.3 |
| Government/other | 9.0 | 8.2 |
| Certification status |  |  |
| Medicare/Medicaid | 78.0 | 84.9 |
| Medicare only | 3.0 | 3.0 |
| Medicaid only | 16.0 | 9.7 |
| Not certified | 3.0 | 2.5 |
| Bed size |  |  |
| Less than 50 beds | 5.0 | 3.9 |
| 50–99 beds | 24.0 | 24.7 |
| 100–199 beds | 51.0 | 51.9 |
| 200 beds or more | 20.0 | 19.5 |
| Census region |  |  |
| Northeast | 22.0 | 23.3 |
| Midwest | 32.0 | 31.0 |
| South | 32.0 | 32.6 |
| West | 14.0 | 13.1 |

*Sources:* Based on G.W. Strahan, *An Overview of Nursing Homes and Their Current Residents: Data from the 1995 National Nursing Home Survey,* No. 280 (Hyattsville, MD: National Center for Health Statistics, 1997), Table 3; and C.S. Gabrel, *An Overview of Nursing Home Facilities: Data from the 1997 National Nursing Home Survey,* No. 311 (Hyattsville, MD: National Center for Health Statistics, March 2000), Table 4.

A 1998 survey of nursing home staffing and compensation for thirty-five salaried (and forty hourly) nursing home staff positions found the median salaried position was paid $34,822.[13] Additionally, the salaried positions received annual bonuses that averaged (median) 5.6 percent and ranged from 2.4 percent to 20.4 percent. In general, bonus arrangements are most commonly found in the proprietary sector. Notable is the fact that the largest bonuses were paid to marketing personnel who are responsible for bringing residents to the homes. The marketing job titles, Di-

Table 12.7

**Employment, Wages, and Earnings, Nursing and Personal Care Facilities, Selected Years**

|                          | 1983      | 1988      | 1993      | 1998      |
|--------------------------|-----------|-----------|-----------|-----------|
| Total employment         | 1,313,900 | 1,463,900 | 1,732,100 | 1,754,800 |
| Average hourly wages     | 7.89      | 9.22      | 9.74      | 10.16     |
| Average weekly earnings  | 276       | 338       | 357       | 377       |

*Source:* Barry T. Hirsch and David A. Macpherson, *Union Membership and Earning Data Book* (Washington, DC: Bureau of National Affairs), various editions.

rector of Marketing, Marketing Representative, and Marketing Coordinator, received bonuses averaging 14.3 percent, 20.4 percent, and 18.3 percent, respectively.

If one separates the salaried positions that are directly health-related from those that are primarily business and management, the fourteen health-related positions had a median salary of $39,073 and a median bonus of 5.6 percent. The positions relating to business and managerial functions had a median of $31,988 with a 6.4 percent bonus that was heavily weighted by the marketing personnel.

The median wage for the forty hourly positions surveyed was $11.89. The highest hourly wages were paid for health-related professional positions that required registration or licensing. Generally, the best paid were professionals involved in occupational, physical, speech, and respiratory therapy that had hourly wages ranging from $16.83 to $27.77. Most therapy professionals are employed on a part-time basis. Registered nurses and registered dieticians earned in excess of $15.00 per hour. Eighteen of the forty hourly positions earned a median wage of under $10 per hour. This group was numerically dominated by nursing assistants. The lowest hourly wages were reported for housekeeping, laundry, and food service aides. Although the latter group and the nursing assistants had a median hourly wage in excess of the legal mini-

mum of $5.15 per hour, many are at or close to the minimum. As proposals have advanced to raise the minimum wage to $6.15 per hour, some legislators have identified the long-term care industry as one of special concern.[14]

In general, wages and benefits in the nursing home industry, even for supervisory personnel, are low and considerably lower than those for comparable positions in hospitals. National averages also conceal a considerable regional variation, with the highest hourly wages usually found in the Northeast or in California. It should be noted, of course, that there are positions—physical therapists, occupational therapists, and speech and hearing therapists—for which nursing homes actually pay more than hospitals. In most nursing facilities, the therapists are usually part-time consultants, especially in the smaller, independently owned operations.

*Turnover Rates*

The few exceptions aside, it is widely acknowledged that disparities like those described above are the cause of the high turnover rates experienced in the industry. The turnover situation is extremely severe among employees that provide direct nursing care, especially among the nursing assistants who provide most of the direct nursing home care. Difficult working conditions, limited training, and few opportunities for advancement (along with low wages and poor benefits) are undoubtedly key factors in the high turnover rate in the nursing assistant job category.[15] In all industries, high turnover rates generate significant costs in lost productivity, recruiting, and training new employees. In the nursing home industry, such high turnover can jeopardize the continuity and quality of the care provided to elderly residents

There are discernable differences in staffing based on ownership. According to the 1995 National Nursing Home Survey, the total number of full-time equivalent (FTE) employees per 100 beds was highest in government facilities and lowest in proprietary facilities. In the crucial area of nursing staff levels, the same pattern is found, not only in total nursing staff but also in each of the nursing subcategories—registered nurses, practical nurses, and nursing assistants. It is worth noting that the highest FTE employee to bed ratios were found in the smallest facilities, those with fifty beds or less. This probably reflects the indivisibility of certain staff positions. Moreover, the highest overall staffing ratios were found in the Northeast census region and in those facilities that had only Medicare certification.

Concerns about nursing home staffing have led to calls for establishment of minimum staffing levels to assure the quality of care.[16] Industry representatives oppose mandated minimums unless the government raises reimbursement rates to cover the additional costs.

*Unionization*

Both the percentage of nursing home industry employees who are union members and the percentage covered by union contracts are shown in Table 12.8 for selected years. The decline over the

Table 12.8

**Percentage of Industry Employees in Unions or Covered by Union Contracts, Selected Years**

|      | Percent union members | Percent covered employees |
|------|-----------------------|---------------------------|
| 1983 | 14.8                  | 17.3                      |
| 1988 | 11.9                  | 13.3                      |
| 1993 | 10.6                  | 12.0                      |
| 1998 | 9.6                   | 10.8                      |

*Source*: Barry T. Hirsch and David A. Macpherson, *Union Membership and Earning Data Book* (Washington, DC: Bureau of National Affairs), various editions.

period in both union membership and nursing facility employees covered by union contracts is apparent. Although the percentages shown are not large, there is considerable state-to-state and intrastate variation. The Service Employees International Union (SEIU) is the largest union in the industry, representing approximately 100,000 industry employees. The nursing home industry is the major target of its organizing efforts. Not surprisingly, the SEIU seeks an augmentation of nursing home staff. As justification, it cites the more intense care needs of a growing subacute resident population and the increased complexity of the care for chronically impaired residents.

**Financing Arrangements**

Table 12.9 shows payments from public sources rose from $44.4 billion in 1995 to $55.2 billion in 1999, an increase of 24.3 percent. Public payments accounted for 61.3 percent of total U.S. spending for nursing home care in 1999. Private payments rose from $30.3 billion to $35.9 billion, an 18.5 percent increase over the period.

Medicaid is the primary payment source, although Medicare payments grew substantially

Table 12.9

**Trends in U.S. Spending on Nursing Facility Care, 1995–1999** (billions)

|                   | 1995 | 1996 | 1997 | 1998 | 1999 |
|-------------------|------|------|------|------|------|
| Medicaid          | 35.4 | 37.8 | 39.8 | 40.7 | 42.4 |
| Medicare          | 7.2  | 8.7  | 10.0 | 9.6  | 10.7 |
| Other public      | 1.8  | 1.7  | 1.8  | 1.9  | 2.1  |
| Out-of-pocket     | 19.9 | 20.1 | 21.4 | 23.2 | 23.9 |
| Private insurance | 5.6  | 6.6  | 6.9  | 7.2  | 7.5  |
| Other private     | 4.8  | 4.9  | 5.1  | 4.3  | 4.5  |
| Total             | 74.6 | 79.9 | 85.1 | 88.0 | 90.0 |

*Source*: Health Care Financing Administration, Office of the Actuary, National Health Expenditures.

between 1995 and 1999. Medicare has increased its share of total payments over this period. The out-of-pocket component of spending was virtually unchanged as a percentage of total spending at about 26 percent. Although private insurance payments rose from 7.5 percent to 8.3 percent of the total, they remain absolutely and relatively small. Together, Medicaid and Medicare offer the primary means of financing nursing home care.

Looked at from the perspective of nursing home residents, Table 12.10 shows that, with minor variation, Medicaid was the primary payer source of about 68 percent of the residents. Overall, approximately 48 percent of nursing home spending was financed by Medicaid. When Medicare is factored in, over 75 percent of nursing homes residents were financed by public payments in 1998.

### Public Payment Options: Medicare and Medicaid

Although it was considered in the drafting of the original Social Security Act, health insurance was not included in the final package. Medicare came into existence in 1965 as an amendment to the Social Security Act. Its purpose was to provide affordable health care for the elderly, primarily at age sixty-five. Medicare is a government entitle-

ment program, a form of social insurance to which all employees and beneficiaries contribute.

Contrary to popular belief with respect to the nursing home industry, many long-term health problems requiring custodial or private nursing care are not covered. Another important exclusion that has received considerable attention in recent Medicare reform proposals has been prescription drug expenses. Deductibles and copayments impose further limitations on Medicare benefits.[17]

Medicaid is a government-funded, means-tested program designed to provide health care to poor people of all ages. To qualify for Medicaid a person must be poor or become poor by spending down assets. The individual states are responsible for the program, designing and administering their respective Medicaid program under broad guidelines established by the federal government, which contributes more than half of each Medicaid dollar spent. State governments contribute the balance, and this is the cause of wide variability in the extent of coverage and the quality of services provided from state to state. Under the law, a core of services must be provided, but each state is able to design a benefit package that meets the needs of its residents through special requests or waivers. Unlike Medicare, many long-term care services can be (and are) covered under Medicaid.

Table 12.10

**Trends in Percentage of Nursing Facility Residents by Primary Payer Source**

|          | 1993 | 1994 | 1995 | 1996 | 1997 | 1998 |
|----------|------|------|------|------|------|------|
| Medicaid | 68.8 | 68.8 | 68.7 | 68.3 | 67.6 | 67.5 |
| Private  | 25.6 | 24.5 | 23.5 | 23.2 | 23.2 | 23.2 |
| Medicare | 5.6  | 6.6  | 8.0  | 8.5  | 9.3  | 9.3  |

*Source*: Joseph A. Giacalone, *The U.S. Nursing Home Industry* (Armonk, NY: M.E. Sharpe, 2001).

## Private Payment Options

As can be seen from Table 12.11, out-of-pocket payments constitute the largest private source of financing for nursing home care, by a large margin. In order to assess the potential for out-of-pocket financing, it is useful to examine the income status of the elderly (age sixty-five plus). The data show a mixed picture of their financial status and their ability to pay for nursing home and other long-term care out-of-pocket. Although the overall financial situation for some of the elderly is strong and while it is improving for most, there are many areas of concern. On average, most financial assets are in the form of housing, which is a necessity and, under normal circumstances, not very liquid. Moreover, the oldest segments of the elderly population are noticeably poorer in both income and assets. Racial minorities and widows living alone are in a similar situation. Such individuals are in a very disadvantaged economic position when it comes to paying for LTC on their own without the help of family or public assistance.

## Long-Term Care Insurance

Although LTC insurance policies have been available since the early days of Medicare, few policies were sold until the 1990s. The early LTC insurance policies essentially had benefit triggers that were similar to those of Medicare. Coverage was provided only to those who received skilled care in a Medicare-certified skilled nursing facility after a three-day hospital stay. There were other significant limitations as well that did not make LTC insurance an attractive insurance option. Ultimately, consumers began to recognize that Medicare was not designed to pay for nursing home care and insurers found that consumers are willing to pay higher premiums for policies that covered additional risks. Currently, LTC insurance typically covers skilled, intermediate and custodial care in state-licensed nursing homes. Policies also offer coverage for home health services provided by state-licensed and/or Medicare-certified homes.

*Tax Treatment of Long-Term Care Insurance.* The Health Insurance Portability and Accountability Act of 1996 provided favorable tax treatment for insurance policies issued after 1999. It created a new class of insurance known as "Qualified Long-Term Care Insurance" or QLTCI. QLTCI is an insurance contract that provides coverage only of qualifying LTC services and that meets additional requirements. For example, the contract must guarantee renewal, must meet certain consumer protection standards, and must coordinate benefits with Medicare.

*Limitations on the Demand for Long-Term Care Insurance.* The risk of falling chronically ill (even for retired people) is relatively low. At the same time,

Table 12.11

**Private Spending on Nursing Home Care, 1995–1999** (billions)

|      | All private funds | Out-of-pocket | Private insurance | Other private |
|------|-------------------|---------------|-------------------|---------------|
| 1995 | 30.3              | 19.9          | 5.6               | 4.8           |
| 1996 | 31.6              | 20.1          | 6.6               | 4.9           |
| 1997 | 33.4              | 21.4          | 6.9               | 5.1           |
| 1998 | 34.7              | 23.2          | 7.2               | 4.3           |
| 1999 | 35.9              | 23.9          | 7.5               | 4.5           |

*Source*: Health Care Financing Administration, Office of the Actuary, National Health Statistics Group.

the cost of LTC is high. This combination of a low risk and a high loss makes such care a classic case for private insurance. However, as has been previously noted, only a small portion of total LTC costs is covered by insurance. Some argue that this low demand is evidence of market failure, calling for government intervention. However, there may be other explanatory factors for the low demand.

One reason for the lack of demand for LTC insurance may be self-insurance. The cost of LTC constitutes a grave financial risk only to the extent that the individual in need of it expects this state to continue for a longer period of time. There is evidence suggesting that the remaining life expectancy of people entering a nursing home is much lower than that of others of the same age.

The demand for private LTC insurance may also be undermined by what may be called free-riding on public welfare. An individual of modest wealth may well prefer spending the wealth on LTC to the point of becoming eligible for public welfare, instead of paying many years of insurance premiums.

Moral hazard and adverse selection constitute additional reasons for market failure in the case of LTC insurance. Moral hazard means that the elderly and their relatives may reduce their efforts to prevent the need for LTC from arising precisely

because they know that the risk is covered by insurance. Adverse selection occurs when the demander of LTC insurance is better able to estimate the probability of loss than the insurer. The private insurer will thus tend to attract the "bad" risks, whereas the "good" ones will prefer to self-insure.

On the other hand, the traditional sales obstacles—the product's high cost and lack of service options—have been mitigated somewhat. As was described above, LTC insurance policies have become more comprehensive since the early 1990s. Premium rates, though not inexpensive, have become more affordable and receive some favorable tax treatment. The greater affordability and tax deductions are expected to stimulate sales and increase private insurance payments to nursing homes. This should benefit providers since private-pay rates for nursing care are higher than for government programs and could improve nursing home profit margins. Private sector funds would help reduce the industry's reliance on federal funds that are increasingly subject to budgetary reductions.

*Long-Term Care Insurance Sales.* The Health Insurance Association of America has been conducting surveys of all known insurance companies selling long-term care policies. The surveys show almost 6 million policies sold by mid-1998. The number of companies that are developing LTC insurance products, the variety of products available, and the number of individuals covered have been growing steadily. However, just nine states accounted for half the policies sold through 1997 and only ten states had market penetration rates of at least 15 percent.[18]

## Home Equity Conversions

It is widely recognized that home equity is by far the largest financial asset held by the elderly—

even those who have little income and may be below the poverty line. If that equity could be tapped, it can provide resources from which not only normal living expenses can be paid but also some LTC expenses. The ability to get cash out of the house while remaining in the house is an attractive option to some of the elderly.

Though some argue that reverse mortgages were not expected to have a very significant impact as an LTC payment mechanism, the Department of Housing and Urban Development remains optimistic about their potential for improving the overall financial status of the elderly. In 1999, new legislation made HUD-insured reverse mortgages a permanent program and increased the amounts of a home's value that can be converted to cash from a range of $86,317–$170,362 to a range of $115,200–$208,800.

## Cost Containment, Regulation, and Quality Issues

Medicaid is the fastest growing component of most state budgets, in large part because Medicaid bears the cost for a significant portion of every state's nursing home residents. Thus, states are faced with the dilemma of how to pay for quality care on a limited budget and use one or more of the following methods.

States often attempt to control their costs by restricting the supply of nursing home beds in order to reduce demand. States can either limit the number of beds they will certify for Medicaid and/or the number of nursing home construction permits they approve. These permits, called certificates of need, restrict development in many states. This creates a situation in which more people are vying for fewer beds.

Payments to nursing homes are based on reimbursement schedules determined by the federal government, but individual states determine the final amount of reimbursement and payment due the nursing home. In order to control rising Medicaid costs, some states do not always reimburse a nursing facility for the full cost of providing care. In other words, non-Medicaid (private pay) residents pay more for their care than the state pays for Medicaid residents. While the industry recognizes Medicaid reimbursement as an important component in their income mix, the majority of facilities prefer to have individuals who can pay their own way. Moreover, Medicaid payments are not always timely. Late payments can weaken the financial stability of nursing homes with small profit margins.

Although the intent of Medicaid has been to provide nursing home and other long-term care services to the poor elderly, the Medicaid rolls have been increased by persons whose fall into poverty was planned by themselves or others such as family members or legal advisors. This shifts the burden of care to the government while preserving an individual's estate. The government has taken several steps to curb this deliberate impoverishment for the purpose of Medicaid eligibility. The Health Insurance Portability and Accountability Act of 1996 (HIPAA) provided for criminal penalties for those people who knowingly and willfully disposes of assets in order to become eligible for Medicaid. Although the maximum penalties for conviction—a $25,000 fine and up to five years in prison—are unlikely to be imposed, the intention of the legislation is to send a strong message.

Another related approach involves delaying an individual's Medicaid eligibility if assets are transferred for less than their market value during a specified "look-back" period. The look-back period is thirty-six months prior to either the date of application for benefits or to the date of entering the nursing home, whichever is later. In the case of the transfer of assets to a trust, the look-back period is sixty months. The ineligibility period is determined by dividing the amount of asset transfer by the average monthly private patient cost of nursing home care in the state.

Federal law requires each state to have an estate recovery program—a way for the state to increase revenues without increasing taxes. These are designed to recover the state's costs from the Medicaid recipient's estate or the spouse's estate. The state can recover an amount equal to the total medical assistance paid.

### Medicaid Managed Care Initiatives

Only a small percentage of the LTC population is currently enrolled in a managed care program. However, both the federal and state governments are exploring managed care options for LTC because they shift some of the financial risks from the government to the managed care companies. The trend toward the delivery of U.S. health services through managed care plans has been most extensive in employment-related health benefits. The growth of such plans has been much slower in the sixty-five plus population. Whether managed care plans can effectively provide care for the more complex medical problems common among the U.S. elderly population is uncertain. Managed care systems require informed health care consumers to be effective. For competition among plans to work, health care consumers must be able to evaluate the services—their quality and cost. When the outcome analysis is performed at the level of a large corporate entity or in a state Medicaid program, it appears that such plans can maintain quality while controlling costs.

However, the record is less sanguine in evaluating the performance of managed care for a program in which individuals, especially individuals with serious medical problems and disability, are the care consumers. To understand this it is useful to recognize that managed care began by providing services to the younger employed population, which is healthier than average.

### The Balanced Budget Act of 1997

The act contained some of the most sweeping changes since the inception of Medicare and Medicaid in 1965. The fiscal objectives of the legislation were to reduce the growth of Medicare outlays by $115.1 billion and the growth of federal Medicaid outlays by $10.1 billion between 1998 and 2002. The act attempted to reduce Medicare's increasing hospital payments by more than $40 billion; physician payments by $5.3 billion; managed care payments by $21.8 billion; home health agency payments by $16.2 billion; and SNF payments by $9.5 billion. All of these changes will impact the nursing home industry both directly and indirectly.

#### Prospective Payment for Skilled Nursing Facilities

The initiation of a prospective payment system (PPS) for hospitals in 1983 led to a significant rise in the demand for skilled nursing services as the hospitals reduced the average length of stay for their patients in order to stay within the cost parameters of PPS. This led to the placement of more acute patients in nursing homes and other components of LTC that remained under retrospective reimbursement systems. However, this time around, Congress considerably broadened PPS to include SNFs and other LTC organizations.

The act required a PPS for SNFs based on per diems to be phased in over a three-year period, commencing with the start of SNF cost reporting in the second half of 1998. The 1998 payment was to comprise a 75 percent facility-specific rate and a 25 percent federal rate. The federal rate was scheduled to rise to 50 percent in 1999, 75 percent in 2000, and in 2001 payments would be based entirely on the federal rate.

Prior to the passage of the Balanced Budget Act, SNFs were slated to receive $83.3 billion from Medicare between the 1998 and 2002 fiscal years, or 6.2 percent of the Medicare budget. The act reduced these numbers to $78.8 billion and 5.9 percent of Medicare outlays. Much of the reduction was targeted to ancillary services, such as therapy. The $9.5 billion reduction amounts to a decrease of 11.4 percent. This substantial reduction was based on the growth in Medicare outlays to SNFs from $456 million in 1983, at the start of PPS for hospitals, to almost $6 billion by 1994. Industry sources believe the growth in Medicare outlays was justified and resulted from an increase in the supply of nursing home beds, the broadening of covered services, and the transfer of patients to less costly service providers.[19]

*Cost Indexes*

The Balanced Budget Act of 1997 mandates the creation of a SNF market basket index that reflects changes over time in the prices of an appropriate mix of goods and services included in covered SNF services. In developing the SNF PPS per diem rates, HCFA used its discretion in adopting an input price index as the measure of annual skilled-nursing facility changes. In the industry's view, that grossly fails to account for actual market conditions among skilled nursing facilities. According to American Health Care Association, the major shortcoming of the HCFA market basket index now being used is that it does not capture changes in costs attributable to changes in the mix

of goods and services produced.[20] The index is incapable of recognizing changes in the intensity of inputs necessary to produce this new mix of goods and services. Since the costs of producing skilled nursing services are directly related to SNF output prices, the industry supports replacing the current HCFA market basket—that measures average changes in the prices of nursing facility inputs—with an index that reflects the average annual change in the prices of nursing facility outputs.

The options include two indexes recently developed by the Bureau of Labor Statistics (BLS): the Nursing Home and Adult Day Care component of the Consumer Price Index and the Producer Price Index for Skilled and Intermediate Care facilities. The American Health Care Association believes that a change in the index would generate an estimated $2.2 billion in additional funding for the industry over a five-year period.[21] Conversely, such an adjustment would add substantial reimbursement sums to the Medicare budget.

### The Balanced Budget Refinement Act of 1999

The political difficulty of trying to hold down the rate of growth in federal health care spending was illustrated by the health care industry's reaction to the 1997 Balanced Budget Act. Though they were unable to stop the legislation in 1997, all industry segments affected by it began a lobbying campaign to roll back the mandated budget cuts and modify other provisions of the statute. The result was the passage of the Balanced Budget Refinement Act in November of 1999.

As it turned out, the Medicare cost reductions originally projected by the Balanced Budget Act were too low. The Congressional Budget Office estimated that instead of an estimated $103 billion in Medicare savings, the total savings were likely to exceed $191 billion.[22] Thus, the major health care providers included in the 1997 legislation were being impacted far more severely than was originally intended. The so-called "BBA Relief Act" restored about $16 billion in the projected Medicare reductions that were scheduled to take effect through fiscal year 2002.

The Balanced Budget Act was intended to reduce Medicare reimbursements for skilled nursing facilities by about $9.5 billion over five years. The Congressional Budget Office revisions brought this to almost $16 billion. Under either scenario, the financial impact on the nursing home industry would be severe. A number of high-profile bankruptcy filings among large nursing home chains (as well as numerous smaller bankruptcies) were the immediate result. The stock prices of the publicly traded companies where Medicare funds were an important part of their revenue stream declined significantly. The reduction of the per diem Medicare rate for the eight largest investor-owned companies declined from 5.3 percent to as much as 36.8 percent.[23]

For the nursing home industry, the Balanced Budget Refinement Act was expected to restore about $2.1 billion in Medicare funding through the 2002 fiscal year. Apparently the refinement did not provide enough "relief." In December 2000, Congress passed the Benefits Improvement and Protection Act that was expected to add an additional $1.5 billion in SNF payments for FY 2002.[24]

## Regulation and Quality

Many of the more egregious cases of quality problems in the nursing home industry have been chronicled in the public spotlight. Currently, the nursing home industry is one of the most highly regulated in the country. It is not clear whether regulation can assure a high level of quality. Some contend that regulation can provide only a quality floor.[25] In the past, facilities that met the minimum regulatory requirements were assured high occupancy rates. Moreover, because the industry was characterized by a relatively small number of competitors in most markets, nursing homes did not compete aggressively against each other. The presence of excess demand for nursing home care, particularly of Medicaid patients, mitigated the need for intense competition. Market segmentation strategies also allowed facilities to avoid direct competition. This may have significantly reduced the pressure to maximize the quality of products or services.

The introduction of prospective payment to hospitals in 1983 encouraged hospitals to shorten length-of-stay by discharging patients to post-acute settings such as nursing homes. To the extent that hospitals did not want to see the discharged patients readmitted, the hospital served as a screening mechanism for the quality of the nursing homes to which it discharged its patients. Furthermore, the transition to managed care created incentives to place patients in lower-cost treatment settings. Nursing homes, which sought to be managed care outlets for discharged hospital patients had to compete on price and quality to a greater degree than previously. State cost containment efforts made publicly funded patients less attractive and thereby made the competition for private paying patients more intense. In this situation, the quality of service became a more important competitive factor.

As a result of continuing criticism of nursing home quality, Congress passed the Nursing Home Reform Act as part of the 1987 Omnibus Budget Reconciliation Act. This legislation mandates that nursing homes provide a broader array of services. The measure also focused on the quality of caregivers by requiring nurses aides, who provide 80 to 90 percent of resident care, to complete seventy-five hours of training and pass a competency exam. In addition, the Resident Assessment Instrument was developed and all Medicare- and Medicaid-certified homes were required to use this instrument to assess all residents annually, both on admission and at the time of any significant change in the resident's status. To assist in resolving disputes and grievances, the act stipulated that states provide advocates in the form of an ombudsman.

Economic theory tells us that the existence of substitute products and services increase the degree of competition. In response to perceived opportunities for expansion in the LTC market, there are now a growing number of substitutes for nursing home care. To the extent that these substitutes provide appropriate services more cost effectively and/or with higher quality, they serve as a direct competitive threat to the nursing home industry, offering what has been referred to as a continuum of LTC. The competitive threat posed by these substitutes is represented not only in the number of potential residents lost by the nursing home industry but also in the types of potential residents lost. Nursing homes are likely to lose lower acuity patients to assisted living and home health settings. The higher acuity residents who remain will require more intensive and complex services, necessitating more staff and equipment. This puts nursing homes in direct competition with hospital-based units that have a client base from their own discharges, a large physician referral network, and a better image than nursing homes. The pressure is on nursing homes to deliver high-quality complex care more cost effectively.

The Nursing Home Reform Act illustrates the dilemma faced by regulators in trying to legislate quality improvements. Although there is evidence that the act has helped to raise the quality of care in nursing homes, the broad array of additional services that the act mandated significantly added to the cost structure of nursing facilities. In an industry where public payment is so widespread, this situation exacerbates budgetary pressures and conflicts with cost containment efforts.

## Competitive Challenges and Opportunities: The Long-Term Care Continuum

The literature of industrial organization provides insights into the evolution of the LTC continuum. The reasons that companies diversify are reasonably well understood, and a common strategy is to vertically integrate, either backward or forward. With respect to the continuum of LTC, backward or forward integration would mean moving throughout the range from short-term acute care to long-term chronic care.

Vertical integration can be achieved through merger, internal growth, or long-term contracts. Markets can be affected by the presence of vertically integrated companies and the competitive position of the nonintegrated firm can suffer. Potential entrants are threatened, effectively raising the barriers to entry. A dilemma faces the potential entrant to any market in which most of the established firms are vertically integrated. Entry as an integrated producer raises capital-cost barriers, while entry as a nonintegrated producer may entail greater risks. The net effects of vertical integration are a balance between moderate anticompetitive effects and moderate net technical economies.

### Long-Term Care Specialization, Diversification and Integration

The demand for greater efficiencies as a result of cost-containment pressures has created significant challenges and opportunities for LTC providers. Recent changes in Medicare reimbursements and managed care initiatives have been instrumental in driving the diversification and specialization of nursing care facilities. This has placed the industry in a more competitive position with regard to other health care providers.

Strategic choices in any market, such as the decision to specialize or diversify, are driven by the need to be responsive to the demands of both consumers and resource providers. As was mentioned above, insurance payers have a particularly strong influence on strategic choices in the health care sector. Service diversification and specialization are mechanisms for marketing to the targeted population.[26] On the one hand, service diversification is aimed at increasing the demand from specific subpopulations of elderly needing institutionalization. On the other hand, specialization of services helps to capture a broader share of an existing resident subpopulation.

The degree of competition for residents faced by nursing facilities has proven to be a strong incentive for both diversification and specialization of services. Greater market competition is reflected in decreases in county level market concentration of nursing care beds. The resulting excess bed capacity increases the likelihood that facilities will develop subacute and other diversified specialty care units.

Competition from substitute products has also encouraged the development of new services within nursing care facilities. The emergence of managed care has led hospitals to develop several post–acute care services that compete directly with nursing care facilities for Medicare recipients. It has also been shown that nursing care facilities are more likely to develop subacute specialty care units in areas with a higher ratio of hospitals to nursing facilities. At the same time, nursing facilities have experienced increased competition for lower-acuity patients from the expansion of home

health programs that receive considerable Medicaid and Medicare support. Home health alternatives serve to delay admission to nursing care facilities as long as possible.

It should be noted that there are various state-level restrictions on growth in the nursing care facility industry. These include certificate of need programs and moratoria on new construction, which are aimed primarily at limiting the number of nursing facility residents who could have a claim to state support. Such restrictions can be a barrier to the development of new services by restricting entry. Furthermore, though originally intended to limit a state's financial liabilities, they may have the unintended consequence of reducing competitive incentives to provide innovative delivery of long-term care services.

### The Continuum of Care and Integrated Provider Networks

The principal elements of the continuum of care are subacute care, home health care, adult day care, assisted living, continuing care retirement communities, and hospice care. Strategically, nursing facilities have been forced to introduce these services in an increasingly competitive long-term care sector as a response to the competition with other health care providers such as hospitals, home health agencies, and retirement living arrangements.

To achieve their objectives, operators of nursing facilities have formed alliances or partnerships with other providers in the post–acute care continuum. Moreover, many operators have pursued a strategy of vertical integration in an effort to become more competitive under PPS. This strategy also expands their ability to compete for managed care business. Its prevalence is evidenced by the extensive merger and acquisition activity that has taken place among publicly traded companies in this sector. These networks are designed to receive capitated reimbursement from managed care payors in exchange for bearing all the responsibility for providing post-acute and rehabilitation services. As a diversified provider, an operator can readily shift managed care and Medicare beneficiaries throughout its system of nursing homes, rehabilitation services, senior housing and home health care to minimize utilization of higher-cost services.

Providers that are members of an integrated alliance and/or are vertically integrated hold a distinct advantage over independent SNF operators. The former have relatively greater access to cost information and clinical data that allows providers to reduce costs successfully and generate better outcomes. Moreover, operators of nursing homes that are not a part of an alliance or a vertically integrated provider will find it difficult to obtain referrals from other care settings, such as acute care hospitals and assisted-living facilities. It is quite likely that the larger, multi-unit providers will continue to acquire the smaller, independent provider population. Given the significant presence of the independent operators in the nursing home industry, the consolidation movement will continue in favorable market situations.

## Public Policy Perspectives

Two primary aspects of any industry are the production of its outputs and the financing of consumption. From a public policy standpoint, a major consideration would be the appropriate role of government in production and financing. It can be argued that there is no economic justification for a large government role in the provision of LTC services, as is the case in many industrialized countries other than the United States.[27] A rationale based on the idea that the industry is a natural monopoly is invalid, as is one based on the assumption that there are significant externalities to be achieved by government provision. In the United States, government provision of nursing home care and other LTC services is a relatively small part of the service provided. Still, government is heavily involved in financing the output of the LTC continuum. The government's role in financing LTC, either in the institutional setting of nursing home care or in another setting in the care continuum, appears to be the primary public policy issue facing this industry in the United States today.

Critics of the current financial arrangements argue that consumers are not adequately protected from catastrophic costs and that the public costs of LTC are unacceptably high. As we have seen, Medicaid, a means-tested welfare approach, plays the lead role in public sector financing, though Medicare's role has been increasing, especially in the areas of subacute care and home care. Neither program was originally designed to finance this type of care and each is hard pressed to keep up with the growing funding requirements. Private funding is largely out-of-pocket with private insurance covering only a small fraction of LTC costs. Various attempts to curtail these substantial public expenditures have been made with only limited success. Some, like the Balanced Budget Act, have been partially reversed. None have been more than short-term measures that have been unable to address the consequences of the demographic trends in the number of elderly who will need LTC services in the next few decades.

## Reforming Long-Term Care Financing: Social Insurance Versus Private Insurance

Some advocate a social insurance model whereby the government would assume primary responsibility for financing LTC services. Gaps in coverage would be filled by an individual's savings or by a supplemental private insurance policy. Others want to see the private sector—individuals and insurance companies—become the primary payers. The government's financing role would be limited to providing supplemental coverage after personal resources are exhausted.

## The Case for Social Insurance

The differential, inequitable treatment of acute care and LTC is the basis on which some advocates of social insurance rest their case.[28] They reject the argument that acute medical care is different from LTC because its goal is to restore health, despite the fact that some acute care has the same objective as LTC—avoiding deterioration and premature death. They also reject the notion that since much LTC is assistance provided by nonprofessionals it is somewhat less deserving than medical services delivered by highly trained professionals. Thus, the proponents of social insurance want to put the illnesses and conditions that result in long-term disability on an equal footing with acute medical illness.

In a social insurance model, participation is mandatory. Those who favor this approach point to Social Security and Medicare as prototypes. The Social Security system provides protection to virtually every working American. There is no risk selection or underwriting, and every individual has access to the benefits regardless of health status or income. Income-based taxation, paid by both the employee and employer, pays for Social Security and Medicare while the employee is the beneficiary. Under such an arrangement, all qualified beneficiaries, especially the disabled elderly, would be entitled to financing for most of their LTC needs. Of course, Social Security and Medi-

care are not without their own long-term financial problems derived from growth in the elderly population, increased life expectancy, and the declining ratio of workers to beneficiaries. These programs may require politically unpopular adjustments such as tax increases and/or benefit cuts. Any social insurance model for LTC would have to address the same issues.

## An Indemnity Approach to Social Insurance

Consideration should be given to an indemnity approach whereby persons with specified disability levels would receive a cash payment. Family resources, private insurance, and a Medicaid-like safety net would supplement the indemnity benefit. The indemnity approach would be similar to Social Security in providing a stipend triggered by age and retirement. It would avoid limiting consumer choice in LTC to a single service package. The nursing home supply restrictions (certificates of need) imposed by states to restrain their public expenditures would then need to be removed to encourage competitive entry. Informing consumer choice with wide dissemination of information on premium costs and policy benefits would enhance the competitiveness of the insurance market. Rather than relying on private insurance as only a supplement to social insurance, its advocates support a much larger role, if not the major responsibility, in the financing of nursing home care and other chronic care needs.

## Private Insurance

Those who oppose government social insurance on ideological grounds see great potential in the evolution of the private insurance market as a means of payment for nursing home care and other

LTC services. The availability of insurance may improve one's access to a higher quality nursing facility as a private paying patient. It might also make it possible to purchase services that public programs like Medicaid do not provide in significant amounts, such as home care.

In an effort to jump-start the sales of private LTC insurance and reduce their Medicaid obligations, a number of states developed so called "partnership" programs as a way for individuals to access Medicaid reimbursement without impoverishing themselves. Their easier eligibility for Medicaid was predicated on the prior purchase of LTC insurance. Under a partnership plan, after individuals collect the maximum benefits under the coverage, they will then qualify for Medicaid and still be permitted to retain assets equal to the amount of insurance benefits they received. However, partnership arrangements have not given rise to a significant expansion of LTC insurance sales as had been hoped.

*Affordability via Tax Incentives*

Throughout the 1990s, the insurance industry has worked to overcome the information problems that limited the development of LTC policies that provided adequate coverage and were affordable. Based on the recommendations of the National Association of Insurance Commissioners, the industry began to offer less restrictive policies that were more reasonably priced though not inexpensive. The result was substantial growth in policy sales to individuals, largely through group associations, life insurance riders and employer-based plans. Though the growth rates of the 1990s were impressive, the base for comparison purposes was low. The market penetration among the eligible elderly was still quite small.

The affordability problem has been partly addressed by the provision of tax incentives (HIPAA)

for the purchase of LTC insurance. Not surprisingly, the insurance industry favors the expansion of these tax incentives. A recent study of an above-the-line tax deduction for LTC policies acknowledged that tax incentives were instrumental in raising the awareness of LTC insurance but claimed that the tax benefits provided are still too limited.[29] Perhaps a more generous tax advantage should be provided to reduce the net cost of policies and stimulate their sales. The analysis concluded that a full tax deduction for LTC premiums would generate an additional 4.2 million policy sales above the current annual growth rate for 2000–2005 and achieve a net reduction in public funding for LTC.

*The Case Against Tax Incentives*

Some argue that the implications of favorable tax treatment for LTC insurance and direct spending on LTC represents an inefficient and inequitable solution to a problem that is poorly defined and probably not of great social importance.[30] For example, it is noted that since tax reductions for some must be made up by tax increases for others, by spending cuts, or by government deficits, someone else in effect pays for part of the cost of the tax-subsidized insurance.

Microeconomic arguments based on efficiency and equitable income distribution notwithstanding, the political trend has been in the direction of increasing the role of private insurance in financing LTC, with tax benefits if necessary. Whether these benefits will be expanded beyond those already provided remains to be seen.

*Vouchers As an Alternative*

Some argue that vouchers are a more effective financing alternative, based on efficiency and equity as compared to a subsidy.[31] A subsidy always distorts the decision by the beneficiary. Under a voucher system, all services and amenities have to be paid dollar-for-dollar by the recipient of the voucher. Therefore, the individual's choices will reflect the true resource cost of formal as compared with informal LTC, a more efficient outcome.

## Alternative Delivery Systems and Incremental Reform

There are several fully or partially integrated approaches to the delivery of care that attempt to cover the acute, post-acute, and LTC needs of the elderly. The distinguishing characteristic of these approaches is that they integrate not only the provision of care but also their financing. Continuing care retirement communities, for example, represent a closed system continuum of residential and health care that residents voluntarily enter, normally when they are healthy. By contract, the system guarantees access to health services, including LTC. There are also several other models that are generally designated as open systems since their users reside in the community. The most promising of these are the PACE (program for all-inclusive care of the elderly) model, the social/health maintenance organizations (S/HMOs), and the community nursing organization (CNO). The 1997 Balanced Budget Act converted the PACE model from a demonstration project to a permanent benefit category for Medicare coverage and reimbursement. The other two are still in the demonstration project stage. All three still require continued testing and evaluation to determine their effectiveness.

Based on history and the current political climate, there is little reason to expect any revolutionary changes in the financing arrangements for nursing home and other LTC services over the short term. There is a strong aversion in the electorate to any major increases in taxation that would be needed to fund a public insurance system. Moreover, as the Clinton administration's failed attempt at major health care reform demonstrated, there are still strong ideological objections to heavier government involvement in the health care system. Another negative political factor is the intergenerational issues raised when proposals that increase the burden on younger population cohorts are introduced. These issues still plague the existing Social Security and Medicare systems. People may say that they want the government to provide more financial support for health care in general or for LTC specifically, but they want others to pay the bill. When it comes to a potentially intrusive government presence in the health care system, there is resistance. These attitudes suggest the future of LTC may involve greater private financing of LTC insurance, encouraged by favorable tax treatment. Experimental delivery and financing arrangements continue to be on the agenda of the HCFA.

A number of incremental proposals for LTC seem to warrant consideration. These proposals emphasize the role of private insurance, family caregiving, home- and community-based care, and improving housing options. They include offering nonsubsidized LTC insurance to all federal employees, tax credits for caregivers, and funding to provide family caregivers with services such as respite care, information about community-based care options, and counseling. Additional funding for increased oversight of nursing homes has been proposed to obtain quality assurance and minimize fraud and abuse. There is interest in adding a costly prescription drug benefit to Medicare while cutting Medicare costs further.

These somewhat contradictory proposals create an impression that both providers and those in need of care are unlikely to see major change in the current financial arrangements. Both groups may have to assume greater responsibility for their respective needs.

## Notes

This chapter is based on the author's book *The U.S. Nursing Home Industry* (Armonk, NY: M.E. Sharpe, 2001).

1. Stephen Heffler, Katherine Levit, Sheila Smith et al., "Health Spending Growth Up in 1999; Faster Growth Expected in the Future," *Health Affairs* 20, no. 2 (March/April 2001): 193–203.

2. Robert J. Newcomer and Marjorie P. Bogaert-Tullis, "Medicaid Cost Containment Trials and Innovations" in Charlene Harrington et al., eds. *Long-term Care of the Elderly* (Beverly Hills: Sage,1985), pp.105–24. Also see James Swan and Charlene Harrington, "Medicaid Nursing Home Reimbursement Policies" in Harrington et al., 125–52.

3. Bruce, C. Vladeck, *Unloving Care: The Nursing Home Tragedy* (New York: Basic Books, 1980).

4. Ibid.

5. Katherine Levit et al., "National Health Expenditures, 1996." *Health Care Financing Review* 19 (1997):161–200.

6. Christopher Murtaugh et al., "The Amount, Distribution, and Timing of Lifetime Nursing Home Use," *Medical Care* 35, no. 3 (1997): 204–18.

7. Burton Singer and Kenneth Manton, "The Effects of Health Changes on Projections of Health Service Needs for the Elderly Population of the United States," *Proceedings of the National Academy of Science* 95 (December 1998): 15618–22.

8. Kenneth Manton, Larry S. Corder, and Eric Stallard, "Chronic Disability Trends in Elderly United States Populations: 1982–1994," *Proceedings of the National Academy of Science* 94 (March 1997): 2593–98.

9. Connie Evashwick and Bonnie Langdon, "Nursing Homes," in Connie J. Evashwick, ed., *The Continuum of Long-term Care: An Integrated Systems Approach* (Albany, NY: Delmar, 1996), 43–59.

10. American Health Care Association, *Facts and Trends: The Nursing Facility Sourcebook* (Washington, DC: American Health Care Association, 1999).

11. Ibid.

12. A.N. Dey, *Characteristics of Elderly Nursing Home Residents: Data from the 1995 National Nursing Home Survey.* Advance data from vital and health statistics. No. 289. (Hyattsville, MD: National Center for Health Statistics, 1997).

13. American Health Care Association, *Facts and Trends: The Nursing Facility Sourcebook* (Washington, DC: American Health Care Association, 1999).

14. Tracy A. Blankenheim, "LTC Workers Deserve Wage Increase, Democrats Say," *McKnight's Long-Term Care News* 20, October 27, 1999, pp. 13–20.

15. Charlene Harington, and Carroll L. Estes, *Health Policy and Nursing* (Sudbury, MA: Jones and Bartlett), 1994 and 1997 editions.

16. Health Care Financing Administration, *Appropriateness of Minimum Nurse Staffing Ratios in Nursing Homes* (Washington, DC: U.S. Government Printing Office, 2000).

17. HCFA Web site: <http://www. hcfa.org>.

18. Susan Coronel, *Long-Term Care Insurance in 1997–1998* (Washington DC: Health Insurance Association of America, 2000).

19. "The Long-Term Care IndustryPerspective," *SalomonSmithBarney* 1, September 21, 1998, pp. 1–31.

20. American Health Care Association, "Changing the Index for Skilled Nursing Facilities," *Regulatory Update* (May 1999): 25–26.

21. Ibid.

22. Congressional Budget Office, *An Analysis of the President's Budgetary Proposals for FY 2000: A Preliminary Report,* March 3, 1999.

23. Andrew Gitkin, *The ABCs of Medicare BBA Relief* (New York: PaineWebber, 1999).

24. Deloitte and Touche, "Final FY 2002 Skilled Nursing Facility Regulations Includes Rate Increase of 2.8 Percent, 0.4 percent Higher than Proposed," *Washington Commentary* (July 2001).

25. Nicholas G. Castle, Jaqueline S. Zinn, and Vincent Mor, "Quality Improvement in Nursing Homes" in Harvey Jolt and Martin M. Leibovici, eds., *Long-Term Care* (Philadelphia: Hanley and Belfus, 1997), 39–54.

26. Ibid.

27. Peter Zweifel, "Guidelines for Policy and a Proposal for Long-Term Care for the Elderly," in Mark V. Pauly and Peter Zweifel, *Financing Long-Term Care: What Should the Government's Role Be?* (Washington, DC: AEI Press, 1996), 1–21.

28. William J. Scanlon, "Possible Reforms for Financing Long-Term Care," *Journal of Economic Perspectives* 6, no. 3 (Summer 1992): 43–58.

29. Marc A. Cohen and Maurice Weinrobe, *Tax Deductibility of Long-Term Care Insurance Premiums: Implications for Market Growth and Public Long-Term Care Expenditure* (Washington, DC: Health Insurance Association of America, 1999).

30. J.M. Wiener, L.H. Illston, and R.J. Hanley, *Sharing the Burden: Strategies for Public and Private Long-Term Care Insurance* (Washington DC: Brookings Institution, 1994); Mark Pauly, "Should Long-Term Care Receive Tax Vouchers or is Medicaid Enough?" in Pauly and Zweifel, pp. 22–40.

31. Zweifel, "Guidelines for Policy and a Proposal for Long-Term Care for the Elderly," in Pauly and Zweifel, *Financing Long-Term Care,* pp.1–21.

## Selected Readings

Giacalone, Joseph A. *The U.S. Nursing Home Industry.* Armonk, NY: M.E. Sharpe, 2001. This is a comprehensive economic and business analysis of the industry, including its history, structure, financing, regulation, and public policy issues.

Jolt, Harvey, and Martin M. Leibovici, eds. *Long-Term Care: Concept and Reality.* Philadelphia: Hanley and Belfus, 1997. This collection of essays includes material on industry diversification as well as several international case studies that provide a comparative perspective not included in this chapter.

Rhoades, Jeffrey A. *The Nursing Home Market.* New York and London: Garland, 1998. This is a full-length review of the literature on the various economic theories and empirical studies that have attempted to explain supply and demand in the market for nursing homes.

Vladeck, Bruce C. *Unloving Care: The Nursing Home Tragedy.* New York: Basic Books, 1980. This is the classic study of the industry that thoroughly covers the industry's historical origins, the serious quality issues, and an agenda for reform.

# 13

# Microcomputer Platforms

## Competition in Software

*Thomas Cottrell*

The rapid development and adoption of microcomputer technology is one of the great success stories of the latter half of the twentieth century. A brand new invention in 1945, the electronic computer has become a vital tool for both work and leisure as the new century begins. Computing technology that was once the esoteric domain of only a few highly skilled technicians has become both broadly accessible and widely used, in part due to the precipitous drop in price that has made computer hardware more widely affordable, as well as the dramatic improvements in software design that have made the technology more easily accessible. The microcomputer hardware segment of the computer market has seen a significant share of this growth, and software firms have greatly profited from it. Success stories of overnight riches falling to small technology start-ups like Lotus, Microsoft and more recently Netscape, have only added to the stature of the microcomputer software industry. Many software companies are known for creating wealth not just for a few key executives, but for hundreds and thousands (at least for Microsoft) of employees. Even early entrants, who might widely be considered visionaries, by far underestimated the eventual size and significance of the microcomputer software industry. In the popular

press, at least, the software industry exemplifies the classic Horatio Alger story of great riches from hard work, determination, and perseverance. But such an account misses important aspects of the fundamental economics of competition in the microcomputer software industry. Although some products became extremely profitable, the path to success was often both hazardous and problematic. Perhaps more important, in an environment where some earned great riches, many found little profit despite technically sound and, in some cases, apparently more competitive products. Firms that were able to prosper appear to demonstrate, either through luck or skill, an understanding of several important points from economic theory as they relate to this industry. Recent developments in economic theory have contributed greatly to our understanding of the nature of competition in the microcomputer software industry. Several of these developments provide key insights into competition and it will prove useful to review them before proceeding to traditional measures of industry performance. The first topic, which is explored in the following section, is the effect of one consumer's decision on other potential purchasers in the market for a similar product. Economic theory concerning "network externalities" has provided exceptional insight into competition and efficiency where markets are subject to this purchasing interdependency. After describing the nature of the network effects, the study examines the role of technological change in the evolution of competition in the software industry. While technological improvements have had a profound effect on competition, their reflection on measures of industry structure may be misleading. Concentration measures of the dominance of leading firms in industry, for example, are not designed to capture dynamics of competition, because they are snapshots. Similarly, turnover measures of the change in the makeup of the leadership group that capture the volatility in rankings must be interpreted with care because, as is discussed below, higher turnover in this industry will not necessarily imply greater consumer benefits. The chapter then examines industry conduct, with particular attention to antitrust interest in Microsoft. Next, the effect of government policy on the industry is considered, as much for what it missed as for what it got right. A brief comment on the future of platform competition concludes the chapter.

## Economic Theory

Today, the market for microcomputers is standardized; the vast majority are "Wintel" machines, descendants of the IBM-PC compatible machines built using IBM-compatible hardware and software. Most computer users are blissfully unaware of the bewildering array of microcomputer platforms available when today's industry giants emerged from small garages to start multibillion dollar firms. (See Table 13.1)

Why the market has come to be dominated by a single platform and how this is likely to evolve in the future are important questions. In order to understand the nature of this narrowing, we turn to recent

Table 13.1

**Microcomputer Platforms Circa 1982**

Platform

Apple II
Digital Equipment Corporation
Digital Research CP/M family
Radio Shack/Tandy
Victor/Commodore/PET
Other Intel family of microprocessors
Atari
Nonspecific BASIC language programs
Hewlett-Packard family of micros
IBM Personal Computer
Northstar family of microcomputers
Other IBM (non-IBM PC)
Altos
Motorola
Texas Instruments

*Source*: Elsevier, 1982.

work in economic theory that has to inform strategy and policy in the industry—network externalities.

## Network Externalities

In some markets, a decision to purchase is heavily influenced by other potential purchasers of the product. In the market for artistic creations, for example, a purchaser looks for works that are, among other things, unique and not easily copied. In contrast, the market for computer hardware and software is characterized by an interest in products that are the same, or that are similar enough that they conform to a "market standard." Economists use the term "network industries" to describe markets where consumers are especially concerned about the purchase decisions of other consumers.[1] (A fine review of the literature is available.[2]) In these markets, the value that a consumer places on a product can be broken into two components: a "stand-alone" benefit that is based on the consumer's own preferences for the product features, and a "network" benefit that is based on the number of other consumers of the same product. When this second component plays a significant role in a consumer's decision, a number of particularly interesting problems arise.[3]

There are many markets where consumers prefer to choose the same product that a large number of other purchasers do. If there are important scale economies in production, purchase of a standardized good is significantly less expensive than that of a customized one. If consumers do not have a strong taste for variety, competitive markets will provide undifferentiated goods at a low price. The effect of providing low-priced, standardized goods results from a "pecuniary externality."[4] But there are other important issues in the purchase of standardized products. The expectation of competitive supply of inexpensive product complements can play an important role in the decision of which product to purchase. If the product is a durable good, assurance of the availability of maintenance and repair services is important. The economic implications of these aspects of standardized products are generally well understood.

Occasionally, however, interest in the number of other purchasers of a similar good is even more significant. In the market for computer software, consumers may have several additional reasons for their interest in the eventual size of the network of other users. Some commonly cited advantages include: the availability of competitively priced product complements, support for learning to use the technology, and the ability to share files with other users. Purists would distinguish this last effect, a "direct network externality," from the former indirect effects. Making this distinction is less important than understanding that both have an impact on competition and industry structure.

Standardization plays a significant role in the development of a number of industries. In some cases, consumers decide only whether to join the network; in others, consumers must also choose which of several competing networks to join. The term "network" is applied to these industries because of similarities with early telephony. The benefits of phone ownership depend on the number of people one can call, something that is alternately called the "size" or "installed base" of the phone network. Generally, the larger the installed base, the better one's chances of finding someone to talk to that will make the investment worthwhile. In the early 1900s, before phones were commonplace, potential purchasers thought carefully about who was already on the network and who would be joining soon. In this situation the concern is primarily over the initial adoption decision. If the expected benefit of adoption (joining the telephone network) was not large enough, a potential adopter might be better off deciding to wait until the network is larger. Since all potential adopters faced a similar decision, it might happen that each would choose to wait, even though they would all be better off if everyone joined the network. In this way, the initial decision to purchase a phone is based on a benefit that is external to each individual's choice.

The phone example illustrates the difficulties arising from simple coordination of timing involved in an individual's decision to join the network or to wait. Frequently, though, the adoption decision includes not only a determination of when but also which network to join: VCRs (e.g., Beta versus VHS),[5] computing platforms (e.g., PC versus Macintosh), high-definition television (a wide variety of competing HDTV standards),[6] AM radio, digital audio (CD-ROM and digital audio tape), quadraphonic stereo,[7] and computer spreadsheets.[8] Where there is competition over several standards, potential adopters evaluate which standard is likely to emerge with the largest installed base. When potential adopters are ambivalent about standards, but all would prefer to use the same one, they face a slightly more involved coordination problem. Coordination is often easily accomplished, as for example when mechanics in the early automobile industry met to agree on common standards for nuts and bolts. Government standards bodies often provide a coordination mechanism for this kind of decision; in the United States, the American National Standards Institute (ANSI) helps set de jure standards.

Frequently, however, consumers have a preference for one standard over another, but would also prefer to be on the larger network. When this decision is resolved in the competitive marketplace, the design that garners the largest installed base is referred to as a de facto standard. Many of the concerns about competition and economic efficiency in networked industries are related to the emergence of a de facto standard. There are two kinds of efficiency problems that result from this standards process: either current adopters rush too quickly to adopt a standard, or the delay in adoption is too protracted.

### Technological Bandwagons

If adopters move too quickly, if everyone jumps on the bandwagon to adopt a particular standard, a number of difficulties can arise. First, current adopters may prematurely standardize on a technology that turns out in retrospect to have been inefficient. This may have been the case in the choice of an HDTV standard in Japan, where NHK was transmitting experimental HDTV signals by 1979.[9] Japanese firms cooperated to select an analog HDTV standard and began producing sets for home use. In the United States, the Federal Communications Commission (FCC) designed a bidding process where competing standards were submitted for agency approval. The competition

process was slow and apparently cumbersome.[10] Eventually, however, a digital design that showed great promise was presented. While the adoption of HDTV standards is still in process, it appears in retrospect that settling on an analog HDTV standard occurred too quickly in Japan.

A second problem from technology bandwagons is that today's potential adopters ignore the effect of their decision on the welfare of those who adopted yesterday, a cost that is external to their own decision.[11] If a large number of adopters enter the market today, they may receive greater benefits from deciding among themselves to purchase today's technology. Those who adopted yesterday may find that they are stranded—stuck with a technology that is no longer supported.

### Delayed Adoption

In contrast to technology bandwagons, standards can also be adopted too slowly. If current adopters choose yesterday's technology when, in the absence of network externalities, they would prefer to choose today's, the adoption of new technology does not proceed quickly enough. A new technology that is superior to current products may not be adopted because the effect of the larger network in the old technology outweighs the stand-alone benefit of the new technology. A potential entrant may not be able to make a profit even though she has superior technology for the same price. The new entrant must compensate adopters of her technology for the effect of a smaller network in comparison to the installed base of the incumbent's technology.

### Complementary Products

The term "product complements" refers to the situation where consumers prefer to combine the

Figure 13.1  **Unit Sales by Platform**

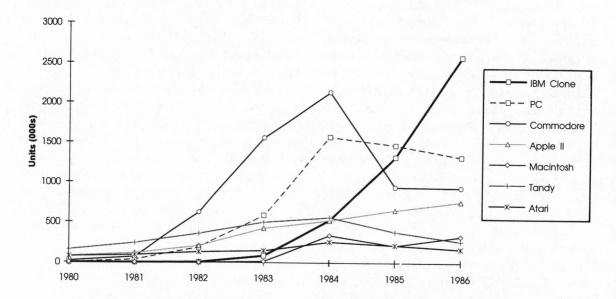

consumption of separate goods. Commonly cited examples include hamburgers and fries or ice cream and cones. When the use of separate products is required under technological constraints but supplied by separate firms, the implications for industry competition and structure can be profound.[12] The consumption of computer hardware and software is an example of technological complements; computer hardware is virtually useless without applications software that provides the user with the solution to some problem (e.g., word processing or spreadsheet).[13] With dramatic improvements in the price and performance of computer hardware, computer hobbyists recognized by 1980 that the cost of owning a computer was becoming affordable. A number of hardware developers entered the personal computer market in pursuit of a profitable slice of that rapidly growing market. Figure 13.1 shows U.S. sales of computer hardware by platform type. The growth of the IBM-PC and the Apple II are important in the

development of a large installed base that will attract the attention of software developers. Sales for the IBM and compatibles by far exceeded the sales for other platforms by the end of 1986, and the battle over a dominant standard appeared to have been won.

With this growth in the installed base of microcomputer hardware, software developers recognized the opportunity to earn significant profits selling shrink-wrapped products to very large markets.[14] By 1986, two platforms attracted the largest number of applications—the IBM-PC and the Apple II. (See Figure 13.2) By 1990, there was an installed base of over 75 million PCs, but only 20 million Apple Macintosh systems. Today, the Wintel standard accounts for over 90 percent of the personal computers in use, while competing platforms are rapidly disappearing. Potential competing application programming interfaces (APIs) in the form of Unix-variants, especially Linux, are emerging.

This large-scale entry of small software devel-

Figure 13.2 **Products by Platform**

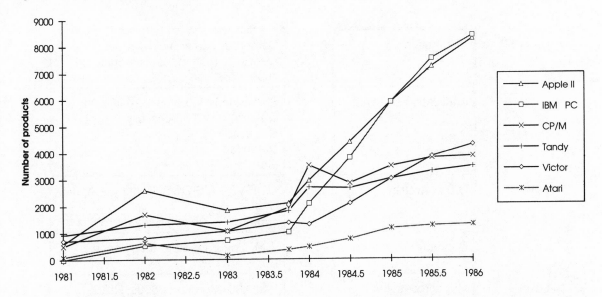

Figure 13.3 **Old (Integrated) Computer Industry Structure**

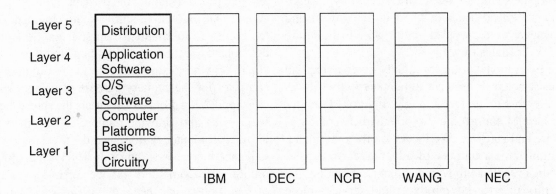

*Source*: Adapted from D. Minasian, "The Computer Industry: Survey," *The Economist*, February 17, 1993.
*Note*: Vendors typically sold complete systems, not components.

Figure 13.4   **New (Less Integrated) Computer Industry Structure**

| Layer 5 | Distribution | Computer dealer, value-added reseller, direct, mass, computer superstore, etc. |
|---------|--------------|-------------------------------------------------------------------------------|
| Layer 4 | Application software | Spreadsheets (Lotus 1-2-3, Excel, Quattro) Word processors<br>Graphics<br>Database<br>etc. |
| Layer 3 | O/S software | *CLIENT* -- MS-DOS, Windows, Apple, Unix ...<br>*SERVER* -- Novell, Banyan, IBM ... |
| Layer 2 | Computer platforms | IBM, Compaq, other Intel-based, Apple Mac ... |
| Layer 1 | Microprocessor | Intel x86, Motorola 6800s, RISC ... |

*Source*: Adapted from D. Minasian, "The Computer Industry:" Survey, © *The Economist*, February 17, 1993.
*Note*: Vendors sell components as well as complete systems.

opers had a profound affect on the vertical structure of the computer industry. Historically, the computer industry was characterized by an integrated vertical structure where both hardware and software were provided by the same firm. Figure 13.3 illustrates this.[15]

Two rationales are commonly given to explain this structure. From a consumer perspective, it was preferable to contact a single, integrated vendor in case of compatibility problems between hardware and software. Producers, on the other hand, might have a number of advantages in a sole-source relationship with customers, including the ability to price key products and services more closely to the consumer's willingness-to-pay. Whatever the advantages of this structure, a less vertically integrated supply has a dramatically different look, as Figure 13.4 indicates.

There are many perceived advantages to this less integrated structure, but perhaps the chief concern is that innovative software development often comes from unanticipated sources. Software developers use the term "killer app" to refer to the condition where consumers decide to purchase a computer for the primary purpose of using a specific application. For business users the spreadsheet was a killer app, drawing millions of customers to the microcomputer platform in order to access a versatile and innovative product. In 1985, sales of 2.7 million microcomputers was accompanied by sales of 2 million spreadsheets; by 1987 over 7.1 million spreadsheets had been sold.[16] Sales of Macintosh were sluggish until Aldus Pagemaker defined a new product segment with the "desktop publishing" killer app. This less integrated product delivery environment appears to facilitate innovation because third parties have an incentive to develop innovative product complements.[17]

### Microcomputer Hardware Example

To understand the effect of network externalities in microcomputer product complements, reflect for a moment on the decision to purchase a microcomputer. The raw computing power of the machines matters a great deal, as does the quality of the input (keyboard, mouse, voice) and output (monitor, printer) devices. These stand-alone features are important, but consumers also care about complementary products and services like training in product use, maintenance and repairs, and, perhaps most important, the availability of low-cost, high-quality software. Without applications software, the hardware is of little use, so a purchasing decision will be influenced by expectations about software availability. Developers of software products are interested in how consumers think about the problem, because before they invest long hours in understanding the hardware and creating the software, they too must form expectations about the payoff from the installed base of computers able to run the software. That is, just as in hardware, while applications software will have certain stand-alone value, there is also a strong interest in the number of other users of compatible software. For software users, a larger installed base increases the probability of realizing advantages like the following: the ability to share data files in collaborative work, the opportunity to learn to use the product from well-written documentation (frequently provided by third parties), and access to expert advice in solving problems or avoiding difficulties in using the software. For this reason, software products that either have a larger number of users or are compatible with a market standard have an advantage over products with similar quality but fewer users.[18]

### VCR Industry Example

Competing standards in the VCR industry illustrate the importance of market dynamics in industries characterized by product complements as they relate to network externalities. Although many considered Sony's Betamax technology to be superior to competing technology, JVC's alliance in the manufacture of VHS has become the de facto standard in VCR technology. It is helpful to see how this occurred since there are several similarities in the VCR market to the market for computer hardware and software. The emergence of VHS as the dominant standard is particularly interesting because performance characteristics of Beta VCR's are often compared favorably with VHS technology. The chief advantages of Sony's Beta during the early stages of standards competition included a sharper picture and the ability to switch quickly between "fast-forward" and "play" because the head could remain close to the tape. Sony was first to market with Betamax in May of 1985. It enjoyed almost a full year's lead over the consortium of VHS producers, which introduced its first VHS machine in October 1986. While the tape playing time of Beta was only an hour compared to VHS's two hours, the network effect would normally tip competition in favor of a first mover. In the first several years of competition, better performance features were important in giving the Beta an early lead in installed base. However, VHS soon caught up in many performance characteristics as Beta and VHS played a game of technological leapfrog in alternately introducing improved features. VHS gained an upper hand, as Table 13.2 shows.

Table 13.2

**VHS Versus Beta–Annual Production**

| Year | Beta | VHS |
|------|------|-----|
| 1975 | 20 | NA |
| 1976 | 175 | 110 |
| 1977 | 424 | 339 |
| 1978 | 594 | 878 |
| 1979 | 851 | 1,336 |
| | | |
| 1980 | 1,489 | 2,922 |
| 1981 | 3,020 | 6,478 |
| 1982 | 3,717 | 9,417 |
| 1983 | 4,572 | 13,645 |
| 1984 | 6,042 | 23,464 |
| | | |
| 1985 | 3,387 | 40,977 |
| 1986 | 1,106 | 29,553 |
| 1987 | 669 | 39,767 |
| 1988 | 148 | 44,761 |

*Source*: Michael A. Cusumano, Yiorgos Mylonadis, and Richard S. Rosenbloom, "Strategic Maneuvering and Mass-Market Dynamics: The Triumph of VHS over Beta," *Business History Review* 66 (Spring 1992): 54.

Perhaps more than any other single factor, however, it was the availability of prerecorded tapes that played the most important role in the emergence of a single standard.[19] While manufacturers of both technologies were focused on the ability to record television programming and replay it at the viewer's convenience, ultimately the VCR was used primarily as a substitute for a visit to the cinema. As major motion picture producers began to offer prerecorded tapes for rental, the choice of VHS or Beta became an important consideration. Providing tapes in both formats was an unnecessary duplication if the majority of the market was standardized on a single format. Not only is there the expense of duplicating the tape, but also that of scarce shelf-space at the video rental store.

These combined costs resulted in a preference for a single format. As VHS began to gain a slight lead in installed base, more studios and video stores turned to VHS for prerecorded rental tapes. The success of VHS over Beta as the market standard was at least partially due to the availability of complementary products. In 1989, Sony acquired Columbia Pictures and CBS records, at least in part in recognition that any future audio and visual hardware technologies would require sufficient software. Sony's motivation comes at least partially from concern that problems like the insufficient number of titles for the Betamax format might recur in other contexts.

The VCR example is important to understanding the market for microcomputer hardware. Although the cost structure of the provision of product complements is different for microcomputer software than for VCR tapes, the pressures for standardization are similar, and a similar standardization resulted. In fact, the VCR and microcomputer stories have other points in common. The eventual dominant standard, the IBM-PC and compatibles, was the product of a coalition of firms, rather than a single monopoly provider. Consumer desire for a single standard follows from a desire for product variety in a complement (software or tapes) rather than preference for the stand-alone performance characteristics of the product itself (hardware or VCR). A number of consumers who guessed wrong were stranded in their investment in the durable good—with microcomputers, the availability of software for non–IBM-PCs dwindled; with VCRs, it became difficult to find Beta format tapes.

### Technological Change

In markets with technological progress, development of a standard is a moving target. Rapid improvements in hardware technology can make one hardware standard obsolete and the software that runs on it worthless. Rapid improvements in hardware technology have played an important role in the way competition in software has evolved. The dramatic price decrease in hardware has increased the demand for software, but the dance between hardware and software producers has not always moved smoothly.

## Decrease in Hardware Price

When economists consider the valuation of a product to be a function of the separate values given to attributes of the product, they use the term "hedonic pricing." Because these attributes are always found bundled in the product, and not for sale separately, a theory for how to distinguish the effect of varying levels of quality in each attribute was needed. The technique that eventually emerged, referred to as hedonic pricing, considers a consumer's willingness to pay for the product as though each attribute could be separately priced. The hedonic pricing approach allows economists to model a quality-adjusted price for a good that is based on separate valuation of product attributes. An hedonic approach is particularly important when the quality of a good increases at a time when the price of the good holds steady or declines.

Applying this approach to the market for computer hardware has helped to provide a model of how the quality-adjusted price of hardware has changed over time. The rapid improvements in computing technology are legendary. The computing power of an early mainframe computer costing millions of dollars and filling a room is now available in a laptop costing less than a thousand. In 1945 the first modern electronic computer, ENIAC, consumed 150 kilowatts of electricity for 18,000 electron tubes and 30 tons of equipment.[20] Now a small laptop computer can be run on the same electricity it takes to turn on a light (books can still be operated on even less electricity). The

fall in the quality-adjusted price of hardware prompted the following: "[I]f the automobile and airplane businesses had developed like the computer business, a Rolls Royce would cost $2.75 and run for 3 million miles on one gallon of gas. And a Boeing 767 would cost just $500 and circle the globe in 20 minutes on five gallons of gas."[21]

This transformation in quality-adjusted pricing is important to understanding competition in the market for computer software. As some have described it, increased computing capability does not just run current programs faster, it makes possible applications that were previously inconceivable.[22] Microcomputer technology improvements made desktop publishing and multimedia documents a reality when only a few years before their introduction to the desktop, the cost of providing a similar capability was on the order of tens or hundreds of thousands of dollars.

## Improvements in Microcomputer Hardware

Innovation in semiconductor technology has had widespread impact on the cost and performance of a range of hardware components—random access memory, hard disk drives, CD-ROMs, sound cards, to name a few. The impact of this is perhaps best illustrated in the performance improvements in Intel's x86 microprocessor chips. These chips serve a vital role as the central processing unit (CPU) for the majority of microcomputers. The following figures illustrate performance improvements in this technology over the past decade. Figure 13.5 shows something of the increased computing performance measured by million instructions per second (MIPS). Faster processing means that software runs in less time, and opens up the possibility of entirely new functionality such as real-time voice and video. Because both this

Figure 13.5 **Microprocessor Performance (MIPS)**

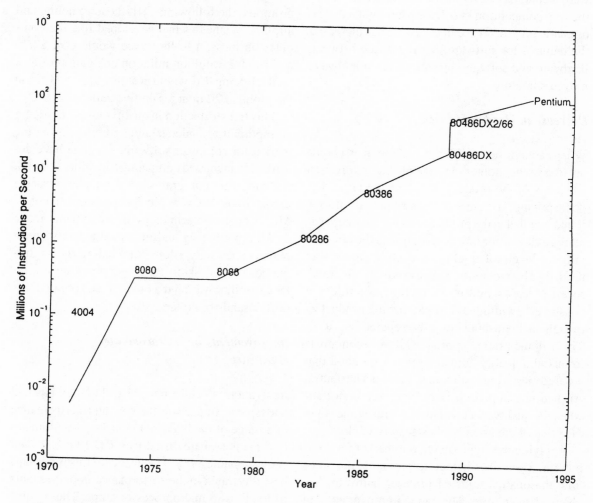

figure and the next are in logarithmic scales, a unit increase on the figures corresponds to a tenfold increase in chip performance.

By the mid-1970s, the cofounder of Intel had identified an important pattern in semiconductor performance now known as "Moore's law"—the number of transistors on a chip doubles every eighteen months (see Figure 13.6), Bill Gates observed this pattern in the early 1980s and declared that "hardware is free." That is, as computing power increased on the desktop, the great detail required in software development for the use of hardware resources such as memory and disk storage was becoming less important than the application's functionality and ease of use. Moore's law holds true despite over three decades of technological development, as Figure 13.6 illustrates.

The rapid and dramatic improvements in processing capability over the past decades, and the likely improvements in the near future, have

Figure 13.6 **Number of Transistors on a Chip**

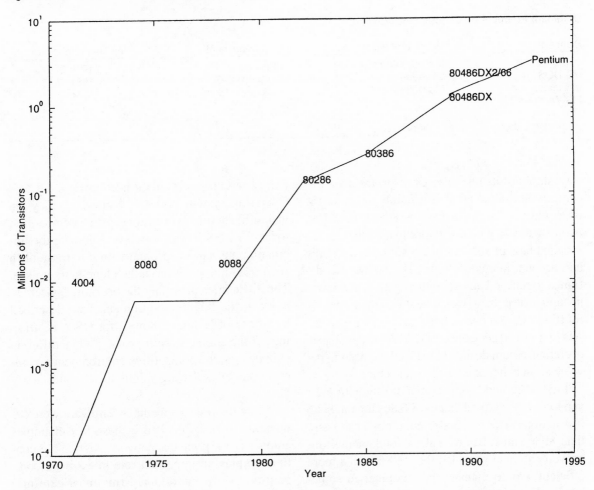

equally dramatic implications for competition between generations of hardware and software. Strategies to introduce new product technologies in the presence of network externalities must take into account the installed base of users and product complements. The introduction of today's new hardware provides both opportunities and threats to software developers. Compatibility between today's new technology and yesterday's old one can be difficult and inefficient because of the need

to coordinate software development, as the following examples show.

### Hardware Generations and Effect on Software

Intel, in its design of x86 microprocessors, routinely has to consider intergenerational effects. Programs written for yesterday's 80486 must run on the Pentium of today and tomorrow. Intel has not al-

Table 13.3

**Dominant Products on Various Platforms**

| Platform | Word processor | Spreadsheet | First year of platform |
|---|---|---|---|
| Apple II | Micropro Wordstar | Visicalc | 1979 |
| MS-DOS | WordPerfect | Lotus 1–2–3 | 1981 |
| Macintosh and | Microsoft Word | Microsoft Excel | 1984 |
| MS-Windows 3.1 | | | 1990 |

*Source*: Industry newletters, various years.

ways designed its microprocessors to maintain this compatibility, although it is certainly aware of the issues today.[23] The change from the 8086 to the 80286 is one example where network externalties of the installed base of software were not taken carefully into account in chip design.[24] The 80286 was designed to run the Unix operating system, and it was not anticipated that it would be used predominantly for IBM-PCs. Yet once a large installed base of PC-ATs (the second generation of IBM-PCs) developed, operating system designers realized the need to develop around the weaknesses in the chip.

First, to provide some compatibility with prior versions, Intel assured that the 80286 chip ran 8086 instructions in "real" mode, and it ran these faster than 8086 chips. But to make a fundamental improvement, Intel provided the 80286 with a more efficient way to manage the computer in something called "protected" mode. To take advantage of this improved performance, however, the computer would either need to start in protected mode, or switch into it (once) during a session. This implementation made it difficult to switch between modes, so that users could not run programs written for the old real mode once the chip was operating in protected mode. This difficulty prompted some software developers to describe the 80286 as "brain-dead." The design made the development of an operating system particularly labored, and

almost certainly delayed the introduction of IBM's Operating System 2 (OS/2). While OS/2 plays an insignificant role in operating system competition today, in 1988 it was poised to dominate the microcomputer landscape, and with it to reestablish IBM's leading position in the clone marketplace. The difficulties in getting the operating system to work in the 80286 environment were described by Microsoft's chief architect for OS/2 as "turning off the engine to shift gears."[25] On a different chip design, the competitive environment for microcomputer software might look significantly different.

While the improvements in hardware were exogenous to software firms, these last examples emphasize the point that network externalities continue to play an important role in evolving competition. More important, firms must carefully manage intergenerational product competition in a market where the hardware environment is improving at a rapid pace. Transitional changes in new platforms are often accompanied by a challenge to the software applications that were dominant on the prior platform. These transitions show that competition in the industry is not the same year after year, but that upon the arrival of a new computing platform the nature of competition shifts dramatically. Table 13.3 shows products that were dominant in various computer platforms.

Another example comes from the development of software for the Apple Macintosh. In 1984, Bill Gates thought that development of the Macintosh was so significant that he put enormous resources into the development of software for the new computer. Apple, perhaps concerned about Microsoft's leverage, resisted Gates's initial request for access to the computer to be able to provide products for the Macintosh product launch. It was not until Gates threatened to drop development of its Apple II products, then a significant portion of Apple's revenues, that Microsoft programmers were allowed early access to Mac development. While Microsoft's MS-DOS applications were mere also-rans, its Macintosh products were immediate hits. The DOS versions of the MS-Word word processor and Multiplan spreadsheet held far less market share than the dominant DOS applications in the United States, while Mac products MS-Word and MS-Excel captured a dominant share in Macintosh. As Microsoft released the MS-Windows operating systems (e.g., 3.0, 95, 98, 2000), Microsoft Office applications were poised to dominate their categories.

## Software Improvements and Generational Effects

While it is clear that hardware improvements have a significant impact on network competition in software products, cheaper hardware has also helped to increase software accessibility dramatically. Some industry analysts observe that what is unique about modern software is the increasingly large percentage of code that is written to support the core functionality of the application, rather than core functionality alone. For example, early microcomputer software developers deemed simple book text sufficient user documentation. Software now includes interactive tutorials, animations, and even multimedia videos to provide users with ex-

tensive introduction to software use. Nearly all of this shift in focus is facilitated by increased microcomputer hardware functionality, but it is clearly user demand for software applications that are easy to learn and use that has determined how this increased hardware power is used.

But software functionality itself, not just the tools that improve its accessibility, has also greatly improved in performance. Software engineering and better theoretical models in mathematics have led to improvements in the performance of software algorithms; it is not just hardware that has shown dramatic improvements over the past several decades. Figure 13.7 shows the processing implications of better algorithm design—in this case a problem in differential equations.

The graph shows a decline in performance in the mid-1970s, not because algorithms became inefficient, but because the significant improvements in processing and coding have made it possible to develop slightly slower code that produces more reliable results. This is an example of the earlier observation that software improvements not only do old processing faster, but also facilitate new functionality.

These improvements are suggestive of the increased capability in software design more generally. The combined hardware and software technological innovation show a significant opportunity for the development of new computer applications. However, there is reason to believe that innovation in the market does not occur as rapidly as it might because there are important switching costs in the development of new technologies.

## Lock-in and Switching Costs

Once there is an installed base of users of a particular technology or standard, a potential entrant

Figure 13.7 **Performance Improvement**

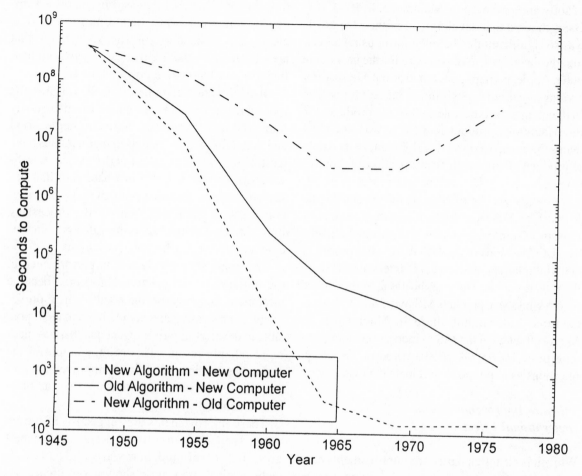

may have to overcome network benefits in order to successfully enter the market. If the installed base of users can inexpensively adopt new technology, then the network effect might not raise the entry cost of new entrants. However, network externalities can have a profound impact on competition when there is lock-in[26] or a switching cost.[27] The installed base of users of an old technology may be reluctant to switch to a new technology even if the new technology is somewhat better. When a user of yesterday's technology evaluates today's competitive alternative, there are three kinds of costs to consider: sunk costs, switching costs, and network benefits. When the product is a durable good, those who purchased yesterday's technology have a sunk cost, the magnitude of which they should ignore in today's adoption decision. But, the ability to use yesterday's technology means that the benefit from the new technology must be significant enough to justify abandoning the old to adopt the new. If the adoption cost falls slowly over time, yesterday's cost to adopt technology, even though it is sunk, is about the same as today's adoption cost. If adoption costs fall rapidly over time, transition from old to new standards is facilitated.

Current adopters are not subject to switching costs, but the adoption decision can be affected by the switching costs of the installed base of users. Any purchase decision must consider the benefit of the new technology along with the benefit of the old, both net of price (i.e., value to consumer in excess of what had to be paid). There is some interest in yesterday's technology because network benefits go along with the installed base. If network benefits are insignificant, the choice is straightforward. Or, if the installed base of users of yesterday's technology is small enough in comparison to those in the market today, current adopters may find the network effect too small to lure them into using the old technology. It is easy to imagine a situation, though, where today's technology must be a very significant improvement before it will make sense for today's purchasers to choose today's technology over yesterday's. If those network benefits are significant, today's buyers may prefer the old technology even though it is not the best stand-alone value available.[28]

The main concern for economic efficiency is that if users incur a switching cost or otherwise become locked in to a certain technology, network effects become all the more important in industry competition. If goods are consumable and there is no cost of adoption, then network effects are important only in that consumers want to coordinate today's purchases. The installed base of yesterday's adopters is unimportant because today's purchase decision is not affected by their earlier choice. If there are switching costs in consumable goods, those who purchased the old technology yesterday have a greater incentive to choose that same technology today. And the size of that installed base, combined with their incentive to choose yesterday's technology, means that today's adopters will have greater network benefits if they are compatible with the old network. If goods are durable, then the installed base that uses yesterday's technology influences the adoption of today's new technology, whether the installed base incurs a switching cost or not.

## Microcomputer Software Example: WordPerfect

It is helpful to apply these ideas to the microcomputer software industry. An example helps to clarify this discussion of lock-in and switching costs. When Satellite Software International (SSI) introduced version 4.0 of WordPerfect in 1984, consumers considered both the performance characteristics of the product as well as the installed base of users.[29] Forward-thinking consumers also considered that by purchasing version 4.0, they were making a commitment to a long-term interest in the success and continuance of SSI. WordPerfect 3.0 was a successful product and had special design features that made it appealing to professional typists. First, the keystroke sequences made it handy to perform commonly required tasks quickly. While there was a menu interface to the product, common functions such as printing a document or saving a file could be executed with a combination of keystrokes. Knowledgeable users could simultaneously hold down a combination of the control-shift-alt and function keys in order to rapidly invoke some functionality such as printing or spell-check. Other programs allowed similar functionality, but it was only available through a tedious menu structure. For typists willing to take the time to specialize their knowledge of WordPerfect, quick keystroke access was a valued time-saver. Second, the program was widely enough known to have third-party writers provide instructional material describing how to learn and use WordPerfect. Third, expectations that a large number of other users would like WordPerfect led more users to adopt this product over competitors like Microsoft Word or Multi-Mate Advantage.

While SSI was concerning itself with a specialized but efficient interface, Multi-Mate was paying attention to a different network of users. Wang Computers, which were very popular in a professional (e.g., law, accounting) office environment, used minicomputer technology to provide word processing functionality. The Multi-Mate Advantage word processor was developed to provide a functional interface on a personal computer that was similar to the Wang. As long as its installed base of Wang users was large, the network benefits and the switching costs might be significant enough to generate sales even if the WordPerfect product were in some way better. Multi-Mate was able to leverage its installed base of Wang users into the PC market, but it was not enough to overtake the eventual dominance of WordPerfect.

One of the most interesting anomalies in the story of market standards and network externalities relates to what happened next in the Word-Perfect story. With a strong product but a moderately difficult-to-learn interface, Word-Perfect sought to improve its market position by redesigning the keystroke sequences. Thus, when WordPerfect 3.0 users learned of the latest version of WordPerfect 4.0, they may have been concerned to discover that they would eventually have to relearn keystroke sequences. The keystroke shortcuts that they had become so attached to were now programmed to deliver completely different functionality. To the extent that the installed base was required to be completely retrained in the use of the software, WordPerfect 3.0 users who wanted to use the latest software were required to incur a

switching cost, although the learning cost for the upgrade to WP 4.0 was less than that for competing products. Reducing the lock-in cost for consumers in a market with network externalities seems inadvisable, yet the difficulty of providing compatibility with the installed base while concurrently attracting new users forces an incumbent to choose.

There are many other examples of intergenerational effects. Delays in the introduction of Windows 95 were attributed to the complexities of providing "plug-and-play" compatibility for thousands of hardware and software products. The installed base of users and the library of software already available for established platforms can be an important constraint on rapid adoption of new technologies. For a number of these reasons, Steve Jobs, cofounder of Apple Computer and founder of NeXT, complains that the high-technology computer industry "moves at a glacial pace." A casual observer may at first think the comment ill founded, particularly in light of the dramatic price/performance improvements in hardware technology. But Jobs's frustration is a result of the inertia of an enormous installed base of users and software that deters the adoption of innovative and powerful, though incompatible, technology. None of Jobs's three computing platforms—the Apple II, the Apple Macintosh, and NeXT—was able to overcome the PC and compatibles, arguably less innovative products.

**Industry Competitiveness**

Traditional measures of industry competitiveness might not be as useful in a market that is characterized by network externalities. Much like the traditional justification for natural monopolies, namely to avoid unnecessary duplication of significant asset investments, an increase in the number of competing standards, and competitors, does

Table 13.4

**Revenues and Employees of the *Soft\*Letter 100* Firms**

|  | Employees | | | Revenue (thousands) | | |
|---|---|---|---|---|---|---|
|  | Median | Average | Minimum | Median | Average | Minimum |
| 1983 | NA | NA | NA | 2,700 | 7,000 | 300 |
| 1984 | NA | NA | NA | 4,200 | 9,325 | 1,000 |
| 1985 | 27 | 83 | 5 | 3,040 | 11,334 | 1,000 |
| 1986 | 35 | 101 | 8 | 3,600 | 14,783 | 1,150 |
| 1987 | 55 | 150 | 7 | 5,800 | 23,278 | 2,250 |
| 1988 | 60 | 187 | 12 | 8,900 | 32,592 | 2,500 |
| 1989 | 80 | 233 | 15 | 10,700 | 39,929 | 3,000 |
| 1990 | 82 | 309 | 8 | 10,000 | 57,049 | 3,020 |
| 1991 | 99 | 391 | 18 | 14,091 | 75,911 | 3,320 |
| 1992 | 100 | 443 | 13 | 15,192 | 92,727 | 3,495 |
| 1993 | 100 | 504 | 17 | 14,400 | 111,433 | 4,000 |
| 1995 | 155 | 602 | 14 | 26,230 | 164,908 | 6,000 |

*Source: Soft\*Letter 100.*

not necessarily benefit consumer welfare. If network externalities are significant, consumers are better off with a single standard, perhaps even with the inefficiencies associated with monopoly. (This view has recently received greater scrutiny in light of the public revelations of Microsoft's aggressively competitive conduct, as reported in the case *U.S. vs. Microsoft.*) If the monopolist cannot capture the additional value related to the size of the installed base, then consumers may be better off coordinating the choice of a single standard in order to maximize the network benefit. Perhaps as important, firms may compete aggressively for a monopoly position in the market, with a resultant high measure of industry concentration, yet without significant welfare loss.

## Structure

Information on software firm revenues and employment is necessary to the analysis of industry structure. Traditional industry reporting by Standard Industrial Classification (SIC) or other government economic indicators rarely anticipate newly emerging market segments. As a consequence, data on microcomputer software and hardware sales is aggregated with older hardware and software service classifications. Fortunately, *Soft\*Letter,* an industry newsletter, produces an annual listing of the largest 100 microcomputer software firms as measured by revenues.[30] To be listed in the report, over 50 percent of a firm's revenues must come from microcomputer software. Data are self-reported, and firms may not pay strict attention to the information they provide. These and other concerns about this report affect the analysis of Table 13.4.

## Concentration

Figure 13.8 shows 4–firm concentration ratios of revenues among the *Soft\*Letter 100.* Since only the largest 100 firms in the industry are used in

Figure 13.8  **Concentration Among the *Soft\*Letter 100* Firms**

the calculation, the true concentration ratio might be significantly smaller if revenues of firms outside of the list are material. The *Soft\*Letter* editor identified over 3,000 firms in the industry by 1995, most with fewer than 30 employees. Because revenue declines significantly with lower rankings, it is unlikely that the sum of revenues outside of the top 100 are significant enough to affect the concentration ratio. On the other hand, because the qualification for listing is that at least half of revenues come from microcomputer software, some microcomputer software revenues are excluded. For example, IBM has significant nonmicrocomputer software revenues, so that its recent acquisition removed Lotus's revenues from the list. If the excluded firms lie outside of the top four, the concentration ratio would decrease. With these caveats, we note that over the past decade (1991–2001), the increase in the Hirschman-Hirfindahl Index (HHI) and four-firm concentration ratio (CR4) are significant.

With the introduction of greater competition on the Internet, companies like Netscape and Sun increasingly compete with Microsoft, and restricting attention to the microcomputer segment alone might cause competition levels to be understated. A later discussion visits the issue of broader platform competition.

## *Turnover*

A second measure of competition frequently used in industry studies is turnover rates. While an industry may be concentrated at any point in time, if firms easily enter the market and grow to displace incumbents, the industry may yet be competitive. Market share alone says nothing about whether the top firms will even survive the next year. Where three or four firms garner a lion's share of the revenues every year, but each year sees three or four different firms at the top, the high rate of turnover in the industry suggests a highly competitive en-

Table 13.5

**Turnover of Top Ten Firms in Software and Hardware, 1985–1995**

| 1985 | 1990 | 1995 |
| --- | --- | --- |
| Software Turnover: *Soft\*Letter 100* | | |
| Lotus Development Corp. | Microsoft Corp. | Microsoft Corp |
| Microsoft Corp. | Lotus Development Corp. | Novell |
| Ashton-Tate | Novell | Adobe Systems |
| Digital Research Inc. | WordPerfect Corp. | Autodesk |
| Micropro International | Autodesk Inc. | Intuit |
| Software Publishing Corp. | Ashton-Tate | Symantec |
| Borland International | Borland International | Attachmate |
| Autodesk Inc. | Adobe Systems | SoftKey International |
| Broderbund Software | Software Publishing Corp. | Borland International |
| Satellite Software International | Aldus Corp. | GE Interactive Software |
| Hardware Turnover: *Datamation 100* | | |
| IBM | IBM | IBM |
| Digital Equipment | Digital Equipment | Hewlett-Packard |
| Sperry | Unisys | Compaq |
| Burroughs | Hewlett-Packard | Digital Equipment |
| NCR | Apple Computer | Electronic Data Systems |
| Control Data Corp. | NCR | AT&T |
| Hewlett-Packard | Compaq | Apple Computer |
| Wang Labs | AT&T | Seagate Technology |
| Xerox | Xerox | Microsoft |
| Honeywell | Wang Labs | Sun Microsystems |

*Source*: *Soft\*Letter* and *Datamation*, various years.

vironment despite the high year-by-year concentration. If rankings seldom change even though concentration ratios are low, the industry might not be competitive. Turnover is a relative measure, and it is important to compare software firms with firms in another industry characterized by network externalities. For comparative purposes, then, the larger, more established hardware firms are included in Table 13.5.

We can measure turnover in these industries in terms of the uncertainty related with a particular ordinal (e.g., first, second, third) ranking by asking "If a firm is ranked in a certain position this year, how likely is it to remain in that position next year?" Ordinal time-series methods help estimate this uncertainty in a measure of entropy. There are several kinds of rank uncertainty—uncertainty about moving up, staying, or having one's rank fall. Figures 13.9 and 13.10 present entropy measures of the likelihood of retaining the current ranking in a subsequent year. For reasons similar to those in the concentration ratio presentation, it is useful to compare these measures with hardware markets. Software firms are more likely to retain their rank.

The uncertainty regarding rank changes appears to be similar between the two industries, which seems quite surprising given that the hardware firms are older and far more established in comparison to the microcomputer software firms.

Figure 13.9  **Cumulative Entropy by Rank**

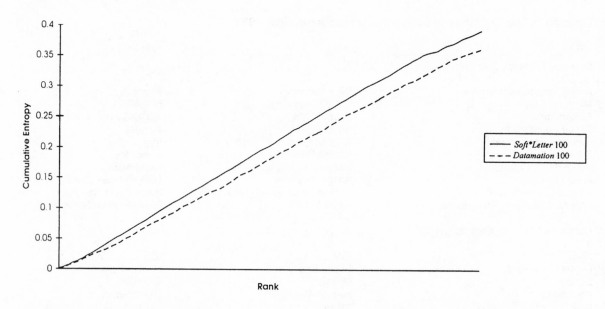

## Entry Barriers and Firm Survival

Industry competitiveness is frequently approximated by measures of minimum efficient scale (MES). If MES is small, any entrepreneur will be able to raise enough capital to enter and compete, as expected in a classical perfectly competitive industry. MES entry costs for software product development have historically been small in comparison with entry costs for many other industries. Almost all costs are development costs, which are fixed rather than variable costs of production. One Harvard case writer estimated that a software entrepreneur required only $10,000 to start a firm.[31] But this is only the required investment in equipment; the entrepreneur must also possess software development skills as well as the marketing and distribution expertise to launch the product. Early industry participants sponsored relatively modest product launches, while later product introductions were accompanied by enormous marketing and

advertising fees. To the extent that advertising has grown to play a more significant role in the industry, entry barriers have become more critical.[32] Compared with many industries where this cannot happen, though, software firms are still known to spring up overnight on a shoestring budget.

## Regionalization

Scholars in economic development occasionally note regional economies from companies locating near one another, such as the concentration of the automobile industry in the midwestern United States, or the semiconductor industry in Silicon Valley.[33] Certain regions may be particularly appealing to industries that require specialized inputs, such as rare minerals or cheap access to power sources. It appears that the software industry does not require that skills be concentrated in a particular region. The primary input to software start-ups is the technical skill in software development that

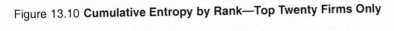

Figure 13.10 **Cumulative Entropy by Rank—Top Twenty Firms Only**

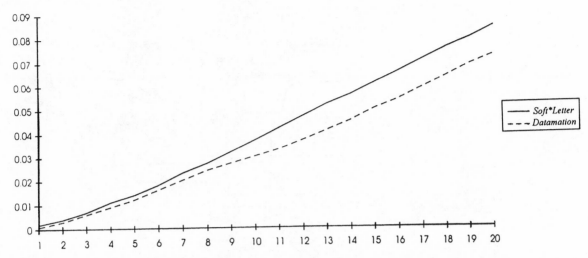

comes from experience with hardware and software. In the early microcomputer industry, this expertise came from engineers working in large computer firms like HP, IBM, and DEC and from computer hobbyists who became interested in starting a company. These characteristics were more common in certain U.S. regions, and it might be expected that early microcomputer software firms were geographically concentrated. Figure 13.11 shows the ranking of U.S. states by *Soft\*Letter 100* revenues in 1990 and 1995.

There is slight evidence of regionalization of the microcomputer software industry, although it is clearly related to population centers. In the western region, the I-5 corridor around Puget Sound has one of the largest concentrations of software developer revenues. Even without Microsoft, a number of firms in the Seattle and Bellevue area play important roles in the industry (e.g., Attachmate, Real Networks, Walker Richer and Quinn). Next, the Bay Area and Silicon Valley in California (Adobe, Autodesk, Intuit, Symantec)

are areas where influential software firms have located. Utah's prominent ranking is due to Novell. Regions of Massachusetts retain the ranking in software development while that in Texas has declined, to be replaced by activity in Pennsylvania. Since revenues are only one basis for ranking, comparisons for revenues, number of employees, and number of firms are presented in Table 13.6.

Data on assets, profitability, employees, market value, and number of firms are available through Compustat (a Standard and Poor's database) for specific SIC codes (Standard Industrial Classification used in the Census of Manufactures) but not separately for microcomputer platforms. Prepackaged software is reported in SIC 7372 (Computer Programming, Data Processing), and augments the above analysis of microcomputer software. (See Table 13.7) Rankings are similar, but the magnitude of asset size and net income provide a perspective on how significant the industry has become.

Figure 13.11 **Ranking by Software Revenue**

*Note:* 1990 rank (regular) followed by 1995 rank (bold); * indicates not ranked that year.

## *Employment*

While the earlier tables list number of employees, they do not distinguish software development work from marketing, accounting, or other functional areas. Measuring the size of the software industry by the number developers is not easily done because the Bureau of Labor Statistics reports employment opportunities by job skill, rather than by sector employment. Although opportunities for programmers have increased over the past decade, it is not easy to determine how closely demand for them relates to microcomputer software development. Furthermore, the unique skill required in software development of shrink-wrapped software is not reported separately, since many software engineers also produce customized products,

maintain large corporate applications, or serve as internal company consultants for solving information systems problems. The concern in some circles is that lucrative careers in software development will disappear if the work can be done cheaply in parts of the world with the requisite labor pool. Some industry observers have noted that telecommunications has reduced the need for face-to-face contact, with the result that many firms have taken the opportunity to access programming skills outside of North America.[34]

## *Industry Conduct*

Casual observers of the software industry attest to the rapid rate of technological innovation, and the apparent availability of investment capital and

Table 13.6

### *Soft*Letter* Rankings by State

| | Revenue | | | | Firms | | | | Employees | | |
|---|---|---|---|---|---|---|---|---|---|---|---|
| | 1990 | 1995 | 2000 | | 1990 | 1995 | 2000 | | 1990 | 1995 | 2000 |
| WA | 2 | 1 | 1 | CA | 1 | 2 | 1 | WA | 3 | 2 | 1 |
| CA | 1 | 2 | 2 | MA | 4 | 4 | 2 | CA | 1 | 1 | 2 |
| UT | 3 | 3 | 3 | WA | 2 | 1 | 3 | UT | | | 3 |
| FL | 8 | 13 | 4 | PA | 6 | 6 | 4 | MA | 2 | 3 | 4 |
| MA | 4 | 4 | 5 | NY | 11 | 5 | 5 | PA | 4 | 5 | 5 |
| PA | 7 | 7 | 6 | OR | 5 | 12 | 6 | FL | 10 | 5 | 6 |
| NY | 15 | 5 | 7 | TX | 7 | 8 | 7 | NY | 10 | 5 | 7 |
| IL | 12 | 9 | 8 | FL | 9 | 15 | 8 | IL | 4 | 5 | 8 |
| ND | | | 9 | IL | 7 | 7 | 9 | ND | | | 9 |
| TX | 6 | 8 | 10 | NH | 17 | 13 | 10 | OR | 6 | 10 | 10 |

*Source: Soft*Letter*, various years.

Table 13.7

### 1996 Activity in SIC 7372 Prepackaged Software, by State

| State | Assets (millions) | Net income (millions) | Employees | Market value (millions) | No. of firms |
|---|---|---|---|---|---|
| California | 9,283 | 687 | 51,670 | 59,874 | 81 |
| Washington | 7,542 | 1,485 | 19,521 | 61,916 | 8 |
| New York | 4,109 | 507 | 10,066 | 19,538 | 15 |
| Massachusetts | 2,629 | 23 | 16,973 | 10,829 | 26 |
| Utah | 2,417 | 338 | 7,272 | 4,889 | 1 |
| Texas | 1,775 | 135 | 11,114 | 7,476 | 15 |
| Illinois | 713 | 40 | 3,532 | 2,008 | 5 |
| Michigan | 603 | 67 | 4,791 | 1,189 | 2 |
| Maryland | 309 | 21 | 2,142 | 525 | 7 |
| Georgia | 195 | (1) | 1,196 | 268 | 4 |

*Source: Compustat, 1997.

human resources for the continued success of the industry. Despite the industry's reputation for innovation and creativity, the recent antitrust action has captured interest in industry conduct as industry insiders appealed to policymakers that venture capital for software development was drying up. Questions of the public interest in industry conduct have centered on Microsoft's business practices in the sale and distribution of Microsoft Windows, and on the "browser wars" in which Microsoft's Internet Explorer displaced industry standard Netscape Navigator. In 1990, the Federal Trade Commission (FTC) began an investigation of Microsoft's business practices. There are two issues that apparently prompted the investigation: product preannouncements and tied sales.

## Product Preannouncements

The earlier discussion of network externalities demonstrates the importance of managing consumer expectations about product performance and new product introductions.[35] Users chronically complain that in the microcomputer software industry, announcements of product improvements come well ahead of their availability. This was one of the early complaints about a number of software firms, and resulted in the term "vaporware" to describe products that either were never launched or that took so long in development that anxious users thought they would never see the launch. The incentive for earlier preannouncements is easily seen in a firm with a dominant but aging product. The firm has two goals in announcing product improvements well ahead of their availability—first, to encourage potential adopters to delay purchasing a competing product, and second, to keep its current installed base from switching to a competitor product. Both of these effects increase the relative size of the installed base, and thus the network benefit, in favor of the incumbent. For the entrant firm, this strategy delays the development of an installed base, and delay may be enough to tip the competitive advantage to the incumbent until the entrant abandons the market. Potential adopters will already be reluctant to choose the entrant product because of the smaller network benefits, and a preannouncement tactic reinforces this. Current users of the incumbent's product will be similarly disinclined to change to the competing product if there is a switching cost, but doubly so if there is a loss of network benefits by moving to a product with a smaller installed base. For the incumbent firm, the strategy deters current users from leaving, and thus maintains both the size of the installed base and the associated network benefits. Both of these effects are important only to the extent that the installed base and the potential adopters believe the preannouncement. Actually, it is more accurate to say that they must believe that everyone else believes the preannouncement.

The FTC investigation of Microsoft included a study of preannouncements, but the eventual consent decree signed with the Department of Justice (DOJ) contains no restrictions on product announcements. The installed base of Lotus 1–2–3 users voiced a similar complaint as release dates for product upgrades dragged on through the 1980s. In Lotus and Microsoft's defense, software development is an uncertain process, and providing specific dates is a difficult task. A developer has a legitimate purpose in preannouncement if users need information on anticipated improvements in coordinating their software purchases. The law requires only that these be "objectively reasonable and in good faith." In some cases, there is only a fine line between legitimate information release and predatory preannouncements.

When Bill Gates began pursuing original equipment manufacturer (OEM) customers for Microsoft Windows in 1983, the development of a graphical user interface seemed close at hand. Apple had introduced the Lisa, and the Macintosh was not far behind. Several hardware manufacturers signed commitments to make minimum quarterly payments to Microsoft in exchange for preferential access to Windows shipping schedules. Much like the 1–2–3 waiting game, however, the calendar moved faster than development, and several firms paid their commitments even though no software was available. While MS-Windows versions 1 and 2 were eventually shipped, it was not until 1990, with the release of MS-Windows 3.0, that a graphical user interface on the PC platform became an effective product. But it is difficult to take Microsoft and Gates to task for this preannouncement. Much like the waiting game for the 1–2–3 upgrade, there is always significant uncertainty in software development, and it is not clear that estimates can ever be reliable in those circumstances.

Still, it is important to note that many users who have wholeheartedly embraced Windows today, or MS-Windows 3.0 and Windows 95 yesterday, waited half a decade for access to a graphical user interface on the PC platform when they could easily have had that under the Apple Macintosh. The long delay in product adoption was at least partially related to the installed base of software for MS-DOS, but it might also be argued that the continual promises of a better graphical user interface from Microsoft must certainly have affected user expectations. Although the evidence regarding product preannouncements is anecdotal, it would seem imprudent to dismiss the implications of network externalities for dynamic market efficiency.

### Tied Sales

The second issue in the FTC investigation was the restrictive nature of Microsoft licensing agreements with OEMs in the sale of operating systems software. In 1993, the FTC panel deadlocked over the decision to proceed to court, and the investigation was closed. The DOJ showed interest in the case and especially in the restrictive nature of OEM licensing agreements, and in 1994 it filed a complaint alleging that the microcomputer operating systems market had come to be monopolized through Microsoft's restrictive business practices. The allegation was that Microsoft established and extended its dominance in operating systems software through a combination of "per processor" charges and required minimum commitment payments in its licensing contracts with OEMs. Microsoft commonly required OEMs to agree to

purchase a copy of MS-DOS for each CPU sold, whether MS-DOS was installed on the computer or not. The potential anticompetitive effect of these "per processor" terms was evident: OEMs, and by implication end users, that have already paid for one operating system (e.g., Microsoft Windows) are unlikely to purchase a second competing one. The effect of this pricing policy is to impose a switching cost on computer users. A potential entrant would have to provide software with so great an improvement over Microsoft's operating systems that users would be willing to pay an additional amount for the new operating system. Perhaps more important, though, to make software applications written for Microsoft operating systems available to a competing operating system would require time and expense. This latter effect came to be referred to in the antitrust case as "the applications barrier to entry." A computer user is interested in the operating system only because of the applications available for it. In the case it was argued that there are over 70,000 applications available for Microsoft Windows. Any new entrant to the operating systems market must also be able to provide consumers with a sufficient variety of applications software. By securing access to the OEM distribution channel, Microsoft assured that both hardware and software manufacturers would have reasonable expectations that their products needed to be compatible with Microsoft operating systems and should make development for Microsoft's operating system first on any application developer's list. Because later "porting" of the software to other operating systems is difficult, expensive, and unprofitable, few applications developers are willing to produce the additional adaptations. The complaint filed by the DOJ in July of 1994 alleged that the "per processor" and the minimum commitment practices were anticompetitive because they diminish the incentives to produce alternative operating systems. In 1995, Microsoft and the DOJ reached an agreement that restrained Microsoft from these practices. In particular, Microsoft was enjoined from tied sales. That is, Microsoft was restricted from licensing agreements for operating systems that are conditioned upon the licensing of other products. However, the consent decree allowed "that this provision in and of itself shall not be construed to prohibit Microsoft from developing integrated products." When Microsoft contractual agreements with OEMs required the inclusion of, and prominent display of the icon for, Internet Explorer with Microsoft Windows 98, the DOJ filed contempt charges and attempted to gain an injunction against the release of Windows 98. In the ensuing DOJ antitrust case against Microsoft, the defendant was accused of abuse of a dominant, near-monopoly position in microcomputer operating systems. Although it is not illegal per se for Microsoft to possess a dominant market share, it is illegal to abuse one's position in order to maintain that dominance.

The challenge to Microsoft Windows as a dominant application programming interface (API) did not come from the products that Microsoft had traditionally identified as rivals, such as the Apple Macintosh, Linux or other Unix variants such as BSD, or a new microprocessor that defined a new computer architecture. Instead, it came from Netscape Navigator, a product providing easier access to the Internet through the World Wide Web. Most industry participants would use API to define a platform, and Netscape was designed not only as an interface to the Internet, but also to provide a sufficient array of APIs to substitute and/or displace Microsoft Windows as the dominant microcomputer platform. There was nothing subtle about Netscape's intent; its founder designed Netscape to run applications in the Java programming language with the purpose of rendering Win-

dows no longer useful. If successful, Netscape and Java would provide a new API that would make Microsoft Windows superfluous, and facilitate software applications that run in virtually any computing environment (e.g., "Wintel," Apple Macintosh, Palm OS, and Unix variants such as Linux, BSD, etc.). This was a direct threat to Microsoft's dominance in operating systems software.

Because Microsoft did not immediately identify Netscape's threat to operating systems dominance when the company was engaged, the effect was abrupt and forceful. The government argued that Microsoft foresaw erosion of its market power by browsers and Java, both of which are capable of supporting software applications that are independent of operating systems. The plaintiff claimed that Microsoft took anticompetitive actions to exclude competition in browsers in order to protect Microsoft's operating systems. Microsoft also took anticompetitive actions to restrain the adoption of cross-platform Java.

According to some, Microsoft weakened competition and harmed consumers with two approaches—exclusionary behavior and predatory conduct. The exclusionary behavior related to restrictive contracts to limit Netscape's access to the computing desktop. For example, Microsoft reduced its development of the part of Microsoft Network (MSN) that was in direct competition with America Online (AOL), in exchange for AOL's promotion and use of Internet Explorer. Microsoft's predatory conduct was evidenced in (1) its free distribution of Internet Explorer, (2) the tied sale of Internet Explorer with Windows 98, and (3) its attempts to promote a "polluted Java," or a Java language that was defined and controlled by Microsoft. On April 3, 2000, Judge Jackson found Microsoft guilty of violations of the Sherman Antitrust Act, and threatened either to impose restraints on Microsoft's business practices (conduct remedies) or to break the company up into separate applications and systems companies (structural remedies). As the case proceeded through the appeals process, it became clear that the government would not seek structural remedies, and instead would settle for a modified final judgment in the consent decree. The modifications, which took effect December 2001, are intended to reduce entry barriers for potential entrants to the operating system market and to reduce the restrictive nature of the OEM licensing agreements. They further require Microsoft to release certain information about the Windows APIs and newly developing communications or interoperability protocols.

## Industry Performance

It is difficult to look at the improvements in desktop computing and complain that the industry has not provided sufficient innovation and adequate performance. While firms in the software industry have historically been profitable, a recent wave of consolidations indicates a change. Firms that played an instrumental role early in the growth of the industry have recently disappeared. VisiCalc's spreadsheet disappeared early as competition from Lotus and internal legal complications deterred its performance. Ashton-Tate's dBASE II, one of the first database products for PCs, became an industry standard for database languages. But by 1990, Ashton-Tate was no longer even in the software development business, and the rights to dBASE had been purchased by Borland. WordPerfect, long the MS-DOS word processing standard, was purchased first by Novell and then by Corel, as larger software firms attempted to assemble integrated product suites. It is interesting to note that in these latter cases the product has continued to be avail-

able. In both instances, industry observers claimed that it was the installed base, and not the product or capabilities, that was being acquired. Yet the recent demise of established firms also suggests that industry competition continues unabated. Newer products, while lacking an installed base for network benefits, also lack many of the constraints that the installed base imposes, most notably intergenerational compatibility.

## Government Policy

Government policy in the form of research and development (in the development of computer programming languages) and infrastructure investment (in the development of the Internet), has served to establish the industry, but it is expected that competition policy will play the more significant role of determining future industry competitiveness. Intellectual property protection and recent antitrust actions are expected to have far-reaching implications for innovation and competition in the industry.

### Copyright Protection

In the late 1970s, after two software patents were overturned, the U.S. Congress debated the merits of stronger intellectual property protection for computer software.[36] The end result of that discussion, documented in a report known as CONTU (Final Report of the Commission on New Technological Uses of Copyrighted Works), determined that copyright protection would be appropriate for computer software. While copyright protects an author's expression of an idea, it does not protect the idea itself. Instead, patents are available to protect novel and nonobvious inventions. The decision to use copyright for protection of intellectual property in software has had a significant impact on the development of the industry.

First, on the hardware side, copyright protection limited IBM's protection on the basic input-output system (BIOS) to the written code rather than the performance of the BIOS. If aspects of the BIOS could have been patented, a clone industry might never have arisen or might have developed far more slowly under the threat of an IBM lawsuit. In 1980, IBM chose the Intel x86 family of microprocessors as the CPU for the PC primarily because the chip was widely used by hardware engineers. IBM had always developed proprietary electronics for its machines in order to protect itself from IBM work-alike products. The decision not to take this approach with the PC was a commitment to an open architecture, where third-party developers could introduce product complements. With a large number of people able to design products around the chip, IBM's open architecture approach facilitated the development of third-party hardware, such as video display cards. This approach was similar to that taken for the Apple II design, since the Apple II provided slots for third-party plug-ins. To facilitate the development of hardware and complementary software products, IBM published a program listing of the BIOS, complete with comments, in its technical reference material. Intimate, detailed knowledge of how the chip and computer architecture operated were essential to the development of fast, useful programs on a product that was built from conventional electronics assembled from third parties. But with only copyright protection, the open-architecture approach and BIOS documentation availability helped to launch the clone industry. When a few firms like AMI and Phoenix were able to develop a BIOS that provided excellent compatibility, the clone industry was born. Thus, machines that a decade ago would have been called IBM-PCs and compatibles are instead referred to as Wintel machines for their compatibility with Microsoft Windows and Intel microprocessors. And IBM, instead of being the dominant force in microcomputers, is merely another producer. When IBM tried to recapture the market with the introduction of the PS/2 and its proprietary Micro Channel Architecture, the large installed base of software users and clone manufacturers respectfully declined to follow. Instead, Compaq, once a clone follower, led a move to adopt an extended-industry standard architecture and IBM's attempt to recapture the PC market failed.

A second significant implication of copyright protection came on the software side. The inventors of VisiCalc, the first spreadsheet, relied on copyright protection for their product. Because CONTU had left only copyright protection for software, only the form of the spreadsheet, rather than the idea itself, was protected. Thus, the developers never patented the basic spreadsheet concepts that were invented and prototyped in 1978. The concept was widely copied and improved upon and, when subsequent developers saw that the spreadsheet could be greatly enhanced with the addition of database, graphics, and a macro programming language, there was little legal protection afforded VisiCalc's original idea. Certainly 1–2–3's launch in February of 1983 was important to the early industry, especially to the dominance of the IBM-PC, since Lotus was at first available only for the PC. However, the fact that few spreadsheet users have ever heard of VisiCalc, and fewer still know of its inventors' names, serves as an important reminder that intellectual property protection has had a profound influence on the evolution of competition. This is not to argue that patent protection would necessarily have altered the outcomes, but one can easily imagine a very different microcomputer hardware and soft-

Table 13.8

**Patent Activity for Major Microcomputer Software Manufacturers**

| Company | 1995–1997 | 1991–1994 |
|---|---|---|
| Microsoft | 211 | 48 |
| Lotus | 5 | 4 |
| Novell | 13 | 4 |
| WordPerfect | 0 | 3 |
| Autodesk | 3 | 1 |
| Ashton-Tate | 0 | 0 |
| Borland | 41 | 3 |
| Adobe | 15 | 18 |
| Software Publishing | 0 | 0 |
| Aldus | 1 | 1 |

*Source*: U.S. Patent and Trademark Office, 1997.

ware industry if patent protection had been efficacious.[37] Recent court cases have suggested that software can be patented, and in June of 1995 the U.S. Patent and Trademark office proposed guidelines.[38] This change in the intellectual property protection regime has already had significant implications for the nature of competition in the industry. Table 13.8 shows the number of patents held by major microcomputer software firms, although only activity subsequent to the 1995 guidelines could refer to software patents.

## *Software Piracy*

Even aggressively litigated patent protection does not guarantee either that competitors do not profit from a firm's innovative ideas or that consumers do not take advantage of the ease of copying software. The Software Publisher's Association estimated software piracy in 1996 of as much as $13.2 billion in lost software revenues, up from $12.2 billion in 1994. Lost revenues are a significant source of concern to the software industry, but weak intellectual property protection has long afflicted the software industry. When Bill Gates and

Paul Allen first introduced Microsoft BASIC for the MITS Altair in 1976, software pirates made thousands of copies of the paper tape, the early equivalent of a floppy disk that was used to store the program. While the MITS Altair was inexpensive, it was also of little use without an accessible tool to develop applications. Microsoft BASIC was the first programming language available for this product, and hobbyists allegedly copied MS-BASIC freely rather than pay for it. This unauthorized copying prompted Gates to formalize the appropriability argument for software developers. In a now famous missive, Gates wrote an open letter to the hobbyist community to point out that if users did not pay for software, programmers would have little incentive to provide it.

Software piracy is a significant problem for the industry's future development, and Gates's argument is clearly important. But there is a particular irony to the piracy story that relates to network externalities and the early development of the microcomputer industry.[39] When IBM determined to produce a personal computer, executives working on the project approached Microsoft for the rights to use MS-BASIC bundled with Digital Research Inc.'s microcomputer operating system, CP/M. IBM executives noted over 50,000 MS-BASIC users and applications. Without such a large installed base of applications for MS-BASIC, IBM might never have noticed Microsoft, and MS-DOS might never have become the operating system for the IBM-PC. Some authors argue that this is an example of a lucky strategy.[40] However, Gates and Allen clearly understood the importance of complementary products in the development of the microcomputer industry, whether luck played a role or not. While the MS-BASIC/IBM connection certainly has an appearance of chance, it is difficult to ignore Microsoft's fundamental insight that early entry and a large installed base had long-term implications for successful network competition. The irony is that the large installed base appears to have come, at least in part, from pirated copies of MS-BASIC. It would not be appropriate to argue that software piracy today is excused by this story, but it is helpful to understand the implications for the development of the industry.

## Network Computers and the Future of Platform Competition

The model of competing hardware platforms may in the end turn out to be an historical anomaly if some industry analysts are correct. Recent products that operate under more platform-independent computing include Netscape or JAVA. To understand how this works, consider the onion model of computer applications. The CPU at the center of the onion is surrounded by layers of systems and application processes that isolate processing power at the center from user applications on the exterior.

A user's request is passed through successive layers finally to receive processing by the CPU. This message-passing analogy allows development of technologies within each layer of the circle to proceed independently of surrounding layers. For example, Microsoft can develop Windows NT for Intel or MIPS chips, and the application user may never need or want to know the difference. Specialized performance across the layers of the onion has been important throughout the history of the microcomputer hardware industry, even when computing power was very limited. As greater raw computing capability appears on the desktop or across the network, specializing applications to a certain chip will become less important. In response to Bill Gates's observation in the early 1980s that "hardware is free," hardware manufacturers might say that "software is also free."

That is, as computers become easier to program and use, applications will focus on content rather than technique. If microcomputer processing performance improvements continue, the craft in software will move from squeezing performance out of the chip to providing intuitive tools. Certainly, this evolution is well underway with the move to graphical user interfaces. But if we see effective distributed computing across the web, the processor and programming language matter less than finding a tool appropriate to the problem at hand. And in that world, hardware platforms and software development environments are likely to be far more generic, and even more competitive.

## Notes

1. N. Economides, "Compatibility and Market Structure," Discussion paper no. EC 91-16 Stern School of Business, New York University (August 1991), pp. 1–16; M.L. Katz and C. Shapiro, "Product Introduction with Network Externalities," *Journal of Industrial Economics* 40, no. 3 (March 1992): 55–83; J. Church and N. Gandal, "Network Effects, Software Provision, and Standardization," *Journal of Industrial Economics* 40, no. 3 (March 1992): 85–103; J. Farrell and G. Saloner, "Standardization, Compatibility, and Innovation," *Rand Journal of Economics* 16, no. 1 (Spring 1985): 70–83; M.L. Katz and C. Shapiro, "Product Compatibility Choice in a Market with Technological Progress," *Oxford Economic Papers* 38 (1987): 146–65; M.L. Katz and C. Shapiro, "Technology Adoption in the Presence of Network Externalities," *Journal of Political Economy* 94 (1986): 822–41; M.L. Katz and C. Shapiro, "Network Externalities, Competition and Compatibility," *American Economic Review* 75, no. 2 (May 1985): 424–40; M.L. Katz and C. Shapiro, "Systems Competition and Network Effects," *Journal of Economic Perspectives* 8 (Spring 1994): 93–115.

2. P.A. David and S. Greenstein, "The Economics of Compatibility Standards: An Introduction to Recent Research," *Economics of Innovation and New Technology* 1, no. 1 (1990).

3. P.A. David, "Clio and the Economics of QWERTY," *American Economic Review* 75, no. 2 (1985): 332–36; S.J. Liebowitz and S.E. Margolis, "The Fable of the Keys," *Journal of Law and Economics* 33 (1990): 1–25.

4. Some economists differentiate pecuniary from network externalities by identifying "direct" versus "indirect" network

effects. A later discussion will clarify these issues. This study will define network effects broadly enough to allow for either effect as long as it plays a role in industry structure.

5. R.S. Rosenbloom and M.A. Cusumano, "Technological Pioneering and Competitive Advantage: The Birth of the VCR Industry," *California Management Review* 29, no. 4 (Summer 1987): 51–76; R.S. Rosenbloom and K.J. Freeze, "Ampex Corporation and Video Innovation," *Research on Technological Innovation, Management and Policy* 2 (1987): 113–85.

6. J. Farrell and C. Shapiro, "Standard Setting in High-Definition Television," *Brookings Papers on Economic Activity: Microeconomics* (1992): 1–77.

7. S.R. Postrel, "Competing Networks and Proprietary Standards: The Case of Quadraphonic Sound," *Journal of Industrial Economics* 39, no. 2 (December 1990): 169–85.

8. N. Gandal, "Hedonic Price Indexes for Spreadsheets and an Empirical Test for Network Externalities," *Rand Journal of Economics* 25 (1994): 160–70; M. Shurmer, "An Investigation into Sources of Network Externalities in the Packaged PC Software Market," *Information Economics and Policy* 5, no. 3 (1993): 231–51.

9. U.S. Congress, Office of Technology Assessment, *The Big Picture: HDTV and High-resolution Systems.* OTA-BP-CIT-64 (Washington, DC: U.S. Government Printing Office, June 1990).

10. Farrell and Sharpiro.

11. For ease of discussion, the terms "yesterday" and "today" refer to periods rather than literal days. If it helps, substitute "last year" and "this year" or "last decade" and "this decade."

12. G.M.P. Swann, "Product Competition in Microprocessors," *Journal of Industrial Economics* 34, no. 1 (September 1985): 33–53.

13. N. Economides and S.C. Salop, "Competition and Integration among Complements," *Journal of Industrial Economics* 40, no. 3 (March 1992): 105–23.

14. R.N. Langlois and P.L. Robertson, "Networks and Innovation in a Modular System: Lessons from the Microcomputer and Stereo Component Industries," *Research Policy* 21, no. 4 (August 1992): 297–313.

15. D. Manasian, "The Computer Industry: Survey," *The Economist,* February 17, 1993, pp. 3–18.

16. E. Schwartz, "Is This Software's Next Kingmaker?" *Business Week,* June 4, 1990, pp. 110D,F.

17. R.N. Langlois, "External Economies and Economic Progress: The Case of the Microcomputer Industry," *Business History Review* 66, no. 1 (Spring 1992): 1–50.

18. J. Church and N. Gandal, "Strategic Entry Deterrance: Complementary Products as Installed Base," *European Journal of Political Economy* 12 (Special Issue, September 1996): 331–54; J. Church and N. Gandal, "Integration, Complementary Products, and Variety," *Journal of Economics and Management Strategy* 1 (1992): 651–75; J. Church and N. Gandal, "Complementary Network Externalities and Technological Adoption," *International Journal of Industrial Organization* 11 (1993): 239–60; J. Khazam and D.C. Mowery, "The Commercialization of RISC—Strategies for the Creation of Dominant Designs," *Research Policy* 23 (January 1994): 89–102.

19. M.A. Cusumano, Y. Mylonadis, and R. Rosenblum, "Strategic Maneuvering and Mass-market Dynamics—The Triumph of VHS over Beta," *Business History Review* 66, no. 1 (Spring 1992): 51–94.

20. K. Flamm, *Creating the Computer: Government, Industry, and High Technology* (Washington DC: Brookings Institution, 1988); K. Flamm, *Targeting the Computer: Government Support and International Competition* (Washington, DC: Brookings Institution, 1987).

21. G.H. Anthes, "Software Pirates' Booty Topped $13B, Study Finds," *Computerworld* 31, January 6, 1997, p. 24.

22. T.F. Bresnahan and S. Greenstein, "The Competitive Crash in Large-scale Commercial Computing," *WP,* January 1994, pp. 1–30.

23. E. Warner, "IBM, Rivals Feel Personal Computer Compatibility Pains," *Computerworld,* September 17, 1984, p. 11.

24. The 80286 was not a significant enough change to induce IBM or its compatible manufacturers to worry greatly about introducing systems based on the chip.

25. G. Letwin, *Inside OS/2* (Redmond, WA: Microsoft Press, 1988).

26. J. Farrell and C. Sharpiro, "Optimal Contracts with Lock-in," *American Economic Review* 79, no. 1 (March 1989): 51–68.

27. J. Farrell and C. Shapiro, "Dynamic Competition with Switching Costs," *Rand Journal of Economics* 19 (1988): 123–37.

28. S.M. Greenstein, "Did Installed Base Give an Incumbent Any (Measurable) Advantages in Federal Procurement?" *Rand Journal of Economics* 24, no. 1 (1993): 19–39.

29. A.R. Nebauer, *The ABC's of WordPerfect 5.1* (Alameda, CA: Sybex, 1990).

30. J. Tarter, *Soft\*Letter 100* (Watertown, MA: Soft\*Letter, 1996).

31. Harvard Business School, *Note on the Microcomputer Software Industry—January 1982* (case study) (Boston, MA: Harvard College, 1985).

32. J. Sutton, *Sunk Costs and Market Structure: Price Competition, Advertising, and the Evolution of Concentration* (Cambridge, MA: MIT Press, 1991).

33. W.B. Arthur, "'Silicon Valley' Locational Clusters: When Do Increasing Returns Imply Monopoly?" *Mathematical Social Sciences* 19, no. 3 (1990): 235–51.

34. E. Yourdon, *Decline and Fall of the American Programmer* (Englewood Cliffs, NJ: Yourdon Press, 1992).

35. J. Farrell and G. Saloner, "Installed Base and Com-

patibility: Innovation, Product Preannouncements, and Predation," *American Economic Review* 76 (1986): 940–55.

36. J. Farrell, "Standardization and Intellectual Property," *Jurimetrics Journal* 30, no. 1 (Fall 1989): 35–50.

37. P. Menell, "An Analysis of the Scope of Copyright Protection for Application Programs," *Stanford Law Review* 41 (May 1989): 1045–104.

38. J. Church and R. Ware, "Network Industries, Intellectual Property Rights and Competition Policy," in *Competition Policy, Intellectual Property Rights and International Economic Integration*, R. Anderson and N. Gallini, eds. (Calgary, Alberta, Canada: University of Calgary Press, 1997).

39. This argument is formalized. L.N. Takeyama, "The Welfare Implications of Unauthorized Reproduction of Intellectual Property in the Presence of Demand Network Externalities," *Journal of Industrial Economics* 42, no. 4 (June 1994): 155–66; R. Rumelt and K.R. Conner, "Software Piracy—An Analysis of Protection Strategies," *Management Science* 37, no. 2 (February 1991): 125–39.

40. W.M. Cohen and D.A. Levinthal, "Fortune Favors the Prepared Firm," *Management Science* 40, no. 2 (February 1994): 227; C.W.L. Hill and G.R. Jones, *Strategic Management: An Integrated Approach* (Boston, MA: Houghton Mifflin, 1995).

## Selected Readings

Cusumano, M.A., and D.B. Yoffie. *Competing on Internet Time: Lessons from Netscape and Its Battle with Microsoft.* New York: Free Press, 1998. Account of the browser wars.

Freiberger, P., and M. Swaine. *Fire in the Valley: The Making of the Personal Computer.* Berkeley, CA: Osborne/McGraw-Hill, 1984. Readable history of the microcomputer industry from the start of the hobbyist fascination with computers and the MITS Altair in 1975 through the introduction of the IBM-PC in 1981.

Grindley, P. *Standards, Strategy and Policy: Cases and Stories.* New York: Oxford University Press, 1995. Provides a framework for standards competition and describes the effect of network externalities in a variety of industries.

Heilemann, J. *Pride Before the Fall: The Trials of Bill Gates and the End of the Microsoft Era.* New York: HarperCollins, 2001. Account of the antitrust trial.

Ichbiah, D., and Susan L. Knepper. *The Making of Microsoft: How Bill Gates and His Team Created the World's Most Successful Software Company.* Rocklin, CA: Prima, 1991. Popular press accounts of the people and products at Microsoft.

Lammers, S. *Programmers at Work: 1st Series.* Redmond, WA: Microsoft Press, 1986. Interviews with programmers who pioneered the microcomputer software industry.

Wallace, J., and J. Erickson. *Hard Drive: Bill Gates and the Making of the Microsoft Empire.* New York: HarperBusiness, 1993.

# 14

# Telecommunications

## Competition and Network Access

*Susan E. McMaster*

The question on everyone's mind on December 31, 1983, was whether the telephones would work in the morning. At midnight on January 1, 1984, the agreement reached by the Department of Justice and AT&T went into effect; it broke "the telephone company" into eight separate parts—AT&T and the seven regional Bell operating companies (RBOCs). This change brought an end to the telecommunications industry as it had been known since the beginning of the century and brought the beginning of competition to long-distance service and equipment manufacturing. Although AT&T was not the only provider of local phone service in the United States, it did provide service to about 80 percent of the local telephones in the nation. Hundreds of independent carriers, the largest of which was GTE, provided the remaining consumers with local telephone service. These independent local carriers were the sole providers of local service in the territories they served.

With the regulatory restrictions on carriers (other than AT&T) offering long-distance service removed, competitors that had begun trying to enter the industry since the 1960s received a boost and began to multiply rapidly. Over the next decade the long-distance part of the industry changed in many ways, with several new companies beginning to provide service and others, which had

been trying to provide service in competition with AT&T, struggling to survive and flourish.

As competition increased, the regulations governing long-distance service were adapted to suit changing overall conditions and market shares. The courts continued to play an important role in the industry, as they had previously. In some ways, the courts undertook a larger role, as both new competitors and the incumbent carriers turned to court proceedings when they were not satisfied with their treatment by the Federal Communications Commission (FCC). Technology continued to evolve, as it had for a hundred years. A variety of innovations and improvements were introduced that brought almost continual change to the industry. Thus, although operating under a revised structural framework, the industry continued to grow and expand throughout the period, offering more products and services for consumers. Each of these matters will be discussed in more detail throughout the chapter.

## The Modified Final Judgment

Over the years since its inception the telecommunications industry had evolved from a monopoly to a competitive local industry and then to a regulated monopoly. Due to changes in the available technologies, in the 1960s competition again began to emerge in long-distance and equipment manufacturing. As a result of this emerging competition and the general attitude in the executive branch, particularly in the Department of Justice (DOJ), an antitrust suit was filed against AT&T during the 1970s, charging violations of the Sherman Act. After several years of preliminary proceedings the case finally went to trial, but AT&T did not want a judge to decide its fate, so although it had fought to remain a single, fully integrated company, management concluded that something would have to change. Late in 1981, seven years after the suit had been filed, AT&T entered negotiations with the DOJ to end the case, cognizant that the final outcome would probably be divestiture. Through negotiations, AT&T felt that it would have more control over the final outcome than if the matter was left to a judge.

After various attempts to negotiate an agreement, the DOJ and AT&T were able to come to an agreement that would see AT&T divest itself of its local operating companies, splitting them off from the long-distance and equipment manufacturing divisions of the company. The two parties also agreed on which other telecommunications services should be assigned to the regulated local operating companies or retained by the long-distance part of the company, based on whether those services could be expected to face competition. By agreeing to split the company among the services that were facing or could face competition and those (natural monopolies) that were not and should not face competition, AT&T and DOJ made the proper distinction (for that time) between services that should be offered by "monopoly" local providers and services that should be provided in a competitive environment. The distinctions made removed the potential for cross-subsidization between regulated and competitive services, thus

making regulation easier for everyone involved.

However, the distinction between monopoly and competitive services that was proposed was difficult to understand. Thus, the final agreement, known as the modified final judgment (MFJ), did not retain the proposed distinction. During the approval process for the agreement, changes were made that granted "monopoly" local providers some competitive services. The distinction was eliminated because Judge Harold Greene, who presided over the case, felt that the agreement should receive public comment before it could be approved. As a result, changes were made to the agreement, such as granting the local operating companies the right to publish the Yellow Pages. By removing the distinction between competitive and monopoly services, the regulation of providers was made more difficult in some ways. In addition, the changes meant that Judge Greene's court would become an ongoing regulator of the industry, thereby affecting how the industry would function over the next decade.

### The Federal Communications Commission

With the break-up of AT&T, the role of the FCC as the regulator of interstate telecommunications changed. First, since the FCC had not been involved in the discussions between AT&T and the DOJ and because they were to lose responsibilities, the FCC asked Judge Greene to explicitly recognize their jurisdiction. Judge Greene agreed and the FCC retained many of its responsibilities, including ensuring universal service and maintaining inexpensive nationwide and worldwide telephone services. In addition, the FCC was to be responsible for ensuring and maintaining the goal of equal access from the MFJ. Moreover, despite the divestiture requirement, AT&T was still seen by those in the FCC and some in Congress as a monopoly, as the company provided 96 percent of the long-distance service in the United States at the time.[1] Thus, the FCC retained the responsibility of regulatory oversight of AT&T and gained similar responsibilities for the newly forming competitive long-distance providers.

One of its first responsibilities was the development of access charges, so that the local carriers could receive payment for use of the local network when a long-distance call was placed. Since the *Smith v. Illinois Bell* decision in 1931, when the court determined that the long-distance calls had to share in the costs of running the local network, long-distance service had been covering its own costs. Following World War II, as the costs of long-distance went down while the costs of local service remained the same or increased, long-distance calls contributed to a greater and greater percentage of the costs of the local network. With the entrance of competitive long-distance providers, the system that had been used since the 1940s to shift revenues from the long-distance part of the industry to the local companies was no longer appropriate. Politically, the FCC had to develop a new system that would allow funds to continue to flow in the new environment. In addition, the restructured AT&T had to determine how revenues would be divided between the RBOCs and the long-distance division of the company. For decades, as a result of regulatory manipulations of the revenues, the long-distance revenues had been shared with the operating companies through the separations process. The high price of long-distance relative to its cost was a major contributing factor in the entry of MCI and others into the long-distance market. At the time of divestiture, the separations process was assigning about one-third of AT&T's long-distance revenues to the local operating companies. With divestiture, there

was no desire on the part of the regulators or those designing the divestiture plan to end the revenue flow to the local companies, as they feared a dramatic increase in local rates without this continued flow of monies. The only change would be that, instead of the funds flowing only from AT&T, they would need to flow from all long-distance carriers.

The MFJ called for the separations process to be replaced by cost-based tariffs to cover the access provided by the RBOCs. The initial access charge system was based on the Exchange Network Facilities for Interstate Access (ENFIA) tariffs that were established in 1978. Under the ENFIA tariffs, AT&T was significantly disadvantaged relative to the new long-distance carriers due to the substantial price discounts received by the other carriers in their access charge rates. Because of the historic relationship between AT&T and the local operating companies, the telephone network was set up to efficiently connect calls from consumers if they chose AT&T as their long-distance provider, but if a consumer wished to choose one of the other long-distance providers they had to dial extra digits in order to access that provider's network. The long-distance providers did not believe this was fair and, as part of the divestiture agreement, the RBOCs were required to convert their systems so that a call could be routed to the consumer's chosen long-distance carrier without the need to dial extra digits. The RBOCs thus began converting their lines to provide such access, known as equal access lines. The percentage of lines offering equal access rose from 3.8 percent in 1984 to 74.3 percent in 1986 to 91.3 percent in 1988 and to over 95 percent by mid-1990.[2] This conversion allowed consumers to select or subscribe to long-distance carriers other than AT&T and allowed the consumer to reach selected long-distance carriers with the standard 1+ dialing, rather than having to dial a five-digit access code. One benefit to the newly emerging long-distance carriers in those areas where they did not have equal access to the local operating company's lines and switches was that, until 1+ dialing was instituted for that area, AT&T paid a 55 percent premium for access services to account for the difference in quality. Although it was written into the rules that AT&T would pay a premium for access in those areas where the other carriers did not have the same level of access to the local switches as AT&T, the new entrants to the long-distance market paid substantially less than AT&T for access to the local switches.

In developing the new rules governing competitive long-distance service, one of the fears was that if the costs were not properly allocated bypass would occur. That is, the largest companies would find it economical to build their own networks and provide their own access to the long-distance network, thus avoiding local access and the associated charges and avoiding the need to pay for the local part of the network. Thus the FCC considered how the revenues would be replaced and how it would keep the large companies from having an incentive to bypass the network. By the end of 1982 the FCC developed a plan to address the issue. The FCC adopted marginal cost pricing for charges assessed on long-distance carriers by the local operating companies for access to their networks. These access charges provided a continuing source of revenue to the local networks and, by setting the rates at marginal cost, removed the incentive for companies to bypass the local operating companies. The use of marginal cost pricing (i.e., setting price at marginal cost) was a radical change for the FCC, which adopted market principles rather than continuing the use of its prior regulatory principles. In addition, the new rules about access charges radically changed the jurisdiction over which the FCC claimed authority, because access charges were local rather than interstate charges.

In providing access to the long-distance network, local carriers incurred two types of costs, those that are incurred when a call is made—traffic-sensitive costs—and those that are incurred regardless of whether calls are made or not—non–traffic-sensitive costs. Due to the concern regarding bypass, the proposed access charges to be paid by the long-distance carriers covered only a portion of the cost that the local carriers incurred in providing access to the long-distance network. The remainder of the cost was not sensitive to the volume of calls that occurred, and thus it was proposed that this cost be covered by a flat monthly charge paid directly by the consumers. Although economically the charges should have been split between traffic-sensitive charges and non–traffic-sensitive charges, the problem was that the non–traffic-sensitive cost was the great bulk of the cost incurred by the local carriers. So rather than impose the full cost on consumers at the beginning, after the divestiture the FCC determined that it would phase in the non–traffic-sensitive (flat fee) charges over a few years, with the difference to be paid via the traffic-sensitive charges. The initial charges were to be set at $2 per residential phone line and $4 per business line. These were to increase gradually to between $6 and $8 per line to cover all of the non–traffic-sensitive charges over several years. The long-distance companies were to continue paying access charges until the customer charges were finally at the rate they should be. This proposal was opposed on a number of different fronts. In the face of the opposition, the FCC postponed the implementation of the end-user (or subscriber line) charges from January to April of 1984. Despite this, the House passed a bill that forbade the imposition of access charges on residential customers. Rather than enacting legislation, however, the Senate requested that the FCC change the order. The FCC complied with this request, reducing the charge to residential customers to $1 per month and delaying its implementation until mid-1985, a year and a half after the divestiture was to occur. Over the next few years the rate was raised to $3.50 per residential line. Despite the fact that this did not cover all of the non–traffic-sensitive cost, the rate was not raised beyond that point for primary lines through the end of the century.[3] Thus, traffic-sensitive charges continued to cover non–traffic-sensitive cost, creating problems with the incentives people had when making long-distance calls, as those charges were incorporated into the charges for long-distance calls.

## The Regional Bell Operating Companies

With the agreement to divest itself of the local operating companies, AT&T determined that the operating companies would be most successful if they were split into multiple units of roughly equal size with assets between $15 million and $20 billion dollars each. Thus the leadership of AT&T offered to divide the twenty-two operating companies among seven RBOCs. This allowed two of the operating companies to remain whole—Pacific Telephone and Southwestern Bell. The other RBOCs were named US West, Ameritech, BellSouth, Bell Atlantic, and NYNEX.[4]

Although the new RBOCs served the local phones in multiple states, under the MJF they were not allowed to provide long-distance service, and thus the calls they would be allowed to carry had to be determined. The leadership of AT&T, working with the DOJ, developed the boundaries between areas AT&T and the emerging long-distance providers would serve, and also between areas the local operating companies would serve. Although it was known that more competition would develop

if the boundaries for the areas split large cities, because of technical concerns AT&T balked at this and was able to get the boundaries set to mirror (in large part) metropolitan statistical areas. The new areas were called Local Access and Transport Areas, or LATAs. The operating companies were to be allowed to provide service within the LATAs, while the long-distance companies provided service across LATA boundaries. LATAs were to be smaller than or equal to a state or an operating company, but larger than just the local calling areas within which consumers could make local calls. This would allow the RBOCs to carry local toll calls. Calls were classified into four different types for long-distance classification purposes: intrastate-intraLATA, interstate-intraLATA, intrastate-interLATA, and interstate-interLATA. The intrastate-intraLATA calls would be made within the state and within the LATA and would be carried by the RBOCs or other local operating companies. Intrastate-interLATA calls would be made within the state but between LATAs and would be carried by the long-distance carriers. Interstate-intraLATA calls would be carried by the RBOCs and would be made within the LATA but between states. This type of call was relatively rare, although there were some LATA boundaries that crossed state lines, such as the LATA for the District of Columbia. The final type of calls would be the interstate-interLATA calls—those that crossed state and LATA boundaries—that were carried by the long-distance carriers. In designing the LATAs and separating local service from long-distance services, it was believed that the local operating companies would have the incentive to serve all the long-distance companies, unlike AT&T, which had historically influenced the local carriers not to interconnect with other companies. This stimulated demand for both long-distance and access services.[5]

## Regulation

### Federal Regulation

In addition to the conversion to equal access and the establishment of a premium that AT&T was to pay for access in those areas in which equal access was not yet available to others, the FCC aided the entry of new long-distance carriers into the market by not encumbering them with all of the regulations AT&T was subjected to. The FCC concluded that these new entrants did not have market power and thus did not have to be regulated. They did have to file tariffs with the FCC, but they could implement them on one day's notice, rather than the ninety days required of AT&T. As a result, over 850 firms were offering long-distance service in 1994.[6] In addition, over the period from 1984 to 1989, the relative size of the companies in the industry changed, with AT&T's share declining by 20 percent and MCI and Sprint's shares increasing by 8 percent and 6 percent, respectively.[7] After 1989, the relative market shares remained fairly stable through 1995.

Although divestiture was expected to prevent AT&T from abusing its unique relationship with the operating companies, it did not lead to the immediate deregulation of AT&T. In fact, initially the regulation of AT&T did not change because of AT&T's market power in the industry and its access to the local operating companies. Thus, AT&T was still required to file tariffs and cost support for those tariffs. In 1986 an FCC commissioner, who later became FCC chairman, suggested that price caps might be a better form of regulation for AT&T than the rate-of-return regulation it was then subject to. Price caps would allow the FCC to regulate prices rather than earnings. By 1987 other carriers began calling for AT&T's deregulation because their relative price was changing as

AT&T adjusted its rates to cover increasing access charges.

Despite the call for changes in AT&T's regulation by firms competing against it, the regulation of AT&T did not change quickly. The first change in regulation was the move from rate-of-return regulation to price-cap regulation in 1989, relaxing the regulation of AT&T and allowing increased flexibility in pricing. Under price-cap regulation, AT&T's services were divided into different groups and AT&T was able to increase its prices for individual items within the groups by an amount (originally 3 percent) less than inflation, as long as the overall price for the group did not change. This allowed AT&T to increase prices for some goods within the group and lower those of others (within certain bounds) without having to go through a rate case. Thus AT&T could better respond to the competition it was facing. Still, AT&T remained subject to regulations different from those of the other long-distance carriers, which limited the competitiveness of the long-distance market, but did not stymie it.

Over the next few years, as competition increased, the FCC moved toward even more relaxed regulation of long-distance services. For those services that were found to be competitive, the FCC reduced AT&T's tariff-filing requirements from ninety days to fourteen days and no longer required the extensive cost back-up of prior years for rate cases. The FCC also began streamlining its regulation of AT&T's business services, as it determined that in general these services had become "substantially competitive." There were some exceptions to this, as private-line analog services and 800-number services were still dominated by AT&T and had to be regulated.

Before the FCC determined 800 service to be competitive, access to all toll-free numbers by all carriers had to be developed. When long-distance carriers first entered the market and began offering toll-free service, they were assigned toll-free numbers in blocks of 10,000. If a customer wanted a specific number, service had to be obtained from the carrier to which that number was assigned. This did not allow for full-fledged competition in the service, as consumers did not have a choice of providers and carriers were able to charge increased rates. Another problem that resulted was that toll-free numbers were stranded in the inventories of various carriers that did not need 10,000 toll-free numbers but had to obtain the whole block regardless of the number needed. Therefore, to encourage true competition in 800 service, the industry first had to develop and implement a means by which customers could take their 800 numbers with them when they changed carriers. Competition in regular long-distance service did not have this requirement, as telephone numbers were assigned to and through the local operating companies rather than the long-distance carriers. To solve the problem of competition in the 800 service market, the industry worked with the FCC and developed a system that allowed 800 numbers to be moved or "ported" to another carrier. The system used a database and capabilities of the digital technology that had been built into the network to determine which long-distance carrier was to receive the call. The call was then sent to the appropriate switch and the carrier could direct the call as required by the customer. With the development of 800-number portability, the industry was also able to offer a number of other features, such as allowing the customer to change which carrier received the call at a particular time of day. The development also slowed the need for additional 800 numbers through the introduction of 888, 877, and 866 toll-free codes. With the implementation of number portability, competition was able to increase and flourish in 800 service. As a result, the FCC

streamlined the regulation of these services as well.

Over the years following divestiture, the new entrants established themselves and gained market share in the general long-distance market. AT&T's market share of toll revenue fell substantially, from 88.3 percent in 1984 to 55.1 percent in 1995.[8] AT&T's share of minutes also fell, from 74 percent to 49 percent of the total long-distance minutes.[9] In addition to these changes, part of the basis for the FCC's decision was the hundreds of other long-distance carriers that provided services. Not all of these carriers truly competed with AT&T at the time, since some were smaller regional carriers that did not provide the same level and quality of service as AT&T and others who truly competed with AT&T. The carriers AT&T generally competed with were those who had annual toll revenues greater than $5 billion. Two carriers met this level and were (still are) generally thought of as AT&T's competition; they were MCI (later MCI-WorldCom) and Sprint. Two other carriers had annual toll revenues between $1 billion and $5 billion and thus had an impact on the top three carriers' pricing. They were LDDS/WorldCom and Frontier.

With the entrance of new carriers, the companies offered a number of promotional programs from January 1989 through June 1994, including AT&T's Reach Out America, the I Plan, AnyHour Savings, True Rewards, True USA, One Rate, MCI's Friends and Family, Sprint Sense, Sprint Select, and others. The companies also introduced a number of other plans targeted at specific customers, in an effort to keep their customers from changing long-distance carriers. Under one type of program that became quite popular, the long-distance carriers offered checks valued from $50 to $100 to return to the particular carrier's service. With the competition that emerged, customers benefited from reduced rates on their long-distance

calls, as rates fell by 70 percent between divestiture in 1984 and 1996.[10]

*State Regulation*

The telecommunications industry has long been
regulated in a two-tiered structure. It is regulated
both at the federal level, as discussed above, and
by state regulatory authorities. State regulation
differs from one state to another, thus carriers are
subject to different rules and regulations depending on which states they are operating in. In addition, within each state regulatory authorities
regulated the RBOCs and GTE differently than
they did the smaller local exchange carriers. The
state regulatory authorities are responsible for
regulating such matters as pricing, competition,
and any general restrictions that may be placed on
the firms in the industry.

For years, state regulators (and the FCC) utilized rate-of-return regulation to regulate prices.
Under this type of regulation, the carriers did not
have any incentive to innovate and further develop
the available technologies, as they were guaranteed a return on their capital investment under the
regulatory scheme. In addition, firms had no incentive to depreciate their capital stock properly,
as they could keep it in their base, thereby raising
the amount of return to which they were entitled.
In the 1980s and 1990s, state regulators (and the
FCC) moved from rate-of-return regulation to
price-cap regulation. Price-cap regulation provides
the company with the incentive to invest efficiently
in new technology, as they are no longer able to hide
inferior technology in their capital base while still
earning a return on it. Those states that began using
price-cap regulation, rather than rate-of-return regulation, were seen as more receptive to competition and experienced higher levels of investment
as the carriers became more competitive.

## The Telecommunications Industry

Although the divestiture of AT&T resulted in major changes in the structure of the industry, certain
basic elements of the industry did not change. The
industry consists of several different parts, including long-distance, manufacturing, local, and cel-
lular/mobile telecommunications.

### *Long-Distance Service*

The long-distance industry saw the most immediate and dramatic effects of the divestiture, as AT&T
changed overnight from a single integrated full-
service telecommunications carrier into a long-
distance carrier and manufacturer. In addition, the
other long-distance carriers had better legal access,
although not initially better technical access, to
the local network. The major entrants to the long-
distance market included MCI, Sprint, and the
resellers.

### *MCI*

MCI had won its lawsuits and hence won the right,
for itself and others, to offer ordinary long-distance
service, but it had a great deal of work to do to
survive and thrive in the market. With divestiture,
MCI was impacted as its environment (and that of
the other long-distance carriers) changed. In 1985,
MCI proposed that its long-distance operations be
broken into seven subsidiaries. Each of the subsidiaries was to be run as a separate company, responsible for its own costs and revenues. By the
time the separate subsidiaries began operating,
MCI was seven times larger than it had been just
three years earlier. This move allowed the company to remain small and entrepreneurial, without
getting caught up in the bureaucracy that charac-
terizes many large companies. In 1986, the com-

pany was restructured again, this time along product (rather than geographic) lines.

In 1987, MCI put its fiber network into service, laying over 150,000 miles of fiber coast to coast. Although costly to install, MCI quickly found that the cost was worth it. Traffic could be carried at higher speeds and maintain better quality than with copper. The company enhanced the network the following year by completing another link that gave MCI two transcontinental fibers. This allowed MCI to better compete with AT&T, carrying over 100 million minutes per day by the end of 1988.[11] MCI's market share was further increased when it introduced its most popular discount plan, Friends and Family. The plan utilized MCI's technological capabilities to identify calls to MCI customers, along with its marketing capabilities, to give discounts for calls that remained on the MCI long-distance network. As a result of this program MCI increased its market share by 3 percentage points, from 14 percent to 17 percent in two years, a significant increase.[12] It also expanded its revenues by 41 percent from $8.4 billion to $11.9 billion.

## Sprint

The other major long-distance carrier that emerged is Sprint Communications. Sprint began as two separate companies, one a local operating company in rural areas of the Midwest, United Telecommunications, and the other a subsidiary of Southern Pacific Railroad. Because United's management felt the firm needed to transform itself to thrive in the changing environment, they sought to achieve a technical advantage over AT&T by building the nation's first all-digital, fiber-optic network, beginning in 1984.[13] The firm used railroad rights-of-way in building its network, as it would have been prohibitively expensive to gain separate rights-of-way or obtain permission from

AT&T to utilize their rights-of-way. Thus, United negotiated with CSX Railroad and was able to reach an agreement that allowed United to utilize CSX's rights-of-way to build its 23,000-mile nationwide network in three years.[14]

The company that eventually merged with United to form Sprint began as a subsidiary of Southern Pacific Railroad. Southern Pacific had installed microwave capacity in order to be able to communicate with its trains. It decided to resell some of this capacity as long-distance service. After suffering substantial losses, Southern Pacific sold the telecommunications capacity to GTE, which renamed the company GTE Sprint.

In the summer of 1985, United and GTE Sprint discussed the possibility of a joint venture between the two companies. The difficult part of the agreement was that GTE would have to write off its microwave assets, which amounted to over a billion dollars.[15] By Thanksgiving of 1985, an agreement was reached that resulted in an equal partnership between the two companies. The merger had to be approved by the FCC and the various state regulatory commissions. In gaining approval for its merger, GTE was not required to divest itself of its local operating companies. Instead it signed an agreement requiring it to adhere to strict separation between the local services offered and the long-distance services. After gaining approval, US Sprint was launched a year after the initial discussions began between United and GTE Sprint. Despite its success, as the long-distance company became profitable, GTE decided to sell its investment in US Sprint to United in 1988.

Sprint's success was aided by its hiring of Candice Bergen, who played the main character in a leading sitcom at the time, as its spokesperson. It also began to offer long-distance for the same rate regardless of the length of the call, which was in stark contrast to service offerings at the time that charged different rates depending on the length of the call. The success experienced by Sprint can be seen in its tenfold growth in revenues between 1980 and 1999, and its over fivefold increase in assets during the same period.[16]

Sprint and MCI-WorldCom attempted to merge at the turn of the century in order to compete better with the RBOCs (which were then merging with one another) and AT&T. Although MCI and Sprint had gained substantial market share, they still had substantially smaller market share than AT&T. The proposed merger between these two companies was heavily scrutinized, as there was fear that such a merger would reduce competition in the long-distance market. Under scrutiny of the DOJ and the commission that oversees European antitrust concerns, MCI/WorldCom and Sprint eventually withdrew their petition and continued to operate as separate companies.

### AT&T Nondominance Proceeding

With the success of the other long-distance carriers, AT&T sought to be more competitive and filed with the FCC to be declared a nondominant carrier under Part 61 of the FCC's rules and regulations. After a thorough review of the record and various studies, the FCC determined that AT&T lacked market power in the (domestic) interstate interexchange market. The FCC therefore felt the precautions that had been taken previously by regulating AT&T more strictly than other long-distance carriers were no longer necessary. Thus, on October 12, 1995, the FCC adopted an order that put AT&T on the same regulatory footing as all other providers of long-distance.[17]

In making its decision, the FCC had to examine and analyze AT&T's market power under the criteria it had established in earlier proceedings.

The FCC had developed its economic definitions of market power in its competitive carrier proceeding—the last order before divestiture—and in so doing incorporated those definitions into the determination of dominance and nondominance for the long-distance carriers. Market power was defined as the ability to control prices unilaterally in the overall (domestic) interstate interexchange market. The FCC also defined the relevant product and geographic markets that it would employ in assessing the market power of the carriers covered by the general proceeding. In regard to the relevant geographic market, the definition adopted was that of a single national market. Using those definitions, the FCC determined that AT&T was no longer dominant in the industry, although there were a few exceptions for some submarkets. In its decision, the FCC stated:

> "[W]e find that the record of evidence demonstrates that AT&T lacks market power in the interstate, domestic, interexchange market, and accordingly, we grant its motion to be reclassified as a nondominant carrier with respect to that market . . . AT&T does not have the ability unilaterally to control prices in the overall interstate, domestic, interexchange market. The record indicates that, to the extent AT&T has the ability to control price at all, it is only with respect to specific service segments that are either de minimis to the overall interstate, domestic, interexchange market, or are exposed to increasing competition so as not to materially affect the overall market."[18]

This reclassification meant that AT&T could file its tariffs on one day's notice like the other long-distance carriers and would be subject to the same minimal regulation as the other carriers.

At the same time that AT&T was being declared nondominant, it made a business decision that (given its history over the prior 100 years) was somewhat surprising. AT&T determined that in the face of increased competition, the most profitable way for the firm to operate was as three separate companies. Having fought the separation of Bell Labs and Western Electric from the long-distance part of the company, AT&T announced that it was again going to break itself into pieces, only this time on a completely voluntary basis. The company split into three parts, the long-distance and cellular phone business formed one part; the network service, including Western Electric, was split into Lucent Technologies (the manufacturing business) and NCR Corporation (the computer business). Thus AT&T ended the century with a completely different look and philosophy than it had at the outset.

*Resellers*

Resellers have played an important role in the development of long-distance competition because they have been able to buy services in bulk and resell them to a variety of customers at discounted prices. At the time AT&T was declared non-dominant in 1995, there were over 300 resellers offering long-distance services. These were relatively small companies, compared with the facilities-based carriers such as AT&T, MCI, and Sprint. The resellers generally earned less than $100 million in annual revenues at that time. The resellers did not compete directly with other resellers in many cases; they often filled competitive niches, providing alternatives to the services of the major carriers. With different resellers offering such services, the facilities-based carriers that offered a full range of services faced competition in all the services they offered.

One of the first resellers of long-distance was Long-Distance Discount Service (LDDS). In November 1983, LDDS was certified by the Mississippi Public Service Commission to operate as a long-distance carrier. Its first customer was the University of Southern Mississippi. The company expanded during the next decade, through both internal growth and mergers, and changed its name to WorldCom. By 1994, WorldCom became much more than a reseller. After installing its own equipment and aggressively expanding through a series of acquisitions, it gained market share that was then about half the size of Sprint's. It merged with MCI after the adoption of the Telecommunications Act of 1996, when other carriers began focusing on offering local and long-distance services.

## Manufacturing Telecommunications Equipment

Although other firms entered the manufacturing market, AT&T was the primary provider of equipment in 1984. But as competition developed in the long-distance market and other types of carriers began to emerge in the industry, many carriers decided not to continue purchasing their equipment from AT&T. In addition, the synergies that had been present between manufacturing and providing service were slowly disappearing. Thus, the manufacturing part of the business and the long-distance part of the business were increasingly at odds with each other. As a result, on September 20, 1995, AT&T decided to split off its manufacturing arm into a separate company, despite the fact that for about a hundred years the company had fought a number of times in a number of different ways to maintain control of manufacturing. This was the largest voluntary break-up in the history of American business.[19]

The manufacturing company, named Lucent, became an independent firm one year after the announcement, on September 30, 1996. As with divestiture, AT&T employees generally were assigned to the company where their work had previously been. Bell Labs, which had contributed so many innovations through the years to telecommunications, went to Lucent.

### Local Exchange Service

In 1984, in addition to the newly formed RBOCs, there were approximately 1,400 local operating companies providing service throughout the United States. These carriers had begun operations early in the century and, like the AT&T operating companies, were the exclusive providers of local service in their territories. As the exclusive monopoly providers, these companies were regulated by the states and, in some cases, also by federal regulators. With the court's approval of divestiture, the local carriers feared the loss of revenue that they could experience if a means of replacing the revenues previously paid by AT&T was not developed. At the time of divestiture, about 14 percent of long-distance revenues were used to subsidize the local phone company.[20] The RBOCs filed for local rate increases of over $10 billion. Resistance to the sought-after increases was minimized through the formation of the universal service funds and subsidies to low-income subscribers. The FCC had also decided to allow for accelerated depreciation schedules, which allows firms to write off the costs of their equipment faster. However, since the rates of the RBOCs were based on the value of their assets, they wanted to increase rates in order to maintain the same level of revenues.

### Wireless

At the time of divestiture, most wireless frequencies were being utilized to provide long-distance services, but as carriers in the long-distance market installed fiber-optic cable, they no longer needed the microwave frequencies for their services. Thus they were available for other services.

The FCC originally assigned frequencies to those who would make the best use of them but, as more frequencies became available, the FCC began to assign frequencies via a lottery conducted among interested carriers. Finally, as a means of raising revenue, in 1993 Congress approved the assignment of frequencies to the highest bidder in auctions. Wireless services had been available for several years but, due to limitations on available frequencies, high prices, and the size of equipment, the services offered were obtained only by a relatively few professionals, such as doctors, who needed to be reachable. As developments in electronics reduced the size of equipment and more frequencies were made available to allow for increased usage, wireless services became more popular, which allowed for price decreases and resulted in increased demand for wireless service.

### Paging

Paging service was the first wireless service to become widely utilized, as the one-way technology was easier to implement and a more cost-effective use of a carrier's frequency. Paging carriers quickly began to compete with each other, resulting in lower prices for consumers and difficulties for many paging companies. Throughout the 1990s, paging evolved as consumers changed to other types of wireless communications and the paging carriers developed two-way paging that allowed messages to be sent as well as received. As paging developed into a mass market product, it experienced rapid growth, with revenues tripling from $670 million in 1994 to $2.2 billion in 1996.[21] Simultaneously, while carriers were lowering their prices in order to obtain more customers, revenues increased even though the revenue per customer fell by about 30 percent, from $13.76 in 1993 to $9.11 in 1997.[22] By 1996, the FCC, due to the number of paging companies operating throughout the United States, had concluded that the paging segment of the market was highly competitive.[23]

## Cellular

Like pagers, cellular phones also improved. Most important, they became smaller, which improved their popularity. Still, the initial growth of cellular service as a mass-market commodity was relatively slow. At the end of 1985, the number of subscribers was only about 200,000, as compared to a potential of about 80 million. Growth in cellular service over the next few years increased dramatically, with the number of cellular customers quadrupling in less than two years, passing 1 million in 1987 and reaching over 6 million in June of 1991. The growth can be explained by increased competition and improvements in technology, which resulted in falling prices. For example, new digital compression technology expanded availability by expanding cellular capacity to fifteen to twenty times the then-current levels. In addition, the improvements in available technology allowed the cellular companies to decrease the size of each cell, which allows more customers to obtain service on the network. Calls must be efficiently transferred from one cell's transmitter to the next without an interruption in order to retain the popularity of the service.

Although carriers were able to increase the number of customers they could serve in an area, they were still limited in the number of places where they could offer service. For various reasons, the FCC had limited the number of areas a carrier could serve and the amount of frequency a company could control. This allowed more companies to obtain frequencies, and simultaneously kept the carriers from developing nationwide service. Since the carriers could not obtain licenses that allowed them to provide service across the nation, they developed agreements with other carriers, referred to as roaming agreements that allowed consumers to utilize their service across the nation, albeit at a cost. With the Telecommunications Act of 1996, there were changes in the restrictions on cellular licenses and by the end of the century carriers were able to obtain the licenses necessary to provide nationwide service without the need for a roaming agreement.

## PCS

Another form of wireless service that emerged in the 1990s was the personal communications system (PCS). PCS operated on a different frequency from cellular service and offered a variety of features that cellular phone service was unable to provide. Under the FCC's rules, there was an initial auction in which carriers bid for the PCS frequencies. The carriers spent substantial amounts of money on these frequencies. In addition, due to the amount of frequency that was made available and the restrictions on how many customers a carrier could obtain within each area, there were multiple carriers offering service in each area.

More than 77 million cellular (and PCS) phones were in use by 1999.[24] With the increased usage, one of the issues that arose was whether people should be able to use their cellular phones while they are driving. Many accidents have been blamed on the use of cellular phones while driving. The convenience of a cellular phone in a person's car offers benefits, but many states are considering regulation that would require the use of a hands-free device while driving. This appears to respond to the concerns and the problems that have arisen because of wireless phone use, but allows for the retention of the corresponding benefits.

## Universal Service

With the changes in the telecommunications market due to divestiture, universal service was formalized to some extent, at least within the regulatory world. Historically, as the only provider of long-distance services, AT&T had provided the funding for universal service. Through the separations and settlements process, AT&T had paid for that portion of the local network utilized by long-distance services, plus an additional amount that had been determined by the state and federal regulators. This obviously had to change, with new carriers offering services. Thus, the FCC, working with representatives from the state public utility commissions, developed access charges to allow for the continuation of universal service funding.

Universal service contributions from both the carriers and the end-user charges allowed for the formation of two programs. One program was to increase telephone penetration by assisting low-income consumers with affordable telecommunications services. The second program sent funds to companies operating in high-cost areas in order to keep the cost of local service reasonable for all of those receiving service in those areas. Within the low-income program, there were two separate programs that the states could offer customers, Lifeline and Link-Up. The Lifeline program allowed for the waiver of the federal end-user charges for low-income individuals, up to an amount matched by the state regulators in their policies. The Link-Up program allowed for the waiver to the end-user of some to all of the local operating company's charges for installing the first new phone for a residence.

Lifeline or support for low-income consumers has four different levels of support, most of which must be matched by programs at the state level. The first level of Lifeline support is a waiver of the federal subscriber line charge, which must be matched by a state level program in order for the company to receive federal funds. The second level allows for a reduction of $1.75 per month from the basic monthly rate of the customer. The third level of support depends on the amount of additional support mandated by the relevant state utility commission. The fourth type of support is available only for eligible individuals living on federally recognized Indian reservations. This program allows those consumers to receive up to $25 per month towards reducing basic local service rates to $1 per month.[25] Although Lifeline is a federal–state joint program, its criteria for eligibility for the programs are established within each state by the state utility commission. Once determined to be eligible for Lifeline, if the state has a Link-Up program (which most states do), the consumer would be eligible for that program as well. Link-Up provides a 50 percent discount up to a maximum of $30 on the initial connection charges consumers face when establishing new phone service at a residence.[26]

The other program was established by the federal–state board designing universal service to assist those companies that provide local service in extremely high-cost rural and insular areas where they are not able to recover their costs through reasonable rates to local customers. Politically, it was felt that local rates should be similar in rural and urban areas and thus some program had to be established. A portion of the funds collected from the access charge was utilized to cover these costs. Because of the two programs, the vast majority (over 95 percent) of Americans now have telephone service in their homes.

Universal service was not truly formalized until Congress passed the Telecommunications Act of 1996 (TA96). Until that time, although the FCC had rules requiring contributions to the funds by the long-distance carriers, there was not a specific rule requiring such a program. TA96 changed universal service in some ways. TA96 directed the FCC to "establish competitively neutral rules . . . to enhance, to the extent technically feasible and economically reasonable, access to advanced telecommunications and information services for all public and nonprofit elementary and secondary school classrooms, health care providers, and libraries."[27] Under TA96, the FCC and state commissions were required to make explicit the mechanisms being used to fund the universal service programs. As before, the funds were to support service to low-income consumers and companies operating in high-cost areas. But Congress added two groups to those that were to be eligible to receive universal service funds—schools and libraries and rural health facilities. The federal–state board can add other groups as they deem necessary. A joint federal–state board determined the mechanism to do this, requiring that all carriers pay a percentage of their total revenues to the fund. It was felt that this would be the most equitable means of collecting funds from all carriers. In another change, the rules codified following the passage of TA96 also required carriers other than the long-distance carriers to contribute to the fund.

Under TA96, the Federal-State Joint Board on Universal Service recommended to the FCC that $2.25 billion per year be collected for the subsidization of schools and libraries. The overall recommendation for all of the universal service programs was between $5 billion and $14 billion annually, with the amount growing each year.[28] This figure was substantially more than had been estimated when the legislation was being considered by Congress. The FCC approved the amount recommended by the Joint Board, plus some additional funds for rural health services, so that the total amount to be collected was $2.65 billion.

## Local Exchange Competition

Although the divestiture was designed to separate the competitive long-distance (and other) services from the local services that were not facing competition at the time, over the period from 1984 to 1996 various pressures emerged on the local network to open the local exchanges to competition as well. Immediately following divestiture, competition in the local exchange market was not foreseen. Technology evolved over the next few years so that carriers could begin providing direct access to the long-distance carriers for some large customers. By the mid-1990s, local markets had begun to resemble the long-distance markets of the 1970s, with a number of carriers emerging as competitive access providers. As with the development of competition in the long-distance market, technology played a role in the emergence of competition in the local market. There were two major advancements: digital technology and fiber-optic cable. With the new technology, carriers that had provided data or media services were able to expand their capabilities to include voice traffic and other services. A number of carriers saw the opportunity for profit and began making inroads to local markets. To do this, the carriers first had to get the regulations changed that prevented anyone but the incumbent monopolist from offering local service in many states. A handful of states had removed the exclusive rights to a franchise by 1994. By February 1996, twelve additional states had removed the restrictions, bringing to sixteen the number of states without exclusive franchises. The passage of the TA96 resulted in the incumbent local carriers facing competition from a number of different types of carriers who entered the market.

After 1996, carriers began to seek various avenues of entry into the local exchange markets.

Although the FCC established rules for interconnection within six months of passage of TA96, there was still a great deal of uncertainty in the rules that carriers were to operate under as various parties filed suit against the FCC's order establishing the interconnection rules. This made entry into the local market more difficult for those trying to enter. With the federal rules and regulations under court review, the companies trying to enter the market entered negotiations with the incumbent carriers in each state. In various state regulatory proceedings, the incumbent carriers sought to charge new entrants for those parts of the network that the new entrants needed to offer services. Basic models were formed in order to develop pricing that would meet the basic requirements of TA96. Using these models, the incumbents and the new entrants established prices within the state proceedings.

## The Telecommunications Act of 1996

The desire for changes in the Telecommunications Act had begun twenty years earlier, when AT&T attempted to get Congress to intervene in the move towards competition in the long-distance market. Due to differences of opinion among regulators, legislators, and the companies offering service, the revisions were not adopted until 1996. TA96 was passed because of four basic factors that defined the need for statutory overhaul. The factors included: the need to give more specific interconnection direction in the statute; the RBOCs desire for relief from MFJ limitations on their entry into long-distance service and manufacturing; the need to reassign jurisdiction between the FCC and the state agencies; and growing public support for deregulation. In advancing TA96, the parties involved in the formulation of the bill held differing beliefs, but they did agree on the basic concept

that competition needed to be encouraged throughout the telecommunications industry. With this basic agreement, the parties were able to reach a compromise that allowed for the passage of TA96.

Congress passed legislation revising the Communications Act of 1934 on February 1, 1996, and President Clinton signed it one week later. This was the first major revision in telecommunications legislation since the passage of the original federal telecommunication legislation more than sixty years earlier; it was designed to address the changes that had occurred throughout the world in technology and communications during the intervening years. In revising the 1934 act, Congress sought to open local telecommunications markets and increase competition in long distance by ending the restrictions on the RBOCs and by encouraging more entrants into telecommunications markets. In passing the legislation, Congress removed the legal obstacles to competition in the local exchange segment of the industry and changed a number of other rules regarding communications. TA96 addressed the need to promote competition and facilitate convergence of the different types of communications, including long-distance, local exchange, cable, and wireless. Competition increased gradually following passage of TA96, as the new entrants slowly overcame various barriers to entry and technology continued to evolve.

Although the new legislation removed the legal barriers to local competition, it did not create competition and, like the implementation of divestiture in 1984, did not remove all of the regulations to which the RBOCs were subject. Competition did not come automatically to the local exchange market, as the RBOCs and the independent local carriers that had been providing service for years were monopolists that held nearly 100 percent of their markets. Just a few large businesses purchased a limited amount of access from competitive providers. Therefore, new entrants had to purchase rights to transport and terminate calls from the incumbents in order to provide services to their customers. It was costly and time-consuming for new entrants to install their own network and facilities, thus carriers often began by leasing facilities from the incumbents and in other cases resold the lines of incumbent carriers.

One of the major revisions of the TA96 was Section 251, which required the RBOCs and other local exchange carriers (LEC) to interconnect with any carriers that request interconnection. The section also dealt with resale, number portability, dialing parity and access to telephone numbers, operator services, directory listings, access to rights-of-way, and reciprocal compensation. Section 251 directed the incumbent LECs to unbundle their networks and allow interconnection at any technically feasible point. In addition, the RBOCs are required to provide nondiscriminatory access to databases and associated signaling necessary for call routing and completion.[29] Section 251 gives competitive providers the right to collocate their equipment on the premises of an incumbent LEC, unless it can be shown that doing so would be impractical. Once TA96 was passed, the FCC had six months to adopt the rules that would interpret Section 251 and guide the carriers in their actions under the new law. The FCC adopted its rules one week before the deadline expired. The length of the order—about seven hundred pages—surprised some observers. Some argued that the order increased the regulatory oversight of the local carriers rather than decreasing it. Moreover, the various parties that were subject to the act did not like some aspects of the FCC's rules and filed suit.

Since suits were filed in a number of circuit courts, they had to be consolidated. The means of doing that involves a lottery in which one of the circuit courts is chosen and assigned the case. In this instance, the Eighth Circuit Court was given the case. The first question to be addressed was whether the FCC had the jurisdiction to make the rules it had made. In adopting the wording of TA96, Congress had made a number of changes regarding the responsibilities of the FCC, but in doing so they did not explicitly give the FCC jurisdiction to regulate local companies in regard to those responsibilities. As a result, the states charged that the FCC was violating their jurisdictional rights and responsibilities. Although many Congressmen believed that explicit jurisdiction need not be written into the act, the lack of explicit direction became one of the many issues the court had to grapple with.

The Eighth Circuit Court determined that in writing its rules the FCC had overstepped jurisdictional boundaries in establishing pricing guidelines and in requiring that the incumbent LECs unbundle their network elements and make them available on an individual basis to the new entrants. In ruling, the Eighth Circuit relied on a prior decision by the Supreme Court in which the FCC had violated the jurisdictional separation between the federal and state regulatory rights. The Eighth Circuit found that "Section 2(b) remains a Louisiana-built fence that is hog-tight, horse-high, and bull-strong, preventing the FCC from intruding on the states' intrastate turf."[30] In overturning the FCC's order, the Eighth Circuit determined that the rules regarding unbundled network elements violated the intent of Congress in TA96. The Eighth Circuit's decision was appealed to the Supreme Court, which overruled most aspects of the Eighth Circuit's decision. The Supreme Court held that the rulemaking power granted to the FCC was expansive rather than limited and as a result the FCC was within its jurisdictional rights to establish national policies regarding interconnection, unbundling, and pricing.

Following the FCC's adoption of rules, the competitive LECs (CLECs) developed a variety of business plans that relied on those rules. Depending on the facilities they had in place at the time, new entrants could consider entering as resellers, as facilities-based carriers using their own facilities, or as partial facilities-based carriers—that is, the new entrant would lease some unbundled network elements from the incumbent carrier and then either combine those with some of their own facilities or combine all of the network elements in order to provide service. Those carriers that intended to combine unbundled network elements had to revise their business plans. The carriers had to install more equipment faster than they had originally expected to. This, of course, required more funding than had been anticipated in the carriers' plans. The resulting court cases that tied the FCC's interconnection rules up in court for over two years also made it difficult for new entrants to make plans to enter the market.

With the Eighth Circuit's determination regarding the FCC's rules, the carriers had to revise their business plans, which slowed their development. Another factor that slowed their entry was the fact that without national guidelines, pricing rules and rates had to be established in each state. Although the states finally adopted similar underlying rules for setting prices for the network elements, their rules do differ in regard to the states' interpretation of the requirement for prices to be just and reasonable—not based on rate-of-return or some other rate-based proceeding. As a result of the Eighth Circuit's short-lived decision, there was a degree of uncertainty about the pricing of various network components the companies would lease or purchase from the incumbent in order to begin providing their own service. This also slowed the pace at which new companies could establish their services and enter the market.

## Section 271 Filings

The other major provision of TA96 that pertained to the local telecommunications providers was Section 271. Entry into the long-distance market was important to the RBOCs—it was a $70 billion dollar market. Section 271 outlined the requirements for the RBOCs' entry into the long-distance market. The process called for each RBOC to be approved on a state-by-state basis and, until approved, the RBOC could not offer long-distance service in the state. Section 271 gave the FCC, in consultation with the appropriate state regulatory commission and the DOJ, the right to review the progress of local entry into that state and grant approval of the RBOC's application for entry into the state's long-distance market. Section 271 included a fourteen-point checklist that the FCC is neither to expand nor contract in reviewing the RBOC's application. (See Table 14.1.) Once the application has been approved for that RBOC in that state, the carrier is also eligible to offer equipment in that state. Section 271 provided two separate tracks under which the RBOCs could apply to the FCC for approval. Track A required that competition be present in the state and that those offering the competitive services be afforded certain competitive rights. Track B did not require that competition exist as long as the RBOC had fulfilled all of the checklist items and had prices in place that would allow carriers to enter the state with relative ease.

In establishing Section 271, the fear of potential entrants (which Congress was reacting to) was that if the RBOCs were allowed access to the long-distance market without meeting the checklist requirements, they would take advantage of their monopoly positions in the local markets to gain monopoly power in the long-distance market as well. Since the provisions of Section 271 applied

Table 14.1

**Section 271 Checklist Items Required to Receive Long-Distance Approval**

| Number | Requirement |
|---|---|
| 1 | Interconnection in accordance with Sections 251 and 252 |
| 2 | Nondiscriminatory access to network elements |
| 3 | Nondiscriminatory access to the poles, ducts, conduits, and rights-of-way owned or controlled by the Bell operating company at just and reasonable rates |
| 4 | Local loop transmission from the central office to the customer's premises, unbundled from local switching or other services |
| 5 | Local transport from the trunk side of a wireline local exchange carrier switch, unbundled from switching or other services |
| 6 | Local switching unbundled from transport, local loop transmission, or other services |
| 7 | Nondiscriminatory access to 911 and E911 services, directory assistance service that allows the other carriers' customers to obtain telephone numbers, and operator call-completion service |
| 8 | White pages directory listings for customers of the other carriers' telephone exchange services |
| 9 | Nondiscriminatory access to telephone numbers for assignment to the other carriers' telephone exchange service customers until the date at which telecommunications numbering guidelines were established, and thereafter compliance with such guidelines |
| 10 | Nondiscriminatory access to databases and associated signaling for call routing and completion |
| 11 | Interim telecommunications number portability (until the commissions established number portability regulations) through remote call forwarding, direct inward dialing trunks, or other comparable arrangements |
| 12 | Nondiscriminatory access to those services necessary to implement local dialing parity in accordance with Section 251 |
| 13 | Reciprocal compensation arrangements in accordance with Section 252 |
| 14 | Availability of telecommunications services for resale in accordance with Sections 251 and 252 |

only to the RBOCs, RBOCs argued that the provisions were unconstitutional, because they singled out that group and did not apply generally to all incumbent carriers. Southwestern Bell Communications Corp. (SBC) filed a claim to that effect in Texas District Court. The District Court agreed with SBC but, on appeal to the Fifth Circuit Court, Section 271 was upheld as valid.

In addition to filing on constitutional grounds, SBC was the first to file with the FCC for approval to offer long-distance services. Their application was for the state of Oklahoma. At the time of the application there was minimal competition in the state, especially in regard to residential services,

where only one company other than SBC offered services (and only to their employees). The FCC denied SBC's application on the grounds that SBC had not met a number of the checklist items. The lack of a significant number of consumers obtaining service from firms other than SBC was the focal point in the FCC's decision. In effect, the FCC determined that a carrier was not "competing" unless it actually offered services for sale to consumers. SBC also did not meet the track B requirements because other carriers had requested the establishment of agreements and services. With its determination, the FCC did not expand on what it would require of an RBOC to grant approval.

The FCC also denied the next several applications for a variety of reasons. Those applications included Ameritech in Michigan, BellSouth in South Carolina, and BellSouth in Louisiana on two separate occasions. In denying Ameritech's Michigan application, the FCC elaborated to some extent as to what was required under Track A of Section 271, suggesting that the requirement to serve was in the aggregate, so both residential and business customers had to be offered service but the exact number was not relevant to the determination of eligibility to offer long-distance services. Still, the FCC felt that Ameritech Michigan had not fulfilled all of the checklist items. The requirements to be approved under Track B were elaborated in the FCC's decision denying BellSouth's application in South Carolina to offer long distance. In their decision, the FCC emphasized the implementation schedules that were required by TA96, but were not necessarily included by states and the carriers in the arbitrated agreements. These had to be in place before approval would be granted.

In 1999, Bell Atlantic (Verizon) of New York was the first company to receive approval to begin offering long-distance services. The FCC determined that there was a significant amount of competition throughout the state of New York and that competition could not be reversed by the actions of Bell Atlantic. In establishing the fact that competition existed in New York and they had met the requirements of the 271 checklist, Bell Atlantic New York used an auditor to show the FCC and the state public service commission that they were meeting the requirements of Section 271 with regard to the operational support systems and other factors. When it became clear what carriers needed to do in order to receive approval, a handful of other carriers filed their applications. These applications, including those of SBC in Texas, Kansas, Oklahoma, Arkansas, and Missouri, and Bell Atlantic in Massachusetts, Connecticut, and Pennsylvania, were subsequently approved. RBOCs in three other states filed applications in the last quarter of 2001, and decisions were pending at the time of this writing.

## Effects of TA96 on Local Competition

Although entry was made difficult by the pricing issues and the difficulties in establishing interconnection, entry did occur at the local level over the five years following passage of TA96. The FCC monitored this entry, in part because of their responsibility in approving Section 271 applications. The incumbent local carriers agreed to and signed more than 5,400 agreements with new entrants regarding the conditions for interconnections. In addition, over 3,000 certificates of public convenience and need have been given to new entrants by the state utility commissions, so that they could offer service in the state assigning the certificate. About 280 companies were offering alternative local service just eighteen months after passage of TA96.[31] Competitors began to see rapid increases in revenues following the passage of federal legislation, with revenues doubling in 1997. The revenues were not large compared to those of the RBOCs, but the growth was significant. By the end of 2000, CLECs reported providing service to about 8.5 percent of the local telephone lines in service to end-user customers across the country, almost double the proportion served at the end of 1999.[32] Tens of thousands of lines were being resold by the incumbent local exchange providers to the new entrants. In addition, carriers had installed over 500 new switches in 1996 and another 270 in the first six months of 1997 in order to provide services over their own facilities.[33] In studying local entry, the FCC found that those states in which the RBOCs had received approval to offer long distance under Section 271 showed the greatest competitive activity at the local level. For example, in New York, where Verizon received permission to offer long-distance services in December 1999, CLECs provided service to 20 percent of the market in the state, serving 2.8 million lines. In Texas, where SBC received permission to offer long-distance services in June 2000, CLECs held 12 percent of the market by the end of 2000.[34] Following the adoption of TA96, there has been an increase in the amount of competition at the local level. Although not as much as some would have liked to see, it has developed at a faster rate than did competition in long distance following divestiture.

As the RBOCs were monopoly providers in their areas, they were formidable competitors to those trying to enter the market. In order to provide access to the same number of new customers, the new entrants had to establish relationships with the incumbents and sign contracts that allowed for the interconnection required. As reported above, a number of these contracts have been signed, but the pace of development in local competition has been slower than desired. Therefore, a number of policies have been developed and instituted in order to promote competition in the local market. The states established prices, some of which were designed to promote competition, especially in residential markets. The states also have assisted the carriers in reaching interconnection agreements. With interconnection agreements in place, competition continued to develop, and, as of December 2000, new entrants reported that they served about 16.4 million (or 8.5 percent) of the approximately 194 million nationwide local telephone lines. This is an increase of approximately 93 percent from 8.3 million (or 4.4 percent) of the nationwide telephone lines in December 1999.[35] Although the revenues of competitors did not ap-

proach the levels reached by the RBOCs and incumbent local carriers, they did double from 1996 to 1997, rising from approximately $1.5 billion to $3 billion, and continued to increase through the end of the century.[36] The CLECs still held less than 5 percent of the market at the end of 1997 and served less than 5 million switched-access lines. It should be noted that the FCC has found that those states in which the RBOC has received approval to provide long distance show the greatest competitive activity. For example, CLECs captured 20 percent of the market in New York, with an increase of over 130 percent (from 1.2 million) between December 1999, when Verizon's application was granted, and December 2000.[37] Texas saw similar rates of increase in the last six months of 2000, with an increase of over 60 percent in customer lines between June and December 2000.[38]

Another matter the FCC has monitored is the method the CLECs use to provide their services—via their own lines, via resale, or via unbundled elements. The FCC has found that CLECs provide about 35 percent of their end-user customer lines over their own facilities. CLECs provide services to another 6.8 million lines via resale and to 5.3 million lines via unbundled elements. Local competition is also dispersing throughout the United States, with at least one CLEC providing service in 56 percent of the nation's zip codes, where 88 percent of U.S. households reside.[39]

## Mergers

With the changes in telecommunications brought about by the passage of TA96, a number of carriers began to pursue mergers with other carriers in order to be better positioned to offer services in other segments of the industry. Table 14.2 lists the major mergers that have been considered by the FCC since the passage of TA96. One of the first merger applications was filed by Bell Atlantic and NYNEX. The carriers originally filed their merger application at the FCC as a merger of equals, but due to certain federal regulations involving mergers within the District of Columbia, the application was changed so that Bell Atlantic bought out NYNEX rather than merging as equals. The application was subject to the review of the FCC as the overseer of national communications regulation, which approved it on August 14, 1997. This merger joined the service providers of the mid-Atlantic states and the northeastern states into one large company and was subject to conditions. There was a great deal of concern on the part of other carriers in the industry that the merger of these carriers would result in less competition. Thus, the FCC required conditions that would create procompetitive benefits for consumers throughout the regions served. The conditions included requirements for Bell Atlantic to provide performance-monitoring reports, to provide uniform interfaces to the company's operations support systems (OSS), to conduct operational testing of its OSS interfaces, to propose rates based on forward-looking economic costs, and to engage in good-faith negotiations to establish performance standards and enforcement mechanisms governing its OSS and network performance.[40] The FCC subsequently examined Bell Atlantic's compliance with the conditions and found them in compliance.

In addition to acquiring NYNEX, Bell Atlantic merged with GTE, the largest independent local carrier, in 2000. As with many of the mergers between the larger carriers, the FCC required that the new company meet conditions that addressed its concerns and the concerns of others regarding the competitiveness of the merger. The major condition in this merger was that the new company had to spin off substantially all of GTE's Internet business to eliminate the potential for monopoli-

zation of these assets. Verizon, the resulting firm, spun off GTE's Internet business into a separate public company named Genuity. Bell Atlantic retained 10 percent interest in Genuity but, in order to develop that interest, it is required to obtain approvals to provide long distance in 95 percent of the region in which Genuity operates for five years. Although GTE was not subject to the Section 271 requirements of TA96, Bell Atlantic (and the merged company) was prohibited from providing long-distance voice or data services in any states in which it had not received Section 271 approval. Thus, Verizon has to obtain approval in each of the states where it operates before it can offer long-distance services in those states.

MCI and WorldCom, the second- and fourth-largest long-distance carriers, were the next to file with the FCC for merger approval. Both carriers had substantial local assets that had been acquired through investment in local assets and mergers with competitive access providers that had been providing local service. Despite the fact that the carriers were two of the largest long-distance carriers, the FCC approved their merger on September 14, 1998. As with other large mergers, the FCC made its approval subject to conditions. In the case of MCI and WorldCom, there were only two conditions—that MCI had to divest itself of its Internet assets and that the transfer of MCI's direct broadcast license was subject to a separate review. The reason for the requirement of divestiture of the Internet assets was that MCI and WorldCom together owned and operated the majority of worldwide Internet assets. As a result, one of the main concerns of those filing comments (and of the FCC) in the proceeding was that if the assets were not divested, the new MCI/WorldCom might have monopoly control over Internet access. The other condition was implemented because MCI's direct broadcast license was then being reviewed in re-

Table 14.2

**Mergers Considered by the FCC Since the Passage of TA96**

| Party 1 | Party 2 | Approval date |
| --- | --- | --- |
| SBC | Pac Tel | January 31, 1997 |
| Bell Atlantic | NYNEX | August 14, 1997 |
| MCI | WorldCom | September 14, 1998 |
| AT&T | Teleport Communications Group (TCG) | September 23, 1998 |
| SBC | SNET | October 23, 1998 |
| AT&T | TCI | February 18, 1999 |
| SBC | Ameritech | October 8, 1999 |
| Qwest | US West | March 10, 2000 |
| Bell Atlantic | GTE | June 17, 2000 |
| MCI | Sprint | Withdrawn |

gard to the initial granting of that license. Whether the initial grant was legitimate had to be determined prior to the FCC approval of its transfer. The merger was approved on the grounds that the FCC believed it would contribute to the development of competition in the overall industry.

Other RBOCs followed the lead of Bell Atlantic and NYNEX. SBC merged with two of its fellow RBOCs, Pac Tel and Ameritech. In addition, it merged with SNET, which, because of AT&T's ownership stake, was not considered to be an RBOC, and thus was not treated as one of the RBOCs during divestiture. The mergers of SBC and Pac Tel and Ameritech were strongly opposed by others in the industry, as it was felt that the RBOCs would strongly compete with one another in the local exchange markets. The RBOCs argued otherwise, and the FCC determined that since the companies were not competing and stated that they were not planning to compete with one another, their merger would not be anticompetitive, again subject to conditions. The conditions, like those in Bell Atlantic/NYNEX, were designed to open the local markets of the RBOCs to competition, stimulate the deployment of advanced broadband services, and strengthen the merged firm's incentives to expand competition outside its service area.

The conditions adopted by the FCC were designed to accomplish five central public interest goals, including: (1) promoting equitable and efficient advanced services deployment; (2) ensuring open local markets; (3) fostering significant out-of-region competition for the first time by an RBOC; (4) improving residential phone service; and (5) ensuring compliance with (and enforcement of) the conditions.[41] It is noteworthy that the FCC found that without the conditions that it imposed the merger would have resulted in harm to consumers and would not allow the merger without acceptance of the conditions.

Although AT&T was divesting itself of some of its activities, it was simultaneously expanding its local capabilities through mergers with two different companies that had facilities that were in some ways more suitable for providing local service. The first company acquired by AT&T was one of the largest competitive access providers that had developed over the prior few years, Teleport Communications Group (TCG). The FCC granted approval on September 23, 1998. Since AT&T held little to no local assets at the time, the FCC believed that the merger would probably create an entity that would increase competition in local markets more quickly than if the two companies had been left to enter the local markets on their own. At the time of the merger, TCG had facilities in a number of cities that would allow AT&T to enter those markets and begin offering local service, and AT&T had the capital to invest to further expand the offerings in those markets.

At the time TA96 was passed, many believed that cable companies had an advantage in entering the local telecommunications market due to their extensive access to consumers via their cable networks. Soon AT&T and Tele-Communications, Inc. (TCI) announced their intentions to merge and filed with the FCC for approval. The FCC approved the merger, but as with some of the other mergers that have occurred in the industry since TA96, the merger between TCI and AT&T was subject to conditions. The conditions required (1) the transfer of TCI's ownership of Sprint PCS tracking stock to a trust prior to consummation of the merger and (2) AT&T's adoption of its proposed policy statement regarding distribution of the proceeds of its ownership of the Sprint stock. In approving the merger, the FCC examined the access available to TCI and AT&T to determine whether the merger would be likely to bring competition to the local market. Unfortunately, the success of the company since merger has not been as great as AT&T would have liked because extensive renovations of the cable networks were needed so the company would be able to provide two-way service via the cable facilities.

US West, one of the more controversial RBOCs because of service quality issues, became a sought-after company as the merger wave proceeded following the passage of TA96. Initially, Global Crossings and US West agreed to merge, but another long-distance carrier, Qwest, which had just acquired another long-distance carrier, LCI, outbid Global Crossings and convinced US West to merge with it instead. The reason for the interest

in US West was that when 271 approval had been gained in each of the states in US West's home territory, there could be a dramatic reduction in the access charges paid by the long-distance part of the company for those consumers who chose to use both the long-distance and the local parts of the company. The FCC approved the acquisition in March 2000. Because of the potential for Qwest to establish monopoly power in the region by serving the vast majority of the local customers until competitors entered the market, the FCC's approval of the merger was subject to the condition that Qwest had to divest itself of all of its long-distance customers in the region, as US West had not received 271 approval in any of its states. With the requirement that it divest itself of all of long-distance customers, the FCC felt that Qwest, as the provider of local service, would have a greater incentive to open its markets to other local providers in order to regain its ability to provide long-distance services. In addition, the FCC determined that the acquisition would promote the goals of TA96 with regard to the deployment of advanced telecommunications services, as US West had expertise in providing digital subscriber line services to the local loop, and Qwest had expertise in high-speed, high-capacity networks.

The FCC approved most of the mergers that were filed during the period following passage of TA96, but one major merger application that was filed was not approved. That filing was by MCI/WorldCom and Sprint—the second- and third-largest long-distance carriers, respectively. Although many filed comments and affidavits in favor of the merger, there were also concerns that the merger would result in antitrust violations. The concerns on the part of the FCC, the Department of Justice, the European Union (which needed to approve the merger because both companies offer service in Europe), and the other carriers ultimately led MCI/WorldCom and Sprint to withdraw their application. Financial mismanagement forced WorldCom into bankruptcy in 2002.

## Telephone Numbers

Local competition is one factor, along with increased use of multiple lines by residential consumers and technologies, that contributes to the exhaustion of telephone numbers available for use. This has contributed to the need to revise the way numbers are assigned to carriers, so that numbers will be available for assignment, rather than being captured in a carrier's inventory. The issue is not that all numbers have been assigned to consumers, but that numbers have been assigned to carriers and therefore could not be assigned to the customers of other carriers, as the network did not have a means of routing the calls for those numbers to any other carrier than the one to which the number was assigned. When telephones were first developed, numbers were not used to route the calls, but after World War II an effort was made to organize the network. AT&T developed a nationwide numbering system for the network, assigning three-digit codes to geographic areas so that the (area) codes could be used to route the calls. When area codes were developed, they were restricted to having either a zero or one as the middle digit and could not start with either a zero or one. This meant that there were 144 area codes available for assignment; 86 were initially assigned across the country. The next three digits of the phone number, the prefix, indicated to the network which local switch a call was to be routed to. In order to differentiate the prefix from the area code, prefixes could not have a zero or one as their middle digit and, for routing purposes, could not start with zero or one. The last four digits of the telephone number indicated which customer was

to receive the call. The information mapping the number to the switch was coded into the switching memory and, due to limitations of the technology available at the time, each area code and prefix could be assigned to only one switch.

As the demand for telephone services increased over time, the demand for telephone numbers increased as well. Over the fifty years following the development of the North American numbering plan (NANP), sixty-one new area codes were assigned to areas that needed new numbers. Thus, the increase averaged about 1.1 new area codes per year. This initial increase in demand for numbers could be maintained without much hardship on the part of consumers and the carriers. However, as new technologies were developed that required telephone numbers, such as facsimile machines, pagers, and cellular phones, and as additional carriers entered to meet the demands for the additional services, telephone prefixes (and hence area codes) were quickly exhausted. Because of the technology in use in the network, each new carrier that wanted to offer service in a market had to be assigned a different prefix, even if the carrier planned to use one telephone number from the prefix, not all 10,000. As more and more prefixes were assigned, and the available supply of prefixes within an area code was exhausted, the initial solution was to assign another area code to the area in question. Over the first fifty years of NANP's existence, the available area codes from the initial 144 were assigned to various locales. The next solution introduced to make more area codes available was to remove the restriction on the middle digit from area codes and prefixes. This did not solve the problem, however, as carriers continued to demand prefixes, leading to the fast deployment of area codes throughout the United States. For example, in 1997 thirty-two new area codes were assigned, almost half the number of area codes assigned over the entire fifty-year period leading up to 1997.[42] Initially the state regulatory commissions continued to assign new area codes by splitting the geographic area assigned to the old area code into two or more different areas. This solution had its pros and cons. It allowed the consumers in the area retaining the old area code to retain their numbers; consumers in the new area code retained their telephone numbers but they now had a different area code. The consumers in the new area code had to change a number of things in order to utilize the new area codes. Some of these included changing business stationery, autodialers, alarm systems, and changing 911 systems and a variety of other systems. The carriers also had to reprogram switches and other large pieces of equipment. This solution was expensive and, in some areas such as Chicago, resulted in requiring consumers to change their telephone numbers several times within a few years. To reduce the number of times consumers were required to change telephone numbers, the state regulatory commissions turned to area code overlays, in which the old area code is retained by all current customers, but those needing new (or additional) telephone numbers are assigned numbers from the new area code. This too had its pros and cons, as customers in such areas had to dial the full ten-digit telephone number for every call, including local calls. These solutions gave the carriers the numbers they required, but they did not decrease the speed with which area codes were being exhausted.

At the rate area codes were being exhausted, there was a fear that the entire NANP would have to be revised to address the problem. The industry and the FCC began working together to find a solution to the problem of area code depletion. After several months of work, the solution adopted by the FCC (with the acceptance of the industry) was number pooling. Number pooling allowed for more efficient assignment of numbers to carriers, as carriers were assigned numbers in blocks of 1,000, rather than in the blocks of 10,000 that had previously been assigned. This left fewer numbers stranded in carriers' inventories that would otherwise never be utilized. Assigning numbers in blocks of 1,000 was made possible by the systemwide implementation of a database that identifies each local call in order to properly route the call to the switch of the carrier chosen to provide service.

The database was implemented to allow for number portability and to meet the demands of the new entrants to the local market. The new entrants to the local market believed that in order to convince current customers of the incumbent LECs to transfer their service, the customers had to be able to retain their telephone numbers when they changed carriers. Working with the FCC, the industry developed two potential methods of number portability. One was a location routing number, in which the next-to-last switch would send a query to the database containing local numbers and the switch to which the number was currently assigned. The other was query-on-release, in which the call would be routed to the switch to which the number was originally assigned—but only if the number was no longer affiliated with that switch would the database be queried. The new entrants felt that the query-on-release method gave the incumbent carriers, who had the majority of the original numbers, an unfair advantage. The FCC ultimately agreed and adopted the location routing number as the method the industry would adopt for number portability.

With the database in place that allows for the transfer of numbers from one carrier to another, the carriers were also able to successfully implement number pooling. Although it would appear that the assignment of numbers could be done on an individual basis, it was felt by many, especially cellular and paging providers, that they needed to be supplied with more than one number at a time because they needed some inventory in place to be able to assign numbers after hours. With the implementation of number pooling, carriers were also required to return unused numbers that were included in the carrier's inventory, but met certain conditions under the number resource optimization plan adopted by the FCC. Prior to adopting the resource optimization plan, only 40 percent of the roughly one billion numbers assigned to U.S. carriers were actually assigned to customers; another 10 percent were being used for administrative and other purposes. The other 500 million numbers were stranded in carriers' inventories. Number resource optimization called for the return of those blocks of 1,000 numbers that could easily be reassigned to other carriers. Most carriers did not want to return any numbers, preferring to retain them in their inventories as long as possible. Thus, no numbers were returned to the pool to be reassigned until the return was required by the FCC's rules, which went into effect in 2000 and resulted in the return of 37 million numbers.[43] With more numbers being available for the carriers, the demand for new area codes has been reduced.

## Technology

One of the driving forces for change in the telecommunications industry has been improvements and innovations in technology. Some of the technology that emerged or was improved in the 1980s and 1990s involves digital switches, fiber-optic cable, and computers with appropriate software. These changes allowed long-distance carriers to improve their service, allowed cellular and other wireless services to become mass-market commodities, and allowed competitive access providers to begin offering services in competition with the incumbent local carriers. The improvements in technology also resulted in improved quality of service as background noise, cross-talk, echoes, and dropped calls were dramatically reduced.

Digital switches had been invented many years before, and by the mid-1980s were serving about half of the customers in the United States, although they were installed in only about one-tenth of the local exchanges operated by the RBOCs.[44] With divestiture and the need to provide all long-distance carriers with access to their local switches, the RBOCs began installing digital switches throughout the system, because the digital switches made such access possible. Another factor that prompted the newly independent RBOCs to install the digital switches was the reduced cost of end-user equipment and central office switching, which reduced their cost of providing service but left them with high asset values. Digital switching increased the speed with which calls were connected and allowed the introduction of a number of services, such as call-waiting, call-forwarding, and three-way calling, among others. This was important to the earnings of RBOCs, since rates (and thus profitability) were determined on the basis of the RBOCs' assets.

Digital technology saw dramatic increases in both usage and application as advances were made in the systems used with digital switches. The adoption of international standards aided the adoption of digital switches as well. The reduction in costs in both digital switching and digital transmission increased its adoption. The costs of digital technology fell by 17 percent during the period from 1988 to 1990. In addition, competition among switch manufacturers led to a decrease in switch costs, with prices falling from $400 to $500 per line to $100 to $200 per line. As the prices of new technology continued to fall, firms continued increasing the amount of digital technology installed.

Fiber optic technology aided both the long-distance carriers and the competitive access providers. The long-distance carriers replaced the microwave technology they had been using in their networks with fiber-optic cable. The use of fiber-optic cable resulted in fewer dropped calls and higher quality voice connections. In addition, fiber allows more calls to be carried on any given line, and this can be increased almost infinitely, depending on the capabilities of the electronics attached to the line. The capacity of fiber is significantly greater than that of wireless at this time, with the theoretical capacity of fiber being over 600 million simultaneous conversations over one strand. Although initially expensive, the introduction of fiber-optics has resulted in the overall reduction of costs to the long-distance carriers and their networks, because the cost of maintenance is relatively low. In competing for business, the new entrants to the long-distance segment of the industry quickly introduced fiber to their networks, with Sprint being the first to complete its all-fiber nationwide network, advertising its benefits with the line, "You can hear a pin drop." There are four national fiber networks in the United States, one each installed by AT&T, MCI, Sprint, and the National Telecommunications Network. Total fiber deployed in the United States by the long-distance carriers was estimated to be 2.4 million miles by the end of 1991, with an estimated capacity of approximately 30 million miles. The newly formed competitive access providers (CAPs) also installed fiber-optic cable. The CAPs installed rings of fiber-optic cable in and around the larger cities, running through the business districts, connecting the buildings. The CAPs installed the fiber cable in rings, so that there was redundancy in the system. If there is a cut in the cable at any one point the call is automatically rerouted in another direction,

so that it is still completed. The major customers of these new fiber providers were the long-distance carriers, accounting for over 60 percent of the CAP's business. By using these services, the long-distance carriers were able to avoid using local operating companies for some of their business, which allowed them to avoid some access charges.

Because of digital switches, fiber-optic cable, and standardization that enables companies to use different brands of equipment in their systems, the adoption of software played an important role in the development of telecommunications during the 1980s and 1990s. The software directs what the switches are supposed to do, thereby ensuring the proper signaling, processing, and routing of calls, along with sending other information regarding enhanced services. The software developed to conform to international standards is known as Signaling System 7 (SS7). Under SS7, a signal is sent ahead of the call to determine the quickest way of routing the call, whether the phone number being called is free, and whether any special services need to be activated. As a result, the efficiency of the network is increased, as the SS7 software requires less capacity to connect any given call. An added feature of SS7 that was beneficial to the carriers has been that SS7 is capable of monitoring maintenance problems.

## Conclusion

With the court's approval of the modified divestiture agreement between AT&T and the Department of Justice, the telecommunications industry entered a new phase of its history in 1984. The structure of the industry was dramatically changed, from that of a monopoly provider of virtually all long-distance services in the United States and about 80 percent of local services, to one employing multiple providers of equipment and long-distance, and eventually multiple providers of local service as well. These changes resulted from changes in all aspects of the industry—regulations, judicial oversight, and technology. Although AT&T still fought for as much market share as possible, it had to do so in a more competitive environment. As technology continued to improve and equal access was gained, the other long-distance carriers were better able to compete with AT&T and thus gained market share. Although there is still some debate as to how competitive the long-distance segment of the industry truly is, it is clear that it is more competitive now than it was prior to divestiture.

In addition to the increased competitiveness in the long-distance segment of the industry, by the end of the twentieth century competition among local services also began to increase as the rules and regulations developed as a consequence of the Telecommunications Act of 1996 were put in place. Although competition is not yet in place uniformly across the country at the local level, it has begun to emerge in the larger cities and in those states with more favorable environments. This competition should continue to develop, and with the falling prices and better service quality seen in the long-distance industry with the onset of competition, local service competition should bring benefits to consumers as well.

The changes seen throughout the industry since 1984 have been rapid and dramatic, with a multitude of new services and technologies being used to provide telecommunications to consumers. The rules and regulations that were in place prior to 1984 (for long distance) and prior to 1996 (for local service) no longer apply. The providers of services have changed as well, with a number of new providers and drastic changes in the business goals of the carriers that remain. The WorldCom episode notwithstanding, the telecommunications industry has been completely transformed in just twenty years, and competition is now a reality. Concurrently, the quality and reliability of the network have improved for the vast majority of consumers.

## Notes

1. Peter Temin, with Louis Galambos, *The Fall of the Bell System: A Study in Prices and Politics* (Cambridge, MA: Cambridge University Press, 1987), p. 284.

2. Federal Communications Commission, Common Carrier Bureau, Industry Analysis Division, *Trends in Telephone Service* (Report), May 1996, Table 14.

3. The rate was increased for second lines following the passage of the Telecommunications Act of 1996.

4. Pacific Telephone served California and Nevada. Southwestern Bell served Texas, Oklahoma, Arkansas, and Kansas. Ameritech served Illinois, Indiana, Michigan, Ohio, and Wisconsin. BellSouth served Florida, South Carolina, North Carolina, Tennessee, Kentucky, Alabama, Mississippi, Louisiana, and Georgia. Bell Atlantic served Virginia, West Virginia, Maryland, Delaware, Pennsylvania, New Jersey, and Washington, DC. NYNEX served New York, Massachusetts, Rhode Island, Vermont, New Hampshire, and Maine. US West served Washington, Oregon, Idaho, Montana, Wyoming, Colorado, Arizona, New Mexico, North Dakota, South Dakota, Iowa, Nebraska, Minnesota, and Utah.

5. Access services supplied by the local operating company connect long-distance calls to the consumer's long-distance provider.

6. Salomon Brothers, "U.S. Telecom Services," *Industry Outlook,* April 17, 1996, p. 19.

7. Paul W. MacAvoy, *The Failure of Antitrust and Regulation to Establish Competition in Long-Distance Telephone Services* (Washington, DC: MIT Press and AEI, 1996), p. 83.

8. Federal Communications Commission, Common Carrier Bureau, Industry Analysis Division, *Long-distance Market Share, Fourth Quarter 1995* (Report), March 1996.

9. Ibid.

10. Lorraine Spurge, *Failure Is Not an Option: How MCI Invented Competition in Telecommunications* (Encino, CA: Spurge Ink!,1998), p. 162.

11. Ibid., p. 136.

12. Ibid., p. 156.

13. John Hoffman, *That Was a Pin* (Leawood, KS: Leathers Publishing, 2000), 19.

14. Ibid.

15. Ibid., p. 27.

16. Ibid., p. 46.

17. Federal Communications Commission, *In the Matter of Motion of AT&T Corp. to be Reclassified as a Non-Dominant Carrier*, FCC CC Docket. No. 95–247, Order.

18. Ibid., pp. 3, 18.

19. MacAvoy, p. 49.

20. Federal Communications Commission, *Telecommunications Industry Revenue: TRS Fund Worksheet Data* (Report), November 1997, p. 4.

21. Federal Communications Commission, *Before the Federal Communications Commission: In the Matter of Implementation of Section 6002(b) of the Omnibus Budget Reconciliation Act of 1993, Annual Report and Analyses of Competitive Market Conditions With Respect to Commercial Mobile Services*, Third Report, FCC Docket. 98–91, released June 11, 1998, p. C-2.

22. Federal Communications Commission, *Before the Federal Communications Commission: In the Matter of Implementation of Section 6002(b) of the Omnibus Budge Reconciliation Act of 1993, Annual Report and Analyses of Competitive Market Conditions With Respect to Commercial Mobile Services*, Fourth Report, FCC Docket. 99–136, released June 24, 1999, p. 5.

23. Federal Communications Commission, *Common Carrier Bureau, Industry Analysis Division, Trends in Telephone Service* (Report), December 2000, p. 7-1.

24 Ibid., p. 7-2.

25. Communications Act of 1934 as amended by The Communications Act of 1996, prepared for the use of the Committee on Commerce, U.S. House of Representatives, March 1996, 47 U.S.C. Section 254(h)(1)(B).

26. Max D. Paglin, Joel Rosenbloom, and James R. Hobson, eds., *The Communications Act: A Legislative History of the Major Amendments 1934–1996.* (Silver Spring, MD: Pike and Fischer, 1999), 76.

27. Peter Huber, "Local Exchange Competition Under the 1996 Telecom Act: Red-Lining The Local Residential Customer," unpublished, November 1997, executive summary.

28. Ibid.

29. Federal Communications Commission, "Federal Communications Commission Releases Latest Data on Local Telephone Competition," news release, May 21, 2001.

30. Federal Communications Commission, Common Carrier Bureau, Industry Analysis Division, *Local Competition* (Report), December 1998, p. 1.

31. Federal Communications Commission, "[FCC] Releases Latest Data."

32. Ibid.

33. Ibid.

34. Ibid.

35. Ingo Vogelsang and Glenn Woroch, "Local Telephone Service," *Industry Studies*, 2d ed., Larry L. Duetsch, ed. (Armonk, NY: M.E. Sharpe, 1998), p. 275.

36. Ibid.

37. Ibid.

38. Ibid.

39. Federal Communications Commission, *Local Competition*, p. 1.

40. Federal Communications Commission, Public Notice, "Commission Seeks Comment on Bell Atlantic's Progress Report on Compliance with Bell Atlantic/NYNEX Merger Order Conditions," File No. AAD 98–24, Released February 5, 1999.

41. Federal Communications Commission, "FCC Approves SBC-Ameritech Merger Subject to Competition-Enhancing Conditions," news release, CC Docket. No. 98–141, released October 6, 1999.

42. Federal Communications Commission, Common Carrier Bureau, Industry Analysis Division, *Numbering Resource Utilization in the United States as of December 31, 2000* (Report), June 2001, p. 1.

43. Federal Communications Commission, "FCC Releases Numbering Resource Utilization Report," news release, June 13, 2001.

44. Richard H.K. Vietor, *Contrived Competition: Regulation and Deregulation in America* (Cambridge, MA and London: Belknap, 1994), p. 188.

## Suggested Readings

Brock, Gerald W. *The Telecommunications Industry: The Dynamics of Market Structure.* Cambridge, MA, and London: Harvard University Press, 1981. A review of the history of the telecommunications industry from its inception to 1980, just prior to AT&T's divestiture.

Crandall, Robert W. *After the Breakup: U.S. Telecommunications in a More Competitive Era.* Washington, DC: Brookings Institution, 1991. An analysis of the divestiture of AT&T and the general trend toward competition in telecommunications in the United States.

MacAvoy, Paul W. *The Failure of Antitrust and Regulation to Establish Competition in Long-Distance Telephone Services.* Cambridge, MA and London: MIT Press, and Washington, DC: AEI, 1996. An assessment of the competitiveness of long-distance services after the divestiture of AT&T and a consideration of the changes in regulation and the role of antitrust procedures in the process.

McMaster, Susan E. *Telecommunications in the Twentieth Century.* Greenwood, forthcoming 2002. A review of the evolution and development of the telecommunications industry from its inception through the end of the twentieth century.

Temin, Peter, and Louis Galambos. *The Fall of the Bell System: A Study in Prices and Politics*. Cambridge, England, and New York: Cambridge University Press, 1987. An analysis of the events that led up to and resulted in the breakup of AT&T.

Vietor, Richard H.K. *Contrived Competition: Regulation and Deregulation in America*. Cambridge, MA, and London: Belknap, 1994, chapter 4. The chapter is a historical overview of regulatory change and the move toward competition in the telecommunications industry.

# About the Editor and Contributors

**Robert M. Adams** is an economist in the Division of Research and Statistics of the Federal Reserve Board. His policy responsibilities include the analysis of the competitive effects of proposed bank mergers and acquisitions. His research centers on issues involving industrial organization, antitrust, banking, and bank productivity. Prior to joining the Federal Reserve Board, Dr. Adams worked as a staff economist at the Department of Justice, Antitrust Division. He received his Ph.D. in economics from Rice University.

**Donald F. Barnett** is president of Economic Associates Inc. (EAI), based in Great Falls, Virginia. EAI provides corporate planning, privatization, acquisition, and business development advice to steel-related industries in the United States and throughout the world. Prior to establishing EAI, Dr. Barnett was a senior economist at the World Bank, where he instigated and implemented restructuring programs in many world steel industries (e.g., Indonesia, Hungary, Peru, Nigeria, Pakistan, and Egypt). While serving as a senior policy adviser in the White House, he played a major role in establishing the trigger-price mechanism. Dr. Barnett is the author of numerous books and articles. His books on the steel industry include *Steel: Upheaval in a Basic Industry* (with L. Schorsch) and *Up from the*

*Ashes: The Rise of the Steel Minimill in the United States* (with R. Crandall). Dr. Barnett received his Ph.D. in economics from Queen's University in Canada, following master's-level training in mining and metallurgical engineering.

**Thomas Cottrell** is an associate professor in the Faculty of Management at the University of Calgary, where he lectures on corporate finance and mergers at the undergraduate and master's levels. His fascination with software began with minicomputers in the 1980s. Prof. Cottrell's research interests are primarily in strategy in software and biotechnology. Dr. Cottrell worked as a Certified Public Accountant for Deloitte, Haskins, and Sells and also worked for Microsoft Corporation prior to completing doctoral work at the University of California–Berkeley.

**Robert W. Crandall** is a senior fellow in the Economic Studies Program at the Brookings Institution. He has specialized in industrial organization, antitrust policy, and the economics of government regulation. He is author of *Who Pays for Universal Service? When Telephone Subsidies Become Transparent* (with L. Waverman); *Talk Is Cheap: The Promise of Regulatory Reform in North American Telecommunications* (with L. Waverman); *The*

*Extra Mile: Rethinking Energy Policy for Automotive Transportation* (with P. Nivola); *Manufacturing on the Move*; *Up from the Ashes: The Rise of the Steel Minimill in the United States* (with D. Barnett); *The Scientific Basis of Health and Safety Regulation* (with L. Lave); *Regulating the Automobile* (with H. Gruenspecht, T. Keeler, and L. Lave); *Controlling Industrial Pollution*; and *The U.S. Steel Industry in Recurrent Crisis*, as well as other books and numerous journal articles. Dr. Crandall has taught economics at Northwestern University, the Massachusetts Institute of Technology, the University of Maryland, George Washington University, and the "Stanford in Washington" program. Prior to assuming his current position at Brookings, he was acting director, deputy director, and assistant director of the Council on Wage and Price Stability. Dr. Crandall received an M.S. and a Ph.D. in economics from Northwestern University.

**Larry L. Duetsch** is a professor of economics at the University of Wisconsin–Parkside. He is a longtime member of the Industrial Organization Society and has done research on topics related to entry conditions and the extent of suboptimal capacity. His articles have appeared in the *Review of Industrial Organization*, the *Journal of Industrial Economics*, the *Southern Economic Journal*, and the *Review of Economics and Statistics*. He has been a reviewer for these and other journals. Dr. Duetsch received his Ph.D. in economics from the University of Wisconsin–Madison.

**H.E. Frech III** is a professor of economics at the University of California, Santa Barbara. He has been a visiting professor at Harvard and the University of Chicago. He is North American editor of the *International Journal of the Economics of Business*. Prof. Frech has published numerous ar-

ticles and written or edited books on many topics, including industrial organization, health economics, insurance, energy economics, land use controls, the Coase Theorem, and the property rights theory of the firm. His most recent book is *The Productivity of Health Care and Pharmaceuticals: An International Comparison*. Dr. Frech's articles have appeared in the *American Economic Review*, the *Journal of Political Economy*, the *Journal of Law and Economics*, the *Quarterly Journal of Economics*, the *Journal of Institutional and Theoretical Economics*, *De Economist*, and the *Revue d'economie politique*. He received his Ph.D. in economics from the University of California–Los Angeles.

**Joseph A. Giacalone** is a professor of economics at the Tobin College of Business of St. John's University, where he also holds the Henry George Chair. Dr. Giacalone received an M.B.A. from St. John's University and a Ph.D. in economics from Columbia University. His research and publications cover the areas of health care, especially the nursing home industry, as well as economic history and collegiate business education. A member of the American Economic Association, the National Association for Business Economics, and the Economic and Business Historical Society, Dr. Giacalone also serves on the editorial board of the *Southern Business Review* and as a referee for various journals and conferences.

**Douglas F. Greer** is a professor of economics at San Jose State University. He is the author of several books and numerous articles in academic journals (including several on the beer industry) and has also served as a consultant on antitrust matters and public utility regulation for private corporations and government agencies. His consulting duties have included work for such brewers as Stroh,

Coors, Pabst, and Schlitz. Under the Fulbright program, Dr. Greer has taught and conducted research in Ireland and New Zealand. He received his Ph.D. in economics from Cornell University.

**John E. Kwoka jr.** is Finnegan Professor of Economics at Northeastern University and is the general editor of the *Review of Industrial Organization*. He has authored numerous articles on issues in industrial organization, regulatory economics, and antitrust policy. Prof. Kwoka has coedited a volume of antitrust case studies entitled *The Antitrust Revolution* and has published a book entitled *Power Structure* that analyzes the performance of electric utilities. He has taught at the University of North Carolina–Chapel Hill and also at George Washington University, and has had visiting appointments at Northwestern and at Harvard. He also has worked in the Bureau of Economics of the Federal Trade Commission, in the Economic Policy Office of the U.S. Justice Department's Antitrust Division, and as special assistant in the Common Carrier Bureau of the Federal Communications Commission. Dr. Kwoka received his Ph.D. in economics from the University of Pennsylvania.

**Susan E. McMaster** is an economic consultant trained in applied microeconomics and industrial organization. She specializes in issues that pertain to the regulation of industries. She has been a consultant on numerous legal and regulatory cases, including cases in telecommunications and a variety of other industries. She also served on the staff of the Federal Communications Commission while it implemented the Telecommunications Act of 1996. In addition, she worked for MCI, when it began entering the competitive local exchange market. Dr. McMaster recently completed a book on the history of telecommunications (from its origins through the end of the twentieth century,

and has also published articles in academic journals. She received her M.S and Ph.D. in economics from the University of Illinois at Urbana-Champaign.

**Lee R. Mobley** is a research economist at the Research Triangle Institute in Research Triangle Park, near Durham, NC. She was previously an associate professor of economics at Oakland University in the School of Business Administration. Her interests include industrial organization, health economics, and spatial modeling. She has published articles in the following journals: *Inquiry*, *Economic Inquiry*, *Applied Economics*, the *Review of Industrial Organization*, *Health Economics*, the *International Journal of the Economics of Business*, *Antitrust Bulletin*, the *International Journal of Healthcare Technology and Management*, and *Advances in Health Economics and Health Services Research*. Most of her published work has involved empirical examination of competition, mergers, and market power in the hospital industry. More recently, she has used GIS software in the examination of access to health care, the impact of managed care on distance traveled, and antitrust market definitions. Dr. Mobley received a M.F.A. in sculpture and a Ph.D. in economics from the University of California–Santa Barbara.

**Steven A. Morrison** is a professor and chair in the Department of Economics at Northeastern University. He is also the managing editor of the *Journal of Transport Economics and Policy*. During 1998–99, he was a member of the congressionally mandated National Academy of Sciences (Transportation Research Board) Committee for Study of Competition in the U.S. Airline Industry. Before joining Northeastern in 1982, he was an assistant professor at the University of British Columbia. He has also held visiting positions at

Harvard, MIT, the London School of Economics, and the Brookings Institution. Morrison is the author of numerous articles on transportation economics and air transportation, and he is coauthor (with Clifford Winston) of *The Economic Effects of Airline Deregulation* (1986) and *The Evolution of the Airline Industry* (1995), both published by the Brookings Institution. He has written many op-ed pieces for newspapers, and he has testified before Congress on airline competition matters on numerous occasions. Dr. Morrison received a B.A. in economics from the University of Florida and a Ph.D. in Economics from the University of California–Berkeley.

**Stanley I. Ornstein** is a vice president at Analysis Group Economics, an economics and financial consulting firm. He specializes in applied microeconomics and industrial organization and their application in the areas of antitrust, intellectual property, regulated industries, and competition in general. Prior to holding this position, he was a research economist and the associate director of the Research Program in Competition and Business Policy, Anderson Graduate School of Management, University of California–Los Angeles. He has been a consultant on antitrust and other lawsuits for over twenty-five years, including cases in motion pictures and a broad range of other industries. Dr. Ornstein has published a number of articles in academic journals on issues of competition and antitrust. Dr. Ornstein's educational background includes a M.S. in business administration from San Diego State University and a Ph.D. in economics from the University of California–Los Angeles.

**David B. Patton** is the president of Potomac Economics, an economic consulting firm specializing in economic and strategic issues in the energy industry. He provides strategic advice, analysis, and expert testimony on deregulation, transmission pricing, asset valuation, market design, and competitive issues. He currently serves as the market adviser and for New York ISO and ISO New England and has been engaged as the independent market monitor for Midwest ISO, Alliance RTO, and Southwest Power Pool. Prior to founding Potomac Economics, Dr. Patton was a senior economist with the Office of Economic Policy at the FERC. Dr. Patton received his Ph.D. from George Mason University, where he concentrated in the fields of microeconomics and competition policy. He has published and spoken on a broad array of topics related to emerging competitive electricity markets, including transmission congestion and pricing, derivatives and risk management, and market power.

**Ronald M. Pavalko** has been a faculty member and administrator at the University of Wisconsin–Madison, Florida State University, and the University of Wisconsin–Parkside, where he is currently an Emeritus Professor of Sociology. His publications in the field of gambling studies include two books, *Risky Business: America's Fascination with Gambling* and *Problem Gambling and Its Treatment: An Introduction*; articles in the *Journal of Gambling Studies* and *National Forum: The Phi Kappa Phi Journal*; and a study of problem gambling among older people. Dr. Pavalko is a member of the National Council on Problem Gambling, the Florida Council on Compulsive Gambling, and the Wisconsin Council on Problem Gambling. He received his Ph.D. in sociology from the University of California–Los Angeles.

**Richard T. Rogers** is a professor in the Department of Resource Economics at the University of Massachusetts–Amherst. Dr. Rogers's interests include marketing and industrial organization, especially issues involving strategic investments, advertising, market dominance, and cooperatives. He is the recipient of a University Distinguished Teacher Award and the winner of a National Excellence in Teaching Award from the U.S. Department of Agriculture. His publications include a coauthored award-winning book, *The Food Manufacturing Industries: Structure, Strategies, Performance, and Policies*, several chapters in books, and numerous articles in professional journals. Dr. Rogers received a Ph.D. in economics from the University of Wisconsin–Madison.

**Robert A. Sinclair** is a vice president at Potomac Economics. He has been an economic consultant since completing his Ph.D. in economics at the University of Pittsburgh in 1993. He has testified in various state and federal jurisdictions on economic matters pertaining to many different industries, but most often the electric power and natural gas industries. Dr. Sinclair has published articles in numerous professional journals on topics relating to regulation and antitrust policy.

# Index